"*Tod Browning's Dracula* situates this landmark film in every historical context imaginable—from the social to the technological, from stage to studio, from directorial concerns to generic ones. Adroitly researched and lavishly illustrated, the book is exhaustive in the best possible sense. With this tome, Gary Rhodes cements his reputation as one of the world's premier historians of horror cinema."
Hugh S. Manon, Professor of Screen Studies, Clark University

"No aspect of the film's origins, pre-production, production, post-production, release, and ongoing fascination for so many remains unexamined, not merely discussed but subjected to serious, scholarly and at all times highly readable analysis. If Gary Rhodes at times seems obsessed with his subject, it is a healthy obsession, evidential of a background that places him firmly on the higher pinnacle of academic scholarship, yet grounded in the world of the true, devoted film enthusiast. He never allows his academic discipline to subvert the love of his subject."
Anthony Slide, film historian and author

"Gary Rhodes correctly takes issue with misrepresentations and myths about this supposedly archaic version of *Dracula*. By setting the film in its cultural, historical, and industrial context he clearly demonstrates how the film functions within its era and not how we would like it to be. This is another of the author's important rewritings of previously accepted film criticism and history supported by important archival detail and close visual and sound analysis."
**Tony Williams, Professor and Area Head of Film Studies,
Southern Illinois University at Carbondale.**

TOD BROWNING'S

Gary D. Rhodes

First published in 2014 by

Tomahawk Press
PO Box 1236
Sheffield S11 7XU
England

www.tomahawkpress.com

© Gary Rhodes 2014
The right of Gary Rhodes to be identified as the author of this work is hereby asserted in accordance with the Copyright, Designs and Patents Act 1988.

Dracula (1931) and any images from that film are copyright Universal Studios

All rights reserved. No part of this publication may be reproduced or transmitted in any form or by any means, electronic or mechanical, including photocopy, recording, or other information retrieval system, without permission in writing from the publisher.

ISBN 13: 978-0-9566834-5-8
Edited by Bruce Sachs
Copy edited by Sheldon Hall
Designed by Tree Frog Communication 01245 445377 www.treefrogcommunication.co.uk
Printed by Gutenberg Press, Malta

**For my dear friend and colleague
Edward "Eric" Eaton.**

**Amongst his many great and varied achievements was helping
to forge Film Studies at the University of Oklahoma.**

ACKNOWLEDGMENTS

I would like to offer my sincere thanks to the various archives, libraries, museums, and universities that kindly offered assistance during the research phase of this project: the American Heritage Center at the University of Wyoming, the Andover-Harvard Theological Library of Massachusetts, the Annenberg Rare Book and Manuscript Library at the University of Pennsylvania, the Ardmore Public Library of Oklahoma, the Bancroft Library at the University of California at Berkeley, the Billy Rose Theatre Division of the New York Public Library, the Charles E. Young Research Library at the University of California/Los Angeles, the Chickasaw Regional Library System of Oklahoma, Cinegraph of Hamburg, the Department of Special Collections at the University of California at Santa Barbara, the Free Library of Philadelphia, the Harry Ransom Center at the University of Texas at Austin, the Louis B. Mayer Film and Television Study Center in the Doheny Library at the University of Southern California, the Margaret Herrick Library of the Academy of Motion Picture Arts and Sciences in Beverly Hills, the Museum of the Moving Image in New York, the National Archives of the United States, the Natural History Museum of Los Angeles, the Newark Public Library of New Jersey, the Special Collections Department at the University of Iowa, the Special Collections Division at the University of Washington Libraries, the Theatre Historical Society of America, and the Wisconsin Center for Film and Theatre Research.

In addition, I want to express gratitude to the following individuals who have helped make this book possible: Jerry Armellino, Marty Baumann, Scott Berman, the late Richard Bojarski, David Bowman, Tom Brannan, Olaf Brill, Mario Chacon, Richard Daub, Michael J. David, the late David Durston, Scott Essman, the late Philip R. Evans, the late William K. Everson, Lawrence Fultz, Jr., the late Richard Gordon, the late Gordon R. Guy, G. D. Hamann, Matt Heffernan, David H. Hogan, Roger Hurlburt, the late Steve Jochsberger, Steve Kaplan, Anthony Kerr, Nancy Kersey, Eugene Kirschenbaum, Logan Kouski, Frank Liquori, Peter Michaels, Mark A. Miller, John Norris, Jim Nye, Marcus O'Brien, Dennis Payne, Victor Pierce, William Pirola, William V. Rauscher, Jeffrey Roberts, Bruce Scivally, the late Richard Sheffield, Don G. Smith, George R. Snell, Brian Taves, Mario Toland, John Ulakovic, the late Stratton Walling, Jon Wang, and Steve Vertleib.

A number of persons have given so much of their time and support that they proved crucial to this book's completion: Meredith Asher, Leonardo D'Aurizio, Buddy Barnett, Doug Bentin, David Bowman, Kevin Brownlow, Bob Burns, Richard Bush, Jeff Carlson, Dr. Donna Casella, Bill Chase, George Chastain, Ned Comstock, Michael Copner, Robert Cremer, Kristin Dewey, Jack Dowler, Dr. Edward "Eric" Eaton, John Ellis, Ted Estes, Sr., Phillip Fortune, Beau Foutz, Fritz Frising, Christopher R. Gauthier, Robert Gitt, Sheldon Hall, Lee Harris, Susan Hart, Clark J. Holloway, Abby Kakeldey, Steve Kirkham, Dr. Robert J. Kiss, Dr. Michael Lee, Bela G. Lugosi, Scott MacGillivray, Scott MacQueen, Gregory William Mank, Mark Martucci, Kathy McLeister, D'Arcy More, Lynn Naron, Henry Nicolella, Ted Okuda, Dr. Desmond O'Rawe, Anthony Osika, Philip J. Riley, William H. Rosar, Bruce Sachs, Gerald Schnitzer, Alexandra Asher Sears, Samuel M. Sherman, John Soister, Dr. Robert Spadoni, Lynne Lugosi Sparks, Billy Stagner, David Stenn, Graham Sutton, the late George E. Turner, Alexander Webb, David Wentink, and Glenn P. White.

My acknowledgments also extend to the many historians who have written about Tod Browning and *Dracula* over the years, as they have helped keep interest in these subjects alive and well. Specifically, I much appreciate the work of my friend David J. Skal. While I generally do not agree with Skal's conclusions, his writing has helped me to sharpen and refine my own positions. Moreover, I believe he deserves much credit for bringing attention to the existence of a particular print of the Spanish-language *Dracula* archived at the Cinemateca de Cuba, as well as for his research into such topics as the role of Harold Freedman in representing the rights to *Dracula* to Universal Pictures, the same studio's acquisition of a print of *Nosferatu*, and the identities of the actresses who portrayed Dracula's wives in Browning's film.

In conclusion, I want to thank a small number of colleagues whose time and advice and encouragement are ultimately responsible for this book reaching publication. My good friends Robert Guffey, Bill Kaffenberger, Constantine Nasr, and Robert Singer spent much time reading drafts of this book, as well as in the pursuit of research materials for it. The same was true of Carter B. Smith, DVM, whose vast communications with me were extremely valuable. Lastly, I would, as always, want to thank Tom Weaver (who carefully analyzed and proofed this book, which is much better for his input), and to my parents Don and Phyllis. All of these individuals deserve my undying gratitude.

Gary D. Rhodes, PhD
Belfast, Northern Ireland
May 2014

Foreword

REMOVE THE CLOAK OF DRACULA!

by Ramsey Campbell

Let me begin with a horrid confession. Until very recently I was no great fan of Tod Browning's film of *Dracula*. Part of the problem may have been that by the time I saw it in the seventies, I was already aware of all the major images and lines of dialogue, having encountered them in *Famous Monsters of Filmland* when I was scarcely even a teenager. As shown on British television, the film seemed not to give them life; the image was too soft to have much presence, the soundtrack was muffled by age, and the whole experience felt antiquated. It wasn't until I watched the recent Blu-ray restoration that I saw and heard how wrong I (or, if you'll absolve me, the television copy) had been. It was like viewing the film not merely for the first time but at its premiere, and I fell in love with it at once.

I'm happy to say that Gary Rhodes' monograph renews the movie for me afresh. He has returned to every source he could find and disinterred secrets of *Dracula* that might have been lost to the grave. Whatever you thought you knew about the Browning version, you'll learn more here. He deserves to rank with Van Helsing as investigator, except he's so much calmer.

He situates the film in the context of the contemporary reputation of the vampire, then traces the complex threads that led the director and producer towards their version of the tale, a route scattered with rediscovered documents of the time. He attunes our senses to the growth of sound on film and in particular Tod Browning's ear for it. He places the production in the context of that era's taste for mystery, from which the film strips away quite a bit of the obligatory broad humour while adding the unambiguous supernatural, virtually giving birth to the horror film. He resuscitates the phantom casting that haunts many movies before they start shooting – the actors who might have been remembered for roles that have survived the test of time, not least several possible incarnations of the vampire Count – and revives the careers of even the most minor players in the film. He shows us the shape-shifting that overtook the tale as it was transformed from novel through stage play into film script, including abandoned ideas that would not take form until Hammer filmed the story and Stephen King united vampirism with air travel. He scrutinises the production as closely as all the evidence allows, especially the improvements the director made during the shoot and those brought about in the editing. Rhodes even turns up comments from the preview, incidentally proving how in every era hostility to horror films uses the same basic language.

He offers an illuminating examination of how publicity molded the image of the film before it was released, and a detailed overview of how it was originally received (including a review that, incredibly, found the early scenes too slow). He traces the growth of "horror" as a positive term for a film – indeed, a selling point – as the film went on general release and spawned a brood of publicity stunts, at least one of which would have made master showman William Castle proud (and, who knows, might even have influenced him). Rhodes also finds a couple of instances of local censorship that are weirder than the film. He celebrates the progeny of

the Browning *Dracula*, both those bearing the Count's name and the one that borrows his uncanny trappings, and shows the film repeatedly rising from its grave, not to mention how for a while it lost some of its character to a new censorship.

Then there's the film's reputation, which sometimes suffers just as much as H. P. Lovecraft's from the repetition of received ideas about the work. Rhodes rescues it with a detailed comparative analysis, and follows this by comparing Browning's film with the (no longer) legendary Spanish-language version. In my view rightly, he finds the Lugosi superior – in fact I'd say that like the *Psycho* remake, it demonstrates that the original director's stylistic choices were the right ones. The entire book brings the film to new life, and I for one am grateful to Gary Rhodes. Like all the best film criticism and analysis, it makes me want to watch the film again.

Ramsey Campbell
Wallasey, Merseyside
September 2014

INTRODUCTION

Having researched and studied the history of cinema for much of my life, I can confidently argue that a number of Hollywood films have been extremely influential, whether on film narrative and style or on film industries and audiences: *The Birth of a Nation* (1915), *The Jazz Singer* (1927), *Citizen Kane* (1941), and *Star Wars* (1977) come to mind, to name but a few. Tod Browning's *Dracula* (1931) has been extremely influential as well, particularly in its effect on popular culture, on the horror film genre, and on the ongoing popularity of the vampire subgenre. And yet, I also believe that Browning's *Dracula* has often been misunderstood.

From the 1950s to the present, critics have often savaged *Dracula*, which is certainly their right, but so often they have (intentionally or not) relied upon blatantly inaccurate descriptions of the film and the era in which it was made in order to generate evidence to support their opinions. Then, during the 1990s, revisionist historians even began to claim that Browning did not even direct part or all of *Dracula*. They relied on an extremely small amount of dubious evidence (specifically the subjective ruminations of one actor), but nonetheless achieved great success in popularizing their views.

These histories are often contradictory, arguing that Browning was largely an absentee director while simultaneously blaming him for every aspect of *Dracula* that is – in their view, at least – poorly conceived or executed. Put another way, they present a paradox rarely presented in film studies: that of the film director who did not direct his or her own film. In response, one could easily propose a counter paradox: that Tod Browning did direct the film, whatever he did or did not do on a film set, as it was his fame (in the industry and the fan press) and, more particularly, his vision (as is apparent in his pre-*Dracula* work) that allowed for the film's creation. In other words, it would be just as easy to argue that Browning directed *Dracula* even if he did not direct *Dracula*.

At any rate, it is important to note that these revisionist accounts feature negative critiques of *Dracula* as a film, and place value on building causal arguments in which an allegedly problematic (or even absentee) director presided over a problematic shoot that went into a problematic post-production phase: thus, the resulting film is problematic. Such a concocted narrative is hardly necessary, as troubled productions have resulted in films regarded as canonical, while other shoots that transpire without difficulty have resulted in bland and forgettable blockbusters.

Nevertheless, many film buffs and scholars have readily accepted these causal arguments about *Dracula*, even though they are fraught with inaccuracies. Perhaps this is due less to their merits than to their sheer repetition, as repetition alone can regrettably breed confidence. The situation calls to mind Michel Foucault's observation that, whereas the monuments of the past once became documents, modern history transforms documents into monuments.[1] In the case of Browning's *Dracula*, the revisionist story has become set in stone, concretized into a monument of film history. Indeed, it is difficult to think of another important film that has suffered such a large number of false premises, incorrect data, and wild speculation.

During the past two decades, it is true that a number of scholars have tried to view Browning's cinematic output (including *Dracula*) in more robust and analytical terms than have, say, film fans writing about movie history. Here I would specifically cite the important work published by such persons as Hugh Manon, Joyce Carol Oates, Andrew Sarris, Matthew Solomon, and others.[2] Despite such efforts, I believe the dominant narrative about Browning's *Dracula* remains deeply flawed and sorely needs to be reassessed.

In this book, I make extensive use of hundreds of surviving primary sources, re-examining those used in prior histories as well as relying on many that have languished unknown in various archives. While some of them have surfaced due to time-consuming detective work, others have been readily available, yet still ignored by previous historians. For example, the *Hollywood Reporter* began publication in September 1930, shortly before *Dracula* went into production. Despite that fact and the publication's ongoing renown, historians writing about *Dracula* in the past have ignored its importance and, as a result, the unique information about the film that it published.

Synthesizing these hundreds of sources, I have constructed a new history of Tod Browning's *Dracula*, one that will I hope provide a much-needed counterargument to the dominant narrative.

Understanding the fact that *Dracula* is a film made by an American director and produced by an American studio for an American target audience, Chapter 1 of this book chronicles the history of vampire lore in the United States in order to provide a relevant context, one that recounts not a mere chronology of events, but rather a succession of different eras, from the focus on imported folklore in the eighteenth century to the convergence of the same with imported fictional entertainment in the nineteenth century.

By the dawn of the twentieth century, vampires in America faced a major disruption due to the renown of Philip Burne-Jones' 1897 painting *The Vampire* and Rudyard Kipling's poem of the same name. Mass media complicated common understandings of the term "vampire," which came to suggest not the supernatural creature, but instead a woman who exerts sexual power over men, bleeding them of their financial resources before moving onto yet another victim. The disruption resulted largely from the popularity and frequency of films featuring this new kind of vampire, as well as of actresses like Theda Bara who became associated with such roles.

What this history means is that for over 150 years the supernatural vampire held sway in America, but – despite the publication of Bram Stoker's *Dracula* in New York in 1899 – the power of cinema and the larger entertainment industry meant a new kind of vampire became the more prominent within the space of fifteen years or less. These two different vampires

struggled for dominance in American culture, with the Broadway success of Hamilton Deane and John L. Balderston's stage adaptation of Stoker's novel in 1927 becoming a key player in the saga.

Importantly, Tod Browning realized that his *Dracula* would have to teach audiences about supernatural vampires, reclaiming them for an emergent sound film genre by restoring the pre-twentieth century definition. Here his task was difficult, not least because (as Chapter 7 will describe), studio publicity for his *Dracula* would draw upon the Burne-Jones/Kipling vampire as part of an effort to lure women to the box-office.

Rumors have persisted that Browning wanted to direct *Dracula* for some years before he had the opportunity, and – thanks to new research uncovered for this book, disclosed in Chapter 2 – we know now with certainty that Browning attempted to do so as early as 1920, pitching a film version to Universal Pictures that very year. While the studio declined to produce it, this information underscores how deeply committed Browning was to the story. It also helps us to re-evaluate his other films, particularly *London After Midnight* (1927) and *Mark of the Vampire* (1935), which should be viewed as his two other (loose) screen adaptations of *Dracula*, their narratives altered in large measure to avoid charges of copyright infringement.

But Browning's ten-year odyssey to direct an official adaptation of *Dracula* was stymied in large measure because studios – in an era before the "horror movie" codified as a coherent genre bearing that name – viewed the story as unfilmable, believing it would be too gruesome for American audiences unaccustomed to serious depictions of the supernatural. As Chapter 2 will show, another important figure proved necessary for Browning's *Dracula* to become a reality: Carl Laemmle, Jr., whose father had named him head of production at Universal when he was only 21 years old.

"Junior Laemmle" (as he was known in the film industry and the press) was a bold and daring studio boss who bravely tried to reinvent Universal Pictures in 1929 and 1930, eschewing low-budget movies in order to produce a smaller number of prestigious films that challenged audience sensibilities, as he did with *All Quiet on the Western Front* (1930), an American war film sympathetic to German soldiers, a movie that featured no female lead or happy ending. Junior Laemmle's production policy seems all the more radical when we consider that he pursued it even after the Great Depression was underway. *Dracula* would come to the screen thanks to Laemmle and Browning, even though the former was nearly three decades younger than the latter.

For Laemmle, choosing Browning as *Dracula*'s director was an extremely important decision. The film became one of the studio's two super-productions of the second half of 1930. Some historians have speculated with no evidence that the studio was worried about Browning's abilities, to the extent that Laemmle may have even had another director ready to take over for him. But such beliefs belie the historical record (including Browning's successful direction of the 1930 Universal film *Outside the Law* only months earlier), just as they defy logic, as no studio boss would have knowingly placed an untrustworthy director in charge of a major production, and certainly not while risking everything to enact a new production strategy when the American economy was crumbling before his very eyes.

Indeed, as Chapter 4 will illustrate, Laemmle took extreme care with the film's screenwriting process, which involved a number of authors over a period of three months, including Pulitzer Prize-winner Louis Bromfield. An analysis of the script's evolution reveals much of value, ranging from the fact that it involved Tod Browning to the important conclusion that the shooting script drew upon numerous texts, including the Deane-Balderston stage play (which some historians have incorrectly cited as its only source), as well as Bram Stoker's novel, F. W. Murnau's *Nosferatu* (1922), and a range of original ideas contributed by the various screenwriters involved.

Histories of *Dracula*'s preproduction, production, and post-production have also relied upon the repetition of problematic evidence and unsubstantiated speculation. For example, the casting has been described as troubled, even though it was in fact a careful and calculated process. In Chapter 3, for example, I divulge newly discovered information that the studio originally intended for a different actress to play the character Mina Seward, the role that eventually went to Helen Chandler.

In terms of the search for an actor to portray the title role, a common perception has been that Junior Laemmle became stuck with Bela Lugosi, an actor that he did not necessarily want. But here again the historical archive does not support such a story. By contrast, it seems clear that the studio achieved an important aim while casting the vampire count, gaining free publicity for it (and for the relatively unknown Bela Lugosi) in newspapers and trade publications over a period of many weeks.

As for *Dracula*'s production process, little has generally been written outside of actor David Manners' memory that he did not recall being directed by Browning, but was instead directed by Karl Freund, the film's cinematographer. Using Manners' brief comments in interviews, some historians have argued the aforementioned case that Browning did not direct the film.

Certainly this argument is problematic for various reasons, the first being that the story defies logic. Had Browning not directed the film, he would have been fired. Had Browning not directed the film, the assistant director would have assumed the role (rather than a cinematographer). And just because a director does not speak to a particular actor does not mean that he is not directing, as he might instead have been coaching other actors or attending to an array of other kinds of duties that involve everything from the film's budget to planning sessions with behind-the-scenes personnel.

Brief memories of one actor who appears only in certain scenes certainly should not be used to detail the days and weeks when he was not present on the set. And the brief memories of one person are finally just that. The lack of extensive interviews with other key cast or crew about the production has elevated Manners' unchecked comments to a status beyond that which even he likely intended. Chapter 5 explores these issues at great length.

Chapter 5 also compares *Dracula*'s shooting script to the completed film and thus reveals dozens of changes that occurred during the production, from individual words spoken by actors to the creation of alternate scenes. Universal founder Carl Laemmle, Sr. was not at the studio for the bulk of the shoot, and Junior Laemmle was away from the studio at one point as well. During the production, *Dracula*'s associate producer E. M. Asher was also overseeing the studio's other super-production, so he could not have been on the set each day. And not even Browning's most virulent critics have suggested that cinematographer Freund was rewriting dialogue – indeed, entire scenes – from the very beginning of the shoot. Forgetting paradoxes and counter-paradoxes, it is possible to determine that Browning directed *Dracula*, whether or not he spoke regularly to one particular actor.

Prior histories of *Dracula*'s post-production have also been beset with problems, relying on one brief and second-hand account of what Browning allegedly said about a television broadcast of *Dracula* in order to construct the completely unsupported assertion that he was hardly involved in the editing process, or, in a related version of events, that Browning edited his own version, which was then taken away from him and re-edited by the studio. Here again contradictions emerge, as some of the same historians who claim Browning did not direct *Dracula* (or most of it) argue that he in fact edited something of a director's cut of it.

As Chapter 6 proves, *Dracula*'s post-production was a complicated process. At least one version was edited, then more footage was shot, then at least a second version emerged, at least one preview screening occurred, more footage was shot, and then more editing occurred. Primary sources suggest that there were at least three versions of the film created during an organic and ongoing editing process that unfolded little different than studio norms of the period.

Amazingly, many prior histories of *Dracula* have also claimed that the film received negative reviews during its original 1931 release, with repeated attention given to a single sentence published in the *Hollywood Filmograph*. As Chapters 8 and 9 prove, *Dracula* actually received overwhelming praise from New York newspaper critics and film industry trade publications immediately after its premiere. The same was true of reviews published in movie fan magazines and newspapers across America. By contrast, the *Hollywood Filmograph* was a minor trade publication that did not critique the film until several weeks after its premiere. This book also reveals for the first time that the oft-quoted review was in fact one of two *different* reviews of *Dracula* published in the *Filmograph*, further evidence of how the known review has assumed much too large a role in *Dracula* histories.

Dracula's box-office success and influence on future films also deserves renewed attention. For example, a hitherto-unknown primary source discovered during the research for this book proves that Junior Laemmle weighed three different possible sequels to *Dracula* within mere weeks of the film's original release. Chapters 8 through 10 explore these various issues by examining the film's premiere, its general release, and its re-emergence in the years that followed in the form of sequels, reissues, and restorations.

Given the sheer volume of errors and problems that exist in prior histories of Browning's *Dracula*, it is necessary for us to pause and consider once again how and why this situation resulted. Certainly many different writers have repeated the same mistakes, and – while I will not ascribe any intentionality to them – it does seem to me that much of what has been written on horror films is not unlike how the genre itself functions, meaning repetition of what has gone before, though in the case of historiography such repetition represents an all-too-trusting faith in the prior written word. In short, mistakes were made and other authors have repeated them.

In some quarters, the zeal to decry *Dracula* is strong, and at times inexplicable. Certainly anyone is entitled to dislike a film, and should do so if they are led to form such an opinion. Works of art deserve detractors as much as they deserve supporters, as their unique qualities will and should keep them from appealing to everyone. Our passion for the cinema and our emotional reactions need not be explained or justified to anyone. Quite the opposite. We should decide what we like and do not like, and we are also entitled to change our minds on such matters, in part or in whole.

As Chapter 11 records, negative critiques of *Dracula* date to the 1950s and continue to the present day. However, to buttress their arguments, such critics have often relied on flawed evidence. They have made numerous mistakes in describing given shots or edits within the film. They have wrongly counted the number of individual musical compositions within the film, and have wrongly claimed that blood only appears onscreen once during its running time (as opposed to *twice*, which it does). They have gone so far as to argue that an improvised cardboard lampshade in one of the film's sets is a sign of Browning's poor direction, even though careful observation reveals its placement to be intentional.

And yet, despite groping for any possible reason to fault the film, no matter how trivial or flimsy, these critics have failed to noticed a quartet of continuity errors in the film, two of which I announced in a previous published essay, and the third and fourth being mentioned for the first time in Chapter 11. As a result, these three errors might not exemplify the film's weaknesses, but rather the fact that sleight-of-hand editing trickery from 1930-31 has eluded modern critics who have actively searched for reasons to disparage the film.

George Melford's Spanish-language version of *Dracula* – produced and edited at roughly the same time as Browning's – has played a major role in critiques of the Browning film. Individual viewers will certainly have different reactions to these two versions of *Dracula*, and they should prefer whichever version they find most compelling. However, *Dracula*'s critics have often provided comparative data about them that is false. For example, despite what has been published, Browning's *Dracula* features fewer continuity errors and less dependence on proscenium framing than Melford's. Browning's version also features a faster pace and a more extensive use of moving camera than Melford's. These mathematical certainties – as well as other points of comparison – are explored at length in Chapter 12.

Like most people, I generally perceive history as a linear succession of events, something akin to links in a chain. However, while considering the trajectory of *Dracula*'s modern criticism, I cannot help but think of Walter Benjamin's discussion of Paul Klee's painting, *Angelus Novus*. For Benjamin, the painting became a visual metaphor for a different perception of history, the angel in the painting witnessing history not as a chain of events, but instead as "one single catastrophe which keeps piling wreckage upon wreckage."[3] I am also reminded of my colleague Robert Guffey's comments about Browning's *Dracula*. The piled wreckage of *Dracula* criticism constitutes a narrative about, in Guffey's words, "perceptual psychology and the fact that human beings (if told something often enough and with great conviction) will simply believe it without examining the matter for themselves. Pretty soon an unsupported rumor becomes a possibility, and a possibility becomes a fact, and a fact becomes common knowledge."[4] Put another way, the documents become monuments.

Despite having written this study of Browning's *Dracula*, I do not propose to change anyone's mind about whether they should or should not "like" the film. However, it would be my aim in these pages to rectify factual errors made regarding *Dracula*'s history and its narrative and aesthetic content, as well as to propose alternative views on the same.

It is my hope that this book will play a worthwhile role in what becomes an ongoing process, reclaiming *Dracula* from a myriad of problematic analyses and incorrect historical data rife in the published record.

1. Foucault, Michel. *The Archaeology of Knowledge and the Discourse on Language*, trans. A. M. Sheridan Smith (New York: Harper and Row, Harper Colophon, 1972): 8-9.
2. See, for example: Manon, Hugh. "Seeing Through Seeing Through: The *Trompe l'Oeil* Effect and Bodily Difference in the Cinema of Tod Browning." *Framework: The Journal of Cinema and the Media*, Vol. 47, No. 1 (Spring 2006): 60-82; Oates, Joyce Carol. "*Dracula* (Tod Browning, 1931): The Vampire's Secret." *Southwest Review* Vol. 76, No. 4 (Autumn 1991): 498-510; Sarris, Andrew. *"You Ain't Heard Nothin' Yet": The American Talking Film, History and Memory* (New York: Oxford University Press, 1998): 80; Solomon, Matthew. "Reframing a Biographical Legend." *Authorship and Film*. Ed. by David Gerstner and Janet Staiger (New York: Routledge, 2003): 235-246.
3. Benjamin, Walter. "Theses on the Philosophy of History." In *Illuminations*, trans. Harry Zohn (New York: Schocken, 1968): 257.
4. Guffey, Robert. Email to Gary D. Rhodes. 29 Sept. 2011.

Chapter 1
THE VAMPIRE IN AMERICA

In April of 1892, a group of men in New York City formed a new society. They called themselves "The Vampires," and held monthly dinners featuring such foods as "fried souls." Prominently featured on their table was a "loving cup filled with 'vampires blood'"; a light inside of it caused its red wine to glow. After drinking their toasts, members sang the following lyrics:

By gravestones cold and white
We spread our wings at night;
Over the mounds we love to dance
And wake a corpse right out of his trance,
His trance, trance, trance.[1]

According to one newspaper account, The Vampires' meeting room sported a "grinning skeleton of Christopher Columbus leaned up in one corner of the room and skulls hung from every chandelier. In the center of the room was a coffin, and at its head a cross and a candelabra, and at its foot an ear of corn standing on end. A large vampire, with burnished wings and big red eyes, perched on a steel slack wire, holding a skull in its beak."[2]

Little else is known about The Vampires, who proclaimed that they were not superstitious, but had banded together to help each other out, after the fashion of most men's organizations of the period. However, the society's existence highlights two important facts. One is that it proves that at least some Americans in the late nineteenth century knew about vampirism. And the second is that some of those same Americans were very much interested in the subject: the society's members were fans of vampire folklore, gathering at regular meetings in the United States some five years before Bram Stoker published his 1897 novel *Dracula* in England.

Chronicles of vampire folklore and literature are many, as are histories of Stoker's *Dracula*. Perhaps the most influential is Raymond T. McNally and Radu Florescu's *In Search of Dracula* (1972), which successfully popularized the (problematic, or at least overly simplified) notion that the fifteenth-century Wallachian prince Vlad the Impaler

Bela Lugosi in a publicity still for Tod Browning's *Dracula* (1931). *(Courtesy of Kristin Dewey)*

was the model for Stoker's Dracula character.[3] Such books have generally offered a global account of the subject, many of them vampirically feeding off of one another, publishing and republishing the same (admittedly fascinating) information (and misinformation), referring repeatedly to important texts like *Varney the Vampyre, or the Feast of Blood* (1847), an often celebrated and yet seldom-read British penny-dreadful.

Collectively, these vampire histories provide important (even if repetitious) background information to Tod Browning's film *Dracula* (1931). However, despite the sheer number of scholars who have tackled the subject, none of them has concentrated solely on the context of vampirism in America, meaning the story of how the vampire and Dracula developed in US history and culture in the years prior to Tod Browning's film.

Such a context is crucial for two reasons. First is the fact that the 1931 version of *Dracula* was an American film produced by an American studio and helmed by an American director. Secondly, a focus on America allows us to understand better American audiences, the key target audience for the 1931 film. For two centuries, if not longer, the subject of vampires regularly surfaced in American culture, creating an evolving understanding of the supernatural character, one that faced a major disruption at the turn of the twentieth century and placed great pressure on the very meaning of the word vampire. It was into this lengthy and complicated history that Tod Browning's *Dracula* intervened.

Folklore and Superstitions

Discussing vampire mythology in 1844, a newspaper in Pennsylvania noted the fact that "so much has been written" on the subject, an indicator of its apparent popularity with readers.[4] Over four decades later, an article in the *Kansas City Times* claimed: "Among weird and unnatural horrors of romance and legend, the vampire has always held the foremost place. The casual wraith, the family ghost, the specter in clanking chains, and even the witch's 'familiar' are nowhere in comparison with this graveyard ghoul, said to sustain its loathsome existence by sucking the blood of living persons."[5]

Excerpt from an article published in the *American Weekly Mercury* of Philadelphia on January 7, 1732.

It is difficult to determine when the American press first tackled the subject of vampires, but it certainly occurred several decades prior to the Revolutionary War. For example, in 1732, the *American Weekly Mercury* published an allegedly non-fiction account from Hungary regarding "certain Dead Bodies (called here Vampyres) [that] killed several persons by sucking out all their blood."[6] Six years later, the *New England Weekly Journal* printed tales of Eastern European vampires, including one discovered in a grave "with his eyes wide open, his countenance fresh and ruddy, with a natural respiration, though dead and utterly motionless."[7]

In the years that followed, various American publications continued to report on vampirism in Eastern Europe and Russia.[8] In 1823, Boston's *New Monthly Magazine and Literary Journal* provided readers with what was perhaps the most extensive treatment of the subject up to that point in American history:

> *The corporeal grossness, the substantially 'palpable to feeling as to sight,' of this monster of superstition, renders it singularly terrific, and lays hold on the mind with a sense of shuddering and sanguinary horror which belongs to few of the aerial demons of imagination, however ghastly or malignant. Fancy (for such tricks will flit across the fancy of the least superstitious) – fancy your friend with whom you are walking, arm-in-arm, or your mistress on whose bosom your head reposes, a spirit – a Gnome or an Undine – or any mere spirit – the idea is startling; if pursued it may lead an active imagination to a disagreeable sense of the possibility of happiness being an imposition, and pleasure 'an unreal mockery,' – but it is not overpoweringly painful; – but let the idea of your companion or your mistress being a Vampyre cross the brain – the blood would run*

chill, and every sense be oppressed by the bare supposition, childish and absurd as it would be felt to be – 'twould shake the disposition With thoughts beyond the reaches of our souls'.[9]

The same author delighted in recounting vampire tales from around the globe, drawing in part on the pioneering research of the French Benedictine monk Dom Augustin Calmet.[10]

Beyond simply reporting stories from other countries, at least one American journalist claimed to have personally investigated the subject during the 1870s.[11] Then, in 1896, the *Boston Globe* described a community in Rhode Island where local citizens believed in vampires, a story that brought the subject much closer to home.[12] Another article published that same year reported, "many people [in Rhode Island] have been digging up the dead bodies of relatives for the purpose of burning their hearts."[13] Such commentaries followed from the "Mercy Brown Vampire Incident" of 1892, in which a corpse was exhumed in Rhode Island to halt the perceived influence of the undead. Novelist Bram Stoker apparently learned of the case when writing his 1897 novel *Dracula*.

Widespread discussion of vampires led various writers to analyze their roots.[14] In 1872, one American newspaper attributed the folklore to three factors: "a sort of epidemic superstition among ignorant persons; some of the phenomena of trance or epileptic sleep; and special monomaniac diseases which it is the province of the physician to study."[15] And yet, even while discounting vampire folklore, journalists conjured memorable descriptions of them. In 1893, L. J. Vance told readers that a vampire "comes at night by your bedside as a horrid shape. It has a human figure and face; its eyes are glassy; its mouth is bloody; its flesh is livid."[16]

Explanations of such folklore in the nineteenth century also focussed on the vampire bat.[17] "There is a bat in South America which sometimes sucks the blood of animals," the *Saturday Evening Post* informed readers in 1874, "and if this species once existed in Europe, it may have given rise to the belief that the dead sometimes rise from their graves and nourish themselves on the blood of the living."[18]

Vampire bats captured the imagination of many Americans in the nineteenth century, so much so that one store in New York displayed a living specimen in its window in 1893:

It is confined in a little wire-grated cage, not more than two feet in height and even less in length and breadth. There it hangs from the top bars, day after day, apparently lifeless, except for the slightest movement of the chest. Now and then it moves its head or sips from the little jar of water placed in a corner of the cage.

… The eyes are small and have an intelligent expression. The tongue is long and sharp and feels as if it were covered with tiny warts. It has six small teeth in the lower jaw and a full row of them in the upper. The little beast is not at all vicious, but rather playful, and seems to know its master well.[19]

In this case, an exhibition of a live vampire bat simultaneously helped to explain the roots of supernatural vampires, as well as to fuel the growing interest in them.

Vampires in Popular Fiction

By the nineteenth century, many Americans understood the concept and mythology of vampires, so much so that journalists regularly adopted the term to use as a metaphor for all kinds of perceived social problems, ranging from slave owners to politicians.[20] By the early 1880s, the term "vampire" even became the name of a famous racehorse.[21]

Americans also learned about and often enjoyed the subject of vampires from the increasing role that such characters played in fictional literature and entertainment. For example, in 1819, the American press excitedly spread news of the publication of Lord Byron's short story *The Vampyre, A Tale*, with newspaper articles conveying the story of Byron's sojourn with "two daughters of William Godwin and a Mr. Shelley," all of whom were induced to write ghost stories, with "Miss Godwin's labours [published] under the title *Frankenstein*."[22]

As for *The Vampyre*, the *Rhode Island American* told readers in April 1819 that, "It is said to be of a most horrifick [sic] nature."[23] Such a description was apt. In the story, the mysterious Lord Ruthven appears in London and befriends a young Englishman named Aubrey, who eventually has a nervous breakdown. Ruthven then marries Aubrey's sister, leaving her for dead on their wedding night before making his escape. As the final line of the story explains: "Lord Ruthven had disappeared, and Aubrey's sister had glutted the thirst of a *Vampyre!*"

Reviewing *The Vampyre* after copies arrived on American soil, the *Ladies Literary Cabinet* dismissed it as being written:

> *…on the spur of the moment, as a catch-penny production, intended to replenish his Lordship's pocket, who has found travelling and the pleasures of Italy somewhat expensive. The Vampyre possesses no merit, unless it be meritorious to frighten young ladies out of their wits, and make them afraid to sleep alone; which, by the way, may produce the good effect of promoting matrimony.* [24]

Portrait of Robert Campbell Maywood, painted by Robert Jacob Hamerton in 1841 (Courtesy of the Victoria and Albert Museum)

Despite some negative reviews, *The Vampyre* seems to have been an immediate success with American readers. And Uriah Derrick D'Arcy quickly published a "burlesque" entitled *The Black Vampyre* in New York, the stated aim being to "ridicule" Byron's tale.[25]

Then – in what was likely the first performance of a vampire play in the United States – the Pavillion Theatre in New York staged *The Vampyre*, an apparently unauthorized and loose adaptation of the story.[26] Robert Campbell Maywood portrayed Lord Ruthven, making him the earliest forebear in America to the likes of Bela Lugosi in the twentieth century. Opening night of the "melo-drama" came in July 1819.

Then, in 1820, the American press divulged the shocking news that Lord Byron

Chapter 1 – THE VAMPIRE IN AMERICA

insisted that he was not the author of The Vampyre, a Tale. His disclaimer made news, as did the identity of the story's actual author: Byron's travelling companion, a physician named John William Polidori.[27] The revelation only served to increase The Vampyre's publicity in America.

By October of 1820, yet another theatrical adaptation of the story appeared in such cities as New York and Washington, D.C. Titled The Vampyre, or the Bride of the Isles, it had originally been written by James Robinson Planché for the London stage. One article in Boston reported than an actor named:

> Mr. Brown was the Vampyre, and when we assert that his contortions and distortions of countenance were even more hideous than the author could have conceived of his subject, we believe we do but express the opinion of a majority of the spectators.[28]

Another article on the Boston performance claimed that the play was "handsomely attended" and was "well-received."[29]

The Vampire, or the Bride of the Isles may well have influenced future stage versions of Dracula. As in Polidori's story, the play's Lord Ruthven appears mysteriously in England and exists for some time without being blamed for the horrible fates that befall those around him, a plot device that would return in stage and screen adaptations of Stoker's Dracula, including Browning's film.[30]

Versions of The Vampire, or the Bride of the Isles continued to be staged for the next several years, making it the key vampire play to appear at American theatres in the nineteenth century.[31] As an article in the New York Literary Journal noted in 1821, "Since the appearance of the story of the Vampire, the conversation of private parties has frequently turned to the subject, and the discussion has been prolonged and invigorated by the pieces brought at the theatres...."[32]

The subject's popularity resulted in vampire characters appearing in other American productions. For example, in 1846, the Boston Academy of Music performed Peter Josef von Lindpaintner's Overture to the Vampire from his opera

An 1856 program for Dion Boucicault's The Phantom.

22   Chapter 1 – THE VAMPIRE IN AMERICA

Artwork published in the *New York Herald* on August 12, 1894.

Der Vampyr.[33] However, the vampire's most notable theatrical appearance after Planché came in Dion Boucicault's two-act play *The Phantom* (originally titled *The Vampire* when it premiered in England). Unfortunately, *The Phantom* remains conspicuously absent from many modern vampire histories.

At its debut at Wallack's Theatre in New York in 1856, Dion Boucicault assumed the title role himself, a vampire named Alan Raby, with the plot unfolding in Wales at the ruins of Raby castle. According to one character, within the castle "dwells a terrible thing – man or fiend." Immediately after he speaks those words a clap of thunder rocks the theatre. From there, he describes careless travellers who wander into the ruins after nightfall. They are later found dead, "each with a wound in his throat in the right side, from which they have evidently bled to death – but no blood is spilt around, the face is white and fixed, as if it had died of horror." Cue another clap of thunder.

Boucicault clearly knew Polidori's tale, as he adopts Polidori's notion that moonlight can revive a vampire. Using that plot device, he created the following scene, which also features a wise character relying on the written word, something that Van Helsing would eventually do in Browning's *Dracula*:

> Col. Stop, Doctor. I command you.
> Rees. [*reading from a book on necromancy*] 'After death, his body must therefore be preserved from the moonlight, lest, by virtue of its rays, he might revive.' See – watching his heaving form – already the life comes back to him, limb by limb!
> Col. Hold! What would you do!
> Rees. Exterminate the phantom – into this black chasm, where the light of heaven never existed, I cast his body! – May his dark spirit sink as low into eternal perdition!

At that, the curtain closes on Act Two and the play abruptly ends. Such brevity recurs in the conclusion of numerous American horror films of the thirties, including Browning's *Dracula*.

In *The Phantom*, we can witness several other elements that reappear in future vampire tales. The vampire attempts to pass himself off as a normal human, much as Ruthven does in Polidori's story. And then – perhaps most notably – Boucicault inverts Polidori, allowing his vampire to be destroyed and his lead female character to survive and be reunited with her true love. Boucicault's conclusion is little different from Stoker's conclusion to *Dracula* in 1897, or, for that matter, Browning's to *Dracula* in 1931.

At least some critical reviews of *The Phantom* were positive. In 1856, one newspaper called it an "an interesting piece, [which] has created a favorable impression upon the audiences."[34] While *The Phantom* never became as successful as Boucicault's Irish-themed plays, theatres did stage it occasionally after its New York premiere. As late as 1870, a version of it appeared in Galveston, Texas.[35]

During the second half of the nineteenth century, the vampire in popular entertainment became a familiar enough character to allow for writers to craft parodies of it. In 1864, a "laughable" farce called *The Vampire, or, A Ghost in Spite of Himself* appeared at the Canterbury Hall in Washington, DC.[36] Other performers drew upon vampires as inspiration for various kinds of theatrical acts. For example, in 1891, a

Cartoon published in the *Omaha World Herald* (Omaha, Nebraska) on May 26, 1895.

24 Chapter 1 – THE VAMPIRE IN AMERICA

minstrel company offered a "Vampire Dance" as one of the "special features" of their show.[37] Such "vampire dance" acts would continue into the early twentieth century.[38]

Perhaps the clearest example of audience familiarity with vampires came in E. Terry's 1872 "burlesque" called *The Vampire*. The title character was "not exactly the demon of the old German legend, but a less dainty monster, who, instead of banqueting on the blood of beautiful maidens, is content to live upon the brains of other men."[39] In other words, the male lead was a plagiarist, with the term "vampire" being used as a metaphor in the world of fiction, much as it had already been used in non-fiction journalism.

Curiously, J. Sheridan Le Fanu's vampire short story *Carmilla* (which appeared in his collection *In a Glass Darkly*, published in London in 1872 and 1884) does not seem to have made any major impact in America in the nineteenth century.[40] By contrast, Stoker's novel *Dracula* became a major success in the United States, thus solidifying the vampire's move into popular American entertainment.

Bram Stoker's *Dracula*

Announcements regarding the publication of Bram Stoker's *Dracula* appeared in the American press in 1897, but it was not until 1899 – when Doubleday and McClure published the novel in New York – that it received widespread attention. And to be sure, its reception was not uniformly positive. "There are but two things of interest about the book," a critic for the *Chicago Tribune* advised. "One is a sense of wonder that any normal mind could conceive of ideas so loathsome, and the other that any one could get it printed."[41]

But various other newspapers heralded *Dracula*'s American publication, with the *Cleveland Plain Dealer* calling it a "romance for people of strong nerves."[42] The *Boston Journal* judged it to be the "grisliest story written in this

Advertisement published in the *Oregonian* on July 8, 1906.

end of the century. … The author has done his work artistically. His fancy never becomes absurdity."[43] Even greater praise appeared in the *Washington Post*, which described *Dracula* as a book of "infinite ingenuity and power."[44]

In addition to reviewing the novel, the American press also mentioned a possible stage adaptation. In late November of 1899, the *Boston Herald* reported the fascinating news: "Since arriving in Boston Bram Stoker, manager of Sir Henry Irving, has received a proposition to dramatize his latest book, *Dracula*. If it is put on the stage, *Dr. Jekyll and*

Mr. Hyde in comparison will, it is said, become a pleasing memory."[45] Discussion of the proposed theatrical version quickly disappeared from American newspapers, but the novel's popularity continued.

Mention of Bram Stoker in the American press during the early twentieth century generally listed *Dracula* as his most notable novel.[46] In 1908, one journalist even declared that *Dracula* placed Stoker "on a par" with Edgar Allan Poe.[47] And in 1911, the *Kansas City Star* informed readers about a "young Englishman" who allegedly became a "raving maniac after reading *Dracula*," adding that "fortunately Stoker has quit that line of literary effort, or he might contribute largely to populating the booby hatches."[48]

In America, *Dracula* soon played a role in other kinds of conversations, including those that revisited the vampire in folklore.[49] The name Dracula also became attached to at least one real-life villain. In 1906, a "wild man" lurked in the woods near one Long Island village, causing residents to shudder in a "state bordering on terror." According to a newspaper account, the local "watchword" became "Dracula, alive or dead."[50]

More commonly, though, *Dracula* became a key text in discussions of supernatural literature and stage plays.[51] Consider the following review of Bertha Kalich's 1914 play *Mariana*:

> *Bram Stoker, in his horrible book,* Dracula, *made believable the most unbelievable of circumstances – simply by absolute accuracy of portrayal and artistic of description – and Bertha Kalich does the same with* Mariana. *She has taken a play that would if only read be interesting only to an alienist – for the plot is as far beyond the pale of reason as was* Dracula.[52]

Three years later, author John Willard was said to be working on a play "in which the mystery and romance of the Orient are tinged with the horror of *Dracula*."[53]

In 1912, a review entitled *Broadway to Paris* featured Gertrude Hoffman as a vampire in the "Dance Dracula."[54] One journalist described the dance as "vampirish," adding that it presented a kind of admirable even if not beautiful form of "grotesqueness."[55] Here the vampire dances of the late nineteenth century merged with the popular currency of Stoker's character.

Without doubt, however, the most consistent Dracula on the American stage in the early twentieth century was a European acrobat who worked in vaudeville as early as 1902.[56] Theatres billed him as Dracula, and – whether or not it was in fact his real name – he was clearly aware of the association to Stoker's character. Year after year he used supernatural descriptions for himself and his act, as can be seen in the following review from 1908:

> *Dracula … 'The Frolicsome Demon,' who presents some surprises in the way of refined acrobatic-contortion exhibitions, performing the most difficult deeds of daring with an ease and grace that amazes and entertains. The stage environments are elegant as is the paraphernalia upon which this wizard of the 'art flexible' disports himself, adding finish, if finish could be added to a perfect performance.*
> *Dracula, in the guise of Mephisto, is seen standing upon a pedestal. Lightning flashes from the point of his sword, disclosing myriads of demons surrounding him. Weird sounds are heard reverberating through the caverns as though calling to the demons to come home, when quick as a flash is the transformation! The demons have disappeared and instead of the dark,*

yawning mouths of the cavern is a beautiful stage setting gorgeous with all the colors of the rainbow in harmonious splendor, and Dracula, divesting himself of his demoniacal garb, presents an astonishing exhibition of the most marvellous feats of flexibility upon pedestals of varying heights and swinging, burnished bars – accomplishments daring and diverting, yet finished and faultless, concluding with a routine of sensational contortion feats upon a swinging trapeze.[57]

It is difficult to determine what became of this particular Dracula. He appeared onstage until at least 1916, and he continued to use stage settings and publicity that drew upon the supernatural.[58] For example, in 1913, he called his act *Mephistopheles at Play*.[59] But at a given point in the late teens, he disappeared from the American entertainment industry.

By contrast, Stoker's *Dracula* remained popular. But with all of its success in America, the novel appeared at a time when the very word "vampire" became applied to a very different kind of character, one that would become the more prominent in American popular culture of the early twentieth century.

Dracula, the "Frolicsome Demon," a contortionist of some repute in the early 20th century.

A Hank of Hair

In 1854, the play *Invisible Prince! Or, the Island of Tranquil Delights* featured four "vampire robbers" named Ruffino, Desperado, Sanguino, and Stiletto.[60] According to a publicity poster, these vampires engaged not in bloodsucking, but instead in a "terrific combat." The occasional use of the term vampire to suggest criminals rather than supernatural creatures continued into the twentieth century, most famously in Louis Feuillade's French film serial *Les Vampires* (1915-16), which was distributed in the United States. However, prior to the serial's American release were such films as *Vampires of the Coast* (Pathe, 1909), *The Forest Vampires* (Domino, 1914), *Vampires of the Night* (Greene Features, 1914), and *Vasco, the Vampire* (Imp, 1914): all of them depicted vampires as non-supernatural criminals.

It does not seem that there was ever a time in American history when the word vampire was predominantly understood to suggest lawbreakers instead of supernatural bloodsuckers; in fact, such usage was relatively rare. However, these examples speak to the potential malleability of the term, which underwent a major evolution at the end of the nineteenth century.

In May 1897, American newspapers announced the "sensational" London exhibition of Philip Burne-Jones' painting *The Vampire*. Some newspapers printed line art drawings of the painting, while others were left to describe it as best they could through words alone. The *Cleveland Plain Dealer* wrote that *The Vampire* "shows a room flooded with moonlight, in which a dying man, with a wound in his breast, lies sleeping. Over him lies a beautiful woman – who has just drained him of his life blood." The newspaper also mentioned that Rudyard Kipling had written a poem of the same name. "Kipling has seen in the female vampire an allegory of the worthless woman," the *Plain Dealer* explained, "who loves a man … until at last he finds she has stolen all or the better part of his life."[61]

Artwork depicts Burne-Jones painting *The Vampire*.
Published in the *Cleveland Plain Dealer* on June 26, 1898.

American newspapers published the full text of Kipling's poem as early as May 1897 and continued to do so during the weeks that followed.[62] Its famous first verse is as follows:

A fool there was and he made his prayer
(Even as you and I!)
To a rag and a bone and a hank of hair.
(We called her the woman who did not care)
But the fool he called her his lady fair
(Even as you and I!)

While some members of the press drew allusions to supernatural vampires, Kipling's poem makes clear that he was conjuring another kind of character. As Burne-Jones said in an 1897 interview published in America, "I intended to paint one of those women who … drain the life blood of a man and Kipling's verses just hit the idea."[63] Though borne out of a metaphorical use of folkloric vampirism, Burne-Jones and Kipling had dispatched a very different creation.

In 1897, the American press covered the story of an "English actress" who threatened to sue Burne-Jones because the woman he painted resembled her.[64] Journalists also wrote about Burne-Jones' visit to America with *The Vampire* in 1902.[65] Shortly after his arrival, rumors spread that Burne-Jones sold the painting to W. K. Vanderbilt, though the story was quickly refuted.[66]

The impact of the Burne-Jones painting and Kipling's poem on American usage of the word "vampire" had an immediate effect. In 1899, the *New York Times* wrote:

> *People nowadays carelessly use the word 'vampire' as a stronger and trifle more loathsome term than 'parasite.' Burne-Jones once painted a picture called the* Vampire. *It was a very beautiful woman leaning over a man she had just slain. And Kipling wrote some symbolic verses about it.*[67]

The journalist added his view that "Probably few persons know what the real vampire is," the Burne-Jones depiction having so quickly displaced the supernatural character in popular culture.

Another example of the shifting definition of vampires can be seen in a *Chicago Tribune* article of 1903:

> *'What is a vampire, anyway?' asked a young woman looking at the Burne-Jones picture now on exhibition.*
> *'A vampire,' [replied] her companion. 'A vampire is the rag and a bone and a hank of hair that Kipling talks about.'*
> *They probably had not spent a portion of their youthful lives in a small town visited occasionally by the 'greatest show on earth' with its sideshow. If they had they would have known all about the 'blood sucking vampire.' They would have dreamed about it....*[68]

A still photograph from Kalem's *The Vampire* (1913).

Actress Theda Bara, the leading "vamp" of American cinema.

Exasperated by the confusion over the term, the journalist proceeded to describe vampires in great detail, both in their folkloric roots and in Stoker's novel.

However, the Burne-Jones/Kipling vampire would not die easily. In 1909, Porter Emerson Brown adapted the painting and poem into a novel published by Grosset and Dunlap. He also wrote a stage adaptation, which opened in New York City the same year. *A Fool There Was* featured Katharine Kaelred as the "Woman," or – as the *New York Times* called her – the "Vampire Lady," who "calls all her victims Fools" and then "asks for more kisses."[69] She ruins the male lead, who is both a husband and a father. At times during the play, characters quote directly from Kipling's poem, drawing a strong link between the two.

Despite some mediocre reviews, the play became a success, and it had an immediate impact on nickelodeon-era American cinema. In 1910, Selig produced a film titled *The Vampire*, which quoted Kipling in its intertitles and attempted to bring the Burne-Jones painting to life. The *Nickelodeon* told readers, "This is the latest embodiment of Kipling's famous poem, and probably the last, for the vampire's vogue is on the wane. We have had her in poetry, in painting, in drama, in the dance, and now in the photoplay."[70]

But the prediction of this kind of vampire's demise was extremely premature. In 1912, another film version of *The Vampire* appeared at American theatres. Kalem produced its own film *The Vampire* in 1913; that same year, Vitagraph touted its film *The Vampire of the Desert* as a "dramatic adaptation of Kipling's well-known poem."[71] Then, in 1914, Kalem released *The Vampire's Trail*, in which a cabaret singer entices a young married man.

Also in 1914, Lubin shot a film entitled *A Fool There Was*, its title drawing on both the Brown play and the Kipling poem. But it would be a film of the same title released the following year that solidified the Burne-Jones/Kipling vampire into the American mind more than any other film, play, or novel. Produced by William Fox, *A Fool There Was* (1915) featured Theda Bara as "The Vampire," and the result remains a classic of early American cinema.[72]

Many audiences and critics responded favorably to the film and – given its publicity, intertitles, and storyline – readily drew the connection to Burne-Jones and Kipling. The *New York Dramatic Mirror* wrote:

Sheet music published in 1919.

> *It is bold and relentless; it is filled with passion and tragedy; it is right in harmony with the poem. For a few moments during the last reel we had fearful premonitions of the approach of a happy ending – the Fool turned into a repentant wise man – but fortunately there is no such inartistic claptrap. He is a wreck, he dies, and the Vampire continues on her path, red with the blood of men. The film, then, remains true to its theme, for which the producers are to be thanked.*
> *…The Vampire is a neurotic woman gone mad. She has enough sex attraction to supply a town of normally pleasing women, and she uses it with prodigal freedom. To come into contact with her is like touching the third rail, and all along the track we see, or hear about her victims.*[73]

The film's impact is hard to overestimate, including on the career of Theda Bara, whose persona as the screen's leading "vamp" still resonates even after the passage of a century.

But Theda Bara – whose first name was an anagram for "death" – was not alone in her particular vampire idiom. Many other screen vamps followed in the wake of Fox's version of *A Fool There Was*, including a Fox remake of the film in 1922. Others included Triangle's *The Wolf Woman* (1916), which caused the *Motion Picture Mail* to comment:

> *So we suppose we shall have to forgive Mr. [C. Gardner] Sullivan for writing* The Wolf Woman, *and granting that the picture public wants photoplays in which a 'wolf woman,' or a 'moth,' or a 'spider,' or some such vampires through five reels of celluloid, ruins men, 'weaves webs,' and all the rest of it, and that [the producing company] Triangle thought its duty to supply the public's demands.*

Chapter 1 – THE VAMPIRE IN AMERICA 31

MOVIE WEEKLY

Page Twelve

How to become a movie vamp
by Jimmie · the janitor's son

Product of the dumbwaiters gives instructions *to would-be screen stars* on how to get that way

As related to Edward Ettinger

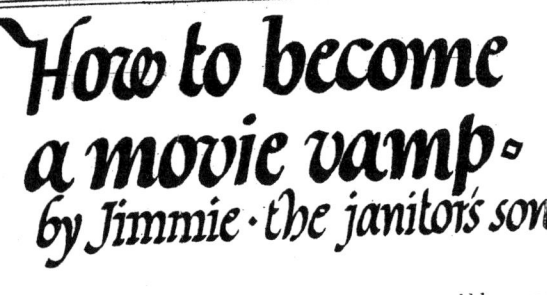

The slant eyes of *Nita Naldi* require no practice in the art of vamping.

When it comes to vamping, *Pola Negri* has a little way that is all her own, and her method will bear studying.

THE FIRST thing what is absolutely necessary for a girl what is got a suppressed desire to become a vampire is, namely, that she must have a pair of silk stockings. Now, I been givin' this here matter considerable attention, and I know from my own personality observation that every girl in these United States is got the first requirement, and therefore is a eligible vampire.

In this business everything is turned upside down. You don't have to be no college graduate at all. You don't have to have nothin' in your head so long as you got somethin' in your stockin', but it's got to have a little better curves than a broom stick.

Right here is a idea for a smart business man. We got schools what cultivates voices, so why shouldn't we have schools what cultivates calfs. (No farmers needed.) Of course, I'd like to be in charge of a school like this here and meet all the applicants personally, but that there sweetheart of mine, Maggie, is so old-fashioned. She ain't a bit broad-minded.

All right, girls, let's start. Now that you got your silk stockings on, you gotta get a dress what is very tight on your form. Your kid sister's dress will surely be tight. The big idea in this is that all the curves should stand out like a house afire. Be liberal with the safety pins, sister, cause you got to be careful you shouldn't come out.

The next and the most important thing is the scenery. Every vamp needs a work bench, a place for action. You gotta get a couch, a sofa, or a chaise lounge. Without this no vampire is complete. It's like fly paper without the glue on it. If you ain't got one of these work benches, you're gonna be outa luck. Take off a hour each day and practice laying down on the sofa in a vampirish way, what means that at least one silk stocking is got to show. The regulation for graduated, experienced vampires is one inch below the knee. Now throw up your arms and clasp them like they is behind someone's neck and draw them down like you is enticing some man from the male sex.

Of course, I'd like to come to all my pupils' houses and give them a regular demonstration, cause I know all the fine points in the game. I know some points what nobody else knows, but like I said before, Maggie is old-fashioned and she ain't a bit broad-minded.

Now for the real experience. That's what counts. If you are a married woman you orter be able to get all the free help you want. You can practice it on the milk man, the ice man, or, in a pinch, even on the cop. From what my pupils write me, you'll find these people very obliging. They'll even take time from their own business to help you with your career. If your husband is a traveling salesman, it will be a great help to you, cause some husbands ain't broad-minded.

If you're a single girl, practice on a dummy or else on one of the boys from the office. One girl writes me that she discovered that one of the boys was a ex-vampire teacher. This bird wasn't satisfied with the work and he had her rehearsin' for four hours. She says she wasn't a bit tired when she got through. He explained everything so nicely. She says it's a pleasure to follow my course. The young man is very interested in her education and promised to teach her even if it took a whole year to do it.

When you goes to Hollywood, it ain't no use taking no written recommendations from your gentlemen friends. These here directors is all imported from Missouri and you got to show 'em. They is all looking for vampires, and they'll give you a chance to show your stockings—I mean your talent.

HERE is a few letters what proves how good my course is:

"Dear Jimmie:
I invited my boss to come down and practice with me. He gave me a $5.00 raise on Saturday. I'm so glad I took your course. Sadie O'Brien."

"Dear Jimmie:
Congratulations on your wonderful work. Your course is a blessing to mankind. Five girls in our office are taking it. The Boys."

"Dear Jimmie:
Five women in the town are taking your course, and it has ruined the milk business. X. Y. Z. Milk Co."

"Dear Jimmie:
My whole family wishes to thank you for the course. I practiced it on the butcher boy with wonderful results. He is leaving me lamb chops now and only charging me for soup meat. Minnie K. Jinks."

If they is anybody that doubts whether this course is on the level, they can look up my poleece record. I been in some of the best jails in the country and I don't care if I do say it myself.

And that ain't all, neither. Once a girl has took my vampire course she is eligible to go in the movies and give such screen stars as Nita Naldi and Pola Negri a race for their money.

Miss Naldi and Miss Negri ain't pupils of mine, but maybe if they was, they'd be better on the film sheets than they are. Cause what I don't know about movie vampires ain't known, that's all.

Why, some of the testimonials I get from my pupils would knock your eye out. That's why I'm not printin' 'em on this here page before you. No, sir; but they've made A Number One Vampires, and that ain't no fable, neither. And a vampire is what every girl wants to be and don't you forget it. That's why I'm in business.

Article published in *Movie Weekly* on July 21, 1923.

… There are people who prefer such films. To these photoplayers this [film] will be a great attraction. And they will talk about it long after the showing. On the other hand, there are many who would consider it – and all pictures of the type – 'shocking' and 'disgusting.' To these we switch on the 'stay away' signal.[74]

Disgusting or not, this kind of vampire film proliferated at movie theatres, to the extent that it quickly became parodied in such comedy shorts as *Vamping the Vamp* (1918), *The Vamp Cure* (1918), and *A He Male Vamp* (1920).[75] "It was [the Burne-Jones] portrait and Kipling's poem that started all of this modern vampire business that has become such a pest on stage and screen," one journalist noted in 1917.[76]

Vampires in the Roaring Twenties
In 1924, an article on Madeline Hurlock, a film actress known for her "vamp" roles, informed readers that:

It really doesn't make any difference what a vamp thinks about. A vamp isn't paid to think, anyway. Her mission is to wear slinky clothes and look mysteriously alluring, or alluringly mysterious, as the case may be.
As a matter of fact, it is all wrong to apply the name 'vampire' to a beautiful young woman. Call her a 'love pirate' or a 'heart bandit' or a 'home wrecker' if you choose, but that's far enough to go. A vampire is a horrible creature that stalks from the grave at midnight, eyes blazing and wolfish teeth champing – but read Dracula *by Bram Stoker (no ad intended) if you want to get the lowdown on vampires and were-wolves and such like demoniacal beings.*[77]

That same year, another journalist also attempted to explain the gulf that existed between the vampire/"vamp" of popular American culture and the "folklore of all ages" that was "replete with legends of true vampires."[78]

Here the use of the phrase "true vampires" designated those of the supernatural variety, who did appear in American culture during the teens, even if in a manner far less prominent than those of the Theda Bara variety. For example, in 1914, David McKay published the American edition of Dudley Wright's book *Vampires and Vampirism*, which compiled folklore from around the globe. Wright also offered a short history of the vampire in literature. In an attempt to clarify different meanings of the term, Wright appropriately even began his book with the question: "What is a vampire?"[79]

Fictional vampire literature continued to appear in the 1910s and 1920s as well, with F. Marion Crawford's short story *For the Blood is the Life* (published by Macmillan in the 1911 short story collection *Wandering Ghosts*) being perhaps the most notable. In it, Crawford graphically depicts both vampire and victim:

…the flickering light of the lantern fell on Angelo's white face, unconscious as if in sleep, and on his upturned throat, over which a very thin red line of blood trickled down into his collar; and the flickering light of the lantern played upon another face that looked up from the feast – upon two dead eyes that saw in spite of death – upon parted lips redder than life itself – upon two gleaming teeth on which glistened a rosy drop.

Despite Crawford's literary prowess, however, the screen vamp continued to reign as the primary vampire in American culture.

By 1921, *The Nation* discussed the growing effort by movie censors to confront the vamp:

What shall be done with the vampires? Do they not obviously corrupt the morals of the young – or have the young of today morals? And if they have no morals – as more than one passionate preacher has hinted – will not the vampires, those black-gowned, sylph-like, cigarette-smoking, eye-rolling enemies of their own sex, keep them from ever acquiring any?[80]

The publication hinted that the censors faced a "hopeless" task given the character's ongoing popularity.

While cinematic vamps gripped the imagination of many filmgoers, particularly younger viewers, Stoker's *Dracula* continued to be popular, far more so than the folklore gathered by Dudley Wright or the vampiric creations of F. Marion Crawford. In 1921, a journalist at the *Baltimore Sun* wrote, "I suppose there is not reader of these musings who does not know Bram Stoker's *Dracula*. In that cheap and flashy book, the terrible soon degenerates into the grotesque, and the reader ends it in weary disgust."[81] According to one American journalist in 1929, the novel *Dracula* had sold an average of 30,000 copies per year since its publication.[82]

Various references to Stoker's *Dracula* appeared during the twenties, as Amy Lowell's 1923 poem *A Dracula of the Hills* attests. Its verse covers "an incident which occurred in what could be any mountain community where superstition and 'signs' still play a part in the life of the simple folk." One review claimed, "The piece smacks of the supernatural quality of Huck Finn's adventures or Hawthorne's stories of the witchcraft days."[83]

But the Stoker novel achieved its greatest success in the 1920s as a stage play. The American press generally made little mention of the 1924 British production of *Dracula*, adapted for the stage by Hamilton Deane. However, what was reported seemed tantalizing, if not scandalous. In July of that year, the *Oregonian* told readers: "*Dracula*, a dramatization of the late Bram Stoker's novel, was produced in a small country town [in England] with remarkable results. Women fainted and men urged the actors to desist from their bloodthirsty conduct."[84]

More news appeared when the play opened in London in 1927, with the *New York Times* noting that its publicity touted "more thrills than the Grand Guignol, including a dark vault wherein reposes a corpse that crumbles to dust when a certain occult treatment is administered; also dire groans, giant bats with glowing eyes, and gibbering maniacs."[85] Another article in the same newspaper declared that *Dracula* was having "such a harrowing effect on the audiences that a trained nurse has been appointed by the theatre management to attend sufferers."[86]

After seeing the play in London, producer Horace Liveright purchased the rights for the American stage and hired writer John L. Balderston to "Americanize" Hamilton Deane's text.[87] After a few tryouts, *Dracula–The Vampire Play* opened on Broadway in October 1927, with Bela Lugosi portraying the title character. Born in 1882, Lugosi was as an actor in his native Hungary for at least fifteen years before moving to Vienna, then to Germany, and then finally to America, where he acted in films and in the theatre for several years prior to *Dracula*.[88]

Publicity for *Dracula–The Vampire Play* on Broadway in 1927.

Shortly after the play opened on Broadway, a newspaper journalist felt compelled to explain once again the difference between the two kinds of vampires: "The word 'vampire,' aside from its current slang significance, suggests superstition, ghosts, werewolves, hobgoblins … and 'horror' based on highly wrought literary imagination rather than any shred of fact." *Dracula*, the writer assured readers, was of the "classical type" of vampire.[89] In short, while Stoker' novel was famous, it was not so ubiquitous as to require no introduction or explanation.

Advertisement published in the *Boston Herald* on October 7, 1928.

The *Boston Transcript* offered a similar distinction, claiming, "Ever since somebody – they do say Burne-Jones, but it's beyond believing – painted that screaming potboiler of a Theda Bara sitting on the end of Mr. Kipling's bedside, the word 'vampire' can be bought for two cents in the Hollywood coinage. *Dracula*, the dramatization now playing to pleasurably scared crowds in the Fulton [on Broadway], will at least remind us that the original vampires buried their fangs into better things than heavy sugar daddies."[90]

In October 1927, the *New York Herald Tribune* published a fictitious interview with the character Dracula, the result of the play's success on Broadway. In it, journalist Whitney Bolton asked the vampire, "Have you ever been to Hollywood?":

> 'Never,' declared the Count Dracula firmly, 'to my certain knowledge!'
> 'Plenty of competition for you, out there,' mused the reporter, as if considering the matter through a glass darkly.
> 'I doubt that,' said the Count Dracula modestly. 'I am the king, you see, of vampires.'[91]

Here the joke revolved around the ongoing confusion between cinematic vamps and folkloric vampires.

Whatever misunderstandings some playgoers may have experienced over the meaning of the word "vampire," the Broadway play was a major success. One critic called it a "pageant of alluring horrors" that provided a "foxy dramatization" of Stoker's novel.[92] Another journalist described his evening at the play:

> Well, next to me, a pretty little thing was sitting. Next to her, a not too handsome gentleman. Now, whenever Bela Lugosi with lips painted vermilion and a face as ghostly white as only

Chapter 1 – THE VAMPIRE IN AMERICA

the 'undead dead' Count Dracula could have, entered the stage, she covered her ears to shut out all possible unearthly screams, and hid her face upon what I have already described as a not too manly bosom.

Her escort, like all men under similar circumstances, undoubtedly would [have] enjoyed the whole thing immensely. Why, of course, he was acting as her King Arthur, as her Parsifal, or what you want.

And if you think that this girl was the only one in the audience who acted so queerly, you are grossly mistaken.[93]

Frightened or not, such audience members bought tickets to the play in large numbers, so much so that by 1928 another journalist referred to any theatregoers seeking mysterious or frightening entertainment as "the *Dracula* crowds."[94]

Those crowds grew in numbers during 1928 and thereafter, as stage productions of *Dracula* took to the road. Consider, for example, the following 1928 review of tennis player William Tilden, who played the title role in a touring version of *Dracula*: "Particularly well fitted to the role in height and build, the tennis champion becomes a menacing figure as he glides about in the shroud of Dracula. His voice,

Advertisement for *Dracula–The Vampire Play* in Seattle, Washington in 1929.

too, takes on the metallic quality of an unearthly being and he succeeded last night in eliciting shrieks of horror from the more impressionable members of the audience."[95]

Bela Lugosi himself appeared in revivals of the play on the West Coast in 1928, 1929, and 1930, appearing in such cities as Los Angeles, Oakland, and San Francisco. In 1929, he performed in the play four times over three days in San Diego, a brief appearance previously unknown to Dracula historians and Lugosi biographers. Of its production, one critic responded:

It is excellently done, and the audience last night got two hours of solid, intense entertainment from it. ... Tall, slender, deliberate in movement and graceful in gesture, [Bela Lugosi] is well fitted to suggest the vampire-like character of the count who has been dead for five centuries but still lives. A remarkable makeup accentuates the unearthliness of the man, and a voice finely modulated, capable of a wide range of tonal inflection value rounds out an impersonation of power.[96]

Reviews such as this underscore Lugosi's effectiveness in the role that he would eventually portray in Tod Browning's film.

Dracula's success onstage also served to bring other vampire tales to the fore. The pulp magazine *Weird Tales* published Everil Worrell's short story *The Canal* in 1927 and Arlton Eadie's *The White Vampire* that same year. Most famous of all was Tod Browning's *London After Midnight* (1927), starring Lon Chaney, an MGM film that will be discussed at length in Chapter Two.

In retrospect, the most important vampire film of the twenties was F. W. Murnau's *Nosferatu* (1922), an unauthorized screen adaptation of Stoker's novel produced in Germany. The judgment of a court case initiated by the Stoker estate nearly led to the destruction of all known copies. Though *Nosferatu* was not released in the US in 1922, the American trade publication *Variety* did publish an extended review of it immediately after its German premiere:

After one of the most expensive publicity campaigns yet waged in Berlin as advance work for the showing of a single feature, the culmination was reached when, March 7 [of 1922], the Prana Film Co. gave a ball in the buildings of the Zoo (strange as it may seem, the most fashionable place to do this sort of thing) solely for the purpose of showing off their film Nosferatu. *They called it The Festival of* Nosferatu, *and expenses were about cleared, which is pretty good when one considers the amount of publicity they raked in.*

The film itself ... was not worth all the shouting; after all is said and done, a still-born Caligari. ... The direction of F. W. Murnau is far from extraordinary, but achieves occasionally an effect of real horror. The best acting is done by a fresh young juvenile, Gustav v. Wangenheim, in the role of Hutter. The make-up used by this actor of the title role is in the right lighting most effective. To those who know German it will be quite amusing to hear that this player's name is Schreck and the scenic designer Grau. Business has been good here, but special publicity must be taken into reckoning.[97]

Despite this lengthy report, *Variety* readers likely paid little attention to a movie that did not receive American distribution.

However, *Nosferatu* did make a brief appearance in the United States in 1929. Few audience members would have seen it, and so its direct cultural impact at the time was extremely limited. *The Billboard*'s critic had mixed feelings after watching *Nosferatu, the Vampire* in New York. As the review has been previously unknown to scholars, it is worth quoting in full:

This German importation is said to be based on the famous vampire story Dracula, *by Bram Stoker. While it holds to some degree to the salient incidents, particularly the beginning of that bloodcurdling novel, it soon loses itself in a slough of strained hocus-pocus proceedings that tend to raise the hair on edge in the worst way. In this respect it succeeds ghoulishly enough.*

Max Schreck as the title character in F.W. Murnau's *Nosferatu* (1922).

> The Count Nosferatu, the blood-sucking human, is made up in the most terrifying screen characterization since Lon Chaney's *Phantom* struck fear in theatregoers' hearts. But the chopped and exaggerated continuity is so amateurish that the count's goose-pimply effect is soon worn off and he becomes nothing more than another bogy man, whose decimation of human souls is at least thwarted by a virgin maid whose blood he desired.
> Naturally the camera is allowed to run riot, what with dark, shadowy angles, scenes that emerge into others and shots of supernatural behavior. These, while nothing unusual, do give a certain unhealthy and mysterious background for the frightful antics of the plot. F. W. Murnau must have directed this in his apprenticeship, for his careful flair for detail and character action is nowhere found.
> Max Schreck gives a splendid performance of the distorted and unhuman [sic] count, his ability as a makeup artist being largely responsible for this. The others register the customary eccentric and foreboding emotions in the best stock traditions.[98]

The critique ends by suggesting that, "cinema patrons will alternately shudder and giggle over it."

Yet another review of *Nosferatu* appeared in the *New York Staats-Zeitung*, a German-language newspaper that took a particular interest in Murnau:

> At the nice Guild Cinema at 8th Road, near 6th Avenue, you could be given the creeps. There you can watch the new German film Nosferatu from the Phoenix company, a story newly told by Henrik Galeen, based on motifs from Bram Stoker's novel *Dracula* which later was made into a stage-play, indeed a symphony of horror. … Without a doubt, many a thing was cut in

the process, but enough hideousness was left to send a chill down our spines and transform our epidermis into the famous goose bumps. A few days ago, we gave a brief sketch of the film's contents, as far as it can be told at all.

It's hard to decide whether the film is meant as an allegory of the Black Death or only spawned by a poet's imagination. Anyhow, it's a deeply disturbing film that affects the viewer in a way which he will not forget soon afterwards.[99]

Like the *Billboard* critic, this writer viewed *Nosferatu* in New York. But the film also seems to have made brief appearances elsewhere in America in 1929, particularly in Newark, New Jersey.

More Americans would have been aware of Montague Summers' 1928 book *The Vampire, His Kith and Kin*, published in the US by E. P. Dutton in 1929. The *New York Times* called it a "mine of out-of-the-way information full of unspeakable tales."[100] In it, Summers surveyed the history of vampire folklore and literature. He drew attention to *Dracula* on Broadway, as well as to its star, mistakenly referring to him as "Bela Lugoni."[101]

Conclusion

In the late twenties, the Deane-Balderston stage adaptation of *Dracula* took America by storm. The *Chicago Tribune* of 1930 underscored this point, claiming that it "has been rolling around the country ever since its first vogue two or three seasons ago, coaxing money into box offices that had abandoned hope of the drama, and of the shriek-and-shudder plays of the last five years it easily leads the list."[102]

More than any other supernatural vampire tales or collections of folklore, and perhaps more than Stoker's own novel, the stage play caused Americans in the Roaring Twenties to reconsider the meaning of the term vampire. Though it did not displace the Burne-Jones/Kipling/Bara "vamp," *Dracula–The Vampire Play* helped in the process of returning the supernatural vampire to a place of prominence in popular culture.

After all, vampires had been regularly present in accounts of legends and folklore published in America even prior to the formation of the United States. The country had witnessed the proliferation of the vampire in literature and on the stage in the nineteenth century, experiencing the character's ability to inspire horror for the sake of audience pleasure. Such gratification had caused many American readers to enjoy tales of the supernatural creature just as the members of "The Vampires" society did in New York in 1892, when they toasted their "blood punch" and dined on "skeleton fodder," "headstone croquettes," and "vampires' wings."[103] Whereas vampire superstitions frightened many Americans in the eighteenth century (some of whom believed in the existence of such creatures), the nineteenth and early twentieth century forged vampire fans who thrilled at the exploits of fictional characters. *A Fool There Was* and its ilk had only temporarily displaced this extensive American experience.

In April 1929, director Tod Browning appeared at a bridge luncheon with numerous other film celebrities. He and his wife often attended social events in the Los Angeles area, regularly becoming fodder for newspaper society pages. Another attendant at this particular party was Theda Bara.[104] As of 1929, her own vampire days were over, having ended in the silent film era. By contrast, Browning's fascination with vampires remained a work in progress, his experiments reaching a pinnacle with the 1931 film version of *Dracula*.

1. "Vampires Hold a Feast." *New York Herald* 2 May 1892: 4.
2. "Vampire's Feast." *Hamilton Daily Republican* (Hamilton, OH) 4 Oct. 1892.
3. McNally, Raymond T. and Radu R. Florescu. *In Search of Dracula: A True History of Dracula and Vampire Legends* (Greenwich, CT: New York Graphic Society, 1972).
4. "The Vroucalaca." *The North American* (PA) 17 May 1844.
5. "The Weird, Romantic Vampire." *Kansas City Times* 14 May 1887.
6. "Medreyga in Hungary." *American Weekly Mercury* (Philadelphia, PA) 7 Jan. 1732.
7. Untitled. *New England Weekly Journal* (Boston, MA) 14 Mar. 1738).
8. See, for example: "Vampyres." *Aesculapian Register* (Philadelphia, PA) 29 July 1824.
9. "On Vampyrism." *New Monthly Magazine and Literary Journal* (Boston) 1 Jan. 1823.
10. Calmet published a lengthy treatise on vampires and other supernatural creatures in 1746 under the title *Dissertations sur les apparitions des anges, des démons et des esprits, et sur les revenants et vampires de Hongrie, de Bohême, de Moravie, et de Silésie*. For a discussion of his work, see Huet, Marie Hélène. "Deadly Fears: Dom Augustin Calmet's Vampires and the Rule Over Death." *Eighteenth Century Life* Vol. 21, No. 2 (May 1997): 222-232.
11. See, for example: "Vampirism in Serbia." *Burlington Free Press* (Burlington, VT) 18 Aug. 1876.
12. "Believe in Vampires." *Boston Globe* 27 Jan. 1896.
13. "Drinking Human Blood." *Oakland Tribune* 27 Mar. 1896.
14. See, for example: "Supernatural Stories." *Eclectic Magazine of Foreign Literature* Vol. 20, No. 1 (May 1850); "The Vampire." *Current Literature* Vol. XXXIV, No. 5 (Nov. 1902).
15. "Vampires and Ghouls." *The Columbian* (Bloomsburg, PA) 4 Aug. 1871.
16. Vance, L. J. "Vampire Lore." *The Open Court, a Quarterly Magazine* Vol. 7, No. 292 (30 Mar. 1893).
17. See, for example: "The Vampire." *New Hampshire Gazette* 21 Feb. 1826; "The Vampire." *The Times* (CT) 31 Aug. 1839; "The Vampire Bat of Brazil." Daily National Intelligencer 6 Sept. 1847; "The Vampire Bat." *The Farmer's Cabinet* (NH) 18 Sept. 1856; "The vampire Bat." *Kalamazoo Gazette* (Kalamazoo, MI) 27 Dec. 1892.
18. "An Old Superstition." *Saturday Evening Post* Vol. LIII, No. 41 (9 May 1874).
19. "A Blood-Sucking Vampire." *Anaconda Standard* (Anaconda, MT) 29 Aug. 1893.
20. See, for example: "Rotary Biography of the Legislation of Wisconsin!" *Madison Daily Patriot* (Madison, WI) 21 Oct. 1856; "Speech." *The M'Kean Miner* (Smethport, PA) 5 Feb. 1861; "The Times on Irish Differences." *New York Daily Times* 31 July 1854.
21. See, for example: "The Sporting Season." *New York Herald* 19 May 1883: 8.
22. This story appeared in the *Philadelphia Union*, and was then reprinted in the *Rhode Island American* (Providence, RI) on 25 June 1819.
23. Untitled. *Rhode Island American* 27 Apr. 1819.
24. "Literary." *The Ladies' Literary Cabinet* Vol. 1, No. 5 (12 June 1819).
25. Untitled. *The Village Record* (West Chester, PA) 18 Sept. 1819.
26. I suggest that the adaptation was loose in large measure because a period advertisement announces the play's three main characters as Lord Ruthven, Aubrey, and Pedro, the latter being a character that does not exist (at least by that name) in Polidori's tale.
27. "Lord Byron." *St. Louis Enquirer* 4 Sept. 1820. Many other American newspapers published this same item.
28. "The Vampyre." *New England Galaxy* (Boston, MA) 3 Nov. 1820.
29. "The Vampire." *Boston Commercial Gazette* 19 Oct. 1820.
30. "The Vampyre," *New England Galaxy* 3 Nov. 1820.
31. See, for example: Advertisement. *Charleston Courier* 14 Jan. 1825.
32. "On Vampires and Vampirism." *New York Literary Journal* Vol. 4, No. 3 (1 Jan. 1821).
33. This performance was held at the Boston Academy of Music on 3 Jan. 1846.
34. "New York Correspondence." *Manitowoc Tribune* 17 July 1856.
35. Untitled. *Flake's Bulletin* (Galveston, TX) 22 Jan. 1870.
36. Advertisement. *Daily National Republican* (Washington, DC) 29 Feb. 1864.
37. "The Amusement Event of the Season." *Centralia Enterprise and Tribune* (Centralia, WI) 11 Apr. 1891.
38. See, for example, "Warm Dance Promised." *Variety* 27 Dec. 1912.
39. "A Burlesque at the Strand." *New York Herald* 14 Sept. 1872.
40. Mention of *Carmilla* does appear in the study "The Supernatural in Nineteenth-Century Fiction." *The Living Age* Vol. 238, No. 3082 (1 Aug. 1903).
41. "Three Faulty Novels," *Chicago Tribune* 30 Nov. 1899.
42. "A Literary Page." *Cleveland Plain Dealer* 26 Nov. 1899.
43. "A Grisly Phantasmagoria." *Boston Journal* 27 Nov. 1899.
44. "Dracula." *Washington Post* 27 Dec. 1899.
45. Untitled. *Boston Herald* 26 Nov. 1899. Similar reportage appeared in "Telegraphic News." *New York Dramatic Mirror* 2 Dec. 1899: 12.
46. See, for example: "Men and Women Who Make Books." *New York Times* 15 Sept. 1906: BR566.
47. "A Remarkable Story." *The Evening Post* (South Carolina) 4 May 1908.
48. Mason, Walt. "Among the Booksmiths." *Kansas City Star* 24 Sept. 1911.
49. See, for example: "The Common Vampire." *Washington Post* 21 Aug. 1904.
50. "Wild Man Roosts in Tree Tops." *Pawtucket Times* (Pawtucket, RI) 14 June 1906.

51. See, for example: "Debates in Progress." *New York Times* 28 May 1904: BR363.
52. "Orpheum." *Oakland Tribune* 24 Aug. 1914.
53. "Chinatown Play Was 'Found' in Oakland." *Oakland Tribune* 11 Apr. 1915.
54. "New York Theatrical Letter." *Colorado Springs Gazette* (Colorado Springs, CO) 1 Dec. 1912.
55. "The Belasco." *Washington Herald* 4 Feb. 1913.
56. "At the Theatres." *The Daily People* (New York) 18 Aug. 1902.
57. "Donnelly and Hatfield's Minstrels." *Fort Wayne Journal-Gazette* (Fort Wayne, IN) 11 Aug. 1908.
58. In 1916, a trade publication referred to an acrobatic performance by "Dracula, aerial frog" ("Sells-Floto Champion Shows" *Billboard* 13 May 1916): 49.
59. "Unusual Bill at Apollo." *Janesville Daily Gazette* (Janesville, WI) 8 Mar. 1913.
60. This information appears on a playbill for the National Theatre in Boston dated 6 Oct. 1854.
61. "The Vampire." *Cleveland Plain Dealer* 23 May 1897.
62. See, for example: "The Vampire." *Salt Lake Tribune* 23 May 1897; "The Vampire, Painting and Poem." *Dallas Morning News* 13 June 1897.
63. "Creation of the Vampire." *Galveston Daily News* (Galveston, TX) 26 June 1898.
64. "Doest Not Like the Likeness." *Steubenville Herald* (Steubenville, OH) 31 May 1897.
65. "Noted Painter Arrives." *New York Times* 27 Feb. 1902: 7.
66. "Denies He Has Sold *The Vampire*." *New York Times* 29 July 1902: 8.
67. "Without Prejudice." *New York Times* 5 Mar. 1899: IMS2.
68. "Vampires." *Chicago Tribune* 25 Jan. 1903.
69. "*A Fool There Was*; No Doubt of That." *New York Times* 25 Mar. 1909: 9.
70. "*The Vampire.*" *The Nickelodeon* 15 Nov. 1910.
71. Advertisement. *Moving Picture World* 10 May 1913.
72. For more information on Theda Bara, see: Genini, Ronald. *Theda Bara: A Biography of the Silent Screen Vamp, with a Filmography* (Jefferson, NC: McFarland, 1996); Golden, Eve. *Vamp: The Rise and Fall of Theda Bara* (Vestal, NY: Emprise Publishing, 1996).
73. "*A Fool There Was.*" *New York Dramatic Mirror* 20 Jan. 1915.
74. "What Our Critics Thought of Them." *Motion Picture Mail* 2 Sept. 1916: 14.
75. "Vamping the Vamp." *Moving Picture Weekly* 19 Jan. 1918: 38; "The Vamp Cure." *Moving Picture Weekly* 13 July 1918: 34; "A He Male Vamp." *Moving Picture Weekly* 26 June 1920: 38.
76. "Playhouse Paragraphs." *Brooklyn Eagle* 13 May 1917: 2.
77. "Wonder What a Movie Vamp Thinks About." *Davenport Democrat and Leader* (Davenport, IA) 27 July 1924.
78. "Romance of Words." *Holley Standard* (Holley, NY) 12 June 1924: unpaginated.
79. Wright, Dudley. *Vampires and Vampirism* (Philadelphia: David McKay, 1914).
80. "Revamping the Vampires." *The Nation* Vol. 113, No. 2927 (10 Aug. 1921): 140.
81. Prospero's Musings." *Baltimore Sun* 20 June 1921.
82. "*Dracula* Popular for Thirty Years." *Seattle Times* 20 June 1929.
83. "The Book Column." *Capital Times* (Madison, WI) 13 June 1923.
84. Baer, Leone Cass. "Stars and Starmakers." *The Oregonian* (Portland, OR) 3 July 1924.
85. "The London Theatre." *New York Times* 20 Feb. 1927: X1.
86. "Two Plays in London Make Many Faint." *New York Times* 11 Mar. 1927: 24.
87. "Digging into Dracula." *New York Times* 25 Dec. 1927: X3.
88. For more information on Bela Lugosi's life and career, see: Rhodes, Gary D. *Lugosi* (Jefferson, NC: McFarland, 1997); Rhodes, Gary D. *Bela Lugosi, Dreams and Nightmares* (Narberth, PA: Collectables, 2007); Rhodes, Gary D. and Bill Kaffenberger. *No Traveler Returns: The Lost Years of Bela Lugosi* (Duncan, OK: BearManor Media, 2012).
89. "Weird New Facts about Vampires: Winged and Human." *Richmond Times-Dispatch* (Richmond, VA) 20 Nov. 1927.
90. "Vampires All." *Boston Transcript* 29 Oct. 1927.
91. Bolton, Whitney. "Count Dracula, Vampire, Admits He Goes on a Bat Every Night." *New York Herald Tribune* 9 Oct. 1927.
92. Hammond, Percy. "Porgy Survives Transition to Stage." *Trenton Times-Advertiser* 16 Oct. 1927.
93. Halasz, George. "*Dracula* is Good, Exciting Vampire Play." *Cleveland Plain Dealer* 16 Oct. 1927.
94. "Play *Hotbed* Raps Hypocrisy in Universities." *Tampa Tribune* (Tampa, FL) 18 Nov. 1928.
95. "*Dracula* Revives Shudder and Chill." *Springfield Daily Republican* (Springfield, MA) 26 Oct. 1928.
96. Hubbard, Havrah. "*Dracula* Gives Evening of Good Entertainment." *San Diego Union* (San Diego, CA) 11 June 1929.
97. Trask, C. Hooper. "Berlin Film News." *Variety* 21 Apr. 1922: 43.
98. "*Nosferatu, the Vampire.*" *Billboard* 15 June 1929: 27.
99. "Theater Und Kino." *New Yorker Staats-Zeitung* 6 June 1929.
100. Field, Louise Maunsell. "Origin and History of the Strange Vampire Tradition." *New York Times* 24 Mar. 1929.
101. Summers, Montague. *The Vampire, His Kith and Kin* (New York: E. P. Dutton, 1929). Summers' book had been published in London the previous year.
102. Collins, Charlie. "The Stage." *Chicago Tribune* 1 Dec. 1930.
103. "Vampires Hold a Feast," p. 4.
104. Collier, Ruth. *Los Angeles Examiner* 7 Apr. 1929.

Chapter 2
TOD BROWNING AND CARL LAEMMLE, JR.

In 1925, a newspaper article lauded Carl Laemmle, Sr., the founder and head of Universal Pictures, for understanding the "tendency of the public to patronize the unusual in motion picture entertainment," a reference to such films as *The Hunchback of Notre Dame* (1923) and *The Phantom of the Opera* (1925).[1] The journalist added:

It is reported that Mr. Laemmle may present Bram Stoker's great thriller Dracula *and that Arthur Edmund Carew, who plays the mysterious, intriguing Persian in* The Phantom [of the Opera] *and who was Svengali in* Trilby [1923], *may play the title role."*[2]

For Universal, producing a film version of *Dracula* in 1925 would have made a good deal of sense, as the novel was well known and its title immediately recognizable to many potential viewers.

There is also the important but little-known fact that Universal had considered producing a film version of *Dracula* ten years earlier. In June 1915, the studio made inquiries about adapting the novel, but determined that obtaining the rights might involve complicated litigation. Given that these plans reached the studio's legal department, Universal must have been serious about the possibility.[3]

Between Universal's attempts to produce films of *Dracula* in 1915 and 1925, the studio undertook discussions for yet another possible version, one that has remained unknown until now. In 1920, the *Oakland Tribune* published news of *Dracula* that involved not only Universal, but also film director Tod Browning:

Will Tod Browning's [sic] attempt to Little-Theaterize the screen? That's what Hollywood is asking since the rumor spread that this courageous young director wants to produce Dracula *as a motion picture.* Dracula *is a daring novel that shocked even New York.*
They say that if Carl Laemmle tells Browning to go ahead, Universal will probably start advertising, 'He's going to shock you if it takes a million of our dollars to do it!'[4]

For reasons that are not entirely clear, nothing came of this 1920 version of *Dracula*. Perhaps the situation was similar to what Browning once said of his 1925 film *The Unholy*

Arthur Edmund Carew, the actor who might have played Dracula onscreen in 1925.

Three: "It wasn't an original story of mine. I read the book several years ago, and I knew it would make a splendid movie. But I couldn't get anybody to agree with me."[5] In the case of *Dracula*, legal issues may have also remained an impediment.

But the reason could also have been the same that Carl Laemmle, Sr. gave to artist Hubert G. Davis in a 1923 letter. In it, Laemmle wrote, "Thank you for ... the book you were kind enough to mention. We have considered *Dracula* by Bram Stoker a little too gruesome to screen well, and we will, therefore, be unable to make use of your suggestion."[6]

At any rate, two important facts can be gleaned from these unmade film versions of *Dracula*. For one, Universal considered producing a version of the novel at least three times during the years 1915 to 1925. Though none of these projects moved beyond the planning stages, Universal did eventually become the first American studio to adapt *Dracula* for the screen. While it was not inevitable that Universal would do so, the trio of unmade versions suggests that the studio gave the possibility more repeated consideration than any of its competitors.

Secondly, and more importantly, is the fact that Tod Browning wanted to direct a film version of *Dracula* for ten years before he was able to do so, if not longer. When he (and William Parker) crafted the scenario to his 1920 Universal film *The Virgin of Stamboul*, perhaps he was already thinking of *Dracula* when writing the following intertitle: "Night again – A black, leering vampire, sweeping down to steal the senses of these three, who could not, would not, trust." According to a 1936 article in *New York Times*, Browning had considered filming *Dracula* with Lon Chaney (who "wanted to act" in it) some "ten years" before finally getting to direct it; that timeline suggests the actor and director might have been discussed the project as early as 1920 when they worked together on *Outside the Law* (1920).[7]

The revelation that Browning attempted to direct *Dracula* at Universal in 1920 makes it crucial to reconsider all of his work prior to 1931, particularly his MGM film *London After Midnight* (1927), which can and perhaps should be viewed as his first effort to translate *Dracula* to the screen, even if in the form of an unofficial variant.

But however crucial Browning became to the eventual and official adaptation of *Dracula* (1931), there was one other man who has never received proper recognition for his role both in that film and in the rise of the horror movie genre. Having already dispensed with *Dracula* on three earlier occasions, Universal may never have finally committed to the project had it not been for Carl Laemmle, Jr., who became the studio's head of production in 1929. Not only did he begin to emphasize major productions over low-budget films, he also took important financial and artistic risks, particularly with *All Quiet on the Western Front* (1930), the success of which paved the way for the younger Laemmle to continue implementing his plans for the studio, plans that – by the summer of 1930, if not earlier – included *Dracula*.

The fact that Universal produced *Dracula* and that it became a lasting contribution to the cinema and to popular culture is due to the tenacity and vision of these two men.

The Edgar Allan Poe of Hollywood

In 1928, *Motion Picture Classic* published a lengthy article on director Tod Browning, describing his work to American movie fans:

> *He is a stylist among stylists. Almost a specialist. The murky, the grotesque, the gruesome, the mystifying, is his stock in trade. Give this man a Lon Chaney characterization, a mystery concoction of his own weaving, and he can tell a story as masterly as one of Poe's. With every chill. With every nerve-racking swing of the pendulum.*[8]

The article implied that Browning the filmmaker was linked with Browning the man, whose personal obsessions spawned his cinematic style.

To the present day, Browning's story continues to exist in a nether region of sorts, with some writers constructing biographies that tell the story of a secretive or mysterious figure.[9] While seemingly an appropriate portrait given the kinds of films Browning made, such an image is limited. After all, as Maurice Rapf (screenwriter and son of MGM's Harry Rapf) once claimed, "Browning was extremely friendly and *not at all* mysterious. He and my Dad and some other fellows used to play cards at our house all the time. It wasn't as if he was some secretive hermit or anything."[10]

What is known of Browning's life? As *Motion Picture Classic* claimed, he had "long experience as an actor on the vaudeville stage and a 'barker' in a circus."[11] Born in Louisville, Kentucky in 1882, Browning's entry into show business came thanks to his work as a magician's assistant and as a showman at carnivals. A 1914 article in *Billboard* described even more of his early career: "Tod Browning, formerly working in front of the kid shows of the K.-W. and Barnum Shows, and also owner of the Deep Sea Diving Show at Riverview Park, Chicago, in 1901 or 1902."[12] At a given point, Browning also worked as a "corpse" who – after being "hypnotized" as part of a sideshow act – would literally be buried alive for hours on end.

Between 1908 and 1910, Browning toured as one half of the comedy team Browning and Jones (the "Jones" being Ray C. Jones). They sang, they danced, and they garnered enough good reviews to get booked throughout much of the United States. One description of their act in 1908 claimed the duo opened each "performance with some good jokes and gave the audience many a good laugh during their turn."[13] Another newspaper article declared that, "Browning and Jones, black face comedians and impersonators ... [have] knowledge [that] is more than mortal. Most gifted artists of the age."[14]

During their first year together (and perhaps longer), Browning and Jones worked in blackface, performing a comedy skit in early 1909 called *14 Minutes in Darktown*. They also scored success by singing such songs as *Sarah Won't You Let Me Serenade You*.[15] Despite their growing stature, by October 1909, the two of them had given up blackface in order to do a "straight act."[16] Then, the following year, they parted ways.

In 1912 and 1913, Browning appeared in a variety show called *The Whirl of Mirth*, singing and acting in such sketches as *Rubbing It In* and *Mutt and Jeff* (in which he played "Mutt").[17] From there, he acted in a number of short comedy films in 1913 and 1914, making the transition from stage to screen thanks to his friend Charlie Murray, the famous Irish comedian who had earlier been one half of the vaudeville team Murray and Mack.

He quickly attracted the attention of the film industry press, with *Motography* noting the following anecdote in September 1914: "Tod Browning of the Komic Company recently told Fay Tichner of the same company to throw a baseball to him. The speed with which the horsehide was delivered was too much for the comedian and a muff resulted in a broken nose. He expects to be back at work within a week."[18]

Browning then began to work behind the camera. In April 1915, the *Photoplayers' Weekly* noted that Reliance and Majestic had "recently" promoted Browning "to the directors' ranks," adding that his "rapid stride in film circles is an assurance of his talents."[19] His directorial debut was *The Lucky Transfer* (1915).[20]

While under contract at Fine Arts in 1917, Browning's publicity emphasized his careful attention to detail. For example, his five-reel film *Jim Bludso* (1917) features a young boy who wears a pair of copper-toed boots that had been popular with children one generation earlier. Having difficulty in finding a pair of them, Browning:

> ...resorted to directing in the daily newspapers in the hope of getting a pair that had been partially worn out. One of the advertisements was answered by a white-haired old lady who

Tod Browning, who attempted to direct a version of *Dracula* at Universal in 1920.

called at the studio to see Director Browning and told him that she had a pair of the boots that had been worn by a son who was killed. Browning would not consent to use them, however, when he learned that the boots were [the] mother's only reminder of her dead boy. It was well he did so, for [the child actor in the film] lost his first pair in the Sacramento River and a second had to be made.[21]

Browning made certain that the first pair that the actor wore and its replacement appeared identical to the original style.

After directing for Fine Arts until "that organization disbanded," Browning went to work for Metro in mid-1917.[22] His film *The Legion of Death* allegedly featured "over two thousand people ... in some of the street scenes depicting the opening of the Russian revolution."[23] Publicity stories claimed that many of the extras were actually Russians, but such accounts may have been inventions designed to build on Browning's reputation for insisting on authenticity.[24] Similarly, the industry press claimed that Browning shot a sequence of *A Love Sublime* (1917) in a real confectionary store rather than on a studio set, all in his drive to capture "realism."[25]

Publicity still for Browning's *The Virgin of Stamboul* (1920).

Increasingly, Browning's work revealed an attraction towards the kinds of mystery and crime subjects that would later make him famous. For example, his film *The Eyes of Mystery* (1918) was a "melodramatic offering in five reels abounding in gunplay, and making use of various appurtenances of mystery such as sliding panels, an entrance to a secret stairway concealed by a revolving portrait from which the eyes can be removed, leaving peep-holes for an observer."[26]

Once again, Browning's publicity promoted his devotion to cinematic authenticity. Of *The Eyes of Mystery*, a journalist claimed:

> *In this fascinating picture ... most of the male characters are rugged, unkempt, full-bearded Virginia mountaineers. Director Tod Browning insisted that his players grow real beards instead of using the usual crepe tonsorial adornment for their roles in the picture. The men were engaged two weeks before the production was started and ordered to let their beards grow. Production began the third week and continued for a month. All this time the men obeyed orders and kept away from the barbers, to their own discomfort and the barbers' loss.*[27]

Another article of the era added, "Tod Browning is a shining example of a sartorial rebel. Browning absolutely refuses to dress like a second lieutenant of the horse marines," meaning the "riding breeches" and "boots and spurs" that some other directors sported. Instead, "Mr. Browning appears for work in a sport-coat, white trousers, white shoes, and a cap."[28]

In 1919, Browning left Metro for Universal, and by autumn of that year he prepared to direct his biggest and most elaborate film to date, one that he had written himself: *The Virgin of Stamboul* (1920), starring Priscilla Dean, told the story of an American soldier who falls in love with a beggar girl in Turkey.

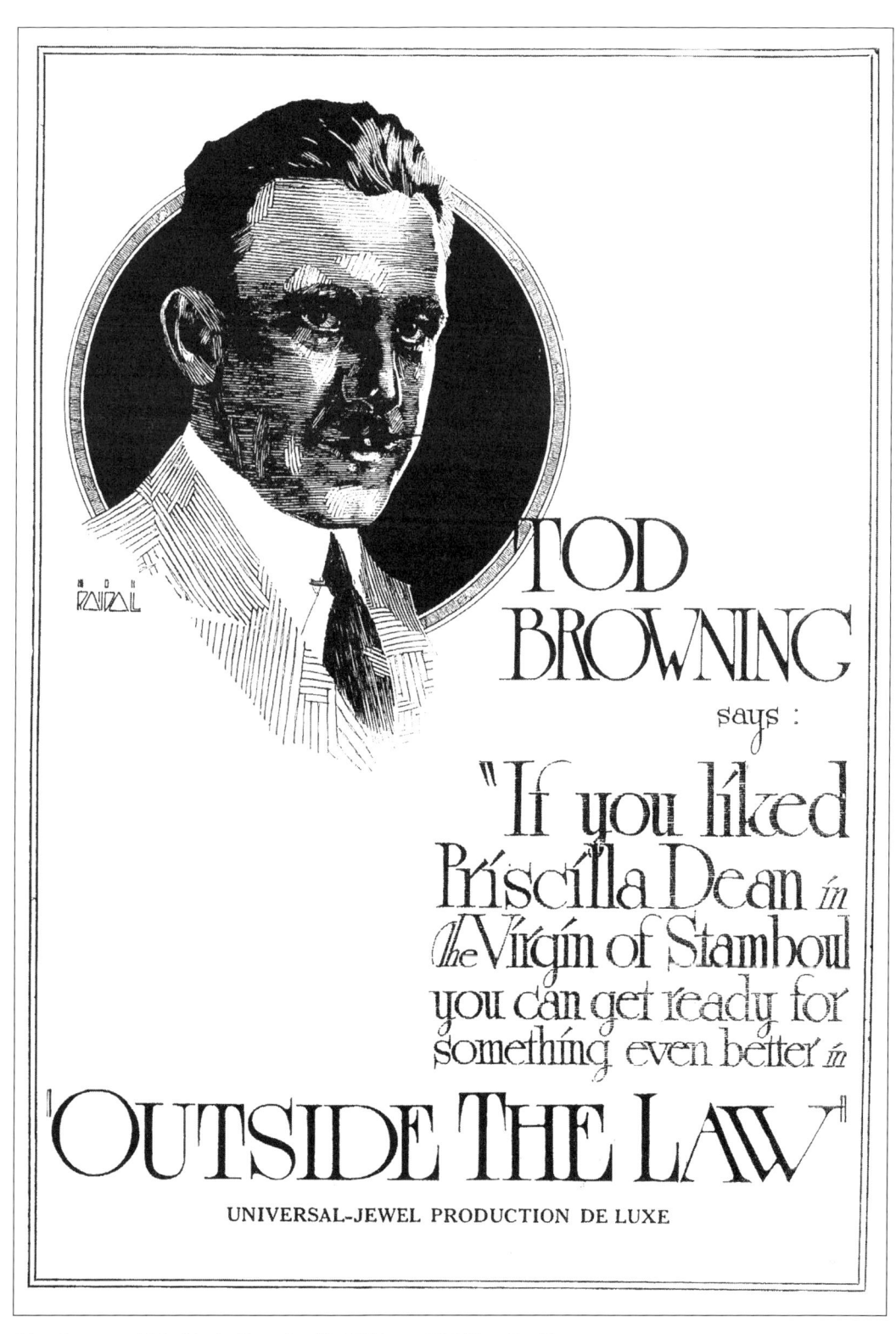

Advertisement published in the December 25, 1920 issue of *Exhibitors Herald*.

Chapeter 2 – TOD BROWNING AND CARL LAEMMLE, JR.

Universal's trust in Browning's ability to deliver a successful, big-budget film was well founded. Theatre manager reports offer insight into how popular *The Virgin of Stamboul* was:

'This is a real special. ... Last reel a knockout.'
– Elite Theatre, Iola, Kansas[29]

'My but this is a puller, and some show.'
–Idle Hour Theatre, Cambridge Springs, Pennsylvania[30]

'Certainly is all that Universal claims it is."
– Short's Theatre, Sulphur, Oklahoma[31]

Thanks to *The Virgin of Stamboul*, Browning's status as a major director was assured.

Soon the trade press announced that Browning was hard at work on writing a stage play, and also discussed his new feature film, *Outside the Law* (1920).[32] The film reunited Browning with actor Lon Chaney, the two having already collaborated on *The Wicked Darling* (1919). *Outside the Law* allowed Browning to explore his interest in the crime genre, including in the clash between villains who either can or cannot reform themselves.

Universal's general manager for film exchanges declared that greater demand existed for *Outside the Law* than for any movie that the studio had ever produced.[33] The film became such a hit that Universal reissued it in 1926.[34] And much of the credit went to Browning.

Advertisement published in *Variety* in 1918.

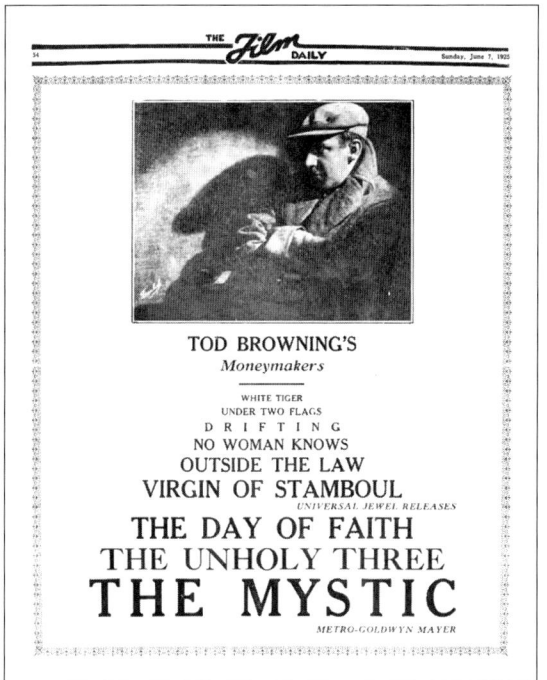

Left: Trade advertisement published in the *Film Daily* in 1925. Right: Trade advertisement published in the *Film Daily* in 1926.

Photoplay told readers that, thanks to Browning's direction, the film featured "practically a thrill a minute guaranteed."[35]

Movement into the upper echelon of Hollywood film directors took its toll on Browning in the early twenties, however. As *Motion Picture Classic* wrote:

> The story of Tod Browning's two sick, inactive years from the screen is too well known to need detailed repetition. He is quite frank in admitting that he could not get a job because he was otherwise occupied in trying to drink up 'all the bad liquor in the world.' Thanks to Irving Thalberg, Browning made a comeback at MGM with The Unholy Three [1925, with Lon Chaney], the boy genius producer putting the story immediately into production after hearing Browning's pitch.

At the time, Browning believed *The Unholy Three* was his "best" film, due to its "spontaneous action" and a plotline that unfolded "logically and smoothly."[36]

His comeback continued at MGM through an array of other successful films, some of which featured Lon Chaney. In 1928, the film industry press reported that Browning and Chaney were celebrating their tenth anniversary together, the result being one of the most important director-actor relationships of the silent film era.[37] At that time, the two were working on *West of Zanzibar* (1928), their tenth and final collaboration.

From that point onward, Browning not only had to direct films without his favorite actor, but he also had to weather the storm wrought by the rise of the talking picture. He successfully made the transition at MGM with *The Thirteenth Chair* (1929), and would continue to direct sound films for another decade before retiring from the screen.

Lon Chaney, Edna Tichenor, and Marceline Day in a publicity still for *London after Midnight* (1927).

Cinematic Trickery

On the battlefield of war amidst exploding bombs, a villainous Asian officer orders his men to nail a woman inside a small coffin that exposes her head and legs, the penalty for passing secrets to the enemy. After revealing that her treachery had led to a bombing in which his own children were killed, the officer proceeds to shoot the coffin with a machine gun. The woman screams before her head falls limp. The officer then kicks the coffin into two pieces. The scene is gruesome and sadistic, particularly by the standards of 1930s cinema.

"Hold it," screams Michael Morgan (Robert Young), standing in front of a poster that says "Professional Magicians' Society." Morgan creates new trick devices for conjurors; the battlefield scene was a fake, nothing more than a stage on which actors demonstrated his newest trick. Thus begins Tod Browning's 1939 film *Miracles for Sale*.

Browning clearly had a love of pranksters and hucksters who were not at all what they seemed to be. Consider, for example, the fake mechanical chess player in *The White Tiger* (1923), the fake spiritualists in *The Mystic* (1925), *The Thirteenth Chair* (1929), and *Miracles for Sale*, the criminal mastermind of *The Black Bird* (1926) who pretends to be his own disabled brother, criminals disguising themselves as old women in *The Unholy Three* (1925) and *The Devil-Doll* (1936), and the magician-turned-voodoo priest in *West of Zanzibar*. Such film characters were all in addition to the fake vampires that populated *London After Midnight* and *Mark of the Vampire* (1935).

In many cases, Browning allows film audiences to understand his tricks even when onscreen characters do not. For example, certain images and intertitles explain how a beheading trick works in *The Show* (1927), information withheld from the bulk of the onscreen audience witnessing the sideshow. By contrast, there are occasions in which characters in Browning's movies eventually learn that they have been conned. Consider for example the natives in *West of Zanzibar* who, by the time of the film's climax, no longer believe in the lead character's fake voodoo magic.

Other deceptions in Browning's films are more complicated. Hugh Manon – whose essay "Seeing Through Seeing Through: The *Trompe l'Oeil* Effect and Bodily Difference in the Cinema of Tod Browning" is one of the most insightful ever published on the director – speaks at length about *The Unknown* (1927), in which Lon Chaney plays an apparently armless character named Alonzo. His paraplegia is a fake, as the film audience learns.[38] But, as Manon describes, audience members may not have realized that the character's feet – which he uses to place a cigarette in his mouth, strum a guitar, and to wipe his brow with a handkerchief – did not always belong to the actor Lon Chaney. Rather, in some shots the feet belonged to Paul Dismute, an authentic "armless wonder" of sideshow acts. Here we can see that Browning's penchant for authenticity existed in a fascinating and complicated interplay with his love of trickery.

Nowhere in Browning's cinema is the simultaneous desire to conceal and reveal a trick more evident than in *The Thirteenth Chair*. In one crane shot, the camera starts near the ceiling of a large room at the Crosby home and moves downward and into the z-axis space to show Inspector Delzante (Bela Lugosi) interacting with other characters. Not only is the shot an attempt to introduce motion into the confines of the main set, it is also one of Browning's most fascinating cinematic tricks. The shot begins with the camera already moving downward. Something is visible in the top of the frame, but it quickly falls out of view. Only a careful viewer will notice a crucial clue that eludes all of the onscreen characters until much later in the film. It is a knife, stuck into the ceiling where the murderer has thrown it during a darkened séance. The clue's presence is obvious and yet hidden, revealed and yet concealed, so much so that even modern critics analyzing the film have failed to notice it.

Alongside Browning's love of all things faked came a parallel obsession towards his aforementioned emphasis on accuracy and authenticity. Consider for example his desire to use the Aya Sophia mosque in *The Virgin of Stamboul*, rather than simply invent a fictional mosque. Likewise, there is the use of the Hungarian language on the sideshow advertising in *The Mystic*. Later, in his talkies, Browning had non-English characters actually speak in other languages, such as the Asian character in *Outside the Law* (1930). Browning also employed authentic footage of Madison Square Garden in *Iron Man* (1931), and, much more famously, he cast real sideshow performers in *Freaks* (1932).

Rather than creating an opposite and contradictory style, the shared emphases on what is real and what is fake features a porous boundary. For example, Browning delights in opening *The Unknown* with a title card that announces: "it's a story that they say is true." Here the mysterious and unnamed "they" have simply *said* that the tale is accurate and honest, a turn of phrase that smacks of the kind of carnival and sideshow publicity that would have been important in Browning's early career.

One of the best examples of Browning blurring the line between fact and fiction appears in *Miracles for Sale*. In it, Michael Morgan exposes fake mediums when he isn't creating new tricks for fellow magicians. But those pursuits hardly keep him from espousing the following view: "For several thousand years the human race has been trying to step across the threshold into the darkness of the unknown. Call it the other world if you like. *Because there's something there*." Morgan *believes*, even while he tries to disprove and disavow and *disbelieve*. Another curious inversion in the same film involves the medium Madame Rapport (Gloria Holden), who does not possess supernatural powers. She derides Morgan for being a "cheap trickster," a term he would no doubt use to describe her own profession

Lobby card for *London After Midnight* (1927).

The emphasis on trickery also allowed Browning to explore his related obsession, irony. In *The Unholy Three*, an older woman takes her grandchild to see the strongman Hercules, promising the little boy that he can grow up to be strong if he doesn't smoke. Shortly after they walk away, Hercules lights a cigarette. At times, Browning founded entire narratives on irony. In *The Black Bird*, a man pretending to be physically challenged becomes just that before his death. More devastating perhaps is the lead character's life in *West of Zanzibar*; he spends years embroiled in hatred, creating revenge plots against a man whom he wrongly believes to have stolen his wife and fathered her child. In actual fact, the child in question is his own daughter.

Intrigued if not obsessed with certain plots and themes, Browning returned again and again to similar storylines. *Under Two Flags* (1922) reminds one of *The Virgin of Stamboul*. *West of Zanzibar* shares important similarities with *The Road to Mandalay*, particularly in that the daughters in both films don't know the identity of their fathers (both of whom having been portrayed by Lon Chaney). Browning remade his silent film *Outside the Law* as a talkie in 1930, keeping the same title. And he famously remade *London After Midnight* as *Mark of the Vampire*.

But Browning also enjoyed altering the past even as he recreated it. In both versions of *Outside the Law*, the lead female characters scold neighbor boys whose tears soon melt their hearts. The scenes are none too different from one another. But in the silent version the boy's damaged kite causes a crucifix-like shadow to appear on a window shade; in the sound version, the shadow beams through the window onto the apartment floor. Similarly, Browning drew upon *The Unholy Three* when he directed *The Devil-Doll*, reworking a scene in which a policeman unknowingly picks up a toy that contains stolen jewels. In such cases, Browning re-imagined his old films rather than merely remaking them.

London After Midnight (1927)

Produced in the autumn of 1927 and released in December of the same year, Tod Browning's *London After Midnight* remains one of the most sought-after of all lost films. It has been the subject of two major photographic reconstructions.[39] And, thanks to a vast array of surviving publicity stills, the image of Lon Chaney as a (fake) vampire ranks among the most memorable in horror film history.

Reviewing the movie in 1927, Richard Watts, Jr. of the *New York Herald Tribune* wrote:

The distinguished talents of Lon Chaney, Tod Browning, and the late author of Dracula *are shrewdly combined in this picture, rather pointlessly known as* London After Midnight, *which is on display at the Capitol this week. Since the screen began some months ago to get itself all worked up over mystery melodramas, no more satisfying, pleasantly grewsome [sic] and, presumably, blood-curdling example of its school has yet been revealed.*

It is not surprising that the Messrs. Chaney and Browning, those two leading exponents of cinema horror tales, should have in time concerned themselves with the fascinating problems of Dracula. *The present picture, however, is not a film version of the Bram Stoker story. Essentially, it is another of those murder mystery affairs in which your old friend, Blake of Scotland Yard, strives to ferret out the guilty man. But a great part, and incidentally, the best part deals with the preoccupation of* Dracula, *an attempt to go into the matter of this legion of the un-dead, of a race of creatures, who, assuming, according to the needs of the moment, the form of man, bat or werewolf, continue their existence by fattening nightly upon the life blood of some helpless victim.*[40]

Watts rightly perceived *London After Midnight*'s similarities to *Dracula*, presumably because he was aware not only of the novel, but also of the Hamilton Deane-John L. Balderston stage adaptation, which had opened on Broadway only two months before Browning's film was released.

Watts was also correct to suggest that *London After Midnight* was not a faithful adaptation of Stoker's *Dracula*. But elements of the novel do appear in it. For example, the Man in the Beaver Hat (Chaney) carries a lantern, just as Dracula does when he first meets Jonathan Harker in Chapter 2 of Stoker's novel. And the film characters' discovery of an empty coffin in a tomb – their presumption being that the corpse has become a vampire – seems similar to Dr. Seward's Diary in Stoker's Chapter 15: "I drew near and looked. The coffin was empty. It was certainly a surprise to me, and gave me a considerable shock, but Van Helsing was unmoved. He was now more sure than ever of his ground, and so emboldened to proceed in his task."

Though Browning had spent seven years or more hoping to direct a film version of *Dracula*, it is difficult to know how familiar he was in 1927 with Hamilton Deane-John L. Balderston's *Dracula–The Vampire Play*. He might have seen it on Broadway in the autumn of 1927, but that is unknown, and even if so, it would have occurred months after he wrote the story on which *London After Midnight* was based. Waldemar Young's surviving scenario based on Browning's story (his "2nd Version") was dated July 16, 1927, meaning a few months before the Deane-Balderston play opened on Broadway.[41] Indeed, what this makes certain is that Browning and MGM clearly intended to make *London After Midnight* prior to the play's success on Broadway

Nevertheless, Browning seems to have been aware of Hamilton Deane's stage adaptation of *Dracula*, which had been a success in London in early 1927, and he (and others at MGM) may have heard about the possibility of a Broadway production in late spring or summer of the same year. At any rate, Browning seems to have been influenced by Deane's play (as staged in London), because his story (and Young's scenario, based upon it) represents a loose variation of it, rather than, say, a loose adaptation of the Stoker novel.

In brief, much of the film's plot involves a vampire (not unlike Dracula) who seems to haunt a decrepit old house in close proximity to the other key characters (not unlike Carfax Abbey). An older investigator (not unlike Van Helsing) tries to protect a young lady (not unlike Lucy, as in the play) with the assistance of her lover (not unlike Harker). To keep vampires at bay, they place a sword inside a wreath of roses on the door (not unlike the use of wolfbane). And, to help offset the horrors, domestic servants provide comic relief (not unlike similar characters in the play).

All that said, Browning and Young crafted a tale marked by a number of clear differences from the Deane (and, for that matter, Deane-Balderston) play, as well as the Stoker novel. As for the vampire, he appeared quite different from Dracula visually, particularly in the fact he wore a beaver hat; he was also different from Dracula in his movements and gestures. Horror film collector Forrest J Ackerman, who saw the film in 1927, later recalled that Chaney's vampire walked in a manner not dissimilar to Groucho Marx. Another viewer who saw the film on its original release – Margaret Brannan of Marietta, Oklahoma – recalled that Chaney's vampire rotated his pupils to create an eerie effect, something that neither Raymond Huntley (who played Dracula in England in 1927) nor Bela Lugosi (who played Dracula on Broadway in 1927) were known to do.

All of the character names in *London After Midnight* are different from their *Dracula* counterparts, save for retaining Lucy as a female character's name (though the film's intertitles at times refer to her as Lucille). The film features not one vampire, but two, the second being a woman. And the film's use of hypnotism – its original title even having been *The Hypnotist* – wrests that power from the (fake) vampire and gives it to the vampire hunter.[42] Moreover, no equivalent character exists for Renfield, and there is no sanitarium.

Instead, *London After Midnight* opens with the murder of Lucy's father, with everything that follows being an elaborate effort to capture the murderer. Browning told a fan magazine:

*In our latest release [*London After Midnight*], we use a lot of ghosts and grave spirits and bats. Now, nobody believes in ghosts and grave spirits except children and some dark-complexioned Southerners. But people would believe in your ghost if they found out later he was a detective solving a murder crime. The plausibility of that doesn't lessen the thrills and chills in the least. On the contrary, it increases them, because the audience is not asked to believe the horrible impossible, but the horror possible.*[43]

In practice, this theory resulted in a narrative in which the two vampires are exposed as fakes, nothing more than a ruse concocted by a detective that successfully scares a murderer into confessing to his crime.

Perhaps Browning believed in the theory he espoused about "ghosts and grave spirits." After all, trickery is the key thread that runs throughout his filmography. But he had also wanted to produce *Dracula* in 1920, a novel that very definitely employs the supernatural. In terms of *London After Midnight*, the non-supernatural explanation (and some of the other plot changes) may have primarily been a narrative device used to prevent lawsuits over copyright infringement of Stoker's novel and/or stage adaptations of it.

At any rate, *London After Midnight* opened in December 1927 and proved successful in many theatres where it was shown, as the following theatre-manager reports from the period attest:

"My people enjoyed two delightfully fearful evenings with this spooky, awesome thing. Chaney has a pleasing role as the detective, and did better business than usual for me."
– Pastime theatre, Mason, Michigan[44]

"First money maker since last April and this run off in the middle of hot August. People evidently like Chaney. Play good, very good."
– Rex Theatre, Salmon, Idaho.[45]

"Mystery entertainment through all seven reels. Give us more like it, Lon."
– Royal Theatre, Kimball, South Dakota[46]

"A shivery mystery drama that scares them to death, but they like to be scared. Drew big Saturday crowd."
– Strand Theatre, Paoli, Indiana[47]

"A good show of mystery, horrors and excitement. Did not please so well on that account. Not a good show for children. All parts well played. Chaney is sure a wonder in this show. Play if you like this type of picture."
– Majestic Theatre, Homer, Michigan[48]

Despite concerns over audience members who weren't interested in "mystery" and "horrors," *London After Midnight* went on to become the most financially successful film that Tod Browning and Lon Chaney ever made together.

London After Midnight also became Tod Browning's first screen adaptation of *Dracula*, even if it was unoffical. Just as the Stoker novel and Deane play influenced it, *London After Midnight* would in some ways influence Browning's 1931 version of *Dracula*, as he would return to certain imagery that he created in 1927, imagery that he may well have been pondering since 1920. The funereal appearance of the (fake) female vampire (portrayed by Edna Tichenor) returns in the costumes and makeup of Dracula's wives in the 1931 film. Armadillos appear in both films, preternatural and nocturnal creatures that Browning apparently believed would add to an otherworldly *mise-en-scène*. And, perhaps most striking of all, the decrepit Balfour Mansion in *London After Midnight* clearly inspired aspects of Castle Dracula and Carfax Abbey in *Dracula*.

Such similarities would not go unnoticed at the time. Reviewing *Dracula* in 1931, Chester B. Bahn provided a particularly adept account of the film for readers: "Mr. Browning's knack for the handling of the eerie, demonstrated in several Lon Chaney productions, approximates genius in *Dracula*. ... Especially effective is Browning's use of fog and atmospheric manifestations; here, the director has gone forward far more than a step from what he first achieved in a Chaney picture, *London After Midnight*."[49]

Tod Browning and Sound Cinema

The fact that some modern critics berate Browning for his limited and unimaginative use of sound is strange, as a close examination of his pre-*Dracula* talkies reveals. Indeed, speaking about the issue as early as August 1928, Browning enthused about the possibilities of sound, believing that the ultimate value of the talkie would be to reproduce sound effects which could "greatly heighten the illusion of the screen drama," adding that "one can have the booming of surf in sea scenes, the roar of the crowd in mob scenes, the mechanical noises in airplane pictures, and all the noises of nature in outdoor pictures."[50]

Browning's grasp of these possibilities can be seen and heard in the first two scenes of *The Thirteenth Chair*, the only two that take place outside the Crosby home. Neither scene exists in Bayard Veiller's play, on which the film is based, and both show a rather careful use of cinematic technique to set the mood. For example, Scene One establishes an exotic locale, in part due to diegetic music (meaning music that both the onscreen characters and the film audience hear): the beating of drums accompanied by a quiet flute and a stringed instrument, perhaps a sitar. Outside of the music played under the opening credits (which is repeated at the happy ending), this is the only song heard during the film.

Shot 1 of Scene 1 is a long shot of the interior of Spencer Lee's home. It is dark; the only light coming into the room is moonlight through the blinds. Edward Wales (John Davidson) enters the room surreptitiously and immediately walks to screen left. Shot 2 cuts on a match-on-action of Wales' moving body as he begins to shut the blinds, making the room even

Promotional material for Browning's first sound film, *The Thirteenth Chair* (1929).

darker; the camera pans right as he moves across the room and turns on a flashlight. Its beam illuminates the closeup of a table in Shot 3, on which sits British tea cups and an exotic tea pot: the first sign of colonialism. Shot 4 shows Wales in silhouette still holding the flashlight, which in Shot 5 illuminates a camera pan of the chalk outline of a man's body man on the floor: the first sign of murder. That the pan is right-to-left (rather than left-to-right) suggests a disruption, made more disruptive when the pan lingers on a bloodstain in the middle of the drawing. Thus far there has been scarcely a sound in the room. As Wales's darkened figure approaches the camera in Shot 6, the loud squawk of a parrot (seen in closeup in Shot 7) jars him, the household, and the viewer. Browning's first talkie thus begins without dialogue, opting instead for exotic background music and a particularly jarring sound effect.

Browning continued to explore sound effectively in his 1930 remake of *Outside the Law*, including its ability to mislead audiences intentionally, an effect that notably extended his cinematic vernacular. For example, one scene finds Fingers (Owen Moore) talking to Connie (Mary Nolan), who is in an offscreen bathroom. We hear the sound of water splashing, with Browning creating the impression that she is bathing. The camera follows Fingers as he moves into the bathroom, but here we learn the sound is nothing more than a trick. Instead of finding Connie in the nude, she is fully clothed, bathing a dog in the tub.

In addition to music during its opening and closing titles, *Outside the Law* also offers an array of fascinating diegetic music and sound effects. A shoeshine boy works on Cobra's

(Edward G. Robinson's) footwear in such a rhythmic manner that Robinson comments on his "tune." A Santa Claus rings a bell, and a boy's little toy wheezes out an odd noise. A pianist pounds out music at the theatre that employs Connie to be one of its living pictures. A bank security guard sings a song, as does Connie in her apartment. And on three different occasions, jazz fills a nightclub set. But perhaps the most notable use of music in *Outside the Law* occurs after Fingers purchases a radio on Christmas Eve. He dials a station that broadcasts peaceful holiday music during an increasingly uncomfortable scene in which Fingers and Connie learn that the neighbor boy's father is a police captain. The friction between the music and unfolding action is palpable.

One can also consider issues of sound in Browning's post-*Dracula* cinema. In the 1931 *Iron Man*, for example, no opening theme is heard under the film's title sequence. Instead, we hear the relentless sound of Kid Mason (Lew Ayres) hitting a punching bag, a device that returns later in the film as part of a montage of newspaper headlines. As for diegetic music, *Iron Man* features a not unexpected scene in a nightclub with a live pianist playing a tune. The soundscape transforms when a female character turns on the radio, announcing to the crowd, "Now we're gonna have some regular music!" The jazz booming from its speaker drowns out the piano music, which returns to prominence later in the scene.

But Browning never lost his ability to create unnerving scenes by avoiding music (and, at times, even sound effects). When the title characters of *Freaks* pursue Hercules (Henry Victor) after he has been knifed, no one speaks and no music is heard; they stalk him against the simple but relentless sound of rain and thunder. Not only is the scene powerful in its articulation, it stands in marked contrast to other scenes, as the film's first eighteen minutes feature an extensive use of diegetic music, something upon which critics have failed to comment. Then, a later film, *The Devil-Doll*, is devoid of non-diegetic music (meaning background music that the audience hears, but that the onscreen characters do not). And in *Miracles for Sale*, a medium conducts a séance in darkness, with a range of onlookers observing her efforts to contact the other side. For over 90 seconds, we see a series of medium shots of the onlookers, as well as a long shot of the medium summoning forth a dead spirit. No music or sounds of any kind are heard. Just deafening silence, an aural – and quite eerie – nothingness that is finally broken when the leading lady recognizes the spirit.

Of course the apparition is yet another fake, another ruse.

Carl Laemmle, Jr.

Born Julius Laemmle in 1908, Carl Laemmle, Jr. – or "Junior Laemmle," as he became known in the film industry and in the press – was the son of the founder of Universal Pictures, one of the men who helped create Hollywood. As an independent film producer, Carl Laemmle, Sr. boldly defied the Edison trust during the nickelodeon era. Then, in 1912, Universal became one of the first studios in California, its success keeping it in business throughout the silent period and beyond. Indeed, Junior Laemmle's rise in power at the studio would coincide with the rise of the talking picture.

As early as 1926, Louella O. Parsons – who became one of Junior Laemmle's strongest supporters in the press – told readers that he was busy writing a story for Jean Hersholt; she quoted a Universal scriptwriter who claimed that he was a hard worker and a "chip off the old block."[51] Four years later, Parsons wrote: "Long, long ago, when he was knee high to a grasshopper, he used to tell his father what was wrong with Universal pictures. His father

The Laemmles, father and son.

listened, too."[52]

During the late twenties, Junior Laemmle was the only member of the second generation of the studio families who followed in his father's footsteps. His father had hoped he would study law at Princeton, but Junior's desire to write dovetailed with his interest in the film business; soon he was scripting Universal's "Collegian" two-reelers that offered fictional stories of university life. Instilling them with "plenty of pep and personality," Junior made a hit of the series, described by one newspaper as "vibrant with excitement and flaming with young love and hilarious fun."[53]

Louella O. Parsons continued to support Junior Laemmle, arguing in 1928 that he was "handicapped by being the son of the owner of Universal," and that he had to "prove that he could make good before his dad would let him supervise any important productions. … He brings into the production a youthful enthusiasm and understanding of the psychology of modern life and an inheritance of business acumen that is invaluable."[54] Perceiving those attributes, Laemmle, Sr. let his son produce such important features as *Lonesome* (1928), directed by Paul Fejos, a man the press referred to as Junior's "discovery."[55]

Given his own age and his belief in his peers throughout America, the youth of America shaped much of Junior Laemmle's outlook on the cinema. Discussing the "unfailing barometer" of audience fan mail, he assured *Film Daily* that, "the humble idea of a high school girl may prove more valuable in some instances than the opinions of all the experts put together."[56]

Near the end of 1928, Universal's General Manager Robert E. Walsh promoted Junior Laemmle to the position of Associate Producer (which allowed him to oversee many productions) after his "expert supervision" of Paul Fejos' *The Last Performance* (1928) and Paul Leni's *The Last Warning* (1929). His first assignment in the new role was *Broadway* (1929), directed by Fejos and starring Glenn Tryon and Evelyn Brent.[57] The result became one of the most impressive of the musicals produced during the late twenties. Gangsters fight backstage while a nightclub presents songs visualized in elaborate crane shots.

As 1929 progressed, Junior Laemmle's importance at Universal increased. In March, it was he who denied rumors about a pending sale of Universal to the press, rather than the general manager, whose power was decreasing.[58] In April, the announcement came that Junior would supervise *King of Jazz*, a major production built around Paul Whiteman and his orchestra.[59] Then, in May 1929, *Film Daily* heralded the news that Junior was "in complete charge of the studio and all production activity. The change is effective at once."[60] By the end of the same year, industry trades reported yet another promotion, claiming Junior Laemmle would "ascend to the command of production in Universal City, where he will be in full executive charge."[61]

John Drinkwater's biography *The Life and Adventures of Carl Laemmle* (G. P. Putnam's Sons, 1931) offers the following description of Junior Laemmle's rise:

> In 1929, Laemmle, daring as usual, made his son, Carl Laemmle Junior, director-in-chief of production at Universal City. The young executive had just passed his twenty-first birthday, and in the gossip of the trade his promotion was attributed to mere family sentiment. But his father though fond was not foolish. He had watched the boy, anxiously, critically, and believed he would be equal to big things in the business. He decided to load him with responsibility early, to give him a leading part in the inception and launching of a policy of which, it was to be hoped, he would one day be in first control. Under parental supervision, which was to become interference only in the case of emergency, Carl Laemmle Junior, therefore, was told to go ahead with the provision of pictures that would meet the demands of the new principle of quality productions.
>
> ... Such opportunities have rarely come to so young a

Junior Laemmle

man. He has immense resources, is gifted with initiative and intuition, and is prepared to back his fancy. His success would be very popular. People like him as they like his father, and the older men in his employment have a genuine respect for him. He will make mistakes, and the best that could be wished him is that they will be mistakes not of timidity and compromise, but of courage and imagination. I think they will be, and if so, few of them will prove really to be mistakes in the end. But every time he releases a picture that is below his own taste, he will be giving an exceedingly dangerous hostage to fortune. His responsibility is greater, perhaps, than he or anyone else at the present time realizes. He has the gifts and the character to bear it. His use of these may have an incalculable influence upon the future of moving picture production.[62]

Those in favor of Junior Laemmle's position continued to see his youth as an asset.

But others were not so sure about the wisdom of placing him in command of an entire studio's production, blaming the decision on the folly of a father blinded by pride.[63] In the words of one columnist, the younger Laemmle had nearly "been juniored to death by the glib hereabouts."[64] And so, as part of an effort to be taken seriously on his own terms, he often put in twelve-hour days and worked not from a large office, but instead from a small bungalow near the back of the studio.[65]

In April 1930, the *Los Angeles Evening Herald* declared that, "Carl Laemmle, Jr. should ... silence his critics with the *King of Jazz*."[66] Shot in color and featuring a large array of musical numbers, comedy sketches, and even animation, *King of Jazz* (1930) remains impressive, particularly in terms of its sets and cinematography. The film also features some striking special effects, including an ending in which Paul Whiteman uses his baton to stir a "melting pot" into kaleidoscopic images of musicians and dancers.

In March 1930, Junior Laemmle took a print of *King of Jazz* to San Bernardino for a "secret" preview at the Fox Theatre, a screening that even few people at the studio knew about. His reasoning: get away from a Hollywood audience and hear what real moviegoers think. Though the film became a box-office flop, he would continue to use the preview as an important component of the editing process.[67]

Junior Laemmle's major success in 1930 came not in the form of a musical, but instead in Universal's adaptation of Erich Maria Remarque's novel *All Quiet on the Western Front*. One period account described its production:

Carl Laemmle, Jr. is responsible for the picture; that is, it is said he is the one who selected the story and was determined to have Universal screen it.

Other companies frowned upon it as pretty nearly impossible screen material, and the story goes that Junior rather lost his nerve as the production on it progressed.

He was courageous enough to see picture possibilities in the book, but most youngsters do wish there were opportunities to retract a little when their elders frown and shake their heads.

He hired Lewis Milestone to direct the picture and gave Milestone a contract which said no one could interfere with this director's work.

Then at the time when Junior began to be a bit worried, he started to confab with Milestone. He had many ideas about the picture, but the uppermost in his mind urged him to fret the director with the idea that the picture should have a happy ending.

It is said that Milestone disagreed with the young Laemmle, but the matter was not solved with that. Then came the final conference when Junior declared that All Quiet *must have a* happy ending.

'What do you suggest?', Milestone inquired.

'We must make this story end happily,' replied Junior.

'All right, then,' Milestone shot back, 'we'll have the Germans win the war!'

Junior's courage shot up again, and he saw the picture through its literal translation to ending the [film the way the book does]. That's the story anyway.[68]

And so Junior Laemmle oversaw the film version of a novel that had allegedly been impossible to produce in Hollywood. Despite its unhappy ending and its lack of a female lead, *All Quiet on the Western Front* became an enormous box-office success, going on to win the Academy Award for Best Picture (and Best Director) of 1929-30.

It is true that Junior Laemmle searched for numerous safe productions in 1930. For example, the press announced he would oversee a sound remake of *The Hunchback of Notre Dame* with Edward G. Robinson in the title role.[69] While that project did not go forward, in June 1930, Laemmle did engage Rupert Julian to direct a sound remake of *The Cat and the Canary* (1927), which would be released in the autumn of that year as *The Cat Creeps* (1930). Here were examples of looking to the hits of the silent era to remake as talkies, a common production tactic.

But there can be no doubt that Junior Laemmle was also taking big risks in 1930, more and more of them. In the spring of 1930, he announced a major policy decision, one in which the studio would largely "discontinue program pictures and just make only great pictures."[70]

Above Top: Trade advertisement published in 1931. Above: Junior Laemmle's film industry predictions for 1932.

Such an approach defied the general logic that his father employed to guide the studio for over fifteen years. And so he was attempting to do something much more than overseeing Universal's productions: he was trying to transform the studio into a company devoted to prestige filmmaking.

As 1930 came to a close, Junior Laemmle explained the chances he took:

Crude melodramatic action is no longer the limitation of screen production, for the recent output of the studios includes numerous examples of subtle and delicate drama translated to the screen without any sacrifice of their spirit or significance. The realization of this has emboldened Universal to undertake the production of a number of splendid stories which would have baffled us a short time ago. Not only have we demonstrated that situations based on psychological reactions can be effectively produced, but we know that the response of audiences thereto will be enthusiastic. All Quiet on the Western Front *is an illustration in point. We defied the judgment of many experienced film people, who predicted that this story could not be told on the screen with any semblance of its original spirit and charm. The result is history. Now we are engaged in a number of other productions in which the attempt to preserve the intangible element of psychological situations has been eminently successful.*[71]

And so, during the spring and summer of 1930 shortly before acquiring the film rights to *Dracula*, Junior Laemmle was steeled by financial and artistic successes that confounded conventional Hollywood wisdom.

Conclusion

In 1926, the American press described a 1925 Soviet film entitled *The Bear's Wedding* (*Medvezhya Svadba*, aka *The Legend of the Bear's Wedding*):

The film takes place in the form of a diary, kept by a German pastor, who, searching for some ancient documents, visits a lonely castle. This castle is tenanted by a beast in human form, the last survivor of an aristocratic family, who on his wedding night turns into a bear, bites the throat of his bride, and drinks her blood.
[One critic has called] attention to the similarity of this theme and that contained in Bram Stoker's famous thriller Dracula. Dracula *also was written in the form of a diary, that of an Englishman who went to a lonely castle in Transylvania where he found himself in the stronghold of aristocratic blood-drinkers.*[72]

Noting that the movie teemed with "extraordinary horror," a journalist added that there was "small likelihood of its ever being exhibited" in the United States. By 1927, however, the film did appear at a small number of American theatres, garnering reviews in *Variety*, the *New York Times* and in *Time* magazine.[73]

In 1926, the press also told readers that "[*Dracula*], incidentally, has been acquired for production by a German film company, but no news has been forthcoming concerning its progress."[74] This story seems not to refer to *Nosferatu* (1922), but rather some unproduced film, a project overlooked by prior historians. Taken together with *The Bear's Wedding*, it underscored the increasing likelihood that a sanctioned version of *Dracula* would reach the screen, even if not in America.

Program for *The Bear's Wedding* (1925, *Medvezhya Svadba*, aka *The Legend of the Bear's Wedding*).

Junior Laemmle's cousin Carla once recalled that, "All the studios, including Universal, considered the story too horrible to film [in 1927]."[75] Her memory was correct, as surviving Universal paperwork prepared for the story department in June 1927 makes clear. One reader claimed, "I cannot possibly see how it is going to make a motion picture." Another wrote, "For a picture it is out of the question – mostly because of the censorship." But perhaps a third reader conveyed the key issues in the following text:

> ABSOLUTELY NO!! In the first place, it would be impossible to transcribe this novel of horrors to the screen. And, if it were possible, who would want to sit through an evening of unpleasantness such as a picture of this type would afford?[76]

Along with questions over censorship and audience interest, a fourth reader noted that the story's complexity would make it difficult to translate into a silent film, uncomfortably joking that it "would take a thousand titles to tell the people what it was all about … and then they [still] wouldn't know!"

That said, a lone fifth reader was positive, seeing in *Dracula* the same traits that likely attracted Tod Browning to the novel in 1920:

> For mystery and blood-curdling horror, I have never read its equal. For sets, impressionistic and weird, it cannot be surpassed. This story contains everything necessary for a wierd [sic], unnatural, mysterious picture.
> I understand it is now being played in London and achieving tremendous success. It is usually the case that if a story can be played upon the stage a screen version can be written from it as

well. It will be a difficult task and one will run up against the censor continually, but I think it can be done.

This reader concluded by stating, "It is daring but if done there can be no doubt as to its making money."[77]

But Universal did not produce *Dracula* in 1927, nor did any other studio, save for Browning's loose adaptation with *London After Midnight* at MGM. It would take different leadership at Universal to proceed with such a project, leadership of the type willing to take major risks, even during the onset of the Great Depression. And it would also require a director who understood the material and who could properly adapt it to the screen.

In November 1929, *Variety* noted that MGM decided not to renew Browning's contract, which was about to expire on the heels of his direction of *The Thirteenth Chair*.[78] Why did they make the decision? Modern writers have suggested Browning's alcoholism as the possible cause, but there is absolutely no evidence (or even rumors) from 1929 to substantiate that view.[79] As Lon Chaney's biographer Michael Blake has quite rightly said, "the truth behind Browning's departure from MGM will probably remain a mystery."[80] Of course it is important to remember that biographical mysteries aren't necessarily borne out of the mysterious (or the scandalous), but often simply out of a lack of surviving information.

In this particular case, it seems extremely *unlikely* that alcoholism caused MGM to drop Browning. After all, in 1930, shortly after leaving MGM, Browning regularly socialized with its key players. At the end of March, he was a guest at a party attended by Harry Rapf, one of the three men who ran MGM.[81] It might be easy to suggest that being joint attendees at an event held by a third party has little meaning insofar as Browning's relationship with Rapf in 1930. But that certainly can't be said of a bridge party that Browning and his wife hosted in their home in May 1930.[82] Guests not only included Harry Rapf, but also Irving Thalberg. Had these men (in tandem with MGM studio chief Louis B. Mayer) just fired Browning from MGM, it is difficult to believe that Browning would have invited them into his own home.

Consider also the modern allegations of Browning's drinking from the standpoint of Universal, who signed Browning shortly after his 1929 MGM contract ended. Had there been rumors of problems with alcoholism in 1929, Universal would likely have heard about it; indeed, Carl Laemmle, Sr. knew Irving Thalberg (the "boy genius" producer at MGM) extremely well, having essentially launched Thalberg's career at Universal before he migrated to MGM in 1923.[83] No, Universal would likely have bristled at any rumors of Browning's drinking, as his alcoholism in the early twenties had caused Laemmle to drop him in 1923. To rehire him on the heels of the expired MGM contract suggests they had faith in his abilities and in his sobriety.

Moreover, MGM would sign Browning again in April of 1931, following the completion of his brief tenure at Universal. If Browning had given either studio major problems of *any* kind, it is difficult to see why MGM would have hired him back after the passage of a mere sixteen months.[84] All of these reasons together suggest that drinking was not the reason that Browning's MGM contract expired.

By contrast, it could well have been Browning who desired a change. He had in fact announced he was leaving in MGM two years earlier, at which time the studio offered him a new and better contract in order to persuade him to stay.[85] In late 1929 and 1930, Junior Laemmle spared no expense at hiring new talent for Universal, and he may have in fact lured

Browning back to the very studio where Browning had become a major director. In addition to money, Browning may have taken great satisfaction at returning to a studio that had once let him go. Indeed, *Billboard* told readers that Browning was rejoining his "first love."[86] After all, the new contract marked his fourth with Universal.[87]

Variety mentioned the Universal contract on 12 February 1930, noting that Browning would "direct a group of features, among which will be a talking version of *Virgin of Stamboul*."[88] Another article claimed Browning's first film would be *The Scarlet Triangle*, which he would write and direct.[89] In March, Universal announced that Browning would direct a film adapted from his own short story *Little Buddha*, which would star Edward G. Robinson.[90] Then, in June, the studio purchased the talking picture rights for Browning's story *White Tiger*.[91] All of these reports imply that the studio that was working hard to please him. Indeed, a Universal advertisement in March 1930 touted the "signing of the famous Tod Browning," calling it "big time news for the trade and for the fans!"[92]

Article announcing Browning's return to Universal Studios in 1930.

And his first film under the contract gave him the chance to cast Edward G. Robinson in a remake of *Outside the Law*, with shooting underway in June 1930.[93] Reviews of the film varied, but many were quite positive.[94] For example, *Exhibitors Herald-World* wrote: "*Outside the Law* ranks as one of the best of the crook dramas. Browning's direction is superb."[95] *Billboard* judged the movie to be "grand entertainment" that was "admirably directed."[96] *Film Daily* called it a "corking underworld drama that should stand up as well as its former silent version. Acting and direction very good."[97] And the *Los Angeles Evening Herald* told readers, "Tod Browning, who acted in the dual capacity of director and co-author with Garrett Fort, has injected originality of plot and vivid detail into a fast-moving story. It is good entertainment for lovers of tenderloin topics."[98]

Films like *Outside the Law* may well have been among the reasons Browning signed with Universal. Though projects like *The Virgin of Stamboul* remake did not come to pass, Junior Laemmle signalled an important opportunity for Browning: he would get to direct films that he wanted to direct, either from stories he had written or that he loved. One of those became *Dracula*. The two men may have even discussed that possibility prior to the execution of Browning's contract, as Browning seems to have been hoping to direct the project at MGM in 1929.[99]

On 3 July 1930, the *Hollywood Daily Citizen* announced that Junior Laemmle "has pointed his finger at Tod Browning to direct Universal's all-talking version of *Dracula*, after having seen with great satisfaction the proof [of] the director's talents in the nearly finished *Outside the Law*." The publication added that Browning's "particular gifts" as the director of "crook dramas" and "Lon Chaney productions" would fit the story "to a T."

However, on 19 August, the *Hollywood Daily Citizen* offered a different report, one that in retrospect seems bizarre, if not unthinkable. Elizabeth Yeaman's column noted that Junior Laemmle was looking for someone to direct *Dracula*. "Tod Browning, of course, has a great deal of experience in directing mystery plays," Yeaman noted, "but on the other hand Hobart Henley, who recently joined the Universal staff, is still without a picture. The decision wavers between these two."[100]

What could explain this account? It was likely a mistake, something that certainly did occur from time to time in Hollywood gossip columns.[101] That fact seems relatively certain given that Universal had excitedly announced Browning as the film's director in a paid advertisement in *Variety* on 13 August, published nearly a week *before* Yeaman's column.

But it could also have represented a moment of disagreement between Laemmle and Browning, perhaps due to differing beliefs about how to adapt the novel and/or play. Or perhaps it was due to their different backgrounds and ages. Browning may have been happy to return to Universal, but he may not have been happy that his boss was at that time a mere 22 years old, someone who had been a child wandering around the lot a decade earlier when Browning was one of studio's key directors.

It is evident that Junior Laemmle at times had to fight in order to show his command of the studio. Consider the following example from March 1930:

Carl Laemmle Jr. is authority for the statement that [actress] Mary Nolan is off the Universal payroll. Junior ought to know, for he is the boy who is in charge of production at Universal City. Miss Nolan chose a bad time to get temperamental, for Universal will not have any more productions until May. If Mary is a good girl by that time, she will be given the lead in Tod Browning's next picture. If she isn't – well – relations between her and Universal are off permanently.[102]

Relations improved, with Nolan signing a new five-year contract with an increase in salary and an opportunity to star in Browning's *Outside the Law*.[103] But Junior Laemmle was clearly able to make his opinions known and to take action when he deemed it necessary. If Browning and Junior Laemmle had any disagreement, the mention of Henley's name could well have been Laemmle's attempt to either infuriate or control Browning, who had indeed been waiting for ten years to direct an official adaptation of *Dracula*.

Whether or not Tod Browning and Junior Laemmle collided personally, which we do not know, they certainly coincided historically. And they did so with a project that forever marked both men. Presumably some other studio and some other director would eventually have produced a version of *Dracula*. With all of its legal problems, F. W. Murnau's *Nosferatu* had already proven that could happen. But for such a project to be mounted successfully as a sound film in Hollywood at the start of the Great Depression required careful thought and experience, as well as great resources and daring. Together, Tod Browning and Carl Laemmle, Jr. provided those necessary components.

1. In this book, I will refer to the studio as "Universal Pictures," as during the time of *Dracula*'s production its official name was "Universal Pictures Company, Inc." Most film viewers and writers use the less precise name "Universal Studios."
2. "Behind the Screen in Movies." *Indiana Evening Gazette* (Indiana, PA) 18 Feb. 1925. It is worth noting that actor Arthur Edmund Carew's name was occasionally spelled as "Carewe," though in the 1920s it more commonly appeared *without* the final "e."
3. Koszarski, Richard. Email to Gary D. Rhodes 26 Apr. 2012. Koszarski made notes regarding 1915 discussion of *Dracula* while examining Universal's legal files in the mid-1970s.
4. "Little Theatre Film?" *Oakland Tribune* 19 Dec. 1920. Here the reference to "Little Theatre" refers to the live theatre movement that was underway in America during the 1910s, with new theatre groups forming in many American cities to produce non-commercial plays in intimate surroundings, at times as an effort to combat the spectacle of the cinema. The usage of the term in this context likely suggests that *Dracula* represented a challenging story of the type that Little Theatre companies often staged, even though there is no indication that any of them specifically produced a stage version of the Stoker novel prior to 1920. Overall, the film industry did perceive the potential effect that Little Theatres could have. For more information, see: "Little Theatre Movement Offers Film Suggestions." *Exhibitors Herald* 1 July 1922: 37.
5. Dickey, Joan. "A Maker of Mystery." *Motion Picture Classic* (Mar. 1928): 33, 80.
6. Qtd. in "Inside Stuff – Pictures." *Variety* 25 Apr. 1951: 14.
7. "Vampires! Monsters! Horrors!" *New York Times* 1 Mar. 1936: X4.
8. Dickey, "A Maker of Mystery," pp. 33, 80.
9. The most extensive Tod Browning biography appears in: Skal, David and Elias Sevada. *Dark Carnival: The Secret World of Tod Browning, Hollywood's Master of the Macabre* (New York: Anchor/Doubleday, 1995).
10. Rapf, Maurice. Interview with Gary D. Rhodes. Norman, Oklahoma. 1997.
11. Dickey, "A Maker of Mystery,"p. 80.
12. "Old Troupers at Hollywood." *Billboard* 24 Oct. 1914: 57.
13. "Excellent Bill at the Crystal Theatre." *Elkhart Truth* (Elkhart, IN) 28 Apr. 1908.
14. "The City." *Eau Claire Leader* (Eau Claire, WI) 15 Apr. 1908.
15. "Chicago Music Notes." *Billboard* 27 Feb. 1909: 49.
16. "Vaudeville Notes." *Billboard* 16 Oct. 1909: 41.
17. "Burlesque Bills." *Philadelphia Inquirer* 2 Mar. 1913; "Whirl of Mirth." *Variety* 23 Aug. 1912.
18. "Bervities of the Business." *Motography* 19 Sept. 1914: 419.
19. *The Photoplayers' Weekly* 30 Apr. 1915: 12.
20. "Tod Browning Rejoins Universal." *Universal Weekly* 15 Mar. 1930: 10.
21. "George Stone Had Pair of Real Copper-Toed Boots." *Tulsa World* 11 Mar. 1917.
22. "Film Flashes." *Jackson Citizen Patriot* (Jackson, MI) 3 June 1917.
23. "Los Angeles Film Brevities." *Moving Picture World* 1 Dec. 1917.
24. "*The Legion of Death* Starring Edith Storey." *Moving Picture World* 22 Dec. 1917.
25. Von Harleman, G. P. "News of Los Angeles and Vicinity." *Moving Picture World* 24 Feb. 1917.
26. "*The Eyes of Mystery*." *Moving Picture World* 9 Feb. 1918: 867.
27. "Strand." *Tulsa World* 12 Mar. 1918.
28. "No megaphone for Tod Browning." *Omaha World Herald* (Omaha, NE) 30 Nov. 1919: 12.
29. "Universal." *Exhibitors Herald* 26 Feb. 1921: 95.
30. "Universal." *Exhibitors Herald* 28 May 1921: 79.
31. "Universal." *Exhibitors Herald* 7 Aug. 1920: 81.
32. "Celluloid Row." *Exhibitors Trade Review* 21 May 1921: 2128.
33. "*Outside the Law* Is Booked in Practically Every City in US." *Exhibitors Herald* 26 Feb. 1921: 79.
34. "*Outside the Law* Is Re-Released." *Universal Weekly* 13 Feb. 1926: 14.
35. "*Outisde the Law*." *Photoplay* (Apr. 1921): 52.
36. "My Best Picture." *Film Daily* 7 June 1925: 19.
37. "Lon Chaney and Director Browning Celebrate 'Anniversary' Week on MGM Lot." *Weekly Film Review* 11 Aug. 1928: 20.
38. Manon, Hugh. "Seeing Through Seeing Through: The *Trompe l'Oeil* Effect and Bodily Difference in the Cinema of Tod Browning." *Framework: The Journal of Cinema and the Media*, Vol. 47, No. 1 (Spring 2006): 60-82.
39. The first reconstruction came in Philip J. Riley's book *London After Midnight* (New York: Cornwall, 1985). The second was Rick Schmidlin's photo reconstruction in film form, which was released on the TCM Archives DVD entitled *The Lon Chaney Collection* in 2003.
40. Watts, Richard, Jr. "On the Screen." *New York Herald Tribune* 12 Dec. 1927.
41. This script appears in: Riley, *London After Midnight*, pp. 41-71.
42. Prior to its release, MGM also considered the title *London After Dark*. See "Chaney Title Changed." *Film Daily* 20 Oct. 1927: 4.
43. Dickey, "A Maker of Mystery," p. 80.
44. "Metro-Goldwyn-Mayer." *Exhibitors Herald and Moving Picture World* 14 July 1928.
45. "Metro-Goldwyn-Mayer." *Exhibitors Herald and Moving Picture World* 29 Sept. 1928.
46. "Metro-Goldwyn-Mayer." *Exhibitors Herald and Moving Picture World* 17 Nov. 1928.
47. "Metro-Goldwyn-Mayer." *Exhibitors Herald and Moving Picture World* 11 Aug. 1928.
48. "Metro-Goldwyn-Mayer." *Exhibitors Herald and Moving Picture World* 21 July 1928.
49. Bahn, Chester B. "*Dracula* Shares Eckel's Honors with Paul Forster; Society Talkie at Keith's." *Syracuse Herald*

(Syracuse, NY) 15 Feb. 1931: 6.
50. "Talkers to Develop Own School, Is Contention." *Film Daily* 26 Aug. 1928: 11.
51. Parsons, Louella O. *Los Angeles Examiner* 14 Sept. 1926.
52. Parsons, Louella O. *Los Angeles Examiner* 6 Jan. 1930.
53. "The Collegians No. 5 at Dixie Theatre." *Uniontown Morning Herald* (Uniontown, PA) 26 Jan. 1927.
54. Parsons, Louella O. "Film Gossip." *San Diego Evening Tribune* 11 July 1928.
55. Ibid.
56. "Along the Rialto." *Film Daily* 18 June 1930.
57. "Laemmle Jr. Made Asso. Producer." *Film Daily* 8 Dec. 1928.
58. "Laemmle, Jr. Denies Deal on for Sale of U." *Film Daily* 11 Mar. 1929: 1.
59. "Laemmle, Jr. in Charge." *Film Daily* 18 Apr. 1929: 7.
60. "Welsh Out of Universal; Laemmle Jr. Takes Helm." *Film Daily* 24 May 1929: 1.
61. "Laemmle to Celebrate 20 Years of Production." *Film Daily* 5 Dec. 1929: 8.
62. Drinkwater, John. *The Life and Adventures of Carl Laemmle* (New York: G. P. Putnam's Sons, 1931).
63. "One Moment, Please!" *Cleveland Plain Dealer* 20 Apr. 1930.
64. Merrick, Mollie. "Hollywood – In Person." *New Orleans Times-Picayune* 6 July 1928.
65. Thomas, Dan. "Declares Movies Won't Let Stage Succumb to Rush of 'Talkies.'" *Sandusky Star Journal* (Sandusky, OH) 27 Apr. 1929.
66. Carroll, Harrison. "*King of Jazz.*" *Los Angeles Evening Herald* 21 Apr. 1930.
67. According to the *Motion Picture Herald* (21 Mar. 1931), Universal "took a loss of $1,000,000" on *King of Jazz*, and "would have lost considerably more but for the fact that European countries received it satisfactorily" (p. 19).
68. Marsh, W. Ward. "Two Big War Films Here." *Cleveland Plain Dealer* 12 June 1930.
69. Parsons, Louella O. *Los Angeles Examiner* 3 July 1930.
70. Merrick, Mollie. "Hollywood – In Person." *New Orleans Times-Picayune* 20 July 1930.
71. Laemmle, Carl, Jr. "The Public Wants the Psychological Story." *Film Daily* 28 Dec. 1930: 3.
72. Dickstein, Martin. "Slow Motion." *Brooklyn Eagle* 19 Dec. 1926.
73. "The Bear's Wedding." *Variety* 1 Aug. 1928: 22; Hall, Mordaunt. "The Screen." *New York Times* 21 May 1927: 25; "Cinema." *Time* 30 May 1927: 35-36.
74. Ibid.
75. Laemmle, Carla. "Preface" to *Dracula (The Original 1931 Shooting Script)*. Ed. by Philip J. Riley. (Absecon, NJ: MagicImage, 1990): 16.
76. Copies of the original reader responses appear in Riley, *Dracula*, p. 30.
77. Ibid., p. 30.
78. "No Renewal for Browning?" *Variety* 30 Nov. 1929: 8.
79. Skal, David J. *Hollywood Gothic: The Tangled Web of Dracula from Novel to Stage to Screen* (New York: W. W. Norton, 1990).
80. Blake, Michael. *A Thousand Faces: Lon Chaney's Unique Artistry in Motion Pictures* (Vestal, New York: Vestal Press, 1995): 273. In *Hollywood Gothic*, Skal notes that it was "widely believed that Irving Thalberg had fired [Browning] from Metro in 1929" over his drinking (p. 116). But Skal provides no evidence for this claim, which – by being written in the passive voice – avoids the need to declare who believed such rumors.
81. Yeaman, Elizabeth. "Society in Filmland." *Hollywood Daily Citizen* 2 Apr. 1930.
82. "Brownings Give Bridge Luncheon." *Los Angeles Examiner* 11 May 1930.
83. Schatz, Thomas. *The Genius of the System: Hollywood Filmmaking in the Studio Era* (New York: Pantheon, 1988): 28.
84. "Browning and Metro." *Variety* 15 Apr. 1931.
85. In November 1927, Browning announced his intentions to leave MGM, his future plans being "indefinite." But then whatever disagreement he had with MGM was resolved when both parties "settled" any "differences." See "Tod Browning Confirms Report of Leaving MGM." *Film Daily* 13 Nov. 1927: 14; "Tod Browning Settles Differences with MGM." *Film Daily* 4 Dec. 1927: 18.
86. "Tod Browning Again with Universal." *Billboard* 15 Mar. 1930: 18.
87. According to "Tod Browning Has Again Signed with Universal" (*Moving Picture World* 19 Nov. 1921: 298), Browning's contract in late 1921 marked his third with Universal. As a result, his 1930 contract would have been (at least) his fourth.
88. "Tod Browning at U." *Variety* 12 Feb. 1930: 10.
89. "Tod Browning Again with Universal," p. 18.
90. Denbo, Doris. *Hollywood Daily Citizen* 27 Mar. 1930.
91. "U Buys Dialogue Rights to *White Tiger*." *Motion Picture News* 12 July 1930.
92. Advertisement. *Film Daily* 25 Mar. 1930: 9.
93. "U Starts *Outside the Law*." *Film Daily* 4 June 1930: 6.
94. In *The Monster Show*, Skal cites a negative review of *Outside the Law* (1930) published in *Variety*, claiming, "Such notices did not bode well for *Dracula*" (p. 116). His use of the plural in "notices" is in error, for he has quoted only the single *Variety* review. More important is what remains absent from his discussion, as many positive reviews of *Outside the Law* appeared in newspapers and industry trade publications.
95. Shreck, Joy M. "*Outside the Law*." *Exhibitors Herald-World* 6 Sept. 1930: 41.
96. Brewer, Conde G. "*Outside the Law*." *Billboard* 6 Sept. 1930: 13.
97. "*Outside the Law*." *Film Daily* 31 Aug. 1930.
98. Porter, Kenneth R. "*Outside the Law*." *Los Angeles Evening Herald* 26 Sept. 1931.
99. Geltzer, George. "Tod Browning." *Films in Review* (Oct. 1953): 415.
100. Yeaman, Elizabeth. *Hollywood Daily Citizen* 19 Aug. 1930.

101 For example, Louella O. Parsons made an error in her column in 1929 about Tod Browning. After first printing he would co-direct *The Thirteenth Chair* with Elliott Clawson, she retracted the claim, admitting her mistake in the *Los Angeles Examiner* on 13 May 1929.

102 Parsons, Louella O. *Los Angeles Examiner* 19 Mar. 1930.

103 Yeaman, Elizabeth. *Hollywood Daily Citizen* 23 May 1930.

Chapter 3
PRE-PRODUCTION

Wall Street crashed on Black Tuesday, 29 October 1929, with the effects being felt by average Americans in 1930. By summer of that year, consumers made cutbacks in their purchasing habits by ten percent or more. Investments declined in number as confidence fell and as deflation began. That was all in addition to a severe drought that wreaked havoc on many agricultural areas.

The American cinema was not immune from the downward spiral. As Donald Crafton has noted, "By mid-1930, the film industry was in a severe recession from which it did not emerge for about four years."[1] Junior Laemmle had begun his emphasis on prestige pictures at Universal prior to the crash, but confidently continued his policy after it happened, apparently believing his strategy would be an effective way to combat declining attendance at the box office. Bigger-budget films that took narrative and thematic risks might encourage audience members to buy tickets to particular Universal films, even if they were overall attending movie theatres with less frequency.

On 27 September 1930 – two days before *Dracula* went into production – *Billboard* told readers that "After turning out such an excellent picture as *All Quiet on the Western Front*, young Laemmle is not taking a chance with any that is even half bad."[2] Such an emphasis on quality included *Dracula*, which the press had already touted as being one of Universal's "most important specials for the coming year."[3] Future studio publicity would put *Dracula* third on a list of Universal's three most important films for the second half of 1930, the other two being Lewis Milestone's *All Quiet on the Western Front* (1930) and Edwin Carewe's *Resurrection* (which, like *Dracula*, would not be released until February 1931).

In different respects, all three of those Universal "super-productions" challenged audience expectations. For example, *All Quiet* explored the horrors of war, not only as embodied in impressive battlefield sequences, but also during one grisly scene in which Paul (Lew Ayres) must remain in a foxhole with the corpse of Duval (Raymond Griffith), a solder whom he has killed. Milestone did not waver from the shock value, including in capturing closeups of the dead man's face.

Dracula represented its own kind of gamble, due in part to the same concerns over censorship and audience interest that had caused Universal to forego producing it during the silent era. But the risk factor may have been mediated to some degree by the ongoing success of the stage adaptation. By March 1930, *Dracula–The Vampire Play* had generated $2,000,000, making as much as $2,000 for appearances in one-week towns. In two different engagements in Philadelphia, it allegedly grossed $150,000.[4] Such success stories could well have steeled Junior Laemmle's resolve.

But the period leading up to the film's production required more than confidence. In part, it relied heavily upon the rise of the talkie, as *Dracula* would be made in the latter stages of the silent-to-sound transition, a complicated and lengthy period that resulted in various challenges, not least of which was the language barrier for Hollywood films in non-English-speaking countries. But the transitional period also fostered audience excitement over many sound mystery films produced between 1928 and 1930, some of which were adapted from successful stage plays.

Consideration of these factors played a role in Junior Laemmle's decision to obtain the film rights to *Dracula*, a complicated process. Once Laemmle put the project into pre-production, he did so with Tod Browning as director, a crew that was well experienced to film such a story, and a partial cast of actors (the rest of whom would be assigned during the production phase). Such choices included Laemmle and Browning's decision to award the title role to Bela Lugosi, a history that – along with the film's entire pre-production phase – deserves careful re-examination.

The Talking Picture

While some Hollywood histories suggest that *The Jazz Singer* (1927) single-handedly convinced studios to forego silent filmmaking, the transition to sound was actually a much slower process that had its roots in the late nineteenth century (as in W. K. L. Dickson's experiments with the Kinetophone) and that found renewed momentum in the mid-twenties.[5] In 1926, Warner Bros. forged an important partnership with Western Electric and released silent features like *Don Juan* (1926) and *The Better 'Ole* (1926) with synchronized music and sound effects using a system ("Vitaphone," as it was called) that reproduced sound on recorded discs; the studio also released sound short subjects featuring George Jessel and Al Jolson. Following their lead, William Fox pursued talking pictures as well, but invested in a technology that recorded sound directly on the 35mm film strip ("Movietone"), rather than on a separate medium.[6]

Bela Lugosi and Helen Chandler in a publicity still for Tod Browning's *Dracula* (1931).

The Jazz Singer excited some audience members, but the film could best be described as a part-talkie, as it still relied on intertitles to convey most of its dialogue. In early 1928, inventor Lee De Forest wrote that Warner Bros. had "struck a real key note" with *The Jazz Singer*, adding: "The day of the complete talking picture has not yet arrived, but I have no doubt that it is not far hence."[7] His prediction was correct, with *The Lights of New York*, the first all-talkie, released in July of that year. Many of the other releases in 1928 were either silent-film issues with recorded music and sound effects, or hybrids that – like *The Jazz Singer* – featured some talking and some silent sequences. In many cases, in other words, sound became an "extra flourish," as Crafton has called it, rather than the driving technology.[8]

Studios complained about the cost of shooting sound films, much as exhibitors did regarding the installation of the equipment to screen them. Nevertheless, the talkie experienced much growth in 1929. Producers quickly shot many films that year to take advantage of the form's growing popularity. Some were all-talkies, but others were still hybrids, including *Prisoners* (1929), which featured Bela Lugosi in a supporting role. Directors continued to be hampered by the demands of recording sound and its impact on other aspects of the production process, such as the limitations it placed initially on blocking (as actors needed to be near the microphone) and cinematography (as moving the camera could create extraneous noise on the soundtrack). Nevertheless, many filmmakers – such as Rouben Mamoulian in his film *Applause* (1929) – quickly began to meet these challenges and experiment with the artistic possibilities that sound provided.

Similarly, projectionists faced challenges with the new equipment installed at theatres. In particular, sound-on-disc technologies like Vitaphone occasionally posed major obstacles for reproducing a synchronous audio-visual experience, as at times the sound could disappear or lose sync.[9] But as with their counterparts at film studios, projectionists quickly adapted to the demands of sound, aided in part by technologies like Movietone that helped ensure a seamless world that integrated a film's aural and visual dimensions.

By June 1929, Jesse L. Lasky (one of the two key founders of Paramount Pictures) confidently announced that "Talking pictures are here to stay – and the public hasn't seen anything yet!"[10] That same month, Sam Katz (President of the Publix Theatres Corporation) told the industry press that audiences had expressed "complete approval of the talking-screen, and a positive rejection of silent film except in novelty form."[11] Such box-office appeal meant that – while many studios had promised to keep producing silent films – their schedules for the 1929-30 season concentrated on sound films. And their remaining silent releases tended to be nothing more than talkies with their soundtracks removed and intertitles added.

Movie fan magazines also devoted much attention to the transition to sound, including the upheaval underway in Hollywood. In December 1929, for example, *Photoplay* wrote about "Mike, the Demon," meaning the microphone that "sends the vocally unfit screaming or lisping from the lots."[12] Some actors' careers continued; others ended. And the door opened to talent with voices suited to the new medium, much of it from the stage.

That same year, the industry press noted that live theatre could also become a source for film narratives. Broadway plays new and old provided narratives replete with dialogue, as well as story titles that in some cases were already famous. The key drawback to this strategy, as *Billboard* described it, was the fact that New York productions of the late twenties regularly featured risqué situations and dialogue that posed potential censorship problems for producers seeking to transfer them to the screen.[13]

In May 1930, the *Film Daily* noted that 6,500 theatres had wired for sound in the previous twelve months, taking the overall total in the United States to over 9,500.[14] By the end of July 1930, *Exhibitors Herald-World* claimed the number had risen to 10,234, which was roughly seventy percent of all American theatres.[15] Despite that fact, audience attendance fell by mid-1930 and continued to do so in the weeks and months that followed. The Great Depression began to take its toll on the box-office, but that did not keep studios from experimenting further with the possibilities and limitations of sound cinema.

Consider, for example, an editorial in an August 1930 issue of *Billboard* that implored filmmakers to return to the "basic quality of the screen." Action was crucial, the journalist wrote. "The musical film, which was nothing more than a photograph of a regularly, stereotyped stage musical show, has passed into the limbo of forgotten things. Straight dialog comedies and dramas are destined to do likewise."[16] In short, studios needed to remember that the word "movie" was a slang corruption of the phrase "moving pictures." Imagery was film's key asset, not sound.

Another editorial published in the summer of 1930 differentiated between the strengths and weaknesses of the talking picture:

> *The talkers are top-heavy and weighted down with realism. They leave practically nothing to the spectator's imagination. Silent pictures did, and therein lay their strength. ... Delighted over the discovery that the screen can make a noise, they can't allow it to be silent or simply musical for so much as a second. They pump talk into a picture as energetically and indiscriminately as though it were solely up to them to demonstrate for the first time that vocal films actually are mechanically possible.*
> *...Nor must it be forgotten that every line of dialogue put into a picture takes its toll in slackened tempo.* [17]

Filmmakers responded to the general call for change, with many talkies produced in 1930 offering an increased use of sequences without dialogue.[18]

Universal Pictures had entered the talking-picture era in 1928, breaking ground for the construction of their new soundstages in July of that year.[19] Three months later, the studio touted plans for sixteen sound films: four would be silent movies synchronized with music and sound effects, and the others being a mixture of all-talkies and hybrids.[20]

Junior Laemmle's ascent at Universal came parallel to the rise of the talkie and thus allowed him to speak regularly on the subject. For example, in 1929, he told the press that he favored sound-on-film systems like Movietone.[21] The following year, Universal announced that studio fan mail had nearly doubled from 1927 (at 800-900 letters per day) to 1930 (at nearly 1,500 letters per day), all thanks to the talking picture.[22]

But the younger Laemmle placed even more focus on the artistic possibilities for the evolving sound film. In mid-1930, he predicted, "The picture of the future will have talk only where talk is needed."[23] In another interview, he spoke at greater length on the subject, declaring:

> *The novelty of mere dialogue has passed, and now that talking and sound pictures have become standard, producers can call upon their past experience to great advantage in developing what might appropriately be termed a 'new screen technique.'*

> *Too many talking pictures have relied upon dialogue to put over necessary business and dramatic punches. In silent films dramatic force and emphasis came from pantomime alone. It is my opinion that in the future we should develop as much of the drama as possible in pantomime … and use the dialogue and sound to give emphasis to the highlights of the production rather than make scenes one continuous barrage of speaking or music.*
>
> *In* Outside the Law, *a crook play, which Tod Browning is directing for Universal, we have employed less dialogue than in any talking picture we have made to date, building big dramatic punches mostly in pantomime and topping them with spoken words. The result is startling. The pantomime proves a fine builder of suspense and the dialogue enhances the climax.*[24]

Here Junior Laemmle cited Tod Browning's film as leading the way for Universal's continued experimentations with sound cinema. Such a mindset was not unique. Edwin Carewe, who directed *Resurrection* at Universal in the autumn of 1930, claimed, "Dialog is bound to be weak, and we must bolster it with pantomime, which is the true art of the motion picture."[25] And so, Browning's directorial approach represented very much the cutting-edge philosophy for sound films in mid-to-late 1930, not – as some writers have contended – an outmoded style bound to an earlier era. And it very much dovetailed with views repeatedly espoused by Junior Laemmle, including in October 1932, when he "ordered" a 25 percent cut in dialogue in all Universal scripts.[26]

For these experimentations with talkies to flourish, Junior Laemmle believed a careful choice of film narratives was paramount. As with so many other persons in the industry, he supported the strategy of transferring stage plays to the screen, but added that, "film producers can't afford to gamble that much money on an original, untried play … Consequently our industry will not permit the stage to die out. We need it as the trial ground for future motion pictures."[27]

The Multi-Lingual Film

During the late twenties, Hollywood studios depended greatly on the successful exportation of their films to other countries. Indeed, by the end of that decade, more than two-thirds of the world's theatres operated outside of the United States, most of them in non-English speaking countries.[28] Whereas silent films could easily traverse changes in geography and language with few if any problems (other than the minor matter of translating and replacing intertitles), a talking picture talked, and it talked in a single language, one that could not be understood across the globe.

And so the rise of the talkie was accompanied by an ongoing discussion about how best to meet the needs of the non-English-speaking marketplace. Trade publications discussed dubbing films into different languages as a possible answer.[29] But the necessary technology was, as Crafton has noted, "inadequate for large-scale application."[30] And so another solution had to be found.

Beginning in 1928, the preferred approach to the foreign-language market was to produce more than one version of particular films, each using the same script, sets, and costumes as the English-language original, but employing different actors who could speak such languages as Spanish, French, and German.[31] In some circumstances, the actors were English-speaking stars who learned their lines phonetically; for instance, Laurel and Hardy appeared in French and Spanish versions of their short subject *Brats* (1930). Most of the time, however, studios hired different casts who were native speakers of the needed languages.

For example, MGM decided to produce "multi-lingual" versions of the "outstanding" films in its 1929-30 season, including a French-language version of *The Unholy Night* (1929) and a German-language version of *A Lady to Love* (1930, aka *Sunkissed*).[32] In the autumn of 1929, Paramount announced that it would focus on Spanish-language versions, given that the "Spanish market, including South and Central America, is the second greatest market in films."[33]

In April 1930, the *Hollywood Filmograph* declared that Spanish-language films were "all the go and producers [were] spending millions of dollars on them."[34] The result also meant that Spanish-language talent in Hollywood was in short supply, more so than actors who could speak German or French. "If you are a leading man and speak Spanish, you can write your own ticket as far as salaries go with the motion picture studios," the *Filmograph* claimed.[35]

PAUL KOHNER
Supervisor
Foreign Production
Universal

"KING OF JAZZ" 19 Languages
"CAT CREEPS" (Spanish)
"EAST IS WEST" (Spanish)
"DRACULA" (Spanish)
"BOUDOIR DIPLOMAT" German Spanish
"RESURRECTION" French German Spanish

Now Preparing Next Season's Output

Advertisement for Paul Kohner, who was in charge of Universal's multi-lingual film department. Published in the *Hollywood Reporter* on December 22, 1930.

And yet Spanish-language Hollywood films experienced greater problems in 1930 than a shortage of actors. Sono Art's Spanish-language version of *Blaze o' Glory* (1929) ignited something of a controversy in early 1930 because "the way the actors are pronouncing their lines in their Mother tongue, isn't at all like it is spoken in their countries, according to some of the folks who have made a study of this sort of language."[36] The sound film may have resulted in greater realism, but it also meant attention had to be paid to regional accents and differing pronunciations. In other words, to speak Spanish was not enough. Someone who learned Spanish as a second language might enunciate differently than native speakers from Mexico or Cuba or Spain or, for that matter, persons from different geographical regions in any one of those countries.

But studios increasingly had to worry about far more than pronunciation. In July 1930, *Variety* described "the headaches of finding talent, sifting out the jealousies and trying to abide by the immigration requisites," which led many studio executives to conclude that multi-linguals were too much trouble to produce in Hollywood.[37] Rather than predict the multi-lingual's demise, the trade claimed that the studios would likely shift production of them to Europe. All that said, some of the studios marched forward with foreign-language talkies scheduled for production during their 1930-31 seasons. For example, in September 1930, Warner Bros. announced it would produce eighteen such films: six in German, six in French, and six in Spanish.[38]

Junior Laemmle was quick to see the possibilities of foreign-language films at Universal, with *Universal Weekly* reminding readers that the studio was the first in Hollywood to produce them. Under the supervision of Paul Kohner, the man who convinced the younger Laemmle of their merit, Universal produced German and Hungarian versions of *The Last Performance*

(1928), but in those instances, the studio opted for dubbing rather than producing entirely new versions with onscreen actors versed in those languages.[39] One of the actors hired was Bela Lugosi, whose voice was (to the extent possible) synchronized with onscreen footage of the film's star, Conrad Veidt, for the Hungarian-language version.

As time went on, Universal entered the multi-lingual market. In February 1930, Junior Laemmle publicized the fact that Kohner would supervise numerous foreign-language productions, including several shot in Spanish with such talent as Lupita Tovar, Nancy Torres, Delia Magana, and Laura de la Puente.[40] These films were all in addition to the use of onscreen hosts speaking various languages for different release prints of *King of Jazz* (1930). For example, a version released in Hungary featured three different Hungarian-language actors, one of them Bela Lugosi.[41]

In September 1930, Universal announced that its 1930-31 season would include a dozen foreign-language films, at least one German and at least one French. But the concentration would be on Spanish-language versions due to the size of the potential market.[42] Junior Laemmle was not yet ready to give up on the multi-lingual, even though its days were numbered.

Mystery Films

However important the foreign-language market was, Hollywood studios wisely continued to choose stories targeted at American audiences. As part of their search for new material suited to the talking picture, Hollywood studios seized upon certain genres, most famously the musical, which seemed in its various manifestations (operettas, revues, and musical comedies) particularly well-suited to the possibilities that sound had unleashed. However, other genres came to the fore as well, notably the mystery, which appealed to studios due to the genre's popularity on the Broadway stage of the teens and twenties. Its appearance in the early days of the talkies proved popular, and its ongoing success on the stage and on film prompted studios to produce even more of the same.

Though it was predated by *Seven Keys to Baldpate* (1913) and *The Thirteenth Chair* (1917), the most notable Broadway mystery play was Mary Roberts Rinehart's play *The Bat*, which opened on New York in 1920.[43] Its success paved the way for many subsequent mystery plays, including *The Monster* (1922) and *The Cat and The Canary* (1922). With regard to the latter, for example, the *New York Times* perceived Rinehart's influence, claiming the new play had "come to town in the pious hope of taking over the business and good-will of *The Bat*."[44]

Many of these plays were set in old dark houses in which horror unfolded alongside comedy. Consider the following description of John Floyd's play *The Wooden Kimono* (1926):

> *It bears all the marks of a successful mystery play, comparable to* Seven Keys to Baldpate *and* The Bat. *It is replete with coffins, shrieks in the dark, groans, disappearances, revolver shots, spiced with liberal admixtures of broad comedy, and baffles the spectators to the last few minutes of the last act.*[45]

The desire to instill comedy into such mystery plays culminated in Ralph Spence's *The Gorilla*, which – rather than offset horror with comic relief – attempted to spoof the mystery genre.[46]

Not surprisingly, some of the successful mystery plays became silent films, including *Seven Keys to Baldpate* (1917), *The Thirteenth Chair* (1919), *The Monster* (1925), *The Bat*

Trade advertisement for Roland West's *The Bat* (1926).

"THE BAT"
A ROLAND WEST Production
A Mystery Melodrama By
Mary Roberts Rinehart and Avery Hopwood
From the stage play produced by Wagenhals and Kemper

Mystery! Melodrama! Millions!

"The Bat," the greatest mystery melodrama ever staged becomes the greatest mystery film melodrama ever made, and March 15th "The Bat's" $10,000,000 legitimate theatre drawing power is available at box offices of picture houses. A lavish production. A superb cast. A picture that will draw big money to the box-office.

NOW BOOKING
UNITED ARTISTS CORPORATION
Mary Pickford Charles Chaplin
Douglas Fairbanks D. W. Griffith
Joseph M. Schenck, Chairman Board of Directors
Hiram Abrams, President

March 15th Release

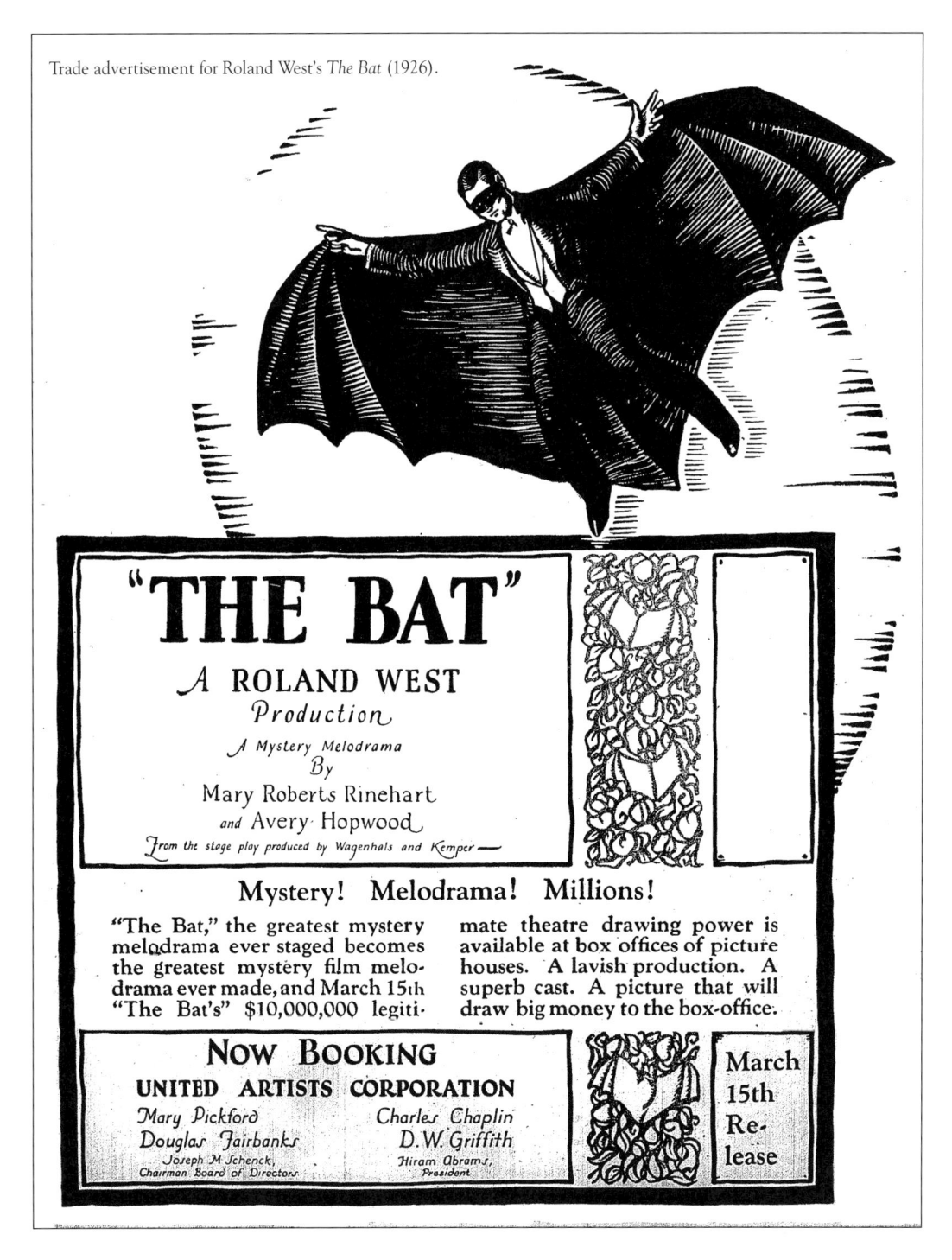

(1926), *The Gorilla* (1927) and *The Cat and the Canary* (1927). But the rise of the talking picture created fresh possibilities for mystery stories. Sound breathed new life into the genre, not only in terms of dialogue, but also by use of key sound effects like the scream of a victim and the creaking of a door. Innovative use of offscreen space came thanks to gunfire and

Left: Publicity for *The Mysterious Dr. Fu Manchu* (1929).
Above: Pressbook advertisement for *The Terror* (1928).

other noises that could originate from an unseen location in an old house or mansion and be heard by the film's characters and by the audience.

Mysteries produced during the transition to the talkie included such films as *Behind that Curtain* (1929), *The Canary Murder Case* (1929), *The Greene Murder Case* (1929), *Seven Keys to Baldpate* (1929), *The Studio Murder Mystery* (1929), *The Unholy Night* (1929), *The Benson Murder Case* (1930), *The Bishop Murder Case* (1930), *The Costello Case* (1930), *The Midnight Mystery* (1930), *Murder on the Roof* (1930), *Murder Will Out* (1930), and *The Second Floor Mystery* (1930). Related films included *Darkened Rooms* (1929), *The Mysterious Dr. Fu Manchu* (1929), and *The Return of Dr. Fu Manchu* (1930).

Roy Del Ruth's *The Terror* (1928), the second all-talking feature film, was at the vanguard of these mysteries. Produced by Warner Bros. and based on a play by Edgar Wallace (which had been staged in England, but not in America), *The Terror* reminded critics of *The Bat* and *The Cat and the Canary*. *Variety* described it as a "mystery thriller on a par with anything of the kind ever produced, but far more effective than any silent picture owing to sound."[47] Key among those sounds were howling winds and the screams of actresses Louise Fazenda and May McAvoy.

When describing the proliferation of the mystery films in December 1928, *Motion Picture Classic* told readers:

> Hollywood is in the midst of an epidemic of sudden and violent death. Almost every day a new murder occurs under mysterious circumstances in one of the movie studios. ... The first result of the talkie panic has been a flood of mystery thrillers on the screen.

Chapter 3 – PRE-PRODUCTION

> ...Plots of murder, mystery and terror offer many chances for the use of sound as part of the story. If sound is what they want, the producers seem to argue, we'll give them plenty of it. As, in the beginning of movies, the players felt duty-bound to keep moving every minute they were before the camera, so at the outset of sound pictures they are making a conscientious effort to provide as many different noises as possible. This coming year will undoubtedly find the fans paying their money to enjoy a restful evening of blood-curdling screams, hair-raising moans, maniacal laughter, shots, and the dull thump of falling bodies.
> ... So every studio lot these days finds foul deeds being committed, quarts of prop blood being shed, bodies being discovered behind secret panels and in haunted houses, and clues scattered about everywhere. Instead of the usual studio orchestra, weird devices for producing uncanny noises have taken their place.[48]

The author concluded by noting that "murder" was the "watchword of the motion picture studios for the moment."

A number of these talkie mysteries drew upon the stage traditions of the teens and early twenties, including Benjamin Christensen's *The House of Horror* (1929) at First National and Tod Browning's *The Thirteenth Chair* (1929) at MGM. By contrast, at least one film eschewed the comic relief present of most mystery plays. According to the *Film Daily*, Edmund Lawrence's *The House of Secrets* (1929) was "one story of a mysterious and spooky house that explains all the terrifying happenings plausibly. ... No comedy, but thrills aplenty."[49]

By contrast, two films of the talkie era drew upon the stage version of *The Gorilla* and used the mystery genre largely as a vehicle for humor. The first was Lewis Seiler's *The Ghost Talks* (1929) and the second was Bryan Foy's *The Gorilla* (1930), a loose adaptation of the original play. Of the latter, the *New York Herald Tribune* noted: "The picture, a shrewd mixture of comedy and mystery, is the most successful case extant of the use of farcical relief to counteract the mood of horror, for in it the comedy is honest enough to appear as an essential part of the entertainment, rather than merely as a self-conscious foil to the macabre side."[50]

Some of the mystery films concentrated on detectives solving crimes and offered little in the way of horror, but others presented fascinating moments that fed into the creation of the thirties horror film. For example, we see and hear the storm at an old mansion in *The Benson Murder Case*. We hear howling wind (which causes the banging of window shutters) and a frightened scream in *Seven Keys to Baldpate*. Bizarre sounds accompany the appearance of a (fake) ghost in *Darkened Rooms*. Thunder, heartbeats, a foghorn, and a locked doorknob being wrenched in the middle of the night by an unknown hand: all of these sounds are heard in *The Bishop Murder Case*, one of the most cinematically sophisticated mysteries of the period.

Such aural possibilities became common enough to merit parody in *The Laurel-Hardy Murder Case*, which was released on 6 September 1930, just three weeks before *Dracula* would go into production. In this short subject (for which a Spanish-language version was also filmed), comedy arises in part out of the incessant and intentional overuse of sound effects like screams, thunder, and howling wind.

Universal engaged in the sound mystery film craze to a degree, most notably in the case of Paul Leni's part-talkie *The Last Warning* (1929). Perceiving it to be similar to previous sound mystery films, one trade publication wrote, "Miss [Laura] La Plante does little or

Above: Publicity still for the English-language version of *The Cat Creeps* (1930). Inset: Advertisement in *Variety* promotes George Melford's direction of the Spanish-language version of *The Cat Creeps* (1930).

nothing except look frightened and scream every so often, the May McAvoy scream of *The Terror*."[51] Already one of the key sounds of film horror had become a known quantity.

In addition to *The Last Warning*, Universal shot *The Charlatan* in 1929, a part-talkie that was also released in a silent version. George Melford directed the "murder mystery," which was adapted from a stage play. That same year, Universal announced that it would produce a talkie remake of *The Phantom of the Opera* (1925), as well as a sequel entitled *The Return of the Phantom*.[52]

Instead, the studio eventually reissued the silent version of *The Phantom of the Opera* with new dialogue sequences, recalling some of the original cast members to shoot the new scenes. Notably absent from that group was Lon Chaney, whose onscreen character remained silent.[53] Thirty-five percent of the resulting film featured spoken dialogue, the rest relying on intertitles.[54] The result was a particularly strange hybrid, one that not only combines silent and sound sequences (sometimes in single scenes, thanks to dubbing), but also new sequences filmed in 1930 edited with old footage from 1925.

By May 1930, *Zit's Theatrical Weekly* believed the mystery – which as a generic term served to encompass everything from detective films to the Fu Manchu movies – was in

Chapter 3 – PRE-PRODUCTION

retreat. Their journalist spoke of the:

> ... *recent flop of the mystery stories, which are following the back stage musicals into the limbo of oblivion. When the backstage stuff grew sour, a switch was made to the mystery yarn, and this, like the backstage stuff, has been run into the ground. The mystery formula is even more inelastic than the backstage stuff, and the changes have been pretty well rung.*[55]

But that prediction did not prove true. In the weeks that followed, for example, Roland West directed a talkie remake of *The Bat*, released in November of 1930 as *The Bat Whispers*.[56]

Universal produced a sound version of *The Cat and The Canary* starring Helen Twelvetrees. Retitled *The Cat Creeps* – a decision presumably made due to the growing audience backlash against the number of sound remakes of silent films – the movie was directed by Rupert Julian in the summer of 1930, finishing with retakes in September of that year.[57] The remake re-imagined the earlier film, particularly in terms of its young male lead. In the silent version, he was the source of much of the film's comedy. In the sound version, he would be more important as one half of its romantic emphasis.[58]

The Cat Creeps also marked the convergence of Universal's production of a sound mystery film with its production of a multi-lingual. Using the same sets and props as the English-language version, George Melford shot a Spanish-language version of the story at night after the Julian cast and crew went home.[59] Originally a stage actor and director, Melford had worked in the cinema from at least as early as 1911. He made the transition to directing sound films with ease, going so far as to write an article on the relationship between the stage and the talkie in 1929.[60]

Junior Laemmle likely chose Melford to direct the film due to his earlier work on *The Charlatan*. At any rate, Melford quickly became an important figure in Universal's Spanish-language films of 1930, including on the Spanish-language version of *East Is West* (1930) in the summer of that year.[61] For his Spanish-language version of *The Cat Creeps*, Melford's leading lady was Lupita Tovar.[62]

Universal Pictures

The year 1930 marked Junior Laemmle's greatest triumphs as head of production at Universal, in part due to the prestige of two films: *King of Jazz*, which premiered in April, and *All Quiet on the Western Front*, which premiered in August. Both films scored with critics, and both would go on to win Academy Awards.[63] While *King of Jazz* became a box-office disappointment, the opposite was true of the much riskier *All Quiet*. Together, the two films were representative of the new Universal that Junior Laemmle was trying to build.

Speaking of Universal's change in production policy, Carl Laemmle, Sr. lauded his son's vision, claiming:

> *For a long time we watched the changing trends in the industry and made up our minds that the moment had come for greater specialization in pictures and concentration on fewer, bigger, and better productions. We were convinced that the change from quantity to quality ought to be made. But were we ready for it?*
> *Without any fanfare of trumpets, we deliberately decided to test ourselves, to find out whether we could, in the midst of a production season on the old plan, produce pictures of the magnitude that would be required by the new.*

Above: Publicity still for the *King of Jazz* (1930). Below: Publicity still for *All Quiet on the Western Front* (1930). John Wray is pictured on the right.

… The result has been complete recognition by the industry that Universal was not only ready for the new plan, but had actually proved its soundness in advance.[64]

For Laemmle, Sr., these changes meant that an important "new day" at Universal was underway.

In April 1930, the studio announced it would cut its 1930-31 product to twenty features, down by nearly two-thirds from the 57 features it produced in 1929-30. "Gone are the U horse operas, serials, and five reelers," *Variety* noted with surprise.[65] The studio also claimed it would produce one-third fewer short subjects during the coming season. The reason was not necessarily to spend less money, but rather to shift money to bigger-budget and more prestigious films, including a planned remake of *The Hunchback of Notre Dame* (1923).[66] Other goals included developing the "remarkable talents of young Lewis Ayres," as well as of John Boles, Jeanette Loff, and Lupe Velez.[67]

A 1930 trade advertisement promoting Junior Laemmle's new vision for Universal Pictures.

The studio outlined fifteen of the proposed twenty films in April 1930, the list including a few films that were eventually produced during the 1930-31 season: *The Boudoir Diplomat, East Is West,* and – in conjunction with Tod Browning's name – *Outside the Law*. Other proposed films (like the remake of *Hunchback* and a sequel to *All Quiet on the Western Front*) did not end up going into production.[68] *Dracula* was not mentioned at that time, nor was it when the studio released a similar list of upcoming films some two months later.[69]

Despite his move to prestige filmmaking, Junior Laemmle attempted to limit the cost of his big-budget productions. In April 1930, Universal claimed it would spend roughly $500,000 on each of its twenty planned productions, the overall expenditure being what it would have spent on fifty films in previous years.[70] But the following month, Laemmle announced that the season's upcoming feature film budgets would only be between $350,000 and $400,000 each.[71]

The reason for the change was financial, some of it resulting from the effect that the Great Depression was having on all Hollywood studios. For the six months' fiscal period ending 3 May 1930, Universal reported a net loss of over $575,000.[72] Here then is a clear explanation for cutbacks to the upcoming film budgets. These losses also found Junior Laemmle instituting various other cost-cutting measures. By the end of August 1930, for example, the studio dropped "as many as 50 employees" in New York. Most of them were stenographers and clerks.[73]

To find more ways to trim the budget, Laemmle tried to remove non-productive "deadwood" from the upper ranks of the studio and instead build up a smaller, high-calibre group of experienced executives.[74] This meant reverting to an associate-producer system with only a few key persons placed in those roles, each looking after particular films.[75] Albert DeMond, and Stanley Bergerman were two of the chosen men.[76] E. M. "Efe" Asher, formerly an independent producer, was the third.[77]

The associate-producer system not only saved money, but it also allowed Junior Laemmle to consolidate his control of studio production by placing a few men that he trusted in key positions. In this way, he organized the studio more to his liking, both through associate producers in charge of particular units, as well as through founding a new unit solely in charge of short subjects, which he created in June 1930.[78]

Despite the cutbacks, Junior Laemmle worked hard not to sacrifice artistic quality, whether it

John Boles and Lupe Velez in Edwin Carewe's *Resurrection* (1931).

was in the stories he purchased or in the talent he hired. In July 1930, for example, *Billboard* discussed the fact that *All Quiet on the Western Front* had allowed Universal to "corner" the directorial market for 1930-31. Having paid a "pretty penny" to hire *All Quiet*'s director Lewis Milestone, Junior Laemmle then proceeded to sign Monta Bell, Malcolm St. Clair, and Rupert Julian. Those were in addition to other directors already on the payroll or already assigned to direct particular films, including the likes of Edwin Carewe and Tod Browning.[79]

That Junior Laemmle continued to take major risks even as the industry suffered from a deepening economic depression is a testament to both his power at Universal and his clarity of vision. Consider for example his decision to produce the film *Resurrection* in the autumn of 1930. In it, a royal soldier named Dmitri (John Boles) woos the peasant girl Katusha (Lupe Velez), but later ignores her when he meets other women during his travels. After losing her job as a maid, Katusha is forced into a life of prostitution and, finally, prison for a murder that she did not commit. Dmitri is powerless to prevent a jury from convicting her, and – out of guilt – he travels with her on an arduous march to Siberia where she will spend the rest of her life. Using his influence, Dmitri is able to get Katusha's sentence commuted to exile. He promises to marry her. But she instead remains with the other prisoners, understanding that her troubled past cannot allow her to wed. At the film's climax, Katusha marches into the snow, leaving Dmitri behind, thus creating another unhappy ending.

Overall, Junior Laemmle successfully reshaped Universal in 1930, supported by a father who seems to have trusted his judgment, even if only temporarily. Indeed, the studio gave Junior Laemmle a ten-year contract as General Manager in June 1930, two months prior to the release of *All Quiet on the Western Front*.[80] At roughly the same time, Junior Laemmle would commit the studio to *Dracula*, the vampire film that Tod Browning had waited one decade to direct.

Dracula

After having considered *Dracula* as a possible film project during the silent era, Universal returned to the story in 1928, presumably due to the success of the Broadway adaptation. In August of that year, *The Billboard* announced: "Universal has bought the screen rights to *Dracula*, stage play."[81] Shortly thereafter, the British publication *To-Day's Cinema* printed a variation of the same story, implying that the studio purchased the novel rather than the play and adding: "No cast has been suggested yet, but the part of Count Dracula, the vampire, is stated to be admirable for Conrad Veidt."[82] Here Veidt's name surfaced for two reasons. One was his success in number of films ranging from *The Cabinet of Dr. Caligari* (1920) to *The Man Who Laughs* (1928). The other was the fact that Veidt was under contract at Universal in 1928.

> ## "Dracula" is Discussed as Picture
>
> Could the motion picture, with the advantage of a broader scope by the camera, out-thrill the stage production of "Dracula?" This has been a subject of spirited arguments among players in the Biltmore Theater cast.
>
> Bela Lugosi, Hungarian actor who is the star of the play, defends the speaking version in its intensity of drama and genuineness of horrors.
>
> With the talking equipment Lugosi believes the screen version could successfully electrify audiences with almost the same effectiveness of the speaking production. But, he contends, the playgoer's state of mind is different than that of the picture viewer. Picture audiences are apt to shake off any alarmed feeling which results when the emotions are excited by reminding themselves they are at a movie, Lugosi believes.

Published in the *Los Angeles Times* on July 22, 1928.

Universal would also have had a director on the payroll particularly suited to *Dracula*: Paul Leni, who directed *The Cat and the Canary*, *The Chinese Parrot* (1927), and *The Man Who Laughs* at the studio, and who had earlier directed such films as *Das Wachfigurekabinett* (*Waxworks*, 1924) in Germany. But neither Leni nor Veidt worked on *Dracula* at Universal in 1928, as the report in *Billboard* was erroneous. Universal had not yet obtained the film rights to either the play or the novel.

Whether due to rumors of the possible film or to mere coincidence, Bela Lugosi spoke to the press about the screen possibilities of *Dracula* in July 1928, while he was starring in a stage production of the same at the Biltmore Theatre in Los Angeles. "With talking equipment, Lugosi believes the screen version could successfully electrify audiences," the *Los Angeles Times* wrote. "But, he contends, the playgoer's state of mind is different than that of the picture viewer. Picture audiences are apt to shake off any alarmed feeling which results when the emotions are excited by reminding themselves that they are at a movie, Lugosi believes."[83] Here Lugosi clearly attempted to connect *Dracula* to the nascent talking picture, as well as to allay fears that the story was too horrifying to translate to the screen.[84]

Much to Lugosi's disappointment, there was no film version of *Dracula* in the late twenties. But Universal – looking to the stage for material during the rise of the talkie

– was more interested in the property than ever before. And that interest grew in 1929 with Junior Laemmle's ascendancy to the studio hierarchy, as there is also some indication that he hoped to produce *Dracula* in 1929 with Lon Chaney portraying both Dracula and Van Helsing.[85]

It is certain that the year 1929 saw negotiations for the screen rights to *Dracula* begin in earnest among a number of different parties. A representative for Bram Stoker's widow Florence worked together with Harold Freedman, a literary agent in New York City, to offer the rights to the novel to a number of studios in 1929 and 1930, including Columbia, Pathe, Paramount, MGM, and Universal. Freedman believed that MGM was a particularly likely candidate, perhaps because Browning and Chaney were both under contract at the studio. The studio declined, presumably for reasons similar to Paramount, where story editor E. J. Montagne told studio boss Ben Schulberg, "At your request, some months ago, I felt out all our supervisors on *Dracula*. We did not receive one favorable reaction."[86] And so Universal purchased the rights in June 1930, despite the fact that the studio had earlier indicated that its interest hinged on signing Lon Chaney as the film's star, a prospect that seemed increasingly unlikely.[87]

Letter from the Bram Stoker estate to John L. Balderston, dated June 24, 1930. *(Courtesy of the New York Public Library, Billy Rose Theatre Division)*

However, the novel *Dracula* was not the only legal problem, as the stage play became the hotter property in the late twenties, and it involved more parties, specifically producer Horace Liveright and writers Hamilton Deane and John L. Balderston. All three had to be included in the sale of the film rights. As late as 24 June 1930 – by which time Universal had already publicly announced that it would be producing *Dracula* – the Stoker estate was still communicating with John L. Balderston, proposing a breakdown of Universal's

Chapter 3 – PRE-PRODUCTION

money, including a "nuisance" fee of $2,400 to Liveright, who by that time was in Hollywood working at Paramount.[88]

At some point in this complicated process, Bela Lugosi claimed to have acted as a representative for Universal in obtaining the rights from Stoker's widow. In 1939, the *New York Post* quoted him in such a way as (supposedly) to preserve his accent:

Den de movies wanted to do it. De Bram Stoker heirs asked $200,000 for de film reidts but Uniwersal didn't like to pay dat much. Zo dey asked me would I correspond wid Mrs. Stoker, de widow, and get it maybe a liddle cheaper.
I wreidt and wreidt until I get cramps, and after aboudt two mondts, Mrs. Stoker says O.K., we can haff it for $60,000.[89]

The exact nature and extent of Lugosi's involvement are difficult to verify. While some persons at Universal knew him (particularly Paul Kohner), Lugosi was hardly in the habit of conducting story acquisitions for any studio. By contrast, there is evidence that he was writing to Florence Stoker in an effort to broker a deal in April 1930 that would include himself as star of the film; the studio in question was MGM, and not – so far as is known – Universal.[90]

At any rate, it seems that Universal (without Lugosi's assistance) paid $40,000 for the rights to the Bram Stoker novel and three different versions of the stage play (including the Deane-Balderston adaptation that had taken Broadway by storm), thus consolidating its control over all of the authorized properties, not only for the purposes of having flexibility for its screen adaptation, but also to avoid future legal entanglements with the playwrights or anyone else.

Universal's complete dominion over *Dracula* onscreen was crucial in part due to the limited theatrical appearance of F. W. Murnau's *Nosferatu* (1922) in America in 1929, as described in Chapter 1. The studio not only wanted to keep Murnau's film out of competition with its own pending *Dracula*, but also hoped to view it for its own purposes, perhaps even believing it might provide another source of ideas. At any rate, the studio finally acquired a copy in August 1930.[91] In the end, Universal's copy of the film helped get one of the rare prints off the market, but it was otherwise of somewhat limited assistance. As Chapter 4 will illustrate, *Nosferatu* became a minor inspiration to *Dracula*'s screenwriters during August and September of 1930.

The press seized on news of Universal's rights to *Dracula*, claiming that Junior Laemmle saw it as a "successor" to *The Cat Creeps*.[92] Indeed, despite earlier reports in other publications to the contrary, the *Los Angeles Examiner* declared in September 1930 that the "vogue of mystery pictures is still going strong."[93] The belief that *Dracula* would be a mystery film was not unusual. Some viewers and critics had categorized the Deane-Balderston stage play as a mystery, and to an extent it was. Characters investigate mysterious activity that largely takes place in a single location, puzzling over the nature of Lucy's illness and its source. Eventually they unravel the mystery. The perception that *Dracula* was a mystery story would continue, despite the novel, play, and film's reliance on the supernatural. Indeed, a critic for *Time* magazine perceived the 1931 film as part of the mystery genre that had arisen with the rise of the talkie.[94]

But Universal envisioned *Dracula* as something beyond that singular genre. "There's more than just mystery to this classic tale and famous stage play," the studio argued in an advertisement in August 1930.[95] The industry press reported that Junior Laemmle and Tod Browning puzzled for over one week as to whether the film "should be a thriller or romance" before finally deciding "to make it both."[96] Laemmle later said much the same in an interview with film historian Rick Atkins: "We decided to hype it as both, and I've never regretted it."[97]

In retrospect, the need for such decisions seem very clear, largely due to the fact that the "horror movie" did not yet exist as a codified genre. It is true that certain kinds of horrific films had been made since the earliest days of the cinema, and occasionally critics did use the word "horror" as a description in their reviews, but the term "horror" had yet to concretize as the genre's name.

By contrast, Laemmle's discussion of the film's "romance" angle had three benefits. For one, it might appeal to female moviegoers. Secondly, it might temper the story's more gruesome aspects, meaning the very reasons Universal avoided producing it during the 1920s. Thirdly, it could build on the Kipling/Burne-Jones/Theda Bara definition of vampires as described in Chapter 1, drawing an unstated link between that tradition and the supernatural creatures rooted in folklore.

Negotiations over the generic categorization of *Dracula* also speak to another crucial issue. Even if Junior Laemmle made the final decisions, he apparently involved Browning for some weeks prior to the shoot, if not longer. And their joint conversations would not only lead to decisions about *Dracula*'s publicity, but also to the formation of its shooting script. As Chapter 2 argued, Junior Laemmle and Tod Browning were the driving forces behind Universal's *Dracula*.

At any rate, in late September, *Variety* announced that Universal was "combing the European stage seeking additional imports [actors] for multi-linguals." Until that point, the studio – unlike its key competitors – had concentrated on Spanish-language multi-linguals.[98] Then, on 23 September, Universal announced that *The Boudoir Diplomat* (1930) would "get Spanish, French, and German treatments." As for *Dracula*, it would be "Spanished."[99]

Dracula's Crew

Laemmle and Browning were the two crucial figures involved in the film version of *Dracula*, but there were other key personnel behind the camera, among them associate producer E. M. Asher. Born in 1888, Asher entered the film business in 1920, operating a film exchange and a chain of theatres before spending five years working in production with Mack Sennett. He joined Universal in 1930.[100]

Dracula's assistant director Scott R. Beal came from a show business family. His father was a director, and his sister was one of Mack Sennett's famous bathing beauties. Beal started his career in 1910 at Selig, spending two decades as an assistant director and occasional actor at various companies.[101] *Dracula* became one of his first films at Universal, where he would finally become a director in 1934.[102] Based upon a production bulletin in the *Hollywood Filmograph*, it would seem Beal was added to the *Dracula* team shortly before filming began.[103] How important he was to the *Dracula* is difficult to assess given a lack of archival materials and lengthy interviews with its cast and crew.

By contrast, the work of some of *Dracula*'s crewmembers is readily apparent from viewing the completed movie. Among them was Karl Freund, the famous German cinematographer

Above: Tod Browning, pictured here in publicity for *The Thirteenth Chair* (1929). Above Right: Karl Freund.

who had shot such films as Paul Wegener and Carl Boese's *Der Golem, wie er in die Welt kam* (*The Golem, How He Came into the World*, 1920) and F. W. Murnau's *Der letze Mann* (*The Last Laugh*, 1924); he was also one of the two cinematographers on Fritz Lang's *Metropolis* (1927).

According to an article published in a 1944 issue of the *American Cinematographer*:

> [Freund] was eventually brought to Hollywood in 1930 by Technicolor, who needed his services in an advisory capacity on a technicolor [sic] matter. ... But things didn't work out that way, and Karl's contract was sold to Universal.[104]

That same year, Freund allegedly gave director Lewis Milestone the idea for how to shoot the conclusion of *All Quiet on the Western Front*, in which Paul (Lew Ayres) dies while reaching for a butterfly.

As of 27 September 1930, the *Hollywood Filmograph* listed the cinematographer for *Dracula* as "unassigned."[105] *Variety* did not announce that Freund would shoot *Dracula* until its 4 October 1930 issue, by which time the film had been in production for five days.[106] As a result, it would seem that Universal did not attach Freund to the film until sometime during late September. At roughly the same time, the studio must have also decided that C. Roy Hunter would act as the film's recording engineer, and that the role of the film's second cameraman would be split between Joseph Brotherton and King Gray (aka King Grey, who had served as cinematographer on the 1926 mystery film *Midnight Faces*).[107]

Dracula's special-effects cameraman Frank H. Booth started his career in 1918 and would eventually spend forty years working with Howard A. Anderson's company, as well as six years as a freelancer.[108] He had previously worked on Universal's *Broadway* (1929) and *All Quiet on the Western Front*, and would also work on *Resurrection* during the autumn of 1930.

Born in 1888, *Dracula*'s art director Charles "Danny" Hall had worked for Charlie Chaplin, designing sets for such films as *The Gold Rush* (1925), before going to work at Universal.[109] In 1929, the *Los Angeles Times* boasted that Hall had already designed "more than 7000 screen sets."[110]

```
KARL FREUND
Cinematographer
European Production
"VARIETY"
"LAST LAUGH"
"METROPOLIS"
"GOLEM"
"BERLIN"
"SYMPHONY OF A CITY"
American Production
"MURDER IN THE RUE MORGUE"
"DRACULA"
"BAD SISTER"
"STRICTLY DISHONORABLE"
"UP FOR MURDER"
"BOUDOIR DIPLOMAT"
Now with Universal Picture Corp.
```

```
COMPLIMENTS

HERMAN ROSSE
```

Top: Karl Freund's advertisement as published in *The Film Daily Yearbook for 1932*. Bottom: Herman Rosse's advertisement as published in *Variety* in 1930.

Working for Hall on *Dracula* were Herman Rosse and John Hoffman. Rosse, who was born in the Netherlands in 1887, studied architecture in London before moving to America. Under contract at Universal since March of 1930, he served as art director on *King of Jazz*, for which he won a 1929-30 Academy Award.[111] As George E. Turner noted, "It was Rosse who saved a chunk of the set budget for *Dracula* by designing the spectacular facade of Castle Dracula so it could be pieced together with portions of disassembled Medieval sets from the silent days."[112] At roughly the same time Rosse worked on *Dracula*, he also acted as art director for Universal's *Resurrection*.[113]

On 19 February 1929, Universal announced having signed Jack Pierce to a two-year contract. Commenting on his history, the *Hollywood Filmograph* wrote:

> The development of the make-up art from its early stages to its present scientific status is said to be largely due to Pierce's experiments and research. The pictures in which he has supervised the make-up of hundreds of players representing various periods of history include The Man Who Laughs, Show Boat *[1929]*, Erik the Great *[The Last Performance]*, and Broadway.[114]

Pierce – who acted as makeup man for *The Cat Creeps* and would do the same for *Dracula* and *Resurrection* – would go on to play a pivotal role in the Universal horror film of the thirties and forties.

Perhaps the most neglected name amongst those who would create *Dracula* is Roman Freulich, a stills photographer who had previously worked on Browning's *Outside the Law* (1930), among many other films.[115] Given that newspapers, magazines, and books generally publish film stills rather than film frames, many movies exist in popular imagination and cultural memory to some degree through still photographs. At times they depict very close approximations of scenes in the film; at times they depict images or events quite different from anything seen in the film. Freulich's stills for *Dracula* would represent a combination of both kinds of publicity stills, and they remain crucial in how many viewers remember the movie, as well as those who have never actually watched the film but can recognize it visually.

Dracula's Cast

Discussions regarding which actors might portray key characters in *Dracula* likely percolated for weeks prior to the final casting. Junior Laemmle, Tod Browning, and others (including E. M. Asher) played pivotal roles in the process. Universal casting director Phil Friedman had taken over from Harry Garson in February 1930 after Garson was promoted to producer.[116] Friedman

LUPE VELEZ, JOHN BOLES, JACK PIERCE, JEAN HERSHOLT and PAUL ELLIS

Publicity montage for Jack Pierce, published in the *Hollywood Filmograph* on March 7, 1931.

underwent an operation for appendicitis during the third week of September 1930, which means he was probably not involved in some of the work on *Dracula*.[117]

But Friedman *was* involved in casting the first two key players. The first seems to have been stage and screen actor Dwight Frye, who was chosen in lieu of Bernard Jukes, the actor who played Renfield on Broadway in 1927. Hollywood photographer Albert Witzel had shot publicity portraits of Jukes as Renfield, though the extent to which Universal actively considered casting him is unknown. At any rate, on 9 September, the *Hollywood Reporter* announced that Frye's agent Al Rosen signed a contract with Universal for the actor to portray Renfield.[118] A veteran of the New York stage – including such productions as *The Devil in the Cheese* (1927), which costarred Bela Lugosi – Frye had arrived in Los Angeles in the autumn of 1929, performing in a six-week run of *The Rope's End* prior to starring in a revival of *A Man's Man* in the summer of 1930.[119]

Dwight Frye in a 1923 publicity photograph.

"FRYE WILL NOT BE TYPED," the *Los Angeles Times* proclaimed in March of 1930. "There seems to be an impression I do one type of thing," Frye complained at the time. "I don't and I haven't. … I don't like specialization. I have no interest in anything but character work, and I have made it a point to vary my roles as much as possible."[120] Before *Dracula*, he had already appeared in such films as *The Doorway to Hell* (1930). After *Dracula*, he would indeed be typecast, to a greater extent than most actors in film history.

On 10 September, *Variety* noted that Universal had also cast Edward Van Sloan in *Dracula*, with the actor leaving New York for Hollywood on 19 September.[121] The Broadway veteran would portray Professor Van Helsing.[122] Born in San Francisco in 1882, Van Sloan became attracted to the theatre while attending the University of California at Berkeley.[123] In addition to appearing in the silent film *Slander* (1916), Van Sloan performed in stock in Canada and throughout America. A review of a 1922 production of *Scandal* in Des Moines called Van Sloan's performance "the high spot in the show."[124] That same year, a critic referred to his work in *Scrambled Wives* (also in Des Moines) by saying: "Edward Van Sloan quite hogs the show as the disillusioned man and later as the successful lover."[125]

Then, most famously, Van Sloan appeared as Van Helsing in *Dracula* in the Broadway production in 1927-28. While Universal could easily have cast any number of Hollywood actors in the same role, the studio opted for Van Sloan specifically because he had been associated with the play, believing that such casting would further connect the film to the successful play.[126] Indeed, his screen test consisted of a reaction shot to Dracula throwing a vase at a mirror hanging on the wall beside him, a scene that exists in the stage play, but not in the film.

The same *Variety* article announcing Van Sloan on 10 September mentioned that the "other principal parts, including the lead, are yet to be filled."[127] In the coming days, however, Universal began to make important announcements. On 23 September, for example, the press noted that Lew Ayres, who had starred in *All Quiet on the Western Front*, would portray Jonathan Harker.[128] As the *Los Angeles Times* mentioned that very same day, Ayres has been loaned recently to other studios, but Universal, it seems, has decided to keep him at home now."[129] The previous month, the *Hollywood Filmograph* touted Ayres as "one of the 'finds' of the year," adding that Universal had "great plans" for him.[130] Given that Universal envisioned *Dracula* as one of its two "super-productions" for the autumn of 1930 (the other being Edwin Carewe's *Resurrection*), the casting of Lew Ayres made sense. It placed him in another major Universal film in what might have been – were it not for script changes that will be explored in Chapter 4 – a large and important role. But after Harker became a dramatically smaller and less important part, Junior Laemmle changed his mind. Later, Ayres allegedly claimed that he was interested in playing Renfield, but there is absolutely no evidence that the studio acively considered him for that part.[131] Junior Laemmle wanted to cast him as romantic leads, not in bizarre character roles; moreover, Frye's contract was executed two weeks before the press first mentioned Ayres in conjunction with the film.

Universal also needed to find a suitable leading lady, one who could not only portray the lead female role Mina Seward successfully, but one who also had some box-office allure. The most logical choice would likely have been Mary Nolan, a popular blonde who was then under contract at Universal. But Nolan's life in 1930 suffered more than one meltdown. As Louella O. Parsons wrote in May 1930, Nolan "had such unexpected outbursts of temperament that Carl Laemmle, Jr., decided she needed disciplining … [she] has come back from the desert or wherever she was. Junior had repeatedly said he would not resume her contract until she agreed to be a good girl."[132] Once the arguments were resolved, Universal announced she would appear in Tod Browning's *Outside the Law*. She

Publicity photograph of Edward Van Sloan.

Lew Ayres in a scene still from *Up for Murder* (1931). The actress is Dorothy Peterson, who had appeared as Lucy in the Broadway production of *Vampire–The Vampire Play*.

had already worked with Browning on *West of Zanzibar* (1928), and – given his penchant for working with the same talent repeatedly – he could well have envisioned her as Mina. But Nolan's problems continued after *Outside the Law* wrapped. Industry trades claimed that she was seeking a release from her contract.[133] And newspapers reported at the end of July 1930 that a federal narcotics inspector interviewed Nolan while she was in a hospital being treated for a "severe case of sunburn."[134] She was cleared of suspicion, but the publicity hardly helped the tempestuous actress. On 3 November 1930, the *Hollywood Daily Citizen* referred to the fact that "unfortunate publicity" had caused her to drop "temporarily" out of sight.[135]

And so Nolan was not a real possibility for a Universal super-production set to go before the cameras in September 1930, even though she was the most famous blonde they had under contract. As a result, the *Hollywood Reporter* announced Universal's plans on 12 September 1930:

> *Jeanette Loff, now back from a week's cruise of southern waters, to prepare for her work in* Dracula *at Universal.*[136]

Though she is now largely forgotten, Loff was a relatively big name in 1930. By the end of that year, the *Hollywood Reporter* touted her as one of Universal's "Box Office Leaders."[137]

Chapter 3 – PRE-PRODUCTION

At roughly the same time, Universal announced that she would "draw several feature stories" during their upcoming season.¹³⁸ Shortly before the start of *Dracula*, for example, Loff finished her work in the studio's film *The Boudoir Diplomat*.¹³⁹ While the *Hollywood Reporter* does not mention the character name Mina, the studio must have intended her for that role (as opposed to the smaller part of Lucy, which would not even be cast until after shooting began). Loff was a new star, and so she would be paired with Ayres and the two would portray the film's young romantic leads.

But like Mary Nolan, Loff seems to have been unhappy at Universal. Her role in *Dracula* would not materialize because at a certain point in September she began fighting for a contract release, one that Universal granted her. Loff immediately signed with Tiffany, where the press originally announced she would star in four Phil Goldstone films.¹⁴⁰ On 4 October, *Variety* wrote that her first film for her new employer would be *Midnight Stage*, costarring Rex Lease.¹⁴¹ Instead, she appeared in William Nigh's *Fighting Thru* (1930) with Ken Maynard. The move to Tiffany essentially ruined her budding career.

Jeannette Loff in the film *Love Over Night* (1928).

With Loff no longer a possibility, Universal decided to borrow a young blonde from Warner Bros. On 24 September 1930, one industry trade announced: "On the strength of her work in *Outward Bound*, Helen Chandler has landed a term contract from WB. An immediate loan to U for *Dracula* followed."¹⁴² Born in South Carolina in 1906, Chandler practically grew up on the stage, working in vaudeville at least as early as 1916.¹⁴³ Two year later, she appeared in such "legit" plays as *Daddy Long Legs*.¹⁴⁴ Critics applauded her appearances on Broadway in *Richard III* (1920), *Daddy Dumplins* (1920), and others.¹⁴⁵ Dubbing her the 'most ingenuous ingénue' of the New York stage, *Billboard* covered her successes at length in a 1925 biographical sketch. By that time, she not only had a string of theatrical triumphs to her credit, but also three published poems.¹⁴⁶ Chandler then began to appear in films like Allan Dwan's *The Music Master* (1927) and *The Joy Girl* (1927).¹⁴⁷

Universal likely cast Chandler for the same reason that Warner Bros. signed her: her work in the critically-acclaimed film *Outward Bound* (1930), which was based on Sutton Vane's stage play of the same name. The story features characters on a boat headed for the underworld. They are dead, but unaware of that fact for much of the narrative. Reviews praised Chandler, with both the New York Times and the New York Herald Tribune selecting the particular word "excellent" to describe her acting.[148] These reviews appeared in print on 18 September, only days before trades announced she would she would appear in Dracula.[149]

Though their names did not appear in the press in conjunction with Dracula, other talent also must have been cast prior to the start of shooting, particularly those actors needed during the first week of the production. For example, Junior Laemmle's cousin Beth Laemmle worked on the first two days of the shoot. Just as she had done for her dance number in King of Jazz, Beth used her screen name "Carla Laemmle"; Film Daily noted that she adopted it "in compliment to her uncle," Carl Laemmle, Sr.[150] Less than one month before Dracula went into production, she entered a beauty contest in Los Angeles; the industry press also announced that she had been cast in Universal's "Leatherpusher" short subjects.[151]

In Dracula, Carla Laemmle would play Sara, secretary to an English woman portrayed by Daisy Belmore, an actress who had moved from England to work on the American stage in 1910.[152] At the time of the Dracula shoot, Belmore was also a member of the Civic Repertory Players at the Los Angeles Music Box. The troupe – which also included actor Alan Mowbray – was readying a production of The Apple Cart to open in November 1930.[153]

Together with Frye's Renfield, Carla Laemmle and Daisy Belmore's characters appear as coach passengers en route to the Transylvanian inn.[154] Also appearing in the same scene is Nicholas Bela, who describes "Walpurgis Night" to Renfield. He was an actor, a linguist, and an author; in 1943, Henry Hull appeared in the lead role in an LA production of

Jeannette Loff, now back from a week's cruise of southern waters, to prepare for her work in "Dracula" at Universal.

Publicity still of Jeannette Loff. Inset: From the Hollywood Reporter of September 12, 1930.

Chapter 3 – PRE-PRODUCTION

Left: Helen Chandler as a young actress. Above: Helen Chandler in a 1927 publicity still.

Bela's horror play *Silver Nails*.[155] More famously, though, Bela detailed his affiliation with the Communist Party to the House Un-American Activities Committee in 1954.[156]

Also cast prior to the shoot were Michael Visaroff, who played the Proprietor of the inn, as well as Barbara Bozoky (the Proprietor's wife) and Anna Bakacs (the Proprietor's daughter). Visaroff, who began his career on the stage in Russia, worked in American films from 1925. During the transition to talkies, he disappeared from the screen for a brief period of time due to language difficulties, reappearing soon thereafter in films like *House of Horror* (1929) and *Disraeli* (1929) with "near-perfect English."[157] Only five months prior to being cast in *Dracula*, he opened a studio of dramatic arts in Hollywood. At the time, Visaroff was also known for his work as a makeup artist.

Given that they appeared in footage shot during the production's first week, it is also possible that Universal cast the three actresses who would play Dracula's wives before filming began. Two of them – Geraldine Dvorak and Cornelia Thaw – were best known in the industry as stand-ins for famous stars. Within days of their work in *Dracula*, the *Los Angeles Times* wrote about both of them:

> *Greta Garbo has a double, Geraldine Dvorak, who has been more fortunate than most. For Greta she just does the 'standing in,' as they call it, but she wears clothes so sumptuously and has such an air with her, that she is used by pretty well all the studios in society scenes, often being given a 'bit.' She was, for instance, in the Monte Carlo scene in* Son of the Gods *[1930]. Then, too, rival studios find it amusing to be apparently using Greta in a minor role.*
>
> *... Corinne Griffith's double was Cornelia Thaw, but now that Corinne has retired to begin raising that family of eight she once promised us, Cornelia, by clever make-up and a change of*

100   Chapter 3 – PRE-PRODUCTION

Above: Carla Laemmle in a publicity still depicting the carriage ride to the Transylvanian Inn. She is in the lap of Dwight Frye. In the middle of the photo with the moustache is Nicholas Bela. On the right is Daisy Belmore. The woman between Frye and Bela remains unidentified. *(Courtesy of Rick Atkins).* Inset: Publicity photograph of actress Dorothy Tree.

hair dress, has become a double for Lila Lee. She also does 'extra' [work] occasionally, chiefly because she need not look like anyone else if she doesn't want to.[158]

Of the two, Dvorak attained the most notoriety in the film business, largely due to her resemblance to Garbo. "Nothing has cost me more roles," she complained bitterly in 1931. "I want them to see me as myself and let me do something on my own. I cannot help how I look. I only wish to do something on my own."[159]

Dorothy Tree portrayed the third of Dracula's trio of wives. Born in Brooklyn in 1906 as Dorothy Estelle Triebitz, Tree worked on the New York stage and then married Paramount publicist (and later screenwriter) Michael Uris.[160] She gained more prominent roles in the years after *Dracula*, when she made the transition from starlet to character actress in such films as *Confessions of a Nazi Spy* (1939) and *Abe Lincoln in Illinois* (1940).[161] However, Tree's

Chapter 3 – PRE-PRODUCTION 101

membership in the Communist Party led to a Hollywood blacklist in the early fifties.[162] Using her married name, she became a speech consultant to the Metropolitan Opera and taught diction classes in New York for more than thirty years. She also wrote four books, among them *Everybody's Book of Better Speaking* (1960).[163]

Count Dracula

Shortly after *Dracula*'s release in 1931, Mordaunt Hall of the *New York Times* wrote, "Mr. Browning had hoped to have Mr. Chaney play the part of Stoker's human vampire, but this was not to be...."[164] Here is the stuff of cinema legends, as one of the great Hollywood myths is that Chaney was to portray Dracula, but the casting was disrupted due to the actor's death. The tale is simultaneously true and false. False, given that Chaney was never cast as Dracula. Indeed, he was not under contract to Universal in 1930. He was also ill prior to his death, which preceded *Dracula*'s production and even the studio's acquisition of the rights to it. Chaney was not Dracula, and due to his health problems and demise, he could never have been, certainly not when the film was produced in the autumn of 1930.

Conversely, it is true that Browning would have liked Chaney to have assumed the role, something evident not only in Mordaunt Hall's comments, but also in the director and actor's collaborative work on *London After Midnight* (1927). Chaney's fame could have greatly assisted the success of the talkie version of *Dracula*, particularly in the eyes of those who viewed the story as too risky to film. And he would likely have portrayed the character in a manner very different from Bela Lugosi, the eventual star. Nevertheless, Browning was unable to work with Chaney on *Dracula*, or for that matter on *The Thirteenth Chair*. Louella O. Parsons reported that Chaney was offered the lead role in Browning's first talkie, but he did not appear in it.[165]

Though he was originally against the idea of appearing in sound films (which might have been why he avoided *The Thirteenth Chair*), Chaney successfully made the transition in *The Unholy Three* (1930), Jack Conway's sound remake of Browning's 1925 silent classic. His continued box-office appeal seemed assured, but tragically he died of throat cancer on 26 August 1930, during a period when Universal was actively considering different actors for the role of Dracula.[166]

As Michael F. Blake, author of three books on Lon Chaney, has noted:

> Many writers have speculated that before his death, Lon was slated to do *Dracula* for Tod Browning at Universal. This is highly unlikely due to Lon's star status at [MGM], as well as his new success in talking pictures. Universal made a request for Lon's services in 1929 to do some dialogue scenes for a part-talking reissue of *Phantom of the Opera*, but Louis B. Mayer turned them down. MGM's only options would have been either to buy the rights to *Dracula* or to simply loan out Chaney and count it as one of his four pictures per his contract. It is improbable that MGM would have done the latter unless Universal paid them much more than Chaney's weekly salary of $3,750.[167]

Put another way, if Chaney had lived, it would have been theoretically possible for him to star in *Dracula*. Loans of major stars did occur occasionally; for example, Universal agreed to loan Lew Ayres to Warner Bros. right after he appeared in *All Quiet on the Western Front* in 1930.[168] However, in the case of Lon Chaney, such a loan would have been quite unlikely.

Indeed, one could add further weight to Blake's argument by noting that Chaney brought suit against Universal in March 1930 over publicity for the sound reissue of *The Phantom of the Opera* that gave audiences the false impression that they would hear his voice in it.[169] Such a disagreement might well have made Chaney at least temporarily unhappy with Universal.

Moreover, even if it was due to his illness, Chaney's name was never mentioned publicly in conjunction with *Dracula*'s casting during the summer of 1930.[170] For example, at the beginning of July 1930, Tod Browning weighed in with his own "definite ideas of how *Dracula* should be produced on the screen," arguing that the role should *not* go to a well-known star. "I favor getting a stranger from Europe," he said, "and not giving his name. It takes away from the thrilling effects of the story."[171] Browning's conception of the character had changed prior to Chaney's death, even if it was the result of Chaney's illness and/or his inability and/or unwillingness to star in a Universal film that year.

Lon Chaney, the "Man of a Thousand Faces." *(Courtesy of George Chastain)*

What names did appear in the press? During the third week of June 1930, the studio initially touted John Wray as their choice for the "neck-biter."[172] *Film Daily* described his portrayal of the dictatorial yet cowardly drill sergeant Himmelstoss in *All Quiet on the Western Front* as "one of the screen's acting achievements."[173] Not only was he associated with Junior Laemmle's hit film, he was also under a long-term studio contract, one that he signed shortly after appearing in Universal's *The Czar of Broadway*, a project filmed in the late winter and spring of 1930 and then released in May of the same year.[174] When Universal announced he would star as Dracula, the 43-year-old Wray was receiving acclaim for his latest role. It is difficult to know why Junior Laemmle decided against Wray, save for the fact that the studio was simultaneously crafting a starring role for him in *Saint Johnson* (aka *St. Johnson*), which would have been shot in the autumn had it not been shelved in late September.[175] Similarly, in early August, *Motion Picture News* mentioned that Wray would costar with Lew Ayres in an "air picture to be directed by Howard Hawks."[176]

Rumors in late June 1930 also suggested that Bela Lugosi, the star of the original New York production of *Dracula–The Vampire Play*, would play the title role. Grace Kingsley of the *Los Angeles Times* argued on 21 June 1930 that, "one cannot imagine anyone else doing it as well as he."[177] As previously noted, Tod Browning spoke on the same matter about ten days later when he declared that he wanted an unknown European to play the role, and that the studio withhold his name from audiences to make him seem more mysterious.[178]

It could be that Browning was already thinking about Bela Lugosi, who had acted in thirteen American films prior to *Dracula*, including a number of talkies in 1930. To Broadway fans and some theatregoers in California, he was well known for portraying Dracula on stage: that limited fame also caused a movie fan magazine to publish an article about him in 1929.[179] Nevertheless, Lugosi remained a virtual unknown to the everyday American filmgoer in 1930, meaning that casting him would add further risk to an already risky production.

Browning and Lugosi had worked together on *The Thirteenth Chair*, in which Lugosi played not a villain but instead a detective in an old-dark-house mystery set in India. Some publicity drew attention to Lugosi's connection to *Dracula–The Vampire Play*, but Lugosi's part in the film was not a vampire or villain of any kind. At least two writers have suggested that Lugosi's role in *The Thirteenth Chair* may have constituted something of a "screen test" for *Dracula*, but there is absolutely no evidence that such was the case.[180] Perhaps Browning saw the film as an opportunity to determine how easy or difficult Lugosi was to work with; indeed, a marker of Browning's career was that he enjoyed working repeatedly with some of the same talent. But as a director who had been interested in *Dracula* for many years, Browning would have known how Lugosi would approach the vampire role simply by seeing him onstage, which he did do on at least one occasion.[181] And to be sure, Lugosi's appearance in *The Thirteenth Chair* does not seem to have influenced the process of *Dracula*'s casting whatsoever.

Moreover, a second examination of Browning's quotation reveals that he may not have been referring to Lugosi at all. Understanding that critics and some New York and California audience members knew about Lugosi's association with the role of Dracula onstage (even if most other audience members didn't), Browning may not necessarily have viewed Lugosi as "unknown," particularly if he really hoped that the actor's name could be concealed from the audience, as he suggested. And indeed, his hope in that regard was not as far-fetched

John Wray, pictured here with Betty Compson in a publicity still for *The Czar of Broadway* (1930).

as it might seem, as Universal and James Whale utilized the same idea when they withheld Boris Karloff's name during the opening credits of *Frankenstein* (1931), replacing it instead with a mysterious question mark.

Regardless, Bela Lugosi was definitely on a mission to win the role of Dracula. Breakfasting with Wood Soanes of the *Oakland Tribune*, he discussed the film version in early July 1930:

> *I am looking forward to the screen production, which is being planned by Universal. As you know, Dracula [on the stage] represents but a small portion of the story as outlined in the Bram Stoker novel. There is one scene in particular that cannot be presented on the stage but would be most effective on the screen.*

Lugosi proceeded to describe that scene, Dracula's voyage to England, adding that, "it should make a most stirring picture."[182]

Then, on 12 July 1930, Lugosi wrote to literary agent Harold Freedman in New York: "[I] wish to thank you very much for your kind effort in suggesting I play the part in *Dracula* when it is filmed. I am sure the success of this enterprise will be largely due to your endeavors, which I very much appreciate."[183] Here Lugosi was trying to stay in touch with someone that he knew had been involved in the sale of the film rights, perhaps in the hope that Freedman might mention him to Universal.

The next key moment in casting the role of Dracula came near the end of July 1930. Associate producer E. M. Asher attended a stage production of *Dracula* starring Lugosi at Oakland's Fulton Theatre. With him were Louis Bromfield and Dudley Murphy, who coauthored a *Dracula* screenplay for Universal (as Chapter 4 will examine). Curiously absent from the Universal delegation was Junior Laemmle, though he may well have already seen the play on one or more occasions. Indeed, Laemmle told film historian Rick Atkins, "After seeing Bela Lugosi successfully do the character on stage, in New York, Browning and I eventually went with Bela."[184] Either the two attended the play in 1927 and/or 1928 when it was still on Broadway and, or – more likely if they actually saw the play together – the two attended the play on the West Coast, perhaps even the Oakland version in 1930.

Bela Lugosi in a publicity still for *Dracula* (1931).

Chapter 3 – PRE-PRODUCTION

At any rate, on 2 August 1930, the *Hollywood Filmograph* quoted the *Oakland Post-Enquirer* as saying: "According to studio announcement following [the Asher/Bromfield/Murphy 'visit' to the Fulton Theatre], Bela Lugosi, who is playing the title role here, will play for the screen the part he has made famous on the stage."[185] The *Filmograph* may have reprinted the quotation from the newspaper because their editor had not yet heard the same directly from Universal. Indeed, it seems to have been a premature announcement, one that Lugosi might have even encouraged the *Post-Enquirer* to publish.

Certainly other members in the press continued to lobby for Lugosi. On 16 August, the *Hollywood Filmograph* reiterated what became its regular refrain that summer: Lugosi was the "greatest living portrayer" of Dracula, and thus should win the role.[186] Three days later, Elizabeth Yeaman at the *Hollywood Daily Citizen* declared that it was "hard to picture anyone [other than Lugosi] in the part." She added, "I suspect that Universal feels that way about Mr. Lugosi, although no definite announcement in this connection has come from the studio."[187]

Given *Dracula*'s importance on the studio schedule for 1930-31, Junior Laemmle and others appear to have labored over the decision of who should play the title role. On 30 August, the *Hollywood Filmograph* told readers that the studio had made a screen test of Lugosi. It apparently consisted of two scenes shot in the space of a few hours. The publication added, "right now Bela Lugosi and a number of others are awaiting the final O K of Carl Laemmle."[188] As Lugosi himself claimed in 1939 (in a quotation that again ostensibly tried to preserve his accent):

> *And who was tested? De cousins and brodder-in-laws of de Laemmles – all deir pets and de pets of DEIR pets! Dis goes on for a longk time and den oldt man Laemmle says, 'Dere's nobody in de family dat can play it, zo why don't you hire an egdor!*[189]

Who were these other persons? Certainly other names were also proposed, including Joseph Schildkraudt, though there is no evidence that Junior Laemmle seriously considered him. An agent suggested Schildkraut's name, the actor having already starred in Universal's *Night Ride* (1930).[190] John Carradine may also have been considered; decades later, he claimed that he was, but – like Schildkraut – his name never appeared in conjunction with the film in any 1930 publications.[191]

Had Junior Laemmle wanted to do so, he could have chosen from a number of Draculas throughout America. Romaine Callender successfully played the role onstage in Washington D.C. in June 1930. Courtney White did the same in Wilmington in September.[192] This is to say nothing of Raymond Huntley, the star of the London production of *Dracula*, who played the vampire again in Philadelphia in 1930.[193] Those were all in addition to Victor Jory, who was getting strong notices as Dracula in a Pasadena production of the play staged in August 1930 at the very time Universal actively sought its screen vampire. The studio certainly doesn't seem to have considered any of these other Draculas, but they did prove one thing: one didn't have to be Bela Lugosi to get applause as the vampire.

The next question then is who did the studio seriously consider other than Lugosi and John Wray? On 11 August 1930, E. M. Asher contacted director Roland West about the availability of Chester Morris, an actor who had just starred in *The Bat Whispers*. Though

The Bat Whispers would not be released until after *Dracula*'s production began, Asher had likely seen Morris' performances in other films, including *Alibi* (1929) and *The Big House* (1930), the latter being released in June 1930. Casting Morris would have meant casting a successful film actor, and it also meant a chance to connect the film directly to the mystery genre. But Roland West – who had Morris under contract – turned Asher down on 12 August, mentioning that he was trying to find a romantic story for the actor.[194] A fan-magazine article published that autumn said much the same, telling readers that West wouldn't let Morris play any more "crook roles," even though they had brought the actor fame.[195] At age 29, Morris was the youngest actor the studio considered as a possible Dracula.[196]

By late August, Universal seems to have moved on to at least two more possibilities. They strongly considered Paul Muni, who remains famous for his work in such films as *Scarface* (1932). Muni made a great deal of sense as a possible Dracula in the summer of 1930, as the press described him as a "new" Lon Chaney after his work in the Fox film *Seven Faces* (1930).[197] Like Chaney, he would have brought a unique quality to the role, one that would have presumably been much less romantic and perhaps more dependent on heavy makeup.[198] From a physical standpoint, he also might have been closer than any other actors under consideration to the shooting script's description of Dracula as a "thick-set" man. Universal did film a test of Muni as *Dracula*, though it does not seem to survive.[199]

At roughly the same time, Universal also shot a screen test of William Courtenay, who had made a great success of playing a magician in a stage version of *The Spider*.[200] While that role may have been one reason the studio thought of him, another was his work in the film *Three Faces East*, which was released in August 1930. In it, Courtenay's tall slender body, large eyes, receding hairline, and commanding presence made him seem like a suitable candidate for the role. In this case, it was Universal's "New York offices" that issued the "demand" that he portray Dracula.[201] Given that fact, his screen test (which also does not survive) may have been little more than an effort to placate some executives. At any rate, Courtenay – who was 55 years old in 1930 – was the oldest possible Dracula of those considered.

Even as the number of would-be Draculas seemed to grow, various persons in the press continued to support Lugosi, perhaps because he had a knack for ingratiating himself to journalists, but also because they had presumably seen him in one of the stage versions. "It seems like everybody that is anybody is pulling for Bela Lugosi to play Dracula," the *Hollywood Filmograph* commented in the issue published on 6 September, adding, "the story

Artwork of Victor Jory as Dracula from a program for his performance in the August 1930 production in Pasadena.

Paul Muni in the film *Seven Faces* (1930).

is made to order for him, since he has the voice along with the appearance that is necessary for the part."[202]

One week later, however, the same trade published what one journalist perceived to be disappointing news: "Dame Rumor has it that Universal has selected Ian Keith [to be Dracula], who just finished a picture on their lot."[203] The film in question was *The Boudoir Diplomat*, in which Keith played the male lead. Immediately prior, Keith played a supporting role in Raoul Walsh's *The Big Trail* (1930) at Fox; he had also portrayed John Wilkes Booth in D. W. Griffith's *Abraham Lincoln* (1930). The 31-year-old actor cut an impressive figure, and would likely have created a romantic Dracula; in *The Boudoir Diplomat*, he played a

Above: William Courtenay (right) with Erich von Stroheim (left) in *Three Faces East* (1930). Below: Ian Keith and Jeannette Loff in *The Boudoir Diplomat* (1930).

ladies' man who flirts with the wives of other characters.

"Maybe we are a bit premature with our announcement," the *Filmograph* said, "but we have every reason to believe that Ian Keith has been selected and unless some unforeseen thing happens will play Dracula."[204] At roughly the same time, however, *Film Daily* told readers that Junior Laemmle was "very favorably impressed" with Lugosi's screen test.[205] Contradictions, apparent or real, abounded.

And then, after nearly three months, Universal announced that a decision had finally been made. On 15 September, *Film Daily* reported that Lugosi would play Dracula; he had in fact signed a contract on 11 September.[206] The news then appeared in various publications over the days that followed. Discussing the choice, Grace Kingsley at the *Los Angeles Times* wrote, "Sometimes certain players who please the dramatic writers really are chosen for certain roles, and that is just what has happened, so far as this writer is concerned, to Universal's production of *Dracula*."[207]

In his book *Hollywood Gothic*, David J. Skal speaks of "Universal's expressed lack of interest" in Lugosi.[208] Then, in his book *The Monster Show*, Skal claims that Lugosi was "the last person Universal wanted in the title role," and reprints as evidence a telegram dated 27 March 1930 from Junior Laemmle to Harold Freedman that reads: "Not interested Bela Lugosi Present Time."[209] While the telegram is of historical importance, questions have to be

Universal bulletins that "all uncertainty about the role of Count Dracula in the Tod Browning production, 'Dracula,' has been dispelled by the signing of Bela Lugesi." Now we'd like to know who suffered all that uncertainty, besides Bela.... Burnet Hershey, writer at the Vitaphone studios, turned out "The Honeymoon Trail" during his honeymoon. Murray Roth says it's very realistic, but imagine a guy, even a gag man, working on his honeymoon!

* * *

Above: Comedian Slim Summerville jokingly attired as Dracula. *(Courtesy of Dr. Robert J. Kiss)*. Inset: From *Motion Picture News* of September 20, 1930.

raised about what its significance actually *is*. Handwriting on it by an unknown person says "Dracula," but that could have been added after the fact for the purpose of filing it, even at a much later date. The telegram itself does not reference *Dracula*. After all, in March 1930, Universal was not seriously interested in *anyone* to star in its film version of *Dracula*, as it had not yet even secured the rights to the property. In other words, the telegram likely refers to something other than the selection of the film's lead actor; to the extent it might have had anything to do with *Dracula*, it could merely have referred to Lugosi's efforts to broker the rights to the story, which (as already noted) he did attempt in the spring of 1930.

The eventual casting of Bela Lugosi actually raises two other possibilities. The first, and most likely, is that Universal considered the role and the film of great importance, and as a result carefully weighed the matter. Numerous persons interjected their beliefs into the process (including E. M. Asher, the man assigned to be the film's associate producer), and so, not surprisingly, an array of different names surfaced as possible Draculas, with John Wray, William Courtenay, Paul Muni, and Ian Keith being logical contenders. And indeed it is easy to see why some persons, such as those in the New York offices who lobbied for Courtenay, formed their position. Some of these other possibilities were safe bets, proven film actors whose marquee value in 1930 far outweighed Lugosi's. After all, if a film version of *Dracula* was a risky proposition, why compound that risk by casting someone unknown to most Americans?

But Lugosi's name kept surfacing repeatedly throughout the entire process, at Universal and in the press, far more than anyone else's. And he did win the role. Perhaps the fact he lobbied so hard for it helped, or perhaps it did not. Perhaps some persons at Universal expressed opposition to Lugosi, or perhaps not. But what is extremely clear is the fact that Junior Laemmle – in conjunction with Tod Browning, as Laemmle himself claimed – cast Lugosi in the role, thus expressing great confidence in him. Too much was riding on the costly project to believe that Laemmle cast someone he did not want in the role.

The other possibility is that Junior Laemmle actually decided on Lugosi earlier than mid-September 1930, perhaps as early as late June or July, such as around the time that the Universal contingent saw Lugosi onstage in Oakland. By not making an announcement until September, Laemmle could have accomplished three goals, one of which was to create the illusion that others at the studio were having real input into a process that was already decided in whole or in part. Secondly, he was able to test reactions in the popular press to different actors mentioned for the part. And thirdly, he created a tremendous amount of publicity over the suspense of who would win the role.

It is important to remember that the *Hollywood Filmograph* called Dracula the "prize role of the season," adding that the question of who would play the role was "the burning question right now in the film industry."[210] Subsequently, the same trade declared "there has been so much said about who will play Dracula for Universal that everybody has sort of watched with interest who the powers that be will select."[211] In her newspaper column, Louella O. Parsons wrote, "Seems to me I never heard so many people mentioned for a part in my life."[212] On 20 September, *Motion Picture News* announced:

> Universal bulletins that 'all uncertainty about the role of Count Dracula in the Tod Browning production *Dracula* has been dispelled by the signing of Bela Lugosi.' Now we'd like to know who suffered all that uncertainty, besides Bela.[213]

Their joking aside, many persons had followed the story of who would be cast in the role, with trade publications and daily newspapers updating readers on a regular basis from late June through mid-September, a span of nearly three months.

More than anyone else, Carl Laemmle, Sr. had helped to create the Hollywood star system, manipulating the press with much skill to generate enormous publicity for the likes of Florence Lawrence in 1910, the first American film star known by name (as opposed to nicknames like "The Biograph Girl" or "The Vitagraph Girl").[214] Perhaps his son was doing much the same in 1930, generating a great deal of free publicity during the pre-production phase of a risky project, repeatedly getting the film's title in newspapers across America (and, by extension, the name of the largely unknown Bela Lugosi), when he in fact planned to cast the actor for weeks prior to making the announcement.

Regardless of exactly *when* the decision to cast Lugosi was made, however, it is simply not credible to claim that the studio did not want Lugosi or was somehow stuck with him, as a variety of other actors could easily have been cast, including those already under contract at Universal. As for the others, it must be said that there is no record of an actual offer being made to Courtenay or Muni, or, by extension, either of them turning the role down. The reality is that Laemmle wanted Lugosi and had faith in his ability to carry the film, or at least to carry it in conjunction alongside the star power of Lew Ayres. To suggest anything else of a major studio producing a risky, big-budget film during the Great Depression would be illogical and baseless in terms of evidence.

Conclusion

In early September 1930, *Motion Picture News* told readers that, "Universal is regarded as having turned the corner as a result of its new production policy, with observers predicting profitable operation next season," something envisioned in no small measure due to *All Quiet on the Western Front*.[215] Junior Laemmle was a risk-taker, but there was a growing impression in some quarters that his youth gave him particular insight into what talking picture audiences at the dawn of the Great Depression wanted. And at least some of his decisions appeared to be paying off.

It is also possible that Laemmle's audacity of spirit simultaneously influenced and was influenced by the Hollywood *zeitgeist* of 1930. Speaking of that fact, *Billboard* noted:

> *As the third year of dialog gets under way, producers have shown a greater daring with their selection of screen material than in the days of the silent picture. They have evidently come to the realization that the motion picture audience has developed a mind of its own that has a greater thinking quality than they supposed. … A glance at the success of* All Quiet on the Western Front *and* Journey's End *[1930] will easily prove that motion picture audiences are willing to accept well-done screen stories no matter what the type.*[216]

Variety added that producers also seemed to be "openly ignoring" the Hays Code (as it then existed) when purchasing "plays or stories for filmization."[217]

Nevertheless, W. R. Wilkerson expressed his increasing trepidation about Junior Laemmle's role at Universal in the pages of the *Hollywood Reporter*. He made no mention of *Dracula*, but worried openly about such movies as *The Boudoir Diplomat* and *Blind Wives* (aka *A Lady Surrenders*, 1930). "It may be that [Junior Laemmle] is accomplishing wonders with the material at hand. However, I doubt it…."[218] His key question was whether Laemmle could really transform Universal into a studio producing prestige pictures, or whether the success of *All Quiet on the Western Front* was due less to his wisdom and foresight than to just being lucky.

At any rate, Junior Laemmle's position at Universal was stronger than ever before during the summer of 1930, even if his recent successes created more pressure to repeat them. Leaving California for New York on 15 September 1930, Carl Laemmle, Sr. would attend his semi-annual meetings with key studio executives, including Phil Reisman, the new sales chief.[219] At that time, they would discuss the fact that Universal bookings were "assuming record proportions" for that stage of the season, and that the sales force was "enthused over the new type of product being produced" and was anticipating its "biggest year" ever.[220] All of it was thanks to Junior Laemmle's production leadership.

And to such pending releases as *Dracula*, so it was hoped, the film being an important component of the studio's strategy for the second half of 1930. In late August, Universal announced that *Dracula* would begin production in the "next three weeks."[221] Other proposed start dates were 22 September and 25 September.[222] In the end, the film's production would not get underway until 29 September 1930, with the younger Laemmle based at the California studio while the elder was on the East Coast.

1. Crafton, Donald. *The Talkies: American Cinema's Transition to Sound, 1926-1931* (Berkeley, CA: University of California Press, 1997): 16.
2. "Scrapping of Bad Films Costly to the Producers." *Billboard* 27 Sept. 1930: 7.
3. "Fox Picks Story for Wayne." *Los Angeles Times* 21 June 1930.
4. "The Mystery Play Took to the Road." *New York Times* 2 Mar. 1930: 118.
5. See Gomery, Douglas. *The Coming of Sound* (New York: Routledge, 2005).
6. Crafton, pp. 10-11.
7. De Forest, Lee. "The Talking Pictures." *American Cinematographer* (Feb. 1928): 4.
8. Crafton, p. 13.
9. "Projection Is Talkies' Foe." *Billboard* 1 June 1929: 20.
10. "Public Hasn't Seen Anything Yet!, Says Jesse L. Lasky: Talkies Widen Screen's Scope." *Exhibitors Herald-World* 15 June 1929: 121.
11. "Public Is Rejecting Silent Pictures Unless They Are in Novelty Form, Says Sam Katz." *Exhibitors Herald-World* 15 June 1929: 125.
12. Lang, Harry. "The Microphone – The Terror of the Studios." *Photoplay* (Dec. 1929): 29.
13. "See Material for Talkies in Many of the Old Plays." *Billboard* 7 Dec. 1929: 38.
14. "6,500 U.S. Theatres Wired in 12 Months." *Film Daily* 1 May 1930: 8.
15. "10,234, or 70 Per Cent of US Theatres Are Wired for Sound." *Exhibitors Herald-World* 26 July 1930: 15.
16. "Talking Pictures Must Get Back to Basic Quality of the Screen." *Billboard* 30 Aug. 1930: 44.
17. O'Connell, J.S. "Talkers 'Producers' Rattles,' Says Pioneer; 'Sound Is No Improvement.'" *Motion Picture News* 7 June 1930: 117.
18. Crafton, p. 16.
19. "U Begins Work on First Unit of Synchronized Film Studios." *Exhibitors Herald and Moving Picture World* 21 July 1928: 38.
20. "Universal Plans 16 Sound Films; Completes First Sound Short." *Exhibitors Herald and Moving Picture World* 15 Sept. 1928: 30.
21. "Sound Track System More Convenient, Says Laemmle Jr." *Film Daily* 21 Feb. 1929: 12.
22. Greene, Walter. "Sound Improved by Universal's New Developer?" *Motion Picture News* 13 June 1930: 66; "Universal Fan Mail Doubled by Sound Films." *Motion Picture News* 26 July 1930: 45.
23. Merrick, Mollie. "Hollywood – In Person." *New Orleans Times-Picayune* 20 July 1930: 2.
24. "U Chief Sees Dialogue Lull." *Los Angeles Evening Express* 11 July 1930.
25. "Star Gazer." *Exhibitors Herald-World* 8 Nov. 1930: 46.
26. "25 Per Cent Dialogue Reduction Ordered for Universal Pictures." *Motion Picture Herald* 29 Oct. 1932.
27. Thomas, Dan. "Declares Movies Won't Let Stage Succumb to Rush of 'Talkies.'" *Sandusky Star Journal* (Sandusky, OH) 27 Apr. 1929.
28. Crafton, p. 418.
29. See, for example: Greene, Walter R. "'Dubbing' Foreign Lines in Talkers, New Coast Practice." *Motion Picture News* 19 Oct. 1929: 26; "C. W. Spain Explains 'Dubbing' in Talkies." *Billboard* 2 Nov. 1929: 21.
30. Crafton, p. 425. See also: Quigley, Martin J. "Dubbing." *Exhibitors Herald-World* 5 July 1930: 16.
31. Crafton, p. 425.
32. "Multi-Lingual Films by MGM." *Billboard* 16 Nov. 1929: 3; "First MGM French Film Will be Unholy Night." *Film Daily* 9 Jan. 1930: 2.
33. "Para. Plans Foreign Language Series of All-Talkie Features." *Billboard* 14 Sept. 1929.
34. "Spanish Pictures Open New Fields to Workers." *Hollywood Filmograph* 12 Apr. 1930: 20.
35. "Studios Are Badly in Need of Spanish Speaking Leading Men." *Hollywood Filmograph* 12 Apr. 1930: 25.
36. "The Latin-American Actors Are Peeved." *Hollywood Filmograph* 1 Feb. 1930: 1.
37. "Move Foreigns to Europe." *Variety* 2 July 1930: 7.
38. "18 Foreign Versions of Warner Talkies in 1930-31." *Motion Picture News* 27 Sept. 1930: 30.
39. "Paul Kohner." *Variety* 8 Jan. 1930: 92; "Universal Takes Lead in Foreign Version Films." *Universal Weekly* 8 Mar. 1930: 26.
40. "Universal Producing Foreign talkies." *Universal Weekly* 22 Feb. 1930: 28.

41. "10 Germans to 1 US Talker in Budapest." *Variety* 15 Oct. 1930.
42. "U's Foreign Language Plans." *Motion Picture News* 27 Sept. 1930: 33.
43. Woollcott, Alexander. "The Play." *New York Times* 24 Aug. 1920: 15.
44. Woollcott, Alexander. "The Play." *New York Times* 8 Feb. 1922: 21.
45. "*Wooden Kimono* Both Lurid and Hilarious." *New York Times* 28 Dec. 1926: 16.
46. "Audience Cheers *The Gorilla* Actors: Much Fun in Ralph Spence's Burlesque of the Mystery Play at the Selwyn." *New York Times* 29 Apr. 1925: 24.
47. "*The Terror.*" *Variety* 22 Aug. 1928: 14.
48. Donnell, Dorothy. "Gorifying [sic] the American Screen." *Motion Picture Classic* (Dec. 1928): 18-19.
49. "*The House of Secrets.*" *Film Daily* 26 May 1929: 8.
50. Watts, Richard, Jr. "*The Gorilla.*" *New York Herald Tribune* 21 Nov. 1927.
51. "Reviews of Recent Releases." *Moving Picture Review and Theatre Management* (Feb. 1929): 18.
52. "U to Remake *Phantom* and *Storm* in Sound." *Film Daily* 3 May 1929: 1, 12; "U to Make *Phantom* Sequel in Sound and Color." *Film Daily* 5 May 1929: 1.
53. "Chaney Still Silent in Talking *Phantom.*" *Variety* 18 Feb. 1930: 8.
54. "*The Phantom of the Opera.*" *Variety* 12 Feb. 1930: 19.
55. Sargent, Epes W. "Talking Pictures." *Zit's Theatrical Weekly* 24 May 1930: 24 May 1930: 11.
56. "Roland West to Direct *The Bat Whispers.*" *Hollywood Filmograph* 5 July 1930: 7.
57. "Hollywood Bulletins." *Variety* 10 Sept. 1930: 25.
58. This issue is discussed in. "*The Cat Creeps.*" *Variety* 12 Nov. 1930: 45
59. "English and Spanish Versions Simultaneously." *Motion Picture News* 2 Aug. 1930: 83.
60. Wilk, Ralph. "A Little from 'Lots.'" *Film Daily* 13 May 1929: 4.
61. "Melford Directs Spanish Version of *East Is West.*" *Hollywood Filmograph* 30 Aug. 1930: 13
62. "Day and Night Production for U's *The Cat Creeps.*" *Film Daily* 31 July 1930: 9.
63. *All Quiet on the Western Front* won Academy Awards for Best Picture and Best Direction; *King of Jazz* won an Academy Award for Best Interior Decoration.
64. Laemmle, Carl, Sr. "Universal's Change in Policy for 1930-31." *Exhibitors Herald-World* 21 June 1930: 63-64.
65. "Universal Cutting Down '30-'31 Product to 20 Features; Shorts Are Cut Way Down Also." *Variety* 2 Apr. 1930: 10. In the end, Universal did produce four serials in the autumn of 1930. See: "Universal Finishes 1930 Serial Schedule." *Billboard* 17 Jan. 1931: 7.
66. "Universal Cuts 1930-31 Features to 20." *Film Daily* 2 Apr. 1930: 1, 8.
67. "Universal Announces New Production Schedule." *Hollywood Filmograph* 5 Apr. 1930: 25
68. "Universal's 1930-31 Lineup Outlined by Laemmle." *Film Daily* 28 Apr. 1930: 1, 6.
69. "20 New Films and 3 Supplementaries on U Schedule." *Motion Picture News* 7 June 1930: 49.
70. "Universal Will Spend $500,000 Per Picture." *Film Daily* 8 Apr. 1930: 2; "Universal to Make 20 Pictures a Year But at a Cost of 50." *Exhibitors Herald-World* 5 Apr. 1930: 26.
71. "U Features to Cost $350,000 to $400,000 Each." *Film Daily* 12 May 1930: 1, 2.
72. "Class Pictures, RKO Deal, 'Break' for Universal." *Motion Picture News* 6 Sept. 1930: 24.
73. "U's 50 Let-Outs." *Variety* 3 Sept. 1930: 5.
74. "U After High Calibre Execs." *Variety* 12 Feb. 1930: 11.
75. In addition to the three associate producers named in the main text, Junior Laemmle later appointed three more in 1930, one of them being Arthur Unger. Then, Laemmle made Erwin Gelsey and Robert Harris associate producers in October 1930. See "Gelsey and Harris Made Assoc. Producers at U." *Film Daily* 12 Oct. 1930: 4.
76. "Garson, Asso. Producer at U, Back to Former System." *Variety* 12 Feb. 1930: 10; "Universal Outlines Production Plans." *Hollywood Filmograph* 5 July 1930: 18.
77. "Universal Names Associate Producers." *Billboard* 15 Mar. 1930: 20.
78. "Special Dep't of U for Shorts; White in Charge?" *Motion Picture News* 14 June 1930: 58.
79. "Universal Corners Directorial Market." *Billboard* 5 July 1930: 21.
80. "10 Year Contract Protects Junior if U Sells Out." *Motion Picture News* 14 June 1930.
81. "Hollywood Activities." *Billboard* 18 Aug. 1928: 20.
82. "*Dracula* to Be Filmed." *To-Day's Cinema* 6 Oct. 1928.
83. "*Dracula* Is Discussed as Picture." *Los Angeles Times* 22 July 1928.
84. Lugosi spoke about sound films again in: "Talkies Will Aid the Stage." *Los Angeles Times* 14 Oct. 1928: B15.
85. See, for example, the reprint of paperwork that suggests this possibility in Riley, Philip J. *Dracula Starring Lon Chaney* (Duncan, OK: BearManor Media, 2010): 10.
86. Schatz, Thomas. *The Genius of the System: Hollywood Filmmaking in the Studio Era* (New York: Pantheon, 1988): 89.
87. An excellent and thorough history of the sale of *Dracula*'s film rights to Universal appears in: Skal, David J. *Hollywood Gothic: The Tangled Web of* Dracula *from Novel to Stage to Screen* (New York: W. W. Norton, 1990): 93-109.
88. Stoker, Irving Noel Thornley. Letter to John L. Balderston. 24 June 1930. Available in in the John L. Balderston Papers, 1915-1950. Series I, Correspondence, 1915-1949. Box 1, Folder 6. The Bill Rose Theatre Division of the New York Public Library.
89. Mok, Michael. "Horror Man at Home." *New York Post* 19 Oct. 1939.
90. Skal, *Hollywood Gothic*, pp. 106-107.
91. Koszarski, Richard. Email to Gary D. Rhodes. 26 Apr. 2012. For an excellent history of *Nosferatu*'s

91. appearance in America and the eventual sale of a print to Universal, see Skal, *Hollywood Gothic*, pp. 100-105, 108-109.
92. Yeaman, Elizabeth. *Hollywood Daily Citizen* 16 Sept. 1930.
93. Ibid.
94. "The New Pictures." *Time* 23 Feb. 1931: 62.
95. Advertisement. *Variety* 27 Aug. 1930: 24.
96. "Universal's *Dracula* to Have Romance and Thrills." *Exhibitors Herald-World* 4 Oct. 1930: 58.
97. Atkins, p. 18.
98. "3-Way Foreign Talent Contest." *Variety* 27 Sept. 1930: 1.
99. "Several Boudoirs." *Variety* 24 Sept. 1930: 6.
100. "E. M. Asher Dies at 50." *Daily Variety* 29 Oct. 1937: 1, 4.
101. "Obituaries." *Daily Variety* 13 July 1973: 15.
102. "Scott Beal Given U Directing Contract." *Daily Variety* 14 Nov. 1934: 12.
103. "Bulletin Board." *Hollywood Filmograph* 27 Sept. 1930: 23. This bulletin shows that an assistant director for *Dracula* was still "unassigned." However, the same column in the 4 Oct. 1930 issue lists "Scotty Beal" in that role (p. 23).
104. Bosco, Wally. "Aces of the Camera: Karl Freund, A.S.C." *American Cinematographer* (Apr. 1944): 124. It seems Freund travelled from England to New York and did some "experimental work" with color film at the Paramount Long Island studio before moving to California. See "Karl Freund Perfecting Color Process in NY." *Film Daily* 2 Jan. 1930: 2. According to *Variety*, Freund was in Hollywood by 1 Apr. 1930. See: "Technicolor's Plant in England Opens June 1." *Variety* 2 Apr. 1930: 7.
105. "Bulletin Board," p. 23.
106. "Assignments." *Variety* 4 Oct. 1930.
107. "Universal Notes." *Hollywood Filmograph* 4 Oct. 1930: 9. This article misspells Brotherton's name as "Bretherton."
108. "Obituaries." *Daily Variety* 20 Jan. 1976: 24.
109. "Obituaries." *Daily Variety* 11 Apr. 1970: 12.
110. "Hall's Sets Aids Screen Production." *Los Angeles Times* 6 Oct. 1929: 31.
111. "Rossi [sic] Set on Coast." *Variety* 19 Mar. 1930: 2.
112. Turner, George E. "The Two Faces of *Dracula*." *American Cinematographer* Vol. 65, No. 5 (May 1988): 37.
113. "Herman Rosse." *Hollywood Filmograph* 29 Nov. 1930: 31.
114. "Jack Pierce." *Hollywood Filmograph* 16 Feb. 1929.
115. For more information on Freulich, see: Buchanan, Sarah A. "The Photography of Roman Freulich from Poland to Hollywood." *History of Photography* Vol. 35, No. 4 (2011): 416-438.
116. "Friedman, U's Caster." *Variety* 12 Feb. 1930: 8.
117. "Hollywood and Los Angeles." *Variety* 24 Sept. 1930: 69.
118. "Frye for *Dracula*." *Hollywood Reporter* 9 Sept. 1930: 2.
119. For more information on Dwight Frye, see Mank, Gregory William, James T. Coughlin, and Dwight D. Frye. *Dwight Frye's Last Laugh* (Baltimore, MD: Midnight Marquee Press, 1997).
120. "Frye Will Not Be Typed." *Los Angeles Times* 16 Mar. 1930: B13.
121. "Comings and Goings." *Film Daily* 19 Sept. 1930: 2.
122. "First Players for *Dracula*." *Variety* 10 Sept. 1930: 32.
123. For more information on Edward Van Sloan, see Bowman, David. "Edward Van Sloan: Universal's House Physician of Horror." *Filmfax* No. 35 (Oct./Nov. 1992): 63-66.
124. "Princess Players." *Billboard* 28 Jan. 1922: 25.
125. "*Scrambled Wives* by Princess Players." *Billboard* 4 Feb. 1922: 25.
126. On 16 September 1930, *Variety* reported that, "those who played original roles in *Dracula* on the stage are being rounded up, wherever possible, for the talker to be done by U."
127. "First Players for *Dracula*," p. 32.
128. See, for example: "Lew Ayres in *Dracula*." *Film Daily* 23 Sept. 1930: 7; "Lew Ayres with Universal." *Los Angeles Times* 23 Sept. 1930: A10.
129. "Lew Ayres with Universal," p. A10.
130. "Universal Has Great Plans for Lew Ayres." *Hollywood Filmograph* 16 Aug. 1930: 11.
131. Skal, *Hollywood Gothic*, p. 126.
132. "Mary Nolan and Universal Bury Hatchet in Row." *Tampa Tribune* (Tampa, FL) 19 May 1930: 12.
133. "Mary Nolan to Leave for Europe Soon." *Hollywood Filmograph* 5 July 1930: 11.
134. "Cleared of Charge." *Tampa Tribune* 1 Aug. 1930: 2.
135. Yeaman, Elizabeth. *Hollywood Daily Citizen* 3 Nov. 1930.
136. "Production Notes." *Hollywood Reporter* 12 Sept. 1930: 4.
137. "Box Office Leaders in Screen Personalities." *Hollywood Reporter* 22 Dec. 1930.
138. "20 Films for U in 1930-'31." *Billboard* 12 Apr. 1930: 22.
139. "Jeanette Loff Back." *Variety* 23 July 1930: 3.
140. "Jeanette Loff Will Make Four Films for Tiffany." *Film Daily* 10 Oct. 1930: 6.
141. "Assignments." *Variety* 4 Oct. 1930: 3.
142. "Hollywood Bulletins." *Variety* 24 Sept. 1930: 12.
143. "Vaudeville Notes." *Billboard* 1 July 1916: 64.
144. "Daddy Long Legs." *Billboard* 30 Nov. 1918: 17.
145. "Richard III." *Billboard* 27 Mar. 1920: 9, 11; "Daddy Dumplins." *Billboard* 4 Dec. 1920: 19.
146. "Helen Chandler, the Most Ingenuous Ingenue on the New York Stage, Says Her Career Was 'Quite Accidental.'" *Billboard* 14 Mar. 1925: 24-25.
147. "Helen Chandler in Pictures." *Film Daily* 14 Nov. 1926: 11.
148. Hall, Mordaunt. "The Screen." *New York Times* 18 Sept. 1930: 28; Watts, Richard, Jr. "On the Screen." *New York Herald Tribune* 18 Sept. 1930.
149. For more information on Helen Chandler, see Mank, Gregory William. *Women in Horror Films, 1930s* (Jefferson, NC: McFarland, 1999): 7-21.

150 "Coast Wire Service: Hollywood Happenings." *Film Daily* 29 Jan. 1930: 4.
151 "Beauties Vie for Honors in Legion Contest." *Los Angeles Times* 8 Aug. 1930: A2.
152 "Daisy Belmore, Stage Actress, Dies at 80." *Los Angeles Times* 13 Dec. 1954: 36.
153 Babcock, Muriel. *Los Angeles Times* 9 Oct. 1930: A9.
154 Another woman in the carriage remains unidentified. Many sources list Donald Murphy as appearing in the carriage ride; however, that could only be accurate if Murphy is the carriage driver. No unaccounted-for male actor or extra appears inside the carriage with Frye and the others. That said, the carriage driver is at times visible through the carriage window.
155 Schallert, Edwin. "Horror Tonight." *Los Angeles Times* 29 June 1943: 13.
156 "Nick Bela Confesses Communist Party Past." *Daily Variety* 15 Dec. 1954: 6.
157 "Michael Visaroff Will Open Establishment Here on May 1." *Hollywood Filmograph* 26 Apr. 1930: 10.
158 Whitaker, Alma. "What Chance Has [a] Double?" *Los Angeles Times* 19 Oct. 1930: B9.
159 "Garbo's Double Acts [as] Cigarette Girl in Comedy." *Los Angeles Times* 14 Mar. 1931: A7.
160 "Dorothy Tree (Uris)." *Daily Variety* 20 Feb. 1992: 14.
161 "Dorothy Tree Runs Wide Range of Character Roles." *Los Angeles Times* 14 Jan. 1940: C4.
162 "Names Listed by Writer in Probe on Film Reds." *Los Angeles Times* 20 Sept. 1950: 8.
163 Uris, Dorothy. *Everybody's Book of Better Speaking* (New York: David McKay, Inc., 1960).
164 "*Dracula* as a Film." *New York Times* 22 Feb. 1931.
165 Parsons, Louella O. *Los Angeles Examiner* 3 May 1929.
166 For more information on Lon Chaney, see Blake, Michael F. *Lon Chaney: The Man Behind the Thousand Faces* (New York: Vestal Press, 1990), and Blake, Michael F. *A Thousand Faces: Lon Chaney's Unique Artistry in Motion Pictures* (New York: Vestal Press, 1995).
167 Blake, *Lon Chaney: The Man Behind the Thousand Faces*, p. 263.
168 "Lewis Ayres Loaned by Universal to Warners." *Exhibitors Herald-World* 2 May 1930: 34.
169 "Chaney's U Suit." *Variety* 5 Mar. 1930: 8.
170 See, for example: "Lon Chaney Better." *Variety* 30 July 1930: 4; "Lon Chaney Recovering." *Film Daily* 5 Aug. 1930: 6.
171 Parsons, Louella O. *Los Angeles Examiner* 2 July 1930.
172 "Wray, the Neck-Biter." *Variety* 25 June 1930: 101.
173 "John Wray Signed for Long Term." *Film Daily* 20 Apr. 1930: 5.
174 "John Wray for U Cast." *Film Daily* 10 Feb. 1930: 9.
175 "U Shelves Pictures." *Motion Picture News* 27 Sept. 1930: 31.
176 "U Plans Air Special." *Motion Picture News* 9 Aug. 1930: 35.
177 Kingsley, Grace. "Fox Picks Story for Wayne." *Los Angeles Times* 21 June 1930.
178 Parsons, Louella O. *Los Angeles Examiner* 2 July 1930.
179 Hall, Gladys. "The Case of the Man Who Dares Not Fall Asleep." *Motion Picture* (Aug. 1929).
180 David J. Skal and Elias Savada proposed this "screen test" argument in their book *Dark Carnival: The Secret World of Tod Browning, Hollywood's Master of the Macabre* (New York: Anchor/Doubleday, 1995). To add weight to their speculation, Skal and Sevada suggest Lugosi's makeup in *The Thirteenth Chair* is "aggressively, unnaturally stylized; his eyebrows are pencil-sharpened precisely as they were for the theatrical vampire role; he wears semiformal attire and seems on the verge of hypnotizing everyone in sight" (p. 129). It is true – due to lighting and his expression – Lugosi arguably appears menacing in one particular medium shot during his first scene at the police station. But major problems exist with Skal and Sevada's description. Lugosi's makeup is actually less pronounced, less stylized than, say, the makeup used for his role in the film *The Veiled Woman* (1929). "Semiformal" attire is hardly the evening dress and cloak of Dracula or indicative of vampirism of course; moreover, the other key male actors at the Crosby home are actually dressed *more* formally than Lugosi. Skal and Sevada also fail to mention that Lugosi's initial costume in *The Thirteenth Chair* is a white suit, again hardly suggestive of Dracula. Lastly, there are no narrative suggestions or visual cues (e.g., extreme close-ups of his eyes) in the film that suggest he is going to hypnotize anyone.

Perhaps in directing Lugosi for *The Thirteenth Chair*, Browning may have begun to consider whether or not to work with him again. But he likely went through that process with every actor, perhaps even having vague thoughts about what kinds of future roles they might fit. But none of this leads automatically to Skal and Sevada's conclusion. After all, the most damning problem for their "screen test" argument is an understanding of how *Dracula* was cast in 1930. As the main text notes, Universal considered other actors for the role. Working with Browning in *The Thirteenth Chair* does not seem to have helped Lugosi get the role of *Dracula* in 1930, nor did it prevent him from having to do a screen test at Universal in 1930. At the same time, the collaboration with Browning on *The Thirteenth Chair* obviously did not preclude Lugosi being cast in *Dracula* either. No, any notion of a Lugosi "screen test" for the 1931 film *Dracula* within a major-studio film made two years earlier at a different studio can be seen as nothing more than unfounded speculation.

Nor was Lugosi's casting in *The Thirteenth Chair* "perversely inappropriate," as Skal and Sevada claim, unless they mean that he is cast interestingly against type. On the cusp of such publicity and after two years of playing Dracula onstage, Lugosi appears in a mystery film, but not as a vampire. Not as a villain or criminal, or even a red herring as he would in various films of the 1930s and 1940s. No, here is a detective, an inspector. In essence, he is a "good guy" who uses tough tactics to try to solve a murder case. Inappropriate? No, but rather cast interestingly against type. Lugosi himself understood this in 1929, as he told Doris Denbo at the *Hollywood Citizen News* (4 Dec. 1929) that he was fearful of becoming typecast in Lon Chaney-style characters. To his mind, *The Thirteenth Chair* importantly gave him a "straight role." The situation is hardly perverse, of course, unless one wants to consider *all* of Lugosi's nonhorror roles perverse, especially those before the 1931 film version of *Dracula*. After all, he appeared in two other films in 1929, *The Veiled Woman* and *Prisoners*. But surely these were not "perversely inappropriate" as well? Certainly no critics believed that at the time, nor is there any surviving reaction of that kind from 1929 audience members.

Of course the bulk of moviegoers would have had no idea who Bela Lugosi was in 1929, making the entire issue largely moot. Many American audience members would likely have labelled Lugosi's accent and appearance as "foreign" and not at all inappropriate to a storyline set in a locale like India, as *The Thirteenth Chair* was. After all, Lugosi would regularly be coded as exotic/foreign in the US stage and film industries, playing Russians and Arabs and Eastern Europeans.

181 Atkins, Rick. *Let's Scare 'Em: Grand Interviews and a Filmography of Horrific Proportions, 1930-1961* (Jefferson, NC: McFarland, 1997): 18-19.
182 Soanes, Wood. "Jane Fooshee Will Open Special Fulton Season Following Lugosi Week." *Oakland Tribune* 6 July 1930: 8.
183 Lugosi, Bela. Letter to Harold Freedman. 12 July 1930.
184 Atkins, pp. 18-19.
185 "Producers Have Their Eyes on Him." *Hollywood Filmograph* 2 Aug. 1930: 13.
186 "Bela Lugosi." *Hollywood Filmograph* 16 Aug. 1930: 19.
187 Yeaman, Elizabeth. *Hollywood Daily Citizen* 19 Aug. 1930.
188 "Universal Has Made Test of Bela Lugosi for *Dracula* Talkie." *Hollywood Filmograph* 30 Aug. 1930: 15.
189 "Horror Man at Home."
190 Skal, *Hollywood Gothic*, p. 120.
191 Weaver, Tom. "*Dracula* (1931)." In Brunas, Micheal, John Brunas, and Tom Weaver. *Universal Horrors* (Jefferson, NC: McFarland, 1990): 10-11.
192 "Theatrical Notes." *New York Times* 19 Sept. 1930: 25.
193 Skal, David J. *Hollywood Gothic: The Tangled Web of Dracula from Novel to Stage to Screen* (New York: W. W. Norton, 1990): 88.
194 Asher, E.M. Letter to Roland West. 11 Aug. 1930; West, Roland. Letter to E. M. Asher. 12 Aug. 1930. Available in the Roland West Papers, Correspondence 1930, 1.f-3, at the Margaret Herrick Library, Academy of Motion Picture Arts and Sciences, Beverly Hills, CA.
195 "It Pays to Be Poor." *Motion Picture Classic* (Oct. 1930): 102.
196 If the John Carradine story is true, he would have been – at age 24 –the youngest actor Universal considered. In any event, Chester Morris was certainly the youngest actor under serious consideration.
"Pasadenans Enact Weird Melodrama." *Los Angeles Times* 21 Aug. 1930: A9.
197 "6 New Univresal Films Start Work This Month." *Film Daily* 12 Sept. 1930: 6.
198 Burton, Stanley. "Don't Call Me Lon Chaney." *Photoplay* (Jan. 1930): 78, 115.
199 On 3 Sept. 1930, *Variety* mentioned that "tests of a number of actors have been made in the part [of Dracula]" before claiming that the selection was "now down" to William Courtenay, Bela Lugosi, or Paul Muni, the implication being that tests would have been shot of all three actors, if not even others.
200 Courtenay's screen test is mentioned in: "Behind the Scenes in Hollywood." *Logansport Pharos-Tribune* (Logansport, IN) 18 Sept. 1930: 10.
201 "Ian Keith to Play *Dracula* For U–Rumored." *Hollywood Filmograph* 13 Sept. 1930: 15.
202 "Pulling for Him." *Hollywood Filmograph* 6 Sept. 1930: 19.
203 "Ian Keith to Play *Dracula* For U–Rumored," p. 15.
204 Ibid., p. 15.
205 Wilk, Ralph. "A Little from 'Lots.'" *Film Daily* 11 Sept. 1930: 6.
206 "To Start *Dracula* Next Week." *Film Daily* 15 Sept. 1930: 6.
207 Kingsley, Grace. "Star and Executive to Travel." *Los Angeles Times* 16 Sept. 1930.
208 Skal, *Hollywood Gothic*, p. 120. Skal claims that, as part of his effort to win the role of Dracula, Lugosi would "donate" his voice services for the dubbing of *The Last Performance* in Hungarian. But the dubbing took place in 1928, and so it seems difficult to believe that his work on that film played any role in the casting for *Dracula* in 1930. Moreover, no evidence has surfaced that Lugosi was unpaid for the dubbing job. Indeed, it seems unlikely that Universal would not have compensated Lugosi for his time, especially given that even a token fee would have allowed the studio to claim legal ownership of Lugosi's recorded voice for the film.
209 Skal, David J. *The Monster Show: A Cultural History of Horror* (New York: W. W. Norton, 1993): 117.
210 "Universal Has Made Test of Bela Lugosi for *Dracula* Talkie," p. 15.
211 "Ian Keith to Play *Dracula* for Us–Rumored," p. 15.
212 Parsons, Louella O. *Los Angeles Examiner* 17 Sept. 1930.
213 Stop Us If We're Wrong." *Motion Picture News* 20 Sept. 1930: 44.
214 Brown, Kelly R. *Florence Lawrence, the Biograph Girl* (Jefferson, NC: McFarland, 1999).
215 "Class Pictures, RKO Deal, 'Break' for Universal," p. 24.
216 "Demands of the Talkie Public Force Changes." *Billboard* 11 Oct. 1930: 3, 89.
217 "Cycle Wheels Right Over Hays' Code." *Variety* 24 Sept. 1930: 4.

218 Wilkerson, W. R. "Tradeviews." *Hollywood Reporter* 29 Sept. 1930: 1.
219 "Carl Laemmle to New York." *Hollywood Reporter* 15 Sept. 1930: 1.
220 "Laemmle Hears Universal Sales Reaching Peak." *Motion Picture News* 20 Sept. 1930: 21.
221 "*Variety*'s Bulletin Condensed." *Variety* 27 Aug. 1930: 32.
222 "To Start *Dracula* Production Next Week." *Film Daily* 15 Sept. 2012: 6; Yeaman, Elizabeth. *Hollywood Daily Citizen* 16 Sept. 1930.

Chapter 4
THE SCRIPT

Parallel to a pre-production phase in which Universal cast key actors and assembled an appropriate crew for *Dracula* was the creation of a shooting script that had to meet the specific needs of Hollywood in 1930, ranging from its length to the depiction of events that, however challenging or horrifying, would avoid potential censorship concerns. The screenwriting phase involved numerous persons from June 1930 to late September of that same year, and became complicated for many reasons, not least because of the fact that Universal writers drew upon both the Bram Stoker novel and the Hamilton Deane-John L. Balderston stage play for inspiration.[1]

In his novel, Bram Stoker related the story of *Dracula* through multiple perspectives thanks to the literary device of presenting diaries, letters, newspaper clippings, and so forth, as if written (or spoken, in the case of phonograph recordings) by different characters. These numerous shifts in point-of-view unfold in 27 chapters and in three major sections. In the first five chapters, Jonathan Harker travels to Transylvania, meets Count Dracula, and becomes a prisoner in his castle.

Chapters 6 to 24 cover Dracula's life in England, during which time Lucy Westenra and then Mina Murray become his victims. Much of the action occurs at Dr. Seward's sanitarium, where a patient named Renfield exhibits a lust for the blood of living creatures. Thanks to Seward's colleague Professor Van Helsing, the key characters learn that a vampire is on the loose. After realizing that Dracula is the villain, they begin their search for him.

But Dracula flees England and returns to his homeland. Chapters 25 to 27 detail the vampire hunters' quest to find and destroy him, which they do at the novel's conclusion. In her journal entry, Mina writes: "on the instant, came the sweep and flash of Jonathan's great knife. I shrieked as I saw it shear through the throat. Whilst at the same moment Mr. Morris's bowie knife plunged into the heart." Thus Harker – with the assistance of a Texan named Quincey Morris – brings an end to Dracula's undead reign. Mina also claims that Dracula's "whole body crumbled into dust and passed from our sight."

Dracula–The Vampire Play, Deane and Balderston's adaptation for the Broadway stage of 1927, also unfolded in three main acts, but the writers made major changes, most of which were likely dictated by the confines of stage settings and the accepted norms of stage narrative duration. Indeed, their adaptation begins *in media res*, thus creating a sense of

Publicity still of Bela Lugosi in *Dracula* (1931).

urgency. Harker speaks the first line of dialogue, asking the maid: "You're sure Miss Lucy is no worse?"[2] She has already fallen under Dracula's spell, and Mina has died even before Act I begins.

Notably, the entire play is set in England. While Harker refers to the fact that he once visited Transylvania, he has only heard of a "famous Voivode Dracula who fought the Turks [and] lived there centuries ago"; he has never met Dracula until the vampire appears at Dr. Seward's home. And rather than chase Dracula back to his home country, a streamlined group of three vampire hunters discovers him in his coffin in England. Harker alone stakes Dracula. The play also implies that Harker will marry Lucy after the end of Act III.

Along with cutting the first and third sections of Stoker's novel, Deane and Balderston also significantly altered the character relationships. The playwrights age Dr. Seward, transforming him into Lucy's father, rather than depicting him as a younger man who loves her (as in Stoker's novel). The result helps limit the number of characters and reduces Lucy's suitors to one man, Harker. What is less clear is why Deane and Balderston chose to invert Lucy and Mina's names, as Stoker writes that Mina is betrothed to Harker.

120   Chapter 4 – THE SCRIPT

Another key relationship that Deane and Balderston transformed is between Dracula and the other characters in the play. In the novel, while Dracula occupies property geographically close to Seward's sanitarium, the other characters remain unaware of that fact for the bulk of the novel. In Chapter 17, Seward writes in his diary: "Strange that it never struck me that the very next house might be the Count's hiding place!" By the time that Seward and some of Stoker's other male characters meet Dracula for the first time, they are already aware that he is a vampire. By contrast, Deane and Balderston construct a story in which Dracula has already befriended the Seward household before Act I starts. Dracula socializes with the key characters, and becomes trusted to the extent that he is allowed to sit with Lucy when she is ill. In fact, in a wicked moment of black comedy, Dracula even offers to undergo a blood transfusion to help her.

In many respects, as has already been noted in Chapter 3, the Deane-Balderston adaptation operates similar to other mystery plays of the twenties. Characters attempt to solve the mystery of Lucy's illness and who is to blame for it. Moreover, the adaptation features a degree of comic relief. For example, Deane and Balderston invented Butterworth, a Cockney attendant at Seward's sanitarium who becomes a repeated source of humor.

Such major deletions and changes still allow for Deane and Balderston to adapt certain aspects of Stoker's novel and its dialogue, even if they had to adjust them somewhat to fit into their new narrative. For example, in Chapter 2 of the novel, Dracula destroys Harker's mirror while he shaves at his castle. His excuse is that a mirror is nothing more than "a foul bauble of man's vanity." In the play, Van Helsing notices that Dracula is not visible in a mirror hanging on the wall. Dracula throws a vase at the mirror, causing it to smash into pieces that fall to the floor. He then suggests that mirrors are "playthings of a man's vanity."

In some cases, Deane and Balderston change minor aspects of Stoker's novel, but still retain a sense of its aims. Whereas Stoker has Dracula journey to England by boat, the playwrights have Dracula journey to England by plane (as described in dialogue that refers to an event which occurred before Act I begins). The incorporation of air travel – which Stoker would not even have had as an option when he wrote *Dracula* in the 1890s – is not at odds with a novel that seems quite eager to incorporate other modern technologies like photography and personal phonograph recordings.[3]

Changes from novel to stage play were necessary, as were changes from both of those to a viable film script. Prior to the start of the film's production on 29 September 1930, at least five different authors attempted to adapt *Dracula* for the screen.[4] Each of them may have produced numerous rough drafts, treatments, or scripts that have not survived (or which were not even submitted to Universal). All that said, two treatments, one partial script, and one complete final shooting script do exist. While it is important to acknowledge that a complete history of *Dracula*'s adaptation to the screen in 1930 cannot be constructed, it is still possible to learn much about how the completed film evolved through an analysis of these surviving materials.

In June 1930, at roughly the same time Universal obtained the rights to *Dracula*, Carl Laemmle, Jr. declared that screenplays could not faithfully adapt all of the action present in the novels or plays on which they were based:

Many stories are stretched over long periods of time, and enacted in widely scattered places, and in handling the plot it is easy to confuse the audience by trying to place too much of the action on the screen. It is surprising how well the action can be cut down to the limit, sparing many scenes that some writers would consider essential.[5]

Here then was the reality facing the many screenwriters who tackled *Dracula*. The entire novel could not be adapted, nor could the play simply be filmed *in toto*.

Much evolution and change occurred in the various attempts to transfer *Dracula* to the screen, but the final result reveals a key fact about its adaptation. The shooting script would not simply try to condense the novel, nor would it faithfully adapt *Dracula–The Vampire Play*. Instead, perhaps due to its evolution in the hands of various writers, Universal's *Dracula* became its own unique story, one that combined elements from the novel and play, but one that also incorporated original narrative and thematic ideas.

Fritz Stephani

Born in Germany in 1903, Frederick "Fritz" Stephani once told the American press that he was a "Baron" and a flying ace during World War I, though the latter claim seems questionable given the fact he would only have been about 15 years old when the Armistice was signed.[6] It is also difficult to determine exactly how and when he became a writer in Hollywood, but he does seem to have been the first person at Universal to provide a treatment for *Dracula* in 1930.[7] Who tasked him with that job is unknown, but his treatment reveals both a knowledge of filmmaking and of the Universal backlot. For example, he suggests that the studio's "Swiss village set" could be used to represent the "little mountain village in Hungary" that his treatment describes.

Stephani opens his treatment in England before Harker departs for (in his version) Hungary. Mina Seward agrees to marry Harker upon his return. This beginning differs noticeably from Stoker (who begins his novel with Harker already en route to Dracula's castle), as well as from the stage play (which does not feature Harker's journey to another country). Though it is possible Stephani arrived at this idea on his own, it is important to note that F. W. Murnau's *Nosferatu* (1922) begins in much the same way. At any rate, Stephani understood that his first scene might or might not be desirable, as he indicates in the treatment that – while it establishes the film's modern setting, the romance between Harker and Mina, and a "normal atmosphere," as opposed to the later "weird developments" – it was still "independent" of everything that follows and could be excised without damaging the rest of the story.

F. W. Murnau's film *Nosferatu* (1922) had a minor influence on the screenwriters of Browning's *Dracula*.

Unlike Stoker's novel, Stephani does not depict Dracula greeting Harker upon his arrival at the castle, but instead has Harker finding a note written by him, promising to appear within the hour. Harker almost

122 Chapter 4 – THE SCRIPT

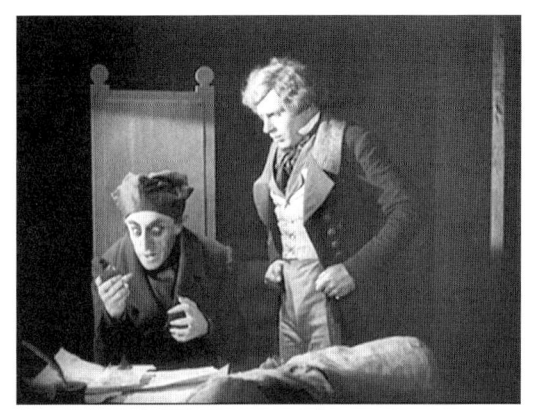

Left: A frame from *Nosferatu* in which the vampire examines a photograph of the film's female lead. Right: A frame from *Nosferatu*, from a scene in which the castle door opens of its own accord, a device repeated in Browning's *Dracula*.

immediately hears a mother's demand that Dracula return her missing child. The scene echoes a similar moment in Chapter 4 of Stoker's novel, but in Stephani's draft, it precedes Harker's introduction to Dracula.

Once the two characters do finally meet, Dracula sees a photograph that Harker owns. It depicts Mina and Lucy. Here again Stephani's treatment features a clear resemblance to *Nosferatu*, in which the vampire sees an image of the young male lead's fiancée and remarks on her "lovely neck." Stephani's treatment also describes the castle's doors as opening "without human assistance," something that does not occur in Stoker's novel or in the play, but which does occur in *Nosferatu*. The same effect would eventually occur on four occasions in the Browning film (thrice at Dracula's Castle and once at Carfax Abbey).

As in Stoker's novel, Stephani's Dracula quickly makes Harker a prisoner in his castle, but then his treatment has Dracula depart for England on an airplane. Some writers have claimed that Stephani describes the plane as something akin to the "batplane" in Batman comics and movies, but that is not certainly what his actual words convey:

> Reaching the court below, the count carries seven coffin-like boxes from a hole in the wall. A short distance away, the immense wings of a big aeroplane can be seen. It looks like a huge bat. The Count loads the big boxes in the plane, then the sound of an engine starting can be heard, and the gigantic plane flies away, accompanied by the chorus of howling wolves.

The description "looks like a huge bat" might well have been meant to describe a normal plane in the dark of night (with mysterious lighting perhaps), rather than an aircraft physically shaped like a bat. Here Stephani might have been recalling his own experience as a pilot, but he might also have been inspired by the Deane-Balderston play. In it, Harker learns that "Dracula arrived at the Croydon airdrome in a three-engined German plane" only three days before Mina becomes ill. Van Helsing deduces that the airplane has given Dracula an opportunity to "cross Europe in a single night" after having been "fettered" to his Transylvanian castle for five centuries.

Once Dracula quietly settles into Carfax Abbey, Lucy and Mina rapidly become ill. As in the play, Dracula befriends the Seward family, Seward being an older doctor with a daughter.

Lucy dies, but Mina regains some of her "vitality" when Dracula visits the Seward home. Here Stephani draws upon Stoker, restoring Mina as the name of the female lead.

At Dr. Seward's request, Professor Van Helsing arrives to investigate the strange illnesses. After her initial hesitation, Mina lets Van Helsing inspect the marks on her neck. Later, Van Helsing shows Renfield some wolfbane, causing the lunatic to recoil and shudder nervously. Both scenes borrow directly from the stage play.[8] Some of Stephani's other ideas did as well:

> *I would like to suggest that the attendant at the sanitarium is played for comedy and that his remarks concerning the escape of Renfield are made in very dry cockney English. This will afford some relief to the intense and dramatic atmosphere of the story. It may even be advisable to take him along to Hungary and through his clumsiness, make the situation of the chase more interesting.*

Stephani drew upon Deane-Balderston's character Butterworth, but was suggesting that his role be even more prominent.

After escaping from the castle, Harker soon reappears in England and destroys Dracula's plane in order to prevent his escape. He is the one who understands that Dracula is the vampire, as opposed to the play, in which Van Helsing deduces that Dracula is (as he calls him) the "King of the Vampires." Then, together with Dr. Seward and Van Helsing, Harker discovers Mina in a near-death state. They save her by means of an emergency blood transfusion.

However, thanks to his hypnotic control over the maid, Dracula returns to Mina's room that very same night. When she screams, Harker rushes to her rescue. "The picture he sees is terrifying. Dracula stands in the middle of the room, his arms about Mina – sucking blood from her throat. … Mina's blood is seen in the corner of his mouth." Dracula escapes, and Van Helsing revives Mina by placing a cross on her forehead, the outline of which sears into her forehead, a fascinating plot device that does not appear in the novel or the play.

The trio of men soon corner Dracula at Carfax Abbey, with Harker attempting to cut the vampire in half with a large blade. Dracula scoffs at their failed efforts, announcing: "Your women are mine and through them, you and others shall be mine! The whole world shall be my creatures!" Here Stephani borrows closely from Chapter 23 of Stoker's novel, in which Dracula declares: "Your girls that you all love are mine already. And through them you and others shall yet be mine, my creatures, to do my bidding and to be my jackals when I want to feed. Bah!"

Soon Harker, Van Helsing, Dr. Seward, and Mina pursue Dracula back to his homeland in a manner similar to the Stoker novel. But Stephani's conclusion offers something uniquely different from Stoker and Deane-Balderston. Rather than having Harker destroy Dracula, Stephani importantly has Van Helsing fashion the broken spoke of a wagon wheel into a stake, which he alone drives through the vampire's heart. Stephani's recasting of which character kills Dracula is likely his most influential innovation, as the 1931 film features Van Helsing staking the vampire.

Stephani's treatment also features one other original idea that was incorporated into the 1931 film. During his carriage ride to Dracula's castle, when Harker:

> *…leans out of the carriage window to shout to the driver to take it easy, he is shocked to see that there is no driver on the seat. The horses seem to be led by unseen hands. A bat is flying ahead of the carriage, and he sees that they are approaching the doors of the Castle estate. Again,*

without human assistance, the huge doors which guard the estate open and the carriage enters the forecourt of the Castle. The big doors close with a bang behind him.

Such a description of a driverless carriage and a bat do not appear in Stoker or Deane-Balderston. The 1931 film offers a variation on Stephani's scene, with the bat driving the carriage. But rather than having it fly ahead of the carriage, Tod Browning positioned the bat above (and slightly in front of) the driver's seat.

Carl Laemmle, Jr. apparently did not find Stephani's treatment compelling, as there is no evidence that Stephani proceeded to write a script or provide any further input on the adaptation. But Stephani's work became an important step in a process that would not only appropriate a few of his specific ideas, but that would also be influenced by his general approach. Stephani had clearly shown that a *Dracula* treatment (and, by extension, a shooting script) could combine elements from the novel and the play, rather than adapting only one of them.

Louis Bromfield:

On 9 July 1930, *Variety* wrote: "Louis Bromfield arrived this week to begin work on the screen treatment for *Dracula*, Universal."[9] At that time, few American novelists were more famous than Bromfield. Born in Mansfield, Ohio in 1896, he studied agriculture and journalism before serving in World War I. All of his novels became bestsellers, including his first, *The Green Bay Tree* (1924), which won rave reviews from both critics and readers.

At the beginning of July, Universal signed Bromfield to a contract, having borrowed him from Samuel Goldwyn.[10] However, he may have been working for Universal earlier than that particular contract suggests, as Bromfield told a friend in mid-July that he had been working on *Dracula* for five months.[11] At any rate, another 1930 account claimed that, "Bromfield planned to abandon Hollywood to the type of workman who can toil by the time clock, but Carl Laemmle, Junior persuaded him to remain."[12] How much Universal paid Bromfield is unknown, but hiring someone of his status underscored the fact that the studio perceived *Dracula* as a prestigious, big-budget production.

By mid-July of 1930, the *Hollywood Filmograph* shed more

Pulitzer-prize winning novelist Louis Bromfield.

Chapter 4 – THE SCRIPT

light on Bromfield's involvement, with Junior Laemmle noting that he specifically selected Bromfield "for this particularly difficult assignment [*Dracula*] after reading *Early Autumn*, a novel which won the author the much coveted Pulitzer award."[13] Rather than being a horror story, *Early Autumn* (1926) explores the many fissures appearing in the foundation of an old and much-respected New England family. The problems reveal themselves when a character who fled years earlier returns, a confident divorcee named Sabine Callendar who has a distinct ability to see through the Victorian veneer of the others:

> *And so the presence of Sabine began slowly to create a vaguely defined rift in a world hitherto set and complacent and even proud of itself. Something in the sight of her cold green eyes, in the sound of her metallic voice, in the sudden shrewd, disillusioning observations which she had a way of making at disconcerting moments, filled people like Aunt Cassie with uneasiness and people like Olivia with a smoldering sense of restlessness and rebellion.*[14]

In *Early Autumn*, the modern world encroaches disturbingly on the old, creating something of an inverse of Dracula's invasion of England. While Junior Laemmle was attracted to Bromfield due to his fame and prestige, he may also have seen in *Early Autumn* Bromfield's gift for creating melancholia and a sustained sense of foreboding.

Louis Bromfield (left) with George Hawkins, Evelyn Laye, and Frank Lawton.

Even prior to his Universal contract for *Dracula*, Bromfield paid close attention to the cinema. For example, in March 1930, he described his views on the talking picture:

> *It is understandable enough that while mechanical difficulties were being worked out the talkers should have used the stage as a source of ready-made material. But new art forms demand their own forms of expression and I look for the great talkers of the next ten years to have been studio-made from the ground up.*[15]

Working on *Dracula* would not provide Bromfield with an opportunity to write a film narrative "from the ground up," but his negative views on adapting stage plays likely shaped his approach to the vampire story.

> **DRACULA**
> There's more than just mystery to this classic tale, and famous stage play. There's the unconquerable love of a man for a maid … his flaming passion bringing light to a city o'er shadowed by evil and dread. Louis Bromfield, famous novelist is adapting it from Bram Stoker's original.
> **TOD BROWNING will direct it!**

Published in *Variety* on August 13, 1930.

Analyzing his *First Treatment of Dracula*, dated 18 July 1930, it is obvious that Bromfield largely tried to avoid the Deane-Balderston play, seeking inspiration instead from Stoker's novel.[16] For example, Bromfield's *Sequence A* presents a segment in which Harker journeys to Transylvania to meet Dracula. *Sequence B* introduces England and the Seward Sanitarium, while *Sequence C* covers Van Helsing's pursuit of Dracula in the same country. Then, *Sequence D* features Van Helsing and his group of vampire hunters chasing Dracula, who has fled back to his homeland.

Along with preserving the key sections of Stoker's novel (such as *Sequence A* and *D*, which are not part of the Deane-Balderston play), Bromfield maintained some of the novel's minor details. For example, he writes that Harker meets Count Dracula's carriage on the eve of St. George's Day. He also has Dracula dispense with Harker's small mirror while Harker is shaving, and he requests that Harker write post-dated letters that attest to his good health. Later, Harker discovers Dracula resting in his coffin at his castle.

But Bromfield also infused the treatment with many of his own ideas. For example, Stoker has an old lady at the inn remove a crucifix from her own neck and give it to Harker, whereas Bromfield's Harker already wears a crucifix, and so instead he accepts a charm from an old woman which can ward off "evil forces." And when Bromfield's Harker arrives at Dracula's castle, Dracula does not formally greet him. Instead, Dracula's "man-servant" silently takes his baggage into a room with a fireplace and a dinner table. Eventually, Harker realizes that the servant (as well as the carriage driver who brought him to the castle) were both Dracula in disguise.

Harker's encounter with the three vampire women in Dracula's castle also features some variations in Bromfield's treatment. With his flair for description, Bromfield depicts the trio

Publicity still from *Dracula* (1931) depicting the Count's introduction to Renfield, a scene on which Louis Bromfield had a profound affect.

as "wild and beautiful, in the costumes of three different periods of history," whereas Stoker does not make specific reference to their clothing, other than the fact they are "ladies by their dress and manner." Bromfield thus implies that Dracula has wed these women in different historical eras. Then, rather than interrupt the women's advance on Harker by Dracula's appearance in the room, as in the novel, Bromfield has Dracula enter through the window and climb down the wall head-first. Here Bromfield describes the action by re-imagining an image that Harker witnesses on three occasions in Stoker's novel, in which Dracula exits through a window and crawls down the castle exterior in a "lizard"-like fashion.

Bromfield's most striking derivation from the Stoker's comes in his depiction of the characters based in England. In his treatment, Mina and Lucy are Dr. Seward's daughters. Making Seward into a father is one of the treatment's few influences from the Deane-Balderston play, another being a British sequence that begins *in media res*. Lucy is already sick by the time *Sequence B* begins, with "gallons of blood" having mysteriously disappeared from her body. Once she dies, Mina becomes ill.

Bromfield relied on one other important plot device in the Deane-Balderston play, the fact that the inhabitants of Seward's household know Dracula socially and do not suspect him of any foul play for most of the story. But Bromfield's treatment offered a notable amendment. The Sewards know Dracula, but only under his pseudonym, Count de Ville; this Dracula/de Ville, thanks to having consumed some of Harker's blood, appears much younger than he did in *Sequence A*. Here Bromfield – who was resistant to the play, even as he borrowed from it – also draws upon Stoker's novel. The name "Count de Ville" appears briefly in Stoker's Chapter 20, it being the pseudonym Dracula used to purchase Carfax Abbey; moreover, Stoker's Dracula appears younger in England than he does in Transylvania.

Bromfield also created an entirely new character, Mrs. Triplett, whose major function was to provide comic relief. She is a "rich neighbor of the Sewards," a fat and coquettish woman of approximately 50 years old. She "behaves as if she were still attractive to men," and "is a good deal of a fool." Bromfield perceived the need for comic relief, but eschewed domestic staff as a vehicle for it, thus avoiding not only the Deane-Balderston play, but also other Broadway stage mysteries that utilized similar characters.

Though Bromfield was relatively new to Hollywood, his treatment occasionally attempts to translate his much-lauded descriptive abilities into cinematic language. For example, consider his account of Dracula and Harker's discussion of the real estate papers for Carfax Abbey:

All this may be shown in close-ups in and out of the speech. One by one Harker examines them. (1) The hands, coarse and covered with hair almost like the bristles of an animal. The nails are long and pointed in needle-like fashion. As one hand turns over you see hairs growing out of the palm. (2) The eyebrows, very dark and bushy. (3) The ears, very pointed at the tips with a suspicion of hair on them.

Similarly, Bromfield instructs the film's director to show Count de Ville only from the back during his initial arrival at the Seward Sanitarium, the camera following him inside and concealing his face from the audience until a given moment when he is revealed to be Dracula. Such instructions were cinematic rather than literary.

Bromfield was also aware of the need for Hollywood films to avoid controversial topics. When Bromfield's Dracula flees England, he leaves on a ship called *The Black Eagle*, rather than the *Czarina Catherine*, a change that at first seems hardly worth noting, but which effectively avoided any reference to Russia in a period following a Red Scare and anti-Communist sentiment in the US.

Bromfield's treatment also describes the vampire-hunters finding a victimized child in the graveyard near Lucy's tomb. But he immediately adds: "There is no special dramatic value in using the child. On the contrary, it rather clutters up the action and may annoy the censors." Here again Bromfield seems quite aware of the studio's need to pre-empt potential trouble.

In general, Bromfield's *First Treatment of Dracula* features much description, save for *Sequence D*, the film's conclusion, on which he strangely spends only one half of a page. Perhaps he was working under time constraints. As a novelist used to taking as much time as he needed to write, Bromfield faced a rapid deadline, one that gave him roughly four weeks to submit the treatment.

If Bromfield accomplished little else, he offered a few ideas that would appear in the completed film. For example, he describes the door of Dracula's castle opening of its own accord, an idea that he either appropriated from Stephani or *Nosferatu* or coincidentally developed on his own. Either way, the description's reappearance after Stephani furthered its chances of becoming incorporated into the completed film.

One of Bromfield's other influential ideas is apparently unique to his treatment. He has Dracula and the three vampire women sleeping in their coffins in the bowels of the castle, with Dracula's being the most "pretentious" of the group (as opposed to Stoker, who describes only "fragments of old coffins" and "great wooden boxes," one of them being Dracula's). The Browning film clearly adopted Bromfield's idea.

Bromfield's treatment also features important advances for Harker's introduction to Dracula. Harker enters the castle and soon looks out a window, with an unseen voice announcing, "It is a long drop, nearly two thousand feet." Harker then asks if he is addressing Count Dracula, with the vampire responding:

I am Dracula. I bid you welcome. My servants have gone to bed. Let me see to your comfort myself. I pray you, be seated and sup when you please. Excuse me if I do not join you. I never sup.

The first two lines are taken from Stoker's Chapter 2, in which Dracula says, "I am Dracula, and I bid you welcome, Mr. Harker, to my house." But here Bromfield breaks them into two clipped sentences, exactly as they became spoken in the completed film (with Renfield's introductory dialogue separating them). After four more dialogue exchanges in Bromfield, wolves howl in the distance. Bromfield's Dracula speaks again, telling Harker: "Listen to them – the children of the night. What music they make." These words are also borrowed from Stoker's Chapter 2. Here Bromfield has isolated and condensed Harker's initial meeting with Dracula from the novel. Refinement would occur in subsequent scripts, but Bromfield provided the basic framework for what would become one of the film's most famous scenes.

Bromfield's *First Treatment of Dracula* was important in the script's evolution, but the bulk of it was finally discarded, presumably due to Junior Laemmle's disappointment. Bromfield apparently continued work after completing the initial treatment, as he indicated on 20 July 1930 that he was having "great fun" writing the project, but was "in a hurry to finish it and go back to Paris to work."[17] That was not yet possible, however, given that the studio soon paired him with another author.

Dudley Murphy

On 24 August 1930, the *New York Times* reported that, "Louis Bromfield and Dudley Murphy, according to Universal, will collaborate on the dialogue for the screen version of *Dracula*."[18] Universal wanted Bromfield to continue his work, perhaps because of the initial investment and Bromfield's name value. However, the great novelist remained in Los Angeles and was now being partnered with another writer. That said, whether the two actively worked together or whether Murphy worked largely in isolation rewriting a Bromfield script is unknown.

It is also difficult to determine when the Bromfield-Murphy collaboration began. On 22 August 1930, *Film Daily* reported:

In making the rounds of Universal offices, one meets up with many of literati's top holers. A recent peak into the story shops revealed Louis Bromfield, Pulitzer prize winner in 1926, John

Wexley, who did The Last Mile, and Dudley Murphy.[19]

It is possible, in other words, that Murphy began working with Bromfield on *Dracula* some days, if not even a week or more, before the announcement of the same in the *New York Times*.

Born in Winchester, Massachusetts in 1897, Murphy served as a pilot in World War I, and moved to Los Angeles after his discharge. After initially trying to enter the film industry as an extra in movies like Cecil B. DeMille's *Male and Female* (1919), Murphy began to raise money to shoot avant-garde projects.[20] *Soul of the Cypress* (1920), his directorial debut, features a composer who falls in love with a Dryad near the seaside cliffs. As one intertitle explains, "Thru the branches of her prison she whispers: 'Give your life to the sea. Become Immortal and I can then join you forever.'" Heeding her call, the composer throws himself into the waters below.

Writer and filmmaker Dudley Murphy. *(Courtesy of Susan Delson and the Murphy Family Collection)*

Murphy's 1922 short subject *Danse Macabre* opens with an animated title sequence of cartoon skeletons that together form the film's title. At midnight in "plague-ridden Spain," Death attempts to seize a young woman from her lover, but the coming of morning causes him to fail. A fascinating film set to Saint Saëns' music, *Danse Macabre* is in some ways prescient of Murphy's involvement in *Dracula*. One image in the film features artwork of a bat hovering near a watchtower, and another depicts a bat flying near Death's head. Artwork of a hilltop castle also seems to anticipate Castle Dracula.

Then, in 1924, Murphy – together with Ferdinand Léger – created *Ballet mécanique*, which remains one of the most arresting films in avant-garde history, its juxtapositions of colorful shapes and black-and-white images of people and machinery still capable of provoking strong reactions. That said, American audiences of the period did not always appreciate its power. In April 1926, *Variety* claimed that *Ballet mécanique* became "one of the few pictures ever to be withdrawn [from a New York theatre] because of the hissing of an audience."[21]

In 1929, Murphy wrote and directed two sound short subjects that explored the synergies between jazz music and the cinema. His *St. Louis Blues* (1929) starred Bessie

Frames from Murphy's film *Danse Macabre* (1922).

Smith, the "Empress of the Blues," and his *Black and Tan* (1929) featured Duke Ellington and his Orchestra. Murphy's films offer unusual depictions of both performers: Rather than being depicted from the front, Smith sings in profile while standing at a bar, while Ellington is introduced from the back, at his piano. Extensive moving camera tries to capture the emotions of an onscreen audience in *St. Louis Blues*, while *Black and Tan* presents the frenetic dancing of Fredi Washington; thanks to a glass dance floor, Murphy even shot Washington from underneath her feet. Most importantly, both films draw upon their respective artists' music to create an overall sense of dread and tragedy.

In December 1930, while *Dracula* was being readied for release, the *Hollywood Reporter* wrote:

> *The director who made two of the best shorts of last year, both in quality of production and gross business, has been knocking at the doors of the studios with but little notice. Black and Tan and The St. Louis Blues, released by Radio Pictures, written and directed by Dudley Murphy, were gems. A director who has such ideas and is able to put them on the screen at a reasonable cost should have no trouble in getting set. But Hollywood is still Hollywood and it still turns out a lot of terrible pictures.*[22]

Despite his best efforts, Murphy found extreme difficulty in penetrating the Hollywood studio system. But Universal did see in Murphy an author who could help Bromfield and *Dracula*.

Surviving pages of their script – *Dracula by Louis Bromfield and Dudley Murphy* – reveals an intermingling of the Stoker novel with the Deane-Balderston play, written in tandem with some of their own ideas. Universal's print of *Nosferatu* might also have influenced the two men, as it seems to have informed Sequence C of their joint script, which features a scene of Harker and Mina together in England before he leaves for Transylvania. While that device may also have been appropriated from Stephani, they incorporate the word "Nosferatu" into the dialogue of their Sequence B; it is heard during a conversation between Van Helsing and an Austrian. The term does "Nosferatu" not appear in either Stoker or Deane-Balderston, and so it is likely that the title of Murnau's film prompted its usage in their script, and – by extension – in the final shooting script as well.

All that said, Bromfield-Murphy began their script with a highly original sequence. The camera moves slowly through a churchyard cemetery at night, creeping towards an old vault. Its door opens slowly and "two or three bats" fly out. The film then cuts to three scenes set in Hungary, France, and England, each depicting cases of inexplicable blood loss among patients. To the audience, the link would be clear. The bats at the beginning have wrecked havoc on the lives of victims in more than one country.

From there, the script shifts to the Seward household, with Mina once again being Dr. Seward's daughter, and – in a change unique to this draft – Lucy being Seward's niece. Harker is Mina's lover, and he is on the verge of leaving for the Carpathian Mountains to meet with Count Dracula.

Harker reaches the inn and travels to Dracula's castle on St. George's Eve. Apparently borrowing from Stephani, Bromfield-Murphy write of the carriage ride, "we see distinctly that Dracula is missing … but above the horses' heads flies a great bat." In another appropriation from Stephani's and/or Bromfield's treatment and/or *Nosferatu*, the script also notes, "the inner door of the castle opens of its own accord." In the completed film, doors open or close without human assistance four times, three at Castle Dracula and once at Carfax Abbey.

In other respects, the Murphy-Bromfield script offers unique ideas that would reappear in the final film. For example, the screenwriters recommend a shot in which the camera tracks through the gate of the Seward Sanitarium to reveal its facade (the film version doing much the same thanks to a crane shot). Drawing on Butterworth in the Deane-Balderston play, the two writers create a comical attendant named Martin, a character who would eventually make its way into the final shooting script.

Harker's arrival in Transylvania also features much that would appear in the final film. An Englishwoman named Sara and her secretary ride with Harker in the carriage, with Sara's secretary reciting a description from a printed travelogue: "Among its rugged peaks are found crumbling castles of a bygone age." Then, at the inn, to instill authenticity, the natives speak some lines in Hungarian.

Once Harker mentions that he will be meeting Dracula, the Bromfield-Murphy script suggests a dissolve into the vampire's castle and its crypt. They write:

> *There is a sinister atmosphere in this crypt, a suggestion of movement of weird animals on the floor.*
> *The camera moves slowly up to the corner of one of the boxes and as it does so, we see the fingers of one of Dracula's hands coming under the lid of the box. As the hand emerges, we pan the camera to the light effect on the wall. The sun goes down and as the light effect disappears, we pan back, and Dracula is discovered with his back to the camera, bending over and closing the box. He straightens up and slowly glides towards camera. We keep him in the lens until his eyes entirely fill the screen as he approaches. He walks right into the camera, fading the picture out.*

Dudley Murphy (far right) visits the set of *Dracula* (1931). From left to right are Tod Browning, Bela Lugosi, and Horace Liveright.

Chapter 4 – THE SCRIPT

DUDLEY MURPHY
Director
♦

"CONFESSIONS OF A CO-ED"
"TWENTY-FOUR HOURS"
"THE MAN WITH RED HAIR"
In Preparation
"S. S. SAN PEDRO"

RKO—"St. Louis Blues"
"Black and Tan"

Dudley Murphy's advertisement in The Film Daily Yearbook *for 1932.*

Some of this imagery appears in the finished film, particularly that of the camera moving towards Dracula's coffin and his hand emerging from within. Moreover, the use of the pan away from and then back to the coffin with Dracula straightening up appears as a visual device used on two occasions in the film's Carfax Abbey scenes.

After Harker's arrival at the castle, Bromfield and Murphy provide the following short description: "Near a gothic window in the upper part of the hallway some bats hang from some tapestry, and suddenly they flutter away." Here again we can see an influence on the final film, which contains a shot of three bats flying just outside the castle window, a minor variation on what the two writers recommended.

The Bromfield-Murphy script also provides an important and unique description of Dracula. Along with suggesting he be tall, thin, and pale, they suggest he should be "dressed in a kind of black officer's uniform or full dress, with a ribbon on his shirt front." This is at odds with Stoker (who writes in Chapter 2 that Dracula is "clad in black from head to foot, without a single speck of colour about him anywhere"). Here the two writers seem to be drawing upon what Stoker's Chapter 3 refers to as Dracula's "warlike" history as part of a "conquering race." While their description of military-style dress did not survive, the idea of the "ribbon on his shirt front" did, becoming an important modification to the costume seen in the Broadway play and something that the final film would use.

More striking is how advanced Harker and Dracula's introduction unfolds in the Bromfield-Murphy script. As in Bromfield's treatment, the vampire says in two short sentences "I am Dracula. I bid you welcome." Immediately thereafter, wolves howl and Dracula speaks the dialogue: "Listen to them – the Children of the Night – what music they make!" Harker then follows Dracula up the stairs. Dracula mysteriously passes through a cobweb without disturbing it, after which Harker "breaks [the] cobweb nervously and continues." The script cuts to a spider that "scurries up the wall." Then the two characters make their way into a "luxuriously appointed and comfortable bedroom" with a large fireplace and a dining table. This script has thus provided the template for the dialogue and narrative action that appears in the final film.

Unfortunately, the surviving pages of the Bromfield-Murphy script end with Dracula offering Harker dinner and wine. The remainder is lost, and with it, an ability to analyze the full extent of the developments and innovations that the two men offered. Nevertheless, what survives shows a marked evolution from the two prior treatments.

There is strong reason to believe that Bromfield and Murphy contributed at least one more draft, as Junior Laemmle wrote responses to a Bromfield-Murphy script that imply he read something different from what exists in the surviving pages. In particular, Laemmle's notes suggest that the two writers (in this apparently lost draft) introduced a significant and lasting change to the story in either late August or early September 1930. No longer did Harker journey to Transylvania, as in the novel. Instead, in the version that Laemmle read, it is Renfield who travels to meet Dracula. The change is profound. Now, there is an extremely clear reason why Renfield goes insane and why he is under Dracula's control: Dracula bites Renfield in Transylvania, and the two travel together to England. Secondly, and also of critical importance, the Harker role shrinks in size and importance, a factor that would eventually influence the film's casting.

Junior Laemmle's comments on this particular Bromfield and Murphy script lends further insight into the line that Universal walked between bringing the story to the screen and yet anticipating what might offend audiences and censors. On the one hand, Laemmle seemed intent on offering horror for horror's sake, writing "keep comedy in picture down," as well as writing that Renfield's carriage ride to Dracula's castle should be "realistic" rather than "fantastic."

At the same time, he worried over a number of particular scenes and lines of dialogue. In the script to which he responded, the three vampire women open Renfield's shirt and bite him on the neck; Laemmle suggested eliminating the "gruesome" scene, and so, in the final film, Dracula prevents the trio from sucking Renfield's blood. Similarly, he judged a scene in which Renfield eats a fly from a lump of sugar to be "awful strong," and so it too disappeared.

Laemmle also believed that an image of Dracula walking through the fog after biting the flower girl should be removed. He said much the same of Dracula's dialogue: "To die – to be really dead – that must be glorious," followed (after a comment from Mina) by: "There are far worse things awaiting man than death."[23]

Garrett Fort

Born in New York in 1900, writer Garrett Fort once told a newspaper journalist that he tried to find work as an attorney in the early 1920s, but grew impatient when a "great lawyer failed to keep an appointment with him." He had studied law at Princeton, where he also wrote "true-confession stories as a sideline."[24] Fort left the lawyer's office that day, initially planning to reschedule the appointment. Walking around the block, Fort accepted employment as a gateman at the Famous Players studio. From there, Fort made a name for himself as a writer under contract to Cecil B. DeMille and, later, at Paramount Pictures.

In his lengthy history of writing for the movies prior to 1930, Fort had not dabbled in the horror genre, though he did write a melodrama called *The Midnight Girl* (1925), which featured Bela Lugosi. By the end of 1931, Fort – who would go on to work on scripts for *Frankenstein* (1931), *The Invisible Man* (1933), *Dracula's Daughter* (1936), *The Devil-Doll* (1936), and *Among the Living* (1941) – referred to himself as a "specialist in sin and jitters."[25] He became one of, if not the, pre-eminent horror-film screenwriters of the classic era.

During the months leading up to *Dracula*'s production, Fort increasingly gained a reputation as an important screenwriter of successful talkies. On 24 February 1930, *Film Daily* wrote that he was:

...rapidly earning the title of 'The Edgar Wallace of the Movies,' judging by the way in which he is turning out scripts and originals that sell. Besides writing the scripts on Paramount's Roadhouse Nights *[1930] and* The Big Pond *[1930], Fort also collaborated with Charles Beahan in writing* Dangerous Nan McGrew *[1930]. Added to this is a play written with Ernest Pascal called* Lessons in French *and an original* The Feat of Fools, *which Crosby Gaige will produce next spring.*[26]

Then, on 18 March 1930, the same publication announced that Universal had signed Fort to a "long term contract."[27]

Beyond the sheer fact he was under contract at Universal, Fort's involvement with *Dracula* likely came as a result of two factors. One was his reputation for adapting novels into scripts with strong dialogue for talking pictures, as he had done for *Roadhouse Nights* and for *Applause* (1929). The second reason was Fort's relationship with Tod Browning. The two had just worked together on the script for *Outside the Law* (1930), and their collaboration on *Dracula* would lead the *Hollywood Filmograph* to refer to them as an important new writing "team."[28]

As Chapter 3 notes, Junior Laemmle apparently involved Browning in the casting of Bela Lugosi as Dracula. He may also have allowed Browning to help read and pass judgment on the treatments and scripts produced by the likes of Stephani, Bromfield, and Murphy. Browning's earlier work with Fort (which Laemmle had praised) may have led the director to push for Fort's participation on *Dracula*, particularly as that also paved the way for Browning to be directly involved in the writing process.

Above: Author Garrett Fort with his bride Mary Stuart. Below: Published in the *Hollywood Filmograph* on August 23, 1930.

GARRETT FORT

Adaptation and Dialogue for

"DRACULA"

In Production

"SCOTLAND YARD"

As a result, it must be said that Universal's decision for Fort to work on *Dracula* is less unusual than the timeline of events that surround it. On 23 August 1930, Fort published an advertisement in the *Hollywood Filmograph* that announced he was doing the "Adaptation and Dialogue for *Dracula*."[29] In some respects, the ad wasn't unusual. Fort regularly bought ads promoting himself in film trades during the twenties, as did many others. Given that various persons at Universal Pictures likely read the publication, it seems difficult to believe that Fort was being untruthful. Indeed, he was under contract at Universal, and very definitely worked on the final shooting script.

However, the *Filmograph* published his advertisement one day *before* the *New York Times* announced that Dudley Murphy and Louis Bromfield would collaborate together on the script for *Dracula*. Here there is an apparent conflict, with more than one possible explanation. Perhaps the *Times* reported information that was already out of date, though that seems unlikely given that Bromfield-Murphy apparently wrote more than one draft.

The more likely explanation is that Laemmle and perhaps Browning were disappointed in the Stephani and Bromfield treatments (as well as perhaps the first draft of the Bromfield-Murphy script, though it may or may not have been read by the time Fort purchased his advertisement). As a result, Laemmle assigned a different writer – one already under contract and on the payroll – to draft a script while Bromfield and Murphy were still working on their own version(s). At any rate, the *Hollywood Filmograph* reported as late as 6 September that Bromfield was *Dracula*'s screenwriter, with Fort's name taking his place in a similar column on 13 September.[30]

What occurred next is even more mysterious, as the title page of the final shooting script (dated 26 September 1930) credits: "Adaptation and Dialogue by Tod Browning and Garrett Fort" and "Continuity by Dudley Murphy." By contrast, John LeRoy Johnston's early draft of the *Dracula* pressbook (dated 15 November 1930), credits Murphy not for continuity, but for "added dialogue."[31]

The shooting script also states that it is the "4th Draft."[32] Four drafts could include one or more by Bromfield and Murphy, and one or more by Browning and Fort. Or the count might refer to the number of scripts that Fort wrote, some or all of which in conjunction with Browning. It is quite possible that Murphy did not collaborate with Fort at all, with his credit on the final script coming as a result of Fort and Browning borrowing heavily from a Bromfield-Murphy script or even an unknown draft written by Murphy alone. Indeed, a still photograph exists of Murphy visiting the *Dracula* set, which might suggest that his involvement outlasted Bromfield's.

At any rate, the final shooting script is fascinating for many reasons, not least of which is that it shows the point the story had reached only three days prior to the start of filming. Also fascinating is the fact that it does not comport with some of Junior Laemmle's worries, as it features comic relief in the form of the attendant Martin, and it includes some of the dialogue that he had wanted removed from a Bromfield-Murphy script ("To die – to be really dead – that must be glorious"). It also features Dracula walking through fog after biting the flower girl, although – perhaps in deference to Laemmle's earlier concerns – the script suggests that the fog is lifting.

By contrast, the Fort-Browning script features one element that evidently stems from Laemmle's responses to the Bromfield-Murphy script. For example, the final script claims Dracula's castle should not be of the "Caligari school," a reference to the German

Expressionist film *The Cabinet of Dr. Caligari* (*Das Cabinet des Dr. Caligari*, 1920), which seems to channel Laemmle's belief that the settings should be "realistic" rather than "fantastic."

The lack of surviving scripts and other relevant paperwork precludes the ability to reconstruct a definitive timeline or, more importantly perhaps, a detailed understanding of exactly who devised what and who borrowed from whom. However, the Fort-Browning final shooting script does offer insight into key influences and innovations that the two men included, even if it is not always certain what ideas they may or may not have developed themselves.

In Stoker, Bromfield, and Bromfield-Murphy, the journey to Castle Dracula occurs on the eve of St. George's Day. By the time of the final shooting script, the date has been changed to Walpurgis Night. Though the two holidays occur at the same time of year, Walpurgis Night has not traditionally been as well known outside of Central and Northern Europe as St. George's Day, with St. George being the patron saint of England. Here the shift might reflect a belief that Walpurgis Night would sound more foreign, more unusual, and – as a result – more frightening. The change might also reflect an awareness of Stoker's short story *Dracula's Guest* (first published in 1914), which takes place on Walpurgis Night, or – for that matter – Goethe's *Faust*, which includes a scene called *Walpurgisnacht*.

The Fort-Browning retains the aforementioned Bromfield-Murphy adjustments to Renfield's character, meaning that it is he who travels to Transylvania, rather than Harker. The script also reveals the influence of *Nosferatu* when Renfield dines at Castle Dracula. He cuts his finger on a knife, thus igniting Dracula's bloodlust. The scenes in the respective films play out quite differently, with the Browning-Fort featuring a vampire who is quickly repelled by the sight of the crucifix around Renfield's neck (as opposed to *Nosferatu*, in which the vampire briefly sucks his guest's thumb before the two move into another room and "sit" together); however, given that no such scene exists in Stoker or Deane-Balderston, *Nosferatu* seems to be the source of this narrative action.

Fort's advertisement in the January 5, 1931 issue of the Hollywood Reporter.

GARRETT FORT

Adaptation, Continuity and Dialogue
" DRACULA "

Lucy's life as a vampire also represents a fascinating evolution in the Fort-Browning script. In Stoker's Chapter 13, for example, the vampiric Lucy is referred to as "the "bloofer lady," as well as "the Kensington Horror," "the Stabbing Woman," and "the Woman in Black." In Deane-Balderston, Dr. Seward calls Mina (rather than Lucy, given the inverted character names) "The lady in white who gives chocolate to little children"; similarly, Lucy (in the play) refers to her as "the woman in white," a name that for some audiences might have conjured memories of Wilkie Collins' 1860 detective novel *The Woman in White*.

Stephani refers to Lucy as the "Hampstead Horror" and – in the words of the children she attacks – a "beautiful lady"; Bromfield's treatment also refers to her as a "beautiful lady." In the final shooting script, however, she is "the Woman in White." Here a minor evolution is present, with the Fort-Browning revealing their awareness of the previous texts. For example, the Deane-Balderston includes a newspaper clipping about the vampire woman's nocturnal activities that features the line, "Narratives of three small girls." Stephani used the same five words; Fort-Browning appropriates them with no change, save for the fact the number of girls is changed to "two." But the final script has the words read aloud not by Harker (as in Deane-Balderston) or by Van Helsing/Seward (as in Stephani, who is not precise regarding which of those two characters he intends to be the reader), but instead by Martin.

The final shooting script also borrows various dialogue from its predecessors, sometimes quite precisely. Consider, for example, the following dialogue from the Deane-Balderston play and the Fort-Browning shooting script:

Renfield (Play): "My cries will disturb Miss Lucy, who is ill. They will give your daughter bad dreams, Doctor Seward, bad dreams."
Renfield (Film): "My cries at night – they might disturb Miss Mina – they might give her bad dreams – bad dreams, Professor, bad dreams!"

Renfield (Play): "Be guided by what he says."
Renfield (Film): "Be guided by what he says."

Renfield (Play): "You know too much to live, Van Helsing!"
Renfield (Film): "You know too much to live, Van Helsing!"

Dracula (Play): "A most distinguished scientist, whose name we know even in the wilds of Transylvania."
Dracula (Film): "Van Helsing – a distinguished scientist whose name we know even in the wilds of Transylvania."

Dracula (Play): "You are a wise man, Professor – for one who has not lived even a single lifetime."
Dracula (Film): "For one who has not lived even a single lifetime, you're a wise man, Van Helsing."

Dracula (Play): "Yes, but only if she dies by day. I shall see that she dies by night."
Dracula (Film): "Ah – the stake – yes! But only if she dies by day! I shall see that she dies by night!"

Beyond such specific dialogue, some scenes in the final script closely echo those in the play. In both texts (and in Stephani), for example, Van Helsing coaxes the lead female character into removing her scarf, after which he asks about the marks on her neck.

The Fort-Browning script also includes an epilogue in the form of a curtain speech, much like the Deane-Balderston play. In both cases, Van Helsing speaks roughly the same words, which end by reassuring the audience that "there are such things" as vampires. A review of the 1931 film would describe the speech as achieving a:

desired effect of a cheerful play on horrors that can be enjoyed in comfort (a technique that is the essence of high comedy). ... His remarks are to the effect that if what happened on the screen comes up to disturb your mind when you get home, don't worry, because such things as the screen showed are possible after all – [a] gentle jest that gives the elaborate horror just the right light touch.[33]

Similar curtain speeches earlier appeared in the stage versions of *The Spider* (1927) and *The Bat* (1920), both of which implored the audience not to reveal their conclusions to anyone who had not yet seen the plays. *The Bat Whispers* (1930), a talkie adaptation of *The Bat*, included such a curtain speech, though that fact would likely have been unknown to Browning and Fort while writing their script, as *The Bat Whispers* would not be released until November 1930. By contrast, *The Terror* (1928) featured two characters giving a curtain speech, the second of whom assures the audience that "there are" villains in real life who resemble the film's murderer.

Despite a number of similarities to the Deane-Balderston play, the Fort-Browning script also illustrates an intentional and repeated desire to distinguish itself from its predecessor. In the play, when Van Helsing warns Dracula that he has something more effective than wolfbane, he reveals the host; in the shooting script, he reveals a crucifix. Likewise, Butterworth and the maid have humorous exchanges in the play, just as Martin and the maid do in the shooting script. But their dialogue is completely different.

The Fort-Browning script also noticeably reassigns what became one of the film's best-remembered lines of dialogue to a different character than in previous texts. In Stoker's Chapter 11, as well as in Deane-Balderston, Renfield speaks the words "The blood is the life," which originally appeared in the Holy Bible (Deuteronomy 12:23). But the shooting script has Dracula enunciating those words.

Beyond dialogue, important differences also occur in how specific scenes unfold.

In Deane-Balderston, Dracula throws a small vase at a mirror on the wall after Van Helsing discovers that he casts no reflection. In the shooting script, however, Van Helsing notices Dracula does not appear in the mirror of an ornate cigarette box. The change allows Van Helsing to be more in control when he surprises Dracula with the "amazing phenomenon" he has discovered; it also allows Dracula to be in closer physical proximity to Van Helsing when he smashes the mirror.[34]

These differences between the Deane-Balderston and the Fort-Browning are important, but others are *monumental*, as the latter was definitely not a mere adaptation of the former, as some historians have wrongly claimed. The play features no Transylvanian section, no scenes of Dracula in London biting a flower girl, no scene at the concert hall, no scene of Dracula biting Lucy (meaning Mina in the play, given the play's inversion of the female character names), and no scene of Dr. Seward examining a body with teeth marks.[35] Together these constitute 53 pages of the Fort-Browning script, meaning Sequences A, B, C, and D.

Such key differences allow the Fort-Browning script to make other alterations as well. For example, in the play, Harker asks Van Helsing (almost on behalf of the audience), "What *is* a vampire?" The Transylvanian section of the shooting script allows a character to describe vampires. And – drawing on the Stephani treatment – it is importantly Van Helsing, not Harker, who stakes Dracula in shooting script.

Some of these variations came due to the artistic beliefs of the writers involved, whereas others were tempered by prevailing morays of the period. After all, it is important to remember that the final shooting script generally comports with the *Code of Ethics for the Production of Motion Pictures* as adopted by the film industry in 1930. For example, the Code said that "The treatment of low, disgusting, unpleasant, though not necessarily evil subjects, should be subject always to the dictates of good taste and regard for the sensibilities of the audience." Here we can see one clear reason why, for example, the shooting script has Renfield describe the many rats he saw, rather than the film depicting them onscreen.[36] (Indeed, fears of possible Code violations and censorship troubles were key reasons why Paramount had passed on *Dracula* when the rights were available earlier in the year).[37]

The Fort-Browning script thus became its own unique narrative, one that hardly explored romance, despite Junior Laemmle having originally envisioned the story as a combination of the romance and thriller genres. By contrast, the Fort-Browning poses Jonathan Harker as a minor and ineffectual male lead, and creates a Dracula interested in women for no apparent reason other than unbridled bloodlust. While the two men could not have anticipated the widespread usage of the term "horror movie," Fort and Browing created a narrative that exemplifies that genre. Indeed, the word "horror" appears twice in their shooting script.[38]

The Hays Office

At the time that Universal obtained the rights to *Dracula*, Charles A. Logue held the position as the studio's "Scenario Chief." A newspaper and magazine journalist early in his career, Logue had himself written film scenarios since at least 1916, ranging from *The Hidden Hand* (1917) to *The Claw* (1927).[39] He assumed his position of what was also referred to as "scenario editor" and "editor in chief" at Universal in April 1930, only a few months before Bromfield began his work on *Dracula*.[40] Then, as of 5 August, Universal announced that Erwin Gelsey would take Logue's place, Logue having resigned on 31 July.[41]

How much of a role that Logue (or Gelsey, for that matter) played in the evolution of *Dracula*'s final shooting script is unknown, but one of Logue's responsibilities had been to liaise with the Motion Picture Producers and Distributors of America (MPPDA), more commonly known as the Hays Office (after the organization's president, Will H. Hays) on treatments and scripts so as to ascertain any possible violations of the *Code of Ethics for the Production of Motion Pictures* prior to shooting particular films. In this regard, the scenario chief also worked hand in hand with a film's associate producer. For example, in May 1930, Logue and E. M. Asher met with Colonel Jason Joy of the Hays Office to discuss the treatment for *East Is West* (1930). Ted Fithian, hired by Universal to serve as the studio's contact person with the Hays Office, assisted them.[42]

In terms of *Dracula*, Logue's name is absent from surviving Hays Office documents, as is Gelsey's. By contrast, it is clear that associate producer E. M. Asher took the lead role.

> 1. In Scene F-8 Martin says: "I am going to find a place with some nice normal loonies--Napoleons, Mussolinis and such like." You will avoid any difficulty which may arise by using characters from ancient history such as "Alexanders" or "Caesars".
>
> 2. In Scene G-33 Renfield calls Van Hesling "A thick headed Dutchman". This epithet should be removed.

Jason Joy's comments to Universal on September 13, 1930.

He contacted Jason Joy about *Dracula* on 26 June 1930, making an initial inquiry about any "censorship angles" on the story, adding that he could provide copies of the novel and play upon request.[43] On 6 July, Joy spent the "whole day" reading Stoker's novel, though there is no surviving record of his response to it.[44]

On 8 September 1930, Asher sent a rough draft of a *Dracula* script (presumably written by Fort-Browning) to Joy, including a note that said:

It is not usual for me to send out an unfinished script, but we are particularly anxious to go into production at the earliest possible moment and [I] am therefore sending it incomplete in order that you may be thoroughly familiar with the production.[45]

Asher concluded by mentioning that he would forward the "polished script" within a few days.

By 10 September, Joy responded to Asher that his staff had found "nothing in it in violation of the Code or which can be reasonably objected to by official censors."[46] However, in a letter Joy sent to Junior Laemmle on 13 September, presumably after examining the "polished" script that Asher had promised him, two minor concerns had surfaced:

1. In Scene F-8, Martin says: "I am going to find a place with some nice normal loonies – Napoleons, Mussolinis, and such like." You will avoid any difficulty which may arise by using characters from ancient history such as "Alexanders" and "Caesars."
2. In Scene G-33, Renfield calls Van Helsing "A thick headed Dutchman." This epithet should be removed.[47]

Here it seems likely that Joy had read a version written by Fort-Browning, as Scene F-8 in the final shooting script is much the same as Joy describes, though Mussolini's name had been eliminated. By contrast, Scene G-33 in the final shooting script does not feature Renfield or Van Helsing, which suggests further drafting had continued to change particular scenes and their sequencing. Indeed, on 19 September, Laemmle wrote to Joy, promising not only to alter the "two points" in the final script, but also to forward the "first complete preliminary draft" in a "few days."[48]

These communications highlight the involvement of the Hays Office in the evolution of *Dracula*'s final shooting script, but also indicate that the office found no code violations, presumably due to Universal's writers having consciously avoided potentially problematic scenes and dialogue. At any rate, the MPPDA's seal of approval clearly appears during *Dracula*'s opening title sequence.

Conclusion

Movement towards the final shooting script for *Dracula* was a complicated process, involving Junior Laemmle, Tod Browning, and a number of different writers, as well as such pre-existing texts as Bram Stoker's novel, the Deane-Balderston stage play, and – even if only to a minor extent – F. W. Murnau's film *Nosferatu*. Moreover, additional viewpoints came from E. M. Asher and, importantly, the MPPDA.

The final shooting script attributes the "continuity" to Dudley Murphy, though the same acknowledgment does not appear in the onscreen film credits. Like Bromfield, Murphy seems to have left Universal after working on *Dracula*. A January 1931 article in the *Hollywood Reporter* announced that MGM had signed Murphy "to work out a scenario based on an original idea submitted by himself."[49] He would have nothing more to do with *Dracula*, to the extent that he did not even mention the film in his memoir.[50] Bromfield does not seem to have spoken about *Dracula* after 1930 either; his name also is absent from the film's onscreen credits.

In December 1930, one press article noted that Browning prepared the screenplay "with Garrett Fort."[51] But, like Murphy and Bromfield, Browning had no onscreen credit for his writing contributions on *Dracula*. (Little can be made of this, as Browning did get an individual screen opening credit of his own for having directed the film.) Garrett Fort alone received credit for a script that was in fact the culmination of ideas from various authors.

Writing about *Dracula* in 1930, the *Hollywood Filmograph* expressed its concern that "Universal would produce its picture from the stage play rather than the novel," adding that such would result in an "ordinary stage thriller." By contrast, "If Bram Stoker's tale is taken, the company will have a motion picture – and the greatest weird motion picture produced. We wait with fear and trembling."[52]

Universal did not respond publicly to the *Filmograph*'s concerns, but had Junior Laemmle done so, his answer would have been complicated, as the shooting script was not an adaptation of the play, nor was it an adaptation of the novel. In varying degrees, Universal's *Dracula* represented an amalgam of both, augmented notably with an array of original ideas that sprang from the imaginations of various persons, including a number of authors on the studio payroll.

1   As Chapter 3 indicates, Universal did acquire the rights to three different stage adaptations of Stoker's novel, but writers at the studio seized upon the Deane-Balderston as it had been a success on Broadway and throughout America. That reason – along with its "Americanized" dialogue – made it the logical version for screenwriters to read.

2   Deane, Hamilton and John L. Balderston. *Dracula–The Vampire Play in Three Acts* (New York: Samuel French, 1933).

3   In Chapter 2 of Stoker's novel, Harker tells Dracula about his visit to Carfax Abbey: "I had not the key of the door leading to it from the house, but I have taken with my Kodak views of it from various points."

4   Historian George E. Turner noted that writer Louis Stevens also "contributed" material to Universal's *Dracula*, though he does not specify whether Stevens merely provided ideas or whether he actually wrote a treatment or script. At any rate, no copy of Stevens' work on the film seems to survive. See: "The Two Faces of *Dracula*." *American Cinematographer* Vol. 69, No. 5 (May 1988): 35.

5   "Carl Laemmle, Jr. Blames Continuity Writers." *Hollywood Filmograph* 14 June 1930: 5.

6   Clippings in the Frederick "Fritz" Stephani file at the Margaret Herrick Library, Academy of Motion Picture Arts and Sciences, Beverly Hills, CA.

7   Stephani's treatment is reprinted in: Riley, pp. 35-40.

8. The Deane-Balderston stage play refers to the herb as "wolf's-bane," whereas the Fort-Browning shooting script refers to it as "wolfbane."
9. "*Variety*'s Bulletin Condensed." *Variety* 9 July 1930: 15.
10. "Bromfield Borrowed." *Variety* 2 July 1930: 39.
11. Bromfield, Louis. Letter to Clare Ryan. 20 July 1930.
12. Merrick, Mollie. "Hollywood – In Person." *New Orleans Times-Picayume* 6 July 1930.
13. "Sign Bromfield to Write *Dracula* Script for Universal." *Hollywood Filmograph* 26 July 1930: 19.
14. Bromfield, Louis. *Early Autumn* (Wooster, OH: Wooster Book Co., 2000): 108.
15. "Bromfield Expects Talkers to Develop Own Material." *Film Daily* 18 Mar. 1930.
16. Bromfield's *First Treatment of Dracula* is reprinted in: Riley, pp. 42-54.
17. Bromfield, Louis. Letter to Clare Ryan. 20 July 1930.
18. "Talking Shadows in the Making." *New York Times* 24 Aug. 1930: X5.
19. Wilk, Ralph. "A Little from 'Lots.'" *Film Daily* 22 Aug. 1930: 6.
20. For more information on Murphy, see Susan Delson's *Dudley Murphy: Hollywood Wild Card* (Minneapolis, MN: University of Minnesota Press, 2006).
21. "Film Hissed Off Screen." *Variety* 28 Apr. 1926: 37.
22. "The Lowdown." *Hollywood Reporter* 1 Dec. 1930: 2.
23. Laemmle's reaction to this particular *Dracula* script can be found in: Riley, p. 56.
24. "He Might Have Been Lawyer If He Hadn't Been Restless." *Los Angeles Times* 23 Jan. 1927.
25. Advertisement. *Hollywood Reporter* 11 Dec. 1931.
26. Blair, Harry N. "Short Shots from New York Studios." *Film Daily* 24 Feb. 1930.
27. Wilk, Ralph. "A Little from 'Lots.'" *Film Daily* 18 Mar. 1930.
28. "Fort and Browning Work on Two Scripts." *Hollywood Filmograph* 18 Oct. 1930: 17.
29. Advertisement. *Hollywood Filmograph* 23 Aug. 1930: 7.
30. "Bulletin Board." *Hollywood Filmograph* 6 Sept. 1930: 24; "Bulletin Board." *Hollywood Filmograph* 13 Sept. 1930: 23.
31. Johnston's draft (dated 15 Nov. 1930) for the *Dracula* pressbook exists in the Universal Pictures collection at the Cinematic Arts Library at the University of Southern California.
32. The final shooting script is available in: *Dracula (The Original 1931 Shooting Script)*. Ed. by Philip J. Riley. (Absecon, NJ: MagicImage, 1990). It begins on page 89, though subsequent pages are not numbered in accord with the book's pagination, presumably so as not to add modern text onto the images of the original pages.
33. "*Dracula*." *Variety* 18 Feb. 1931: 14.
34. Given that the trailer uses footage of Edward Van Sloan as Van Helsing in a scene in which the mirror on the wall is smashed (apparently his screen test filmed in September 1930), it would seem quite possible that the change with the cigarette box came late in the scripting process.
35. When I suggest the Deane-Balderston play includes no scene of Lucy being bitten, I more specifically mean – given the inversion of character names in the play – a scene of Mina getting bitten.
36. "Code of Ethics for the Production of Motion Pictures." *The Film Daily Yearbook for 1931* (New York: Film Daily, 1932), p. 659.
37. Schatz, Thomas. *The Genius of the System: Hollywood Filmmaking in the Studio Era* (New York: Pantheon, 1988): 89.
38. In Scene G-7, Van Helsing promises Mina that Lucy's soul would be "released from this horror." Shortly thereafter, in the same scene, Mina refers to her condition as "this horror."
39. "Charles A. Logue Will Direct Screen Adaptation of Own Story." *Exhibitors Herald* 28 Dec. 1919: 75.
40. "Weisenthal Leaves U." *Variety* 2 Apr. 1930: 4; "Logue Services Will Be Held in Venice (Fri)." *Variety* 4 Aug. 1938: 7.
41. "Gelsey at U Studios." *Variety* 6 Aug. 1930: 17. Logue returned to Universal in October 1930 to prepare a story based upon W. R. Burnett's novel *Saint Johnson*. See "Universal Notes." *Hollywood Filmograph* 25 Oct. 1930: 12.
42. Jason Joy mentions this meeting in a note preserved in the PCA file for *East Is West*. Available in the Motion Picture Association of America, Production Code Administration collection at the Margaret Herrick Library in Beverly Hills, CA (hereinafter abbreviated).
43. Asher, E. M. Letter to Jason Joy. 26 June 1930. PCA file for *Dracula*, Herrick.
44. Joy, Jason. File note. 6 July 1930. Ibid.
45. Asher, E. M. Letter to Jason Joy. 8 Sept. 1930. Ibid.
46. Joy, Jason. Letter to E. M. Asher. 10 Sept. 1930. Ibid.
47. Joy, Jason. Letter to Carl Laemmle, Jr. 13 Sept. 1930. Ibid.
48. Laemmle, Carl, Jr. Letter to Jason Joy. 19 Sept. 1930. Ibid.
49. "Dudley Murphy at MGM." *Hollywood Reporter* 16 Jan. 1931: 3.
50. Delson, Susan. Email to Gary D. Rhodes. 29 Sept. 2012.
51. "Weird Drama Being Filmed for Picture." *San Diego Evening Tribune* 5 Dec. 1930.
52. Pictures – Reviewed and Previewed." *Hollywood Filmograph* 23 Aug. 1930: 20.

Chapter 5
PRODUCTION

Two factors are surprising in terms of previous historical accounts of *Dracula*'s production. For one, little has been published on the shoot's day-to-day activities and progress, which has largely been due to a limited amount of surviving studio paperwork. That said, it has been possible to uncover and reclaim a surprising amount of data for this book, ranging from previously unknown clippings from such publications as the *Hollywood Reporter* to an exacting comparison of the final shooting script and completed film against the shooting schedule, which fortunately does exist.[1]

The second remarkable fact about histories of *Dracula*'s production is how little access they have had to the memories of its cast and crew. Few persons who were on the set were interviewed about the film, particularly those who were heavily involved in the process, rather than merely watching it unfold. Nicholas Webster, the son of *Dracula*'s script girl Aileen Webster, later relayed how – despite the fact he was scared of the cobwebbed sets – he used one of the film's coffins as an impromptu desk to study his homework; he also recalled his mother travelling to Lugosi's residence to assist the actor with his lines.[2] Geraldine Chandler, sister-in-law of *Dracula*'s leading lady Helen Chandler, visited the set and noticed that Lugosi seemed "very distant. He didn't want to meet somebody's kid sister. I guess he had more important things to do." She also remembered Chandler describing a woman that she presumed to be Lugosi's wife, though Lugosi was unmarried at the time. "[The woman] thought she was extremely important, and tried to boss people around. The people on the set didn't like her."[3]

But whomever that woman was, she apparently did not always accompany Lugosi, as the actor became entranced with Frances Dade, who would portray Lucy. On more than one occasion during the shoot, Lugosi asked Dade to date him. She refused, mainly because he frightened her.[4] "He made her very uncomfortable," Frances Dade's daughter Dade Moran later revealed. "She didn't like it when the two of them were alone together."[5]

These memories are helpful in building a limited picture of the persons involved in the film, but they have not factored into earlier accounts of *Dracula*'s production history in any major way, in part because two of the interviewees (Geraldine Chandler and Dade Moran) did not share their memories until recent years. Unfortunately, *Dracula*'s key personnel – its director, producer, screenwriters, cinematographer, and assistant director – died before any historian conducted thorough thorough interviews with them about the film. The same

Bela Lugosi on the set of Tod Browning's *Dracula* (1931).
(Courtesy of Jack Dowler)

was true of much of the cast, save for David Manners, who portrayed Jonathan Harker. His recollections have played a major role in modern histories of *Dracula*, despite the fact that his comments were brief and in some respects problematic.

Of *Dracula*, Manners said: "To be quite honest, Tod Browning was always off to the side somewhere. I remember being directed by Karl Freund, the photographer who came from Germany and had a great sense for film. I believe that he is the one who is mainly responsible for *Dracula* being watchable today."[6] Manners also recalled that Browning was "back in the shadows" during what he perceived to be an "extremely disorganized" shoot.[7] From Manners' statements, writer David J. Skal has confidently pronounced that, "Karl Freund, nominally the cinematographer, actually directed much of the film, and everything that involved Manners."[8] Here Skal actually goes further than Manners, but provides no other evidence.[9] After all, Manners never claimed that Browning was absent from the set or that Freund directed scenes not involving Manners.

While Manners made similar remarks to me in 1985, he importantly added that his years in Hollywood were extremely unhappy; he also implied that he did not care for either Tod Browning or Bela Lugosi, dismissively describing Lugosi as someone who kept repeating "I am Dracula!" between takes. Herein lies one important problem. No other star or crewmember was formally interviewed about the film in the decades that followed (save Edward Van Sloan, who was hardly asked any questions about it), and so Manners became the key source of such information.[10]

The dangers of relying on Manners as sole support for claims that Tod Browning did not direct the film (or most of it) are manifold. First, his memories seem to have been biased against Browning, as well as in favor of Freund, whom he apparently befriended or at least admired. As early as November 1930, Manners enthused to the *Los Angeles Times*, "We have a marvelous cameraman [for *Dracula*], a German. ... It is amazing to watch him work."[11]

Even if Freund did discuss certain issues with Manners, they may well have concentrated on blocking and camera movement, as there is a good deal of camera movement during the scenes involving Manners, more than has generally been acknowledged. It would not have been unusual for the cinematographer to describe matters of frame lines and blocking vis-à-vis the timing of camera moves, for example. Moreover, Freund might well have conferred with Browning on the specifics of such shots prior to any conversations that Freund had on the set with Manners. (After all, had Freund actually directed the film or "much" of it, he would likely have wanted credit for doing so, if not more money, but no evidence suggests that he ever claimed to have directed *Dracula* in part or whole.)

Secondly, Manners seems to have been unhappy about the entire production and, most particularly, the role he played: he was the third actor cast as Harker, a character that had greatly diminished in importance by the time of the final shooting script. He shared his feelings about the film in the press in 1930:

I don't appeal to myself in this [film], because I'm the only sane one of the lot, though I don't think I will be long. Really, I suppose I'm the voice of the audience, for all I do is wander about and say, 'But you can't do that. Things like that don't happen today.' And then they do to show me, so after all I'm pretty useless.[12]

Later, in 1931, he told a fan magazine that he disliked the roles he played in *most* of his films, save *The Right to Love* (1930) and *Journey's End* (1930), the latter being the film that had brought him fame. He even went so far as to condemn *Kismet* (1930) as "badly directed."[13]

Thirdly, while it is difficult to determine the precise number of days that Manners worked on *Dracula*, it is fair to say that – given his role in the script as compared against the surviving production schedule – he was on the set for no more than half of the shoot, if even that much. Building an argument that Tod Browning did not direct the film (or most of it) based on the brief memories of someone who was not on the set the entire production (or a majority of it or even half of it) is extremely problematic, not least because of the fact that Manners made no reference in his interviews to Scott R. Beal, *Dracula*'s assistant director. Had Browning chosen not to speak to Manners, or had he for some reason not actually directed the film, Beal would likely have done so (not Freund), at least until such time that the studio formally removed Browning.

This was as opposed to the 1932 film *The Mummy*, which Karl Freund *did* direct as per his contract and as that film's onscreen credits attest. Manners acted in *The Mummy* as well, playing a role similar to Jonathan Harker. Here it is not difficult to imagine that – when speaking to interviewers decades later – Manners could even have conflated his memories of Freund on the set of *Dracula* with his memories of having actually been directed by Freund on the set of *The Mummy*. In any event, it must be acknowledged that Manners himself has not been served well by historians who have applied his comments to either the entirety or majority of *Dracula*'s production, something that goes far beyond anything he seems to have intended.

Fourthly, the problems of oral history are well-known. Decades after an event, an individual may well forget some aspects of it, and in this case, it is crucial to note that Manners did make one key error when recalling *Dracula* to an interviewer, one that is completely at odds with surviving primary sources. Though the specifics will be discussed later in this chapter, it is worth mentioning in brief that, while Manners claimed to have made $2,000 per week for acting in *Dracula*, a surviving contractual agreement indicates that was definitely not the case: he actually made much less money. It is always worthwhile to question

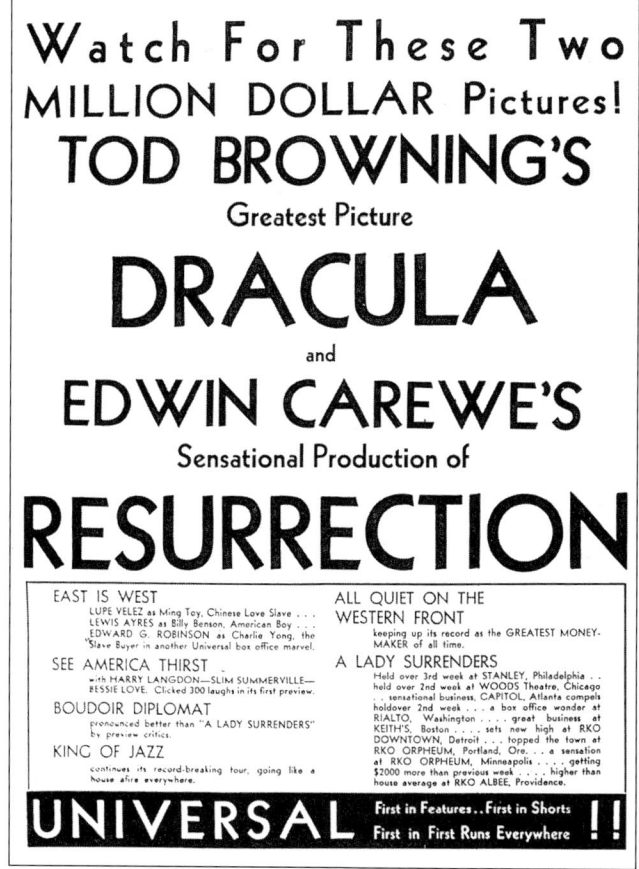

Advertisement published in the October 25, 1930 issue of *Motion Picture News*.

148   Chapter 5 – PRODUCTION

the unchallenged assertions of a single person, but in this case, it is particularly necessary, as Manners was clearly incorrect on that issue and may well have been on others.

What do these four points tell us? At a minimum, they suggest that Manners' recollections have assumed far too large a place in histories of *Dracula*'s production. While valuable, they must be considered with appropriate caution for all of the aforementioned reasons, and they should also be judged against an interview that Bela Lugosi gave about the production while it was still underway. On 18 October 1930, the *Hollywood Filmograph* quoted Lugosi as saying:

> *I played the role of Dracula for two years on the stage, but I found in playing in the picture that there was a great deal I had to unlearn. In the theatre I was playing not only to the spectators in the front rows, but also to those in the last row of the gallery ... I 'took it big,' as the saying is. But for the screen, in which the actor's distance from every member of the audience is equal only to his distance from the lens of the camera, I have found that a great deal of repression was an absolute necessity. Tod Browning has continually had to 'hold me down.' In my other screen roles, I did not seem to have this difficulty, but I have played Dracula a thousand times on the stage, and in this one role I find that I have become thoroughly settled in the technique of the stage, and not of the screen. But, thanks to my director, I am 'unlearning' fast.*[14]

Here Lugosi makes absolutely no mention of being directed by Freund, even though he had known Freund since 1920, when he appeared in F. W. Murnau's *Der Januskopf* (1920), a film that Freund shot. By contrast, Lugosi praises his director, Tod Browning. One could suggest that Lugosi's remarks were merely meant for publicity purposes; however, it should be noted that they appeared in the *Filmograph*, a trade publication, not a movie fan magazine.

Of course the apparent contradictions between Manners' later interviews and Lugosi's 1930 interview might not be contradictions at all. Tod Browning could well have spoken a great deal with Lugosi, and yet hardly talked to Manners, preferring instead to convey his communications to him through Freund or Beal. In other words, even if Manners was not biased against Browning and was as completely accurate and honest as he could possibly have been during his interviews, which is possible, his memories offer little concrete information beyond the fact that Browning was not speaking to *him* at length (the resulting appearance being that Browning was "back in the shadows"). However, just because a director opts not to communicate with one particular actor does not at all that mean he didn't direct a film, including in all the vast array of responsibilities and decisions that one single actor might not notice or necessarily understand, particularly an actor who had – like Manners – only recently made a transition from the stage (and, by extension, from a world in which he was used to theatre directors).

Perhaps the discrepancy can be explained to some degree by Browning's directorial style. As *Motion Picture Classic* noted in 1928:

> *[Browning] directs briefly. Conveying his ideas in succinct comments and isn't overly dependent on soft music and boxed-in sets for inspiration. His particular type of production would be excuse enough for the average director to affect all sorts of temperamentalism from a Sherlock Holmes hat to a gun-guarded camera. But quite the contrary, it is easy enough for the most casual studio visitor to drop onto a Chaney-Browning set and watch them create mystery in a businesslike way.*[15]

E.M. Asher, unit producer for *Dracula*. (Courtesy of Alexandra Asher Shears)

In short, the sheer fact that a director does not speak at length with one actor does not mean that the director is not overseeing the shoot with a guiding artistic vision that begins in a pre-production phase (long before a given actor is ever hired) and continues with a multitude of duties that have nothing to do with that given actor, ranging from grappling with budgetary concerns and dealing with studio executives to overseeing crewmembers to create a particular *mise-en-scène*, one that might be informed by analyzing the dailies after that same actor has left the studio for the day.

Browning's myriad responsibilities might have made it appear to Manners that he was "back in the shadows," but in those "shadows" he could have been making key decisions about the production in talks with Junior Laemmle, E. M. Asher, the crew, and/or actors that he believed required personal attention, such as Lugosi. And so Browning likely had larger issues on his mind than lavishing attention on an actor cast after filming began, who portrayed a straightforward and uncomplicated supporting role. After all, Manners never suggested Browning was actually absent from the set.

To be sure, many film directors working in the Classical Hollywood period did not necessarily spend a great deal of time directing individual actors on their performances. For example, John Huston famously talked about the fact that most of his direction of actors occurred through his choice of casting, rather than in giving specific verbal direction during a film shoot. And, for that matter, consider what actress Frances Drake said of Karl Freund's own direction of the 1935 film *Mad Love*:

Director Karl Freund kept wanting to be the cinematographer at the same time – and Gregg Toland was a marvellous cameraman! He was such a dear little man, sort of slender, and he looked rather hunted when this wretched big fat man would say, 'Now, now, we'll do it this way!' You never knew who was directing. The producer was dying to, to tell you the truth, and of course, he had no idea of directing.[16]

Given events on one film set (such as *Mad Love*) should not necessarily shape our opinion of what happened on another film set (such as *Dracula*), and a singular quotation about any production represents only one perspective (whether it comes from Frances Drake or David Manners).[17] But taken together, the memories of Drake and Manners might suggest to us even another possibility: if directors were generally happy with the work of particular actors, they might have perceived little value in discussing their characters or portrayals with them. In other words, what the actors saw as a lack of communication could have been a director's silent endorsement.

To return to the specific case of *Dracula*, the juxtaposition of the Manners and Lugosi quotations underscores how little has actually been known about its production, and also reveals how contradictory oral histories can be, particularly when few interviews exist about a shoot that lasted for 36 days over the span of more than three months. In short, it would be unwise to place too much emphasis on Manners, and much more unwise somehow to apply his version of his singular experience to a film shoot that featured days and weeks when he wasn't even present.

Nevertheless, I believe prior emphasis on the Manners quotation has helped some scholars use the subject film's production to explain the flaws they perceive in the completed film. Consider again the work of David J. Skal, who has written at length on *Dracula*.[18] Rather than praise the film, Skal usually critiques it quite negatively. At times, his work seems predicated on the need to connect the problems of the finished film (as he sees them) with problems during the shoot (as he sees them, mainly through the perspective of Manners).

Beyond his uncritical acceptance of Manners' recollections and his resultant claim that Freund "actually directed much of the film," Skal also raises other issues that are worth noting, including the statement: "In one story that circulated around Hollywood – possibly apocryphal, since it has no firm attribution – Freund became so fed up with Browning's static ways that he finally just turned on the camera and let it run unattended."[19] Skal acknowledges the story has trafficked without evidence, but simply publishing it arguably serves to further the bias against Browning, as the tale could readily be dismissed on technological grounds. It simply would not have been possible to leave a 35mm camera of the period running without an operator and obtain usable takes; moreover, a crewmember walking on/off set during filming would likely have made noise that would have disrupted the recording of clean audio. Any cinematographer resorting to such nonsense would have been relieved of duty; *Dracula*'s crew also featured assistant camera operators who would have been ready to take over for him, and in fact it is quite possible (as Chapter 6 will note) that a second camera filming footage for the eventual silent version was also rolling. Needless to say, the story of Freund walking away from his camera (and thus becoming an absentee cinematographer) is also *greatly* at odds with depictions of Freund the impromptu director.

Skal also tries to build an argument that Universal might not have trusted Browning, claiming:

> One piece of evidence suggesting that the studio was unhappy with Browning, even from the time of preproduction, was the caption that appeared on at least one batch of early publicity photos, distributed by Universal before shooting began, identifying Dracula as 'Edwin Carew's superproduction.' Carew … had just produced two blockbusters for Universal, Ramona *and* Resurrection, *and would have been a natural choice to replace Browning if the studio felt the production was in trouble. But Carew was also one of the most expensive directors in the business, making at least $200,000 per production on a percentage basis. Did Universal really plan to dump Browning from* Dracula, *only to reconsider in light of finances? The truth may never be known.*[20]

But in this case, the truth is very much known, as primary sources make clear that Edwin Carewe – his last named was spelled thusly, despite Skal's srepeated elimination of the final "e" – could *never* have served as *Dracula*'s director or as a replacement for Tod Browning.

To be sure, Carewe and Browning were under contract at Universal at the same time, meaning that they were *both* being paid. And Carewe's *Resurrection*, a film that Skal mentions, was a Universal "Super-Production." But Skal's timeline is factually incorrect. Carewe had *not* "just produced" *Resurrection* for Universal before the studio proceeded with *Dracula*.

Chapter 5 – PRODUCTION

Junior Laemmle personally assigned Carewe as director of *Resurrection,* with the shoot beginning on 22 September 1930, just one week prior to the start of *Dracula's*.[21] Indeed, Laemmle specifically sought out Carewe for *Resurrection* because Carewe had already directed a silent version of the same story in 1927. A surviving telegram from early 1930 reveals that Laemmle was even worried that Carewe might shoot a talkie version of the story for another company.[22] On 17 April, Laemmle telegrammed William H. Hays: "IT IS OUR INTENTION TO PRODUCE CAREWE'S VERSION OF RESURRECTION COMMENCING WORK AT AN EARLY DATE STOP."[23] Months later, Laemmle finally got his wish.

According to the *Hollywood Reporter*, Carewe's *Resurrection* shoot lasted for approximately six weeks.[24] That meant it wrapped at roughly the same time as principal shooting on *Dracula* came to an end or perhaps one week earlier. In other words, given the fact he was working on one of the two biggest films then underway at Universal, Carewe would have been the very *last* director to whom Laemmle would have turned as a replacement for Browning. Nor could this have been Laemmle's hope at some earlier stage, as he had formally announced that Carewe would direct *Resurrection* at least as early as 1 July 1930, and had actively sought his services months earlier.[25]

By contrast, an important Universal director like John Murray Anderson (who had helmed *King of Jazz*) was sitting idle during the *Dracula* shoot.[26] As the *Hollywood Filmograph* wrote in August 1930, "it cannot be said at this time whether the veteran stage producer will select a musical or dramatic offering as his next Universal picture."[27] But Junior Laemmle did not choose Anderson or anyone else to direct *Dracula*, even though he easily could have: instead, he chose Browning. Carewe's name on the *Dracula* publicity photos was nothing more than a typographical error, as both Carewe's *Resurrection* and Browning's *Dracula* appeared together in numerous advertisements for Universal in the autumn of 1930, with Browning's name and *Dracula* sometimes even listed *above* Carewe's. One could go further and say that it is a typographical error none-too-different from the repeated misspelling of Carewe's last name in Skal's book.

More important is the fact that there is *no* evidence that Junior Laemmle believed that he needed a stand-by director for Tod Browning. Indeed, for a studio undergoing a major strategic change and facing huge financial problems, it is rather bizarre to imagine Laemmle assigning a director he did not trust to *Dracula*. Skal has also raised another possible spectre with the director, claiming, "The effect, if any, of Tod Browning's drinking on *Dracula* is not known."[28] But there is absolutely no indication that Browning (who had faced problems with alcoholism in the early 1920s) drank to excess during the *Dracula* shoot, or that he had any other personal or professional difficulties of any kind that impaired his work on the film.

As noted in Chapter 2, Junior Laemmle took quick action against film star Mary Nolan in the summer of 1930. Then, as Chapter 4 explained, Junior Laemmle removed the famous novelist Louis Bromfield from *Dracula* at a given point prior to its production. Later, on 8 November 1930, while the *Dracula* shoot was underway, *Billboard* announced that Laemmle would add a number of sequences to Malcolm St. Clair's "completed" film *The Boudoir Diplomat*, recalling key cast members to shoot "elaborate" scenes for the "present production." All of that was in spite of the fact that director St. Clair had already left California for a European vacation.[29]

Taken together, these three examples depict a studio boss who was quite capable of taking decisive action, even if the talent that it affected – Bromfield, Nolan, and St. Clair – might have been displaced. It is difficult to believe Laemmle would ever have assigned Browning to such an important and risky film as *Dracula* if he had even the slightest hesitations about his ability to direct it successfully. And if there had been indications that Browning was not directing the film – allowing, for example, a cinematographer to direct it, something Laemmle would have learned from visits to the sets, or through communications with the associate producer or the assistant director or others – Laemmle would have fired Browning for violating his contract. Or E. M. Asher, in charge of that production unit, would have done in Laemmle's absence. But that certainly did not happen, nor is there any indication whatsoever that the studio was ever displeased with Browning's work on the film.

To denigrate the production process further, Skal notes that Browning shot the film "roughly in sequence – an odd and inefficient way to work, then as today…."[30] But problems exist with this statement, not least of which is that it represents an example of a scholar alleging that Browning did not direct "much" of the film while simultaneously giving him credit for controlling the schedule of the entire shoot. More to the point, it is necessary to accentuate Skal's word "roughly," as the film was definitely *not* shot in sequence. By contrast, the shooting schedule – which will be discussed at length in this chapter – reveals that Browning shot the film by location, meaning that he shot all narrative scenes in a given location over the space of one or more days before moving on to another location, a highly efficient and logical plan of action that comported with Hollywood norms of the time.

For example, Dr. Seward's library appears as a location periodically throughout the second half of the narrative, but Browning shot all scenes within it over a series of consecutive days, rather than, as Skal implies, shooting the first scene in the library, then moving to other locations that appear next in the narrative chronology, and then later returning to shoot the second scene in the library. By way of another example, Browning did not shoot the interiors of the London theatre (where Dracula first meets Dr. Seward, Mina Seward, Jonathan Harker, and Lucy Weston) until near the end of the production, by which time he had already shot all of the narrative action that occurs subsequent to that scene in the edited film (save for the film's climax at Carfax Abbey).

It is true that Browning shot the Transylvanian sequences prior to those that take place in England, but the key reason is quite clear. The cast and sets were ready, as opposed to those needed for the scenes set in London and Whitby, with the casting of two English characters – Jonathan Harker and Lucy Weston – not yet finalized. Moreover, it is quite possible that Browning – a director who had worked in the industry for many years, including at Universal – intentionally decided to shoot the Transylvanian scenes first given the elaborate sets they required. Browning was likely aware that the studio was facing financial troubles, as they had been reported in the trade press. As a result, he might cleverly have chosen to shoot scenes requiring the most expensive sets first, knowing that cutbacks might occur later.

Given the various problems inherent in many prior histories of *Dracula*'s production, it is important to construct a history out of all known primary sources, meaning available studio paperwork from 1930, reportage in film industry trade publications, and articles printed in the popular press. It is true that such sources did make errors on occasion, but reliance on them importantly avoids the anti-Browning and anti-*Dracula* biases that arose decades later.

In addition, the final shooting script and the released film are pivotal primary sources. Dated 26 September 1930, the shooting script importantly features the words "Approved by

Carl Laemmle, Jr." on the title page. A surviving title page also features the handwritten words, "Send Lugosi c/o Hollywood Athletic Club," a reference to the actor's then-current residence. Given these comments and the fact that the production began less than three days later, it seems apparent that the script is exactly what it purports to be: the "final draft."

And yet the finished film features quite a number of changes and additions to that final draft. Tod Browning once described his work as a director in this way:

> [The director] must photograph all the dramatic scenes called for by the script and any additional scenes that may occur to him. Scripts are no more than rough working sketches and the director is expected to elaborate on them as he goes along.[31]

Here Browning operated quite similarly to standard procedure in Hollywood. For example, in October of 1930, an article in the *Exhibitors Herald-World* claimed that, "new ideas and better methods of telling the story present themselves very frequently" during the production process, and added that the "director does not dare to ignore these new ideas."[32]

By the time that *Dracula*'s production began, Carl Laemmle, Sr. was on the East Coast, far from Hollywood. And, as will be shown, Junior Laemmle was ill during part of the shoot; he was also facing a number of challenges in the autumn of 1930, particularly the studio's mounting financial problems. For example, on 4 September 1930, the studio reported a net loss of $578,848.23 for the six-month period that ended on 3 May 1930.[33] This is all in addition to the fact that Junior Laemmle stopped supervising individual films during the period from August 1930 to February 1932.[34]

In other words, it is unlikely that either of the two Laemmles was involved with the myriad changes made to *Dracula*'s script during its production, many of which were extremely minor. Nor is there any shred of evidence to suggest that Karl Freund was rewriting the script once the production began. Associate producer E. M. Asher supervised *Dracula*, and next to Browning would have been the person watching over its production more closely than anyone else, which means he would assuredly have noticed if Browning was not directing the film. He also might well have made important contributions to *Dracula*, including in the form of discussions regarding what was and was not possible given its budget and eventual budget cutbacks. That said, Asher also oversaw other films under production at roughly the same time as *Dracula*, including *Resurrection*. Whatever his contributions, Asher was not in charge of the day-to-day, hour-by-hour responsibilities and artistic decisions made for *Dracula*, responsibilities that involved far more than conversations with (or without) David Manners.

And so who was responsible for the creative decisions that occurred on a daily and hourly basis? The likely explanation is that Browning did on the *Dracula* shoot what he described in the aforementioned quotation: he "elaborated" as he went along, even if in consultation with a variety of other persons, including perhaps Asher, Freund, Beal, and Fort. Such "elaborations" are apparent by a close comparison of the shooting script to the completed film. Plumbing the depths of the finished film in a kind of cinematic archaeology reveals not only changes to the script, but particular changes that *had* to have been made during the production process, rather than during post-production.

Here I would highlight the fact that it is not possible to know exactly who is responsible for conceiving of each of the large number of changes, but that is of course true of the productions of most movies. Filmmaking is a collaborative art, which has led to arguments regarding various important movies, whether they be Pauline Kael's criticism of Orson Welles for taking too much credit for *Citizen Kane* (1941) or artist Saul Bass' claim that he – not Hitchcock – directed the shower scene in *Psycho* (1960). But without even delving into these examples, it is safe to say that Welles directed *Citizen Kane* and that Hitchcock directed *Psycho*. There are many reasons why we can confidently make such assertions, ranging from analyzing a director's style over a body of work (auteur theory) to understanding the hierarchal administration of studio film sets in which – regardless of who developed particular ideas – the director ultimately decided, "Yes, we will do that," or, "No, we won't," save perhaps for intervention by studio producers, though such intervention did not normally occur in an ongoing manner over small matters like, say, extremely minor dialogue changes. In other words, studio directors directed their films, and Browning was no exception.

As a result, in the following production history, I will note changes that Browning made (or at a minimum approved) and use his name to recount them. Quite likely some ideas originated with the cast and crew (or others like Asher, for that matter). But the sheer numbers of these changes suggest a consistent directorial control. The same can be said of their uniform goals, including a concerted effort to build up Herbert Bunston's role as Dr. Seward (sometimes, it should be noted, to the disadvantage of David Manners' character), a desire to clarify key subjects like vampirism and wolfbane and thus ensure audiences understood them, an attempt to avoid potential censorship problems, and an aim to shorten the narrative by eliminating unnecessary dialogue.

In other words, rather than being a collection of random alterations, the changes suggest that a director was working with particular goals in mind. These changes began during the first two days of the shoot and continued thereafter with much regularity.

Shooting *Dracula*
29-30 September 1930: The Transylvanian Inn

On 29 September 1930, the first day of the shoot, Browning shot interiors and exteriors at the Inn.[35] The following day, he shot the interior of the coach that Renfield takes to the Inn, as well as footage of the coach at the Inn's courtyard. The crew shot these images on a hill at the Universal backlot, near what film historian George E. Turner once described as a "deeply rutted old wagon trail."[36] Universal rented the needed horses from Moore & Boyle Live Stock. For these scenes and indeed the entire film, Karl Freund shot 35mm using a silent-film aperture, perhaps because he knew that the studio would release a silent version of *Dracula*; for prints featuring an optical soundtrack, however, the image would have to be slightly cropped.[37] Frank Booth likely photographed the effective glass shot of the coach travelling to the Inn at roughly this same time; it seamlessly combined footage filmed at Vasquez Rocks northeast of Los Angeles with striking and quite believable mountainous peaks.

As filming began, *Dracula –The Vampire Play* appeared onstage at the Teck in Buffalo, New York for 29 September-4 October.[38] And on 29 September, the *Hollywood Reporter* announced that Lupita Tovar and "Carlos Villar" (as Carlos Villarias would be billed onscreen) had arrived at Universal to prepare for the Spanish-language version of *Dracula*.[39]

Carla Laemmle, niece of studio mogul Carl Laemmle, Sr., appeared in the coach ride and at the Inn; she was not yet 21, which made her slightly younger than her cousin, Junior

Publicity still depicts the arrival of Renfield (Dwight Frye, left) at the Transylvanian inn. The Proprietor (Michael Visaroff) stands at his immediate right. *(Courtesy of Kristin Dewey)*

Laemmle. She speaks the first dialogue heard in the edited film. In the coach, she reads aloud from a travel guide: "Among the rugged peaks that frown down upon the Borgo Pass are found crumbling castles of a bygone age."

Her memories of the scene are among the few that have surfaced regarding the film's shoot:

> *I was taken to the wardrobe department where I was fitted with the outfit of the secretary that you see in the movie. I was cast to play a rather timid, comic little secretary to a sour-faced English woman. It just so happened to be the opening coach scene in* Dracula. *I thought the eyeglasses would be a good prop.*
>
> *… I sat across from Dwight Frye in the scene to read the dialogue and fall over his lap to give the illusion of a rough and treacherous ride. The property men were juggling the coach out of camera range. There were at least four prop men. Otherwise, it was a stationary coach, a prop with an open front.*
>
> *There was another scene that I was aware of and that was the village Inn where I was standing*

outside the coach at the Inn alongside Dwight Frye and a couple of other actors. If you look close, you'll see me running into the Inn as the coach leaves in a long shot.[40]

Carla Laemmle appeared in no scenes other than those she describes, the result meaning that her memories of the film shoot are few. When asked about Tod Browning in 2012, she said she had no memory of him.[41] When asked about him in 2014, she said much the same, but suggested she had a vague memory of meeting him.[42] Either he did not introduce himself, given that she was such a minor player, or, during the ensuing eight decades, she forgot any discussions that they had.

Once shooting began, Browning immediately began to make numerous changes to the shooting script. Given that Junior Laemmle had already approved the script, the young studio boss would probably not have been involved in the minor changes that occurred thereafter. For example, the script calls for a four-year-old girl to be in the coach, but in the footage she is not present, perhaps due to space limitations in the set. The Englishwoman's dialogue "And why?" became "And why, pray?", perhaps to sound more English or aristocratic. And after the characters arrive at the Inn, Renfield speaks dialogue not in the script ("I say, porter" and "No, no, please put that [luggage] back up there").

Actor Michael Visaroff, as depicted in the March 14, 1931 issue of the *Hollywood Filmograph*.

In other cases, Browning seems to have made changes to clarify and heighten narrative information. For example, the final shooting script treats the discussion of vampires quite differently than the final film. The script has the Proprietor of the Inn converse with the Secretary about vampires in search of blood from their "victims." But Browning likely did not even shoot the Proprietor's conversation with the Secretary, as he instead filmed a new, important exchange between the Proprietor and Renfield, one that does not exist in the final shooting script. In it, the Proprietor says: "We people of the mountains believe at the castle there are vampires! Dracula and his wives, they take the form of wolves and bats. They leave their coffins at night, and they feed on the blood of the living." In this way, Browning redirects the information about vampires to Renfield, a major character (unlike the Secretary).

The discussion was necessary to define vampirism for members of the original audience, some of whom – as Chapter 1 indicates – might have understood the term somewhat differently. Indeed, as the *Los Angeles Times* told readers in 1930, *Dracula* was a "different kind of vampire."[43] Similarly, a review of the film in the *Los Angeles Examiner* claimed: "*Dracula*, in case you don't know, is all about vampires. Not the Theda Bara sort, but people who are dead and yet walk the earth between sunset and sunrise."[44] The impromptu exchange

Chapter 5 – PRODUCTION 157

Inside a home at the Transylvanian village. (Courtesy of Buddy Barnett)

between the Proprietor and Renfield is a clear example of Browning distancing *Dracula* from the Burne-Jones/Kipling/Bara tradition (and, with it, the "romance" genre), something the shooting script had already tried to do.

The new dialogue also presents information not present in the final shooting script, information regarding the inhuman forms that vampires take and the fact that the women at the castle are Dracula's "wives." The changes also allowed for an extra to shout dialogue that warns the sun will soon be setting while simultaneously lighting a lamp. Browning was quite happy with the result, later claiming that he could not have "see[n]" anyone playing the role [of the Proprietor] other than [actor Michael] Visaroff."[45]

By contrast, Browning sometimes deviated from the script to discard unnecessary narrative information. Consider Scene A-4 in the final shooting script, an interior sequence that shows three villagers in a "Peasant Hut" preparing for Walpurgis Night. The script suggests that the camera begin on a man placing the wolfbane in the room, then pull back and follow him as he places an oil lamp above the door. The camera would then move further back to show one woman praying at a fireplace and another woman lifting a baby to place a crucifix around its neck. But in the finished film, the scene eliminates the oil lamp, and the other action is depicted in a static shot, one that as a result places the greatest emphasis on the praying woman, not only because she is nearest the camera with an audible voice, but because the camera's distance from the others makes it difficult to determine precisely what they are doing. Her prayer connects nicely with the subsequent scene, in which an old woman

158   Chapter 5 – PRODUCTION

gives Renfield a crucifix. Here Browning rightly regarded the other action as unnecessary, as Renfield's new crucifix negated the need to show the child's crucifix; similarly, any emphasis on wolfbane in this scene would have been hard for the audience to understand, as it is only later in the film that wolfbane is verbally defined.

By contrast, Browning added an image of two worried villagers staring through a window, as well as of another woman crossing herself at the mention of Dracula's name; here the image is unique, though the basic idea may have been inspired by *Nosferatu*, in which an old woman at an Inn crosses herself while seated with two other women. At any rate, the final shooting script – which provides a thorough description for shots in this sequence – does not mention either image.

1 - 4 October 1930: Dracula's Castle and the Borgo Pass

On 1 October, Browning directed exteriors at the courtyard of Dracula's castle, as well as interiors at Dracula's chambers, continuing to work at the latter during 2-4 October. He also shot exteriors of the courtyard gates on 3 October, and night exteriors at the Borgo Pass on 4 October, the crew relying on a mountainous area on the west side of the Universal lot.[46] Here the film uses black horses for Dracula's coach, just as the shooting script suggests. It could also be that Browning shot the footage of Dracula emerging from his coffin at some point during these same four days, though that is unknown.

The press soon described the elaborate sets that Universal had built for Dracula's castle. In early October, the *Los Angeles Evening Express* wrote:

> *A great stone fireplace, its mantel higher than a man can reach, is one of the architectural features of a magnificent set just erected at Universal City, and now being used for some of the opening scenes of* Dracula, *the strange drama which is being directed by Browning.*
> *This enormous setting is the largest 'interior' ever constructed at the studio, entirely filling one of the new sound stages and representing a great-room in the mountain castle of Count Dracula. Carved stone pillars 14 feet in diameter support the vaulted ceiling, and the entire construction is of stone, including even the flagging of the floor.*[47]

The *Exhibitors Herald-World* also described Dracula's Chambers to members of the film industry, repeating the line that the set's fireplace was "higher than a man can reach."[48]

During this time frame, the press also announced news that Junior Laemmle and Tod Browning presumably knew a few days earlier.[49] On 3 October 1930, Louella O. Parsons wrote:

> *Lew Ayres has been taken out of* Dracula, *the creepy mystery play which Universal is producing. No, Lew hasn't been a bad boy, quite the contrary. He is needed for an important role in* Mississippi, *an original story by Ben Lucien Burman, which goes into production shortly. Robert Ames, who has been one of the talkies' white-haired boys since his success in* Holiday *[1930], replaces Ayres in* Dracula.[50]

The role in question was that of Jonathan Harker. As *Mississippi* did not start production during the *Dracula* shoot (indeed, it was never made), it could well be that Universal did not want to relegate Ayres – who had scored such a triumph in *All Quiet on the Western*

Above: Publicity still of Dracula and Renfield at the Borgo Pass. Below: Dracula and Renfield in "Dracula's Chambers." (*Courtesy of Jack Dowler*)

Front (1930) – to a role that had in fact become relatively small and unimportant.[51] As for Ames, Junior Laemmle and E. M. Asher had attended a preview screening of *Holiday* in the summer of 1930, and were apparently impressed with him.[52]

The industry trade press also announced that Universal had finalized its cast for the Spanish-language version of *Dracula*:

Carl Laemmle has signed up Eduardo Arozamena, Manuel Arbo, and Carmen Gerro [sic], thereby completing the cast for the Spanish version of Dracula *in which Lupita Tovar and Carlos Villar [sic] are featured. [Pablo] Alvarez Rubio rounds out the cast, which George Melford will direct for Universal.* [53]

This report noted that the production would not start for approximately ten more days.

More generally, on 5 October, the press quoted a proud Junior Laemmle describing his belief that the cinema had made important strides to eliminating crude melodramas, opting instead for subtler drama:

The realization of this has emboldened Universal to undertake the production of a number of stories which would have baffled us a short time ago. Not only have we demonstrated that situations based on psychological reactions can be effectively produced, but we know that the response of audiences will be enthusiastic.[54]

Here Laemmle may well have been thinking of several films, but given the timing, *Dracula* was likely on his mind.

At any rate, the scenes shot during these four days illustrate Browning's effort to improve upon the atmosphere and mood by making further changes and additions to the shooting script. For example, after Renfield's arrival at Dracula's castle, Browning adds an image of three bats flying outside the window: Dracula's wives in inhuman form.

And then there was Dracula's first appearance. Bela Lugosi allegedly insisted on applying his own makeup; at least four still photographs show him doing just that. But makeup artist Jack Pierce – who was also working on *Resurrection* – likely helped apply a small hairpiece that Lugosi wore, which created a more pronounced widow's peak.[55] Pierce might also have given Lugosi some advice on the rest of his makeup or even applied some or all of it, as it was far less overt in the film than what Lugosi had used as Dracula onstage. In fact, Pierce apparently had a green-tinted makeup created for the film by Max Factor.[56] At any rate, it is difficult to imagine that Pierce did not have some voice in Lugosi's makeup given his important role at Universal, as opposed to Lugosi's complete lack of film stardom in 1930. Those who might suggest otherwise would likely point to the publicity stills of Lugosi applying makeup, but it must be said that those were publicity stills for public dissemination in a period when Universal and others sought a "second Chaney," the "Man of a Thousand Faces" who applied his own makeup. In other words, the publicity stills were posed; they do not necessarily indicate reliably that Lugosi applied the entirety of his makeup himself.

The final shooting script recommended visually introducing Dracula in a single shot that moves inward to show his hand opening his coffin lid, then moving to a wide shot revealing the rest of the crypt, then moving back to a "full shot" showing Dracula's back; after surveying two coffins, he finally turns towards the camera and ascends a staircase.

Chapter 5 – PRODUCTION

In Browning's film, the camera does move inward towards Dracula's coffin in Shot A, but the shots that follow feature far more narrative and thematic information than the script describes. Strange fog lifts from ground near Dracula. In Shot B, a possum moves near another coffin, while one of Dracula's wives opens the lid to another coffin in Shot C. An insect crawls out of a wooden container (perhaps a coffin) in Shot D, which helps initiate a visual link between the vampires and other night crawlers. In Shot E, Dracula's wife sits upright in her coffin, while in Shot F we see yet another coffin, one containing a skeleton and a possum. We hear the possum moving against the bones.

Then, in Shot G, we see Dracula, standing upright. Unlike the description in the script, his back is not to the camera. Instead, he is staring directly into the camera, which tracks inward towards him. Shot H then offers a long shot of all three of Dracula's wives, visually introducing the women that the Proprietor has already mentioned. In Shot I, Dracula ascends the stone staircase.

During this time frame, Browning also filmed Dracula and Renfield in Dracula's Chambers, meaning the space where Renfield sits down at a dinner table. According to a

Dracula's wives inside of "Dracula's Chambers."
(*Courtesy of Anthony Osika*)

story printed in the film's pressbook, the fireplace crackled so loudly that the actors and crew had to wait for it to die down before shooting could begin.

For this scene, Browning made numerous changes to Dracula and Renfield's conversation, reordering some of it for thematic purposes (as the actors' blocking makes clear, rather than these changes being a later product of editing). In the film, after mentioning that he has "taken the liberty of having [Renfield's] luggage brought up," Dracula literally takes Renfield's cane, hat, and coat. He then leaves the room with Renfield's belongings through a door that opens on its own, thus removing all visual signs of Renfield's ability to travel or flee. Instead, it is Dracula who will control Renfield's movements. Here Browning added dialogue for Dracula's conversation with Renfield about their pending journey, words that do not appear in the script: "I have chartered a ship to take us to England."

Browning even changed minor aspects of the sequence in which Dracula pours Renfield a glass of wine. Instead of "I trust you will like it," as in the script, Dracula instead says, "I hope you will like it," perhaps in an effort to avoid what would have become a repetition of the verb "trust" in the scene (as Dracula earlier says, "I trust you have kept your coming here a secret"). In the script, Renfield sips the wine but offers no reply, whereas in the film he responds, "It's delicious."

The script then has Dracula say "And now, I'll leave you. I may be detained elsewhere most of the day tomorrow – in which case we will meet here – at sundown." But Browning eliminated the second sentence, instead having Renfield say "Well, goodnight," as the camera encircles him in the very same shot, which proves the change occurred during the production, rather than in editing. The result leads nicely into the final shooting script's closing line for Dracula, which did make it onscreen: "Goodnight, Mr. Renfield." Given the timing of the camera movement, the aforementioned changes were made during the shoot, rather than during editing.

But perhaps the most striking alteration occurs after Renfield faints in Dracula's Castle, his wine having been drugged. Dracula silently commands his wives to leave Renfield alone; the scene ends with Dracula crouching down onto the floor to bite Renfield, though a fade-to-black prevents us from seeing the actual penetration. The final shooting script does not describe either action. Instead, Renfield becomes dizzy after looking out a window and seeing a "drop of hundreds of feet to a dark chasm below." He then sees a bat and hits his head against the window, which causes him to collapse "unconscious, upon the floor."

Browning's decision was likely made due to a set that did not allow for that chasm to be visualized, but it also helps to clarify Dracula's control over Renfield for the rest of the film. It also directly contravenes Junior Laemmle's suggestion on a Bromfield-Murphy draft of the script that Dracula should "go only for women and not men."[57] And, rather bravely, the implications of the new narrative action ignored the *Code of Ethics for the Production of Motion Pictures* as adopted in 1930, which claimed, "Sex perversion or any inference of it is forbidden."[58]

Perhaps near this same time frame, Karl Freund secured the services of William Davison to build a model of the exterior to Dracula's castle. Recalling his work, Davison implied that Freund approached him prior to the production; if so, their meeting likely happened in late September, as Freund's involvement came close to the start of the shoot. Davison also claimed that Freund brought him a drawing of the castle:

I studied the drawing, and then I said, 'How soon do you need it?'
'Well,' he smiled, in Europe we wait for weeks and then the work is not completely satisfactory. I don't want to rush you, but I would like it as soon as it is convenient.'
I smiled myself. He didn't know I had a day and night crew.
'I'll have it for you in 24 hours.'[59]

Freund was surprised by Davison's speed and was excited by the results. Davison's crew created a castle that was "about 5 feet tall on a one inch scale. The whole set extended seven to eight feet in length and width. It cost around $2,000."

6 - 7 October 1930: The Main Hall at Dracula's Castle

Following a break on Sunday, 5 October, Browning spent two days shooting the Main Hall at Dracula's Castle, with an effective glass shot adding vast expanse to the already impressive sets.[60] The footage of Renfield and Dracula aboard the *Vesta* may have been shot during the period as well.

Edward Churchill of the *Exhibitors Herald-World* visited the set while Browning filmed Dracula's introduction to Renfield. His report represents the key production anecdote published in the press in 1930:

… the company has designed magnificently weird sets which form a background for the stoop-shouldered menacing [Bela Lugosi] who moves through the product[ion] like a wolf stalking his victim.
I arrived on the Universal stage one day in time to see him walk up the dingy stairs of his deserted castle, and down again, holding a candle. … The candle flickers eerily as the camera cranks. The dull tread of his feet echoes through the silent stage.
Few men can walk up and down a flight of stairs and tell a story while doing it – but he has accomplished it.[61]

Churchill also had lunch with Lugosi, and was thus able to give his readers a small amount of biographical information about him.

Some weeks later, a trade-publication article offered yet another description of the main hall of Dracula's Castle as follows: "The entire interior is festooned with cobwebs, one of these great silken meshes being more than 18 feet in diameter and extending entirely across the grand stairway. The wall hangings droop in tatters, blackened with age and dust. Fallen blocks of granite litter the floors, and enormous trees thrust their dead branches in at the window openings. The scene is one of utter desolation."[62]

8 - 9 October 1930: Lucy's Bedroom and Van Helsing's Lab

On 8 and 9 October, Browning shot footage in Lucy's Bedroom, apparently finishing early enough on the second day to begin shooting interiors at Van Helsing's Laboratory. These scenes marked the first time that key actors other than Lugosi and Dwight Frye appeared before the camera. Here is also the first clear instance of Browning shooting footage out of chronological narrative order.

On 8 October, John Zinn of Universal Pictures sent a courier to deliver a contract for actress Frances Dade to Samuel Goldwyn, who had her under an exclusive contract at that

Dracula (Bela Lugosi) in the castle's "Main Hall." *(Courtesy of Buddy Barnett)*

time.[63] Zinn's accompanying letter noted, "Our driver is waiting to return our copy of this agreement."[64] What this means is that – while Universal had a verbal agreement to cast Dade as Lucy – the final contract was being executed on the first day that she appeared on the set. Beginning 10 October, trades announced Dade's addition to *Dracula*, claiming that the cast was "completed."[65]

That turned out to be incorrect, however, as Robert Ames was still listed as playing Harker, even though David Manners soon replaced him. On 8 October, the *Los Angeles Examiner* noted that Manners had just accompanied Elsie Janis to Lawrence Tibbetts' supper party. Among the others in attendance were Roland Young, Michael Curtiz, and Ramon Novarro.[66] That same day, another society column announced that Mrs. Tod Browning would co-direct a children's show for the Assistance League at the Ambassador Hotel with Mrs. John Ford.[67]

With regard to footage shot in Lucy's Bedroom, Browning made important dialogue changes between Lucy and Mina. In the finished film, the scene starts with Mina imitating Dracula's voice and his description of how Carfax Abbey "reminds" him "of the broken battlements" of his Transylvanian castle. The shooting script begins the scene with Mina laughing at Lucy's "romantic" nature, but does not have her imitating Dracula. Moreover, Browning added dialogue for Lucy, which she recites mysteriously and longingly while staring off into space: "Castles. Dracula. Transylvania."

The additional dialogue underscores Lucy's infatuation with Dracula, which becomes important given that he bites her in her bedroom only a short time after Mina departs. When he does, Dracula bites her offscreen, as he does with Renfield at his castle, a flower girl on the streets of London, and Mina in Whitby. Browning may have opted for this approach for several reasons, ranging from artistic preference to concerns over potential censorship. Indeed, he may well have considered the 1930 *Code for the Production of Motion Pictures*, which warned that, "brutal killings are not to be presented in detail."[68]

Browning also made a notable change to the scene in Van Helsing's

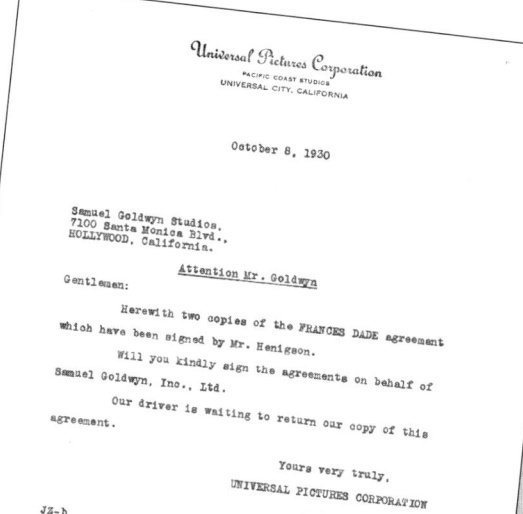

166　　　　　　　　　　　　　　　　　　　　　　　　　　　　　Chapter 5 – PRODUCTION

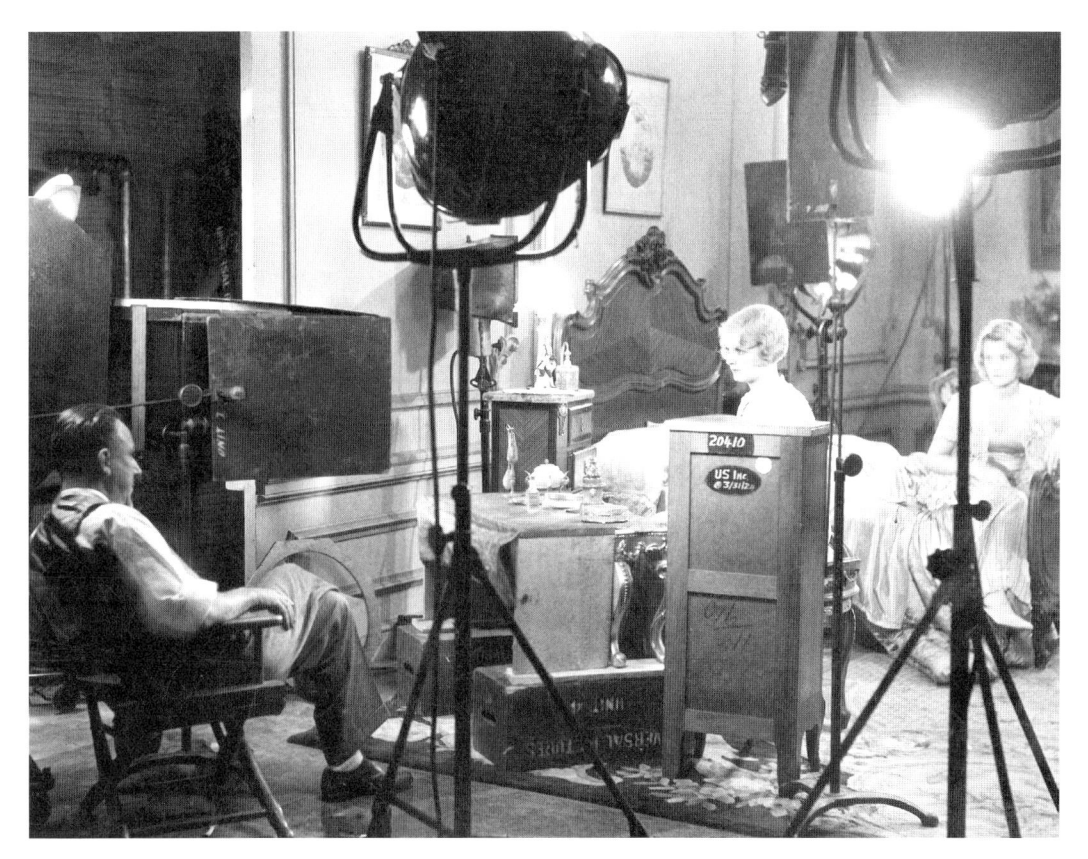

Above: Tod Browning directs Frances Dade and Helen Chandler on the set of Lucy's Bedroom. *(Courtesy of Photofest).* Opposite Top: The letter which accompanied Frances Dade's contract for *Dracula* (1931). Opposite Bottom: Actress Frances Dade, here depicted in January 1930 beside a photograph of Ronald Colman.

Laboratory. In the script, even though Dr. Seward is present in the room, he has no dialogue. In the scene that Browning filmed, Seward speaks lines originally meant for another doctor: "But Professor Van Helsing, modern medical science does not admit of such a creature. The vampire is a pure myth. Superstition." The result gives actor Herbert Bunston more screen time and dialogue, and also highlights the fact that the two characters know each other, which more clearly explains why Van Helsing appears at the Seward Sanitarium immediately thereafter.

It is difficult to determine exactly when Universal cast Herbert Bunston, the stage actor who reprised his Broadway role of Dr. Seward for the film, though they had certainly done so by 6 October.[69] Born in England in 1874, Bunston had appeared on the London stage in such plays as *A Run for His Money* (1916).[70] He also made a name for himself in New York theatre circles, acting in such plays as *That Awful Mrs. Eaton* (1924) and *Simon Called Peter* (1924).[71] Shortly before working in *Dracula*, Bunston appeared in the film *The Lady of Scandal* (1930).[72] Given that he was already in Hollywood, Bunston provided Universal with a great opportunity. Here was a chance to cast another original member of the Broadway version of *Dracula*, but in the form of a local actor who likely did not command a high salary. Universal valued his contributions enough that his name appears above Frances Dade's on *Dracula*'s onscreen credits, even though Dade had received much more publicity during

Chapter 5 – PRODUCTION

1930 due to her connection with Sam Goldwyn and her appearance in *Raffles* (1930) with Ronald Colman.

10 October: Renfield's Room and the Upper Hall

On 10 October, Browning shot Renfield in his cell (or "Room," as the production schedule calls it) at the Seward Sanitarium. The footage included the extremely impressive crane shot that begins at the sanitarium gates and floats gently through the air until Renfield's offscreen scream causes the camera to move upwards and reveal Renfield and Martin through the barred window to Renfield's cell. It is clear that Browning made a decision to go beyond the shot description as detailed in the script, as he gave another inmate the following new line of dialogue: "He probably wants his flies again!" The movements of the crane shot are carefully coordinated not to move immediately screen left and upwards to Renfield's room at the sound of his scream, but rather to move first towards screen right in order to capture the other inmate speaking this new dialogue.

That same day, Browning directed the two brief scenes that take place in the sanitarium's "Upper Hall," meaning the small office where Martin reads the newspaper story about the "Woman in White" to two nurses. Again, it is clear that Browning made changes to the script. After Martin reads from the newspaper account, he speaks dialogue that is not present in the final shooting script: "Vampires," he says, which briefly summarizes the narrative he has just read. Irish-born actor Charles Gerrard – who had appeared in films since 1916 – portrayed Martin. In 1927, *Motion Picture Stories* magazine labeled him a "persistent" screen villain.[73] Gerrard's name first appeared in print in conjunction with *Dracula* on 6 October.[74] By mid-November, having completed his work on the film, he would act in *The Man Who Came Back* (1931) at Fox.[75]

On the night of 10 October, director George Melford began directing the Spanish-language version of *Dracula*. Paul Kohner – who was then in charge of all of Universal's foreign-language productions – supervised the film. Melford's crew shot at night while Browning's crew shot

Renfield (Dwight Frye, left) and Martin (Charles Gerrard, right) in "Renfield's Room." (*Courtesy of Buddy Barnett*)

168   Chapter 5 – PRODUCTION

Publicity still of Bela Lugosi depicts him putting on his makeup. The choice to shoot these photographs might have been an effort to connect Lugosi to Lon Chaney, Sr., the "Man of a 1000 Faces."

in the daytime. At times they would be filming on the same sets; at times, they would not. At roughly the same moment, Universal was preparing the short comedy *Scared Stiff* for release. In it, two inspectors search for diamond thieves, one of whom is dressed in "gorilla garb." To add to the comedy, a real gorilla is also on the loose until it ends up handcuffed to one of the detectives.[76]

11 - 14 October: Dr. Seward's Office, the Theatre Exterior, the Weston Home, and the Hospital

On 11 October, Browning directed interiors at Dr. Seward's Office, as well as the exteriors of the theatre (including, presumably, Dracula biting the flower girl) and of Lucy's home (meaning the shots of Dracula on the street looking up at her bedroom window). After breaking for Sunday, 12 October, Browning spent 13 October directing more interiors at Dr. Seward's Office, as well as at Seward's Laboratory (meaning the room where Van Helsing first meets Renfield, who appears polite before sharply warning the professor to keep his "filthy hands" to himself. This room appears to be litle more than an office, given Seward's desk, but the script refers to it instead as a "Laboratory"). Then, Browning shot interiors at the hospital and of Dr. Seward's library terrace on 14 October.

As for changes to these particular scenes, Browning elected to make one key modification in an apparent effort to pre-empt trouble with censors. When Dracula bites the flower girl before going to the theatre, the film does not show – as the final shooting script suggests – Dracula's "fang-like teeth," a physical feature regularly noticeable in *Nosferatu*. Actress Anita Harder, born in 1905, portrayed the flower girl, and was presumably cast only days before Browning directed this scene.

With regard to the hospital, actor Wyndham Standing, who had worked in films since 1915, portrayed the surgeon. Coincidentally, his sister Joan Standing would also appear in *Dracula*, playing a maid at the Sanitarium.[77] During the hospital shoot, Browning likely filmed a closeup of the bite marks on Lucy's neck that did not make it into the final edit. Such a closeup appears in the Spanish-language version of *Dracula*; the actress in the image has blonde hair (as opposed to the dark hair of Carmen Guerrero, who portrayed Lucia Weston in that film), and so it was likely filmed by Browning's crew.[78]

Numerous minor dialogue changes occurred during the filming at Seward's Laboratory. Among them was a new line for Dr. Seward. After Renfield warns Van Helsing that he knows "too much to live," Seward scolds him by saying, "Now, now, Renfield!" Once again, Herbert Bunston received more dialogue.

On 11 October, the *Los Angeles Evening Express* printed a brief anecdote about the *Dracula*'s production:

'I'll be there with my hair in a braid!'
 This is a common crack, but a certain person at Universal City was startled to hear director Tod Browning had put the idea into practice.
An Eastern newspaperman, hunting for the director, asked directions of a man carrying 'props.'
'Mr. Browning is over on the Dracula set,' said the workman; 'the man with the barette [sic] on.'
'With the barette on?' gasped the reporter.
'Sure!' answered the other. 'A barette on his head.'

The story's punchline was that the newspaperman 'finally found Browning, wearing a blue beret!'

That same day, the *Hollywood Filmograph* published a story that also seemed to be the product of a studio publicist. "So horrible is this grotesque monster [Dracula] that everyone on the Big U lot is terrified whenever Bela Lugosi emerges from his dressing room."[79] More believable was *Film Daily*'s announcement on 13 October that "Carl Laemmle, Jr. has signed Bela Lugosi to a long term contract. … Young Laemmle, it is learned, has instructed his scenario department" to find appropriate stories for Lugosi's next films.[80]

15 -18 and 20 - 24 October 1930: Dr. Seward's Library

For eight days (divided by a break for Sunday, 19 October), Browning filmed scenes at Dr. Seward's Library, the set where Mina tells Harker about her dream, where Van Helsing discovers the marks on Mina's throat, where Renfield describes the rats he has seen, where Van Helsing shows Dracula the mirrored cigarette box, and where Dracula attempts to hypnotize Van Helsing.

On 22 October 1930, *Film Daily* noted that *Dracula* and the Spanish-language version of the same represented two of the eleven units currently in production at Universal. Three other feature films were underway: Edwin Carewe's *Resurrection*, Hobart Henley's *Half Gods* (re-titled *Free Love* for its release), and Vin Moore's *The Cohens and Kellys in Africa* (1930).[81]

A publicity still of Conrad Nagel and Genevieve Tobin for Universal's film *Free Love* (1930). Its shooting schedule overlapped with *Dracula*'s.

Chapter 5 – PRODUCTION

During *Dracula*'s first two weeks of production, Universal also completed the ten-chapter serial *Finger Prints* (1931); the studio then began work on two-reel comedies starring Slim Summerville.[82] *Film Daily* also noted that approximately twelve of the studio's productions for 1930-31 were adaptation of Broadway stage plays, *Dracula* among them.[83]

One week earlier, on 15 October, trade publications announced that David Manners had replaced Robert Ames in the role of Jonathan Harker.[84] A newspaper article claimed that the reason was the fact that Ames was busy working on another film, which was certainly accurate, as he was costarring in *Millie* (1931), a film that RKO would release only days before *Dracula*. Another reason for the change might have been Ames' personal troubles, though that is by no means certain.[85] His drinking and "arguing" led to a divorce from his wife in November.[86] At any rate, on 16 October, the *Los Angeles Evening Herald* joked:

> As fast as you print leading men in *Dracula*, Universal changes them. First it was Lew Ayres. Then it was Robert Ames. Now, David Manners, the nice young chap of *Journey's End*, will do the honors.[87]

The following day, Louella O. Parsons column added, "On a moment's notice, young Manners was rushed into the part...."[88] Though Manners had never previously worked with Browning, he had costarred with Helen Chandler in the Warner Bros. film *Mother's Cry* (1930) only a few months earlier.[89]

Much has been made of the fact that Manners made $2,000 per week, particularly in two books written by David J. Skal, who claims the actor pocketed "four times" Bela Lugosi's salary.[90] Why this would have seemed necessarily peculiar to any historian is difficult to understand, given that in 1930 Lugosi was a virtual unknown to American moviegoers, whereas Manners had just appeared in *Journey's End*. And there was the also the issue of Manners' last-minute casting. Perhaps here was an apparent opportunity for historians to decry (or lament, as the case may be) Lugosi and/or *Dracula*'s production process.

But the key issue is that – as the introduction to this chapter already noted – Manners certainly did *not* in

Actor David Manners, who replaced Robert Ames in the role of Jonathan Harker.

> **FIRST NATIONAL PRODUCTIONS CORPORATION**
> FIRST NATIONAL STUDIOS
>
> TELEPHONE: GLADSTONE 4111   CABLE ADDRESS: "FIRNATEX"
>
> BURBANK, CALIFORNIA
>
> October 14, 1930.
>
> 2. You agree to pay us for the artist's services the sum of Five Hundred Dollars ($500.00) per week, said compensation to start on the date of the commencement of the term hereof and to continue thereafter until the expiration of said term. Compensation for the last weekly period of said
>
> Yours very truly,
>
> FIRST NATIONAL PRODUCTIONS CORPORATION
>
> By _____
> Assistant-Secretary

Excerpts from the contract covering First National's loan of David Manners to Universal.

fact make $2,000 per week for *Dracula*. In October 1930 (and since 14 March of the same year), Manners was under contract at First National at a salary of only $300 per week.[91] In a surviving legal agreement at the Warner Bros. archive at the University of Southern California, First National loaned Universal "the services of DAVID MANNERS hereinafter referred to as the 'Artist' to portray the juvenile lead in the photoplay entitled *Dracula* to be produced by you." The text continues as follows:

> *You agree to pay us for the artist's services the sum of Five Hundred Dollars ($500.00) per week ... the artists [sic] engagement with you hereunder is to be for a period of no less than four (4) weeks, and you guarantee that the weekly compensation to be paid by you to us underunder shall aggregate not less than Two Thousand Dollars ($2,000.00).*[92]

The agreement also required Universal to "reimburse" First National an additional "sum of Fifteen Hundred Dollars ($1,500.00) [that] shall be payable to us concurrently with the execution thereof," the purpose being what we would expect: reimbursement for "salary accumulation." Manners absolutely did not make $2,000 per week, nor even did First National. In fact, Manners apparently received no more than his standard weekly salary of $300 as per his First National contract, with First National pocketing the overage, a very common practice in studio loans at the time. It is an unsubstantiated and

Chapter 5 – PRODUCTION

sadly repeated myth that Manners made more money per week than Lugosi. Indeed, he likely made no more than $1,500 total for what became no more than five weeks of work. Indeed, it is possible he made less than that amount, as the same agreement between Universal and First National allowed for Universal to pay a pro-rated salary for any final week that became less than six days of shooting. What is certain is that Manners made less money than Lugosi for *Dracula*.

The same day that the Manners story appeared in the press, *Variety* reported that Universal was already planning Tod Browning's next film, an adaptation of the play *The Up and Up*, which had scored a success in New York after opening in September 1930. Junior Laemmle purchased the rights to adapt the play sometime during the third week of October.[93] Such an announcement hardly suggests Browning was not actually directing *Dracula* or that the studio in any way held him in contempt, as by that time the film was at least three weeks into production.

The studio expected Browning go into production on *The Up and Up* in only three weeks' time, meaning immediately after the *Dracula* shoot ended.[94] The rush came from the fact Universal's agreement for the property allowed them to produce the film while it was still appearing on Broadway, a somewhat rare provision that presumably cost the studio more money.[95] Universal's choice of Browning was obvious given his work on crime melodramas like *Outside the Law* (1930), as *The Up and Up* depicted the "under-world" by revealing the "seamy side of speakeasy life."[96] Then, only days later, *Hollywood Reporter* announced that Browning would likely direct Universal's adaptation of the Charles G. Norris novel *Seed*, another important project.[97]

On 15 October, *Film Daily* printed a front-page story praising both Junior Laemmle and Universal, the journalist having just visited the studio:

> Under his direction have just been completed two enormous new sound stages and a modern laboratory costing about a quarter of a million. We made a tour of Universal City under his personal guidance. Never have we seen this historical old lot more finely trimmed for action. Never was there less confusion and more spirit in evidence.[98]

The story ended by acknowledging Junior Laemmle's record of accomplishments, which at that time seemed to be getting more impressive.

Only one week later, Universal ran a full-page "Straight from the Shoulder Talk" advertisement in which the studio reminded readers of its recent box-office success with such films as *All Quiet on the Western Front* and *Outside the Law*. The studio predicted that *Resurrection* and *Dracula* were "looming as two of the biggest and finest pictures ever produced."[99]

The industry press also reported information specific to *Dracula*. For example, on 19 October, *Film Daily* announced that Charles "Danny" Hall's drawings for the sets of *Dracula* (and *All Quiet on the Western Front*) were on exhibit at Hollywood's Knickerbocker Hotel.[100] Then, the *Exhibitors Herald-World* described a fire "of unknown origin" that destroyed the Transylvanian Inn set on 23 October. Browning's crew had already used the set, but it had to be rebuilt "at once" for the Spanish-language *Dracula*.[101]

News of *Dracula*'s stars also appeared in the press. On 18 October, Louella O. Parsons' column told readers: "An interesting piece of news brought to our ears is the happy marriage of Helen Chandler, New York actress, here in Hollywood, to Cyril Hume, well known author. Everyone in Hollywood seems to know that pretty little Miss Chandler and the author of *The Centaur* are man and wife. I just happened to hear it today. Miss Chandler is now at Universal playing the lead in *Dracula*. It's about a year ago that she came out here to make talkies and it was at that time that she was married."[102]

As for the scenes filmed in Dr. Seward's Library, Browning made numerous changes, ranging from many minor alterations to the dialogue to larger narrative modifications. When Renfield pleads with Harker and Seward to be "guided" by Van Helsing, it seems clear that Browning cut some three pages of dialogue in which there is much discussion of Van Helsing saving Renfield's "soul" and whether "God" would condemn a lunatic or whether he will be "damned forever." It is quite likely that some of this dialogue was shot and later cut in editing, as the scene in the released film shows Renfield talking directly to Harker, then – after a brief and somewhat unnecessary cutaway of Van Helsing – Renfield is talking directly to Seward, the geographical shift happening within the space of approximately two seconds

Edward Van Sloan and Bela Lugosi appear in the set known as "Dr. Seward's Library." *(Courtesy of Anthony Osika)*

But the bulk of the dialogue was definitely eliminated during the production, as a single shot of Renfield imploring Harker to take Mina away from the sanitarium also includes Renfield's recognition of Dracula in bat form at the terrace doors. In the final shooting script, two pages of dialogue occur in between those exchanges. Browning clearly discarded that dialogue on the set, presumably in an effort to speed up the action. The same was also true of other dialogue that Browning eliminated during the production process, as he replaced Van Helsing's line "I want you to help me prove something," with the single word "Look" when confronting Dracula with the mirrored cigarette box.

Other changes may have occurred to ensure that given dialogue was befitting a particular character. Browning had Lugosi's Dracula ask Mina if he can "call later" to inquire after her health, whereas the script's Dracula simply states that he will return at a later time. Similarly, Browning did not have Lugosi read the shooting script's dialogue "It was unavoidable" after smashing the cigarette box. Instead, Lugosi says, "I dislike mirrors. Van Helsing will explain," which is more polite and reserved, more in keeping with Dracula's earlier dialogue to the same characters. and thus creating a greater contrast to his animal-like anger when he first sees the mirror.

After Dracula smashes the cigarette box and departs, the script has Harker exchange dialogue with Van Helsing. But in the film, Seward – who is framed in a two-shot with Harker – speaks dialogue not present in the script: "Wild animal? Like a madman!" He also spoke a variation on what was intended to be Harker's dialogue ("What on earth caused that?") and a replacement for another of Harker's lines ("Follow?", in response to Van Helsing's comment as to why Dracula left through the window). These changes have little narrative purpose, but they do feature Seward in a way that the script did not. Here are additional examples of Herbert Bunston receiving more dialogue than the script gave him, perhaps as part of an effort to make one of the play's original cast members seem more present in the film. By contrast, of course, these are also further examples of David Manners losing dialogue.[103]

Browning also made an important change to Dracula's encounter with Van Helsing. The script finds Van Helsing unable to get wolfbane out of his vest pocket because of Dracula's hypnotic powers. Van Helsing struggles, but cannot overcome Dracula's command to place the wolfbane into a drawer. Dracula's control is finally broken when the two lose eye contact, and then Van Helsing produces a crucifix. Dracula flees, with Van Helsing nearly collapsing from mental exhaustion.

But Browning did not shoot this footage, or if he did, he also chose to shoot a wholly different conception of the scene. In the released film, Van Helsing breaks from Dracula's hypnotic control and then reaches for his vest pocket. Dracula presumes it will be "more wolfbane," but Van Helsing advises him that the object is "more effective." Dracula lurches forward, scoffing "Indeed!" before being repelled by a crucifix. The new dialogue speeds up the narrative action and also makes Dracula more physically assertive.

Browning did much more than change dialogue, however. He also added new narrative situations, sometimes in an effort to clarify particular plot developments. For example, in terms of Seward's Library, Browning created an exchange between Van Helsing and Seward that does not exist in the script. In it, Van Helsing explains: "Dracula boasts that he has fused his blood with that of Miss Mina. In life she will now become the foul thing of the night that he is."

He also modified some of Renfield's dialogue as well, perhaps to clarify how Renfield has broken out of his barred room. After Seward threatens to put him in a strait-jacket, the script finds Renfield responding, "I'm afraid it will do no good now, doctor," but in the film Renfield instead says, "You forget, doctor, that madmen have great strength." Van Helsing interjects: "Dracula has great strength, eh Renfield?", to which Renfield (in more new dialogue) dismissively repeats, "Words, words, words."

Other changes to scenes in the library could have been made to prevent accusations of religious impropriety. In the script, Dracula boasts to Van Helsing that Mina will "live though all Eternity, as I have lived!" Browning changed the dialogue to have Dracula say that Mina would "live through the centuries to come, as I have lived." The minor change removes Dracula's invocation of a Christian afterlife as embodied in Psalms 90 in the Holy Bible, which specifically uses the possessive phrase, "God's Eternity." Such might have been particularly wise given the fact that Renfield seems to draw an uncomfortable parallel between Dracula and Moses, who parted the Red Sea in Exodus in the Holy Bible. That dialogue remains in the final film: "A red mist spread over the lawn, coming on like a flame of fire, and he parted it…"

25 October-3 November 1930: Mina's Bedroom

For seven days, Browning shot footage in Mina's bedroom, his work being broken up by two Sunday breaks (26 October and 2 November); he may have shot some of the footage on the terrace during these days, though there is a brief mention of "terrace" on the shooting schedule's earlier notations for 14 October. At any rate, it is certain that Browning also shot exteriors at the sanitarium during this phase of the production (25 and 27 October), with the surviving production schedule specifically noting that the first exteriors were shot at night. Such footage likely included the outdoor scene in which Dracula wraps his cape around the hypnotized Mina. At roughly the same time, *Dracula–The Vampire Play* appeared onstage at Detroit's Lafayette Theatre.[104]

On 28 October, *Film Daily* mentioned that Josephine Velez – sister of Lupe Velez, then starring in Edwin Carewe's *Resurrection* – had joined the *Dracula* cast.[105] The following day, the same publication announced that Moon Carroll would also appear in *Dracula*.[106] Both would portray nurses, though Carroll had the larger role as Briggs. In fact, the *Los Angeles Times* published an article on Carroll shortly after she was cast, drawing attention to the fact that she had worked with Browning and Lugosi on *The Thirteenth Chair* (1929).[107]

That same day, *Film Daily* told readers that, "Universal executives are said to be highly enthusiastic over the performance of Bela Lugosi in *Dracula*, which Tod Browning is directing as one of the company's big feature productions."[108] The following day, the publication added that – as a "reward for his excellent work in *Dracula*" – Lugosi would likely star in *The Red Mystery*, a German novel that Junior Laemmle had recently acquired.[109] Whatever his precise involvment, Laemmle was paying enough attention to *Dracula*'s progress to watch Lugosi, on the set and/or in rushes. By extension, he was likely aware of Browning's progress in some detail, meaning once again that he would have known if Browning was not directing the film.

Also on 28 October, *Film Daily* published a column entitled "Picture of the Month Club," a list of current productions that represented the "best-from-each-lot." The trade heralded *Dracula* for Universal (rather than Carewe's *Resurrection*), the rest of the list including such films as *Sin Takes a Holiday* (Pathe), *Morocco* (Paramount), *Dirigible* (Columbia), *Kismet* (First National), *The Life of the Party* (Warner Bros.), and *Cimarron* (RKO).[110]

By the end of October, the *Hollywood Reporter* noted that Universal would shoot three multi-lingual versions of *The Boudoir Diplomat* – one in Spanish, one in French, and one in German – in eight-hour shifts around the clock.[111] At that point, the Spanish-language version of *Dracula* was still underway. In fact, on 25 October, *Variety* wrote: "Torba Avalos, Professor of Spanish at Mexico University, is here directing dialog on U's Spanish *Dracula*."[112] The same trade also claimed that Universal had just given Paul Kohner a "fat bonus check," not specifically due to the Spanish-language *Dracula*, but instead because he had just "completed ten years at Universal."[113]

Then, on 3 November, the *Hollywood Daily Citizen* described a problem involving Mary Nolan, Universal's troubled star:

Since Mary Nolan's unfortunate publicity in the newspapers some weeks ago, she has temporarily dropped from sight, as far as her professional career is concerned. She holds a years [sic] contract with Universal, and I understand that Junior Laemmle is planning to star her in The Up and Up. *This is the racetrack story that Tod Browning will direct. Her contract with the studio has four more months to run, and I hear that Carl Laemmle is thinking of retaining her for another year with a possible increase in salary. He has great faith in her acting ability, and leading ladies are so scarce in Hollywood right now that the producers are loath to let them go, especially when they have built up a fan following.*[114]

Here Universal again linked Browning's name to *The Up and Up*, with the studio expressing enough faith in him to believe he should helm one of their valuable new properties.

During the days leading up to the Nolan story, Browning continued to direct *Dracula*, making changes to scenes that take place in Mina's Bedroom, and to those that feature references to it. For example, Browning added dialogue in which Van Helsing says, "Miss Mina, both this room and your bedroom have been prepared with wolfbane. You will be safe if Dracula returns." In this case, Browning's addition helps explain the power of wolfbane to an audience that may never have heard of it.

But the key change with regard to these scenes is the number of onscreen visits that Dracula makes to Mina's bedroom. The final shooting script includes only one such visit, whereas the edited film shows two. While it is indeed possible that this change occurred entirely during editing, there are two reasons to suspect this decision was made during the production phase.

The first is Renfield's dialogue when he implores Harker and Seward to be "guided" by Van Helsing's wisdom. This scene comes immediately after the scene in which Dracula summons Mina outside into the night and envelopes her in his cape. In the shooting script, Renfield speaks the following dialogue:

I begged you to send me away – but you wouldn't! Now it's too late – it's happened –

But in the film, Renfield's dialogue importantly ends with an extra word that had to have been added during the production: "it's happened *again*." The addition of that single word suggests that Browning knew that viewers would already have witnessed Dracula visiting Mina's bedroom, which – together with Dracula and Mina's outdoor encounter – marked the need for the dialogue amendment. True, Mina does discuss her "dream" with Van Helsing, both in the script and in the completed film, which – together with Dracula and Mina's outdoor encounter – would possibly have merited Renfield's usage of the word "again." But the script – which features the dream discussion and outdoor encounter – does not include the word. It was added, presumably for some reason.

More importantly is the fact that the lighting and blocking in Mina's Bedroom are different in the two scenes, which also suggests that the decision to have Dracula visit the room twice occurred at some point during the production. In his first nocturnal visit, Dracula seems to be entering the room through the bedroom doorway (certainly that is implied in his bodily placement), and as he approaches Mina, he does so towards what would be the screen-left side of her body and neck (as opposed to Van Helsing's discovery of marks on the screen-right side of her neck). The lighting in the scene – while dim enough to suggest that Mina is sleeping – is fairly even and high-key.

By contrast, on his second nocturnal visit to her bedroom, Dracula enters very definitely through the terrace door, his movements in no way connecting with footage used for the first visit. In the shot depicting his entrance, the bedroom is much darker than any image used for the first visit, its key light source being from Mina's bedside lamp, which throws an unusual pattern onto the wall. Hence, the footage does not appear to have any similarity to that used in the other scene, a possible indication that the two visits were planned during the production phase. (Further consideration of this issue will occur in Chapter 6, which covers the film's post-production.)

4 November 1930: Carfax Abbey and the Seward Sanitarium

Browning directed interiors in the main hall at Carfax Abbey on 4 November, as well as nighttime exteriors at the sanitarium. During the same basic time frame (3 to 8 November), *Dracula–The Vampire Play* appeared in Cincinnati.[115]

Early November looked bleak at Universal Pictures. On 4 November 1930, the *Hollywood Reporter* announced that Universal posted a net loss of $146,340 for the quarter ending 2 August of that year, whereas the studio had posted a profit of $73,790 for the corresponding period in 1929.[116] Junior Laemmle was not at the studio when the news broke, however. Instead he was "directing the production activities from his home," where he had been "confined with a cold" since approximately 3 November.[117] Then, only a few days later, he denied rumors of a pending temporary shutdown at Universal, reassuring the press that the studio had "enough pictures on the prepared list to keep them working to capacity until March."[118] But his statement was not enough to quell the gossip, which erupted again in mid-December.[119]

As already noted, Carl Laemmle, Sr. left California prior to the start of *Dracula*'s production. As late as 8 October, *Variety* reported that he would travel to England with his biographer John Drinkwater; their trip was scheduled for sometime "around Thanksgiving," with the studio founder's planned return to Hollywood not coming until "around Christmas."[120] But those plans changed. On 18 October, Laemmle, Sr. announced that he was heading from New York to Hollywood, his intention being to "stay west for several months."[121] The stated reason was to see his new granddaughter, which could have been true, at least in part.[122] But financial concerns likely led him to cancel the European trip. In late October, for example, *Variety* announced:

> Universal's home office [did] some more shearing. About 50 are estimated to have been included in the shake-up. … Reason for the let-outs, second batch within a few months, is that the policy of Universal is not to cut salaries, but to reduce the working force during such economy moves.[123]

Here one has to wonder if Laemmle, Sr.'s presence was being felt at the studio even before he physically returned to it.

It was likely during late October and early November that the studio made financial cutbacks to *Dracula*'s budget. Discussing the shoot, Bela Lugosi once remembered: "Everything Tod Browning wanted to do was queried. Couldn't it be done cheaper? Would it be just as effective if …? That sort of thing. It was most dispiriting."[124] Similarly, John L. Balderston claimed in 1934 that he had understood budget cutbacks had occurred to

Van Helsing (Edward Van Sloan), Mina (Helen Chandler), and Harker (David Manners) on the terrace of the Seward Sanitarium. *(Courtesy of Anthony Osika)*

Dracula's 1930 budget as well.[125] But how much the film suffered is hard to know with any exactitude. What is clear is that Universal spent $2,000,000 more on productions during its 1930-31 season than it originally planned.[126] And cutbacks to film budgets were hardly rare, particularly during the Great Depression. Moreover, *Dracula*'s budget remained dramatically higher than the average budget for Universal films produced from August 1930 to February 1932, which was only $237,000 per picture.[127]

Given that he was shooting Carfax Abbey and nighttime exteriors at Whitby in early November, Browning likely intended to film the destruction of Lucy, the Woman in White, around the same time frame. In the shooting script, Fort and Browning wrote:

An eerie, awesome view of the churchyard at Whitby, as it lies beneath the wan light of a cloud-flecked moon. Ground mists curl, wraithlike, about the ancient and moss-covered tombstones, and in immediate fore., a melancholy willow droops sweepingly over a headstone. In b. g., and dotting the churchyard here and there are the more pretentious mausoleums and family vaults. The Weston vaults, one [of] which looks as if it had served as the final resting-place of the Westons for generations, is [sic] prominently established.

In the background, slowly approaching, is the figure of a woman in white – Lucy Weston. As Lucy draws closer to the floor of the open vault, we see it stands partly open. Lucy comes

walking slowly, as if in a trance, eyes staring straight ahead, and enters the vault. As the door of the vault closes slowly, with a faint creaking sound, behind Lucy and from somewhere near at hand, an owl hoots. CAMERA SWINGS AROUND TO MED. CLOSE SHOT [OF] HARKER AND VAN HELSING, crouched behind a nearby tombstone, and we get over Harker's reaction to Lucy's appearance, which has left him speechless and shaken.
He stares at the closed door of the vault with an expression of complete stupefaction – [he] can't credit his senses – there is a pitiful look in his eyes as if he almost suspected his own sanity. Van Helsing does not speak. He studies Harker gravely, watching to see the effect this will have upon him, his manner paternal. One hand goes out, steadying, to Harker's trembling shoulder. For the first time, we see that Van Helsing is carrying an oblong, paper-wrapped parcel. He indicates [the] parcel – pointing to [the] vault, [and he] says gravely,
VAN HELSING: *I would have spared you this, but I wanted you to see for yourself.*
Harker hesitates for a moment, the horror of the situation almost overcoming him. Then he braces himself and says through his teeth,
HARKER: *Come on!*

The final shooting script then cuts to the scene in which Dracula exerts hypnotic control over Briggs the nurse, who removes the wolfbane from the terrace door so that he can visit Mina's bedroom. Along with explaining the discovery of the Woman in White, the scene's chronological placement indicates why Van Helsing and Harker are not in the sanitarium and guarding Mina's bedroom themselves when Dracula visits it.

The narrative chronology of the final shooting script then returns to the vault to offer the conclusion of Lucy's destruction. After mentioning the scene should be framed in a medium long shot, Fort and Browning wrote:

Vault in fore. Through the open door there comes the sound of a heavy blow being struck – followed by a piercing, unearthly scream. An owl, disturbed by the sound, flutters across [the] scene. For a moment there is absolute silence, then slowly the figure of Harker appears, a ghastly stricken look on his face – he emerges and leans limply against [the] door of the vault, head bowed, [and] body sagging. Van Helsing follows after a moment, backing out, his eyes looking back into the darkness of the vault.
VAN HELSING: *Driving that stake in her heart was an act of mercy   may her soul rest in piece!*
[Van Helsing] crosses himself and starts to draw [the] door of [the] vault shut – Harker watches him in silence – then we see his horror give place to [the] cold fury of destruction, and he says harshly,
HARKER: *Let's go to the abbey!*

Absolutely none of the action in the churchyard cemetery appears in the Browning film, and it is extremely likely that the set was never built.

The key reason was presumably budgetary, as the churchyard set would have cost a good deal of money. Fort and Browning had intended for Lucy to walk through the same set when the bicycling bobby hears a child's scream, describing a "low ground-mist curling about the white headstones" while she walks "staring straight ahead, with unseeing eyes," passing by the camera and in "between the headstones." And yet in the Browning film (and in the

Chapter 5 – PRODUCTION

Spanish-language *Dracula*, which relies on an alternate take from Browning), Lucy walks through a simple wooded area in one single shot. No church or churchyard, no tombstones and no vault.

Here it would seem that Browning not only had to eliminate a scene from the script, but that he also had to improvise as a result, which he did in a manner differently than the Spanish-language version would. In the latter, the Van Helsing and Harker characters stand in front of an existing set – the gate to Carfax Abbey – and recount having killed Lucia (as she is called in that film). Director George Melford likely chose that set because Browning had used it when he shot the bicycling bobby. By his use of the set, Browning made the (perhaps necessary) decision for Lucy to be stalking children near Carfax Abbey, the implication being that she resides in the crumbling building, much as Dracula's wives reside in his Transylvanian castle. Likely this decision came as a result of being unable to build the churchyard set and the Weston family vault, which would instead have located Lucy in London rather than in Whitby.

Unlike Melford, Browning may not have filmed Van Helsing and Harker in front of the gate describing Lucy's destruction, even though the gate itself is not a cemetery gate. At any rate, Browning opted to leave Lucy's fate somewhat unclear. Speaking to Mina on the terrace, Van Helsing promises that, by the end of night, Lucy's "soul" would be "released." Later, in the script, Van Helsing's final dialogue to Harker and Mina at the film's conclusion was: "I shall remain – and fulfill my promise to Renfield." In the finished film, Van Helsing also remains behind at Carfax Abbey, but his rationale is more vague, as Browning changed the dialogue during the production: "Not yet. Presently," he tells Harker and Mina. By removing Renfield's name, Browning seems to imply that Van Helsing might also remain behind to destroy Lucy.[128]

5-6 November: The Theatre

On 5 and 6 November, in yet another example of how the film was not shot in narrative sequence, Browning directed the interiors of the concert hall, built over five years earlier for *The Phantom of the Opera* (1925) inside Universal's Stage 28.[129] Then, on 6 November, Browning shot material described as the "Interior of a Boudoir" (meaning the small room adjacent to Mina's bedroom, which features a vanity table), as well as exteriors of a road and graveyard. The latter likely included Lucy's aforementioned nocturnal walk, as well as the bobby hearing a crying child near the same location.

On 5 November, the Los Angeles press noted that David Manners had just attended a supper for Ruth Chatterton. Others present included Ronald Colman, Lois Wilson, and Paul Lukas.[130] Manners and Lukas had recently appeared together with Chatterton in the film *The Right to Love* (1930). That same day, *Variety* wrote that Dudley Murphy – who had worked with Louis Bromfield on the second draft of the *Dracula* script, and who would be credited on the shooting script for his "continuity" – had been "engaged by Pathe to direct shorts."[131] The *Hollywood Reporter* also noted that John Drinkwater's biography of Carl Laemmle, Sr. was "almost ready" for publication.[132]

As part of his ongoing changes to the script, Browning gave Dracula an additional word of dialogue after hypnotizing the usherette. After giving her instructions, Dracula commands her to "obey," which underscores his mental control over her.

Browning also sought to make certain that given characters were not bereft of dialogue in particular scenes. In the shooting script, Harker, Mina, and Lucy silently nod when

Mina (Helen Chandler) and Harker (David Manners) at the theatre. *(Courtesy of Buddy Barnett)*

Seward introduces them to Dracula at the concert hall; in the film, all three characters offer verbal greetings, which helps introduce the trio to the film's audience, as they have not been previously depicted. Moreover, Seward speaks an additional line of dialogue not present in the script; following Mina's line that it will be a "relief" to see lights burning at Carfax Abbey, Seward agrees: "It will indeed."[133]

7-14 November 1930: Carfax Abbey

On 8 November, George Melford completed his direction of the Spanish-language *Dracula*, having spent a total of 26 working nights on the film. Its total cost was $68,750, the film having benefited from the use of so much that was charged against Browning's larger budget. In other words, a comparison of the two budgets is highly problematic, as the Browning budget included the costly literary rights, the sets, and the props that the Spanish-language film relied upon. It is also worth noting that at $68,750 the film was far beyond Kohner's promise to Junior Laemmle in 1930 that Spanish-language versions of Universal's films could be made for "about $35,000 each."[134]

That said, the studio was likely pleased with Melford's work. Within a few days, Universal announced that he would direct the Spanish-language version of *The Boudoir Diplomat* (1930).[135] At roughly the same time, Carl Laemmle, Sr. encouraged other Hollywood studios to keep producing multi-linguals, warning that foreign markets would otherwise be lost.[136]

Dracula–The Vampire Play continued to be staged during the film's production. From 10-15 November, the Shubert Rialto presented a version in St. Louis.[137] The play also appeared in San Francisco on 9 November.[138]

Whether Junior Laemmle was at the studio during the final days of *Dracula*'s shoot is difficult to say with certainty. On 8 November, the trade press wrote that Laemmle ailed from "a combination of cold and overwork," and added that he would "probably go away for a fortnight's rest next week."[139]

All that said, on 9 November, the *Los Angeles Examiner* noted that Junior Laemmle had recently attended a surprise dinner for Sue Carol, other guests including Bing Crosby and Pandro S. Berman.[140] Then, on 13 November, the *Hollywood Daily Citizen* noted:

> Mr. Laemmle [Sr.] proved something … important when All Quiet on the Western Front was selected for first place by the Academy of Motion Picture Arts and Sciences. He demonstrated that a 21-year-old boy [Junior Laemmle] can be placed in charge of a studio and come through with flying colors.
> Last night when he discussed the proud triumph which has come to him and to Universal Pictures, Mr. Laemmle had but one thing to say, "All credit goes to Junior." The lifelong ambitions of the father had found fulfillment in the son!
> Over a year ago when Carl Laemmle decided to retire from active management of Universal Studios, he placed his son, who had barely reached his seniority, in charge of production. There were many who smiled indulgently, thinking that Uncle Carl was a bit mad to shift so much responsibility on a mere boy. There were some who scoffed openly at the idea of a lad being able to direct the destiny of a talking picture studio.
> Father and son were practically the only persons who had confidence in the arrangement. In the face of a critical world, they went about their business, and within one year they had turned the scorn of their competitors to praise.[141]

Mina (Helen Chandler), Dracula (Bela Lugosi) and Renfield (Dwight Frye) on the staircase inside the "Crypt" of Carfax Abbey. *(Courtesy of Anthony Osika)*

While accurate, the story neglected to mention the financial problems then plaguing the studio.

As for Tod Browning, his crew spent seven days filming Carfax Abbey, their progress interrupted for a break on Sunday, 9 November. Such work included the "Door of Crypt" (7-8 November), the interior of the "Crypt" (10, 13 and 14 November), and the interior of the "Catacombs" (11-12 November). These terms borrow from the shooting script, the "Crypt" being the area of the abbey that contains the staircase where Dracula kills Renfield, and the "Catacombs" being the area where Van Helsing stakes Dracula.

Browning made various changes to these scenes, one of which possibly occurred in an effort to avoid offending religious groups. In the final shooting script, Renfield pleads with Dracula on the crypt staircase, saying, "I can't face God with all those lives on my conscience, all that blood on my hands." But in the completed film, direct mention of God disappears, with Renfield instead crying: "I can't die with all those lives on my conscience, all that blood on my hands."

The other key change in this sequence involved Renfield's death. The script suggests that: "As Renfield's limp body comes slithering and rolling to the bottom [of the staircase],

Chapter 5 – PRODUCTION

where it lies in a broken, twisted heap." But Browning altered this plan during the shoot, having Renfield instead fall from the staircase before reaching its base, his body being hidden by some rubble. As with the other death scenes in the film, Renfield's occurs (or at least culminates) in an offscreen space.

Shortly after the Crypt and Catacombs shoot, the *Exhibitors Herald-World* described the Crypt to its readers: "Perhaps the most beautiful setting in the picture is the steep, narrow stairway leading down into the crypt – a seemingly endless succession of steps in a single unbroken curve. As an example of architectural beauty, this set is said to constitute a veritable triumph for Danny Hall, art director of the picture."[142]

During the same period as the Crypt and Catacombs shoot, Browning also filmed at the Borgo Pass (9 November) and at a location referred to as the "Proscenium Arch" (13 November). The latter is likely Van Helsing's curtain speech. Surviving frames make it appear that he is standing in a theatre in front of a movie screen, and that the speech was filmed as a single crane shot.

In addition, Browning shot at the "Boat" on 13 November, presumably a reference to Renfield in the hold of the ship that he and Dracula take to England, as well as the harbor scene after the ship has docked). In the shooting script, Fort and Browning envisioned a miniature of a boat encountering rough waters, which would serve as a metaphor of the

Harker (David Manners), Mina (Helen Chandler), and Van Helsing (Edward Van Sloan) in the "Catacombs" of Carfax Abbey. *(Courtesy of Anthony Osika)*

problems aboard ship. The script also describes Dracula emerging from his coffin, the horrified faces of two sailors, Dracula approaching the camera into a "huge closeup," and another sailor laughing maniacally before jumping overboard into the "surging seas."

From there, the script suggested brief shots, some "dissolving into others" and "some quick cuts" to create an intensifying pace. The images themselves would be of:

> CLOSEUP CAPTAIN AT WHEEL, screaming … SUPERIMPOSE FACES OF SAILORS, five or six, dissolving in and out – all wild with fear – screaming, staring – driven beyond the bounds of human endurance…
> LARGE CLOSEUP DRACULA, fangs bared.
> MED. SHOT SAILOR, vaulting over the rail … CLOSEUPS ad lib, to be worked out in detail later – ending with huge and impressive shot of Dracula, arms upraised, dark coat billowing in the gale, about to close in upon a screaming, helpless wretch he has cornered. And he does so.[143]

From there, the scene ends with a closeup of Renfield through the cabin window, "screaming and laughing and gesticulating, a stark, raving maniac."

There is no evidence that Browning shot this footage, perhaps due to time and budget constraints, but also perhaps due to two other reasons. For one, at some point after the completion of the shooting script, it is clear that a decision was made not to depict Dracula's fangs. Secondly, the scene might have been changed or cut due to Junior Laemmle's aforementioned suggestion that Dracula should "go only for women" While Browning did not take that advice in terms of Dracula biting Renfield, he might have insofar as an overt attack on the ship's crew. At any rate, the footage in the released film shows Dracula surveying stock footage of a ship's crew from a distance, the implication perhaps being that he will feed on them, but that is only loosely implied.

Despite cutting so much of the action, Browning shot footage of Renfield aboard ship that does not appear in the script, perhaps as part of improvising a wholly new conception of the scene. In it, Renfield kneels before Dracula, imploring the "master" to let him have lives once they arrive in England, "not human [lives], but small ones, with blood in them."

By contrast, Browning shot the harbor scene using the script as a clear guide, including its suggestion for a fascinating reliance on offscreen space, as voices without faces comment on the fate of the ship and captain. In an uncredited cameo, Browning supplied one of the voices himself, another indicator that he was not always "back in the shadows," as Manners had claimed. And here again, new dialogue appears as the scene ends, with a voice describing Renfield as being "mad" and "crazy," words that neatly introduce a full-screen newspaper clipping about the ship, an image that is not mentioned in the script.

15 November 1930: Pick Ups

On 15 November, Browning filmed "pick ups," though it is difficult to know what they were. One of them could well have been footage of the Proprietor (Michael Visaroff) describing vampires to Renfield. Browning clearly decided to make the aforementioned change (meaning the Proprietor speaking to Renfield about vampires, rather than to the Secretary) when the scenes were shot on 29-30 September 1930. But in the edited film, the scene unfolds as if it has been filmed over two, if not three, different days. One of them was likely in September. Another could well have been on 15 November. The third might have been shot during one day of filming in 9 December (or even on the single day of filming in January, though that seems unlikley given that notations of the January retakes do not mention the Transylvanian Inn).

At any rate, the initial two-shot of Renfield and the Proprietor looks in every way similar to all previous footage in the same scene. [See Figure 5A.] At a clearly coordinated moment, the two characters look towards offscreen space, creating an eyeline match to a village woman, depicted in a single medium shot. Curiously, when the film cuts back to a two-shot of Renfield and the Proprietor, important changes are visible. The angle of the shot has changed such that the background does not show any of the village buildings; this could be due to the set burning and being rebuilt. What is much more clear is that the Proprietor holds a *different* handkerchief than in prior shots. [See Figure 5B.]

Shortly therafter, a medium single shot of the Proprietor is intercut with the two-shot; here the Proprietor looks noticeably different than in either previous shot. In addition to continuity errors in this shot (such as the fact that his pipe erroneously appears in his right hand), the lighting is different. Indeed, Visaroff's makeup appears different, particularly in terms of his eyebrows, than in the aforementioned shots.[144] More importantly, a comparison of the background words on the wall of the Inn indicates that the set is neither the original set nor the rebuilt set as it appears in the Spanish-language version of *Dracula*. Entire words are missing from the advertisement, which in this medium shot also appears to be painted inside a recessed section of a wall. [See Figure 5C.]

Figure 5A

Figure 5B

Figure 5C

Whatever pick ups were filmed on 15 November, they did not require Helen Chandler. The day before, the *Los Angeles Times* noted:

> After staving off an operation for appendicitis for more than six weeks in order that she might finish her role in Universal's screen drama Dracula, *Helen Chandler, blond screen actress, entered Hollywood hospital last night and is scheduled to go under the knife this morning.*[145]

188   Chapter 5 – PRODUCTION

The article added that she had developed appendicitis "soon after" being cast for her role, and that she had been receiving daily treatments during the shoot from her doctor. The following year, Chandler told a movie fan magazine about the operation: "In *Dracula*, I played one of those bewildered little girls who go around pale, hollow eyes and anguished, wondering about things … I was wondering about when I could get to a hospital and part with a rampant appendix without holding up the picture."[146]

On 15 November, the *Hollywood Filmograph* printed Bela Lugosi's plea for "notable actors and artists" in the film community to take part in the "civic theatre movement" in Los Angeles.[147] One week earlier, the same publication quoted him as arguing that the developing talkie needed to recruit "stage trained people" in order to feature real artists.[148]

During this same time frame, *Dracula–The Vampire Play* continued to appear in numerous cities. From 17 to 22 November, it was staged at the Shubert in Kansas City, and from 22 to 27 December, it appeared at the Hanna in Cleveland.[149] The play also had an extensive and very successful run in Chicago in December 1930.[150] But producer Horace Liveright – who had brought the play to America – was not experiencing equal success with his own career. Paramount hired him in 1930 to supervise some of its film productions, but in November the studio announced that he was "through."[151]

The premiere of Universal's Spanish-language version of *The Cat Creeps* also took place during this period, with star Lupita Tovar in attendance at a theatre in Mexico City on 20 November. Broadcast inside the theatre via telephone were the voices of Junior Laemmle, Paul Kohner, and George Melford.[152] However, Universal halted production of the French version of *The Boudoir Diplomat* at roughly the same time, being unsatisfied with the French players "imported" to appear in the film.[153]

Conclusion

According to the production schedule, Tod Browning completed *Dracula*'s production at nearly $14,000 *under* the original $355,050 budget, which requires us to question once again David Manners' assertion that the shoot was disorganized.[154] While Browning may not have been able to shoot everything he wanted, particularly the destruction of the Woman in White at her vault, he had completed principal photography successfully, even if he did so roughly one week over schedule. His crew filmed for 42 days instead of the planned 36.[155]

To conclude the argument that Tod Browning directed *Dracula* and in such a way that the studio appreciated his work, it is worth examining the immediate path his career took after November of 1930. For example, on 8 December, the studio announced that it had just purchased the rights to W. R. Burnett's novel *Iron Man*, which Browning would "probably" direct in the "near future."[156] The studio already held the rights to Burnett's novel *Saint Johnson*, and Warner Bros. had earlier acquired the rights to his *Little Caesar*, which became a major film release starring Edward G. Robinson in early 1931.

Though the boxing drama might have little appeal to horror film fans of future decades, *Iron Man* was a prestigious property, causing Universal to cast Lew Ayres in the lead role. By mid-December, Ayres was taking boxing lessons in order to give a realistic performance.[157] After first considering Dorothy Burgess for the female lead, Universal cast Jean Harlow, the platinum blonde.[158] Browning directed the film in January of 1931, its production halted briefly when Ayres walked out during a salary dispute with the studio.[159]

Had Universal or either of the Laemmles believed that Browning did not direct *Dracula* for any reason, they would have fired him. Here was a studio in deepening financial difficulty, struggling to stay afloat amidst both the strategic changes that Junior Laemmle had instituted and the economic travails of the Great Depression. If Universal had any qualms about Browning's directing, the studio would certainly not have immediately put him in charge of another important property featuring two major stars.[160] But Browning did direct *Iron Man*, a film that received numerous positive reviews.[161] "Nicely made," *Variety* said.[162] *Motion Picture Herald* went much further, calling *Iron Man* "head and shoulders above the average story of fights and fighters," adding that it was a "thrilling and enthralling picture" handled "intelligently" by Browning.[163]

Jean Harlow in a publicity still for Tod Browning's film *Iron Man* (1931).

Following the production of *Iron Man* (and at a point when *Dracula* was scoring huge successes in American theatres, a subject that will be covered in Chapter 9), Browning's contract with Universal ended. The next one he signed was for an even larger salary, as well as a triumphant return to MGM. Here is yet another reason to dispel notions that MGM had fired him in 1929, as they would scarcely have hired him back if there had been major problems. Likewise, here is another reason to believe that Browning directed *Dracula*. Even unsubstantiated rumors of Freund directing *Dracula* would not only have made it to the office of Junior Laemmle – who stated in November 1932 that Universal had just cultivated Freund as a director "in recent days," not months – but such rumors would also have circulated to other studios.[164]

And yet Browning did sign an important contract with MGM in March 1931. The *Hollywood Reporter* described the situation as follows:

> *Tod Browning was put on the spot recently by two of our best producers, Irving Thalberg and Ben Schulberg. It seems that Tod had finished his Universal contract, went out to MGM to see some old friend, [and] ran into Thalberg who inquired: 'Would you like to come back to MGM?'*
> *They talked things over and Irving offered $50,000 a picture. Tod said: 'I will let you know later.' While this was going on, Browning's manager had extracted an offer from Paramount for $80,000 a picture. Browning goes to MGM as Irving told Ben he spoke first, with Tod asking himself 'Is there no justice?'*[165]

And so Browning celebrated his new long-term contract before heading to Europe for a two-month vacation.[166]

As he did, *Dracula*'s box-office gross continued to climb. Browning could take heart in that fact, as he did indeed direct the film. Claims to the contrary simply do not withstand scrutiny.

Chapter 5 – PRODUCTION

1. The original production schedule exists in the Universal Pictures collection at the Cinematic Arts Library at the University of Southern California. It is reproduced photographically in: *Dracula (The Original 1931 Shooting Script)*. Ed. by Philip J. Riley. (Absecon, NJ: MagicImage, 1990): 62.
2. Skal, David J. *The Monster Show: A Cultural History of Horror* (New York: W. W. Norton, 1993): 121.
3. Mank, Gregory W. and Gary D. Rhodes. "A Very Lonely Soul: A Tribute to Helen Chandler." *Monsters from the Vault* Vol. 10, No. 19 (Winter 2004): 29.
4. Moran, Frances Dade Van Every. Email to Gary D. Rhodes. 3 May 2011.
5. Rhodes, Gary D. Interview with Frances Dade Van Every Moran. 21 August 2012.
6. Norris, John. Interview with David Manners. 1974.
7. Skal, *The Monster Show*, p. 121.
8. Ibid., p. 121.
9. I perceive minor (if not major) contradictions in Skal's various accounts of *Dracula*'s production. While he has relied upon Manners' recollections to pronounce that Freund "directed much of the film," he has also on another occasion claimed (with his coauthor Elias Savada), "Browning's experience making *Dracula* may well have been stressful" (*Dark Carnival: The Secret World of Tod Browning, Hollywood's Master of the Macabre* [New York: Anchor, 1995], p. 153), an odd statement if Browning allegedly did not direct the film, or did not direct "much" of it.
10. Unfortunately, the published interview with Van Sloan has him saying nothing about the film other than that he believed Dracula smashing a hanging mirror with a vase (as in *Dracula–The Vampire Play*) was more effective than having the character break a mirrored cigarette box (as in the film version). See "Great Horror Figure Dies." *Famous Monsters of Filmland* 31 (Dec. 1963): 40-51.
11. Boland, Elena. "Manners Stands Apart." *Los Angeles Times* 16 Nov. 1930: 15.
12. Ibid., p. 15.
13. Nagle, Edward. "Dave To His Mother – Perhaps." *Picture Play Magazine* (Mar. 1931): 52-53, 107.
14. "Bela Lugosi Praises Director Tod Browning." *Hollywood Filmograph* 18 Oct. 1930: 12. The same quotation appears in "Timely Topics." *Film Daily* 20 Oct. 1930: 9.
15. Dickey, Joan. "A Maker of Mystery." *Motion Picture Classic* (Mar. 1928).
16. Mank, Gregory William. *Women in Horror Film, 1930s* (Jefferson, NC: McFarland, 1999): 339.
17. With regard to the fact that anecdotes from one film production do not necessarily have meaning to another, I recall my own interviews and conversations in the 1980s with actress Carroll Borland, who appeared in Tod Browning's *Mark of the Vampire* (1935). At times, she mentioned that she really didn't know what it was like to have been directed by Browning, as he hardly spoke to her (which hardly seems odd, given the fact she played a minor part and had extremely limited dialogue). But on other occasions, she spoke about how he devoted a huge amount of time to a special effect that allowed Borland's character to appear to fly with bat wings. She also described a conversation with him involving her idea that her character should hiss like a cat. Together, her memories seem somewhat contradictory, as two of the three comments suggest Browning did direct her.
18. In addition to the previously-cited books *The Monster Show* and *Dark Carnival* (with coauthor Elias Savada), Skal also covered the 1931 version of *Dracula* in *Hollywood Gothic: The Tangled Web of* Dracula *from Novel to Stage to Screen* (New York: W. W. Norton, 1990).
19. Skal, *Hollywood Gothic*, p. 130.
20. Skal, *The Monster Show*, p. 125.
21. "*Herald-World*'s Production Directory." *Exhibitors Herald-World* 18 Oct. 1930: 54.
22. Hays, Will H. Telegram to Carl Laemmle, Jr. 18 Apr. 1930. Available in the file for *Resurrection* in the Motion Picture Association of America, Production Code Administration collection at the Margaret Herrick Library in Beverly Hills, CA.
23. Laemmle, Carl, Jr. Telegram to Will H. Hays. 17 Apr. 1930. Available in ibid.
24. "Production Activities." *Hollywood Reporter* 13 Oct. 1930.
25. *Hollywood Daily Citizen* 1 July 1930.
26. "Dramatic Plus Music for Anderson at U." *Variety* 18 Oct. 1930.
27. "John Murray Anderson Prepares Next Picture." *Hollywood Filmograph* 16 Aug. 1930: 18.
28. Skal, *The Monster Show*, p. 124.
29. "Laemmle To Make Special of *Command to Love*." *Billboard* 8 Nov. 1930: 7.
30. Skal, *Hollywood Gothic*, p. 130.
31. "Cutting No Cinch, Browning Avers." *Exhibitors Herald* 25 Dec. 1920.
32. Clark, L. E. "Sound Reproduction." *Exhibitors Herald-World* 18 Oct. 1930: 55.
33. "U Shows Half Million Loss; Warner, General Theatres Up." *Exhibitors Herald-World* 6 Sept. 1930: 31.
34. Schatz, Thomas. *The Genius of the System: Hollywood Filmmaking in the Studio Era* (New York: Pantheon, 1988): 86.
35. These shooting dates stem from the shooting schedule, recorded daily by studio personnel. See Riley, p. 62. The original paperwork exists at the Universal Archives at the University of Southern California.
36. Turner, George E. "The Two Faces of *Dracula*." *American Cinematographer* Vol. 69, No. 5 (May 1988): 38.
37. Turner, p. 40.
38. "Dramatic and Musical." *Billboard* 4 Oct. 1930: 74.
39. "Production Notes." *Hollywood Reporter* 29 Sept. 1930: 2.
40. Atkins, Rick. *Among the Rugged Peaks: Carla Laemmle, An Intimate Biography* (Baltimore, MD: Midnight Marquee Press, 2009).

41. Nasr, Constantine. Interview with Carla Laemmle. 26 Oct. 2012.
42. Rhodes, Gary D. Interview with Carla Laemmle. 9 Apr. 2014.
43. "Here's Another Kind of Vampire." *Los Angeles Times* 9 Nov. 1930: H3.
44. Busby, Marquis. "*Dracula*." *Los Angeles Examiner* 28 Mar. 1931.
45. "Director Commends Visaroff Character." *Hollywood Filmograph* 4 Apr. 1931: 8.
46. Turner, p. 38.
47. "Huge Fireplace in Eerie Drama." *Los Angeles Evening Express* 9 Oct. 1930.
48. "Most Unusual Sets in U History Used to Film *Dracula*." *Exhibitors Herald-World* 29 Nov. 1930: 37.
49. See, for example: "Robert Ames in *Dracula*." *Hollywood Reporter* 2 Oct. 1930: 3; Wilk, Ralph. "A Little from 'Lots.'" *Film Daily* 2 Oct. 1930: 6.
50. Parsons, Louella O. *Los Angeles Examiner* 3 Oct. 1930.
51. In *Hollywood Gothic*, Skal claims that Universal turned to Ames "in desperation" (p.126), but there is no surviving evidence to support that statement. Rather, as the main text of this chapter claims, it seems Universal removed Lew Ayres from the cast of *Dracula* for rather logical reasons.
52. Wilk, Ralph. "A Little from 'Lots.'" *Film Daily* 25 June 1930: 6.
53. "Spanish *Dracula* Cast Completed." *Film Daily* 1 Oct. 1930: 6.
54. "Universal Finds Film Limitations Fading." *Los Angeles Times* 5 Oct. 1930.
55. "Jack Pierce." *Hollywood Filmograph* 29 Nov. 1930: 31.
56. Taylor, Al and Sue Roy. *Making a Monster* (New York: Crown, 1980): 13.
57. Riley, p. 56.
58. "Code of Ethics for the Production of Motion Pictures." *The Film Daily Yearbook for 1931* (New York: Film Daily, 1932): 655.
59. Davison, William, as told to Raymond Lee. "Hollywood in Miniature." *Classic Film Collector* (Fall 1972): 53-54.
60. Turner, p. 38.
61. Churchill, Edward. "Star Gazer." *Exhibitors Herald-World* 18 Oct. 1930: 52.
62. "Most Unusual Sets in U History Used to Film *Dracula*."
63. For more information on Frances Dade, see: Rhodes, Gary D. "Frances Dade: Universal's Unearthly Woman in White, Part I." *Filmfax* No. 131 (Summer 2012): 36-41; "Frances Dade, Universal's Unearthly Woman in White, Part II." *Filmfax* No. 132 (Fall 2012): 34-39 and 102-104.
64. Zinn, John. Letter to Samuel Goldwyn Studios. 8 Oct. 1930.
65. "*Dracula* Cast Completed." *Film Daily* 19 Oct. 1930.
66. Parsons, Louella O. *Los Angeles Examiner* 8 Oct. 1930.
67. Rubin, Rachel. "Society in Filmland." *Hollywood Daily Citizen* 8 Oct. 1930.
68. "Code of Ethics for the Production of Motion Pictures," p. 655.
69. Wilk, Ralph. "A Little from 'Lots.'" *Film Daily* 6 Oct. 1930: 4.
70. "In London." *Variety* 13 Oct. 1916: 4.
71. "*That Awful Mrs. Eaton*." *Billboard* 11 Oct. 1924: 36; "*Simon Called Peter*." *Billboard* 22 Nov. 1924: 36.
72. "*The Lady of Scandal*." *Billboard* 21 June 1930: 22.
73. Rombo, Ramon. "And the Villain." *Motion Picture Stories* 20 Sept. 1927: 10.
74. Wilk, Ralph. "A Little from 'Lots.'" *Film Daily* 6 Oct. 1930: 4.
75. "Gerrard Cast." *Film Daily* 20 Nov. 1930: 8.
76. "*Scared Stiff* Is Well Sustained Comedy." *Hollywood Reporter* 8 Dec. 1930: 2.
77. "Joan Standing in Von Stroheim Cast." *Los Angeles Times* 10 June 1923: III31.
78. A cut occurs in the film immediately before mention is made of the marks on Lucy's throat. Viewing the scene, it is easy to see that the closeup of the marks might well have been intended immediately to precede and/or overlap with the dialogue about them.
79. "Bela Lugosi." *Hollywood Filmograph* 11 Oct. 1930: 17.
80. "Hollywood Flashes." *Film Daily* 13 Oct. 1930.
81. "11 Units, 7 Stories Readying, at Universal." *Film Daily* 22 Oct. 1930: 1, 2.
82. "Production Activities." *Hollywood Reporter* 13 Oct. 1930.
83. "Universal Will Talkerize Dozen Broadway Stage Plays." *Film Daily* 16 Oct. 1930: 1.
84. See, for example: "Manners in *Dracula*." *Hollywood Reporter* 15 Oct. 1930: 3; "David Manners Given Lead." *Film Daily* 15 Oct. 1930: 6.
85. Carroll, Harrison. "Screenographs." *Los Angeles Evening Herald* 16 Oct. 1930.
86. "Los Angeles." *Variety* 19 Nov. 1930: 46.
87. Carroll, Harrison. "Screenographs." *Los Angeles Evening Herald* 16 Oct. 1930.
88. Parsons, Louella O. *Los Angeles Examiner* 17 Oct. 1930.
89. "Henley for *Mississippi*." *Variety* 6 Aug. 1930: 28.
90. Skal, *Hollywood Gothic*, p. 127; Skal, *The Monster Show*, p. 118.
91. Boland, p. 15; Nagle, p.53; Hunt, Dick. "David Manners Hesitates." *Los Angeles Evening Herald* 12 Apr. 1930.
92. I am very grateful to Gregory William Mank, who found this information at the Warner Bros. Archives housed at the School of Cinema-Television at University of Southern California in Los Angeles. The two-page contractual letter of agreement is dated 14 October 1930, typed on the letterhead of the First National Productions Corporation, signed by the studio's Assistant-Secretary, and then approved, accepted, and countersigned by a representative of Universal Pictures.
93. "Universal Is Strong for Broadway-Produced Plays." *Billboard* 25 Oct. 1930: 6.
94. "U. Rushing *Up and Up*." *Variety* 18 Oct. 1930.
95. "Hollywood Bulletins." *Variety* 22 Oct. 1930.

96 "The New Plays on Broadway." *Billboard* 20 Sept. 1930: 31.
97 "Production Notes." *Hollywood Reporter* 24 Oct. 1930: 2.
98 Alicoate, Jack. "Mr. Laemmle, Jr. – Has Made the Grade." *Film Daily* 15 Oct. 1930: 1-2.
99 Advertisement. *Variety* 22 Oct. 1930.
100 Wilk, Ralph. "A Little from 'Lots.'" *Film Daily* 19 Oct. 1930: 4.
101 "Set for U's *Dracula* Is Wiped Out by Fire." *Exhibitors Herald-World* 25 Oct. 1930: 48.
102 Parsons, Louella O. *Los Angeles Examiner* 18 Oct. 1930.
103 Similarly, Herbert Buston received new dialogue in a subsequent scene in the library involving Seward, Harker, and Van Helsing: "John, I know you love her. But don't forget, she's my daughter, and I must do what I think is best."
104 "Dramatic and Musical." *Billboard* 1 Nov. 1930: 74.
105 "Josephine Velez in *Dracula*." *Film Daily* 28 Oct. 1930: 6.
106 Wilk, Ralph. "A Little from 'Lots.'" *Film Daily* 29 Oct. 1930: 8.
107 "Moon Carroll to Play Here." *Los Angeles Times* 9 Nov. 1930: B22.
108 Wilk, Ralph. "A Little from 'Lots.'" *Film Daily* 28 Oct. 1930: 6.
109 Wilk, Ralph. "A Little from 'Lots.'" *Film Daily* 29 Oct. 1930: 8.
110 "Picture-of-the-Month-Club." *Film Daily* 28 Oct. 1930: 2.
111 "Foreigns in Work at U in 8-Hour Shifts." *Hollywood Reporter* 30 Oct. 1930: 4.
112 "Local Chatter." *Variety* 25 Oct. 1930.
113 Ibid.
114 Yeaman, Elizabeth. *Hollywood Daily Citizen* 3 Nov. 1930.
115 "Dramatic and Musical." *Billboard* 8 Nov. 1930: 76.
116 "Universal Shows Loss in Quarterly Report." *Hollywood Reporter* 4 Nov. 1930: 1.
117 "Junior Laemmle Ill." *Hollywood Reporter* 5 Nov. 1930: 1.
118 "Laemmle Denies Shutdown Rumors." *Hollywood Reporter* 8 Nov. 1930.
119 "No U. Shutdown." *Variety* 17 Dec. 1930.
120 "Laemmle Biog. Trip." *Variety* 8 Oct. 1930.
121 "Laemmle West." *Variety* 18 Oct. 1930.
122 "Laemmle Cancels Sailing to See Granddaughter." *Exhibitors Herald-World* 25 Oct. 1930: 23.
123 "U Lets Out 50." *Variety* 29 Oct. 1930: 5.
124 Qtd. in Hutchinson, Tom and Roy Pickard. *Horrors: A History of Horror Movies* (Secaucus, NJ: Chartwell, 1984), 15-16.
125 Balderston's comment appears within the text of his 1934 treatment for *Dracula's Daughter*.
126 "U Is Budgeting New Releases in New York." *Variety* 2 June 1931: 7.
127 Schatz, p. 86.
128 In *Dark Carnival*, Skal and Savada suggest that "trims" occurred to *Dracula* that included the "merciful staking of Lucy in her crypt," but there is no evidence such footage was ever filmed (p. 153). Indeed, the surviving production schedule and the production changes to other scenes (including the Woman in White footage that does appear in the film, as well as to Van Helsing's closing dialogue) mitigate against that speculation, as does the absence of the set and scene in Melford's Spanish-language version, which instead features an improvised discussion about Lucia's death in front of the gates to Carfax Abbey.
129 Turner, p. 39.
130 "Supper Honors Ruth Chatterton." *Los Angeles Examiner* 5 Nov. 1930.
131 "Hollywood Bulletins." *Variety* 5 Nov. 1930: 4.
132 ""Uncle Carl's Biog Almost Ready." *Hollywood Reporter* 5 Nov. 1930.
133 Browning also gave new dialogue to the Seward character during the shooting of Mina's boudoir, shortly after Mina admits having seen the Woman in White. The script notes Seward's presence, but he has no dialogue in it. In the finished film, he responds "But John!" after Harker suggests contacting the police, and affirms Van Helsing's statement that he "must be master here" with the single word "Quite!"
134 Turner, p. 37. In *Dark Carnival*, Skal and Savada draw a direct comparison between the budgets of the Spanish and English-language versions of *Dracula*: "[Melford's] $68,750 versus Browning's $355,050" (p. 150). Such a comparison is very problematic because, as discussed in the main text, Melford's budget did not include such major costs as the literary rights and the sets, even though Melford's cast and crew utilized them.
135 "Hollywood Bulletins." *Variety* 12 Nov. 1930.
136 "Producers Must Fight to Hold Foreign Market, Says Laemmle." *Exhibitors Herald-World* 15 Nov. 1930: 22.
137 "Dramatic and Musical." *Billboard* 15 Nov. 1930: 76.
138 "*Dracula* to be Shown at President." *San Francisco Chronicle* 4 Nov. 1930: 7.
139 "Making Junior Rest." *Variety* 8 Nov. 1930.
140 "Birthday Fete Offered to Sue Carol." *Los Angeles Examiner* 9 Nov. 1930.
141 Yeaman, Elizabeth. "Carl Laemmle, Sr. Delighted with Success of Jr." *Hollywood Daily Citizen* 13 Nov. 1930.
142 "Most Unusual Sets in U History Used to Film *Dracula*," p. 37.
143 Riley, unpaginated.
144 Here I would like to thank my friend Carter B. Smith, DVM for drawing my attention to this particular shot.
145 "Film Actress Goes Under Knife Today." *Los Angeles Times* 14 Nov. 1930: A1.
146 Rankin, Ruth. "A Child of the Theatre." *New Movie Magazine* (Jan. 1932): 78-79.
147 "Bela Lugosi Boosts Civic Theatre Idea." *Hollywood Filmograph* 15 Nov. 1930: 18.
148 "Bela Lugosi Discusses Stage and Screen." *Hollywood Filmograph* 8 Nov. 1930: 16.
149 "Dramatic and Musical." *Billboard* 22 Nov. 1930: 79; "Dramatic and Musical." *Billboard* 27 Dec. 1930: 72.

150 "Dramatic and Musical." *Billboard* 6 Dec. 1930: 113; "Dramatic and Musical." *Billboard* 13 Dec. 1930: 80; "Dramatic and Musical." *Billboard* 20 Dec. 1930: 73; "Annual Slump Cuts into Chi." *Variety* 24 Dec. 1930.
151 "Liveright Out." *Variety* 22 Nov. 1930.
152 "Staging a Hollywood 'Opening' by Telephone." *Variety* 26 Nov. 1930.
153 "French Imports Fail; U Halts Diplomat." *Variety* 22 Nov. 1930.
154 Riley, p. 62.
155 Ibid, p. 62.
156 Yeaman, Elizabeth. *Hollywood Daily Citizen* 8 Dec. 1930.
157 "Hollywood Chatter." *Variety* 17 Dec. 1930: 42.
158 "Dorothy Burgess–U." *Variety* 31 Dec. 1930: 9; "Hollywood Bulletins." *Variety* 28 Jan. 1931: 12.
159 "Ayres Walks, Returns." *Variety* 21 Jan. 1931: 2.
160 Skal and Savada call *Iron Man* "a picture obviously finished to complete a contract and nothing more" (p. 157), a description that seems very much at odds with primary sources regarding the acquisition of the story, its production, and its release.
161 Despite receiving several good reviews, *Iron Man* was lambasted by *Billboard* on 25 Apr. 1931, whose reviewer called it a "lethargic-paced piece of celluloid" (p. 20).
162 "Miniature Reviews." *Variety* 22 Apr. 1931: 19.
163 "*Iron Man*." *Motion Picture Herald* 28 Mar. 1931: 37.
164 Laemmle, Carl, Jr. "Why I Choose Cinematographers as Directors." *American Cinematographer* (Nov. 1932): 11, 35.
165 "The Lowdown." *Hollywood Reporter* 26 Mar. 1931: 2.
166 Wilk, Ralph. "A Little from 'Lots.'" *Film Daily* 5 Apr. 1931: 4.

Chapter 6
POST-PRODUCTION

In December of 1930, Universal Pictures generated publicity by announcing that it was going to increase its production budget for the 1931-32 season to a total of $18 million.[1] That same month, *Film Daily* declared that Junior Laemmle was lining up new properties to shoot in the coming months, adding that the head of the studio's New York story department had arrived in Los Angeles with "about 100 plays, books, and original stories."[2] From the various options, Universal would select 32 features to produce.[3]

Within the space of one month, however, a different picture emerged. On 5 January 1931, *Hollywood Reporter* informed readers that, "Carl Laemmle, Sr. has taken actual physical charge of all production and business operation of the Universal studios and a general slash in the payroll is being made."[4] The decision was likely the consequence of poor financial returns, as well as resulting questions over the studio's recent emphasis on prestigious, big-budget films. To be sure, Universal lost $2.2 million in 1930.[5] Even Junior Laemmle may have had second thoughts about his own strategy, as he wrote a lengthy article in December 1930 about how film serials were making a comeback.[6] Only months earlier, he had tried to eliminate them from Universal's production schedule.

These changes occurred during *Dracula*'s post-production, which began at some point in mid-November and continued for approximately two months. Describing the "picture of the future" in July 1930, Junior Laemmle stated: "Action will be edited closely – as closely as the dialogue. There will be no wastage in camera or sound in the telling of tomorrow's stories. Song will come in where it is befitting. Music will have its place necessarily, but we are through with the heterogenous mixage of the two."[7]

Here was perhaps a guiding, or at least overarching, artistic vision behind the editing of *Dracula*, one that Tod Browning probably shared. Both men likely played prominent roles in *Dracula*'s editing, which could also have received input from such persons as associate producer E. M. Asher. Changes at the studio might have meant that Carl Laemmle, Sr. also provided feedback and oversight. Unfortunately, no studio files have surfaced that detail *Dracula*'s post-production phase, and so it is necessary to rely on other kinds of primary sources, specifically reports printed in trade publications and in newspapers, as well as on the edited film itself.

Publicity still for *Dracula* (1931), which was edited between mid-November 1930 and early January 1931.

At the time of *Dracula*'s production, Maurice Pivar – born in Manchester, England, in 1894 – served as Universal's Supervising Film Editor (or "Editor-in-Chief," as he was sometimes called). According to one account, he had "grown up in Carl Laemmle's employ," having worked as the Accessories Manager before spending several years in "charge of the cutting and editing department."[8] He resigned from the studio in late 1929, at which time Del Andrews took his place. But Pivar returned to Universal in March of 1930, and was Supervising Film Editor at Universal when *Dracula* entered its post-production phase.[9]

Working under Pivar's supervision (and perhaps even his specific wishes about particular edits) was editor Milton Carruth. Born in Colorado in 1899, Carruth was one of two editors who worked on Universal's *Night Ride* (1930) and *Captain of the Guard* (1930); he also edited the silent version of *All Quiet on the Western Front* (1930). That same year, Carruth – who was still in the early stages of his career – edited Tod Browning's *Outside the Law* (1930).

A few modern writers have suggested that Browning disliked the final edit of *Dracula* and that he was either not involved in the film's post-production or his views were not heard or implemented. However, there is no evidence to support these claims. By contrast, a newspaper account in January 1931 claimed that, "Edwin Carewe, who directed *Resurrection*, and Tod Browning, who directed *Dracula*, are personally supervising the cutting and editing of their respective films."[10]

It is true that William S. Hart, Jr., a friend of Browning's, once claimed that the director told him that a print of *Dracula* broadcast on television was not his original version, but rather "a thing put together and sold to television out of the scraps on the cutting room floor."[11] But this quotation is highly problematic for more than one reason, as it ostensibly refers to a version aired on TV, not the 1931 release print.

While it is true that Universal does not seem to have changed *Dracula*'s continuity for TV distribution, it is also true that television stations sometimes trimmed running time from movies to force them to fit into certain broadcast schedules. Such schedules had to allow time for television commercials, as well as (at times) for onscreen hosts to provide their own commentary or comedic skits. Indeed, it is possible that some of Browning's angst about a television broadcast of *Dracula* resulted from comments or jokes made by a horror host. Certainly that was the case with actress Mae Clarke, who took legal action against a horror host who made fun of her during a broadcast of *Frankenstein* (1931) in 1957.[12]

And then there is the fact that Browning must have made his comments about the television version of *Dracula* sometime in the late fifties or early sixties prior to his death in 1962, as the film's inaugural broadcast did not occur until 1957. By that time, George Geltzer had already written his essay on Browning for the October 1953 issue of *Films in Review*, claiming: "Today *Dracula* seems weak, but its opening sequences of Count Dracula's castle still create an eerie atmosphere."[13] Then, in January 1954, William K. Everson published his essay on horror films in which he damned *Dracula*'s post-Transylvanian sequences as "plodding" and "talkative."[14] Browning definitely knew about Geltzer's essay, and he may well have read Everson's. In short, his discussion of "scraps on the cutting room floor" in 1957 or thereafter could have even been a way for him to shift blame for *Dracula*'s perceived shortcomings onto others at Universal.

But the problems with Hart's comment become even greater when considering what he said in 1980 to a *different* interviewer. Asked whether or not Browning watched his films on television, Hart replied: "Yes, but he complained that they had been re-edited. He said specifically that a lot of stuff he cut out had been restored and that the picture was not as he left it. He said he cut out some broad, hokey shots that were put back in."[15] Here the reference is not specifically to *Dracula* having been re-edited for television, but to a number of Browning's films. (In the same interview, Hart also mistakenly claimed – either due to his own error or to incorrect information Browning gave him – that Browning went to Germany in 1930 to negotiate the film rights to *Dracula* with Bram Stoker's widow. He added that Browning met Paul Von Hindenburg during the same trip.)

William S. Hart, Jr. also claimed to have seen Browning's preferred edit of *Dracula* as a young boy, noting that it featured fewer images of *Dracula*.[16] At the time, Hart would only have been about seven years old. While his memories are important, they should not assume too large a position in the story of *Dracula*'s post-production. Decades passed before he articulated this story in an interview, and it is worth considering how well anyone remembers specifics about a single film screening after the passage of several decades, particularly when the screening occurred during one's youth. More importantly, it is worth remembering that the final shooting script that Browning himself coauthored features *more* dialogue and screen time for Dracula than that which appears in the edited film.

At any rate, numerous other sources suggest that Browning took a great deal of interest in the editing of his films. Consider, for example, the memories of set director/art designer A. Arnold Palmer:

Of Harry Reynolds, the film editor of most of Tod's efforts, I recall little. He must have been patient and always willing to share his Movieola with his director because Browning wielded a film editor's scissors with aplomb and authority. You remember, Tod was a complete director.[17]

Reynolds edited the six MGM films that Browning directed before he moved to Universal in 1930: *The Unknown* (1927), *London After Midnight* (1927), *The Big City* (1928), *West of Zanzibar* (1928), *Where East Is East* (1929), and *The Thirteenth Chair* (1929). It would seem that Browning not only played an active role in the editing process, but also sought to work with the same editor repeatedly.

Similarly, it is true that Browning took a great interest in the post-production of *Freaks* (1932), to the extent that he spent a great deal of time working with the editor, Basil Wrangell, who later complained: "We were working until four o'clock in the morning every goddamn day. And he would go off for dinner sometimes in the afternoon, and then we'd sit around and wait until two in the morning for him to get back."[18] Wrangell's memories suggest he had a disliking for Tod Browning, but they also underscore the extent to which Browning was directly involved in the post-production of that particular movie.

Browning's interest in film editing goes back to his direction *The Virgin of Stamboul* (1920), if not earlier. In 1920, he told the *Exhibitors Herald*: "The director does the real writing of his story in the cutting and projection rooms. But he must select and prepare his entire vocabulary before he considers the actual piecing together at all."[19]

For Browning, the editing process on *Dracula* involved a working relationship with Milton Carruth. It is possible to presume that – if Browning had had earlier difficulties dealing with Carruth on *Outside the Law*, and did not want Carruth to edit *Dracula* – he could have pressured Laemmle or Pivar to assign a different editor to the film. After all, Carruth was at an early stage in his editing career, and as a result likely had little power at the studio. Moreover, there is also the important fact that, after *Dracula*, Carruth also edited *Iron Man* (1931), Browning's next film with Universal. Had Browning disliked Carruth's editing on *Outside the Law* and *Dracula* – or just *Dracula*, for that matter – it is also probable that Browning could have argued for someone else to edit *Iron Man*. Instead, the two men worked together on three consecutive films.

In terms of *Dracula*, as Chapter 5 proved, numerous changes were made to the script during the production process. As a result, no one could *ever* have edited *Dracula* to follow the Fort-Browning shooting script precisely. The larger issue is whether Browning intended for *Dracula* to unfold onscreen as it does. In other words, did he approve of the release print? Unless period documentation surfaces, that question cannot be answered. He may have been happy or unhappy with the final edit. But Browning probably experienced more complicated emotions than complete happiness or complete unhappiness. His feelings about the release print could have varied from scene to scene, and might also have been shaped by regrets over a production process that did not allow him to shoot all of the scenes that he likely wanted to include (such as the destruction of Lucy, the Woman in White), scenes that as a result could not be edited at all.

Likewise, there is absolutely no evidence that there was one "Director's Cut" and a second "Studio Cut."[20] Indeed, surviving evidence about *Dracula*'s post-production does not at all support such a simple explanation, one likely shaped in the minds of latter-day writers by modern studio publicity about "Director's Cuts" sometimes employed to sell more copies of particular films on home video after their theatrical releases. Rather, a strong knowledge of the raw footage and plans towards editing led to the (certainly not unexpected or unusual) need to film "pick ups" on 15 November 1930. Then, a *Dracula* work print of some kind led to the perceived need for "added scenes" to be shot in December 1930, which were apparently edited into a second version that was screened at a preview that same month. Then, "retakes" filmed in January 1931 were incorporated into what by that point was at least a third version. The fact that added scenes and retakes were shot also means that it is not possible to draw a clear line between the end of the production phase and the beginning of the post-production phase; rather, there was some overlap and interplay between them.

Indeed, *Dracula*'s post-production was likely more complicated than the creation of three different edits. After all, editing is an organic process, one that can alter films in an ongoing manner. Each day that passed could have seen the

This publicity still for *Dracula* (1931) depicts Bela Lugosi in action not represented in the finished film. However, that does not necessarily mean that footage of this kind was actually filmed. *(Courtesy of Anthony Osika)*

Chapter 6 – POST-PRODUCTION

Here is another publicity still showing action that does not appear in the finished film, this time between Lugosi's Dracula and Frye's Renfield. *(Courtesy of Jack Dowler)*

film change in large and small ways. In the case of *Dracula*, the editing process may well have been influenced not only by Browning and Carruth, but also by Pivar, both of the Laemmles, others at the studio (such as feedback from the film's associate producer), journalists who critiqued the preview version in print and/or in conversation to studio personnel, preview audiences who may have given formal and informal feedback, and representatives of the Hays Office who saw the film before its release.

    Such a complicated process probably cut some footage that was filmed in the production phase. However, sparse information exists on this topic, and past speculation has little basis in fact. For example, in his 1974 biography of Bela Lugosi, writer Arthur Lennig suggests that "photographs do exist that show Dracula standing by the boxes [of Transylvanian soil], near a wagon that will transport the strange cargo to the ship, but this episode has been completely cut."[21] However, there is no evidence *whatsoever* for Lennig's claim, which seems particularly spurious given that other publicity stills also depict action not included in the film's script or its running time. For example, one photograph shows Renfield kneeling before Dracula in the catacombs of Carfax Abbey. Two others show Dr. Seward searching Carfax Abbey with Van Helsing. None of these illustrate action in the final film *or* in the script. What can we make of these stills, rather than immediately jumping to the conclusion that they represent moments that have been "cut" from the film? In all likelihood, none of them was filmed. Rather, following the common practice of so many Hollywood publicity stills of the era, actions are represented that are different from those that appear in the film itself.

Two more publicity stills illustrating action that does not appear in the finished film, in these cases with Van Helsing (Van Sloan) and Seward (Buston) at Carfax Abbey. In the script and in the completed film, Seward never ventures to the abbey. *(Courtesy of Anthony Osika and Buddy Barnett)*

Chapter 6 – POST-PRODUCTION

One of the film's most iconic publicity photos depicts Dracula about to bite Lucy (Frances Dade); Andy Warhol used it as the basis of *The Kiss* in 1962. The image is yet another instance of a publicity still depicting action not in the script or film. (*Courtesy of Anthony Osika*)

Here it would seem Lennig's book is unaware that publicity stills are vastly different from actual frames from a given film.

Later, in his book *The Immortal Count: The Life and Films of Bela Lugosi* (University of Kentucky, 2003), Lennig confidently states footage of sailors aboard the *Vesta* was "cut" and that footage of Van Helsing and Harker dispatching the Woman in White was "trimmed."[22] But there is absolutely no evidence of any kind that such cuts were made, just as there is no evidence that such material was even filmed. Indeed, it seems clear that not only was the destruction of the Woman in White not filmed, but that the sets were not even constructed. (Lennig is quite incorrect to say that footage in the completed film depicts Van Helsing and Harker at the "cemetery"; rather, they are at the gate of Carfax Abbey.)

What *do* we know about the editing of *Dracula*? It is certain is that its post-production phrase took place over the period of approximately two months, resulting not only in a talkie release print, but also in a silent version prepared for theatres that had not yet converted to sound. Tod Browning was clearly involved in the editing phase and in at least some of the changes that transpired (given that he directed the added scenes and retakes). Whether he agreed with all of the changes or fought against some of them is impossible to say with any confidence, but various changes certainly occurred as part of a broader process that also involved the addition of music to the film's soundtrack.

The First Rough Cut

Precisely when *Dracula* entered a post-production phase is hard to pinpoint. The *Hollywood Reporter* claimed that *Dracula* was in "final editing" as of 20 November 1931, as was the "Spanish version," which was being assembled by Arthur (Arturo) Tavares, the man who had previously edited Universal's Spanish-language versions of *The Cat Creeps* (1930) and *East Is West* (1930).[23] According to *Film Daily*, he had worked for First National for "several years" and had spent two years "with the Gainsborough Company in London."[24] Along with his editing experience, Tavares was also a film actor.

On 3 December 1930, the *Hollywood Reporter* once again claimed that both versions of *Dracula* were in "final editing."[25] That process generated ideas for some changes, as Browning directed "added scenes" for *Dracula* on 13 December 1930. Only one week earlier, *Film Daily* told readers that Browning had been spotted having lunch at Universal with Karl Freund, *Dracula*'s cinematographer. The two men may already have been discussing their upcoming shoot.[26]

However, it is difficult to determine what the "added scenes" might have been, as the film features only a minor amount of footage that is not mentioned in the script. Moreover, the fact that the footage was filmed in only one day likely suggests that it was limited in scope. Such new footage may have included two brief shots of Dracula at Carfax Abbey. In both of them, the camera pans to the left and tilts upward towards a window after the lid of his earth box begins to open; the camera then pans back to the right and tilts downward to reveal Dracula standing.

And then there is the additional visit that Dracula makes to Mina's bedroom. As suggested in Chapter 5, Browning could well have made the decision to include the scene during the original production schedule. However, it is also possible that the Browning and/or others (e.g., Junior Laemmle, E. M. Asher) made the decision after viewing a rough cut, which could have led to filming some of the needed images for it on 13 December.

One reason to suspect this was the case is that Carruth seems to have had limited footage from which to construct the scene, although that fact alone does not provide a definitive answer. Indeed, one can examine a range of other films of the thirties that rely on similar editing decisions, including Browning's *Mark of the Vampire* (1935), which twice relies on footage from the same two shots (a bat flapping at some terrace doors and a female vampire peering through a window), even though the scenes in which the shots reappear come at distinctly different moments in the film's narrative.

At any rate, Dracula's additional visit to Mina's bedroom became chronologically his first visit. Shot A is of Mina in bed [See Figure 6A]. Wolfbane is on her neck, even though Van Helsing has not yet ordered wolfbane be used in the home; Carruth has borrowed this image from footage shot for use in what eventually became Dracula's second visit to her room. Shot B is of a bat flying at a window. The image actually depicts Lucy's apartment window; Mina's does not even have a window, but instead terrace doors [See Figure 6B]. Then, Shot C returns to the image in Shot A [See Figure 6C].

Shot D is an image that seems to have been filmed with the intention of becoming part of the additional visit Dracula makes to Mina's room [See Figure 6D], as it features

Figure 6A

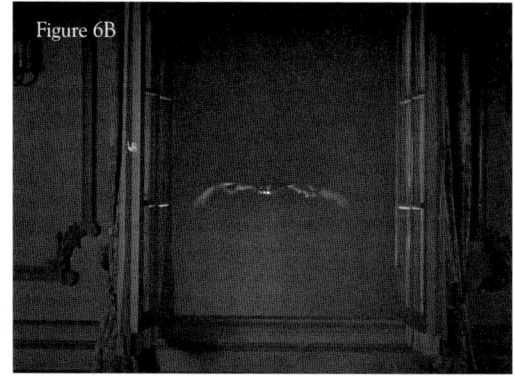

Figure 6B

Figure 6C

Figure 6D

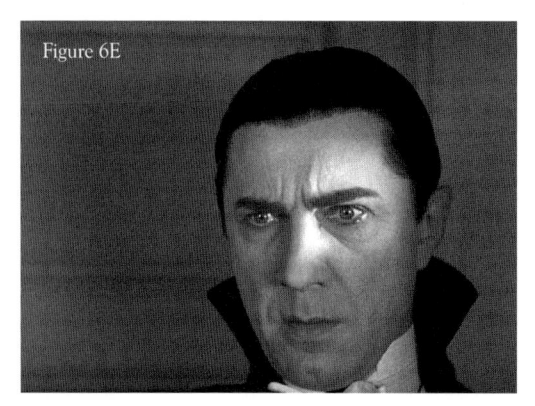

Figure 6E

Figure 6F

Figure 6G

Figure 6H

Chapter 6 – POST-PRODUCTION

different lighting and blocking from footage used to construct what became chronologically his second visit. Here Dracula lowers his cape, as if he has just appeared, presumably after having transformed from a bat. Shot E is another image not seen elsewhere; it is a closeup of Dracula staring at the offscreen Mina [See Figure 6E]. Shot F returns to Shot D, picking up the narrative action as Dracula approaches Mina's bed [See Figure 6F]. Shot G returns to the image depicted in Shot A, and then Shot H ends the scene as Dracula's face nearly fills the screen before moving downwards to Mina's offscreen neck [See Figures 6G and 6H]. Shot H became one of the most striking images of Dracula in the film.

Browning might have made the decision to create this new scene during the production phase, or he and/or others could have made the decision during the editing process. Not enough evidence exists to prove when the decision occurred, or whether or not Browning agreed with it. At any rate, the scene works only due to Carruth's imaginative repurposing of some images originally filmed for two other scenes, so much so that no critics or historians seem to have noticed that fact until I discussed the issue in an essay published in 2012.[27]

The Preview Screening

Hollywood had relied on previews for many years prior to *Dracula*. As *Film Daily* wrote in 1925, "Often pictures are tried out two or three times" in order to observe "audience reactions," to determine "weaknesses," and to know "where changes and cuts should be made."[28] On 20 September 1930, *Motion Picture News* wrote that Universal intended to preview its own films in a new manner:

> A system which has proved successful with other studios is being tried by Universal with hopes of beneficial results. The plan is this: Talkers are previewed in a very rough form with a [sic] lengthy footage. Scenes which are not even planned to be used are judged and scenes that are expected to go over well and fail are remade. The policy is retaking scenes that are weak and in some cases adding sequences in places that will bolster up the film. … When finished, it is expected the talkers will show about fifty percent improvement.[29]

Advertisement on the cover of the January 31, 1931 issue of the *Film Daily* quotes from the *Motion Picture Herald*'s coverage of *Dracula*'s preview screening.

Dracula's preview thus followed from standard studio practice, one reiterated just prior to *Dracula*'s production phase.

On 20 December 1930, the *Hollywood Filmograph* claimed that *Dracula* was still in the "cutting room"; the following day, *Film Daily* reported that Universal had "completed" three new movies, one of them *Dracula* (the other two being *Resurrection* and *Many a Slip*).[30]

Dracula's preview seems to have come at roughly the same time. Both the *Hollywood Reporter* and the *Motion Picture Herald* reviewed the film, their journalists watching it with a full audience just before 24 December 1930. Presumably the version projected included footage from the "added scenes" shot on 13 December.

In response, the *Hollywood Reporter* predicted that the "spooky" film would "draw well." Its critique – published nine days before *Motion Picture Herald*'s and nearly six weeks before the film's premiere – offered only moderate praise:

> Dracula *is entertainment. … They will say 'good,' but they won't rave. … There is much excitement to see when and where and how [Dracula's] going to get that stake through the heart. [But] Count Dracula should be able to do more terrifying things as head vampire than to give his intended victims a cold and deadly stare.*
> *… There is enjoyment here, but the picture isn't the melodramatic smash that anyone who has read the book or who has seen the play might anticipate.*[31]

While such a response is none-too-different than many critics would give to *Dracula* decades after its premiere, this reviewer would find himself in a minority by the time of its original release.

On 3 January 1931, *Motion Picture Herald* published its own critique, one that was more sympathetic to the film:

> *Universal has presented something unusual to the screen in* Dracula. *To appreciate just how unusual it is, you must see it, for it deals with vampires who are 'half-deads' [sic], wolves who howl in the night, bats who suck blood, insane men, and red mists which sweep over lawns just before dawn. And all of these things, mind you, without mentioning castles in which spiders spin their webs, homes for the mentally incompetent, and wild rides through the mist in driverless carriages, are part of the campaign to make your hair stand on end.*
> *At the end of the product, rather an unusual departure, Edward Van Sloan, the technically minded research worker who solves the mystery of the strange count, Dracula, tells you from the screen that vampires really exist, which makes the evening even more terrifying.*
> *But, after all is said and done, Carl Laemmle, Jr., Tod Browning, and others who have given their time and talents to the production have done an excellent job. The photography, the settings and the backgrounds show extreme care. Not only that, but the sound effects rank among the unusual in the production of photoplays. You are bound to get a 'kick' out of* Dracula.
> *… Bela Lugosi, who created the original role and played it on the stage for three years, does his job well. Frye, as the madman, scores equally, with screams and scenes which will make the hair stand on end. The preview audience, at any rate, allowed its hair to stand thus and so.*
> *… All in all,* Dracula *has been handled well and thoughtfully. The preview audience was so entertained that it gasped and thrilled without stint, and that is the reason* Dracula *was made.*[32]

Obviously happy with the response from the critic and the preview audience, Universal quoted from this review in an advertisement published in *Film Daily* on 11 January 1931.

Colonel Jason Joy of the Motion Picture Producers and Distributors of America (MPPDA) previewed the film at a different screening in early January, one presumably arranged specifically for the Hays Office. Joy informed Junior Laemmle that he "enjoyed" watching it

> Comments of previewers on "Dracula"
>
> "I am sorry that I cannot see one redeeming feature in this picture. It is the most horrible thing I have ever seen. The author must have had a distorted mind and I cannot understand why it was produced. I cannot speak too strongly against this picture for children. It would be a crime to allow a child to see such a gruesome, hidious, ghastly, horrible nightmare!"
>
> "This film in my opinion is wholly bad and with no redeeming features worth mentioning. It is unwholesome and ghastly, morbid, inhuman and pointless. In this day of high pressure living, strained nerves and constant excitement it seems too bad that such pictures with the strong influence upon the emotions should be allowed a showing anywhere. I feel that it is completely undesirable for adults and very harmful in its influence over children or young people. It has nothing of beauty or educational value to recommend it and is without humor, entertaining quality or moral value. There seems to be no real reason for its production."
>
> "It is mo honest opinion that this picture should be protested by every previewing organization. Its insane horrible details shown to millions of impressionable children, to adults already bowed down by human misery, will do an infinite amount of harm. To the better balanced it holds not one element of entertainment."
>
> "The only value this film has lies in the acting, direction, photography and sets – It is impossible for children, the sensitive, nervous woman and few men enjoy myths. The story does not justify the outlay of money which it represents for it is not of universal appeal.
> We enjoyed its technic. Perfectly done." Mrs. Leo M. Hedges.
>
> "I would like to add my protest to these. I know the theme of the picture and saw the first fifteen minutes of it and felt I could stand no more of it. I feel that it should be withdrawn from public showing, as children, weak minded and all classes attend motion pictures indiscriminately." Marjorie Ross Davis. P.T.A. Report Chairman.

Feedback to *Dracula* compiled by the Motion Picture Producers and Distributors of America (aka, the Hays Office).

and believed it was "quite satisfactory from the standpoint of the Code."[33] Within days, the MPPDA noted that *Dracula* was suitable for a "family audience."[34] The question, though, is whether Joy would have approved of the version of *Dracula* previewed in December, or whether some potentially problematic material had been cut prior Joy's viewing in January.

At any rate, the MPPDA file on *Dracula* contains notes regarding several viewers who responded quite negatively to the film after seeing it at an advance screening, perhaps the one that Joy attended, though perhaps not:

> *'I am sorry that I cannot see one redeeming feature in this picture. It is the most horrible thing I have ever seen. The author must have had a disturbed mind and I cannot understand why it was produced. I cannot speak too strongly against this picture for children. It would be a crime to allow a child to see such a gruesome, hidious [sic], ghastly, horrible nightmare!'*
> *'It has nothing of beauty or educational value to redeem it and is without humor, entertaining quality or moral value. There seems to be no real reason for its production.'*
> *'The only value this film has lies in the acting, direction, photography, and sets -- It is impossible for children, the sensitive, nervous woman, and few men enjoy myths.'*
> *'It is my honest opinion that this picture should be protested by every previewing organization. Its insane horrible details shown to millions of impressionable children, to adults already bowed down to human misery, will do an infinite amount of harm. To the better balanced it holds not one element of entertainment.'*[35]

Chapter 6 – POST-PRODUCTION

To these complaints, a representative of the Parent-Teacher Association added her contention that *Dracula* should be "withdrawn from public showing."

Though it is difficult to understand the reasons for them, Universal made further changes to *Dracula*. Unfortunately, critiques of the preview screening do not list a precise running time that can be compared against the length of the release print. At any rate, on 2 January 1931, Browning shot retakes in "Dracula's Chambers" and "Seward's Office," though what these constituted is unknown, outside of the fact that the production schedule recorded them as retakes, rather than as added scenes. Some of these shots might have filmed to correct continuity errors, including those created in the editing process as a result of shortening the same scenes, as the major change made after the preview screening seems to have been decreasing the film's running time. That said, such reshoots may also have created new continuity errors. For example, in Dracula's Chambers, Dracula's right hand is on a wine bottle during the dialogue "I trust you have kept your coming here a secret." But in the very next shot, Dracula's right hand is on Renfield's briefcase. Later in the same conversation, after Dracula folds the lease to Carfax Abbey in half, it appears unfolded in one shot, when he tells Renfield, "I have charted a ship to take us to England. We will be leaving tomorrow evening."[36]

At any rate, the basic process of studios shooting retakes was certainly not unusual. On 10 September 1930, for example, *Variety* noted that Universal was going to do some re-shoots for *The Cat Creeps*.[37] Moreover, Browning again was involved in the process, whatever his (unknown) feelings about it were.

The Final Edit

As already noted, it is not possible to identify exactly what changes occurred at particular stages of the editing process, or to determine who approved or did not approve of them. The versions that emerged relied largely on Browning's raw footage, but also drew upon a few pre-existing images. In an apparent effort to save money, Milton Carruth repurposed footage of a ship at sea from the 1925 Universal film *The Storm Breaker* (which *Film Daily* had once called "one of the most realistic sea stories ever screened") in order to visualize Dracula and Renfield's voyage to England.[38]

More importantly, editing *Dracula* allowed for various refinements to occur, including what seems to have been the deletions of particular scenes and dialogue (assuming Browning shot them, a fact that cannot always be known with certainty). Carruth may well have cut some dialogue so as to prevent moral outcries from religious groups. For example, shortly before Dracula hypnotizes Briggs and she removes the wolfbane from Mina's door, Briggs tells a "night nurse":

We've had to keep [Mina] under opiates all night – the minute she smells that wolfbane, she goes out of her head and starts to fight us.

This scene may well have been cut to remove any mention of drugs or sedation, as well any hint of Mina's animal-like (and thus sexualized) behavior. Such a cut could even have resulted from feedback at the December preview screening.

Carruth made other changes in an apparent effort to use editing to augment the film's cinematic style. For example, in the final shooting script, the first shot of Dracula at his castle is intercut with Renfield at the Transylvanian Inn, but Carruth eschewed that approach, preferring instead to withhold Dracula's initial appearance until after Renfield's carriage leaves for the Borgo Pass. The result means the audience hears about vampires from the Proprietor of the Inn, but does not yet see any of them. The decision also wisely avoids a potential problem in that the conversation at the Inn occurs prior to sundown, with the delay keeping the vampires in their coffins until the sun has definitely set.

Other changes of this type are more pronounced and affect the film's continuity. In the shooting script, Van Helsing announces in his own laboratory that a vampire is at large. The next scene introduces the Seward Sanitarium, with a crane shot culminating in an introduction to Renfield and Martin; the following scene has Van Helsing and Seward talking together in Seward's laboratory, the two of them are soon joined by Renfield. But Carruth re-edits the order of these three scenes. He begins the trio with the introduction to the sanitarium, then cuts to Van Helsing's laboratory, and then cuts to Seward's laboratory (as the script calls it). The change creates a much more fascinating transition to the scene in Seward's laboratory, in which we see Van Helsing and Seward deep in conversation about Renfield's bloodlust. It is as if their basic conversation from Van Helsing's laboratory has continued, despite the change of geography and the passage of time, a common tactic in Hollywood cinema that allows for dialogue on a singular topic to continue even as the setting changes.

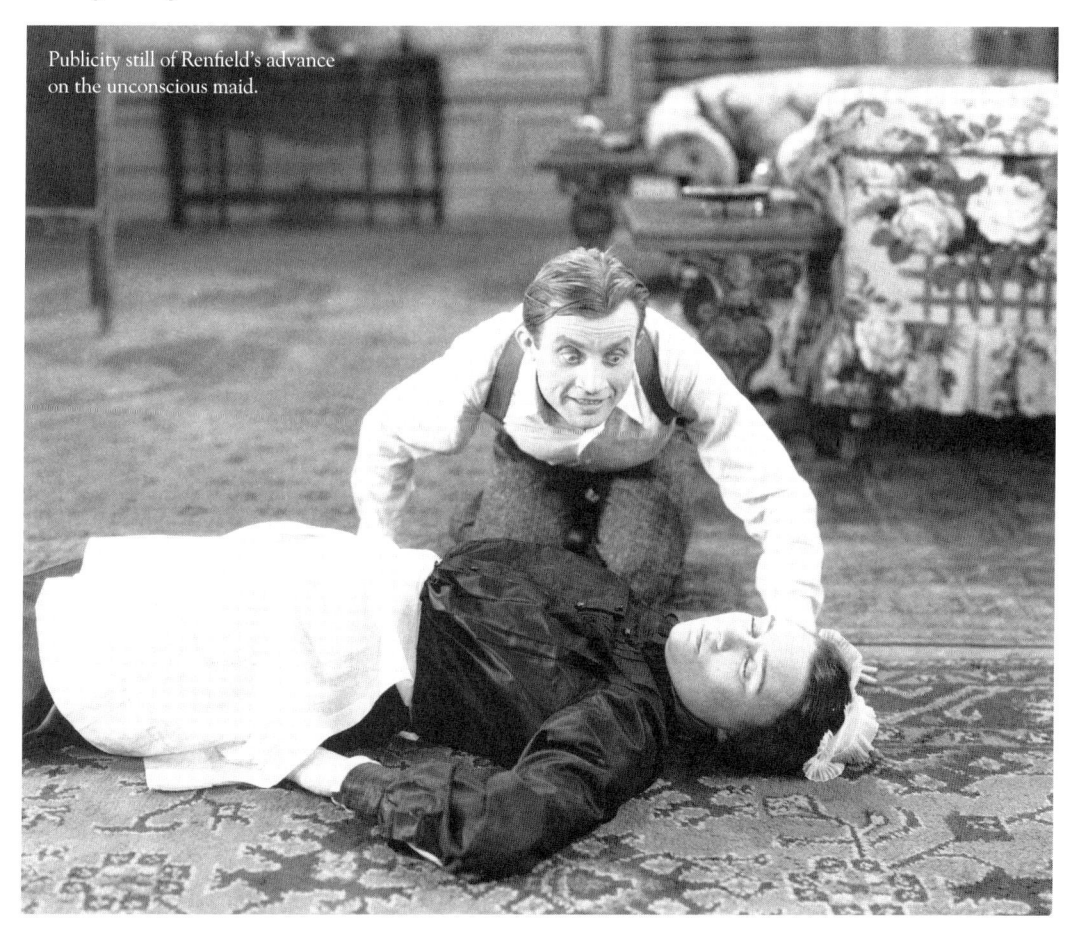

Publicity still of Renfield's advance on the unconscious maid.

And then there is the scene of Renfield crawling towards the maid after the other characters have left the room to search for Mina. The shooting script has Renfield attempt to catch a fly on the maid's cheek after she falls to the floor unconscious. He misses, and then "sits back upon his haunches with a frustrated air and starts to snivel." While it is difficult to know why Browning changed the narrative action – indeed, it could have been as simple as the problem of getting a fly to light on her face – the alteration results in a far more disturbing scene. Renfield grins eerily as he crawls towards the maid. Carruth cuts the scene before we see what Renfield does, but he certainly has not withdrawn from her body. Here the audience is left to question whether or not Renfield intends to graduate to human blood, just as he has already graduated from flies to spiders. Whoever made the decision to cut the scene short, the result is a brilliant use of editing to create horror, as the audience is left to wonder exactly what, if anything, Renfield does to the woman's unconscious body. After all, cutting away from the action echoes the scenes in which Dracula bites Renfield and Lucy.

More commonly, however, Carruth seems to have deleted footage in an effort to shorten the film's overall running time, which at its eventual (and approximate) 74 minutes and thirty seconds comported with norms of the period. For example, he cut a brief and arguably unnecessary scene between Harker and a nurse, at least assuming that Browning shot it. But most of Carruth's work came within scenes that do appear in the final cut. For example, dialogue in the opening carriage ride begins with the Secretary's line "Among the rugged peaks that frown down upon the Borgo Pass…." But the edited film does not include the Secretary's other dialogue in the scene (as it appears in the shooting script), or a brief exchange she has with her employer, the Englishwoman, and Renfield. (That said, Carruth retains the Translyvanian passenger's dialogue "To the Virgin we pray" as the closing dialogue for the carriage ride; as intended in the Fort-Browning shooting script, the dialogue marks a relevant transition into the next scene at the "Peasant Hut," where a native is praying aloud.)

Similarly, it is possible that Browning filmed all of the shooting script's dialogue for Dracula when he first meets Renfield: "The walls of my castle – the shadows are many – but, come – I bid you welcome." But in the completed film, a shot of Renfield cuts to Dracula speaking only the final four words. Another cut eliminated the dialogue that followed Dracula's line "I trust you have kept your coming here a secret":

RENFIELD: *Oh, yes, indeed – just as you requested.*

DRACULA: *And you've destroyed all our correspondence – ?*

Carruth cuts directly to Renfield's next line, "I've followed your instructions implicitly," thus eliminating two unnecessary lines of dialogue, even while creating a minor continuity error in that Dracula's hand in the second shot is no longer on the wine bottle, as it was in the first shot [See Figures 6I and 6J]. Here the minor continuity error suggests that Browning probably did shoot the dialogue, and that it was excised in editing.

Carruth also apparently eliminated footage during Van Helsing's first onscreen meeting with Renfield. The shooting script finds the two characters discussing Oxford University, as well as the merits of eating flies, which on the one hand Renfield dismisses as "a low form of life beneath my notice," but which on the other hand he applauds

Figure 6I

Figure 6J

for having "wings [that] typify the aerial powers of the psychic faculties." By using a cutaway of Dr. Seward seated at his desk, Carruth bridges the jump cut that would otherwise have occurred by deleting some of the conversation. As a result, he is able to move immediately ahead with Van Helsing's dialogue, "I am here to help you. You understand that, do you not?"

Another example comes during Dracula's visit to the Seward home when Van Helsing discovers the Count casts no shadow in a mirrored cigarette box. Cutting seems to have removed two dialogue exchanges in the shooting script that might well have been filmed. One is between Dracula and Mina; learning she is unwell, Dracula suggests he should depart, but Mina requests that he stay. Later in the same scene, Carruth also omitted an exchange in which Harker apologizes for having been rude and Dracula "smiles courteously" and offers a brief response. In these cases, Carruth shortened individual scenes in an apparent effort to speed up the film's pacing.

Major changes made during either the production and post-production phase prompted some of the other editing decisions. For example, prior to the scene of Dracula's additional visit to Mina's bedroom (which, as already noted, chronologically represents the first visit he makes), Carruth inserted a scene of Renfield in his second-floor room, talking through the iron bars on his window to a silent Dracula standing on the ground below. In the shooting script, the scene comes immediately after Van Helsing instructs Briggs to make certain that Mina wears wolfbane when she goes to bed.

As shot, the Renfield-Dracula scene features *more* dialogue than the shooting script, a key reason to believe that Browning may have decided to change this aspect of the continuity during the production. However, the altered continuity results in a minor continuity error. Renfield wears gray tic trousers during the scene in Seward's laboratory, but in one shot he wears darker trousers in his cell, which – given the altered continuity – takes place only minutes or hours later in the narrative.[39] While continuity errors can and do happen during the production process, especially when footage might stem from retakes and pickups shot days or weeks apart, the different trousers might suggest that the decision to move the scene came during post-production. By contrast, Renfield's pertinent dialogue occurs in a medium shot filmed through the bars of his window; in it, his trousers cannot be seen. But it is apparent that his hair appears quite different from the immediately prior shot with the darker trousers, suggesting that the two shots *may* have been filmed at different times or even on different days. After all, as Dracula's first visit to Mina's room indicates, it is not impossible or even improbable that brief scenes in this film can and – at least in that case – have been constructed out of footage filmed at different times for different purposes.

At any rate, however, the most notable change during the scene is not the new dialogue created during the production phase, but instead the deletion of Renfield's line: "You're not angry with me?" In the original order of events, Dracula would have had reason to be upset with Renfield, who by that point had advised Harker and Seward to be "guided" by Van Helsing's wisdom. Once moved into the earlier section of the film, the scene would have made no sense if Dracula was angry at Renfield, and so the line was eliminated.

After the decision was made to have Dracula make two visits to Mina's bedroom, dialogue in the scene of Mina explaining her dream also needed to be cut, lest it confuse the timeline:

VAN HELSING: *When did you have this dream, Miss Mina?*
MINA: *Why, I – it was the night Father left for Switzerland – the night after Lucy's funeral.*

Assuming that Browning shot it, Carruth eliminated this dialogue. Likewise, Carruth deleted an earlier exchange between Harker and Mina in which Harker bemoans the fact that she was left alone while her father was "away," a reference to the Switzerland trip.

Eliminating references to Seward's journey to Switzerland condenses the overall Whitby narrative. Rather than taking place over many days if not longer (as such a round trip to the continent would have required), the story unfolds over a much briefer time frame. This change includes Van Helsing's laboratory. While Van Helsing's nationality (to which Dracula obliquely refers when he suggests the professor should return to his "country") might imply that his lab is in another country (as could the scenery visible through its window), that much is not stated in the released film. Nor is the lab explicitly linked to Switzerland in the shooting script, though that might have been the intended implication, with Seward's trip occurring so that he could deliver the vampiric blood sample to Van Helsing.

In the script and film, Seward appears in the scene in Van Helsing's laboratory, perhaps to strengthen the narrative connection between Seward's trip to Switzerland and the location of Van Helsing's lab (as well as to give actor Herbert Bunston more screen time). But the elimination of all references to Switzerland and Van Helsing's appearance at the sanitarium in Whitby immediately after the scene in his own lab hardly suggests that the two have just spent time together in Switzerland. Rather, their contact in the final film seems to occur entirely in England.

Publicity portrait of Dwight Frye in the gray tic trousers.
(Courtesy of D'Arcy More)

Despite his best efforts, however, Carruth seems to have been unable to remove every vestige of Seward's trip to Switzerland. Shortly after a maid announces Dracula's arrival in the scene that leads to him smashing the mirrored cigarette box, Dracula speaks the following line: "It's good to see you back again, Doctor. I heard you have just arrived." Dracula speaks the second sentence while a cutaway of Mina appears onscreen. Importantly, the shooting script uses the word "returned," rather than "arrived." The reason for the cutaway was likely due to the word "arrived" being replacement dialogue that tried to modify the meaning of the original dialogue.[40]

Viewers might understand this dialogue to mean that Seward has just arrived from London or some other (in the context of the film's geography) nearby location, rather than returning from a lengthy journey to the continent. In any event, the removal of Seward's Switzerland trip represents one of the key narrative changes that occurred during the post-production phase. Indeed, the only other change of the same magnitude would be Dracula's additional visit to Mina's bedroom, if it did in fact originate during the post-production phase. With the elimination of Switzerland, the film's running time decreased and its pacing increased, the result being a Seward household under siege by a vampire with onscreen images of clocks and sunsets underscoring the relentlessness of each passing hour.

Music

In April 1930, Universal purchased a half-interest in the music publishing company of Handman, Kent, and Goodman.[41] Frank Goodman, the firm's general manager and president, also helped Universal expand its musical staff, which, according to *Billboard*, would "compose special numbers" for forthcoming Universal films. At that time, David Broekman acted as the studio's musical director.[42]

Above Top: Heinz Roemheld, General Musical Director at Universal during *Dracula*'s post-production. *(Courtesy of William H. Rosar).* Above: Roemheld's advertisement in *Variety* for Christmas 1930.

By August 1930, however, Universal appointed pianist and composer Heinz Roemheld to be Broekman's successor, with the title General Musical Director.[43] Born in Wisconsin in 1901, Roemheld had served as musical director at Universal's Alhambra Theatre in Milwaukee in the mid-1920s.[44] His original score for *The Phantom of the Opera* (1925) caused Universal to move him to the more prominent Rialto Theatre in Washington, D. C. for two years; the studio then sent him to Germany to manage two Laemmle-owned theatres.[45]

Under Roemheld's direction, Universal developed a new strategy for film music in September 1930, shortly before *Dracula* went into production. Given that few movies on the

Lugosi's Dracula and Dade's Lucy at the theatre, depicting moments in the film shortly before Schuber's *Unfinished Symphony* is heard for a second time. *(Courtesy of Jack Dowler)*

autumn schedule needed original songs, staff composers began to write special compositions that Universal planned to "keep for future use in musical scoring." As a result, the studio hoped to build up a library of original scores, thus preventing it from having to pay large royalties for copyrighted material.[46] The strategy would also prove helpful in January 1931, when Laemmle, Sr.'s cutbacks at Universal resulted in the music department being slashed to just three persons, with Roemheld becoming "boss of what's left."[47]

At the time, the norm in the film industry was to avoid non-diegetic film music, meaning background scores heard by the film audience, but not by the onscreen characters. However, it is worth noting that the Warner Bros. film *The Terror* (1928) features an

```
                                              February 14, 1931
                                              No. Pages 1

     There follows a list of the compositions recorded in connec-
tion with the Photoplay entitled

                         "DRACULA"

Production No. 109-1, Erpi No. 2-Wc-104, as reported to this office
by Universal West Coast.

                                   D.S. PRATT              VL
Recorded Oct.10,1930
                                                         Extent
   Title of Composition    Composer        Publisher     of use

 *1  Le Lac Des Cygnes     P.Tschaikowsky  Public Domain   P
 *2  Unfinished Symphony   Schubert        Fischer         P
 *3  The Miestersingers    Wagner          Public Domain   P
       Von Nuernberg
 *4  Unfinished Symphony   Schubert        Fischer         P
 *5  Old French Folk Song                  Public Domain   P
```

Universal's compilation of musical cues used for *Dracula*, prepared on February 14, 1931. *(Courtesy of William H. Rosar)*

almost constant usage of background music for its entire running time, save for three scenes that use diegetic organ music (diegetic meaning music that stems from an onscreen source that the characters hear).[48]

By contrast, Roemheld's soundtrack for *Dracula* concentrated on music for the opening titles, as well as solely on diegetic music heard within the narrative. *Dracula* would not feature a background score, but that was also true of its important predecessors at Universal, including *All Quiet on the Western Front* and *The Cat Creeps*, the latter of which featured absolutely no music of any kind (diegetic or non-diegetic) during its narrative.[49] Roemheld followed the same approach for *Resurrection* (1931), which he supervised in late 1930.[50]

While adhering to general norms of Hollywood at the time, it is must be said that Roemheld (perhaps in tandem with others) definitely made artistic choices about the music for *Dracula*, as well as the lack of the same. To eschew background music – as had been used in *The Terror*, for example – was in fact a decision, and it was not a decision based on financial concerns, as scholar Michael Slowik has incorrectly speculated.[51]

For example, the decision to use Tchaikovsky's *Swan Lake* over the opening credits for *Dracula* remains a distinctive choice, and it was indeed a choice. While Universal would reuse this music for opening credits of future films like *Murders in the Rue Morgue* (1932) and *The Mummy* (1932), *Dracula* was the very first time it was heard in one of their talking pictures, horror or otherwise. It is worth noting that *Swan Lake* was still under copyright in 1930, which meant its selection would have required payment to the rights holder. What all of this means is that, rather than using in-house music composed by a member of staff already on the payroll, Roemheld (or one of the persons working under him, such as Sam Perry) specifically selected

Swan Lake for *Dracula*, likely due to its common usage as a mysterious theme in live silent-film music.[52] Indeed, for the opening title sequence to Universal's *The Cat Creeps*, which had been released while *Dracula* was still in production, Roemheld quoted J. Bodewalt Lampe's *Misterioso Pizzicato*, another theme popular with those musicians who accompanied silent films.[53] In short, paying for *Swan Lake* meant intentionally choosing it, rather than repurposing music that Universal owned or having a staff composer write something new as part of his salaried position.

This frame from *Dracula* depicts Lucy's music box.

Dracula's second and third musical compositions are heard during a scene at the theatre in London, with the key characters gathered at an evening's concert. Schubert's *Unfinished Symphony* accompanies Dracula's entrance to the lobby, while the coda to Wagner's *Meistersinger* prelude plays while Dracula is ushered inside the auditorium. After the intermission, Schubert's *Unfinished Symphony* returns.

The fourth musical composition heard in *Dracula* (and the fifth selection, given the two uses of Wagner) is heard in Lucy's London apartment, while she discusses Count Dracula with Mina. Following from a suggestion for the same in the final shooting script, Browning used a music box that is also a perfume bottle. A list of music cues prepared by Universal in February 1931 refers to the film's fifth musical selection as *Old French Folk Song*.

The shooting script also offers advice for music to be heard at *Dracula*'s conclusion: "the sound of organ music starts to accompany for final rounding off of fade. Then it is suddenly cut off as we hear a voice command." The voice was Van Helsing's (Edward Van Sloan's). According to the script, he shouts, "Wait!" and then proceeds to give his curtain speech. From the standpoint of the film's soundtrack, the script's idea was quite clever. Fort and Browning intended Van Helsing's intrusion into the final moments of the film to be jarring, as if it was an impromptu speech; the actor disrupting the organ music would have added to that effect. It is difficult to say with certainty whether Roemheld used such organ music for the film's original ending, though it is extremely likely; organ music can certainly be heard at the end of the Spanish-language *Dracula*. Given that Van Helsing's voice was intended to interrupt and overlap with the closing music in the Browning version, it is quite likely that Universal had to remove the music for the 1938 re-release; otherwise, when they excised the curtain speech, the organ music would have ended abruptly.

At any rate, surviving prints from 1938 and thereafter feature a brief use of chimes, which aurally imply the future marriage of Mina and Harker. Universal's 1931 list of music cues in *Dracula* makes no mention of either organ music or of the chimes. The probable reason is that the list chronicles only pre-existing music for legal reasons, whereas the organ music (if it was used in the original 1931 release prints) and the later chimes were likely composed by Universal staff for the film.

Roemheld's department recorded all of Dracula's original music on 10 October 1930, some time before editing began, which indicates how carefully he and his colleagues made their choices. They were not working under the duress of time, but instead operating far ahead of the post-production schedule, during which sound man Jack Foley would record a range of sound effects for Dracula that ranged from howling wind and howling wolves to a scream for the flower girl, a sound that the shooting script notably did not suggest. Along with the music, the sound effects would be added to the edited film in the post-production phase.

Title Sequences

During the post-production phase, Universal's art title department prepared Dracula's opening and closing title sequences. By 1930, artist Max Cohen had spent over a decade as the department's manager, working on everything from film prologues to special effects and trick photography.[54] And as one trade publication noted, he "art-titled all the big [movies] during that time."[55] Born in Pittsburgh in 1889, Cohen began his career as an actor in vaudeville and then motion pictures before finding work as an artist and a technician. He was also the director of the 1923 film *The Mystery of King Tut-Ankh-Amen's Eighth Wife*.

Only four days before Dracula's premiere in New York City, the *Los Angeles Times* wrote:

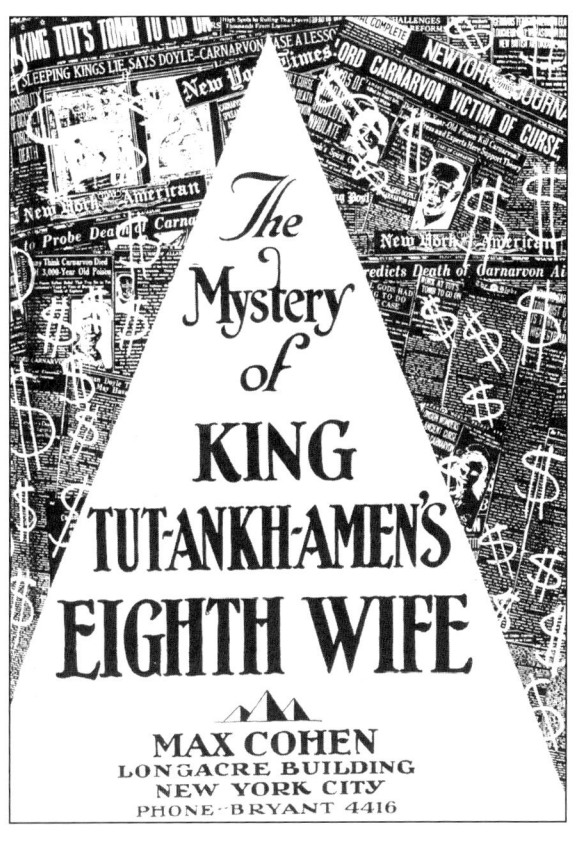

Advertisement for Max Cohen's film *The Mystery of King Tut-Ankh-Amen's Eighth Wife* (1923).

> Max Cohen, whose strikingly original and often futuristic backgrounds adorn many of the main titles that go all over the world on motion pictures, took his job naturally, showing an inherent interest for art even in his kindergarten days.
> It was in this stage of his career that his mother, noting a very unusual sketch, ventured to ask him what it was.
> 'That's heaven,' replied little Max without looking up from his labors.
> 'But good gracious!' exclaimed his mother. 'You don't know what heaven looks like. Nobody knows what heaven looks like!'
> 'They will though,' returned the youthful artist with conviction, 'when I get this picture finished.'

Figure 6K

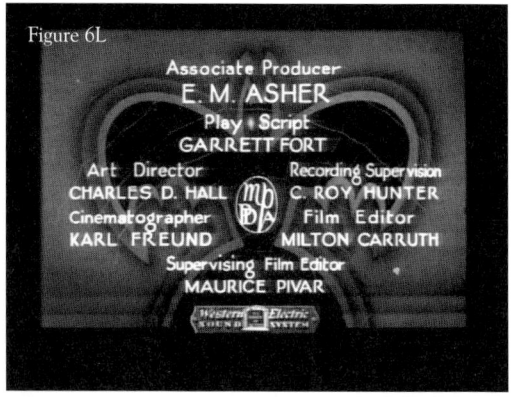

Figure 6L

Figure 6M

Figure 6N

Cohen's paintings were regularly exhibited in the Los Angeles area in the late twenties, including at his own gallery in North Hollywood.[56]

Dracula's opening credits feature Cohen's striking art deco bat and spider-web, which appear behind all of the onscreen text. Regrettably, a misspelled word appears on the first set of titles ("Carl Laemmle, President" is printed as "Presient" without the "d"). Then, after the first set of text dissolves into the second, the size of the bat decreases for no apparent reason, an error that may have occurred in post-1931 reissue prints. [See Figures 6K and 6L].

In all available prints of the film, the closing credits unfold as a single title card that announces "The End," while a turning globe in the lower right corner reminds the audience, "It's a Universal Picture" [See Figure 6M]. Given that Universal cut Van Helsing's curtain speech for a 1938 re-release, it is quite possible that the film's closing credits were altered as well. On 17 December 1930, the *Hollywood Reporter* announced that:

> Universal is going to rehash an old system of screen credits by carrying at the end of each production the names and pictures of each character in the story so that the patrons will remember these players more definitely. The regulation main title of credits will remain the same as before.
> The new system will go into effect with the release of *Resurrection* and continue with all subsequent releases until voted down or disapproved by the exhibitors.[57]

Resurrection was released on 2 February 1931, ten days prior to *Dracula,* and surviving prints of Carewe's film do in fact show the names and pictures of each main character at the end of the film [See Figure 6N]. Universal did implement the plan, which means that *Dracula*'s original end credits might well have featured images of the film's stars and their names after Van Helsing's curtain speech.

In addition to the opening and closing credits, *Dracula* features two onscreen titles during the narrative. The first reads, "Aboard the *Vesta* -- bound for England," and the second reads, "London." Both of them give viewers basic geographical information, similar to many other such titles used in the early talkie period and, for that matter, throughout the history of classical and post-classical Hollywood. For example, *Resurrection* features five intertitles, which offer geographical information ("On the Russo-Turkish Frontier") as well as temporal details ("For seven years Katusha Maslova was forgotten, and then --").

In terms of *Dracula*, the most fascinating onscreen title is perhaps the one that mentions the *Vesta*. The final shooting script does not name the ship, whereas Stoker's novel refers to it as the *Demeter*, after the Greek goddess of fertility and the harvest. Stoker likely selected the name due to the famous mythical story in which Hades abducts Demeter's daughter Persephone to the underworld. By contrast, Vesta was the Roman goddess of the home, hearth, and family, with her closest equivalence in Greek mythology being Hestia; the Vestal Virgins were a priesthood devoted to her. Here the film creates an ironic, even if unintentional, metaphor. Dracula sleeps deep inside a ship named for a virgin goddess as he journeys to violate three virgins in England.

The Silent *Dracula*

The transition from silent film to sound was fraught with many concerns, ranging from the financial to the technical. And, as Chapter 3 suggested, it was a slow transition, with some movie theatres in smaller towns and rural areas delaying the installation of sound equipment, due in part to problems borrowing money once the Great Depression began.

As a result, major American studios released silent versions of many of their talkies. In the spring of 1929, for example, MGM told the industry press that it would offer silent versions of the majority of its sound features for the 1929-30 season.[58] During the summer of that same year, Fox organized a "silent pictures department" to prepare silent editions of its new talkies.[59] And by November of 1929, United Artists announced that it would release silent versions for all of its sound films.[60]

Universal was no exception, with Carl Laemmle, Sr. deciding in April 1929 to make "pictures for both markets," meaning silent and sound.[61] The studio continued to produce silent versions of some of its sound product during the 1930-31 season, a choice that was not surprising. As of January 1931, over 12,000 American theatres had installed sound equipment, but over 3,100 had not.[62]

For the silent version of *Dracula*, the process necessary to achieve a silent version could well have meant what it did for at least some other Hollywood film shoots of the time: a second camera rolled near the main camera and shot similar footage of each take. It is difficult to say with certainty that this occurred, but it certainly would explain how Universal constructed the silent negative for *Dracula*, as making an inter-negative from the print used for the sound version and simply adding intertitles to it in order to strike positive prints would not have yielded a quality image. One could invoke the fact that Freund shot a

> Here's Wishing You a
> Greater Thrill Year
>
> BELA LUGOSI

Above: Bela Lugosi's advertisement in the January 3, 1931 issue of the *Hollywood Filmograph*. Opposite: Tod Browning's Christmas advertisement, published in the *Hollywood Reporter* on December 22, 1930.

silent-aperture image with his camera, which is true, but that still does not necessarily speak to the silent version. Indeed, industry press mention of King Grey and Joseph Brotherton acting as second cameramen might suggest that a second camera *was* present (rather than necessarily meaning that one or both of the men shot footage elsewhere while Freund was at work on set).

At any rate, Universal tasked Gardner Bradford with writing approximately two hundred intertitles to explain the film's narrative. Bradford's career included work as a journalist and publicist, but he was also well-known for writing silent film intertitles, which he had done since at least 1913.[63] He had worked in the same capacity for Universal for years, with Tod Browning's *Outside the Law* (1920) and *Drifting* (1923) among his many credits.

Given that *Dracula* was a talkie, it is perhaps not surprising that all of Bradford's titles represent dialogue. The only descriptive intertitles listed are those that also appear in the sound version (such as "Aboard the *Vesta* -- bound for England"). Many of Bradford's intertitles draw directly from the film's dialogue, including such famous lines as "I am Dracula," "The blood is the life, Mr. Renfield," "I never drink – wine," and "To die – to be really dead – that must be glorious!" Bradford also attempted to mimic Martin's Cockney accent in such intertitles as: "'E thinks they're wolves! 'E thinks they're talking to him! 'E's crazy!"

Indeed, it seems clear that Bradford used the sound film as a guide, rather than the final shooting script, as some of his intertitles indicate changes made during the production process. For example, Bradford's intertitle has Dracula telling Van Helsing: "She will live through the centuries, even as I have lived!" Here Bradford shortens Dracula's dialogue in the film, as he does elsewhere to limit the number of intertitles and the number of words on each. But he was clearly aware of Browning's changes, as opposed to repeating (or abbreviating) the dialogue from the final script, which reads: "She will live through all Eternity, as I have lived!"

By contrast, some of Bradford's dialogue intertitles vary noticeably from the sound film. For example, he changed the secretary's opening dialogue to: "-- approaching Bistritz, the road crosses the Carpathian Mountains, one of the wildest parts of Central Europe." No reference is made to the "rugged peaks that frown down," which became one of the most famous lines of dialogue spoken in the classic American horror film.

Three of Bradford's intertitles even alter the narrative, at least to a minor degree. At the climax of the sound film, Harker spots Renfield heading for Carfax Abbey. He exclaims: "That's Renfield. What's he doing at the Abbey?" By contrast, Bradford's intertitle makes Harker more deductive and assertive: "That's Renfield heading for Carfax Abbey! He may lead us to Dracula's earth-boxes!"[64]

More notably, two intertitles that appear after Van Helsing stakes Dracula are quite different from any dialogue spoken in the sound version. Both occur when Van Helsing appears alongside Harker and Mina, and both were likely meant to convey Van Helsing's dialogue, given that his lips are moving in the shot while the other two characters embrace. The first intertitle says: "At last Dracula is really dead – a stake through his heart – his soul is at peace." The second reads, in a reference to Mina: "And for you too, the horror is over –." In the sound film, the final discussion of Dracula (who is not a particularly sympathetic character) comes in the form of Mina's dialogue; she recalls the

Chapter 6 – POST-PRODUCTION

"look on his face" when "the daylight stopped him." By contrast, Bradford's intertitle mentions that Dracula's "soul [is] at peace," thus presenting a more gentle description of the vampire's end.

Universal prepared and released the silent version of *Dracula* near the end of the American cinema's transition to sound. As early as the spring of 1930, RKO, Paramount, and Columbia announced that they were ending the practice of releasing silent versions of sound films, with Columbia blaming the decision on "meagre returns available from unwired accounts."[65] Similarly, MGM declared in June 1930 that it would no longer offer silent versions of its talking pictures, a marked contrast to the studio's practice the prior year.[66] In the autumn of 1930, two articles in *Billboard* argued that a market still existed for silent films in both America and abroad, but with each passing day, that was less and less true.[67] And so *Dracula* became one of Universal's final silent film releases.

Conclusion

At approximately 74 minutes and thirty seconds, the final edit of Universal's *Dracula* was within a very acceptable range of running times for 1931. Universal's hit *All Quiet on the Western Front* ran a lengthy 145 minutes, but the studio's *Free Love* (1930) ran 70 minutes, *Resurrection* 81 minutes, and *Many a Slip* (1931) 64 minutes, all three being films edited at roughly the same time as *Dracula*. To offer another example, *The Cat Creeps*, released while *Dracula* was in production, ran approximately 75 minutes in length, with only seconds separating its duration from *Dracula*'s.

The editing phase tightened *Dracula* considerably over the story that unfolds in the shooting script, creating a faster pace by abbreviating particular scenes and cutting others in their entirety. The result features three very brief appearances by Dracula that the shooting script had not envisioned, but at the same time deletes a good deal of screen time that he had in other scenes.

The final edit also condensed the narrative time at Whitby, transforming the story from one that takes place over a period of weeks to a small number of days, the result more clearly creating a tense situation at a sanitarium/residence under siege by the attacks of a vampire and the incessant ramblings of a maniac who manages to escape his cell at will. Here is arguably a major improvement to the film's narrative.

As for Tod Browning, the exact role he played in post-production remains unknown. He could have been less involved in its latter stages, particularly as he began directing his next film *Iron Man* in mid-January 1931, though that certainly would not have prevented him from viewing changes to *Dracula* in the evenings.[68] Also unknown are his true feelings about a post-production process that involved numerous persons working on what became at least three versions of the film, if not more.

What is certain is that by the end of January (if not even sooner), *Dracula* was ready for its premiere. While a production log noted a total cost of $355,050, Junior Laemmle's account of the final negative cost of *Dracula* was $441,984.90, the higher figure likely resulting from expenditures and salaries related to pre-production and post-production.[69] That figure might also have included a studio overhead charge and costs associated with the preparation of publicity materials.

1. "Universal Increases Budget for Next Year." *Film Daily* 17 Dec. 1930: 1.
2. "Universal Lining Up Next Season's Stories." *Film Daily* 3 Dec. 1930: 1.
3. "Universal Plans for 32 Next Year." *Hollywood Reporter* 3 Dec. 1930: 1.
4. "Laemmle, Sr., Slashes Payroll at Universal." *Hollywood Reporter* 5 Jan. 1931: 4.
5. Schatz, Thomas. *The Genius of the System: Hollywood Filmmaking in the Studio Era* (New York: Pantheon, 1988): 87.
6. Laemmle, Carl, Jr. "The Serial Makes a Comeback." *Billboard* 6 Dec. 1930: 70.
7. Merrick, Mollie. "Hollywood – In Person." *New Orleans Times-Picayune* 20 July 1930.
8. "Maurice Pivar, U Film Editor, Marries on Coast." *Universal Weekly* 14 Aug. 1926: 29.
9. "Pivar Returns." *Variety* 12 Mar. 1930: 4; "Pivar Returns to Edit 'U' Pictures." *Hollywood Filmograph* 5 Apr. 1930: 15.
10. "*Resurrection* is Nearing Completion." *Seattle Times* 11 Jan. 1931: 28.
11. Skal, David J. and Elias Savada. *Dark Carnival: The Secret World of Tod Browning, Hollywood's Master of the Macabre* (New York: Anchor, 1995): 151.
12. The "host" in question was actress Ottola Nesmith, who pretended to be Mae Clarke on a KTLA broadcast on 1 Oct. 1957. Gregory William Mank has written about this incident in his essay "Shock! Theatre, 'The Half-Witch and Half-Fairy,' and Dr. Lucifer." At the time of this writing, Mank's essay has not yet been published.
13. Geltzer, George. "Tod Browning." *Films in Review* (Oct. 1953): 415.
14. Everson, William K. "Horror Films." *Films in Review* (Jan. 1954): 15.
15. Buster, Alan. Interview with William S. Hart, Jr. 10 Aug. 1980. Transcript exists at the Margaret Herrick Library, Academy of Motion Picture Arts and Sciences, Beverly Hills, CA.
16. Skal and Sevada, p. 151.
17. Qtd. in Riley, Philip J. *London After Midnight* (New York: Cornwall, 1985): 24.
18. Skal and Savada, p. 171.
19. "Cutting No Cinch, Browning Avers." *Exhibitors Herald* 25 Dec. 1920: 209.
20. Indeed, it seems likely that there were at least three versions of *Dracula*. One work print apparently led to the perceived need for the "added scenes," which then led to a formal preview screening, which then led to "retakes" and thus what became a third version. However, it is important to note that this would be the *minimum* number of versions, as the process of editing over a period of weeks likely produced ongoing changes and evolutions.
21. Lennig, Arthur. *The Count: The Life and Films of Bela "Dracula" Lugosi*. (New York: G. P. Putnam's Sons, 1974): 96.
22. Lennig, Arthur. *The Immortal Count: The Life and Films of Bela Lugosi* (Lexington, KY: University of Kentucky, 2003): 113, 120.
23. "Production Activities." *Hollywood Reporter* 20 Nov. 1930: 3.
24. Wilk, Ralph. "A Little from 'Lots.'" *Film Daily* 30 Nov. 1930: 4.
25. "Production Activities." *Hollywood Reporter* 3 Dec. 1930: 4; "Pictures Now in Production." *Hollywood Reporter* 2 Jan. 1931: 4.
26. Wilk, Ralph. "A Little from 'Lots.'" *Film Daily* 7 Dec. 1930: 4.
27. Rhodes, Gary D. "The Curious Undead Life of Tod Browning's *Dracula* (1931)," *Monsters from the Vault* (Summer 2011): 4-33.
28. "Los Angeles Previews." *Film Daily* 18 Oct. 1925: 4.
29. "Universal Adopts 'Overhaul' System." *Motion Picture News* 20 Sept. 1930: 57.
30. "Universal Has Plenty of Work Outlined." *Hollywood Filmograph* 20 Dec. 1930: 18; "Universal Completes Schedule for 1930-31." *Film Daily* 21 Dec. 1930: 1, 12.
31. "Spooky Film Will Draw Well." *Hollywood Reporter* 24 Dec. 1930: 3.
32. Churchill, Edward. "New Product." *Motion Picture Herald* 3 Jan. 1931: 71-72.
33. Joy, Jason. Letter to Carl Laemmle, Jr. 9 Jan. 1931. Available in the file for *Dracula* in the Motion Picture Association of America, Production Code Administration collection at the Margaret Herrick Library in Beverly Hills, CA.
34. Fisher, James. Notation on *Dracula*. 14 Jan. 1931. Available in ibid.
35. "Comments of Previewers on *Dracula*." Available in ibid.
36. Moreover, as will be discussed in Chapter 11, the edit point on the first two shots in Dracula's Chambers features a continuity error in which the door closes of its own accord is in two different stages of shutting.
37. "Hollywood Bulletins." *Variety* 10 Sept. 1930: 25.
38. "The Storm Breaker." *Film Daily* 20 Sept. 1925: 4.
39. Here I would like to acknowledge the work of Clark J. Holloway, who noticed Renfield's different trousers after viewing Universal's 2012 restoration of *Dracula*.
40. Replacement dialogue can be heard elsewhere in *Dracula*. Aurally, it is clear that such was the case with Van Helsing's lines: "Doctor, this time we can do no harm. This time we are ready for him." The dialogue was added with ease, as Van Helsing's back is to the camera for those lines, thus avoiding any problems of the audio being out of sync with his lips.
41. "U Joins Music Publishing Ranks." *Exhibitors Herald-World* 19 Apr. 1930: 58.
42. "Laemmle Buys in on Music Publishers." *Billboard* 12 Apr. 1930: 22.
43. "New U Musical Chief." *Motion Picture News* 9 Aug. 1930: 9.
44. "Variety Revue in Milwaukee." *Variety* 7 Apr. 1926.
45. Rosar, William H. "Music for the Monsters: Universal Pictures' Horror Film Scores of the Thirties." *The Quarterly Journal of the Library of Congress* Vol. 40, No. 4 (Fall 1983): 393.

46 "U Writers Kept Busy." *Hollywood Reporter* 22 Sept. 1930: 5.

47 "Hollywood Bulletins." *Variety* 28 Jan. 1931.

48 Surviving sound discs of *The Terror* actually include four scenes using organ music, though aural evidence is not sufficient to determine whether the music in one of those four scenes is diegetic rather than non-diegetic.

49 Rosar, p. 392.

50 Wilk, Ralph. "A Little from 'Lots.'" *Film Daily* 3 Nov. 1930: 6.

51 Slowik, Michael. "Diegetic Withdrawal and Other Worlds: Film Music Strategies Before *King Kong*, 1927-1933." *Cinema Journal* Vol. 53, No. 1 (Fall 2013): 1-25.

52 Ibid., p. 394.

53 J. Bodewalt Lampe's *Misterioso Pizzicato* was published in the *Remick Folio of Moving Picture Music* in 1914. A similar, though different, theme appeared the prior year in *Sam Fox Moving Picture Music* by J. S. Zamecnik. As a result, it is possible that the origins of *Misterioso Pizzicato* date to an earlier period, even to the nineteenth century.

54 Quigley, Martin, ed. "Cohen, Max." *The Motion Picture Almanac, 1931*. (New York: Quigley Publishing, 1932): 106.

55 "Universal Notes." *Hollywood Filmograph* 13 Dec. 1930: 11.

56 See, for example: "Good Short Stories." *Los Angeles Times* 23 Dec. 1928.

57 "Universal to Use Credits at End." *Hollywood Reporter* 17 Dec. 1930: 3.

58 "Silent Versions Available for 50 New MGM Audiens." *Exhibitors Herald-World* 27 Apr. 1929: 41.

59 "Fox to Make Silent Negatives; Stone to Head New Department." *Exhibitors Herald-World* 5 Aug. 1929: 32.

60 Silent Versions Available on All U.A. Product." *Film Daily* 18 Nov. 1929: 1, 14.

61 Vischer, Peter. "Industry's Pace Dooms Self-Satisfied Company, Declares Laemmle." *Exhibitors Herald-World* 20 Apr. 1929: 34.

62 "More Than 12,000 Houses in US Are Now Wired to Show Talking Pictures." *Motion Picture Herald* 31 Jan. 1931: 13.

63 Price, Guy. "Coast Picture News." *Variety* 14 Dec. 1917.

64 In the sound film, Harker speaks his dialogue in a two-shot with Van Helsing, who responds, "Come, Mr. Harker." As a result, it is extremely likely that Bradford's intertitle refers to dialogue spoken by Harker, rather than reassigning it to the much wiser Van Helsing. I suggest this not only because it follows from the sound film, but also because Van Helsing's lips move so little in the shot.

65 "Silents Are About Washed Up; Not Enough Income in Sight Outside of the Foreign Market." *Variety* 2 Apr. 1930: 13.

66 "Silent Versions Off MGM List for New Season." *Motion Picture News* 21 June 1930: 19.

67 "Boosting Silent Films Brings Bigger Business." *Billboard* 13 Sept. 1930: 6; "Market for Silent Films." *Billboard* 22 Nov. 1930: 34.

68 "Five New 'U' Pictures Start Work This Month." *Film Daily* 12 Jan. 1931: 12

69 *Dracula (The Original 1931 Shooting Script)*. Ed. by Philip J. Riley. (Absecon, NJ: MagicImage, 1990): 62.

Chapter 7
PUBLICITY

On 21 January 1931, *Variety* announced that Harry Wilson, formerly a publicity man for director Edwin Carewe, had joined Universal to lead the advertising campaigns for *Resurrection* (1931) and *Dracula*.[1] His new position came just prior to the February premieres of both movies. Wilson would have had little input into the lengthy process that led to the creation and design of Universal's printed matter for those films, but he would have been well aware of the controversies surrounding Hollywood's publicity materials during the second half of 1930.

In June 1930, publicity man Frank Whitbeck described the problem in the pages of *Motion Picture News*:

A recent poster on a certain picture had a girl stretched out on a couch, was naked up to the hips and down to her navel. If that poster sold tickets, it wasn't apparent in Los Angeles. The picture did a flop. In another spot, maybe it would sell tickets. But either way, that poster was damned dangerous for this business of ours. It was offensive to good taste. It must have been downright repulsive to the women who interest themselves in the P.T.A., Women's Clubs and Better Films, not alone the fussy men in Better Business organizations and the Civic Beauty committee of any town.[2]

Whitbeck was particularly concerned about the fact that so much studio publicity was posted in places other than movie theatres, meaning billboards, store windows, as well as on empty buildings, fences, and so forth.

Will H. Hays, President of the Motion Picture Producers and Distributors of America (MPPDA), had earlier declared a need to eliminate "lurid, sexy advertising" from the motion-picture business, but by November of 1930, it seemed to some observers that nothing had really been accomplished, despite the industry's adoption of a "Code of Advertising Ethics" some five months earlier.[3] "Mr. Hays, we believe, should take another look at screen advertising. It is working much harm," judged a writer for *Billboard*.[4] One month later, the same trade publication returned to the issue:

The growth of cheap, lurid, and sensational advertising in connection with motion pictures has become a real menace. Will Hays and his organization had better do something to check it

7A – Publicity shot of Bela Lugosi, David Manners, Helen Chandler, Dwight Frye, and Edward Van Sloan for *Dracula* (1931). *(Courtesy of Jack Dowler)*

immediately. … Irreparable damage is being done [to] the good name of the entire industry, and unless action is taken soon the infection may prove fatal.
The principal difficulty seems to be that the advertising is written in New York. What the picture companies fail to consider is that Broadway's likes and dislikes are peculiar to that thorofare [sic].[5]

Declaring the problem to be one of the "most serious confronting the industry," *Billboard* warned that the ongoing use of salacious ads would "spell nothing but disaster."

By the end of December 1930, *Motion Picture Daily* headlined its front page with the story "Smutty Ads Boomerang," claiming that twelve state legislatures planned to consider new censorship laws for motion pictures the following month. "Sexy advertising is entirely responsible," the trade claimed, for "the worst censorship situation in recent film history and, perhaps, in the history of the business."[6]

The situation quickly grew worse. By early January, newspapers in Washington DC began censoring "sexy ads" for film releases.[7] That same month, an editorial in *Film Daily* implored studios to eliminate "hot" advertising, arguing that such "smut" was "building a wall of needless resentment" in the minds of some moviegoers.[8] And it was occurring during an economic depression.

Universal Studio's reaction was not one of fear. On 30 January 1931, *Film Daily* wrote: *Efforts to dignify theatre advertising have hurt attendance, according to Carl Laemmle [Sr.]. A timely warning is sounded in the Laemmle statement. There's much talk of fumigating advertising copy. Very likely sensible talk, too. But copy, although it should be kept out of the offensive class, shouldn't be dry-cleaned. That is, rendered so colorless that it makes dry, uninteresting reading.*[9]

Despite Laemmle's position, theatre chains proceeded to "warn managers" to "be good" in their advertising campaigns in early February.[10]

On 17 February 1931 – only five days after *Dracula*'s premiere in New York City – *Motion Picture Daily* printed Frank Whitbeck's response to Laemmle's philosophy, claiming he was "off on his wrong foot again."[11] Whitbeck not only disagreed with Laemmle on the need for dignity in film advertising, but also on where such ads should be posted. Universal continued to advise exhibitors to post heralds on every "fence and barrel" near their theatres.

It is difficult to determine the extent to which the furor over studio publicity affected *Dracula*'s advertising copy. Outwardly, Universal does not seem to have been intimidated by those who wanted to clean up movie advertisements, but the studio also likely wanted to avoid any negative publicity or unnecessary controversies. What is clear is that some of the pre-release advertisements for *Dracula* in the autumn of 1930 were somewhat more provocative than publicity materials printed for the film's premiere and the start of its general release in February 1931.

Aside from such controversies, *Dracula* posed other challenges to Universal and those persons who designed its advertising copy. The studio did not call the film a "horror" movie, despite the fact that at least one journalist had used that word to describe it in the autumn of 1930.[12] Universal eschewed "horror" in part because it had not yet experienced widespread, repeated usage as the name of a genre. Moreover, as Chapter 3 detailed, Junior Laemmle had envisioned *Dracula* as a combination of the romance and thriller genres. In the end, while Browning's film could be described loosely as a thriller with sexual undertones, it did not feature romance. Despite that fact, however, the studio continued to perceive *Dracula* in those terms, following from how Laemmle's original vision would appeal to various potential ticket-buyers, particularly women.

Representing the thriller and romance genres adequately in advertisements and proposed ballyhoo efforts was not easy, particularly when these goals involved the simultaneous need for studio publicity to promote *Dracula* without generating unhelpful accusations of being too "lurid." The result yielded a campaign that generally adhered to the needs of a key tagline, "The Story of the Strangest Passion the World Has Ever Known." But while this idea provided something of an anchor to *Dracula*'s publicity materials, it curiously invoked both the supernatural vampire and the Burne-Jones/Kipling/Bara "vamp," the latter being a connection that the film's own narrative sought to avoid.

Pre-Release Advertisements

In November of 1930, industry trade publications announced that Universal – despite making cutbacks elsewhere in its operation – intended to spend more money on publicity during the upcoming six months than it had ever spent during any similar

A comical publicity photo of Edward Van Sloan and Bela Lugosi taken for *Dracula* (1931). *(Courtesy of Buddy Barnett)*

time frame.[13] Carl Laemmle, Sr. said: "Universal is increasing its advertising space in trade papers, in newspapers, and in every other form of advertising. Good goods deserve more advertising than any other kind, and they deserve it during a business depression more than at any other time."[14] One example of this approach came in the form of the studio's "colorful brochure" that contained 44 pages of advertisements for films in the 1930-31 season.[15]

Ed Thomas' early draft of the *Dracula* pressbook, dated 15 November 1930, helps clarify the fact that Universal's vision of how to promote the film changed noticeably from the time of its production to the time of its release. In its pages, Thomas suggested a number of "catchlines," including:

> *Nameless horrors of the night.*
> *Shuddering horrors! Shrieks in the night! Death!*
> *The terrifying story of the weirdest character in fiction.*
> *The shuddering terrors of the blood-sucking vampires.*
> *Moldering graveyards, and the drip-drip-drip of blood.*
> *Dripping blood, and the dismal howling of wolves!*
> *The crowning mystery drama of the screen.*[16]

Universal's advertisement in the November 8, 1930 issue of *Motion Picture News*.

But none of Thomas' many catchlines survived the autumn to appear in the final studio pressbook or any of its publicity materials in 1931. As will be seen, the studio generally avoided all mention of words like "horror," "terror," "blood," and "mystery" in conjunction to *Dracula* in 1931. Perhaps the change in strategy came because such words did not meet with Junior Laemmle's belief that the film belonged to the romance and thriller genres, and/or as a result of the controversies over movie advertising in the autumn of 1931.

Other evolutions can be seen in Universal's advertisements for *Dracula* in the trade press from late 1930 to early 1931. For example, in two different issues of *Film Daily* in November 1930, Universal presented numerous small ads that featured only text:

> *Who is* Dracula? *What is he? Where is he?*
>
> Dracula *is coming!*
>
> *What is a Vampire Kiss? Only* Dracula *knows!*[17]
>
> *Do human vampires actually exist? See* Dracula
>
> *Wait for it! Watch for it!* Dracula, *world famous vampire picture is on the way!*
>
> *Was it a blessing or a curse? The kiss of* Dracula.
>
> Dracula *will get you if you don't watch out!*[18]

```
PRESSBOOK...
DRACULA
ET

                          CATCHLINES
                          ──────────


THE TERRIFYING STORY OF THE WEIRDEST CHARACTER IN FICTION.

A STORY OF VAMPIRES, AND THEIR NIGHTLY FEAST OF BLOOD.

NAMELESS HORRORS OF THE NIGHT.

THE SHUDDERING TERRORS OF THE BLOOD-SUCKING VAMPIRES.

A TERRIFYING FIEND --- IN THE FORM OF A MAN.

REVEALING THE HORRIBLE SECRETS OF THAT STRANGE HALF-WORLD LYING
     BETWEEN LIFE AND DEATH.

MOLDERING GRAVEYARDS, AND THE DRIP-DRIP-DRIP OF BLOOD.

"AND A STAKE MUST BE DRIVEN THROUGH HIS HEART!"

A STORY OF VAMPIRES, NEITHER WHOLLY DEAD FOR ENTIRELY LIVING --
     TERRIBLE "UNDEAD" CREATURES OF THE DARKNESS.

SHRIEKS IN THE NIGHT --- AND A MONSTER IN THE FORM OF A MAN SLINKS
     INTO THE SHADOWS.

THE STORY OF A HUMAN VAMPIRE --- NOW A MAN, NOW A WOLF, NOW A
     REPULSIVE BAT FLUTTERING OFF INTO THE DARKNESS.

SHUDDERING HORRORS!  SHRIEKS IN THE NIGHT!  DEATH!

INTRODUCING THE TERRIFYING "DRACULA KISS" OF DEATH.

DEMONSTRATING THAT HUMAN VAMPIRES ACTUALLY EXIST.

COUNT DRACULA HAS BEEN DEAD FOR 500 YEARS, BUT EACH NIGHT HE
     WALKS AMONG HIS FELLOWS, SEEKING THEIR BLOOD.

THE STRANGEST STORY EVER TOLD.

A STARTLING STORY OF HUMAN VAMPIRES.

DRIPPING BLOOD, AND THE DISMAL HOWLING OF WOLVES!

A WEIRD TALE OF HUMAN VAMPIRES WHO RETURN FROM THE GRAVE AT NIGHT.

THE STORY OF AN ABIDING LOVE --- AND A STRANGE PASSION.

CHILLING HORRORS OF THE NIGHT!

                          Continued
```

Taglines prepared by Ed Thomas for *Dracula* in November 1930 which did not appear in the final pressbook. (*Courtesy of George E. Turner*)

Collectively, these taglines conveyed three ideas. The first was to invoke the pre-existing popularity of the novel and play. The second was the idea of mystery, and the third was the idea of romance and perhaps sexual passion.

Also in November, Universal ran an advertisement for *Dracula* on the cover of *Film Daily*, offering for the first time the tagline that intentionally combined supernatural vampires and the "vamp" tradition: "The Story of the Strangest Passion the World Has Ever Known."[19] In this case, the ad illustrates a woman who is fast asleep in her bed. Due to her dark hair and facial features, she resembles neither Mina (Helen Chandler) nor Lucy (Frances Dade). Her gown is low-cut, and the artwork clearly depicts her right nipple as being erect. Descending from above is Dracula, his face – evidently designed to look like Bela Lugosi – staring intently at her. Dracula's hair flows upward, which accentuates his downward movement, and his hand reaches out for the woman's face. Overall, the image seems influenced by Fuseli's famous 1781 painting *The Nightmare*, as well as by artwork used to promote at least one American stage version of *Dracula* in 1928, though in the case of the latter, the vampire is present only in the form of two eyes.

Instead of drawing on Bela Lugosi's name (or any other actors in the film), the ad refers to Tod Browning and, in larger type, *All Quiet on the Western Front* ("World's Greatest Moneymaker") and *Resurrection* ("Ranking in the Big Money Class with *All Quiet on the Western Front*"). *Dracula* appears as the third film in a list of the studio's important achievements, even though *Resurrection* was not yet released. But it is clear that the list tried to link box-office success with prestige filmmaking. "First in First Runs Everywhere," another tagline claimed. In short, Universal was promoting *Dracula* as a big-budget and dignified film, rather than as a new mystery picture. Noticeably absent from discussion are Universal's sound version of *The Phantom of the Opera* (1930) and *The Cat Creeps* (1930).

Above Top: The provocative advertisement used on the cover of *Film Daily* of November 9, 1930. Above: The "Style C" one-sheet for *Dracula* (1931), which features notable changes to the earlier artwork, specifically in the elimination of the woman's erect nipple.

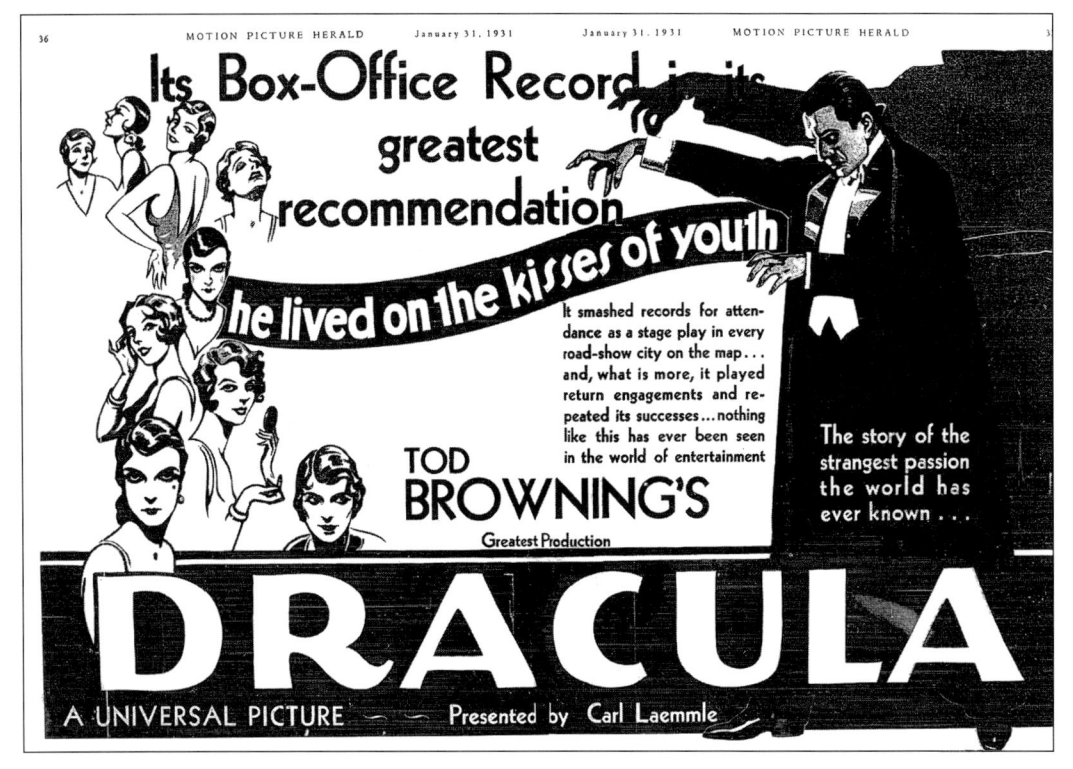

Advertisement published in *Motion Picture Herald* on January 31, 1931.

This particular advertisement (featuring a vertical aspect ratio) and a variation of it (with a horizontal aspect ratio, published in film trades in the autumn of 1930) would not reappear during *Dracula*'s general release.[20] The "Style C" one-sheet movie poster reused the artwork of the woman sleeping, but it featured two key differences. The image of Dracula was deleted, an artist replacing him with two large eyes in the darkness, harkening back to the aforementioned publicity for the stage play. Though the eyes represent a male presence, they suggest that the presence is watching the woman, rather than on the verge of touching her. Moreover, the artist noticeably altered the depiction of the woman's breast by eliminating the erect nipple. (This is at odds with the cover of the Grosset & Dunlap "photoplay" edition of Stoker's novel. Released in early 1931, the book featured a cover with the eyes replacing the face, but kept the erect nipple, further evidence that the change made for the "Style-C" poster was a conscious decision.)

Why the changes from November 1930 to February 1931? They may well have resulted from the controversy over "sexy ads" and "gutter copy" raging in the industry press, which was at its peak during those very months. The alterations may also have stemmed from personnel changes in Universal's publicity department. On 12 December 1930, the *Hollywood Reporter* announced that the Universal publicity department was "in the throes of a general re-organization, with Jack Proctor, Johnny Mitchell, and Junior Mace being let out, and Bob Donaldson and Jimmy Carrier added."[21]

Other pre-release advertisements for *Dracula* were less explicit than the *Film Daily* cover, but were still provocative in their own way. For example, a two-page trade advertisement showed a photograph of Lugosi's Dracula clutching the neck of Chandler's Mina. The largest tagline declares: "The kiss no woman can resist," while another repeats "The Story of the Strangest Passion the World Has Ever Known." Dracula smiles, whereas Mina looks as if she is asleep, perhaps in a trance. His cape conceals her chest.[22]

Another ad announced, "He Lived on the Kisses of Youth!" In it, Dracula looms over Mina and Lucy, his hands poised to grab both of them.[23] Given the inclusion of both women, the message seems to be far less one of romance than of unbridled sexual passion.[24] A more daring exploration of the same theme appears in artwork created for a two-page trade advertisement published in *Motion Picture Herald* on 31 January 1931. Dracula stands with his arm extended, as if to hypnotize nine women on the opposite page. They look young and confident, standing in elegant poses with one of them even applying makeup. "He lived on the kisses of youth," the key tagline suggests, implying sexuality and again linking supernatural vampires with those of the Theda Bara variety, though in the form of a gender inversion, with a male taking Bara's place. Another tagline announced: "The Story of the Strangest Passion the World Has Ever Known."

The Mainstream Press

In addition to touting *Dracula* within the film industry, Universal attempted to generate publicity for the film in the mainstream press of late 1930 and early 1931. As of 19 November 1930, the studio decided to promote Bela Lugosi's name "in larger type in all advertising" for *Dracula* as part of a plan to build him into a star.[25] The increased emphasis on Lugosi quickly extended to publicity in newspapers and fan magazines.

By the end of 1930, two different fan magazine articles featured stories about Lugosi and his connection to *Dracula*. Published in *Silver Screen*, one of them asked the pointed question "Is HE the Second Chaney?" Referring to Lugosi as a "man of mystery and a master of make-up," the story printed a trio of photographs of the actor, one of them depicting him in front of a makeup mirror.[26] Here the discussion seemed appropriate, as Chaney's death only months earlier created a perceived gap in the film industry, with various actors mentioned in the press as his possible successors.

At roughly the same time, *Motion Picture Classic* gave Lugosi even more coverage, with author Gladys Hall attempting to link his role of Dracula to his belief that women were more interested in horror and death than men. She quotes him as saying:

> *But it is women who love horror. Gloat over it. Feed on it. Are nourished by it. Shudder and cling and cry out* – and come back for more.
> *... When I was playing* Dracula *on the stage, my audiences were women. Women. There were men, too. Escorts the women had brought with them. For reasons only their dark subconscious knew. In order to establish a subtle sex intimacy. Contact. In order to cling and to feel the sensuous thrill of protection. Men did not come of their own volition. Women did. Came – and knew an ecstasy dragged from the depths of unspeakable things. Came – and then came back again. And again.*[27]

The rest of the article features Lugosi elaborating on the subject, including his claim that women thrive on attending Lon Chaney movies, cemeteries, freak shows, séances, executions, and even lynchings due to their insatiable lust for all things macabre. While Lugosi may

AFRAID OF HIMSELF

By LILLIAN SHIRLEY

Mr. Lugosi hates the character of Dracula. But his fascinating portrayal of it dooms him to go on playing it despite this hate.

Bela Lugosi is haunted by the horrible character he has created on the stage and screen—Count Dracula

IMAGINE the feelings of a man who for more than one thousand times has played a part which he hates with all his soul and yet is compelled to go on playing because his very hatred of the rôle makes it so convincing that no other man can give a satisfactory portrayal of it!

Bela Lugosi is the man and "Count Dracula" is the rôle in the play of that name. On the streets, men who don't know Lugosi stare unpleasantly when they recognize him, and women experience anticipatory shivers. Say "vampire" to almost anyone in Hollywood and they will reply, "Lugosi."

At this writing "Dracula" is being filmed into a talking picture at Universal City. You may remember "The Phantom of the Opera" with its mystery, gruesomeness and the horrible make-up of Lon Chaney. It was a trifling bug-a-boo tale to frighten infants compared to this "Dracula." It gives me a crawling spine just to think of it, and it produces shudders and backward looks over the shoulder in everyone connected with the making of it. So—I went off to Universal City, and carefully chose a terrifically hot day with plenty of bright sunlight to talk with Bela Lugosi, the mystery man of Hollywood.

"I AM a Hungarian by birth and education," he told me very quietly, almost sombrely. "I was reared in the town of Lugos, named for my family. I began stage work at the age of twenty, entirely by accident, and until after the war I had never been more than a few kilometers away from my native land. Most of the time I spent in Budapesth. Then I left—suddenly, to avoid being shot or hanged."

"In heaven's name—why?" I gasped, for young leading men do not usually make that kind of confession.

"It was the post-war penalty for being on the wrong side of politics," he replied with a faint smile. "I'm told they use the same method in Chicago occasionally. Well, I didn't wish to be 'taken for a ride.'"

Without doubt Bela Lugosi is Hollywood's prime mystery, but behind the mystery lies something that first attracts women to him before it makes them gasp and shiver. And looking at him in his make-up for the part of Dracula I wouldn't doubt it for a moment. To begin with, the story of Bram Stoker's gruesome novel which was first made into a stage play and is now being made into a moving picture is a terrible, supernatural story. It it a tale of vampires—the "undead"—who lived on human blood—an incredible tale for this twentieth century. No need to go deeply into it for this is not the story of the story, but of the man who for several years has lived the story, week in and week out.

Dracula is a blood curdling being with a dreadful fascination. Bela Lugosi has played the part so often he is afraid he is permanently absorbing the horrible creature's personality.

AS I understand it, an actor is a man who tries to make you believe that the character he shows you on the stage or screen is a real character. If he makes you believe it he is called a good actor. Sometimes he lives his part so thoroughly that he becomes the character he portrays—that is, if he plays it long enough and intensely enough. There was Joseph Jefferson in "Rip Van Winkle," and here in Hollywood is an old man who played one rôle for forty years—typifying a man who limped with his left leg—and now he needs no make-up and cannot help limping though there is nothing wrong with his leg.

This Count Dracula is a horrible, unnatural, repulsive super-fiend. Bela Lugosi, underneath the make-up and between scenes, is a gentlemanly, quiet, studious, courteous person. But we shiver—we women—because he's the kind of actor who can't do a trifling job of acting, and—here's the unpleasantness again—he comes from that part of Hungary where they believe in human vampires; resurrected creatures able to transform themselves into huge bats. Mr. Lugosi was brought up on those vampire tales, and he has made such a terrible success of the part because he has *(Continued on page 106)*

From *Modern Screen* of March 1930.

well have spoken to Hall (rather than his quotations being created by the studio's publicity department), his emphasis on women enjoying horrifying events and movies dovetailed with Universal's concerns over whether or not *Dracula* would appeal to women. As a result, the interview may have been little more than a publicity effort to convince female readers to see the film.

Soon thereafter, in early 1931 shortly before *Dracula*'s release, *Modern Screen* also published an article on Lugosi. Journalist Lillian Shirley claimed to have interviewed him during the making of *Dracula*, though unfortunately she offered no specific information about its production.[28] Instead, she tried to exoticize Lugosi by recounting stories of how he learned about vampires while he was a boy in Hungary. During the interview, Lugosi admitted that he hated the role of Dracula. "When I finish this picture, if it is possible to avoid it, I shall play Dracula no more. No. Never!"[29]

Studio Posters

Movie posters acted as the cornerstone of Universal's publicity materials for *Dracula*'s release. All of them were "printed in color combinations that throw an eerie spell," or so the pressbook claimed. The studio continued to push the tag line "The Story of the Strangest Passion the World Has Ever Known," but the imagery was generally safe, at least insofar as its overt sexual suggestiveness.

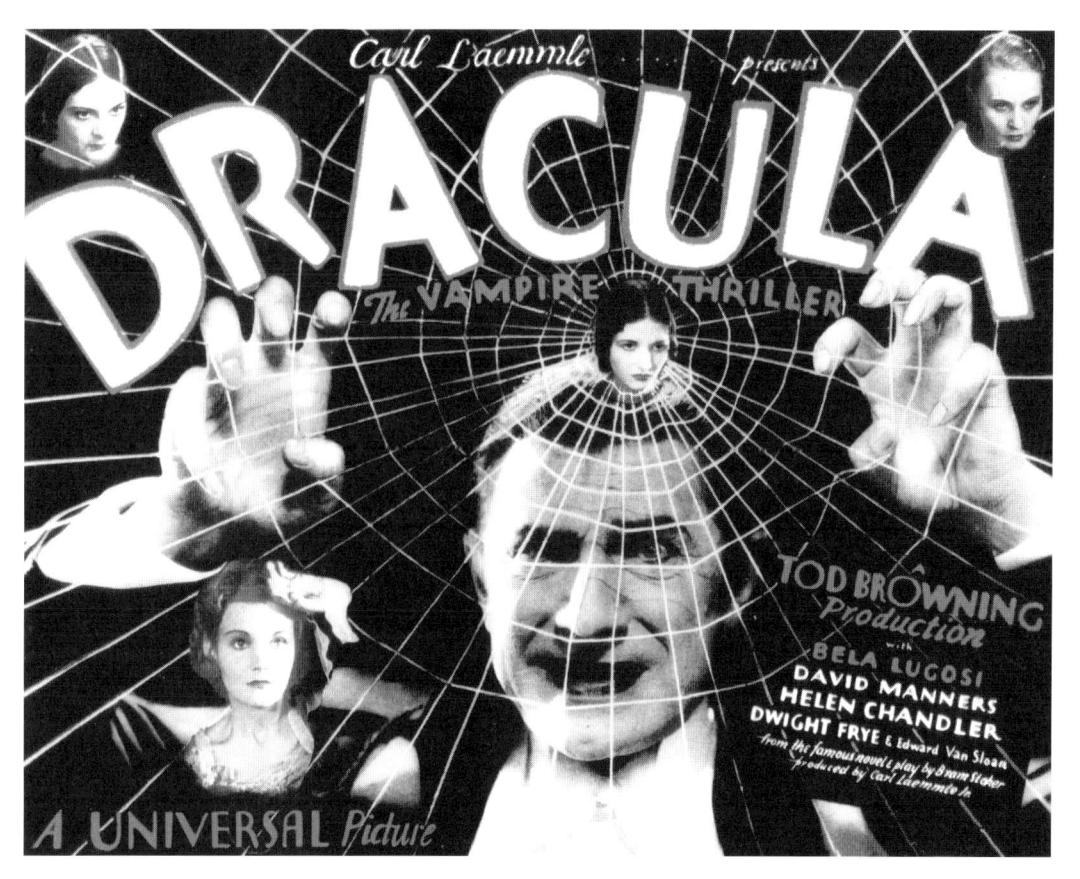

The title lobby card for *Dracula* (1931). *(Courtesy of Kristin Dewey)*

The Style A one-sheet features a closeup of Dracula, whereas the Style B three-sheet – as well as one of the two- 22x28 half-sheets, one of the two window cards, and the (only) six-sheet – offers an image of Dracula and a hypnotized Mina; the same was true of one of the two advertisement slides for *Dracula*. The twenty-four sheet finds Dracula hovering over a sleeping Lucy, though her nightdress is not low-cut. Like the aforementioned Style C one-sheet, the image is a tame variation on the aforementioned *Film Daily* cover.

The most complicated poster image appears on the Style B one-sheet and on one of the two window cards. A horizontal variation of the same can be found on the title lobby card, on one of the two 22x28 half-sheets, and on one of the two advertising slides. All of them depict an image of Dracula clawing at a superimposed cobweb and at the various women who appear to be trapped in it, ranging from his three Transylvanian wives to Mina. (Universal's 14x36 insert poster for *Dracula* offers a variation of this image. In it, Dracula gestures towards Mina, the only woman who is pictured; the spider web motif appears prominently.)

"AN INCUBUS"

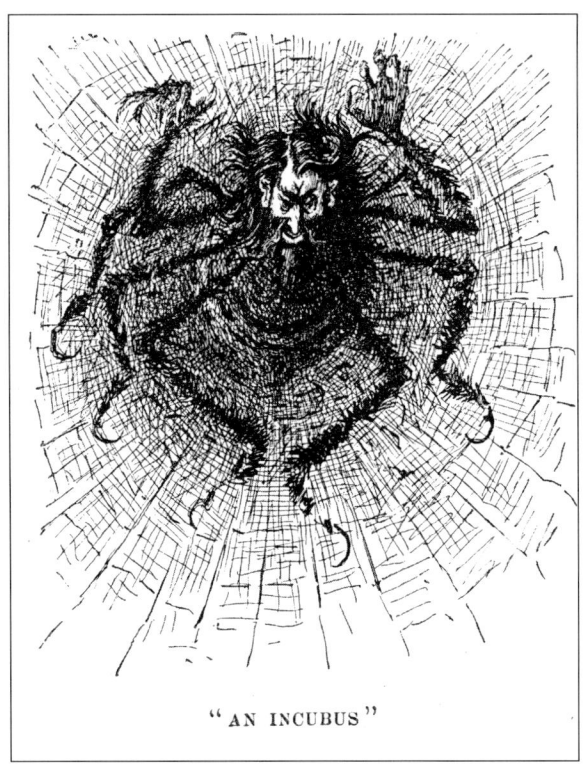

Artwork from the first edition of Du Maurier's novel *Trilby* (1895).

These particular *Dracula* posters bear the influence of artwork used in the original editions of George Du Maurier's novel *Trilby* (1895), specifically a drawing of Svengali as a spider that bears the caption *An Incubus*. As Trilby says in the novel, "He reminds me of a big hungry spider, and makes me feel like a fly!" In the 1931 version of *Dracula*, the title character speaks similar dialogue: "The spider spinning his web for the unwary fly." Here the Universal artist(s) echoed the *Trilby* artwork to visualize the metaphor of Dracula as spider, with various women caught in his web. These poster images were not the first time the studio had employed such imagery. Years earlier, Universal released the Rex two-reeler *The Spider and Her Web* (1914); its artwork is quite similar to the Dracula spiderweb.

The Style D three-sheet for *Dracula* is the only poster that employed the overt sexual imagery of the pre-release advertisements. Here an artist depicted Dracula immediately behind a female victim who is being enveloped in his arms and cape. Both of Dracula's hands are on Mina. One of them is positioned immediately under her right breast; the other seems to be on Mina's right hip, or just slightly above it. The artwork appeared on no other posters, and so the Style D might well represent the curious position that Universal took regarding "sexy" and "lurid" advertisements. The studio simultaneously wanted to be provocative while avoiding backlash.

A contrast to the Style D three-sheet came in the form of two other studio posters that offered no images whatsoever, but instead a range of text. A 3x10 foot banner and a block three-sheet shouted the words: "Weird! Wild! Breath-taking!" The banner called *Dracula* a "vampire thriller," whereas the three-sheet asked, "Do Vampires Really Exist?", a variation on a question that appeared in the film's trailer and in the small, text-only *Film Daily* advertisements in November 1930.[30]

Suggested Theatre Ballyhoo

Universal provided exhibitors with a range of suggestions and materials for theatre ballyhoo exploitation, which included the promotional coming-attraction trailers created by other companies. For example, Universal contracted Famous Artists of the Air to create radio trailers for *Dracula*. Supervised by Eddie Dowling and Monte Brice, the aural trailer was released on electrical transcription discs. At a certain point in the recording, the trailer featured a break for live announcers to insert the name of the local theatre screening *Dracula*.[31]

National Screen Service edited a theatrical film trailer for *Dracula* out of unused takes from the film. The trailer also incorporated footage from Edward Van Sloan's screen test, in which an offscreen Dracula hurls a vase that crashes into a mirror hanging on the wall. In addition

One of Universal's lobby cards for *Dracula* (1931).

to this trailer (which was available in both silent and sound versions), Universal also provided exhibitors with text for a trailer that they could create themselves.

As for theatre décor, the studio pressbook for *Dracula* advised exhibitors to "keep it weird" without becoming too "gruesome."[32] To achieve that goal, the studio suggested that theatre staff make bat "cut-outs" from paper and hang them in their lobbies. After hanging the bats, blue lights could illuminate them in an eerie fashion. A second idea had staff marking up any mirrors in the lobby so that they would appear to have been broken by Dracula.

Another plan suggested that exhibitors write each letter of Dracula's name on different cards for a window display and then placing a burning candle behind each letter. Free passes could be given to those patrons who guessed which candle would burn the longest. While promoting contests as a form of ballyhoo, the pressbook warned against allowing children to be contestants, because *Dracula* could "hardly [be] classed as a child's picture."[33]

The "Style-A" one-sheet for *Dracula* (1931).

Universal also encouraged exhibitors to promote *Dracula* outside of their theatres. To assist in that regard, the studio offered two different roto heralds featuring still photographs from the film with relevant text. Published in either four colors or two ("soft brown" and "mystery blue"), the heralds could be easily slipped into daily newspapers if exhibitors made proper arrangements with "local newsdealers." Heralds could also be distributed at "hotels, big stores, and transit centers."[34]

Similarly, the studio also prepared two products featuring *Dracula* artwork and text that exhibitors could use as giveaways. One of them was a small envelope allegedly containing wolfbane; another was a bookmark, which merged nicely with the pressbook's suggestion that exhibitors join forces with local bookstores to promote *Dracula* as both a film and novel. As with the heralds, exhibitors could obtain these envelopes and bookmarks at regional film exchanges, and then add their own theatre's name and address before distributing copies to potential ticket-buyers.[35]

Conclusion

Universal's publicity for *Dracula* evolved during late 1930 and early 1931, featuring an increasing emphasis on actor Bela Lugosi and offering less provocative imagery than appeared in the film's pre-release advertisements. But despite these changes, the general thrust of *Dracula*'s publicity remained the same, its key remit being to avoid emphasis on the mystery genre and instead link the ideas of romance and thrills. In large measure, Universal's publicity department succeeded, though sexual passion would better describe the release posters and other advertising ephemera than the word "romance."

At the end of January 1931, Carl Laemmle, Sr. strangely fluctuated from the studio's carefully considered approach to *Dracula*, running a "Straight from the Shoulder Talk" advertisement in *Motion Picture Daily* in which he alluded to the film's horrific elements in far starker terms than the studio's prepared publicity materials. After giving a brief mention of the film's "strange kind of love" story, Laemmle proudly announced that Tod Browning:

> Produced it ruthlessly, Boldly, Brutally.
> He deliberately made it to shock!
> And it will shock. It will stun. It will stick in your memory.[36]

While Laemmle told exhibitors not to advertise the film as a "mystery," he warned them not to "pussyfoot" about describing the film as a "straight, blunt, direct, and vivid story on a subject that every living man, woman and child thinks about and wonders about."

In some ways, Laemmle, Sr.'s comments were prescient, because – even though he did not use the word "horror" – they are not dissimilar to the manner in which many exhibitors, critics, and audience members viewed the film in 1931 and certainly in the years that followed. But at the same time, they were not in keeping with studio publicity that presented a largely coherent message, particularly by the time of the film's premiere and general release. For the sake of its official studio publicity, *Dracula* was a film that combined romance and thrills. It was, in short, "The Story of the Strangest Passion the World Has Ever Known."

1. "Hollywood Bulletins." *Variety* 21 Jan. 1931: 12.
2. Whitbeck, Frank. "Choice Locations and Good Taste Outdoor Advertising Requirements." *Motion Picture News* 7 June 1930.
3. Quigley, Martin J. "Editorial." *Exhibitors Herald-World* 25 Oct. 1930.
4. "Lurid Screen Advertising." *Billboard* 22 Nov. 1930: 53.
5. "A Stop Must Be Put to Lurid Motion Picture Advertising." *Billboard* 27 Dec. 1930: 44.
6. "Smutty Ads Boomerang." *Motion Picture Daily* 29 Dec. 1930: 1.
7. "Sexy Ads Being Censored by All Newspapers at Capital." *Motion Picture Daily* 5 Jan. 1931: 1, 3.
8. Alicoate, Jack. "Hot Advertising Has Got to Go." *Film Daily* 13 Jan. 1931: 1.
9. "The Mirror–A Column of Comment." *Film Daily* 30 Jan. 1931: 1.
10. "Industry Cleaning Up Its Ad Copy as Chains Warn Managers to 'Be Good.'" *Motion Picture Herald* 7 Feb. 1931: 42, 46.
11. "Frank Snipes Laemmle for Sniping Idea." *Motion Picture Daily* 17 Feb. 1931: 16.
12. "Barrymore Has Vulture in His Group of Pets." *Brooklyn Eagle* 5 Oct. 1930: 3. This article quotes an unnamed Hollywood correspondent of the Associated Press as saying: "A real test of the comparative effectiveness of stage and talking screen may be had in the projected film version of the horror *Dracula*."
13. See, for example: "Universal to Boom Business with More Advertising." *Film Daily* 14 Nov. 1930: 1, 7; "U Will Spend Plenty for Adv." *Hollywood Reporter* 15 Nov. 1930: 1; "U Spends More on Ads; Laemmle Asks Exhib Aid." *Motion Picture News* 15 Nov. 1930: 24.
14. Advertisement. *Motion Picture News* 8 Nov. 1930.
15. "Universal's Colorful Brochure on 1930-31 Product Catches Eye." *Exhibitors Herald-World* 25 Oct. 1930: 29.
16. The original copy of Ed Thomas' draft pressbook for *Dracula* dated 15 Nov. 1930 exists in the Universal Pictures collection at the Cinematic Arts Library at the University of Southern California.
17. These quotations formed three different small advertisements in *Film Daily* on 10 Nov. 1930.
18. These quotations formed four different small advertisements in *Film Daily* on 12 Nov. 1930.
19. Advertisement. *Film Daily* 9 Nov. 1930: 1.
20. Another example of this advertisement in the film industry press of 1930 appears in *Variety* 17 Dec. 1930: 30.
21. "Universal Publicity Dept. Is Shaken Up." *Hollywood Reporter* 12 Dec. 1930: 2.
22. Advertisement. *Motion Picture Herald* 3 Jan. 1931: 72-73.

23 Advertisement. *Variety* 31 Dec. 1930: 279.
24 Similarly, Universal published an advertisement for *Dracula* on the cover of *Film Daily* on 11 Jan. 1931. It depicts an image of Dracula looming above a photograph of Mina (Helen Chandler) and Lucy (Frances Dade).
25 Wilk, Ralph. "A Little from 'Lots.'" *Film Daily* 19 Nov. 1930: 6.
26 "Is HE The Second Chaney?" *Silver Screen* Jan. 1931: 51-52. [Though it bears a January 1931 date, the contents of this magazine suggest that it was on newsstands by December of 1930, if not earlier.]
27 Hall, Gladys. "The Feminine Love of Horror." *Motion Picture Classic* (Jan. 1931): 33, 86. Though it bears a January 1931 date, the contents of this magazine suggest that it was on newsstands by December of 1930, if not earlier.
28 Shirley, Lillian. "Afraid of Himself." *Modern Screen* (Mar. 1931): 61, 106-107. Though it bears a March 1931 date, the contents of this magazine suggest it was on newsstands prior to *Dracula*'s release, likely as early as January 1930.
29 Shirley, p. 107.
30 The same text also appeared on a cut-out hanger that depicted Dracula and Mina.
31 "Bert Muller to Handle Famous Artists' Sales." *Film Daily* 14 Jan. 1931: 8.
32 The pressbook for *Dracula* is reprinted in *Dracula (The Original 1931 Shooting Script)*. Ed. by Philip J. Riley. (Absecon, NJ: MagicImage, 1990).
33 Ibid.
34 Ibid.
35 Ibid.
36 Advertisement. *Motion Picture Daily* 21 Jan. 1931.

Chapter 8
PREMIERE

In the days and weeks leading up to *Dracula's* premiere in February 1931, the vampire seemed to be increasingly present in American culture, as did the persons who brought him to the screen. *Dracula–The Vampire Play* appeared in Boston and Cincinnati in January 1931. That same month, both Horace Liveright (who produced the 1927 Broadway version of *Dracula*) and Dorothy Peterson (who starred in that same production) appeared at a party together that made the society pages in the Los Angeles press.[1]

Trade publications kept the industry up to date regarding *Dracula*'s onscreen cast. Just before Christmas 1930, *Film Daily* claimed that David Manners would portray Billee in Warner Bros.' movie *Svengali* (a role that would eventually go to Bramwell Fletcher).[2] *Billboard* announced the birth of Dwight Frye's son in January 1931.[3] Then, in late January, *Variety* informed readers that Helen Chandler would appear in James Cruze's *Salvation Nell*, a role that she did enact.[4]

As for Bela Lugosi, in December 1930, he told a newspaper journalist: "I can't say what I am going to do now that *Dracula* is finished. I have heard rumors that I am to make this and that picture, but I don't know for sure. It seems that a person who is going to do something always is the last one to find out about it. I might even go back on the stage again sometime, but I'm not certain about that. I would like to stay in pictures at least long enough to live down the reputation I earned in *Dracula*."[5] On 10 January 1931, *Motion Picture Herald* revealed that Universal had not taken up the option on Lugosi's five-year contract, and so Fox signed him for a role in *Women of All Nations* (1931).[6]

Discussion of *Dracula* unfolded while other horror and mystery dramas gripped America. During January and February of 1931, many theatres screened *The Bat Whispers* and Universal's own *The Cat Creeps* (both released in November 1930). Then, on 9 February of that year, the stage play *Doctor X* opened on Broadway; the following day, reviews of *Drums of Jeopardy* (1931) began to appear in the trade publications.[7]

At roughly the same time, Universal found itself in more than one quandary. In early February, the studio announced that more cutbacks would soon occur, with employees who weren't laid off required to accept mandatory pay cuts. The cuts were due to take effect the very week that *Dracula* was scheduled to open in New York City.[8] Such financial

Publicity still for *Dracula* with Bela Lugosi as the vampire and Helen Chandler as Mina (1931). (Courtesy of Anthony Osika). Inset: Paul Kohner, head of Universal's "Foreign-Language Department."

difficulties may well explain the apparent oddity of Universal not taking up the option on Lugosi's five-year contract.

Universal's "foreign-language department" also seemed under threat. On 2 January 1931, the *Hollywood Reporter* wrote that the studio was planning to increase its multi-lingual production, with Paul Kohner (head of that department) attempting to tie-up as much "foreign talent" as he could.[9] But only five days later, *Motion Picture Daily* announced that the studio would likely eliminate "foreign talker versions" of its English-language films after those currently in production were finished.[10] The Spanish-language version of *Dracula* was a key example of such productions on the studio's 1930-31 schedule.[11]

Studio founder Carl Laemmle, Sr. had intended to leave California for New York in early February, but trades announced his change of plans, a decision that allowed him to remain on the West Coast to

PAUL KOHNER
In charge of foreign production department at Universal studios, was the first to see the value in foreign versions of the present day talkers and the first to persuade his employers to install a special department for this work.
Kohner has been associated with Universal for the past five years.

242   Chapter 8 – PREMIERE

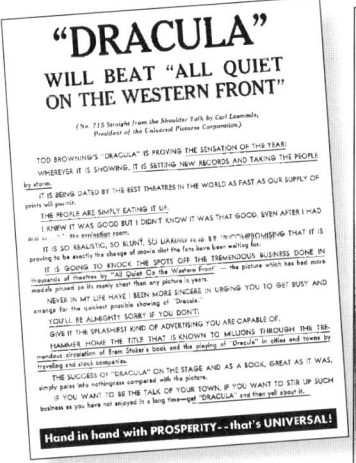

Above: Universal's advertisement in the *Motion Picture Daily* of January 29, 1931. Right: Advertisement published in the February 11, 1931 issue of the *New York Evening Journal*.

be feted for the anniversary of his twenty-fifth year in the film business.[12] In early February, the Hollywood film industry celebrated Laemmle, Sr.'s jubilee, with such luminaries as Irving Thalberg, Cecil B. DeMille, Mary Pickford, and Will Rogers saluting him at a special event. From there, Universal planned a lengthy series of tributes to Laemmle, culminating at yet another celebration on 24 February.[13]

But there seem to have been other reasons Laemmle stayed at the studio. The *Hollywood Reporter* claimed that he needed to oversee the start of the 1931-32 production program during April,[14] Given Universal's poor financial reports in the autumn of 1930, this choice might suggest a growing concern over Junior Laemmle's leadership.

Then, on 12 February 1931 – the very day of *Dracula*'s premiere – trades announced even more news. Laemmle, Sr. named Al Szekeler as Universal's new General Manager, with his headquarters in New York. Szekeler had been with the studio for seventeen years, and would provide leadership alongside Laemmle, Sr., as well as Junior Laemmle (head of all production) and Phil Reisman (general sales manager).[15] The announcement of Szekeler's new role was well-timed, coming prior to a studio shutdown that would last from 21 February to 15 March, until the new season of production was set to begin.[16] At any rate, Szekeler was

Chapter 8 – PREMIERE

Above Left: Advertisement published in the February 12, 1931 issue of the *New York Evening Journal*. Above Right: Advertisement published in the February 12, 1931 issue of the *New York Herald-Tribune*. Opposite: Advertisement for *Dracula–The Vampire Play* starring Courtney White at Brooklyn's Majestic Theatre.

the highest-ranking Universal employee on the ground in New York when *Dracula* opened. Likely he phoned or telegrammed the Laemmles after its premiere.

If so, he would have had much good news to report, as *Dracula* scored a major financial success during its opening week, which proves – along with a small number of recorded audience responses – that the film was a hit with most New York viewers. Similarly, an investigation of critical responses published in both New York newspapers and the film industry press reveals that *Dracula*'s premiere received largely favorable reviews.

Opening Night

As late as 29 January 1931, the *Hollywood Reporter* reported that Universal was searching for a legitimate Broadway theatre to open *Dracula*, a prestigious "long-run house" that would charge up to two dollars per ticket.[17] Possible venues included the Hollywood, the Central, and the Criterion.[18] But the studio quickly discarded this idea, instead holding *Dracula*'s premiere at New York's Roxy Theatre, a movie palace that would charge 50 cents, 75 cents, and one dollar per ticket for the film, the three prices reflecting different seating options: orchestra, mezzanine, and balcony. "De Luxe Performances" occurred five times per day, at 1:30PM, 3:30PM, 7:45PM, 9:30PM, and a "Midnight Performance Nightly."[19]

Opened in 1927, the Roxy deserved its moniker, "The Cathedral of Motion Pictures." S. L. "Roxy" Rothafel put $10,000,000 into the theatre and proudly told the press that it was "way ahead [of the competition] in acoustics, lighting, and general stage mechanics."[20] A massive organ sported three consoles and 21 chimes; the theatre also featured an orchestra comprised of over 100 musicians. Architecturally, Rothafel described the Roxy as being "Roman, with a quick journey into Africa, or Spanish Renaissance. It has therefore a touch of the Oriental." He was also proud of the color scheme, dominated as it was by a single amber tone.[21]

The 6,300-seat Roxy hosted numerous Universal films in the autumn of 1930, including *All Quiet on the Western Front* and *The Cat Creeps*.[22] The theatre also screened the studio's "super-production" *Resurrection* in January 1931.[23] Indeed, *Variety* revealed that the decision

244   Chapter 8 – PREMIERE

to premiere *Dracula* at the venue came as a result of a "contract Roxy signed six months ago … [and] Roxy made known his insistence for the picture, Feb. 13."²⁴ In short, Universal was required to let the Roxy open *Dracula* based upon a longstanding contractual agreement.

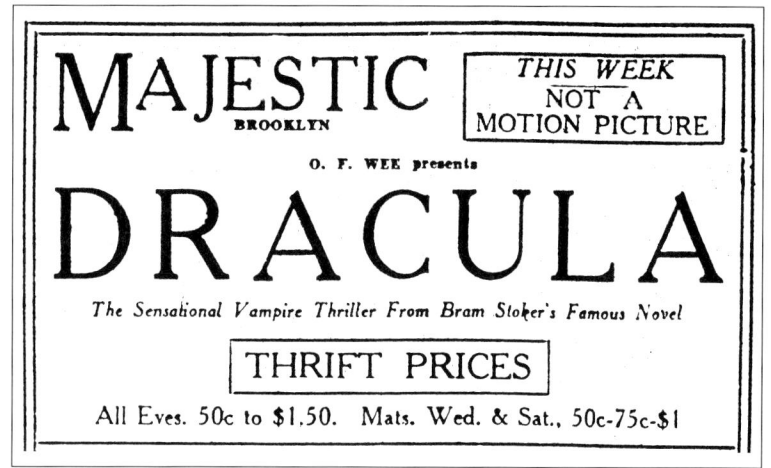

At the time of *Dracula*'s opening, the New York press noted that *Dracula–The Vampire Play* (starring Courtney White) was returning to Brooklyn's Majestic Theatre, the timing clearly intended to coincide with the film's opening.²⁵ Another version of the play was being staged at Baltimore's Maryland Theatre from 9-14 February.²⁶ That same week, *Viennese Nights* – which includes Bela Lugosi in a bit part– was playing at New York's Strand Theatre.²⁷

But *Dracula* on film commanded far more attention than any of these other productions. One of the key publicity schemes involved the launch of Grosset and Dunlap's "photoplay" print edition of Bram Stoker's novel *Dracula*, which featured still photographs from the Universal film. More than one hundred stores in the New York metropolitan area promoted the book at the time of the film's premiere. According to *Billboard*:

> *Complete windows, each carrying copies of this special photoplay edition and large displays of enlarged photos and advertising matter on the picture, have been arranged. The tieup includes department stores, 40 circulating libraries, besides displays to be carried by over 75 important drug stores thruout [sic] New York City.*²⁸

The trade also reported that plans were already underway for similar tieups between the book and the film in other key cities.

Rothafel created two different advertisements that newspapers ran on the two days leading up to *Dracula*'s premiere. Both republished a telegram featuring the following text:

> *Dear Roxy Don't blame me but I was born superstitious STOP Just heard you are opening Dracula Friday STOP That bad enough but Friday the Thirteenth is terrible STOP I have put everything I have into the picture and as a favor to me can't you open your presentation Thursday STOP Best wishes Tod Browning*

Faked for the sake of publicity, the telegram was quoted not only in Rothafel's ads, but also in the New York papers and film industry press.²⁹ *Billboard* speculated that the real reason for rescheduling *Dracula* to open on 12 February may have actually had to do with the Roxy's prior film, *Girls Demand Excitement* (1931), which – at a $45,000 gross for six days – represented a "new [financial] low" for the theatre.³⁰

The Roxy's advertisements for *Dracula* also promoted two other key ideas. One was the fact that the story had "held two generations in fascination and suspense," with additional mention of "First a best-selling book – then a sensational stage play – now, still greater as a talking picture!"[31] Here the publicity tried to build on the kind of historical context of *Dracula*'s previous renown in America as described in Chapter 1.

The other key theme in the advertisements stemmed from Universal's own publicity department: "The Story of the Strangest Passion the World Has Ever Known." While *Dracula* did not open on St. Valentine's Day, its first week coincided with it. At least some ticket-buyers likely made a connection between the ad copy and the holiday, particularly the many persons who actually viewed it on 14 February 1931.[32]

At any rate, it is clear that audiences saw far more at the Roxy than just *Dracula* during the week of the premiere. Before the projectionist screened the new film, the house lights dimmed. Two organists played music through the theatre's impressive pipes. Then the curtain opened. Conductor Erno Rapee waved his baton, and the Roxy Orchestra presented a special arrangement of Gershwin's *Rhapsody in Blue*, featuring Harry Perrella at the piano. A recording artist, Perrella had once worked in Paul Whiteman's orchestra, which had debuted *Rhapsody in Blue* in 1924.

The back cover of the Grosset and Dunlap "photoplay" edition of Bram Stoker's novel.

Immediately thereafter, an elaborate new live show entitled *Hello New York* appeared on the Roxy's stage.[33] It featured seven scenes of "color, dance, and song," with an array of performers and an orchestra of 125 musicians.[34] *Billboard* called the production:

> Quite a departure this week from the usual run of stage shows here. Not that there has been a change in the elaborateness, artistic quality, and cast performances of the show, but this

The Roxy's program for *Dracula*'s premiere.

production smacks more of Broadway than the usual coverage. Show runs 63 minutes, including the splendid nine-minute Rhapsody in Blue *overture.*[35]

Largely impressed, *Variety* added that the Roxy had "hit on a gold mine of an idea as the central thread of a presentation review, an idea that is capable of endless variation."[36]

Hello New York began with *The Bowery*, a dance routine in which performers appeared as silhouettes against "an impressionistic setting of fire escapes, fluttering clothes lines, and a lamp post, all blacked out against a semi-luminous eye of blue." Next was *Greenwich Village*, which featured a nightclub set with "a line of banquet tables in sharp perspective, before which the dancers in gosh-awful arty draperies and grotesque Benda masks, do a series of lackadaisical interpretative dances, a smart touch of witty satire."[37] Accompanying music came from a group of vocalists singing, *Three O'Clock in the Morning*.

Critics judged *Harlem*, the third sketch, to be the most provocative of the show; *Variety* expressed surprise about how "high voltage" it was for the "polite Roxy." In it, a number of African-American tap dancers, including women "in [a] typical Harlem undress," performed "high speed and acrobatic winging." Their act – which *Billboard* called the "biggest punch" of the show – took place on a terraced set constructed above the stage level.[38]

Rapid Transit supplied the fourth segment, a humorous bit staged on a subway set with the

Roxy Chorus and the Roxy Ballet Corps. *Times Square* provided the fifth and final sketch, in which the Roxyettes and the Ballet Corps combined forces to become an ensemble of sixty dancers onstage at the same time.

In between the five key sketches came "two mild bits" that helped allow time for stagehands to change the sets. One featured a ballroom dance staged against a projected slide of a clock face. The other was a "quartet ... doing casual harmony until the new set was ready."[39]

At that point, the stage lights dimmed again and the projectionist began the film selections. Rothafel programmed *Dracula* and a compilation of newsreel images in a short subject entitled *Today–and Yesterday*.[40] According to *Zit's Theatrical Weekly*, the newsreel material "conclude[d] the bill," a decision made likely to end the show on a more upbeat mood than *Dracula* would have created.[41]

How did viewers react to *Dracula* as juxtaposed against *Hello New York*? Unfortunately, only one comment exists on that particular point. *Variety* noted, "Feature is *Dracula* (U), which gave another novel twist to an all-around novel entertainment."[42] That said, a number of responses specific to *Dracula* at the Roxy survive from critics and audiences.

Audience Response

At least a few critics who saw *Dracula* at the Roxy immediately advised adults to keep their children away from the film. *Harrison's Reports* warned readers that the film would give children under the age of 14 nightmares.[43] Similarly, a review in the *New York Daily Mirror* claimed, "*Dracula* isn't a picture to insure tranquil sleep to impressionable little children, but it is good entertainment for adults to whom it offers plenty of dandy, pleasurable scares."[44]

Photograph capturing the crowds at one of *Dracula*'s first performances. (*Courtesy of Robert S. Birchard*)

Describing viewers in attendance at the premiere, Mordaunt Hall wrote in the *New York Times*: "It is a production that evidently had the desired effect on many in the audience yesterday afternoon, for there was a general outburst of applause when Dr. Van Helsing produced a little cross that caused the dreaded Dracula to fling his cloak over his head and make himself scarce."[45]

Nine days later, Hall once again described the audience response to the film. It is unknown whether his comments refer to viewers at a different screening, or whether he was simply restating his earlier anecdote. At any rate, he wrote: "At the Roxy it is safe to assert that most of those in the audience were quite affected by the eerie happenings, and it was a decided relief to many when Dr. Van Helsing defeated the intentions of the fiendish Count by exhibiting a small cross. There was no uncertain round of applause – handclapping such as is rarely heard during the showing a motion picture."[46]

Other indicators of the film's success with New York audiences are various data reported by the industry trade press. *Film Daily* reported that approximately 50,000 viewers bought tickets to *Dracula* during its first two days at the Roxy.[47] Seeing those numbers, the *Pacific Coast Distributors Bulletin* predicted the film would be "one of the biggest box office attractions the Roxy has ever played."[48] After four days, the Roxy had generated $73,781.95 on the film.[49] By the end of eight days, that amount climbed to $112,119.[50] Ultimately, the industry press believed that *Dracula*'s gross yielded a greater financial success than any other film playing in New York City during February 1931.[51]

By all indications, *Dracula* would have continued to draw large crowds to the Roxy, with the *Hollywood Reporter* declaring that its business had been "unusually good."[52] However, for reasons that had absolutely nothing to do with *Dracula*, the Roxy soon opened a new movie, *East Lynne* (1931).[53] *Dracula* ended a seven-film agreement between Universal and the Roxy.[54] The termination of the agreement – planned in advance – meant that Rothafel had already booked *East Lynne* to open on the exact day that it did, the film being part of his new deal with RKO.[55]

The New York Critics

Dracula's premiere in New York garnered largely positive critical reviews, a fact that has never been properly examined and understood. Consider the "Cream Puffs and Slams" column in the *Hollywood Reporter* of 17 February 1931. Reprinting a few brief lines from eight different New York newspaper reviews of *Dracula* at the Roxy, the publication offered insight into how critics in Manhattan viewed the film. The trade's selection suggests five very favorable reviews, and one moderately favorable review. The other two grumbled that the film could have been better than it was, but they were largely favorable in their other comments.

However, to understand the overall critical response to *Dracula*'s premiere, it is important to know that there were twelve different reviews of the film published in the following daily newspapers in New York City: the *American*, the *Daily Mirror*, the *Daily News*, the *Evening Journal*, the *Evening Post*, the *Graphic*, the *Herald Tribune*, the *Morning Telegraph*, the *Sun*, the *Telegram*, the *Times*, and the *World*.[56] All of them were printed on 13 February 1931, except for the *American*'s review, which was published on 14 February.[57] As a result, while it is possible one or more of these critics could have conferred with each other about the film immediately after viewing it on 12 February, the greater likelihood is that at least eleven of them wrote their reviews without necessarily having read the work of their colleagues.

Artwork published in the *New York Telegram* on February 14, 1931.

Of these twelve newspapers, eight of them praised Tod Browning, among them the *New York Times*, whose reviewer Mordaunt Hall called his direction "imaginative."[58] The *Daily Mirror* judged Browning's work to be "excellent," and the *Morning Telegraph* congratulated him on his subtlety.[59] The *American* declared he was "at his best" with the film, and the *Herald Tribune* said he imbued *Dracula* with "his gift for pictorial suggestion and almost Poe-like horror."[60]

The remaining newspapers featured one review that praised Browning, but also argued that he did not "quite capture all the dread gruesomeness of the Bram Stoker novel."[61] Another critic compared him unfavorably to director F. W. Murnau, mentioning not *Nosferatu* (1922), but instead another film: "Where, for example, are the mists of Murnau, who caught more of the atmosphere of *Dracula* in the swamp scenes of *Sunrise* [1927] than [Browning's] talkie does in all departments?"[62]

As for Lugosi, nine of the twelve newspapers responded to his performance favorably. For example, the *Daily News* called him "simply grand," and the *Morning Telegraph* told readers that he was "superb."[63] Two other critics claimed he was even better in the film version than he was on the stage.[64] As for the three reviews that did not speak about Lugosi in favorable terms, two of them simply made no comment about him at all, positive or negative.[65] The third of the group – the only negative notice Lugosi received – dismissed his work as being "of the old clutching hand school of acting."[66]

With regard to the overall film, seven of the twelve New York reviews were completely positive. It is possible that an eighth review was completely positive as well; the full text of the *Graphic*'s review does not seem to have survived, but what does exist is wholly favorable.[67] "Brrrrr! We enjoyed it!" exclaimed the *Daily News*, for example.[68] Four other reviews were largely positive, but included some minor comments that limited their praise.[69] Of this latter group, the *Times* did not actually voice complaints, but qualified its comments, perhaps in order to avoid heaping too much praise on a movie about vampires: "This picture succeeds to some extent in its grand guignol intentions. … [It] can at least boast of being the best of the many mystery films."[70]

Two of the other reviews in that group of four acknowledged the film's power, but maintained that it could have been better than it was. For example, the *Telegram* wrote that:

… although Mr. Browning has, for the most part, told his story skillfully and turned out an exciting and thrilling picture, it is a picture that is good enough to make you wish it were better. When it is good, it is very good, indeed. When it isn't, it is still so much better than the average picture that we wish it were more consistent – as good throughout as it is in spots.

Likewise, while questioning whether *Dracula* was "half as good as it might have been," the *Sun* confessed that it achieved a "curdling effect" and was still the best new film of the week. The final newspaper of the four that offered qualified praise was the *Morning Telegraph*:

The weakness of [Dracula's] opening episodes, which lag, are more than counterbalanced by the compelling action of the last three-quarters of the picture. Director Tod Browning was apparently in no hurry to get at the substance of the story, but he redeemed himself in the effective climactic scenes.[71]

This reviewer lauds the very sections of the film that some critics in the second half of the twentieth century would perceive to be its weakest.

All that said, the *Morning Telegraph*'s review did congratulate Browning for:

resorting to the use of only a minimum of those devices which one expects in a mystery picture. The vampire bat does not flap too often; screams are inserted only when in all reason there should be screams; the wolf howls not too many times. Even so, there were too many of these things for me. It would be interesting to see a picture in which nothing of the sort is used.[72]

Here again the critic's response is somewhat surprising, as modern writers have sometimes complained that the film does not feature enough sound effects or scenes depicting onscreen horror.

The only largely negative review of *Dracula* was published in the *World*, which claimed the film was a "pretentious effort" with a story told in "jumps and fidgets," the result producing "few thrills."[73] And yet, with all of these negative comments (and others, including clear disdain for Helen Chandler's performance), the *World* still felt obliged to admit that *Dracula* was a "somewhat effective telling" of the novel and play.

What then, does this information mean? *Dracula* received reviews that were either completely or largely positive from eleven of twelve different New York newspapers, which can lead to only one clear conclusion: it was a major critical success in New York City.

And the praise did not stop with those twelve reviews. On 22 February 1931, Mordaunt Hall – who had reviewed *Dracula* for the *New York Times* only nine days earlier – wrote a second piece about the film for the same newspaper. As previously noted, it is unknown whether Hall saw the film a second time, or whether he was swayed to write about *Dracula* again due to its box-office success. At any rate, he expressed greater enthusiasm in his second article, claiming: "The result is quite an exciting Grand Guignol production … It is a far superior film to the ordinary mystery drama … It is a film with superior performances throughout."[74]

Later, P.S. Harrison – best known as the editor of the film industry trade *Harrison's Reports* – reviewed the film for the *Irish World*, an ethnic newspaper published on a weekly basis in New York. He was extremely impressed, telling readers that *Dracula* was:

> Excellently produced. The picture is extremely weird, fantastic and morbid. ... Most of the situations are so terrifying that they send chills up and down one's spine, especially those in which Dracula, the vampire, overpowers his victims by hypnotizing them. ... Bela Lugosi, in the role of Dracula, makes the part extremely convincing and horrible.[75]

Harrison's review is yet another example of how well *Dracula* was received in New York City, where the dominant critical response was positive.

The Trade Press

Seven different film industry trade publications critiqued *Dracula's* New York premiere, all of their reviews published within ten days of its opening.[76] And like the predominant number of New York newspaper critics, these reviews offered significant praise for *Dracula* and those persons who worked on it.

Five of the seven publications gave unqualified praise to Tod Browning, with one of the other two (which was completely positive) not mentioning him by name.[77] For example, *Motion Picture Daily* claimed that Browning's direction "is his best in this one"; *Film Daily* referred to Browning's "expert direction," adding that he "knows how to get the most out of the weird and spooky effects."[78] Only *Billboard* limited its approval, but still acknowledged that Browning had "directed [the film] creditably."[79]

Lugosi received unanimous praise from six of the seven trades, with the seventh (which was completely positive about the film) not mentioning the actor by name.[80] For example, *Billboard* called Lugosi's performance "brilliant," *Motion Picture Daily* said he was "exceptionally good," and *Film Daily* declared that he had created "one of the most unique and powerful roles of the screen."[81]

As for the overall film, only *Billboard* raised any hesitations, noting: "At times the film is faulty in photography and sound recording. Poor work on that end often causes one to strain to get what is flashed and heard on the screen." Here again a negative comment from a 1931 critic seems completely at odds with modern complaints, which often praise Karl Freund's cinematography while decrying Browning's direction. Nevertheless, *Billboard* still admired *Dracula* to a degree, claiming: "Universal has done a good job of this thriller, making the story proceed in a manner conducive to holding [audience] interest and providing innumerable thrills."[82]

The six other trade reviews heaped unqualified praise on the film. *Motion Picture Daily* assured readers it was "eerie, spooky, and entertaining." *Film Daily* judged that there was "no denying its dramatic power and tingling thrills." And *Zit's Theatrical Weekly* called *Dracula* a "decided improvement on the stage version of the same opus ... The whole thing is done with a fine hand drawing a close line between grim realism and exaggerated fantasy."[83]

Similarly, *Film Curb* wrote about *Dracula* with great enthusiasm, calling it a "most excellently produced melodrama, splendidly mounted throughout," adding that, "no expense has been spared to make this popular play and widely circulated book a tremendously appealing screen attraction." Commending the film's "thrills and comedy," *Film Curb* concluded by referring to *Dracula* as a "splendid and fascinating production."[84]

No trade publication spent more time on *Dracula* than *Variety*, which devoted nine paragraphs to heralding the film's acting, its settings, and its story development:

> Such a treatment called for the utmost delicacy of handling, because the thing is so completely ultra-sensational on its serious side that the faintest excess of telling would make it grotesque. Nice judgment here gets the maximum of shivers without ever destroying the screen illusion ... The atmosphere makes anything seem possible. ... some of the horror tricks of sound and sight are full powered. ... Story is cunningly developed like the fireside ghost tale, and with just the right twist that it couldn't possibly happen to give it the true flavor. It took the resources of the studio to get the story right.[85]

Advertisement published in the *Motion Picture Daily* of February 17, 1931.

In addition to providing an extensive analysis of the film, *Variety*'s critic understood that the shooting script had resulted in a unique story: "Treatment differs from both the stage version and the original novel."

Conclusion

Surprisingly, given *Dracula*'s successful premiere, mainstream American magazines generally ignored the film. The key exception was *Time*, which printed a response to it on 23 February 1931:

> *Director Tod Browning, who had charge of the best Lon Chaney pictures, has a talent for creating macabre atmosphere by the use of 'interiors.' ... He had done a good job with it, especially with the settings in a madhouse and in cellars. ... Dracula is an exciting melodrama, not as good as it ought to be but a cut above the ordinary trapdoor-and-winding-sheet type of mystery film.*[86]

Though somewhat tepid, this critic still offered a degree of praise, something that marked nearly every published at the time of *Dracula*'s premiere.

Chapter 8 – PREMIERE   253

Curiously, one of the most insightful of those reviews was printed not in Manhattan, but instead on the West Coast. Norbert Lusk wrote his critique after seeing the film's premiere in New York, but it was published in the *Los Angeles Times*:

> *Plainly a freak picture, [Dracula] must be accepted as a curiosity devoid of the important element of sympathy that causes the widest appeal: an interesting example of production values and direction, but failing to qualify as a challenge to the emotions.*
>
> *Favorable as the majority of reviews are, no critic goes so far to indorse [sic] the film for a long run or to nominate it as a picture that everyone should see. In the praise bestowed upon it, the name of Tod Browning, the director takes first place. It is a tribute to his mastery of the morbid and perverse, of his extraordinary use of shadows to establish a mood and sustain it without monotony, or his surpassing skill in atmosphere detail, or his ability to provoke terror without overdoing it to the extent of making the effort laughable.*
>
> *These gifts manifested in his direction of Lon Chaney are here even more apparent than usual, for he has material that is more macabre than any starring Chaney. ... To Mr. Browning's further credit it should be said that the film version is considered superior to the successful play, and Bela Lugosi is thought to exceed the effectiveness of his work on the stage in the same role. Other characters are well played, on the whole, though the reporter wonders at the hardwood of some actors in maintaining their ego in view of the scathing estimates of their work that appear from time to time in newspapers [in New York].*[87]

Even the title of Lusk's article – "*Dracula* Hit on Broadway" – provides succinct and helpful information, underscoring just how well the film performed during the week of its premiere.

Not surprisingly, Universal seized upon news of the successful opening, touting *Dracula*'s New York grosses in various trade advertisements.[88] The studio also ran ads that quoted from a range of different New York newspaper reviews.[89] And, within four days of the premiere, Carl Laemmle Sr.'s "Straight from the Shoulder Talk" spoke even more plainly: "The people are simply eating it up. I knew it was good, but I didn't know it was that good, even after I had first seen it in the projection room."[90]

But the response to *Dracula* was still just beginning, with the film's national release beginning immediately after its premiere at the Roxy.

1 Nye, Myra. "Society of Cinemaland." *Los Angeles Times* 11 Jan. 1931.
2 Wilk, Ralph. "Hollywood Flashes." *Film Daily* 23 Dec. 1930.
3 "Births." *Billboard* 17 Jan. 1931: 72.
4 "Hollywood Bulletins." *Variety* 21 Jan. 1931.
5 "Political Upheaval Sent Bela Lugosi to Hollywood." *Niagara Falls Gazette* 11 Dec. 1930: 9.
6 "Option on Lugosi Not Taken by Universal." *Motion Picture Herald* 10 Jan. 1931: 40.
7 Smith, Alison. "Another Play." *New York World* 10 Feb. 1931: 14; "Seitz Turns Out Real Thriller." *Hollywood Reporter* 10 Feb. 1931: 3.
8 "New Slash Coming at Universal Studios." *Hollywood Reporter* 6 Feb. 1931: 44.
9 "More Foreigns for Universal in 1931." *Hollywood Reporter* 2 Jan 1931: 3.
10 "U May Drop Foreign Films." *Motion Picture Daily* 7 Jan. 1931: 1.
11 During World War II, Universal pursued the Spanish-language market with dubbing, rather than return to the use of multi-lingual productions. See: "Dubbing Plans at Peak; Universal to Go to Spain." *Motion Picture Herald* 15 July 1944: 50.
12 "Scroll Signed by 249 Film Leaders Presented by Hays to U Head." *Film Daily* 4 Feb. 1931: 1, 8.
13 Laemmle's twentieth anniversary in the film industry had also been recognized. See "Carl Laemmle's 20th Anniversary to be Celebrated Throughout Industry." *Weekly Film Review* 30 Jan. 1926: 14.

14. "Uncle Carl to Stick Around Here Awhile." *Hollywood Reporter* 5 Feb. 1931: 1.
15. "Al Szekeler Made Gen. Mgr. of 'U.'" *Hollywood Reporter* 12 Feb. 1931: 1.
16. "Universal Closes Feb. 21 to Mar. 15." *Hollywood Reporter* 9 Feb. 1931: 1. Universal had earlier announced a longer closure of four to six weeks. See "U to Close Down Studio?" *Motion Picture Daily* 6 Jan. 1931: 1.
17. "*Dracula* for B'way $2 House." *Hollywood Reporter* 29 Jan. 1931: 3.
18. *Variety* 28 Jan. 1931.
19. *Roxy Theatre Weekly Review*. Theatre Program for *Dracula*. 12 Feb. 1931: 11.
20. "A Trip Through the New Roxy Theatre." *New York Times* 27 Feb. 1931: X7.
21. Ibid., p. X7.
22. "4 U's at Roxy." *Variety* 17 Sept. 1930: 33.
23. "U Special for Roxy." *Billboard* 17 Jan. 1931: 7. As with *Dracula*, Universal had originally planned to roadshow *Resurrection*, but contractual obligations with the Roxy kept it from doing so. See "*Resurrection* into Roxy." *Motion Picture Herald* 10 Jan. 1931: 47.
24. *Variety* 4 Feb. 1931.
25. "Beau Ideal Heads Bill at 4 Theatres." *New York Evening Journal* 12 Feb. 1931: 56.
26. "Dramatic and Musical." *Billboard* 14 Feb. 1931: 76.
27. Advertisement. *New York World* 13 Feb. 1931.
28. "*Dracula*." *Billboard* 14 Feb. 1931: 12.
29. See, for example: Johaneson, Bland. "Ina Claire Signs 5-Year Contract for Goldwyn." *New York Daily Mirror* 11 Feb. 1931; "Superstition Wins." *Film Daily* 10 Feb. 1931: 1.
30. "Better the Day, Better the Deed." *Billboard* 21 Feb. 1931: 11.
31. See, for example, advertisements in the *New York Evening Journal* (12 Feb. 1931) and the *New York World* (12 Feb. 1931).
32. In *Dark Carnival: The Secret World of Tod Browning, Hollywood's Master of the Macabre* (New York: Anchor, 1995), David J. Skal and Elias Savada claim that suggestions of *Dracula*'s "marketing tie-in with St. Valentine's Day" is "completely without basis" (p. 153). While I agree that the Roxy's publicity campaign did not specifically refer to the holiday, it seems inconceivable to me that viewers who read taglines referring to the "story of the strangest passion the world has ever known" during the film's opening weekend did not draw a connection to the holiday, particularly those viewing it between 12 February and 14 February 1931.
33. According the *Roxy Theatre Weekly Review*, a Fox Movietone newsreel would be screened between *Rhapsody in Blue* and *Hello New York*. However, a published review of the film's premiere claimed the newsreel concluded the bill. See: "Film Reviews." *Zit's Theatrical Newspaper* 21 Feb. 1931: 9.
34. Advertisement. *New York Herald Tribune* 12 Feb. 1931.
35. "Roxy, New York." *Billboard* 21 Feb. 1931: 13.
36. "Roxy." *Variety* 18 Feb. 1931.
37. Ibid.
38. "Roxy, New York" p. 13.
39. Ibid.
40. Pelswick, Rose. "*Dracula* at the Roxy." *New York Evening Journal* 13 Feb. 1931.
41. "Film Reviews," p. 9.
42. "Roxy, New York," p. 13.
43. "*Dracula*." *Harrison's Reports* 21 Feb. 1931: 31.
44. Johaneson, Bland. "*Dracula* Ever Scarey [sic], a Thriller as Talkie." *The Daily Mirror* (New York) 13 Feb. 1931.
45. Hall, Mordaunt. "The Screen." *New York Times* 13 Feb. 1931: 21.
46. Hall, Mordaunt. "*Dracula* as a Film." *New York Times* 22 Feb. 1931: 98.
47. "*Dracula* Draws 50,000 in Two Days at Roxy." *Film Daily* 16 Feb. 1931: 1.
48. "50,000 People See Universal's *Dracula* in Two Days." *Pacific Coast Distributors Bulletin* 1 Mar. 1932: 2.
49. Advertisement. *Motion Picture Daily* 17 Feb. 1931.
50. "$89,271 Wows 'B'way 4 Days on *East Lynne*." *Motion Picture Daily* 25 Feb. 1931: 7.
51. "Theatre Receipts." *Motion Picture Herald* 28 Feb. 1931: 27.
52. "*Dracula* Doing Well in New York Roxy." *Hollywood Reporter* 19 Feb. 1931: 2.
53. Ibid. In *Hollywood Gothic: The Tangled Web of Dracula from Novel to Stage to Screen* (New York: W. W. Norton, 1990), David J. Skal claims that the Roxy "dropped" *Dracula* (p. 144), which is factually incorrect. Rothafel's agreement with RKO meant that he was unable to book a holdover for *Dracula*, and instead contractually had to screen *East Lynne* when he did. Moreover, it is also possible that relations between Rothafel and Universal were poor at the time, given Universal's efforts to circumvent their agreement with Rothafel and not allow him to premiere *Resurrection* and *Dracula*.
54. "*Dracula* Ends Roxy-'U' Pact." *Motion Picture Daily* 14 Feb. 1931: 1.
55. "Universal Deal with Roxy Terminates; Reisman on the Coast." *Motion Picture Herald* 21 Feb. 1931.
56. Crewe, Regina. "Shivery Cinema on View at Roxy is Capably Acted." *New York American* 14 Feb. 1931; Johaneson, Bland. "*Dracula* Ever Scarey [sic], a Thriller as Talkie." *The Daily Mirror* (New York) 13 Feb. 1931; Thirer, Irene. "Roxy's *Dracula* Spine Chiller." *New York Daily News* 13 Feb. 1931; Pelswick, Rose. "Hair-Raising Tale Better on Screen Than on Stage." *New York Evening Journal* 13 Feb. 1931; Delahanty, Thornton. "The New Film." *New York Evening Post* 13 Feb. 1931; Watts, Richard, Jr. "On the Screen." *New York Herald Tribune* 13 Feb. 1931; Cheavens, David. "Bela Lugosi Brings Creeps." *The Morning Telegraph* (New York) 13 Feb. 1931; Cohen, John S., Jr. "The New Photoplays." *New York Sun* 13 Feb. 1931; Boehnel, William. "Pushes Opening Ahead to Avoid Double Hoodoo." *New York Telegram* 13 Feb.

1931; Hall, Mordaunt. "The Screen." *New York Times* 13 Feb. 1931: 21; Gow, James. "The New Films." *New York World* 13 Feb. 1931: 10.

57. Sadly, the full text of the *Graphic*'s review does not seem to exist. The New York Public Library considered the newspaper to be a poor example of journalism, and as a result it did not preserve a complete run. Nor did any other library, so much of the newspaper's history is lost. However, Universal quoted the *Graphic*'s review of *Dracula* (as written by Julia Shawell) at some length in a two-page advertisement published in *Film Daily* on 16 Feb. 1931. She wrote: "Shivers and thrills at the Roxy. One of the creepiest mystery melodramas ever screened. *Dracula* is the best talking picture of its type yet exhibited. Bold, vivid presentation, leaving the audience fascinated, but shivering. Lugosi is remarkable as the strange Count Dracula." More text from the review appears in an advertisement that Lugosi himself ran in the *Hollywood Filmograph* on 21 Feb. 1931: "And the acting, with Bela Lugosi's work outstanding, is all splendid. Lugosi is remarkable as the strange Count Dracula, who proves to be a deathless corpse turned vampire and living on the lifeblood of his victims. He transforms himself into a bat or wolf and his awful howls in the night are enough to make any viewer leary [sic] of the dark for a while. Not satisfied with his own horrible plight he goes around getting recruits who likewise become vampires and the reels in which he plunders on life and is finally killed are certainly worth viewing if you like that sort of thing" (p. 2).
58. Hall, "The Screen." As the full text of the *Graphic* review is unavailable, it is unknown whether or not critic Julia Shawell praised Browning by name.
59. Johaneson, "*Dracula* Ever Scarey [sic], a Thriller as Talkie."; Cheavens, "Bela Lugosi Brings Creeps."
60. Crewe, "Shivery Cinema on View at Roxy is Capably Acted"; Watts, "On the Screen."
61. Pelswick, "Hair-Raising Tale Better on Screen Than on Stage."
62. Cohen, "The New Photoplays."
63. Thirer, Roxy's *Dracula* Spine Chiller"; Cheavens, "Bela Lugosi Brings Creeps."
64. Crewe, "Shivery Cinema on View at Roxy is Capably Acted"; Watts, "On the Screen."
65. Johaneson, "*Dracula* Ever Scarey [sic], a Thriller as Talkie."; Gow, "The New Films."
66. Cohen, "The New Photoplays."
67. Here I am referring to: Crewe, "Shivery Cinema on View at Roxy is Capably Acted"; Delehanty, "The New Film"; Johaneson, "*Dracula* Ever Scarey [sic], a Thriller as Talkie"; Pelswick, "Hair-Raising Tale Better on Screen Than on Stage"; Watts, "On the Screen"; Thirer, "Roxy's *Dracula* Spine Chiller."
68. Thirer, "Roxy's *Dracula* Spine Chiller."
69. Here I am referring to: Boehnel, "Pushes Opening Ahead to Avoid Double Hoodoo"; Cheavens, "Bela Lugosi Brings Creeps"; Cohen, "The New Photoplays"; "Hall, "The Screen."
70. Hall, "The Screen."
71. Cheavens, "Bela Lugosi Brings Creeps."
72. Ibid.
73. Gow, "The New Films."
74. Hall, "*Dracula* as a Film."
75. "Reviews of the New Motion Pictures as Seen by P. S. Harrison." *The Irish World* (New York) 28 Mar. 1931: 12. It is worth noting that this review is a shortened version of the same text that Harrison published in *Harrison's Reports*.
76. The seven reviews are: Harris, Sidney. "*Dracula*." *Billboard* 21 Feb. 1931: 10; "*Dracula*." *Film Curb* 21 Feb. 1931: unpaginated; "*Dracula*." *Film Daily* 15 Feb. 1931: 11; "*Dracula*." *Harrison's Reports* 21 Feb. 1931; "*Dracula*." *Motion Picture Daily* 21 Feb. 1931: 3; "*Dracula*." *Variety* 18 Feb. 1931: 14; "Film Reviews." *Zit's Theatrical Newspaper* 21 Feb. 1931: 9. It is my presumption that *Hollywood Reporter* and *Motion Picture Herald* did not review the film in February due to the fact that both trades had – as noted in Chapter 6 – already reviewed the film's preview screening.
77. *Film Curb* did not mention Browning by name, but its review of *Dracula* was uniformly positive.
78. "*Dracula*," *Film Daily*, p. 11.
79. "*Dracula*," *Billboard*, p. 10.
80. *Film Curb* did not mention Lugosi's performance specifically, but its review of *Dracula* was uniformly positive.
81. "*Dracula*." *Motion Picture Daily*, p. 3; "*Dracula*," *Film Daily*, p. 11.
82. "*Dracula*," *Billboard*, p. 10.
83. "Film Reviews," p. 9.
84. "*Dracula*." *Film Curb* 21 Feb. 1931: unpaginated.
85. "*Dracula*." *Variety*, 14.
86. "Cinema." *Time* 23 Feb. 1931: 62.
87. "*Dracula* Hit on Broadway." *Los Angeles Times* 22 Feb. 1931: B9.
88. See, for example, the two-page advertisement in *Motion Picture Herald* of 21 Feb. 1931.
89. See, for example, the two-page advertisement in *Film Daily* of 16 Feb. 1931.
90. Laemmle, Carl, Sr. "Straight from the Shoulder Talk." No. 715, published as an advertisement. *Film Daily* 18 Feb. 1931.

Chapter 9
GENERAL RELEASE

In May of 1930, Universal announced that it would be renting its films for the 1930-31 season to exhibitors in either groups of five or as singles, with the studio making a percentage of each theatre's gross and guarantees that required minimum payments regardless of the receipts. The new system drew upon Junior Laemmle's production policy, the emphasis being on prestige pictures that exhibitors could book without any requirement to block-book other films they did not want.[1]

The Universal sales force underwent a number of changes during the 1930-31 season. Phil Reisman succeeded Lou Metzger as Sales Manager in July 1930, moving to Universal after a three-year successful run at Pathe.[2] Within weeks, the studio created a new sales promotion department as well, presumably at Reisman's request.[3] In the autumn of that year, rumors of a "shake-up" in his sales department appeared in the industry press. Waiting until just before the Christmas holiday to make his announcement, Reisman reconfigured the administration of his team, the result of which meant that eight district managers oversaw all film sales in the U.S. and Canada.[4]

Reisman also oversaw two major distribution deals in the autumn of 1930, both of which would have a major impact on *Dracula*'s release. The first was a deal to book Universal's entire output for the 1930-31 season into 800 Warner Bros. theatres situated throughout New Jersey, New York, New England, the Atlantic seaboard, and in such Midwestern territories as Chicago and Omaha. *Billboard* specifically named *Dracula* as one of the many films included in this agreement.[5] Similarly, Reisman signed a contract with RKO, whose theatres would screen *Dracula* in other territories across America. Those two major deals were in addition to a large number of bookings for other, smaller chains and "mom and pop"-owned single theatres. As per usual, Universal adhered to prevailing zoning rules that prevented two competing theatres within a certain geographical proximity from screening the same film until a given amount of time had passed.

Responding to *Dracula*'s general release were a large number of film critics, including those working at movie fan magazines and a small number of industry trades that did not review it immediately after its New York premiere. However, the largest number of reviews published during the film's release came in the form of daily newspapers across the country, most of which were positive. In some cases, such reviews presented little more than plot summary and even borrowed text from *Dracula*'s pressbook. However, others were carefully considered and thoughtful. For example, a critic in Canton, Ohio believed the film was at its peak during the Transylvanian sequences, but quickly added that the film did not suffer from a "lack of action" during the scenes set in England.[6] And a critic in Springfield, Massachusetts claimed that Browning had "done a thoughtful piece of work, keeping a nice balance between the horrific and ridiculous; at no time, when the actions of *Dracula* are supposed to be taken seriously, is there manifested an audience tendency to discredit them."[7]

Exhibitors recorded numerous responses to *Dracula*, mainly in terms of its gross at their individual theatres, including how it compared to other films they had recently screened in both qualitative and quantitative terms. They shared their successes and failures with the marketing strategies and ballyhoo campaigns they devised, which sometimes augmented or even ignored prepared studio publicity.

Audience members also responded to the film, while it was being projected and afterwards, in the form of word of mouth. A small number of these responses from 1931 survive thanks to journalists who recorded them in newspapers and to the moviegoers who wrote letters to fan magazines. Who were these persons? Certainly both studio personnel and theatre managers targeted women in their approach to advertising *Dracula*.[8] They also hoped the film would attract children, whose lack of attendance at movies in late 1930 and early 1931 was the cause of much concern. *Dracula* posed particular challenges for selling ticket to children, however, as many journalists warned parents that the film was unfit for them.[9]

What is clear is that these three groups – critics, exhibitors, and viewers – wrested power from Universal once the studio released the film. Despite suggestions in the prepared studio publicity and pressbook, numerous theatre advertisements referred to *Dracula* as a mystery, as did some critical reviews.[10] Others used such adjectives as "creepy" and "terrifying," and even publicized particular screenings of *Dracula* as "spook shows."[11] Most notably, journalists and exhibitors increasingly used the word "horror" to describe the film during its general release.[12]

Indeed, the gradual rise of the term "horror" as the nascent genre's name during the period from February to April 1931 (and thereafter) represents one of the key legacies of *Dracula*'s original release, with the term coming to the fore not as the result of Universal's marketing strategy, but rather in spite of it, thanks to its organic usage among many persons throughout America.

Trade Publications

While the major film industry trade publications reviewed *Dracula* in February immediately after its New York premiere, four others published critiques during the film's general release. In March, the *National Board of Review* magazine praised Lugosi's "brilliant" performance and deemed the film suitable for "mature audiences."[13] That same month, the *Exhibitor's Forum* predicted *Dracula* would become a "box-office sensation" because it was even more "hair-raising" than the book or play.[14]

In late March, Welford Beaton offered a particularly positive review in the pages of the *Film Spectator*:

> A *box-office success is being scored by* Dracula *because it is a production that is honest with itself. It makes no pretense at being anything but a horrible and impossible conception offered for the sole purpose of making its audiences gasp.*

...*Dracula* is a successful picture because it has mixed its elements more intelligently than we find them generally in screen entertainment. ... Tod Browning never did a better job of directing.[15]

Not perceiving *Dracula* to be a romance film or even a thriller, Beaton chose the phrase "creepy horror" to describe it.

The most quoted of these later trade publications comes in the form of Harold Weight's review in the 4 April 1931 issue of the *Hollywood Filmograph*, particularly in his remark "we cannot believe that the same man was responsible for both the first and latter parts of the picture," a judgment that fits neatly with many critiques of *Dracula* in the later years of the twentieth century. Indeed, some authors have used this particular trade review to imply that overall critical response to the film was negative and even the cause for Universal to be worried.[16]

However, major problems exist for such a use of Weight's review. For one, it was not published until nearly seven weeks after the film's premiere and indeed long after the major (and largely positive) critical reviews appeared in print. And the *Filmograph* was certainly not among the most important trade publications, as opposed

Top: Advertisement promoting Bela Lugosi published in the *Hollywood Filmograph* on February 21, 1931. Bottom: Universal Studios placed this advertisement in the *Film Daily* on February 18, 1931.

Chapter 9 – GENERAL RELEASE

259

Watch This Column
Universal Chat

BELA LUGOSI
as "Dracula"

When Bram Stoker's book, "Dracula," was published, the whole world gasped. The thrilling tale of the worst of all the human vampires was eerie, spooky, tingling and emotional and held the reader spellbound. In picture-form, just produced by **UNIVERSAL**, the story is immeasurably intensified because of the limitless possibilities of the camera. "Count Dracula," the leading character, enacted by BELA LUGOSI, the man of mystery, a master-actor whose portrayal of intense roles has won him world-wide fame, is the greatest of all the vampires and rises from his grave at night to feast on the living. He has the power to change himself into any character or thing and exerts his devilish influence on all with whom he comes in contact. Those whom he destroys become vampires like himself.

THIS PICTURE HAS BEEN PRONOUNCED BY REVIEWERS TO BE ONE OF THE MOST AMAZING PRODUCTIONS IN PICTURE HISTORY. BE ON THE WATCH FOR IT.

My Silver Anniversary this month has brought me scores of fine letters from exhibitors everywhere who volunteer to make this a **UNIVERSAL** month and to show only **UNIVERSAL** pictures. To be the oldest active pioneer in the industry is a distinction I prize most highly. To have furnished entertainment to the world's millions for twenty-five years is satisfaction enough for any man. This is my means of expressing my unbounded appreciation of your confidence and support.

A good picture, like a good story, is worth repeating. How often have you seen *"All Quiet on the Western Front?"* You cannot possibly appreciate this picture by seeing it only once. By all means see it again and again at the very first opportunity. I will not be satisfied until <u>FIFTY MILLION AMERICANS</u> have seen this picture.

ASK YOUR THEATRE TO SHOW *"Free Love," "King of Jazz," "Resurrection," "Dracula," "Little Accident," "A Lady Surrenders,"* and that marvelous mystery *"The Cat Creeps."* Also don't forget *"Many a Slip," "See America Thirst,"* and *"Cohens & Kellys in Africa"* — all three made principally for laughing purposes.

Your **FREE** copy of the beautifully illustrated booklet describing the new **UNIVERSAL** pictures is ready. **WRITE** for it.

Carl Laemmle

UNIVERSAL PICTURES
CARL LAEMMLE, President
"The Home of the Good Film"
730 Fifth Ave.   New York City

to, say, *Variety* and *Film Daily* (both of which reviewed *Dracula* in positive terms immediately after its premiere).

Moreover, Weight's review was not as wholly negative as the single quotation suggests. He did believe that the second half of the film was disappointing, that the setting should have been the Victorian era, that the battle between Van Helsing and Dracula should have been "longer, harder," and that the film's "dialogue should have been much sparser." But these comments result from Weight's overall belief that the screenwriters should have solely used the Stoker novel for its adaptation.[17] And it must be said that Weight does praise Lugosi at length, claiming he "outdoes any of the performances ... which we have seen him give on the stage." In the end, Weight also admitted that, "Universal has made an entertaining thriller."

But there is another reason that it is *crucial* to limit the importance of Weight's *Filmograph* review in the history of *Dracula*'s release. Approximately one month later, on 9 May 1931, the *Hollywood Filmograph* published a *second* review, one that has remained unknown until now. Written by Bertrand Calmson, it was not a brief synopsis or capsule review, but a lengthy and somewhat positive critique:

Opposite: Another advertisement for *Dracula*, this time bearing Carl Laemmle, Sr.'s signature. (*Courtesy of George Chastain*).
Above: Universal's advertisement on the cover of the *Film Daily* of February 22, 1931.

> *For sheer eeriness,* Dracula, *directed by Tod Browning, is masterful in its gripping subtlety. Bela Lugosi's performance as Count Dracula is even better than his stage characterization. ... While the screen version of* Dracula *does not come up to the standard set by the stage production, it is effective enough in spots to a point bordering upon the repulsive.*[18]

This second review praised the other cast members, particularly Chandler, Frye, Van Sloan, and Gerrard, as well as Karl Freund's cinematography. Exactly why the *Filmograph* published it remains unknown (other than the fact its appearance at the Hollywood Pantages might have merited the same, though trades were not in the general habit of reviewing the same film twice). At any rate, Calmson's views clearly temper those of Weight, and together they suggest differences of opinion amongst the writers of the same publication.

Fan Magazines

During the period of *Dracula*'s general release, the key movie fan magazines critiqued it. While their covers generally sported dates that were anywhere from four-to-twelve weeks

Photo montage from the *Graphic* of February 28, 1931.

after their physical appearance on most newsstands, it seems clear that their reviews appeared during the first few months that *Dracula* was in theatres. And they were read by far more persons than the industry trade reviews, with their key audience being moviegoers rather than members of the film industry.[19]

In terms of critical response to *Dracula*, *Modern Screen* declared it was a "first-rate adaptation of both Bram Stoker's chiller-thriller novel and the stage play in which Bela Lugosi created the role he plays in the picture."[20] *Motion Picture* advised its readers to "see this super-thriller," adding that, "Tod Browning and the cameraman divide credit for sustaining the eerie atmosphere."[21] *Silver Screen* rated the film as "good" and praised the acting of Bela Lugosi.[22] And *Picture Play* wrote, "it's just a spectacular fantasy cleverly directed and brilliantly mounted, interesting because of the pains extended on it rather than for any terror it evokes. ... of all the mystery melodramas, this probably is the best because it is more outlandish than the others."[23]

Six other fan magazine reviews were positive, but advised only adult moviegoers interested in mystery and scares to see the film. "If you are looking for hair raising thrills, through believing what you see and hear, then don't fail to attend," *Screen Book Magazine* wrote, adding, "It is not for children."[24] The *New Movie Magazine* claimed the "rather well done" *Dracula* would be a "delectable repast" for viewers who "prefer to enjoy their nightmares in the theatre, rather than in bed," but also warned parents to "leave the children at home."[25] *Screenland* said *Dracula* was "just a real, good scare!"[26] *Film Fun* commended the movie to moviegoers who "like mysteries."[27] Similarly, *Screenplay* and *Hollywood* offered praise, but – to quote a word that appeared in both publications – recommended the film only for those who enjoyed "shivery" entertainment."[28] The latter publication (which ran two reviews of *Dracula*) even used the words "terror and horror" while praising the film's "photography and settings."[29]

By contrast, a few other fan magazines were not convinced. *Photoplay* recommended *Dracula* for the "mystery minded" and praised Helen Chandler's acting, but added that the film "could have been better."[30] A second review in *Picture Play* dismissed *Dracula*, which "tries to be too thrilling and is a bit funny in the portrayal of the eye-rolling corpse."[31] And *Motion Picture Classic* complained that it "isn't so chilling on the screen."[32]

Roughly two-thirds of the fan magazine reviews of *Dracula* were positive, which is an important point and one that continued the overwhelmingly positive response critics writing for all manner of publications gave to the film. That said, it is difficult to determine what effect such reviews had in terms of motivating readers to buy tickets at their local theatres.

Theatre Ballyhoo

Advertising and exploitation campaigns for *Dracula* varied from city to city and theatre to theatre. Some exhibitors followed advice from the film's pressbook, ranging from a liberal use of heralds to staging the burning candle stunt, in which patrons could win prizes by guessing which candle behind a given letter in the word "Dracula" would burn the longest.[33] Other exhibitors created their own unique ballyhoo efforts, or combined their own ideas with suggestions from the studio.

Advance publicity for *Dracula*'s arrival in movie theatres came in various forms, including the use of radio trailers. For example, the Publix-Ellanay Theatre of El Paso, Texas had an announcer on KTSM break into broadcasts of dance music to mention *Dracula* and advise listeners that every tenth person at the theatre who mentioned the station's call letters would receive a free ticket to the show.[34] Then, on the day of *Dracula*'s local

Theatre ballyhoo for *Dracula* (1931) features the faked Tod Browning telegram about February 13. *(Courtesy of D'Arcy More)*

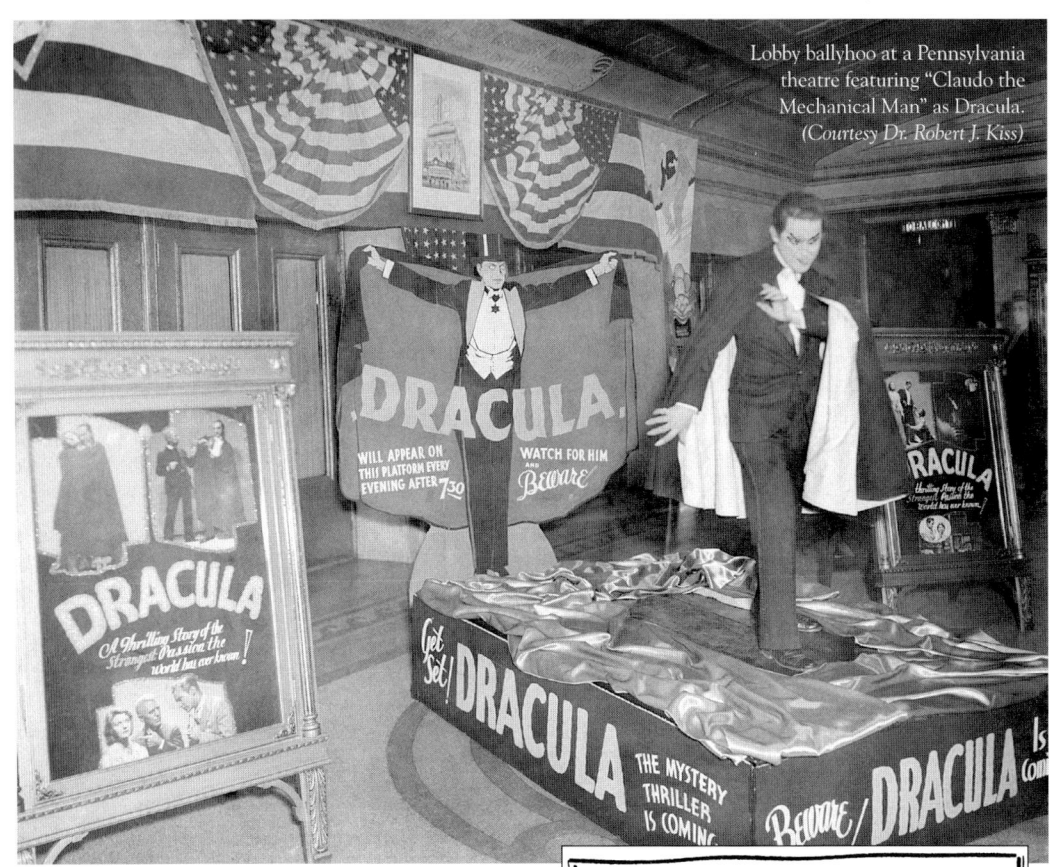

Lobby ballyhoo at a Pennsylvania theatre featuring "Claudo the Mechanical Man" as Dracula. (Courtesy Dr. Robert J. Kiss.)

premiere, KTSM broadcast a special program about the film, likely using the prepared radio trailer described in Chapter 7.[35]

More commonly, theatres relied on film trailers, using both the coming attraction edited by National Screen Service as well as (in some cases) their own creative additions. The Granada in Olyphant, Pennsylvania, followed the film trailer with a green spotlight that moved all around the house until finally stopping on a man onstage who wore a Dracula cape and a skull mask; a deep voice bellowed out "Beware of Dracula" while the costumed man walked across the stage, his claw-like gloves grasping at the air around him.[36]

By contrast, the York Theatre of Athol, Massachusetts, integrated their own effects during the film trailer. After closing their stage curtain midway through it, a camera was flashed from the side of the orchestra pit. A

Why Don't You SWAP?

Surely you have some things around the house you are no longer using—things other people really want and need, for which they will trade you something you want. Write an ad now, phone or bring it to The Observer, and receive two courtesy passes to the Broadway Theater.

SWAP CONTEST

If you are clever in writing the ad, you may win the first prize of $15 in gold The Observer is offering for the most novel and interesting ad, or the second prize of $10 in gold. Swap ads are charged at regular want ad rates.

NOW PLAYING AT
WARNER BROS.
Dial 6530 **Broadway** Dial 6530
DRACULA
Thrilling—Startling—Unforgettable.

Advertisement in the Charlotte Observer of North Carolina (March 13, 1931).

264   Chapter 9 – GENERAL RELEASE

A roving "Dracula" promoting the Browning film on the streets of Olyphant, Pennsylvania.

green spotlight then hit an image of Dracula onscreen in the trailer. The theatre blinked the house lights on and off rapidly, with someone dressed as Dracula appearing onstage. Wearing a black hat and cape, he skulked across the stage in a crouched position, apparently imitating (at least to a degree) Lon Chaney's movements in *London After Midnight* (1927). Then there was diabolical laughter and a voice that declared, "It's Dracula!"[37]

Other theatres eschewed the prepared trailer and wholly invented their own form of coming attractions. The Rialto in Phoenix, Arizona, created large letters that spelled "Dracula" and "No Woman Could Resist His Kiss" and hung them on a set of lines in front of their stage curtain. Just before the start of the feature film screened the week prior to *Dracula*, the theatre turned off the house lights. Organ music accompanied about fifteen seconds of darkness, after which a beam of purple light shot from the projection booth to illuminate the letters. The organ music came to a climax, after which the spotlight was turned off and the house lights were restored.[38]

Advance publicity also included a "whispering campaign," as in the case of the Capitol Theatre in Hazelton, Pennsylvania, where ushers quietly informed patrons that "Dracula [was] Coming" one week before the film opened. Other theatre employees used the same stunt elsewhere in the city, including at public schools. According to the exhibitor's account, "by the end of the week, most everybody and especially the kiddies were whispering to one another, 'Dracula is coming!'"[39]

Borrowing ideas from *Dracula*'s pressbook (as well as from longstanding practices in film exhibition), many theatres ran contests in advance of their film screenings. In Rocky Mountain, North Carolina, the Carolina Theatre and the local *Evening Telegram* joined forces to give twelve prizes to those writers who could best describe their "creepiest experience" in

Chapter 9 – GENERAL RELEASE

the space of 75 words or less.[40] In Sandusky, Ohio, a local newspaper offered thirty free tickets to readers who could find words pertaining to Dracula buried in its classified advertisements and assemble them into a complete sentence.[41]

In many cases, street ballyhoo featured men dressed as Dracula, walking in front of the theatre or in the nearby area.[42] In Louisville, Kentucky, a theatre (working in tandem with a newspaper) offered rewards for those who could "capture" Dracula, a costumed man roaming the city streets; similarly, a theatre in Aberdeen, South Dakota, awarded five dollars to anyone who could recognize a local "Dracula" on the prowl.[43]

The Egyptian Theatre in Falls, South Dakota, attempted what was perhaps the most elaborate version of this stunt, its tie-up including the support of 21 local stores and radio station KSOO, which made daily reports regarding the five-day hunt for a man dressed as Dracula. Twenty-five dollars was awarded each day to the person who found him in a store, tapped him on the shoulder, and said: "I have been looking for you, Dracula. By day you are dead. By night you come forth to haunt youth and beauty."[44]

A "mirror" gimmick used at the Smoot Theatre in Parkersburg, West Virginia.

During both the days prior to screening *Dracula* and during its run, some exhibitors promoted the film at various locations in their cities and towns, the most common approach being the use of window cards in local stores and other locations. Other exhibitors tried unique publicity stunts, such as the Eagle Theatre in New York City, which convinced a nearby store to put a coffin and a skeleton in its window.[45] A manager on the West Coast staged a version of the same, placing a *Dracula* display in a furniture store window with a humorous caption pretending to be the vampire's dialogue: "Ah, the beauty slumbers...I cannot awaken her...She must be sleeping on an Ostermoor mattress."[46]

At their own theatres, exhibitors tried a range of other exploitation efforts, including an extensive use of Universal's movie posters for the film. Theatre lobbies also became important, as in the case of one theatre that gave out "magic potions" to keep patrons from having nightmares; these packets contained nothing more than oolong tea, but they served to generate word of mouth.[47]

Show times provided another source of publicity, with numerous exhibitors screening *Dracula* at midnight. Some theatres began their programs at 11:30PM, starting with short subjects so that *Dracula* would unreel at 12AM.[48] In a number of cases, *Dracula* even made its local premiere at midnight shows.[49] While midnight shows were not uncommon in some cities in 1931, the timing of them meshed nicely with *Dracula*'s more mysterious and horrifying elements.

Other gimmicks occurred in theatre auditoria while *Dracula* was projected onscreen. The most common gag was to have women planted in the audience to scream or even pretend to faint during the film, a practice that borrowed from a similar trick used at some performances of *Dracula–The Vampire Play*.[50] Less common was the stunt used at the Spreckel's Theatre in San Diego, in which a "huge [fake] bat with luminous lighting" swung over the viewers' heads. According to the *San Diego Union*, "one old lady screamed, another female patron made a dash for the exit, and for a second all was commotion," resulting in what the newspaper called a "riot."[51]

When *Dracula* opened in New Haven, a group of Yale students released a number of bats stolen from a university laboratory into a local theatre auditorium. Rather than incite a small degree of panic, as had happened in San Diego, patrons believed the college prank was an intentional publicity gag, and "complimented" the theatre staff on their effective ballyhoo.[52]

Above: Newspaper advertisement for *Dracula* that emphasizes the vampire bat. Below: This advertisement for *Dracula*'s appearance in New Haven, Connecticut uses artwork from the studio pressbook.

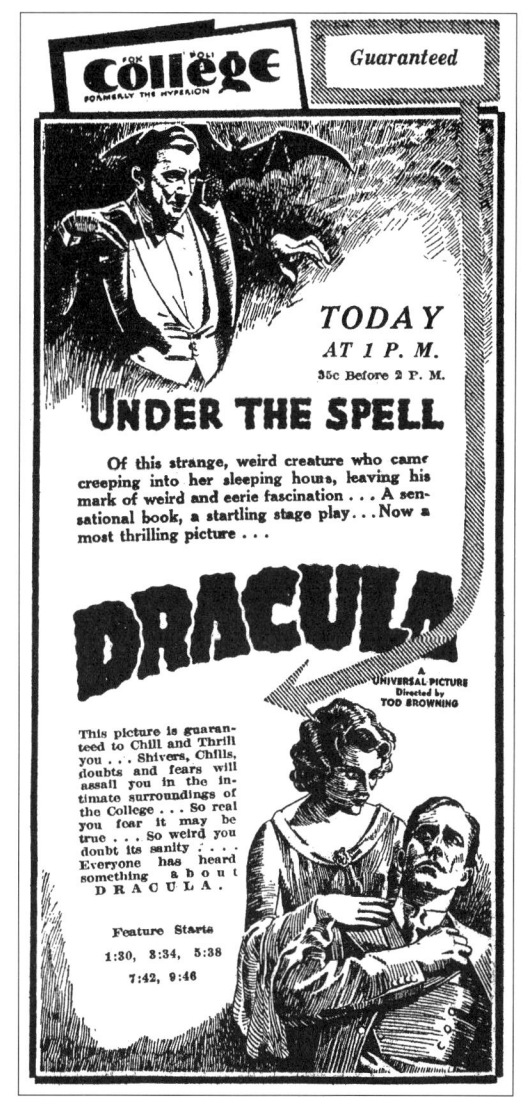

Audience Responses

Reconstructing audience responses for *Dracula* is extremely difficult, as millions of viewers saw the film in 1931 and no records exist to convey how the bulk of them responded. Even a single moviegoer might have experienced varying emotions throughout the film. Indeed, audiences are fragmentary and temporary coalitions of persons who watch a film and are quickly replaced with another group who view the same during a subsequent screening.

Fortunately, a small number of specific responses to *Dracula* were recorded. For example, a newspaper critic in New Orleans claimed that "gasps, screams, and startled exclamations came from the lips of scores who saw this uncanny drama."[53] While fascinating, these kinds of reported viewer reactions tend to suggest an entire audience (or at least a large section of it) responded to *Dracula* in much the same way, something that might have been the case, but it is also possible that these "gasps" came from only a small number of persons in the auditorium, or possibly even from a theatre employee instructed to scream at given points in the film.

Other recorded responses are specific to particular viewers. A newspaper in Brooklyn published the story of a man in Astoria, New York, who found himself menaced by a dog while he was walking home. The dog not only growled at him, but also tried to prevent his escape. After he finally got inside his house, the dog remained only a few yards from his front door. The newspaper reported that the man had recently seen *Dracula*, and experienced "disturbing recollections" of the film during his encounter with the dog.[54]

In other cases, moviegoers preserved their own reactions by writing to movie fan magazines. For example, a viewer in San Diego wrote to the *Motion Picture Classic*, claiming that he had just seen the film:

> *Dracula* effectively absorbed my attention. It made me feel I was there in the scene, hushed and still, while horrible things were being done, while drama and tragedy and life flowed past. It made me realize the artistry of acting so flawless that I forgot it was acting.
> It was not too grim, however. Clever interpolations throughout relieved the plot, keeping it from morbidness.
> Direction must have been nearly perfect to be so self-effacing, and the same can be said about the performance of the characters. They seemed to have in mind always that maxim of Shakespeare's – 'The play's the thing.'
> I've knocked around the world considerably … done nearly everything from flying a plane to being Secretary of a Christian Endeavor group – had enough experience of all sorts to make me think that I was fairly blasé against movie 'spooky' plays – but *Dracula* folks, really and truly gave me a thrill![55]

Not all moviegoers responded the same way, of course, as exemplified in the following two letters which were published in *Photoplay* in June 1931:

> Give us more pictures like *Dracula*. It is the best murder mystery I've ever seen. Bela Lugosi was magnificent. He almost hypnotized the audience.

> Why can't pictures of frenzied horror such as *Dracula* be eliminated entirely from the screen? Life is hectic enough without tormenting us with pictures of this kind.[56]

These two letters reveal extreme views on the film, and so it is not difficult to speculate that, while some moviegoers might have agreed with one or the other, many more might well have situated their response somewhere in between the two.

Prior to *Dracula*'s release, one journalist asked the important question, "Will feminine movie-goers return to see this scene, as did feminine stage audiences?"[57] Then, on 18 February

1931, only days after *Dracula*'s premiere, *Variety* confidently declared that the "femme angle looks all right" for the film.[58] One surviving anecdote along these lines is the case of Annie Mood, Annie Mabry and Mrs. Perry Price, who travelled with one Mr. Price from Barnwell, South Carolina to Columbia specifically to see *Dracula* during its original release.[59]

Based upon responses from various public groups, the *Motion Picture Monthly* declared in May 1931 that *Dracula* was suitable for adults only, a belief which has already been noted.[60] The *Los Angeles Record* issued a similar statement:

> A very strenuous warning is issued to parents that it is important to keep all children, however unimaginative, away from this film. It is not like the ordinary mystery thriller, to which youngsters of high school age can go without undue excitement. There are implications in it that might haunt an unformed mind for years. It seems to me that the Orpheum would win a great deal of respect if it refused admittance to those children who might be taken to the show by parents who are not familiar with the tale.[61]

Similarly, the *Richmond Times-Dispatch* told parents "you will be wise if you leave the children at home" when seeing *Dracula*.[62] And a review in one Chicago newspaper described a woman having to reassure one youngster in the audience that, "It's only a picture."[63]

However, many children did see the film, and it is clear that many, if not most, exhibitors wanted their business. Indeed, the *Motion Picture Monthly* noted that *Dracula* received the highest response in a 1931 survey among pupils who had to write about their favorite films.[64] And one sociological study recorded the story of children enacting the plotline of *Dracula* during their playtime.

February 1931

Immediately after *Dracula*'s New York premiere, the film opened in other cities, its general release underway. *Dracula–The Vampire Play* continued to appear at various theatres during the film's run as well. For example, the Arthur Casey Players staged a version of the play in Houston, and the Hayden Players did the same in Dallas.[65] Roadshow versions also continued their successes, appearing in Baltimore and Brooklyn that month.[66] In the same way the film fed off the play's renown, so too did the play off the film once it was at movie theatres.

Examining the film's general release in February of 1931 (and in the months that followed) allows for a clearer understanding of its geographical movements, its advertising and ballyhoo, its critical reception, and its box-office success. Unfortunately, a reconstruction of those events must focus on the particular theatres for which theatre manager reports exist, while acknowledging that the film did appear in many other cities and towns and that those under review herein may not be particularly representative of all of the United States. Despite the limitations of such a reconstruction, much can still be learned.

In some cities the film *Dracula* opened on 13 February 1931, but in other cities it opened on St. Valentine's Day, with the tagline "The Story of the Strangest Passion the World Has Ever Known" dovetailing nicely with the holiday.[67] In addition to a number of urban centers, *Dracula* also played in some smaller towns during the weekend of 13 February, including Big Spring, Texas.[68]

The Rialto Theatre in Washington, DC booked *Dracula* on its first weekend with a newsreel, a two-reel comedy, and a live organist.[69] According to the *Post*, the theatre was "crowded from early morning until late at night," with the management "seriously considering starting earlier than usual each morning to accommodate the crowds."[70] *Dracula* grossed a better-than-expected $17,800, its manager calling the film "A winner. Miles ahead of average business."[71]

Other theatres opening *Dracula* that same weekend included the Midwest in Oklahoma City, which booked it alongside the short subjects *With Pleasure* and *One Hour to Go*. Advertisements promoted *Dracula*'s thrill and romance angle, but added other words like "Haunting."[72] "Just the picture for this house," a theatre manager's report later noted as a result of its "above average" gross of $8,500.[73]

With help from Universal's publicity department, the Alhambra in Milwaukee sponsored a contest with a local newspaper. For the three best ghost stories featuring local legends, the Alhambra offered $50 in cash; other winners received free tickets and transportation to see *Dracula*.[74] The stunt generated a "fine amount of publicity," which was aided by a publicity campaign featuring ads with an emphasis on the horrific, far more so than most other theatres in February 1931.[75] Positive reviews may have helped as well, with the *Milwaukee Journal* praising *Dracula* as an improvement over the stage play.[76] The Alhambra management later wrote about the film's "good appeal," which translated into a "big" $11,000 gross.[77]

By 20 February, *Dracula* moved on to a number of other theatres, including the RKO Orpheum in Tacoma, "doing fairly" against local competition from such films as Chaplin's *City Lights* (1931).[78] In Atlanta, the Capitol Theatre went further with the "strangest passion" angle in newspaper ads that claimed *Dracula* "Loves Woman to Insanity!" and "Loves Women to Death!"[79]

Thanks in part to its publicity in New York City, *Dracula* generated $40,000 at Brooklyn's Albee when it was paired with a vaudeville bill featuring a European clown, a fourteen-piece girl orchestra, and a musical comedy star.[80] The

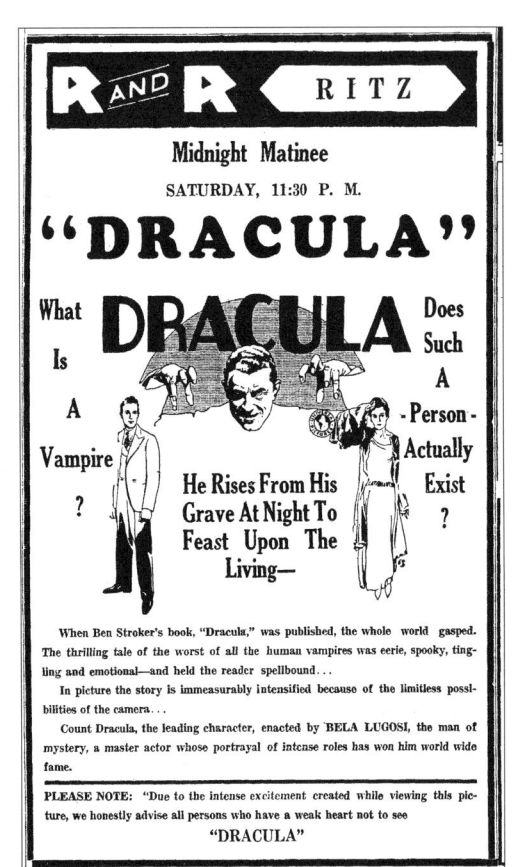

Above Top: Advertisement for *Dracula* published in the *Big Spring Daily Herald* on February 12, 1931. Above: Advertisement published in the *Rocky Mountain Telegram* (Rocky Mountain, North Carolina) on February 25, 1931 eschews studio artwork, presenting instead unique imagery.

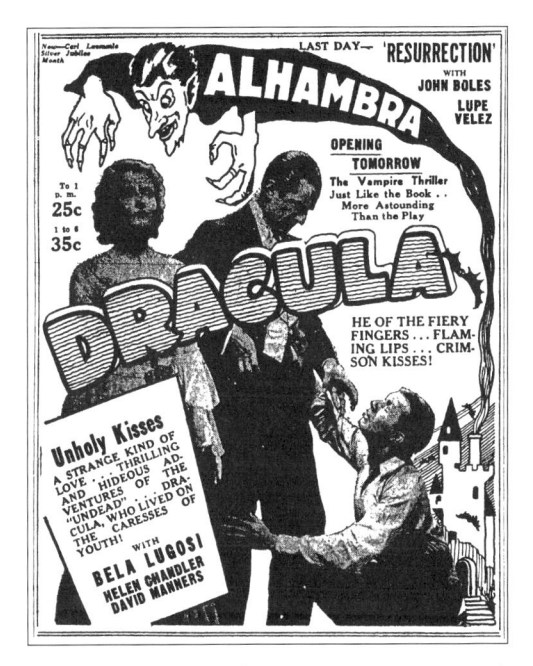

Top Left: Advertisement for *Dracula* in Milwaukee, Wisconsin, published in the *Milwaukee Journal* on February 12, 1931.
Left: This advertisement in the February 21, 1931 issue of the *Atlanta Constitution* uses artwork from the studio pressbook
Above: Advertisement for *Dracula* published in the *Milwaukee Journal* on February 15, 1931.

film became the city's biggest hit that week and even broke the Albee's record for Monday ticket sales.[81] Writing in the *Brooklyn Eagle*, Martin Dickstein praised *Dracula*'s "artistic and atmospheric use of the camera and a number of striking sets," but also found it "disappointing in achieving the weird fascinating and heart-clutching spasms that were expected."[82]

Dracula then opened at a number of theatres during the last weekend of the month, including at the RKO St. Louis in St. Louis, Missouri (where the ballyhoo featured a "mammoth" banner stretching across one street and the distribution of "Don't Dream" envelopes after each screening), and at the Stanley in Pittsburgh, Pennsylvania, where it became "the biggest thing in town" with a total gross of nearly $35,500.[83]

That same weekend, *Dracula* made its Portland, Oregon, premiere at the RKO Orpheum alongside a vaudeville bill that included a comic singer, five female jugglers, and a harpist.[84]

Chapter 9 – GENERAL RELEASE

The city's censor board required one cut in the film, though the specifics of the offending footage is unknown. As a local journalist wrote, "as soon as the last curtain falls [on the vaudeville show], you get to thinking again about that darned *Dracula*."[85] Positive critical response appeared in the *Oregon Daily Journal*, which viewed *Dracula* as a mystery reminiscent of *The Bat*; their critic called the film a "big picture" and praised both its visuals and sound effects.[86] Along with *Reaching for the Moon* (1931), *Dracula* became one of the two "big winners" in the city, making around "$15,000," an increase over the previous week's $11,500 with *Millie*.[87]

Seattle's Orpheum screened *Dracula* on a bill that included a newsreel, a band, and a vaudeville show. Borrowing a story from the studio pressbook, local publicity claimed that fifty real bats had been captured inside a Nevada cave for use in the production of *Dracula*.[88] The *Seattle Times* called it a "weird, creepy drama on [an] unusually big scale," and *Post-Intelligencer* drew particular attention to the subtleties of Bela Lugosi's performance, adding that the "gay and gladsome" vaudeville bill helped offset the film's "eerie atmosphere."[89] The bill grossed a "good" $13,000.[90]

At Philadelphia's Stanley Theatre, *Dracula* gained enormous support from the city's five newspaper critics, who unanimously praised it. The *Evening Ledger* wrote that, for those who enjoyed "their dash of horror," *Dracula* was "recommended in no uncertain terms." The *News* and the *Bulletin* believed the film an improvement over the stage version, and the *Record* judged it to be "easily one of the best" films in the city.[91] Viewers apparently agreed in large numbers, as it broke all weekend records for the Stanley and grossed a "very good" $25,000 for the week.[92]

During the last weekend of the month, *Dracula* made a triumphant return to Manhattan, opening at the Hippodrome Theatre.[93] February also saw the film rating holdovers at numerous other theatres, including the Fox Eckel in Syracuse, the Alhambra in Milwaukee, the Rialto in Washington, D.C., and the RKO Granada in South Bend, Indiana.[94] The Albee

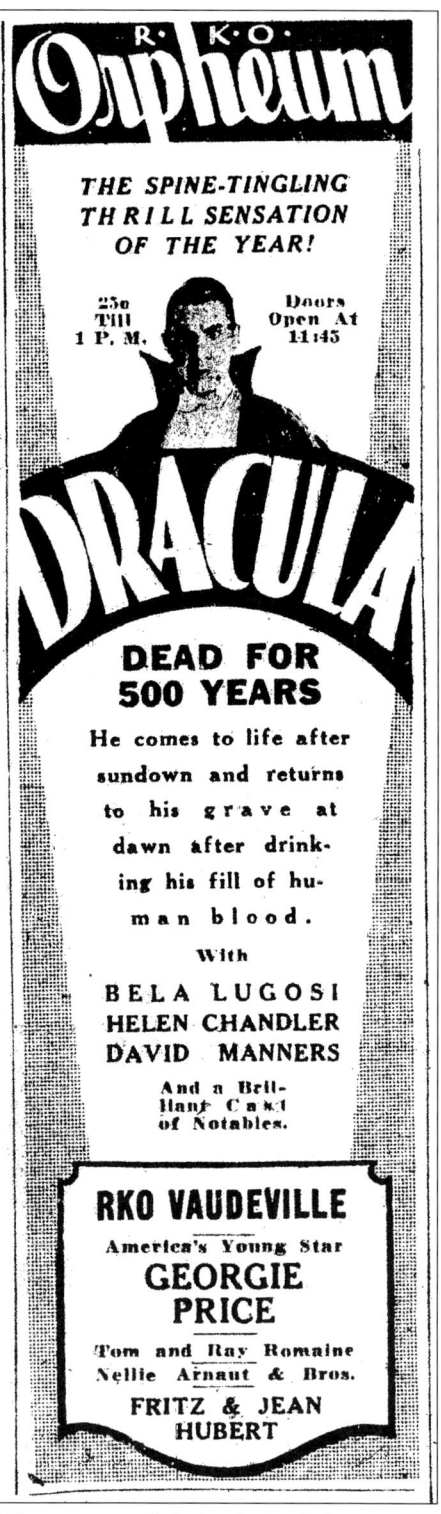

Advertisement published in the *Seattle Post-Intelligencer* on February 28, 1931.

272   Chapter 9 – GENERAL RELEASE

in Brooklyn also booked the film for a second week, where it brought "the crowds in" to add another $24,000."[95]

In late February, after *Dracula*'s premiere and its first two weeks in general release, Universal's sales manager Phil Reisman proudly declared the film to be a "domestic sensation" and "one of the outstanding box office attractions of all time."[96]

March 1931

In March, Universal released numbers from their annual fiscal report for 1930, revealing a loss of $2,047,821, as opposed to a profit of $491,358 posted for the prior year.[97] Carl Laemmle, Sr. tried to instill confidence in the company by noting that the full production costs of films like *All Quiet on the Western Front* (1930) were charged against that year, even though they made a good deal of their money subsequent to November 1930.[98] Along with formally welcoming Al Szekeler to his new position as Universal's General Manager in March, Laemmle also hired film producer Sol Lesser that month.[99] Though trades claimed Lesser would act as Laemmle's executive assistant for the "business end" of Universal, the new personnel suggests that Junior Laemmle had lost some power at the studio.[100]

By the middle of March, Universal announced plans to produce a version of *Frankenstein*.[101] Within two weeks, the studio also announced plans for *Murders in the Rue Morgue* to be the third film in their cycle, with *Film Daily* using the word "horror" as a description for those two films and for *Dracula*.[102] The studio had good reasons to proceed with their plans, not least of which was the concern that competitors might encroach on their terrain, which – thanks to *Dracula* – was continuing to generate large profits. Here is an important point in *Dracula*'s evolution to becoming understood primarily as a "horror" film.

Universal's advertisement in the *Motion Picture Daily* on March 5, 1931.

During the first weekend of March, Baltimore's Auditorium reported a gross of $7,600 after screening *Dracula* for six days, a sizeable increase over the previous week's $4,900 for *Cimarron* (1931).[103] It became their box-office leader for the first three months of the year, with the manager calling *Dracula* a "stand out."[104] Theatre ballyhoo included prizes awarded for the best local ghost stories, with the winning tales publicized in local newspapers and on radio station WCBM.[105]

The Mainstreet Theatre in Kansas City opened *Dracula* that same weekend, the film appearing on a bill that also featured a live show titled the *20th Century Revue*.[106] The *Kansas City Star* promised moviegoers that *Dracula* was "scary," much more so than either the play or the novel. The same critic heaped praise on Tod Browning and the cast, save for David Manners, who "does not do much for himself or the film."[107] According to *Motion Picture Daily*, *Dracula* "wow[ed]" audiences in the city, with its "excellent" gross of $21,000 making it the city's top-earning film.[108]

Cleveland audiences also saw *Dracula* the same week, with the RKO Hippodrome opening it at a midnight show.[109] Augmenting the studio publicity materials were newspaper ads that featured the word "terror," a noticeably stronger term than the studio's preference for "thrills."[110] A local review assured readers that Browning had directed the film "unusually well," creating a movie that bested the stage version.[111] The same critic also declared that *Dracula* was a "horror story."

Advertisement published in the *Kansas City Star* of March 6, 1931.

Local audiences seemingly agreed with his recommendation, as the film grossed a successful $30,000 during its first week in Cleveland, a dramatic increase over the previous week's $14,000 from *Stolen Heaven* (1931).[112] One newspaper account claimed that a woman fainted while watching the film, likely the result of having been paid to do so by the management.[113] Despite the film's local success, one viewer took great exception to it, writing a letter to the editor in which he decried the movie – as well as the "stupidity" and "ignorance" of Bela Lugosi – for depicting Transylvania, Romanians, and the historic Dracula in such an inaccurate manner.[114]

The film then premiered on Friday the 13th of March at the RKO Albee in Providence, Rhode Island, the timing specifically chosen by the theatre's managing director to frame an advertising campaign that relied on such descriptions as "terrifying."¹¹⁵ To ballyhoo *Dracula*, the Albee hired boys to wander about the streets wearing capes; theatre staff wore masks, with the ticket-taker costumed as Dracula.¹¹⁶

The *Providence Journal* warned readers that *Dracula* "brings terror," while the *Evening Bulletin* praised Tod Browning's direction of the "fine and intelligent and completely scarey [sic] study in the supernatural."¹¹⁷ Many local moviegoers agreed, with the film generating a solid $12,000 gross for one week before the same chain immediately moved it into Providence's RKO Victory. Advertising at that theatre headlined the phrase "We Dare You To See It!", but gross revenues there only amounted to a "so-so" $5,500.¹¹⁸

Dracula opened at the State-Lake Theatre in Chicago on 19 March without any cuts from the city's censorship board, something of a victory for the film, which appeared alongside the short subjects *Wine, Woman, and No Song* and *She Went for a Tramp*.¹¹⁹ Building on the studio publicity, advertisements in Chicago added the tagline, "Good to the Last Gasp!" Ballyhoo efforts included tying the front of the theatre with a huge spider web made of rope; at its center was a large image of Dracula's face, his green eyes flashing on and off.

Other publicity stunts included a Chicago radio station broadcasting a serialization of the novel *Dracula* over a six day period, using talent from a local dramatic school. Bricks with the film title and theatre name were given to newsstands as temporary paperweights. And Chevrolet collaborated with the State-Lake on a street ballyhoo, supplying one of their new models so

Above Top: Advertisement published in the *Providence Journal* on March 13, 1931. Above: Advertisement published in the *Providence Journal* on March 16, 1931.

Chapter 9 – GENERAL RELEASE

Left: Advertisement published in the *Sheboygan Press* (Sheboygan, Wisconsin) on March 16, 1931. Right: Advertisement published in the *Sandusky Register* (Sandusky, Ohio) on March 19, 1931.

that a local actor could portray Dracula by riding around the city in a mask. Chevy also published photographs of the gimmick in the auto sections of Chicago newspapers and even gave the film a two-minute plug on the company's national radio hour.[120]

Reviews in the city varied. The *Chicago Evening Post* praised *Dracula*, drawing particular attention to Lugosi's performance.[121] The *Tribune* called it "quite a satisfactory thriller," but also argued that its "attempts to frighten" were too "evident," making the film "not as scary as the play."[122] More harsh was the *Daily News*, which – after drawing the distinction between "ladies of swell figures and no morals" like Theda Bara and "real vampires" like Lugosi's Dracula – complained the film was "uneven," with some scenes not being "in the best of taste" and others "so overdone as to be ridiculous and evoke a chortle in the place of a chill."[123]

Nevertheless, an exhibitor report in *Variety* claimed that *Dracula* "clicked solidly" with Chicago audiences, resulting in "extraordinarily big biz."[124] The total gross for the week was a "smashing" $40,000, with $26,000 generated over the first three days, an achievement that broke an eight-year record at the State-Lake.[125] A subsequent account happily proclaimed *Dracula* brought "gold" into the theatre's box-office, a vast improvement over the previous week's paltry $17,850 from the film *Millie*.[126]

Advertisement published in the *Chicago Tribune* of March 27, 1931.

While appearing in Chicago, *Dracula* also played Detroit's RKO Downtown Theatre. Though the city did not have a censorship board, the police had forbidden any theatre from screening *Dracula* in February, but apparently experienced a change of heart soon thereafter.[127] As a goodwill device, the theatre advertised that they would offer no children's prices for tickets, something they normally did for other movies. Analyzing this tactic, *Variety* concluded that the theatre accentuated the film's "gruesomeness" rather than concealing it behind a safer publicity campaign.[128] The result brought $26,000 to the theatre's box-office, their average business at the time being $24,000.[129]

During the last week of March, the RKO Orpheum in San Francisco premiered *Dracula*, booking it with a "huge stage show" called *La Fiesta* that featured 75 performers and with two short subjects, *The Stolen Jools* and *Golf*. Ads in newspapers like the *San Francisco Chronicle* used words like "terrifying" to describe the film, which grossed a strong $18,000 for the week, a major improvement over the $10,000 generated by *Millie* the week prior, but still far behind their high for the year, which was $30,000 from *Cimarron*.[130]

Dracula's biggest opening at the end of March came at the RKO Orpheum in Los Angeles on 27 March.[131] On the stage was a revue entitled *The World of Pleasure*, featuring 75 performers in a range of musical sketches that included Gershwin's *Rhapsody in Blue*.[132] Local publicity included a newspaper story describing the ingenuity of Universal technicians who created *Dracula*'s elaborate cobwebs out of rubber cement, fashioning the substance into shape thanks to an electrically operated rotary gun.[133]

Most notably, Bela Lugosi apparently gave a speech over LA radio station KFI on 27 March.[134] A surviving transcript in one of the actor's scrapbooks shows that the speech – likely written or at least approved by Universal – featured his description of growing up in "almost the exact location of the story," and having played the role of Dracula onstage in New York. "I think that the picture will be no less effective than the stage play," he told listeners. "In fact, the motion picture should even prove more remarkable in this direction, since many things which could only be talked about on the stage are shown on the screen in all their uncanny detail."[135]

Such detail brought forth a range of different opinions amongst critics in Los Angeles. The *Evening Herald* wrote, "*Dracula* is a swell nightmare, perhaps as grand a one as you will ever see," and the *Illustrated Daily News* praised the "adeptness" of the film's "execution."[136] Drawing a connection between *Dracula* and the mystery genre, the *Examiner* noted, "The cat has crept, the bat has whispered, and the ghost has walked, but *Dracula* would make the hair rise on a brass monkey," adding that it "is a better motion picture than it was as a stage play."[137]

By contrast, the *Los Angeles Times* complained that many of the shots seemed "posed," particularly:

> ... those of Count Dracula – who, of all the company, should have been the most elusive, steeped as he is in the tradition of the undead. Then, too, the dialogue is particularly artificial, although I admit that 'modernizing' it would have robbed it still further of its claim to illusion. Music, perhaps, would have helped, but that is something to concern its creators more than the casual spectator, who can only report his own responses to the finished version.[138]

Trade advertisement published on March 25, 1931.

And the critic for the *Los Angeles Record* claimed, "I would like to have seen [Dracula] actually change into a bat or wolf, but I suppose we can't have everything."[139]

Overall, *Dracula* experienced great success in March, with the film generating large grosses and rating holdovers in such cities as Baltimore, Chicago, Cleveland, Detroit, Philadelphia, and San Francisco. It was also a major triumph in Cincinnati and Columbus that month.[140] Such news helped bolster Universal's argument in March that its financial condition was beginning to "assume [a] healthier position after [an] 'off' year."[141]

April 1931

In early April, *Variety* described the industry's "surprise" over *Dracula*'s box-office success in February and March, claiming that it had been well received in most theatres, more so in some cases than *All Quiet on the Western Front*, including at a number of African-American theatres.[142] As a result, Universal forged ahead with plans to produce versions of *Frankenstein* and *Murders in the Rue Morgue* during their 1931-32 season, with *Variety* declaring that the studio had the "horror cycle" all to itself.[143] But other studios had noticed *Dracula*'s success; Paramount announcing in early April that it had acquired the rights to the novel *Murder by the Clock*.[144] And the *Hollywood Reporter* warned exhibitors that same month that they

Above: Advertisement published in the *San Francisco Chronicle* of April 1, 1931.

would get a "flock" of "horror pictures" in the near future from a variety of studios.[145] Key to this discussion was the increasing use of the word "horror" to describe *Dracula* and a burgeoning cycle of films in the works.

But *Dracula* also remained tied to its stage predecessor. Producer O.W. Wee staged a version of *Dracula–The Vampire Play* at the Royale in New York, bringing the play back to Manhattan with a run that opened on 13 April.[146] The *New York Times* noted that Courtney White portrayed the part of Dracula "with relish."[147] As productions of the play continued in April, so too did screenings of the film. *Dracula* made inaugural appearances at many theatres, including in such cities as Hollywood, where it grossed a disappointing $10,000 at the Pantages, as well as in Houston, where it made an acceptable $10,500 at the Majestic.[148]

The RKO Keith's in Boston screened *Dracula* the week of 3 April on a bill with the short subjects *Golf with Johnny Farrell* and *The Stolen Jools*. Ads in local newspapers largely adhered to Universal's publicity materials. The *Boston Herald* informed readers that Browning had "expertly handled" the film, which went on to be the top box-office performer in the city.[149] But viewers in Boston did not see shots of a skeleton in a casket or of an insect during the opening sequence in Dracula's castle: the Massachusetts Board of Censors had required their deletion.[150]

On 10 April, the RKO Orpheum in New Orleans paired *Dracula* with a vaudeville bill consisting of a singer, a harmonica player, an impressionist, two slapstick dancers, and a group of "bike-robatics." Ads promised viewers "thrills," "chills," and – perhaps in an effort to avoid scaring off possible ticket-buyers – "laughs."[151] Though unimpressed with the live show, the critic at the *Times-Picayune* praised *Dracula*: "Until such time as a movie producer manages to descend into the pit of Acheron and emerge with a film depicting home life along the banks of the Stygian creek will *Dracula* remain the most amazingly weird chronicle of gruesome horrors ever to thrill a theatre audience."[152] An exhibitor's projection for the theatre's box-office receipts for the film was $10,000, a noticeable increase over recent weeks.[153]

In April, news also began to appear from other countries. On 19 April, *Film Daily* reported that the P.C.T.-Gaumont British circuit booked *Dracula* to screen in more than 300 theatres in Great Britain.[154] As for Australia, the *Motion Picture Herald* announced that:

> … not for years has a picture cleaned up Sydney as spectacularly as Dracula has done. Its success has been phenomenal. Opening in mid-summer weather, and going into the Capitol, which boomed one time but which now is satisfied with a weekly gross of $6,000 to $6,500, Dracula pulled in a little in excess of $16,250 in its first week, and, at that, turned the crowds away.[155]

Above: Advertisement published in the *Riverside Daily Press* (Riverside, California) on April 20, 1931.

The same article noted that the "horror cycle" seemed to have started successfully in Australia, another sign of the increasing use of that term in relation to *Dracula*.

When April began, *Variety* published a Universal advertisement promoting *Dracula* as the "greatest held over picture," and – while that phrase was certainly an exaggeration – the film did continue to play second week runs at numerous theatres that month, including in Los Angeles and San Francisco.[156]

Summer and Autumn 1931

In May, Universal reassured its sales force (and, by extension, the film industry) that its production policies and decisions of 1930 would definitely result in a successful annual gross for 1931.[157] Carl Laemmle, Sr. stressed the fact that the studio was in "splendid financial condition" thanks to a number of recent succeses.[158] But the studio also touted its upcoming emphasis on a number of serials and "action films," which hardly suggested a strict adherence to Junior Laemmle's production strategy of the prior year.[159] And despite the studio's positive rhetoric, *Variety* reported in May that all executives and departmental heads at Universal suffered pay cuts of 25 percent.[160] The pay cuts even extended to Junior Laemmle, who remained as head of production and was also elected in May as Universal's

Dracula played many theatres in particular cities following its local premieres in first-run houses. While the film had opened at the RKO Albee in Brooklyn, it subsequently appeared the RKO Prospect. (*Courtesy of the Michael R. Miller Collection, American Theatre Architecture Archives, Theatre Historical Society of America*)

"second vice president," which could have been the result of various power struggles in the studio hierarchy.¹⁶¹

Dracula continued its box-office success, increasingly moving into small towns where it had not previously appeared. For example, Oklahoma City played *Dracula* on the St. Valentine's Day weekend, but it would not be until June that the film would appear in Ardmore, a town located in southern Oklahoma.¹⁶² During the same time frame, neighborhood theatres began screening *Dracula* in the same cities where it had already played movie palaces and deluxe first-run houses. In June, Universal even initiated a drive to convince exhibitors to book revivals of some of its biggest budget talkies, including *King of Jazz* (1930), *All Quiet on the Western Front*, and *Dracula*.¹⁶³

Publicity for other films also began to refer to *Dracula*. Advertisements for *The Dangerous Affair* (1931) – a mystery film featuring a character who believes she can communicate with the dead – labeled it a "companion picture to *Dracula*" and used artwork of a spider web and a mysterious claw to bolster the comparison.¹⁶⁴ Similarly, some publicity for Paramount's *Murder by the Clock* (1931) touted its villain as a "Female Dracula."¹⁶⁵

Then, on 8 May, the Spanish-language version of *Dracula* debuted at the California Theatre in Los Angeles, paired with a newsreel showing the Cinco de Mayo celebrations in Mexico. Less than one year earlier, the Fox Coast West chain had reopened the theatre to screen only Spanish-language talking pictures.¹⁶⁶ The *Los Angeles Times* praised George Melford's direction as "unusually good, except for some parts, which tend to be slightly episodic in form."¹⁶⁷ The theatre manager reported a box-office take of $5,600 for the film, which was somewhat less than the previous week's $6,600 from Paramount's *Gente Alegre* (1931).

As the year progressed, Hollywood noticed a dramatic decrease in the demand for Spanish-language multi-linguals.¹⁶⁸ "The foreign versions of American pictures have been an out-and-out flop in every country, due to a thousand and one reasons," the *Hollywood Reporter* complained.¹⁶⁹ To overcome the language barrier, studios increasingly viewed

An advertisement for *Murder by the Clock* (1931) that makes direct reference to Browning's *Dracula* (1931).

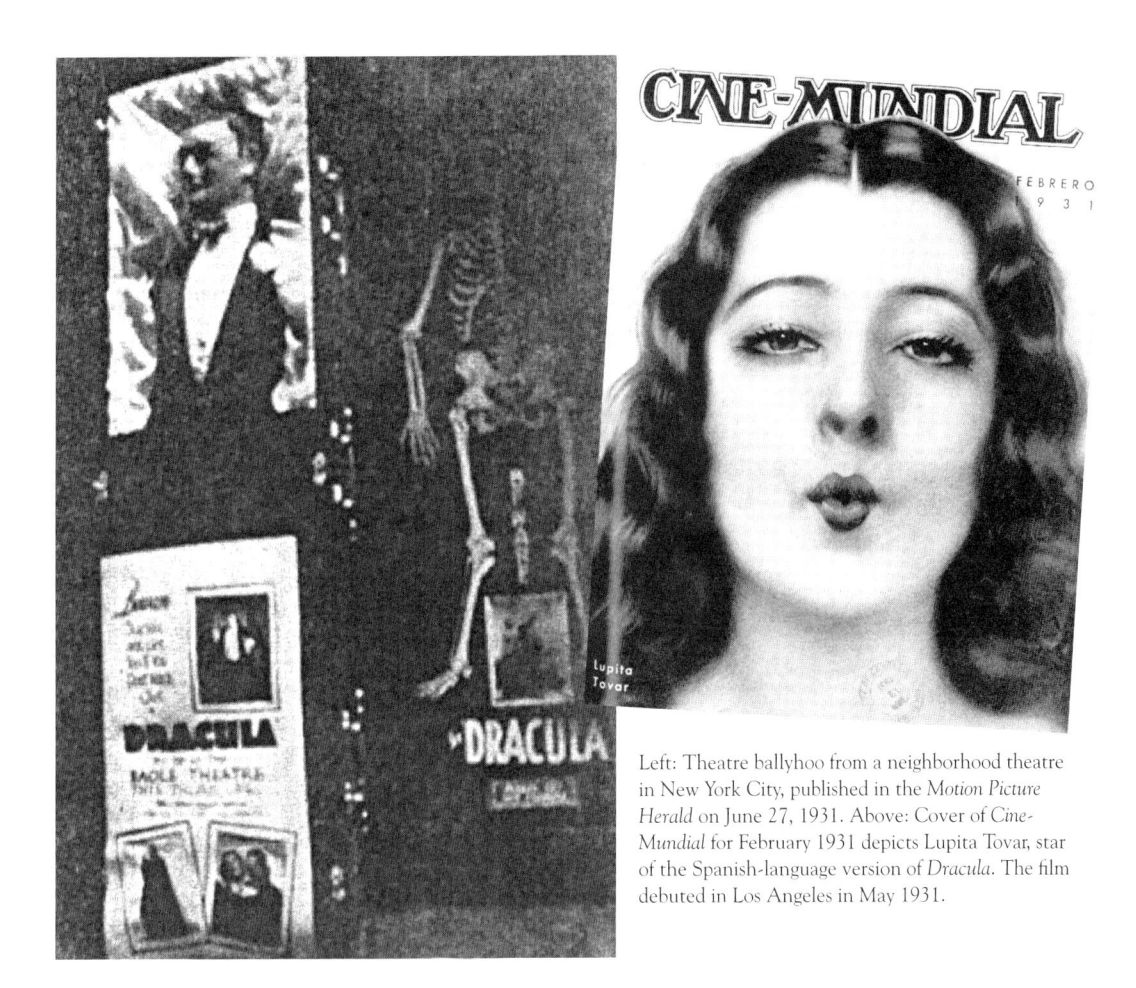

Left: Theatre ballyhoo from a neighborhood theatre in New York City, published in the *Motion Picture Herald* on June 27, 1931. Above: Cover of *Cine-Mundial* for February 1931 depicts Lupita Tovar, star of the Spanish-language version of *Dracula*. The film debuted in Los Angeles in May 1931.

dubbing as the way to conquer non-English-speaking markets.[170] The Spanish-language *Dracula* had thus premiered near the end of Hollywood's production of multi-linguals.

Conclusion

In July 1931, Universal posted a net profit of $255,783 for the quarter ending 2 May, by which time *Dracula* had already been screened in the major urban areas of the United States.[171] Eventually, the studio declared a net profit of $615,786 for the fiscal year ending 31 October 1931, a period that included the bulk of *Dracula*'s general release.[172] Later Universal cited a net profit of $400,000 for the calendar year of 1931, making it the only studio in Hollywood to have improved its situation over calendar year 1930.[173] *Dracula* grossed approximately $700,000 domestically, almost double its production cost, though its net profits are difficult to determine with any exactitude given the complexities of studio accounting processes. Nevertheless, there can be no doubt that the film was a major success in 1931, and it was key to the growing health of Universal's finances.

Credit for *Dracula* went not only to Bela Lugosi, who became a Hollywood star as a result of the film, but also to Tod Browning and Carl Laemmle, Jr. As *Photoplay* wrote of Laemmle in October 1931, "The darn fool kid set out to make *Dracula*, that weird, fantastic, and blood curdling stage play. How can that goofy thing sell as a picture? Goodbye, Junior. Again the dice came out as a natural."[174] Laemmle's gamble had indeed paid off, and that included his reliance on Tod Browning.

Though it would not win any major film awards in 1931, *Dracula* did receive numerous critical accolades. *Motion Picture Herald* included it in a list of the twenty films that received the greatest amount of exploitation during a six-month period ending on 25 April 1931.[175] When asked to list the Ten Best Pictures of 1931, seventeen critics named *Dracula*, more than enough to secure its placement on *Film Daily*'s "Roll of Honor."[176] And Tod Browning received "Honorable Mention" in a poll of critics regarding the best directors of the year.[177]

As Chapter 10 will explore, *Dracula*'s success and ongoing influence is manifold, ranging from its own cinematic reissues in the years after 1931 to the various ways in which it has been refracted in mainstream culture, a process that was already underway during its original release. But in many respects, it was America's impact on *Dracula* in 1931 that needs to be better remembered, as critics and audiences increasingly reassigned the film into a genre fast becoming known as the "horror movie."

Dracula's success was hardly limited to the United States. Here the film appears on the cover of a Belgian publication. *(Courtesy of George Chastain)*

1 "Universal Has New Selling Plan." *Billboard* 14 June 1930: 18.
2 "Reisman Goes with U, as Gen. Sales Mgr." *Variety* 30 July 1930: 15.
3 "Grimm Back at U." *Variety* 27 Aug. 1930: 31.
4 "U Realigns Its Sales Crew." *Motion Picture Daily* 26 Dec. 1930: 1, 2; "Universal Re-Aligns Its Sales Department." *Hollywood Reporter* 29 Dec. 1930: 1, 3.
5 "Entire Universal Output Is Purchased by Warners." *Billboard* 11 Oct. 1930: 31.
6 Marriott, Robert H. "Fantastic Mystery Film Thrills Fans at Palace Program." *Canton Repository* (Canton, OH) 2 Mar. 1931: 8.
7 Mace, Louise. "News of the Theatres." *Springfield Republican* (Springfield, MA) 2 Mar. 1931: 8.
8 In terms of industry analyses of women and their cinematic interests, see: Quigley, Martin J. "Feminine Interest." *Exhibitors Herald-World* 13 Sept. 1930: 24.
9 For more information on the decreased patronage of movie theatres by children in late 1930 and early 1931, see: "Children Will Come Back, Say Exhibitors – and They Get 'Em." *Exhibitors Herald-World* 26 July 1930: 27; "Solve Problem of Child Patron in New Talking Film Product." *Exhibitors Herald-World* 20 Dec. 1930: 15"Saturday Show Used by Many Houses in Effort to Regain Lost Kiddie Patronage." *Motion Picture Herald* 24 Jan. 1931: 71.
10 For examples of ads using the term "mystery," see: Advertisement. *The Courier-Journal* (Louisville, KY) 28 Feb. 1931; Advertisement. *State Center Enterprise* (State Center, IA) 5 Mar. 1931: 5; Advertisement. *The Chronicle-Telegram* (Elyria, OH) 15 Apr. 1931: 4. For examples of journalists using that term, see: "Dracula Rated Hit as Wierd [sic] Mystery Drama." *Woodland Daily Democrat* (Woodland, CA) 29 July 1931.
11 For an example of the word "creepy" used in conjunction with *Dracula*, see: Advertisement. *Sunday Times-Signal* (Zanesville, OH) 17 May 1931: 9. For examples of the word "terrifying," see: Advertisement. *Seattle Times* 2 May 1931: 2; Advertisement. *Twin Falls Daily News* (Twin Falls, ID) 26 June 1931: 4. For examples of the term "spook show," see: Advertisement. *Coshocton Tribune* (Coshocton, OH) 25 Apr. 1931: 6.
12 For examples of the word "horror" used in conjunction with *Dracula*, see Keavy, Hubbard. "Hollywood Screen

Life." *Washington Post* 5 Jan. 1931: 9; "Plain Dealer Critics Give You Tips on Current Programs." *Cleveland Plain Dealer* 22 Sept. 1931: 20.

13. "Dracula." *National Board of Review Magazine* (Mar. 1931): 18.
14. "Picture of the Week." *Exhibitors Forum* 17 Mar. 1931: 14.
15. Beaton, Welford. *The Film Spectator* 28 Mar. 1931: 13.
16. For example, David J. Skal relies heavily on this particular *Hollywood Filmograph* review of April 1931 in three of his books. See: Skal, David J. *Hollywood Gothic: The Tangled Web of* Dracula *from Novel to Stage to Screen* (New York: W. W. Norton, 1990): 173; Skal, David J. *The Monster Show: A Cultural History of Horror* (New York: W. W. Norton, 1993): 121; Skal, David J. and Elias Savada. *Dark Carnival: The Secret World of Tod Browning, Hollywood's Master of the Macabre* (New York: Anchor, 1995): 154. These books seem completely oblivious to the Calmson review mentioned in the text.
17. Weight also suggests that the film should have "closed with that mad race over the roads of Transylvania, when Van Helsing struggled with upcoming darkness, and Count Dracula sought to reach his ruined castle and safety."
18. Calmson, Bertrand. "Dracula." *Hollywood Filmograph* 9 May 1931: 21.
19. For more information on the history of American movie fan magazines, see: Slide, Anthony. *Inside the Hollywood Fan Magazine* (Jackson, MI: University Press of Mississippi, 2010).
20. "The *Modern Screen Magazine* Reviews." *Modern Screen Magazine* (May 1931): 92.
21. "Dracula." *Motion Picture* (Apr. 1931): 62.
22. "Dracula." *Silver Screen* (May 1931): 46.
23. "Dracula." *Picture Play* (May 1931): 71, 96.
24. "The First Nighter." *Screen Book Magazine* (Apr. 1931): 6.
25. "Dracula." *New Movie Magazine* (May 1931): 92.
26. "Critical Comment on Current Films." *Screenland* (May 1931): 85.
27. "Talkie Tips." *Film Fun* (June 1931): 58.
28. "Dracula." *Screenplay* (June 1931): 88; "A Brief Guide to Current Pictures." *Hollywood* (June 1931): 42.
29. "Dracula." *Hollywood* (May 1931): 36. [The words "terror and horror" appear in this review, which was longer than the "brief" review *Hollywood* ran in the June issue. Then, in the September issue, the magazine ran another "brief" review, which praised the "capable" cast (p. 64).]
30. "The Shadow Stage." *Photoplay* (Mar. 1931): 56.
31. "A Confidential Guide to Current Releases." *Picture Play* (June 1931): 72.
32. "Ten-Second Reviews." *Motion Picture Classic* (May 1931): 106.
33. "Goldsmith's Efforts on *Dracula* Clicked Very Well for House." *Motion Picture Herald* 2 May 1931; "Greene's Campaign on *Dracula* Thrilled Brooklyn Play-goers." *Motion Picture Herald* 25 Apr. 1931: 92.
34. "Special Radio Program on *Dracula*." *Film Daily* 27 Apr. 1931: 4.
35. "Hemphill Uses Gag with Radio Station to Boost *Dracula*." *Motion Picture Herald* 6 June 1931: 50.
36. "Exploitettes." *Film Daily* 31 May 1931: 3.
37. "Hesse Uses Trailer to Good Advantage on *Dracula* Film." *Motion Picture Herald* 27 June 1931: 65.
38. "Cut-Out Letters on Stage Helped Weaver Put *Dracula* Over." *Motion Picture Herald* 2 May 1931.
39. "Whispering Ushers Was Stunt Used by Cohen in Hazelton." *Motion Picture Herald* 2 May 1931.
40. "Winners Chosen in Contest for Theatre Prizes." *The Evening Telegram* (Rocky Mountain, NC) 20 Feb. 1931. In March, the Paramount Theatre in Baton Rouge, Louisiana sponsored a similar contest. See "Biggest Fear Contest Being Conducted Here." *The Morning Advocate* (Baton Rouge, LA) 6 Mar. 1931: 7.
41. Advertisement. *Sandusky Register* (Sandusky, OH) 19 Mar. 1931: 1.
42. "Street Ballyhoo for *Dracula*." *Film Daily* 3 Apr. 1931: 5;
43. "Trying Everything." *Variety* 18 Mar. 1931: 20; "Helen Ward Winner in *Dracula* Contest." *Aberdeen Evening News* (Aberdeen, SD) 21 Apr. 1931: 8. [The Publix-Egyptian Theatre of Sioux Falls, South Dakota staged a stunt similar to the Aberdeen gimmick. See "Ableson and Beecher Promoted Ace Ti-Up in Sioux Falls, N.D. [sic]." *Motion Picture Herald* 2 May 1931.
44. "*Dracula* Can Offer a Variety of Stunts." *Exhibitors Forum* 21 Apr. 1931: 14.
45. "Phillips Gag on *Dracula* Raises Hair on East Side." *Motion Picture Herald* 27 June 1931: 64.
46. Cunningham, James. "Asides and Interludes." *Motion Picture Herald* 9 Apr. 1932: 19.
47. Daly, Phil M. "Among the Rialto." *Film Daily* 2 Mar. 1931: 4.
48. See, for example. Advertisement. *Big Spring Daily Herald* (Big Spring, TX) 11 Feb. 1931: 2.
49. See, for example: Advertisement. *The Rhinelander* (WI) 26 June 1931: 2.
50. "Women Fainting Gag." *Variety* 18 Mar. 1931: 20.
51. "Huge 'Bat' Starts Riot at *Dracula*." *San Diego Union* 4 Apr. 1931: 3.
52. "Bats in Theatre." *Variety* 11 Mar. 1931: 22.
53. "Asbestos." *The Times-Picayune* (New Orleans, LA) 11 Apr. 1931: 10.
54. "Seen and Heard." *Brooklyn Star* 5 Mar. 1931: 20.
55. "Thrilled by *Dracula*." *Motion Picture Classic* (June 1931): 6.
56. "Brickbats and Bouquets." *Photoplay* (June 1931): 146.
57. Undated clipping in the author's collection.
58. "Miniature Reviews." *Variety* 18 Feb. 1931: 14.
59. "Social News in Georgia and South Georgia." *Augusta Chronicle* (Augusta, GA) 1 Mar. 1931: 5.
60. "List of Previewed Pictures." *Motion Picture Monthly* (May 1931): 6.
61. Miller, Llewellyn. "Dracula." *Los Angeles Record* 28 Mar. 1931.
62. Keats, Emma. "The New Films." *Richmond Times-*

63. Harris, Genevieve. "A Weird Story Is Skillfully Filmed." *Chicago Evening Post* 20 Mar. 1931.
64. "The Judgment of Youth." *Motion Picture Monthly* (Aug.-Sept. 1931): 2-3.
65. Untitled. *Billboard* 7 Feb. 1931: 28; "Season of Good Profits for Hayden at Dallas." *Billboard* 14 Feb. 1931: 28.
66. "Dramatic and Musical." *Billboard* 13 Feb. 1931: 76; "Dramatic and Musical." *Billboard* 21 Feb. 1931: 75.
67. In *Dark Carnival: The Secret World of Tod Browning, Hollywood's Master of the Macabre*, David J. Skal and Elias Savada claim that suggestions of *Dracula*'s "marketing tie-in with St. Valentine's Day" is "completely without basis" (p. 153). While I agree that publicity campaigns at theatres in 1931 did not specifically refer to the occasion, it seems inconceivable to me that viewers who read taglines referring to "The story of the strangest passion the world has ever known" during the film's opening weekend did not see a connection, particularly if they viewed it on 14 February.
68. Advertisement. *Big Spring Herald* (Big Spring, TX) 13 Feb. 1931: 8.
69. "What the Pictures Are Doing." *Billboard* 28 Feb. 1931.
70. "Vampires Are Abroad Again in Odd Drama." *Washington Post* 15 Feb. 1931: A4.
71. "*Dracula* and *Paid* Capitol Bell-Ringers." *Motion Picture Daily* 28 Feb. 1931: 6. *Dracula*'s total gross in Washington, D.C. was higher than projected in *Variety* on 18 Feb. 1921.
72. Advertisement. *Daily Oklahoman* (Oklahoma City, OK) 15 Feb. 1931.
73. "What the Pictures Are Doing." *Billboard* 28 Feb. 1931: 9; "*Cim* Breaks O.C. Record; Is Held Over." *Motion Picture Daily* 25 Feb. 1931: 6.
74. "*Dracula* Ghost Stories." *Variety* 18 Feb. 1931: 19.
75. "*Dracula*." *Billboard* 28 Feb. 1931: 12.
76. "*Dracula*." *Milwaukee Journal* 15 Feb. 1931.
77. "What the Pictures Are Doing," p. 9; "*Reducing* and *Cim* Hog Coin in Milwaukee." *Motion Picture Daily* 28 Feb. 1931: 4.
78. "Chaplin $5,900–Tacoma." *Variety* 25 Feb. 1931: 10.
79. Advertisement. *Atlanta Constitution* 21 Feb. 1931.
80. "Albee Theatre." *Brooklyn Eagle* 22 Feb. 1931: B9.
81. "*Dracula* Sweeps Brooklyn at $40,000 and Will Hold Over." *Variety* 25 Feb. 1931: 19.
82. Dickstein, Martin. "*Dracula*." *Brooklyn Eagle* 16 Feb. 1931: 19.
83. "St. Louis Theatre, St. Louis." *Billboard* 7 Mar. 1931: 10; "Feb. Comparisons." *Variety* 18 Mar. 1931: 27.
84. Advertisement. *Oregonian* (Portland, OR) 26 Feb. 1931: 6.
85. Truebridge, John K. "Picture at RKO Orpheum Sets Record as Thriller." *Oregonian* 27 Feb. 1931: 6.
86. "*Dracula* Found Fascinating Thriller." *Oregon Daily Journal* 27 Feb. 1931: 11.
87. "P'tland Doing Well, 3 Are Beating $12,000." *Variety* 4 Mar. 1931: 10. [In the 18 Mar. 1931 issue of *Variety*, a survey of February grosses listed *Dracula* as having grossed $13,000 during its week at the Orpheum.]
88. "Fifty Huge Bats Caught for Part in *Dracula* Film." *Seattle Times* 2 Mar. 1931: 5.
89. "At the Theatres." *Seattle Times* 1 Mar. 1931: 20; Armstrong, Everhardt. "Ghostly Classic Finely Pictured." *Seattle Post-Intelligencer* 28 Feb. 1931.
90. "*Body & Soul, Dracula* Win the Seattle Race." *Motion Picture Daily* 9 Mar. 1931: 11. [The film's $13,000 was less than the projected $16,000 in *Variety* on 4 Mar. 1931.]
91. Qtd. in "Cream Puffs & Slams." *Hollywood Reporter* 5 Mar. 1931: 2.
92. "Record for *Dracula*." *Hollywood Reporter* 3 Mar. 1931: 3; "*Lynne* Off with a Rush at Philly." *Motion Picture Daily* 9 Mar. 1931: 10.
93. "*Dracula* Going Big." *Motion Picture Daily* 26 Feb. 1931: 12.
94. Advertisement. *Variety* 25 Feb. 1931: 26.
95. "*Lovers* on Way to $55,000 at B'klyn Par." *Variety* 4 Mar. 1931: 9.
96. "Universal 'Up in the Air' on Foreign Films." *Motion Picture Herald* 28 Feb. 1931: 14, 16.
97. "U 1930 Loss $2,047,821." *Motion Picture Daily* 16 Mar. 1931: 5.
98. "Uncle Carl Issues Optimistic Statement." *Hollywood Reporter* 13 Mar. 1931: 2.
99. "U Home Office Welcomes Szekler [sic]." *Motion Picture Daily* 6 Mar. 1931: 2.
100. "Lesser Joins U as Laemmle Asst." *Hollywood Reporter* 25 Mar. 1931: 1; "Lesser Joins U as Aide to Laemmle." *Motion Picture Daily* 26 Mar. 1931: 1.
101. "*Frankenstein* Will Be Next Universal Thriller." *Hollywood Reporter* 16 Mar. 1931: 2; "Production Activities." *Hollywood Reporter* 20 Mar. 1931: 5.
102. "*Murders in [the] Rue Morgue* Third U Horror Film." *Film Daily* 27 Mar. 1931: 10.
103. "Theatre Receipts." *Motion Picture Herald* 28 Mar. 1931: 52. A report in the 11 Mar. 1931 issue of *Variety* projected *Dracula* would take $10,000 in Baltimore, whereas this later report is probably more accurate, even though it is for the film's first six days, rather than a full week.
104. "2nd *Lynne* Week at $11,000 – Balto; *Dracula*, $10,000." *Variety* 11 Mar. 1931: 9.
105. "*Dracula* Can Offer a Variety of Stunts," p. 14.
106. Advertisement. *Kansas City Star* 6 Mar. 1931.
107. "Mainstreet–*Dracula*." *Kansas City Star* 8 Mar. 1931.
108. "$19,500 Wows Kansas City on *Dracula*." *Motion Picture Daily* 16 Mar. 1931. On 18 Mar. 1931, *Variety* offered revised final figures on the Kansas City gross at $21,000, an increase over the original announcement of $19,500.
109. Advertisement. *Cleveland Plain Dealer* 4 Mar. 1931.
110. Advertisement. *Cleveland Plain Dealer* 5 Mar. 1931.
111. Marsh, W. Ward. "*June Moon* Is a Nice Comedy; *Dracula*, Well Done, Is Horror Story." *Cleveland Plain Dealer*, Women's Magazine and Amusement Section 8

Mar. 1931: 11.

112 "Theatre Receipts." *Motion Picture Herald* 21 Mar. 1931: 53.

113 Marsh, W. Ward. "Comparing the Fates of Gray and L. Tibbett." *Cleveland Plain Dealer* 31 Mar. 1931: 22.

114 Stanley, Gabriel Stanciu. "Roumanian Protests." Letter to the Editor. *Cleveland Plain Dealer, Women's Magazine and Amusement Section* 22 Mar. 1931: 12.

115 "Scared?" *Motion Picture Herald* 4 Apr. 1931: 74.

116 "Draculas and Cowboys Scare Prov. Public." *Motion Picture Daily* 21 Mar. 1931: 2; "Duplicating Count Dracula." *Variety* 25 Mar. 1931: 20.

117 "Albee." *Providence Journal* 15 Mar. 1931: 7; "Dracula–Albee." *Providence Evening Bulletin* 14 Mar. 1931: 13.

118 "W Plan in 2 Breaks, One Good—Other Holy Week; Will Do $5,000 in Prov." *Variety* 1 Apr. 1931: 9. *Motion Picture Herald* published a smaller gross for the RKO Victory screening of *Dracula*, claiming in its 4 Apr. 1931 issue that the film made only $5,000 (p. 55).

119 "Censors Disagree, but Chi. Ok'd Dracula 100%." *Variety* 18 Feb. 1931: 4.

120 "*Dracula* Can Offer a Variety of Stunts," p. 14.

121 Harris, Genevieve. "A Weird Story Is Skillfully Filmed." *Chicago Evening Post* 20 Mar. 1931.

122 Tinée, Mae. "Awed Stillness Greets Movie About *Dracula*." *Chicago Tribune* 21 Mar. 1931: 21.

123 Rodenbach, Clark. "A Recipe for the Heebie-Jeebies." *Chicago Daily News* 20 Mar. 1931: 32.

124 "*Dracula* Loop Big; May Get $40,000; *Man Word*, Chi, $48,000, Not So Hot; *Parlor, Bath*, Very Light at $16,000." *Variety* 25 Mar. 1931: 8.

125 "Loop Starts New Week with Storm; *Dracula* Strong, 2d Wk., to $24,000; *Lights* Looks $23,000; 3d Big Week." *Variety* 1 Apr. 1931: 8; "U's *Dracula* Smashes 8-Yr. State-Lake Record." *Film Daily* 25 Mar. 1931: 8. A report in the *Hollywood Reporter* on 2 Apr. 1931 claimed that the State-Lake's gross for *Dracula* was $39,000, as opposed to the $40,000 that *Variety* claimed initially, or the $39,800 that *Variety* claimed on 15 Apr. 1931. By contrast, on 4 Apr. 1931, the *Motion Picture Herald* claimed the amount was $41,875.

126 "Comedies' Strong Loop Stride, Rose Back in Form – $29,000; Duo on Oriental's Stage $38,000." *Variety* 8 Apr. 1931: 10; "Theatre Receipts." *Motion Picture Herald* 4 Apr. 1931: 50.

127 "Censors Disagree, but Chi. Ok'd Dracula 100%," p. 4.

128 "Making It Tougher." *Variety* 25 Mar. 1931:

129 "$23,000 Big for Chaplin in Auto City." *Motion Picture Daily* 1 Apr. 1931: 18.

130 "Theatre Receipts." *Motion Picture Herald* 11 Apr. 1931: 57.

131 "U in Two Houses." *Hollywood Reporter* 23 Mar. 1931: 3.

132 Advertisement. *Los Angeles Times* 27 Mar. 1931.

133 "Large Spider Web Is Strange 'Prop' in *Dracula* Film." *Los Angeles Illustrated Daily News* 2 Apr. 1931.

134 No mention appears of Lugosi's speech on KFI in newspaper radio logs for March 27, 1931, but given its brevity, that may not be surprising, as it was probably spoken as part of some larger program. It is worth noting that Universal had long relied on radio to generate publicity for its films.

135 Lugosi, Bela. Speech for Radio Station KFI. 27 Mar. 1931. Lugosi kept the original copy in one of his personal scrapbooks, once in the possession of Lugosi's friend Richard Sheffield and, later, in the possession of the collector Forrest J Ackerman.

136 Oliver, W. E. "*Dracula*." *Los Angeles Evening Herald* 28 Mar. 1931; Barnes, Eleanor. "*Dracula*." *Los Angeles Illustrated Daily News* 28 Mar. 1931.

137 Busby, Marquis. "*Dracula*." *Los Angeles Examiner* 28 Mar. 1931.

138 Scheuer, Philip K. "Adventures of *Dracula* Now in Film Form." *Los Angeles Times* 30 Mar. 1931.

139 Miller, Llewellyn. "*Dracula*." *Los Angeles Record* 28 Mar. 1931.

140 "Slump Can't Dim *Dracula* at Cincinnati." *Motion Picture Daily* 11 Mar. 1931: 10; "B.O. Picks Up in Columbus." *Zit's Theatrical Newspaper* 28 Mar. 1931: 12.

141 "$1,000,000 *Jazz* Loss and *Abie* Suit in U's Drop of 2 Million." *Motion Picture Herald* 21 Mar. 1931: 19.

142 "U's Full Program Set; Surprise of *Dracula*." *Variety* 8 Apr. 1931: 7;

143 "U Has Horror Cycle All to Self." *Variety* 8 Apr. 1931: 2.

144 "Mystery for Para." *Hollywood Reporter* 2 Apr. 1931: 4.

145 Wilkerson, W. R. "Tradeviews." *Hollywood Reporter* 16 Apr. 1931: 1.

146 "*Dracula* Stages Return." *Billboard* 18 Apr. 1931: 5.

147 "*Dracula* Returns." *New York Times* 14 Apr. 1931: 35.

148 "Secret Six Terrific with $27,000 Take." *Motion Picture Daily* 9 May 1931: 6; "Theatre Receipts." *Motion Picture Herald* 25 Apr. 1931: 63.

149 "The Screen." *Boston Herald* 4 Apr. 1931: 6; "*Dracula* in Second Week Tops Boston." *Motion Picture Daily* 23 Apr. 1931: 6.

150 Joy, Jason. Letter to Carl Laemmle, Jr. 20 Feb. 1931. Available in the file for *Dracula* in the Motion Picture Association of America, Production Code Administration collection at the Margaret Herrick Library in Beverly Hills, CA.

151 Advertisement. *The Times-Picayune* (New Orleans, LA) 10 Apr. 1931.

152 "Eerie Adventures of Vampire Count Make Thrilling Film." *The Times-Picayune* 11 Apr. 1931: 10.

153 "Page O.K in N.O.–Points for $16,000." *Variety* 15 Apr. 1931.

154 "Big British Booking for *Dracula*." *Film Daily* 19 Apr. 1931: 9.

155 "*Dracula* Triumphs in Sydney." *Motion Picture Herald* 23 Apr. 1931: 21.

156 Advertisement. *Variety* 1 Apr. 1931; "Nothing Special in LA, Now Tho *Skippy* $25,000 at Par; Hollywood 2d Runs Hold Up." *Variety* 8 Apr. 1931.

157 "U Is Winning Place in Sun, Salesmen Hear." *Motion Picture Daily* 8 May 1931: 1, 7.

158 "U Financial Strength Is Meet Keynote." *Motion Picture Daily* 11 May 1931: 1, 7.
159 "8 Serials on Coast Lists." *Variety* 15 Apr. 1931: 32; "U Adds 14 Action Films to New List." *Motion Picture Daily* 13 May 1931: 1.
160 "U Cuts Pay Checks of All Over $100 Wkly." *Variety* 20 May 1931: 5.
161 "Laemmle, Jr. Made Vice President." *Motion Picture Herald* 2 May 1931: 20.
162 Advertisement. *Daily Ardmoreite* (Ardmore, OK) 4 June 1931.
163 "Universal Starts Drive for Revival Bookings." *Film Daily* 15 June 1931.
164 Advertisement. *Seattle Times* 25 Oct. 1931: 27.
165 See, for example: Advertisement. *Aberdeen Daily News* (Aberdeen, SD) 29 Oct. 1931: 12.
166 "To Reopen and Show Only Foreign Versions." *Exhibitors Herald-World* 23 Aug. 1930: 39.
167 "*Dracula* in Spanish Next at California." *Los Angeles Times* 6 May 1931; "*Dracula* in Spanish Opens at California." *Los Angeles Times* 11 May 1931.
168 "Spanish Film Interest Dives." *Variety* 3 Nov. 1931: 15.
169 "Inability of American Producers to Produce Satisfactory Foreigns May Cause the Abandonment of Field." *Hollywood Reporter* 17 Oct. 1930: 1, 3.
170 "Hollywood Sets Foreign Policy." *Variety* 3 Nov. 1931: 15.
171 "Profit of $255,783 Reported by Universal." *Film Daily* 13 July 1931: 1, 12.
172 "Universal Shows $615,786 Profit Netted in a Year." *Motion Picture Herald* 5 Mar. 1932: 35.
173 Schatz, Thomas. *The Genius of the System: Hollywood Filmmaking in the Studio Era* (New York: Pantheon, 1988): 87.
174 Quirk, James R. "Close-Ups and Long-Shots." *Photoplay* (Oct. 1931): 26.
175 "The Exploitation Check-Up!" *Motion Picture Herald* 13 June 1931: 59.
176 "Ten Best Pictures of 1931." *The Film Daily Year Book for 1931* (New York: Film Daily, 1932): 63.
177 "Ten Best Directors of 1930-31," *The Film Daily Year Book for 1931*, p. 11.

Chapter 10
REAPPEARANCES

In 1947, the famous newspaper columnist Jack O'Brian recalled an incident from his childhood: "I chilled to Bela Lugosi in *Dracula* and was almost too frightened to walk home through the winter dusk after a matinee."[1] Here O'Brian remembered an event that occurred some sixteen years earlier, when *Dracula* gripped his imagination. He never forgot the film's effect on him, or its importance in entertainment history.

As early as 1932, many newspapers and trade publications declared that *Dracula* had initiated the nascent horror movie, easily forgetting or ignoring other such talkies as *The Cat Creeps* (1930) or *The Terror* (1928).[2] For example, the *Washington Post* described *Dracula*'s "overwhelming box office success" as causing a cycle of related films.[3] And the *National Board of Review Magazine* wrote that an "avalanche of horror pictures" fell into movie theatres after *Dracula*.[4]

Though referencing some silent films, a history of horror films published in the *New York Times* in 1936 maintained that the "real triumph of the spectral thrillers was reserved for the arrival of sound," with *Dracula* acting as the catalyst.[5] Then, in 1944, the same newspaper claimed Universal "gave celluloid birth to the original 'horror' pictures [thanks to] *Frankenstein*, *Dracula*, and sundry tales of werewolves and invisible men."[6] During the decades that ensued, most accounts tended to repeat and emphasize the chronology, anchoring *Dracula* firmly to the genre's inception, or at least to its launch in the sound era.

Dracula not only survived after 1931, but also flourished in various forms, ranging from cinematic sequels and follow-ups to a myriad of reissues, reappearances, and restorations on theatre screens, television broadcasts, and home-video releases. Throughout the twentieth and early twenty-first centuries, Tod Browning's *Dracula* has been ubiquitous, its influence manifold through revivals and through subsequent cinematic refractions.

Sequels and Followups

Within three weeks of *Dracula*'s premiere in February 1931, Universal Pictures considered ideas for no fewer than three sequels to it, registering their titles with the Hays Office on 7 March of that year: *The Modern Dracula*, *The Return of Dracula*, and *The Son of Dracula*.[7] Though no notes exist regarding possible story content, each of the three illustrate the problem of the 1931 film's ending. Should the original Dracula return, or should he instead

Edward Van Sloan and Bela Lugosi in a publicity still for the 1931 *Dracula*. *(Courtesy of Kristin Dewey)*

reappear in the form of some descendant? While Universal did not produce any of these sequels in 1931, the studio did return to similar questions in future years.

Universal eventually produced five subsequent films during the classic era that featured Dracula or his vampiric relations. In various respects, all of these films referenced the character's depiction in the 1931 film, as well as its basic approach to screen vampires. None of them featured actors wearing fangs. And all of them posited Dracula as a pre-existing character, one that audiences presumably knew from either viewing or simply being aware of the 1931 film.

That said, these five Universal films undertook two clear missions. One increasingly Americanized the Dracula character in various respects, most obviously in the casting of American-born actors to play the role. The other was to de-emphasize and de-center the character in each narrative, the result (however unintentional) offering deference to the 1931 film.

While Universal originally planned to star Bela Lugosi in the first sequel, *Dracula's Daughter* (1936), the final shooting script did not feature Dracula, save for his corpse (played

Gloria Holden in a publicity portrait for *Dracula's Daughter* (1936), in which she portrayed the title character.

by a dummy in a coffin), which his daughter burns as part of a failed effort to end her own bloodlust. Nevertheless, the Dracula of the 1931 film is curiously more present in this first sequel than in any of Universal's subsequent efforts. In some measure, this is due to the production team, the film's story having been written by John L. Balderston (of the Deane-Balderston team who coauthored the 1927 Broadway play). Garrett Fort, co-author of the final shooting script to *Dracula*, returned as the screenwriter, and E. M. "Efe" Asher was the associate producer, as he had been for the 1931 film.

Another reason that *Dracula's Daughter* closely echoes its predecessor is the decision for its narrative to begin immediately after the climax of the 1931 film. At Carfax Abbey, two policemen arrest Van Helsing (portrayed once again by Edward Van Sloan) for Dracula's murder. They also discover Renfield's corpse on the castle floor. The opening scenes thus attempt to connect the two films plausibly and continue the same narrative. Later scenes also recall *Dracula*, particularly the Main Hall of Dracula's castle in Transylvania, which closely (even if not precisely) recreates the *mise-en-scène* of the original. *Dracula's Daughter* even repurposes footage from its predecessor: a high-angle long shot of a teaching space in a hospital in which a physician discovers punctures in the neck of a victim.

But a number of limitations emerged in *Dracula's Daughter*. The Carfax Abbey set appears noticeably different than in the earlier film, particular in its much less grand staircase. Dr. Seward, Mina Seward, and Jonathan Harker do not appear in the sequel, even though – in a faithful continuation of the first film – they should have been somewhat nearby when the policemen arrive and thus been able to attest to Van Helsing's innocence. And while actor Edward Van Sloan once again portrays Van Helsing (who in this film is rechristened "Von Helsing"), his hair is darker than in the earlier film, and his eyeglasses (which he wears at Carfax Abbey, something he does not do at the conclusion of the 1931 film) are of an obviously much lower magnification. Van Sloan also employs a different speaking style, his voice not being nearly as slow and deliberate as in *Dracula*.

Not surprisingly, some of the modern discussion of *Dracula's Daughter* concentrates on the absence of both Lugosi and Dracula. However, in many respects Dracula is the central focus of the sequel. Dracula appears in his Transylvanian castle in the form of artwork on a billowing tapestry, its appearance more closely recalling Lugosi's appearance than the dummy corpse in the coffin. More importantly, Dracula looms over the entire storyline, as his daughter seems convinced that he remains responsible for her cravings. Such beliefs lead her to bemoan her fate and seek a cure, making much of the film into a lengthy exploration of Dracula's dialogue in the 1931 film: "To die – to be really dead. That must be glorious!"

Dr. Niemann (Boris Karloff, left) and Dracula (John Carradine) in a publicity still for *House of Frankenstein* (1944).

As portrayed by Gloria Holden, Dracula's daughter echoes Lugosi's portrayal. With her dark hair, hypnotic eyes, mannered speaking voice, and generally slow movements, Holden becomes an onscreen avatar for the absent Lugosi. Though presenting a somewhat less "foreign" persona (due to a less pronounced accent), she nonetheless seems closer to Lugosi's 1931 depiction than any of Universal's subsequent actors. Here again Dracula seems present through his absence.

Universal's next revival of the Dracula character came in 1943 with *Son of Dracula* (a film title first considered in 1931), with the title character regularly referred to as Count Dracula (and Count Alucard, his pseudonym). Indeed, a page from Bram Stoker's novel *Dracula* even fills the screen at one point. One character briefly mentions that Alucard might be a descendant of the original Dracula (hence the use of "son" in the film title), but otherwise little distinction is drawn between the two, presumably due to the desire to return Dracula to the screen without the narrative burden of having to explain how he survived being staked at Carfax Abbey.

At its core, *Son of Dracula* repeats *Dracula*'s narrative. Dracula travels to another country in search of fresh blood (America, in this case, rather than London). A fatherly figure (Dr. Brewster, rather than Dr. Seward) tries to look after two different women, one of whom (Katherine, much like Lucy in the 1931 film) is predisposed to Dracula's charms. That same fatherly figure relies on expertise from another country (Professor Laszlo instead of Van Helsing). In these basic respects, the early sections of the film represent a loose remake *Dracula*. However, in a manner opposite to the 1931 film, which leaves Lucy's story unfinished, the second half of *Son of Dracula* focuses on the Lucy character, having its vampiric Katherine attempt to double-cross Dracula after marrying him and obtaining everlasting life.

Lon Chaney, Jr.'s portrayal of Dracula was strikingly different from Lugosi's, not only due to his wearing a moustache, but also as a result of his physical size and visage. Though a physically larger and lesser talented actor than his own father, the younger Chaney's appearance in this film resembles some photographs of Lon Chaney, Sr., resulting in an admittedly inexact, but still fascinating indication of how the elder Chaney might have looked if costumed as Universal's Dracula.

More importantly, though, is how much more American the character looks and sounds in *Son of Dracula*, the result of an American actor who makes absolutely no effort to alter the accent of his voice. This Dracula also seems less regal, both in his sheer physicality (as when he fights with the film's leading man at the climax), as well as in his readiness to embrace modernity (riding as he does as a passenger in an automobile). As a result, *Son of Dracula* thus became an important marker, with Universal initiating what would become a pattern: Dracula's otherworldliness would increasingly be depicted not through an actor's portrayal, but instead through special effects. *Son of Dracula* features numerous onscreen vampire transformations, whether from human form to bat or human form to mist (or vice versa). Even his death by sunlight provided the impetus for special effects, with his hand and arm becoming skeletal right before the audience's eyes.

In 1944, Universal redeployed the Dracula character in *House of Frankenstein*, a film that was in some ways a sequel to both *The Ghost of Frankenstein* (1942) and *Frankenstein Meets the Wolf Man* (1943). In this narrative, Dracula exists as a famous character, his skeleton being a key exhibit in a travelling "Chamber of Horrors" sideshow. Once a stake is removed

Bela Lugosi (as Dracula) and Glenn Strange (as the Frankenstein Monster) relaxing on the set of *Abbott and Costello Meet Frankenstein* in 1948. (Courtesy of Kristin Dewey)

from Dracula's remains (presumably the one hammered into him in the 1931 film), special effects allow his entire body to reappear. As portrayed by John Carradine (whose performance and accent are more suggestive of a southern gentleman than a Transylvanian count), the moustachioed Dracula continues his new life as a physically active character, at one stage ferociously driving a team of horses in a carriage that careens off an old path. Thanks to more special effects, Dracula's prominent ring glows, and his own body returns to skeletal form when sunlight destroys him. His death occurs within the first half hour of a film that features numerous other monsters; Dracula's screen time totals less than fifteen minutes.

The following year, Universal released *House of Dracula* (1945), a film in which Dracula is a composite of his previous appearances in the studio's sequels. Sporting another moustache, John Carradine returned to portray the vampire; the character is again reliant on special effects to create a sense of exoticism and to inspire fear. Here the special effects draw closely on *Son of Dracula* and *House of Frankenstein*, meaning onscreen human form-to-bat transformations and an onscreen death in which Dracula once again metamorphoses into a skeleton.

While he is alive, this Dracula is somewhat sympathetic, seeking – much like the title character in *Dracula's Daughter* – a cure for vampirism. *House of Dracula* even features a scene in which a female character unwittingly plays bizarre piano music that captures the morbid world of vampirism, much as Dracula's daughter does in the 1936 sequel. But, as in *House of Frankenstein*, Dracula is soon destroyed, leaving other monsters like the Wolf Man and Frankenstein's Monster to live and fight in his absence. A kindly doctor also outlasts Dracula; infected by the vampire's blood, the doctor goes mad, having become a curious amalgam of both Dracula and Renfield.

Then, in 1948, Universal produced *Abbott and Costello Meet Frankenstein*, a movie that in some respects ended the classic horror-film era that had arguably started with the 1931 version of *Dracula*.[8] It was only fitting that Dracula would appear in this final film, even if it was a comedy and even if it meant sharing screen time once again with the Wolf Man and Frankenstein's Monster. The casting of Bela Lugosi as the vampire further highlights the fact that the character Dracula book-ended the start and conclusion of the classic horror era.

While age had changed Lugosi's physical appearance, it is ironically the Dracula of *Abbott and Costello Meet Frankenstein* who is the more physically agile. In the 1931 film, Lugosi's Dracula speaks and moves slowly, in a manner befitting royalty. Such methodical gestures served to underscore the rare moments when he does move quickly, as when he sees a crucifix or a mirror.

In the Abbott and Costello film, Dracula speaks more rapidly and with a less peculiar rhythm. He is much less regal, including in the fact that he does not wear the medallion seen in the 1931 film. He is also profoundly active, ranging from helping the Monster stand up to engaging in battle with the Wolf Man at the film's climax. In the 1931 movie, it would seem inconceivable for Dracula to run, to crash through a door, or to throw a flowerpot, but he does all of that in the 1948 film.

Mark of the Vampire (1935)

In 1939, Bela Lugosi's friend Manly P. Hall wrote a treatment for an unmade *Dracula* sequel that attempted to pick up where the 1931 film ended, bringing Dracula back to life thanks to the fact that – according to Hall's reworking of events – Van Helsing had staked the vampire one minute after sundown.[9] Nearly ten years later, Universal discussed a remake of *Dracula* with Lugosi, with the industry press claiming a deal was in the "negotiation stage."[10] The studio never made either film, nor did it produce *Wolf Man vs. Dracula* in 1943, which might also have starred Lugosi as the vampire. Instead, Universal opted to produce the aforementioned sequels and follow-ups.

And so, perhaps not surprisingly, director Tod Browning became responsible for the closest attempt at a *Dracula* remake mounted during the classic horror era. Having wanted to bring *Dracula* to the screen as early as 1920, and having directed both *London After Midnight* in 1927 and *Dracula* in 1930, Browning returned to the subject matter at MGM in 1935. Ostensibly, *Mark of the Vampire* is a remake of *London After Midnight*, but to end with that description would be unfair to Browning and to the film, as it builds directly on his work in *Dracula*, and represents a re-imagining of it, a fact that even Universal noticed, as the studio considered legal action against MGM.[11]

In an apparent attempt to avoid such copyright concerns, Browning retained the storyline of his 1927 film, in which a detective uses fake vampires as a ruse to scare a criminal into a confession. But that basic framework also repeats key elements of *Dracula* and *Dracula–The Vampire Play*. Here a wise elder (Professor Zelen, much like Van Helsing) works with the

Luna (Carroll Borland) and Count Mora (Bela Lugosi) as depicted in a publicity still for *Mark of the Vampire* (1935).

help of two other older men (Dr. Seward splintered into two other characters, Inspector Neumann and Baron Otto) to protect a young woman (Irena Borotyn, much like Mina) from a vampire (Count Mora, much like Count Dracula) who lives in the nearby decrepit Barotyn residence (not unlike Carfax Abbey). And Professor Zelen struggles to convince the young woman's paramour (Fedor, not unlike Harker) of the potential danger she faces. A female vampire also lurks nearby (Luna, not unlike the Woman in White). These characters are all in addition to domestic servants who supply comic relief (not unlike Martin and the maid in *Dracula*).

But *Mark of the Vampire*'s similarities to *Dracula* extend beyond its narrative. Consider, for example, the opening scene, in which gypsies prepare for vampire attacks. One prays in an Eastern European language, with an infant protected by bat thorn (this film's version of wolfbane) in its crib. Nearby, an innkeeper describes the "demons of the castle" to tourists who – like Renfield – dismiss vampirism as mere superstition. Actor Michael Visaroff reprises his role as the Proprietor from *Dracula*, sporting here a costume, moustache, and pipe similar to the earlier film. An Eastern European woman crosses herself in an insert edit; another cutaway features a character silently watching the unfolding conversation. Both shots assist the film in simultaneously recreating and reworking the same scene in *Dracula*.

Several other scenes in *Mark* feature variations on particular moments in *Dracula*. When Count Mora first appears, he carries a lit candle and walks down the steps of the Borotyn mansion. Luna's costume resembles the clothing worn by Dracula's wives (and, by extension, the Bat Girl of *London After Midnight*). Count Mora enters Fedor's room to bite him, much as Dracula bites Renfield; here the male vampire attacking a male victim has no real narrative purpose other than to repeat an action that Browning had used in *Dracula* despite initial hesitation from Carl Laemmle, Jr. Then, after Irena sees Luna on the castle grounds, her behavior changes noticeably from a frail, sick woman to one who is cheerful and suddenly alive; the scene strongly resembles one in *Dracula* featuring Mina after seeing Dracula, in terms of both its narrative content and terrace setting.

Various sets in *Mark of the Vampire* also echo *Dracula*, such as the interior of the Borotyn mansion, its main hall being a mirror-opposite recreation of the Carfax Abbey set; inside of it, doors open of their own accord, a device Browning used in the earlier film. And Baron Otto's home is quite similar to the Seward residence, particularly Irena's bedroom (to the extent that it features a lamp that projects an eerie light upwards, like Mina's), as well as its adjacent boudoir and terrace.

But Browning does not merely repeat himself in *Mark of the Vampire*; he clearly tries to make improvements on *Dracula*. A fake spider climbs the wall of the Borotyn home, much as happens in Dracula's Transylvanian castle, but in this film Browning provides far more creatures, ranging from numerous bats, rats, possums, and insects to a Russian wolfhound, all of them linked to undead vampires. In place of the armadillos seen in *Dracula* and *London After Midnight*, a bizarre crab-like spider scuttles across the floor of the crypt; the studio prop represents no known creature. Similarly, while Browning employs no music in *Mark of the Vampire* other than a limited use of gypsies singing and a character playing the organ, he went much further than *Dracula* in his repeated use of sound effects that range from howling wind to rats squeaking and crickets chirping.

Mark of the Vampire also allowed Browning to delve deeply into narrative situations that he was not able to cover fully in *Dracula*. For example, Zelen, Neumann, and the Baron explore the castle and its crypt at length, something that Van Helsing and Harker are not able to do at Carfax Abbey during *Dracula*'s brief conclusion. And then there are the vampires, who appear repeatedly, so much so that we might well question once again the assertion that Browning originally wanted to keep Dracula's scenes to a minimum in the 1931 film.

Beyond merely showing the vampires, *Mark of the Vampire* features two original and successful uses of special effects for them. One shows a bat that becomes Count Mora: here Browning offered Hollywood's very *first* onscreen transformation of a vampire from bat to human form. Another highly memorable shot depicts Luna as part-human, part-bat as she flaps downward to the floor of the Borotyn home. Here she is not unlike the aforementioned crab-like spider creature, which is also locked between two forms.

Browning also seized upon his opportunity to explore the Lucy character anew through Luna. In *Dracula*, there are accounts of the Woman in White stalking children and visiting

Above: Professor Zelen (Lionel Atwill, left) and Baron Otto (Jean Hersholt) appear in a publicity still for *Mark of the Vampire* (1935). Below: Tod Browning (in the beret) directs Bela Lugosi and Carroll Borland on the set of *Mark of the Vampire* (1935). *(Courtesy of Gregory William Mank)*

Mina, but these are not visualized. By contrast, Luna pursues Irena onscreen, observing her from a distance on two occasions and attacking her on two others. Luna also appears at length roaming through the foggy nighttime exteriors, something that Lucy does in only one shot.

Indeed, for budgetary reasons, Browning was unable to build the churchyard cemetery set he wanted for *Dracula*, which meant that a scene at Lucy's vault was not filmed. And so he created an extremely memorable version of the same in *Mark of the Vampire*. Its foggy cemetery features wonderfully askew tombstones and grave markers, reminiscent of Fort and Browning's description in the shooting script for the 1931 *Dracula*:

> *Ground mists curl, wraithlike about the ancient and moss-covered tombstones, and in immediate fore[ground], a melancholy willow droops sweepingly over a headstone. In [background], and dotting the churchyard here and there are the more pretentious mausoleums and family vaults.*[12]

The vault in *Mark of the Vampire* belongs not to Luna, but rather to the Borotyn character whose murder has inspired the fake-vampire scheme. Nevertheless, the cemetery set more fully realizes Browning's intentions for *Dracula* as preserved in *Dracula*'s shooting script, even down to its inclusion of a shot of an owl.

Mark of the Vampire thus became the third entry in Browning's *Dracula* trilogy, giving him the opportunity to return to some of his favorite narrative situations, rethinking their potential, as well as the opportunity to explore new ground, ranging from the use of innovative special effects to the creation of sets and scenes that it had not been possible to include in *Dracula* and *London After Midnight*.

Theatrical Reissues

In late 1951, Bela Lugosi told an interviewer "Dracula never ends. I don't know whether I should call it a fortune or a curse, but it never ends. I don't know whether I should brag or complain about it, but *Dracula* is the only picture in existence in all the world … since it was made in, I don't know, 1931, it is the only picture which is revived in every city in America every year." Perhaps his comment resulted from the fact that *Dracula* was then on the verge of a national re-release, but, whatever its motivation, Lugosi overstated *Dracula*'s frequency at American movie theatres.

Nevertheless, his comment was not entirely without merit. In March 1948, *Daily Variety* noted that *Dracula* "has been playing constantly since it was first released, and never has been out of circulation."[13] Indeed, a few theatres played *Dracula* for Halloween that very year, a period outside of a national reissue.[14] In fact, *Dracula* reappeared over and over again during the thirties and forties, including on a double bill in New York City in 1933.[15] *Motion Picture Herald* reported a screening of the film in 1940, which suggests that it was available at times through film exchanges for individual bookings.[16]

In addition to movie-theatre revivals, *Dracula* returned in other fora. For example, a "travelling exhibitor" appeared in at least a few rural towns with a battered *Dracula* print. A press account in Utah spoke about how *Dracula*'s "final triumph" was that everyone in the audience loved it even though the ragged print "was so cut up that no one knew what it was all about."[17] That particular exhibitor may have had a sound print, or he might possibly have been carrying a copy of the silent version of *Dracula*, which remained in circulation as a

16mm rental for many years. A 1945 catalog for Mogull's, Inc. described it as: "Ranking with the leading classic[s] of silent movie days, this is a film everyone will enjoy."[18]

Despite its ongoing availability, *Dracula*'s most notable reappearances on theatre screens came during three particular years. Its first national re-release started with little aplomb. Searching for a cheap program to screen, the Regina Theatre in Beverly Hills, California programmed *Dracula*, *Frankenstein* (1931), and *The Son of Kong* (1933) on a triple bill in 1938, running advertisements daring audiences to withstand so "much horror in one show."[19] The triple bill had much to commend it, ranging from an admission price of only thirty cents to the fact that Hollywood studios had arguably not produced or released any horror films since 1936. Their absence created a hunger for horror, and the Regina Theatre reaped the rewards. Lines on opening day stretched for two blocks, and the theatre played the films to capacity audiences for 21 hours a day over the course of several weeks, with ticket buyers coming from as far away as Fresno and San Diego.[20]

John Hamrick's Blue Mouse Theatre in Seattle quickly booked *Dracula*

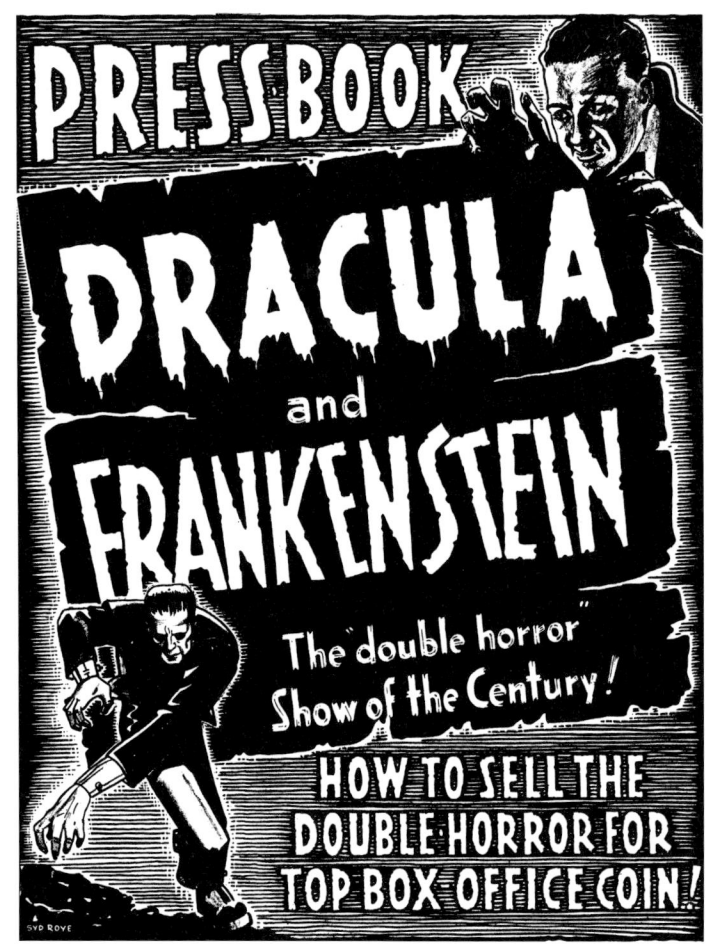

Above: Universal's pressbook for the 1938 reissue of *Dracula* (1931) and *Frankenstein* (1931). Below: A frame of Edward Van Sloan's closing speech in *Dracula* (1931), deleted for the 1938 reissue. (*Courtesy of George E. Turner*)

and *Frankenstein* as a double bill, refining the Regina's program into the form that most audiences would experience in 1938. In a telegram that year, Hamrick described his success: "Unable to handle crowds opening day and second day yesterday equaled first day's business … Combining these pictures [is a] showman's dream of good times here again."[21] As with the Regina, the Blue Mouse built an advertising campaign on the idea of daring audience members to see the two films together.

Universal rapidly placed *Dracula* and *Frankenstein* on a double bill for national reissue, ordering 500 new prints of both films. These new prints featured three key changes, all of them requests made in 1938 by the Production Code Administration (PCA), which had formed in 1934:

> [T]here are two sequences in which it seems to us deletions from the soundtrack are desirable in order to avoid a violation of that section of the Code which forbids excessive gruesomeness.
> The first instance is in reel 8 in the scene where Dracula attempts to kill the insane lawyer. It seems to us that the lawyer's groans and moans are excessive. Kindly shorten this on the sound track [sic] as to leave only one or two groans.
> The second instance is in reel 9. Please delete the groans of the vampire as the stake is being driven through his heart.
> … We [also] suggest the deletion of the closing comment of the scientist where he tells the audience that "after all there are such things."[22]

The PCA conveyed this message to Universal in March 1938, which proves the studio was contemplating a reissue of *Dracula* months prior to its revival at the Regina. Universal made all of the requested cuts.[23]

When the double-bill reissue of *Dracula* and *Frankenstein* played New York's Rialto, the theatre experienced better business than it had for over twelve months, as well as the second-best opening in its entire history.[24] In St. Louis, Newark, and many other cities, *Dracula* and *Frankenstein* doubled the average business of the theatres screening them.[25] The reissue became a major event in the film industry in the autumn of 1938.[26]

Ballyhoo efforts included a range of stunts designed to entice potential ticket-buyers. Some theatres had ambulances parked in front of their doors in case frightened patrons needed medical assistance; at least one of those theatres used actors who "fainted" at pre-arranged moments during each screening. Other stunts included hiring actors dressed as the Frankenstein Monster and Dracula (who arrived at one theatre in a coffin, "coming alive" when the show began), as well as suspending phosphorescent skeletons on wires and dangling them above audiences during show time.[27]

Exhibitors occasionally programmed the two horror films separately.[28] But their overall success was a joint venture, one commemorated in the poem *Dracula, Frankenstein, & Co.*, published in December 1938:

> *Hush my baby; look and listen*
> *Through this double-feature show;*
> *Watch the Karloff eyeballs glisten*
> *When he rolls them to and fro*
> *Nestle, baby, warm and cozy,*

*While the woodwinds eldritch moans
Mark the time for B. Lugosi
Gnawing flesh from human bones.*[29]

While such literature placed rightful emphasis on the double bill, perhaps the larger impact of the 1938 reissue was that it illustrated the ongoing cultural and financial value that both films possessed. Rather than being a successful film of 1931 only remembered in the past tense by those who viewed it on its original release, *Dracula* successfully grasped at the present and, by extension, the future.

Dracula's next formal re-release came in 1947. Universal announced the plan in February of that year, once again pairing it with *Frankenstein*. Here the studio's decision came as part of a larger strategy of double bill reissues, which included *Destry Rides Again* (1939) and *When the Daltons Rode* (1940), as well as *You Can't Cheat an Honest Man* (1939) and *I Stole a Million* (1939).[30]

Dracula and *Frankenstein* appeared in Los Angeles in April of 1947, with the two being booked at other theatres throughout the summer and autumn. As one exhibitor reported:

> Played this double feature one day to capacity business. It will scare them, especially *Dracula*.
> –Roxy Theatre, Hinckley, Minn.[31]

Some exhibitors programmed the dual bill as a midnight show; others scheduled screenings during the Halloween season.[32] Not surprisingly, some exhibitors staged elaborate ballyhoo efforts. For example, one newspaper joked about a ten-year-old "skeleton" advertising *Dracula* in Tennessee; his costume featured an unintentional slit that revealed the "solid expanse of [his] blue jeans."[33]

At least a few theatres booked *Dracula* without *Frankenstein*.[34] And, though the account is difficult to verify, *Daily Variety* of 10 December 1947 even claimed that Bela Lugosi made live appearances at a number of *Dracula* screenings:

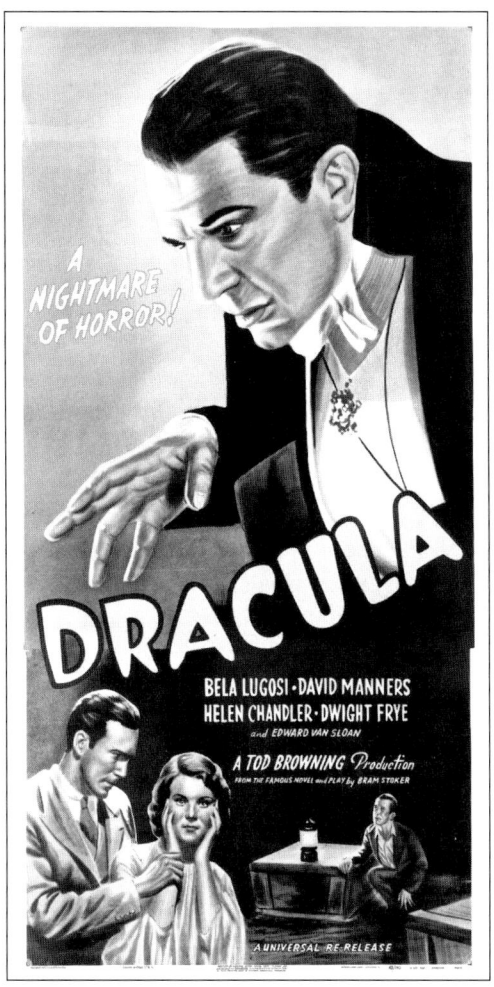

Above: Universal's three-sheet for *Dracula*'s reissue in 1947. *(Courtesy of D'Arcy More)*. Below: Advertisement published in the August 26, 1948 issue of the *Daily News* (Ludington, Michigan).

302   Chapter 10 – REAPPEARANCES

A 1951 poster heralding yet another reissue of *Dracula* (1931).

> *For the last two months the vet film menace has been touring the mid-west putting on midnight shows in film houses, booking himself in at 50-50 slice of gross, charging $1.50 per head and unspooling a print of the old Universal release, Dracula. Midway in picture, Lugosi inserted an eight-minute act, in which he used a girl partner and re-enacted a chill sequence from the footage. The actor himself rented the print from Universal, and on this stunt has been netting around $4,000 weekly....*[35]

It is certain that Lugosi appeared in a brief tour of Poe's *The Tell-Tale Heart* in late 1947. At the opening show in Rockford, Illinois on 19 and 20 November 1947, the theatre paired Lugosi's "powerful dramatic sketch" with the 1931 film.[36]

Dracula's next major theatrical reissue came in 1952. In March of that year, Jack Broder's company Realart released the film nationally as part of yet another double bill with *Frankenstein*.[37] It seems likely that Broder intended to release the duo at least a few months before he did, as some publicity materials carry a 1951 date. At any rate, the two films appeared on theatre screens throughout America, including (apparently for the first time) at drive-ins.[38]

Realart and its franchise holders used the two films to initiate a four-month exploitation contest offering cash prizes to theatre managers for the best ballyhoo campaigns.[39] Such stunts included one theatre ending each screening of *Dracula* and *Frankenstein* with an advertising trailer called *Help Your Blood Bank*.[40]

More commonly, exhibitors focussed on publicity that tried to draw attention to the status that age had brought to *Dracula* and *Frankenstein*. For example, many newspaper advertisements heralded the fact that audiences would see the "original" films, as opposed to sequels.[41] Touting their horror elements, some ads also promised viewers that they would see the "uncut" versions of *Dracula* and *Frankenstein*, even though that was not true.[42] Prints of *Dracula* in 1952 (and 1947) featured the same changes as those struck in 1938.

The double bill experienced varied success in 1952. In Louisville, the two films generated "nice takings" at a weekly gross of $4,500.[43] Cincinnati's Lyric Theatre made "no complaint" after grossing $5,000, and Chicago's Grand pronounced their $8,000 "okay."[44] By contrast, San Francisco's Golden Gate complained that ticket sales were "only $8,000," the theatre having generated $13,500 the previous week from screening *Macao* (1952).[45] Baltimore's Stanley bemoaned its "blah" gross of $5,500, and Cleveland's Palace reported a "disappointing" $8,500.[46]

Advertisement published in the April 25, 1952 issue of the Syracuse *Post-Standard*.

Television

During the fifties, *Dracula*'s greatest triumph came thanks not to a theatrical reissue, but instead to television. In the summer of 1957, WABC-TV in New York signed a $750,000 deal with Screen Gems – a television subsidiary of Columbia Pictures, which had acquired broadcast rights to Universal's complete pre-1948 catalog – that allowed them to air a large number of Universal horror and mystery films, one of them being *Dracula*. An ABC official told the press, "We're hoping to create a new 'program identity' to crack entrenched viewer habits."[47] That identity became the "Shock!" package, which the flagship ABC channel advertised heavily in the weeks leading up to its premiere at the end of September 1957. *Dracula*'s inaugural broadcast on WABC came on 4 October 1957 at 11:15PM EST.[48]

Variety worried that those stations planning to air the "Shock!" films were taking a "highly flexible attitude" toward the Television Code of the National Association of Radio and Television Broadcasters (NARTB), which declared that the "use of horror for its own sake" had to be eliminated from programs. In addition, the Code's section on "Responsibility Toward Children" decreed that broadcasters needed to avoid "material which is excessively violent or would create morbid suspense, or other undesirable reactions in children."[49] But many TV stations believed that openly advertising the movies as "shockers for shockers' sake" would properly prepare adult viewers. They also believed that late-night schedules for films like *Dracula* would prevent children from seeing them.

Dracula's initial telecast in New York drew an impressive 8.8 percent rating and a 41.7 percent market share, which represented an amazing 450 percent hike in the station's rating.[50] Another figure calculated that one station broadcasting *Dracula* saw its ratings lifted by 1,225 percent over the same time slot in the previous month. *Variety* reported that, "In their first two weeks on the air, the thrillers, represented thus far by *Frankenstein* and *Dracula*, have turned local rating pictures topsy-turvy, boosted late night sets-in-use to well nigh unbelievable levels and made some top star-name feature film programming look like kid stuff."[51]

Such success continued in other markets. A first-run broadcast in Providence in 1958 found *Dracula* taking 54 percent of the share for its time slot.[52] One year later, John Zacherle (aka Zacherley) hosted a broadcast of *Dracula* as part of what he declared "National Vampire Week."[53] And, as time went on, some broadcasters brazenly programmed some horror films outside of their original late-night schedule. In 1963, for example, *Dracula* obtained 31 percent of the share in one market after being shown in a 5:00-6:30PM time slot.[54]

But *Dracula*'s success on TV did not occur without minor controversy. The Television Code Review Board of the NATRB argued that "Shock!" pictures needed to be banned from television only six weeks after the first broadcast. The organization also threatened to deny usage of their "seal of good practice" to all stations that did not heed its warning.[55] By 1960, 19.7 percent of households confessed that their children had experienced "upsetting programs" like *Dracula*, *Frankenstein*, and other movies in the "Shock!" package.[56]

Such concerns hardly forced *Dracula* off the air. Subsequent broadcasts of the film occurred repeatedly in the years that followed, including as part of an MCA-TV package of 77 Universal horror and mystery films in 1971. Stations purchasing the rights to that group included WGN in Chicago, KTLA in Los Angeles, WJW in Cleveland, and WDCA in Washington.[57]

It is difficult to chart any changes or edits that stations made to *Dracula* for its television broadcasts. The need for the film to fit into particular time slots – which also generally required a certain amount of time for TV commercials, as well as (in some cases) bumpers featuring onscreen horror hosts like Zacherle – suggest that individual stations may well have occasionally trimmed seconds or even minutes from the film's running time. Moreover, some television prints borrowed music from Universal's *The Frozen Ghost* (1945) to use under *Dracula*'s closing credits.

Other television prints may well have featured even more alterations. A curious English-language print housed at Universal features somewhat generic background music and added sound effects. No new onscreen credits appear, which make it difficult to determine the music's origin, but it was certainly not written for the film. Even in such crucial scenes as Renfield's first meeting with Dracula, cues end at ill-timed moments and then immediately restart, thus stitching together a new and decidedly awkward soundscape. Apparently the print was prepared for television screenings (allegedly for broadcast in France) in a cheap effort to modernize the film.

Home Video

For most audiences prior to the late 1970s, viewing *Dracula* meant buying a ticket for a theatrical screening or carefully monitoring television guides to watch a broadcast of the film at home. To own a full-length version of *Dracula* was not possible, short of purchasing a pirated print. Though not legal, such prints weren't hard to find. According to a 1974 issue of *Variety*, a bootleg of *Dracula* could be bought for as little as $75.[58]

The first legal release of *Dracula* to the home market came courtesy of Castle Films, Inc. In 1963, the company sold a heavily condensed optical-sound version on 16mm (at approximately 300 feet in length) and a magnetic-sound version on 8mm (at approximately 150 feet in length). It offered the film (catalog number 1023) from 1963 to 1977, though by 1971 it had deleted the standard 8mm version (which was also available as a silent film), offering instead a Super 8mm edition.[59] In addition to these versions (which were publicized as "Complete Editions," even though they included only about one-tenth of *Dracula*'s running time), Castle also released silent "Headline Editions" on 8mm that were mounted on 50-foot reels.[60]

Approximately eight minutes in length, Castle's "Complete Edition" not only condensed *Dracula*, but also made some notable changes to it. This version retained *Swan Lake* for *Dracula*'s opening theme, but presented new onscreen credits, simple text over a hypnotic spiral in the background. The narrative begins with Dracula biting the flower girl in London and then walking away. Instead of attending the concert, Castle's editing makes it seem as if Dracula proceeds directly to Lucy's apartment, rather than attending the concert. The film then cuts to Mina describing her "dream," after which Van Helsing discovers bite marks on her neck. Viewers familiar with the full-length film would view such a cut as a narrative ellipsis, but others could easily conflate the biting of the character Lucy (whose voice is not heard) with the character Mina, who describes having been bitten.

From there, the condensation finds Harker and Mina on the terrace, with Mina responding to a bat as if she can understand it. After she tries to bite Harker, the film cuts to Dracula on the sanitarium grounds. Mina joins him and becomes enveloped in his cape. Castle's editing makes it seem as if they immediately leave together for Carfax Abbey, which is not the case in the full-length film. Harker and Van Helsing pursue the duo, with the condensation's final three minutes devoted to a re-edited version of Dracula's death and Mina's restoration. In many respects, the Castle version features effective transitions between scenes, allowing a coherent narrative to emerge. But curiously absent is the sound of Lugosi's voice, as there are no scenes in which Dracula talks.

The first authorized presentation of the full-length version of *Dracula* on a home-viewing format came in 1978, when MCA/Universal Home Video released a Discovision copy for the Magnavox Magnivision players; the studio continued to offer the same product until October 1980. Though cropped slightly, the film was well transferred from an original nitrate print.⁶¹ MCA/Universal Home Video subsequently released *Dracula* on VHS and Betamax home videotape formats in 1980 and 1985, and then released the film again on VHS only in 1988.

Understanding *Dracula*'s ongoing potential to generate revenue, Universal hired the YCM Laboratory in Burbank undertake the first restoration of *Dracula* in 1988. As technician Peter Comandini would later complain, Universal's original negative existed in such bad shape as to be unusable, so YCM struck a new negative from a lavender protection print. By using Impact Noise Reduction, YCM impressively cleaned up the film's audio, the result allowing viewers to hear sound effects of wind that had been aurally obscured in previous circulating

A retouched publicity still of Lugosi in *Dracula* (1931), dating to the 1960s. In this instance, the key alteration is to the fingernails, which are changed to appear more like claws.

copies. Of great importance was the fact that YCM also relied on a print of *Dracula* at the British Film Institute, which helped the company to restore audio of Renfield's scream and Dracula's groan, absent from American screenings since 1938.⁶² YCM also attempted to restore Van Helsing's curtain speech, but finally deemed surviving footage to be too far gone. Its efforts were further hampered by the fact that the speech unfolds in a single moving-camera shot. MCA/Universal released this restoration on a 1991 laser disc and on a 1992 VHS tape; it also appeared at select movie theatres in October 1991 alongside *Frankenstein* to commemorate their shared sixtieth anniversaries.⁶³

Universal released an inaugural DVD copy of *Dracula* in 1999, with such bonus features as the documentary *The Road to Dracula*, an audio commentary by David J. Skal, the Spanish-language version of *Dracula*, and a special audio feature that allowed viewers to hear Philip Glass' new musical score for *Dracula* (as played by the Kronos Quartet) while watching the film. That same year, Universal released a final VHS version of *Dracula* in a clamshell case; it also featured the Philip Glass score. Such versions eliminated *Swan Lake* and all music from the concert hall scene, as the Glass score plays almost continuously during the film.

Commenting on his work, Glass wrote, "Many films have been made based on *Dracula* since the original in 1931 – however, none is equal to the original in eloquence or the sheer power to move us. … The film is considered to be a classic. I felt the score needed to evoke the feeling of the world of the 19th century – for that reason, I decided a string quartet would be the most evocative and effective. I wanted to stay away from the obvious effects associated with horror films. With Kronos, we were able to add depth to the emotional layers of the film."[64]

In addition to the general excitement surrounding the DVD format at the end of the nineties, the Philip Glass connection brought *Dracula* to a new group of audiences. The Nonesuch label released a CD soundtrack of the Glass score, which the Kronos Quartet performed at various live screenings in 1999, including the Telluride Film Festival, the Brooklyn Academy of Music, and Royce Hall at UCLA. The Glass score proved a success at Telluride, though some other performances received unenthusiastic reviews.[65]

Sadly, Universal's 1999 release of *Dracula* on DVD and VHS did not use the 1988 restoration, but instead relied on mediocre source material and a transfer that was too dark. The same was true of a reissue of the film in a 2004 DVD set entitled *The Legacy Collection*, which also included the Spanish-language version of *Dracula*, *Dracula's Daughter*, *Son of Dracula*, and *House of Dracula*. The only key difference between the two releases came in the form of separate mistakes regarding *Dracula*'s audio track. The 1999 DVD accidentally and quite unforgivably erased the pivotal usage of Schubert's *Unfinished Symphony* at the end of the concert hall scene, whereas the 2004 version strangely eliminated the sound of Renfield's scream and Dracula's groan, which had been so carefully restored in 1988. Neither release did service to the film.

Universal then touted its 2006 DVD, released under the grammatically suspect title *Bela Lugosi Dracula: 75th Anniversary Edition*. This edition recycled bonus features from previous releases, but importantly added a new audio commentary by Steve Haberman. While Skal's audio commentary (which was also included on this release) tends to decry the film, Haberman's offers a more positive approach. Together, the two create a sense of critical balance sorely lacking in the previous DVDs.

Happily, this version of *Dracula* presents a complete and accurate representation of the film's music and sound effects, something that could not be said of any of the prior DVDs. However, the overall sound quality suffers in this version, and the visual appearance is highly problematic. Heavy in grain, this release features noticeably incorrect black levels, and is quite inferior to the 1991 laser disc.

The question logically arises as to why Universal Home Video would not rely upon superior materials that should have been within easy reach. The only answer can be carelessness. Indeed, this version nearly used a transfer of the aforementioned print of *Dracula* with the new music score and sound effects, the one apparently created for French television. Fortunately, Constantine Nasr – who produced the Haberman audio commentary – noticed the print was incorrect and thankfully prevented it from being used.[66]

In 2012, Universal mounted a major restoration of *Dracula*, the film being part of a company centennial project in which numerous other films – including the Spanish-language version of *Dracula* – were also restored. The key purpose was for a Blu-ray release, though the company struck new 35mm negative and positive prints as well. For the first time since 1988, technicians paid extremely careful consideration to the audio and video of the entire film, relying on a nitrate lavender positive housed at the Library of Congress, a print apparently struck in 1938. Following a wet gate scan, in which a liquid bath removed dirt and filled in some scratches, digital artists carefully painted out some scratches and corrected numerous flaws, at times isolating particular areas of individual frames in order to restore their luster and to correct problems with brightness and contrast. The entire process illuminated much detail that was lost in prior releases.

Restorationist Peter Schade has noted, "By using high resolution film scanners and the digital tools that we have at our disposal, we were able to ... provide more detail than ever seen before. Viewers can now experience the story and presentation as the filmmaker wanted ... Subtle differences in shades of gray, subtle differences in the texture of clothing, and fine detail in the backgrounds on set, like curtains, bookcases, walls and fireplaces are now evident." Schade is certainly correct, as the image clarity is oustanding. Various details emerge that were lost in earlier home video releases. One example of many is that we can now clearly see that Dracula does appear in the long shot of London that features the city name as onscreen text. We can also see the evil, shimmering eyes of the bat that appears at Lucy's window.

A retouched publicity still of Frances Dade and Bela Lugosi in *Dracula* (1931). The addition of blood is one of the changes that has been made, apparently to modernize the image.

The restoration also corrected a jump cut present in *Dracula*'s opening credits since at least 1938, in which an art deco bat in the background becomes larger for no apparent reason. According to Schade, "In the case of the change in size of the art deco bat in the credits, we felt the jump to a different size in addition to the image movement was not the way those credits were originally intended. That jump is printed in to the lavender positive but we believe it is the result of an attempt to fix some kind of damage in the original negative before this particular positive element was printed. Therefore, we chose to smooth it out."[67]

Audio specialists also undertook a major restoration of the film's soundtrack, working to correct various sonic problems in the source material, ranging from cleaning up occasional pops to de-noising the entire film, thus eliminating the amount of hiss present in prior releases. Perhaps the most notable change occurs in the film's opening titles, which purges *Swan Lake* of the garbled sound present in earlier versions, though whether the problem dates to 1931 or only to 1938 is unknown. Here there is a benefit perhaps, in that the music plays clearly, but there is also a potential problem, as the restoration team simply borrowed the music from a print of the Spanish-language version of *Dracula*, and so – however close it may be – the music is not original to Browning's film. Nevertheless, the restoration presents an amazingly clear soundscape, even more so than audiences experienced in 1931.

Advances in technologies may allow for other future improvements to *Dracula*, and perhaps a print featuring Van Helsing's curtain speech will someday surface. However, it is more likely that the 2012 version of *Dracula* will remain the definitive version. And this is a happy outcome, because the restoration is truly remarkable.

Conclusion

While the 1931 film *Dracula* remains the key referent, the character Dracula evolved during subsequent Universal horror films, not least through his subjugation into narratives concentrating on other monsters. But these depictions operated not in a vacuum, but rather in an ongoing interplay with the 1931 film, not only due to its original impact, but also to its reappearance at movie theatres thanks to revival screenings and national reissues. *Dracula* also re-emerged quite clearly in the form of Tod Browning's *Mark of the Vampire*, a film that marked the director's third effort to bring the Dracula story to the screen.

As influential as *Dracula* became as a result of its theatrical screenings, television breathed new life into it, causing its cultural impact to widen. Shortly after the film's initial TV broadcast in 1957, Gabriel Dell began imitating Lugosi's Dracula (in full costume) on *The Steve Allen Show*. At roughly the same time, Lenny Bruce began incorporating a Lugosi-Dracula impression into his stand-up comedy act. In 1958, television horror host Zacherle scored a top ten hit with his novelty song *Dinner with Drac*. Even jazz drummer Philly Joe Jones entered the dialogue with his 1958 album *Blues for Dracula*; directly inspired by Lenny Bruce, Jones offered his own Lugosi-Dracula impression on the record.[68] The convergence of these salutes and imitations of *Dracula* extended to Andy Warhol's *The Kiss* (1962), a silk-screen painting that depicts repetitions of Lugosi from the 1931 film against a silver background.

The popularity of these imitations and references alongside the original 1931 *Dracula* resounded into cultural echoes that reverberated in the years that followed, ranging from the mascot for General Mills' Count Chocula breakfast cereal, which launched in 1971, to the Count von Count (voiced by Jerry Nelson), a character that first appeared on *Sesame Street* in 1972. To chronicle all of them would take an entire book, one that would have to address everything from comic books and video games to Halloween decorations and greeting cards.

These cultural echoes are all in addition to the many vampire films produced after the classic horror era. Whether in the Hammer Dracula movies featuring Christopher Lee, or in the Universal film *Dracula* (1979) starring Frank Langella, or in comedy films like *Love at First Bite* (1979) with George Hamilton and *Dracula: Dead and Loving It* (1995) with Leslie Nielsen, the influence of the 1931 film can readily be felt. Indeed, so strong is the 1931 *Dracula*'s cultural impact that it is present even when it is absent. Consider *Bram Stoker's Dracula* (1992), in which Gary Oldman's portrayal stands out as different not on its own terms, but rather by comparison to the 1931 film. Hearing Oldman's rendering of "Listen to them! The children of the night. What sweet music they make!" immediately invokes Lugosi's version, with Oldman's addition of the word "sweet" standing out precisely because it is different from the original dialogue.

The reason is not merely the lasting influence of Tod Browning's *Dracula*, but its ongoing availability. Never has it been more accessible to own, to view, and to review, than in the twenty-first century with numerous versions available in a variety of formats.

1. O'Brian, Jack. "Broadway." *Sandusky Register-Star-News* (Sandusky, OH) 11 Nov. 1947.
2. Shaffer, George. "Movie Studios Busy with New Horror Films." *Chicago Tribune* 22 Feb. 1932. It is true that at least one newspaper article attributed the genesis of the horror film cycle to *Frankenstein*. See: "Frankenstein Stars Era of Terror Films." *Los Angeles Times* 12 Jan. 1932.
3. Bell, Nelson B. "Thoughts on Horror Era, Renaissance, and Miss Ulric." *Washington Post* 21 Feb. 1932.
4. "Freaks and Monsters." *National Board of Review Magazine* (Mar. 1932).
5. "Vampires, Monsters, Horrors!" *New York Times* 1 Mar. 1936.
6. Stanley, Fred. "Hollywood Flash." *New York Times* 16 Apr. 1944: X3.
7. Kelly, J. Interoffice Memo to Mr. McKenzie, copied to Colonel Jason Joy. 7 Mar. 1931. Available in a file entitled *The Return of Dracula* in the Motion Picture Association of America, Production Code Administration collection at the Margaret Herrick Library in Beverly Hills, CA.
8. I do not personally believe that the horror film ended in 1948, but I do believe that the particular kinds of horror films popular from 1931-1948 largely come to a close in the late forties, specifically in the reliance on monsters like Dracula, Frankenstein's Monster, the Wolf Man, the Mummy, et al.
9. Schallert, Edwin. "Lewis Stone to Play Chief Executive Role." *Los Angeles Times* 12 July 1939: 13.
10. "UI Plans Remaking Lugosi's *Dracula*," p. 8.
11. Koszarski, Richard. Email to Gary D. Rhodes. 26 Apr. 2012. Koszarski made notes of the possible legal action against *Mark of the Vampire* while examining Universal's legal files in the mid-1970s.
12. The Browning-Fort shooting script appears in: *Dracula (The Original 1931 Shooting Script)*. Ed. by Philip J. Riley. (Absecon, NJ: MagicImage, 1990).
13. "UI Plans Remaking Lugosi's *Dracula*." *Daily Variety* 9 Mar. 1948: 8.
14. Advertisement. *The News-Palladium* (Benton Harbor, MI) 9 Oct. 1948: 2; Advertisement. *The Rolfe Arrow* (Rolfe, IA) 28 Oct. 1948: 5; Advertisement. *Maryville Daily Forum* (Maryville, MO) 29 Oct. 1948: 7.
15. "Theatre Receipts." *Motion Picture Herald* 6 May 1933: 38.
16. "Universal." *Motion Picture Herald* 6 Jan. 1940: 62.
17. "C. C. C. Chatter." *Garfield County News* (Utah) 26 Jan. 1934.
18. Mogull's Camera and Film Exchange, Inc. *Catalog of 16mm Silent Motion Picture Film Library*, 1945: 7. Accessed 3 Nov. 2012. Available at http://mediahistoryproject.org/nontheatrical/.
19. "Three Horror Pix for 30c Fills Local Theatre to Capacity 21 Hours a Day." *Hollywood Reporter* 6 Aug. 1938.
20. Ibid.
21. Qtd. in Advertisement. *Motion Picture Herald* 3 Sept. 1938: 49.
22. Harmon, Francis S. Letter to J. D. Miller of Universal Pictures Co., Inc. 17 Mar. 1938. Available in the file for *Dracula* in the Motion Picture Association of America, Production Code Administration collection at the Margaret Herrick Library in Beverly Hills, CA.
23. As these PCA documents prove, writer Arthur Lennig is quite incorrect in his book *The Immortal Count: The Life and Films of Bela Lugosi* (Lexington, KY: University of Kentucky, 2003) when he claims that the curtain speech was "omitted from later releases because decades later audiences would likely find these final words campy, yet another example of Hollywood's cornball taste" (p. 121).
24. "Horror Pix, *Suez* and *Sisters* Give Broadway Big Biz." *Hollywood Reporter* 18 Oct. 1938: 3.
25. "U Horror Revivals Double Average Biz." *Hollywood Reporter* 7 Oct. 1938: 1.
26. "'Space Ships,' 'Death Rays,' 'Terror' Trend Brings New Theatre Business." *Motion Picture Herald* 17 Dec. 1938: 17.
27. These ballyhoo efforts were undertaken at some of the first theatres booking the 1938 double bill; they are described in the pressbook that Universal hastily prepared for the reissue.
28. Such an example is described in "Universal." *Motion Picture Herald* 8 Oct. 1938: 55.
29. B.W.W. "A Line O' Type or Two." *Chicago Tribune* 17 Dec. 1938.
30. "U Reissuing Eight for Double Bills." *Daily Variety* 25 Feb. 1947: 2.
31. "Universal." *Motion Picture Herald* 25 Oct. 1947.
32. Advertisement. *The Record-Argus* (Greenville, PA) 7 November 1947; Advertisement. *Oak Park Oak Leaves* (Oak Park, IL) 16 Oct. 1947: 66.
33. "Street Scenes." *Kingsport Times* (Kingsport, TN) 12 Nov. 1947: 1.
34. Advertisement. *Kingsport News* (Kingsport, TN) 11 Nov. 1947; Advertisement. *Biloxi Daily Herald* (Biloxi,

MS) 30 Jan. 1948: 5. In a curious example of theatre programming, the West End in Chicago booked *Dracula* on a double bill with *House of Frankenstein* in September 1947. See: *The Garfieldian* (Chicago, IL) 11 Sept. 1947.

35. *Daily Variety* 10 Dec. 1947.
36. Advertisement. *Rockford Register-Republic* (Rockford, IL) 15 Nov. 1947.
37. "Reissuing *Dracula* and *Frankenstein*." *Daily Variety* 4 Feb. 1952: 5.
38. See, for example: Advertisement. *The Evening Observer* (Dunkirk, NY) 17 June 1952: 16; Advertisement. *Cleveland Plain Dealer* 8 Oct. 1952: 29.
39. "New York." *Variety* 16 Apr. 1952: 20.
40. Graham, Sheilah. *Daily Variety* 3 June 1952: 2.
41. See, for example: Advertisement. *Fitchburg Sentinel* (Fitchburg, MA) 29 May 1952: 4.
42. See, for example: Advertisement. *Boston Daily Record* (Boston, MA) 28 Apr. 1952: 49.
43. "L'Ville Limps; *Carbine* Lean 9G, *Flesh* Oke 4G." *Variety* 28 May 1952: 8.
44. "*Jack* Gigantic $26,000 in Cincy." *Variety* 13 Aug. 1952: 12; "Chi Climbs; Autry Ups *Aaron Slick* to Fine 35G, *Skirts*-Vaude Okay 37G, *Mountain* Big 18G, *Eagles* Mild 11G." *Variety* 4 June 1952: 9.
45. "*Express*, *North* Each Hot 16G to Pace Frisco B.O." *Variety* 7 May 1952: 8.
46. "Baltimore." *Variety* 2 July 1952: 22; "*College* Hefty in Cleve. at $15,000, *Atomic* $11,500." *Variety* 23 July 1952: 9.
47. "WABC-TV Ratings to Get 'Shock' Therapy." *Billboard* 19 Aug. 1957: 10.
48. "On Television." *New York Times* 4 Oct. 1957: 47.
49. "Stations Flock to 'Shock' Pix." *Variety* 4 Sept. 1957: 33.
50. "Huge Ratings Jumps Show Dialers Flocking to 'Shock!'" *Billboard* 14 Oct. 1957: 8.
51. "Late Nite Chiller-Diller Ratings Open Up Whole New Vistas for TV." *Variety* 16 Oct. 1957: 27.
52. "*Variety* Pulse Feature Chart." *Variety* 24 Dec. 1958: 26.
53. "Tonight's Pick of the TV Best." *The Herald Statesman* (Yonkers, NY) 2 Mar. 1959: 16.
54. "*Variety* ARB Feature Film Chart." *Variety* 3 July 1963: 36.
55. "NARTB Would Bar All Horror Films on TV." *Variety* 20 Nov. 1957: 30.
56. "Pulse Beat." *Broadcasting* 27 Jan. 1960: 26.
57. "Program Notes." *Broadcasting* 13 Dec. 1971.
58. "Pirated Print Fees." *Variety* 31 July 1974: 31.
59. MacGillivray, Scott. *Castle Films: A Hobbyist's Guide* (Lincoln, NE: iUniverse, 2004): 188.
60. Okuda, Ted. Email to Gary D. Rhodes 12 Nov. 2012.
61. "*Dracula* (1931) [23-001 Discovision]." http://www.vivalaserdisc.com/dracula-1931-23-001-discovision. Accessed 10 Nov. 2012.
62. Turner, George E. "The Two Faces of *Dracula*." *American Cinematographer* 69.5 (May 1988): 41.
63. "MCA Retros Monsters for Promo Push." *Daily Variety* 3 Oct. 1991: 4.
64. "*Dracula*." http://www.philipglass.com/music/recordings/dracula.php. Accessed 12 Nov. 2012.
65. Higgins, Bill. "Light Mood Reigns at Wet Telluride Fest." *Variety* 6 Sept. 1999: 16; Kozinn, Allan. "Dracula Hears Philip Glass and Gets Thirsty." *New York Times* 28 Oct. 1999: E5; Rich, Alan. "*Dracula*." *Variety* 2 Nov. 1999: 11. For an unethusiastic review, see: Turan, Kenneth. "Live Musical Accompaniment Drains *Dracula* of Its Scariness." *Los Angeles Times* 1 Nov. 1999: 11.
66. Nasr, Constantine. Email to Gary D. Rhodes. 11 Feb. 2013.
67. Schade, Peter. Email to Gary D. Rhodes, forwarded by Aaron Rogers, Director of Advertising & Publicity for NBC/Universal. 16 Mar. 2013.
68. "Reviews and Ratings of New Jazz Albums." *Billboard* 29 Dec. 1958: 35.

Chapter 11
CRITICAL BACKLASH

Dracula's life has not only been extended by various sequels, restorations, and imitations, but it has also continued to thrive thanks to the work of the numerous historians and theorists who have written about it. The first time that a serious film critic tackled the 1931 film version of *Dracula* in print seems to have occurred in October 1953, when George Geltzer published an article on Tod Browning in *Films in Review*, which was referenced in Chapter 6. "Today *Dracula* seems weak," he wrote, "but its opening sequences of Count Dracula's castle still create an eerie atmosphere."[1] Soon thereafter, in January 1954, William K. Everson's essay "Horror Films" appeared in the same publication, echoing Geltzer's praise for the opening sequence, but damning the rest of the film as "plodding" and "talkative."[2] Both men published their views soon after Realart's theatrical reissue of *Dracula* in 1952, and in an era when Tod Browning and Bela Lugosi were still alive. At that time, horror films arguably featured much technological progress; for example, *House of Wax* (1953) was filmed in color and 3-D.

Geltzer and Everson became the model for subsequent criticism. In the same way vampire movies – like all genre films – are founded on repetition, subsequent writers discussing Browning's *Dracula* have tended to reiterate what has already been said. Everson himself returned to *Dracula* in his landmark book *Classics of the Horror Film* (1974), calling it "stilted" and "pedestrian."[3]

Perhaps some or all of the film's detractors have wholeheartedly believed every word they have written, but they repeat one another nonetheless, sometimes even to the extent of specific word choice: words like "pedestrian" and "stolid" appear over and over again. Taken together, the best case is that these critiques are links in the same chain of thought. The worst case is that they represent reverberations in an echo chamber. Witness, for example:

> …as soon as the action moves to London, the picture betrays its origins 'on the boards,' becoming talky, pedestrian, and uncinematic. We are told, when we should be shown, about the 'red mist' that heralds the arrival of the vampire and about the werewolf seen running across Dr. Seward's lawn. Marvelous opportunities are ignored – like the episode of Lucy (Frances Dade) turning into a vampire herself – and the ending is curiously half-hearted. A powerful villain like Dracula surely deserves a more impressive demise than an off-screen groan.
> –Carlos Clarens, An Illustrated History of the Horror Film (1967)[4]

Publicity still of Bela Lugosi in Dracula *(1931).*

The main fault with the film lies in the fact that it was mainly adapted from the play and not from the novel. As a result it was a very static and talkative film, apart from the early scenes set in Transylvania. Lugosi's performance attracted the praise of many of the critics, but seen today it seems too theatrical and even a little ludicrous.
–John Brosnan, The Horror People (1976)[5]

The 1930 [sic] Dracula has not maintained its original impact. That it is watchable at all is most probably due to the strange tricks which Bela Lugosi performs with the English language, and to the absurd exaggerations that pass for acting with him and Dwight Frye. It is the Hollywood equivalent of a Tod Slaughter film, but even more stagily presented. Tod Browning had some sort of reputation as Lon Chaney Snr's favourite director, but this may have been merely because he did not interfere when the star felt like showing off. Certainly in Dracula he shows no command of pace, or editing, or composition, or camera movement, and only because the story itself was so odd can the film have fascinated those early talkie audiences as it did; even for aficianados [sic] Browning's handling makes it hard to follow. The almost total absence of music doesn't help, and a sense of strain is evident in the attempt to turn Dracula's few appearances and scant dialogue into a star part.
–Leslie Halliwell, The Dead that Walk (1988)[6]

The flaws in *Dracula* are so self-evident that they are outlined in nearly every critique; only Lugosi freaks and the nostalgically inclined still go through the motions of praising and defending the film. The main problem is that it hews too closely to the play, abandoning many potentially exciting scenes delineated in the novel. Browning is slavish in his faithfulness to the stage production, indulging in wearisome long takes and filming scenes in long and medium shots as though the audience were viewing the proceedings through the proverbial proscenium arch.
–Tom Weaver, Universal Horrors: The Studio's Classic Films, 1931-1946 (1990)[7]

The film's first two reels are without question its strongest, and provide the main reason for the film's enduring fascination. The Transylvania sequences have, however, been routinely overpraised in terms of their direction and cinematography.
–David J. Skal, Hollywood Gothic: The Tangled Web of Dracula from Novel to Stage to Screen (1990)[8]

With all their repetitions, these comments – which represent a very small selection of the many that could be quoted – do reveal a gradual escalation of negativity. By 1990, as if both to agree with and surpass his predecessors, Skal even argued against praising *Dracula*'s opening scenes.

That many persons do not appreciate Browning's *Dracula* places the film in a wonderful position. Any important work of art provokes various responses, and everyone is entitled to their opinion. The trajectory of *Dracula* criticism exemplifies a school of thought, one apparently marked by some of its members closely reading and being influenced by the work of writers who have gone before.

All that said, a distinct problem with these stated opinions is the evidence – or lack thereof – that some of these authors have used to promote their views. A viewer can dislike *Dracula*, or even despise it, for no stated reason. But it is curious that some writers, in their zeal to decry the film, have committed a number of factual errors. Some of these are relatively minor. For example, Leslie Halliwell claims, "a few shots cover the voyage of the *Demeter*," when in fact *fifteen* shots cover the voyage of a ship that in the film is actually named the *Vesta*.[9] In *Dark Carnival: The Secret World of Tod Browning, Hollywood's Master of the Macabre*, Skal and coauthor Elias Savada note, "The film is devoid of music, save for a generically mysterious theme from Tchaikovsky's *Swan Lake* under the titles, and a few snatches of Wagner when the vampire visits a concert hall."[10] But only one selection of Wagner is heard at the concert hall (*Die Meistersinger*); the other selection is Schubert's *Symphony No. 8*, which is excerpted twice in the scene, thus book-ending the Wagner. Skal and Savada also fail to mention the music box playing in Lucy's bedroom.

Other mistakes are more pronounced. Various writers claim that *Dracula* adheres too closely to the Deane-Balderston stage play, but – whether or not one likes the film, or the play for that matter – a cursory comparison of the two illustrates how widely they diverge. Their differences are stark enough that I wonder how many writers who have confidently made this claim have actually seen or read the play. Notably, the film's Transylvania sequence, ship journey, and London sequence (the death of the flower girl, the concert hall, and Lucy's apartment) occupy approximately 29 minutes of a film that runs approximately 74 minutes and thirty seconds, resulting in nearly forty percent of its running time. None of these scenes appears in the play. Moreover, though it is only mentioned in retrospect, the Dracula of the play journeys to England by plane, not by ship.

In the play, Dr. Seward has a larger role, and even accompanies Harker and Van Helsing in their journey to stake Dracula. Harker has more to do as well, and is more intelligent than his film counterpart; it is he who has heard of a "Voivode Dracula who fought the Turks" while he was once in Translyvania, and it is he who figures out how a Translyvanian vampire can live in England, so far from his native earth. These are but a few examples of many that could be cited, and perhaps distract from the larger point that the play operates as a mystery in which the lead characters attempt to determine who the vampire is, an issue that is treated only briefly in the film. In short, as Chapter 4 illustrates, the Fort-Browning shooting script borrowed from *many* sources, with the stage play being only one of them.

Aesthetics and CineMetrics

In his book *Monsters and Mad Scientists: A Cultural History of the Horror Movie* (Basil Blackwell, 1989), Andrew Tudor wrote the following of *Dracula*'s critics: "They observe, rightly, that even by the standards of the day the film is slow and stagy...."[11] Such an observation appears repeatedly in literature on *Dracula*; here again is an ingrained belief about the film that is bereft of concrete evidence.

How can one determine the extent to which a film does or does not adhere to the norms of a given period of time? Aside from mere guesswork (which has plagued *Dracula*, certainly to the extent that its historians and critics seem not to have studied other Hollywood films produced in 1930), the best approach is quantitative, neo-formalist analysis of the type employed by Barry Salt, David Bordwell, Kristin Thompson, Yuri Tsivian, and other scholars, which we can herein refer to as "CineMetrics" following from the name of software developed by Yuri Tsivian and Gunars Civjans.[12] By compiling statistical data regarding key aspects of *Dracula*'s cinematography and editing and then comparing the same to other films produced at roughly the same time, it is possible to determine the extent to which *Dracula* was or was not in keeping with the "standards of the day."

For this chapter, I have made exacting notations of twenty Hollywood films that appeared in theatres at the time of *Dracula*'s general release (five of them playing at first-run New York theatres the very same week as *Dracula*'s premiere). The twenty films represent different genres released by the major studios.[13] As a result, they are an adequate sample from which to draw data.

Scholars undertaking such studies often focus on the Average Shot Length (ASL) of particular films. Calculating an ASL in mathematical terms helps us to understand the overall pacing of a single film, or, for that matter, groups of films made in given eras and/or in given countries. Consider, for example, Yuri Tsivian's research, which revealed that the cutting tempo of Russian films moved from the slowest in the world to the fastest between 1917 and 1918.

Individually, the twenty films considered for this study feature ASLs that vary from as fast as approximately 6.9 seconds in *Dirigible* (1931) to as slow as 16.5 seconds for *No Limit* (1931). Together, the films – which feature a combined total of 8,917 shots – have an average shot length of 11.29 seconds each.[14] The ASL of Browning's *Dracula* is approximately 9.4 seconds, which suggests at a minimum that it is very much within the norm of Hollywood films produced in late 1930. Indeed, it could easily be argued that it is in fact faster-paced than the average.

With regard to specific edits in *Dracula*, David J. Skal has complained about a "jarring jump cut" in the second reel when "Dracula's wives glide across the flagstones toward their unconscious victim."[15] Most scholars in Film Studies draw distinctions between jump cuts, which feature temporal ellipses, and other types of disjunctive edits, the word "disjunctive" being a more accurate description of the cut Skal describes, as the editor has carefully ensured that the two shots advance the narrative without resorting to the elimination of *any* action.[16] In the first shot, Renfield falls unconscious to the floor. In the second shot, Dracula's three wives advance on Renfield, whose body remains unconscious in the same position. In other words, continuity editing is in fact carefully preserved by the cut.

The edit is disjunctive, however, because it represents a cut of approximately fifteen degrees to screen left (though it should be noted, the second shot also repositions the camera ten or fifteen feet behind the position used in the first shot). One could easily argue that this cut represents a violation of the thirty-degree rule in the Classical Hollywood Style. But considering the cut in view of the period in which *Dracula* was edited results in a very different conclusion. Of the twenty films under review for this study, *all* of them without exception feature cuts of less than thirty degrees, sometimes ten or twenty or more within the *very same* film.[17] Occasionally, these edits feature a change of focal length, but no change of degree at all, simply cutting inward into a closer shot (or outward from one). However, the bulk of these cuts offer angle changes of only ten or twenty degrees.

What this means is that the particular cut in *Dracula* under review was by no means unusual in the period, nor would it have been seen as an error or mistake in the context of 1930 and 1931. Indeed, if modern same critics viewed *Dracula* more closely, they would notice other cuts of less than thirty degrees elsewhere in the film. The edit of two shots depicting Renfield's approach towards the door of Dracula's Castle is one example (which is arguably mollified somewhat by the fact that Renfield makes a clean entrance into screen right of the second shot). [See Figures 11A and 11B.] Two shots depicting a conversation between Van Helsing and Seward at the Sanitarium also represent a change of less than degrees, and without any clean entrance or exit. Most notably, such a cut occurs between the first two shots of Dracula and Renfield once they are inside Dracula's Chambers. In addition to cutting at an angle of less than thirty degrees, the door (which closes of its own accord) is at a noticeably earlier stage of closing in the second shot. A continuity error emerges, though no prior historian or critic has mentioned it, perhaps because the edit also represents a match-on-action cut of the tilting of Dracula's head, where the eyes of most audience members would be focussed. [See Figures 11C and 11D.]

The duration of another specific shot in *Dracula* has also elicited criticism. The shot (which begins at approximately 50:15) appears in a scene featuring Van Helsing, Mina, and Harker on the terrace at the Seward residence. Soon after it begins, Karl Freund pushes the camera inwards, creating a two-shot (Van Helsing and Mina), with Harker exiting screen right. Then, in the same shot, Freund moves the camera backward to allow for Harker's return to the frame. Then, in the very same shot, Freund tilts upward for Van Helsing's exit on screen left and then tilts downward, thus creating another two shot (Mina and Harker). Van Helsing's offscreen voice soon beckons Mina to come indoors, with the camera moving backwards to follow her and soon revealing Van Helsing. She exits screen right, leaving Van Helsing and Harker alone in the center of the frame to converse while Van Helsing shuts one of the terrace doors.

Writer Arthur Lennig complains about the length of this shot and notes the fact that it runs 251 feet, meaning approximately three minutes, but strangely and quite regrettably he fails to mention the sheer number of camera moves it contains, all of which had to be timed carefully in terms of actor dialogue and blocking.[18] Drawing on Lennig, Skal adds that the shot was "clearly meant to be broken up with closeups and reaction shots," but he also fails to mention the number of camera moves it features, which collectively mitigate against any speculation regarding an intention to insert reaction shots.[19] I believe such unfounded opinions have resulted in egregious misrepresentations of the Browning film.[20]

Indeed, such a complicated and repeatedly mobile shot presenting action in a manner impossible for a viewer to witness in live theatre makes it difficult to understand why critics have condemned *Dracula* for being "stagy." As for the suggestion of reaction shots, it should be noted that the twenty films reviewed for this study feature a minimal use of the shot-reverse shot structure; in fact, some of them present extended shots of characters in conversations that are devoid of any camera movement. Examples can be found in such films *The Devil to Pay!* (1930), *Reaching for the Moon* (1931), *Ten Cents a Dance* (1931), and *Dance, Fools, Dance* (1931).

Figure 11C

Figure 11D

More generally, complaints against *Dracula* argue that Freund's camera was not particularly mobile. The twenty films under review for this study collectively feature 473 examples of moving camera. On average, that means each film contains 23.65 camera moves. By contrast, *Dracula* features 43 camera moves, far more than the norm of the period. This is to say nothing of the fact that *Dracula* features an impressive crane shot to introduce the Seward Sanitarium, one that – unlike many crane shots of the period – includes an onscreen character speaking dialogue.[21] By contrast, the bulk of the films under review for this study do not use any crane shots whatsoever.[22] Indeed, it is clear that Universal was the leader in crane shots in the early sound period, the studio having constructed the first modern camera crane in Hollywood for Paul Fejos' film *Broadway* in 1929. Both *Dracula* and *Resurrection* (1931) feature impressive uses of the same crane, though *Dracula*'s combination of the same with onscreen dialogue places it at the forefront of films using the device.[23]

Dracula's reliance on offscreen space to avoid depicting scenes of graphic horror has also drawn criticism, but other films examined for this study operate in much the same way. *The Bat Whispers* (1930) features offscreen murders, and *Little Caesar* (1931) features two offscreen shootings. It is true that *Little Caesar* also features an onscreen murder, but nevertheless *Dracula* does not operate noticeably differently from other films of its time in this regard.

As mentioned in Chapter 6, *Dracula* uses two onscreen titles during its narrative, both of which inform the audience of geographical information ("Aboard the *Vesta* -- bound for

England" and "London"). While at first they may appear to be relics of the silent-film era, the fact is that *many* of the movies examined for the current study also relied on onscreen titles, most of them conveying similar kinds of narrative information. For example, *Morocco* (1930) uses one onscreen title, *Dirigible*, *Kept Husbands* (1931), *Little Caesar*, and *Millie* (1931) use three onscreen titles each, and *Cimarron* (1931) and *Resurrection* use five each. Such onscreen titles have of course continued to be used in the decades since *Dracula*'s production as well.

The issue of *Dracula*'s ratio of dialogue to silent sequences also deserves investigation. As Chapter 3 indicated, Junior Laemmle and Tod Browning viewed the need to limit dialogue in the sound films Universal produced during mid-to-late 1930 as an important remedy to the constancy of the same in the Hollywood talking picture of 1928 to 1930. Rather than looking backward, the two men envisioned progress for the cinema in which the best of silence and sound could be combined into a new kind of moving picture. They were not alone in their thinking. In August 1930, for example, Phil Goldstone, head of Tiffany Productions, announced his opinion that the "public today is tired of an excess of dialogue and music, even of incidental sound effects." He added:

> *It has become increasingly evident in the past year that the primary purposes of motion picture entertainement were being violated. Pantomime has been relegated in many scenes to a detail of performance not worthy of special attention. Voice, lines, sound recording – these have occupied so much attention that often directors have lost sight of the fact that they should be making scenes.*[24]

Such views indicate that silent passages in *Dracula* represent a then-current filmmaking philosophy during the second half of 1930, one that Junior Laemmle continued to profess in print at least as late as October 1932.[25] While it was not a view adopted by all Hollywood filmmakers, it is possible to see the strategy at work in films other than *Dracula*. For example, Frank Capra's *Dirigible*, which was in production at roughly the same time as *Dracula*, features numerous non-dialogue passages as well.

Music is another key subject that arises in discussions of *Dracula*. The film features five musical selections, six if we count – as we should – the brief use of chimes heard during its conclusion in at least some prints. (One could also argue six musical selections if, as it certainly seems, the original 1931 release prints featured organ music prior to Van Sloan's closing speech, as opposed to the chimes that were likely added in 1938.) The twenty films under review for this study feature an average of nine examples of music per film.[26] Here is perhaps one instance where *Dracula* seems at odds with the norms of the period, but it should be added that some of the films under review feature numerous scenes in nightclubs and dance halls and so forth, meaning that their narratives required an extensive use of music. And it is important to note that a number of films in this study featured *less* music than *Dracula*. For example, only two examples of music are heard in *Parlor, Bedroom and Bath* (1931). *The Bat Whispers*, *Hook, Line and Sinker* (1930), and *The Drums of Jeopardy* (1931) each feature only three examples of music, and *Kept Husbands* and *Illicit* (1931) each feature only four.

Despite its inclusion of various music, viewers occasionally bemoan *Dracula*'s lack of a background score. However, absolutely *none* of the twenty films under review for this study features a background score. Moreover, only two of the twenty films feature non-diegetic music of any kind. *Dance, Fools, Dance* and *Little Caesar* each feature single scenes in which music plays in the background with no apparent onscreen source (such as a live orchestra, a radio, a phonograph, etc.).

Overall, it would be very reasonable to argue that in some respects *Dracula* was visually progressive by comparison to many films produced in Hollywood during the same time period, whether in the amount of its moving camerawork, its use of crane shots, and its conscious desire to create an interplay between sound and dialogue with silence and pantomime. But even if one rejects that argument, the statistical data prove that *Dracula* was certainly not regressive or outmoded by the production standards of its day. And I would argue that the quantitative data, rather than being revelatory, merely serves to reinforce the qualitative reaction that most careful viewers of films released in the period would have experienced. It also serves to underscore the limited knowledge that most of *Dracula*'s modern critics seem to have of Hollywood filmmaking as it existed in 1930.

One can also compare *Dracula* to the other horror films produced in Hollywood in 1931, specifically *Svengali* (released in May), *Murder by the Clock* (released in July), *Frankenstein* (released in November), and *Dr. Jekyll and Mr. Hyde* (released in December). To be sure, such comparisons are somewhat unfair to *Dracula*, given that Hollywood filmmaking evolved during the year 1931, ranging from the use of sound to the use of the optical printer (as can be seen in *Dr. Jekyll and Mr. Hyde*'s wipes for split-screen effects and transitions). Moreover, subsequent horror films were able to use *Dracula* as a template of what to do or not to do. After all, despite the year of its theatrical release, *Dracula* is best understood as a film produced in the second half of 1930. That said, previous scholars have often discussed *Dracula* in relation to these later films, particularly *Frankenstein*, and so it is worthwhile to revisit these comparisons.

The four major post-*Dracula* horror films of 1931 feature an ASL of approximately 10 seconds, as opposed to *Dracula*'s at approximately 9.4 seconds.[27] The same four films feature a combined total of 169 camera moves, which as a simple average results in 42.25 per film, as opposed to *Dracula*'s 43 camera moves. In short, *Dracula*'s pacing and use of camera movement are very much in keeping with its immediate generic successors. (It might also be worth adding that Browning also made extensive use of moving camera in his first horror film after *Dracula*. *Freaks* [1932] features 56 camera moves during a running time of approximately 61:07.)

Like *Dracula*, these four horror movies avoid depicting certain moments of graphic horror onscreen. For example, *Murder by the Clock* features two offscreen murders. *Frankenstein* uses the Monster's body to block a direct view of Little Maria when she crashes into the water in which she drowns. And *Dr. Jekyll and Mr. Hyde* reserves a number of its horrors for retellings (as when Champagne Ivy recounts being whipped and raped); the film also has Hyde murdering Ivy on the floor behind a bed, thus hiding the action from the audience's field of vision.

In terms of music, it is not surprising that a film like *Svengali* – in which the title character is a composer and pianist who hypnotizes a woman and transforms her into a great singer – features nineteen examples of music (including its opening and closing themes); more impressive is the fact that it also uses a limited amount of non-diegetic music. At the same time, it is also important to note that *Murder by the Clock* features absolutely *no* music other than its opening and closing themes. And *Frankenstein* features six examples of music, two being its opening and closing themes, and the other four stemming from the very same narrative situation: villagers celebrating a pending wedding. That said, *Frankenstein* uses only five *different* musical selections (one of the villagers' songs is heard twice).[28] This is equivalent to *Dracula*'s six uses of music, which in fact stem from five different musical selections (Schubert being heard twice). And yet it must be said that *Dracula* features diegetic music in two clearly different scenes and contexts (the concert hall and Lucy's apartment), as opposed to *Frankenstein*'s sole reliance on the villagers' celebration for its use of diegetic music. Moreover, it would not be incorrect here also to invoke Dracula's own dialogue about the howl of wolves in Transylvania ("What music they make!").

Occasionally viewers bemoan the presence of comic relief in *Dracula*, particularly as embodied by the sanitarium's attendant and maid. However, it should be noted that, of the four subsequent horror films produced in 1931, three of them feature comic relief to offset the horror. Here I would specifically cite the title character of *Svengali* (whose bathing and thievery early in the narrative provide humor); the Irish maid and Irish cop in *Murder by the Clock*, and Baron Frankenstein in *Frankenstein*.

Of Cardboard and Continuity

Perhaps the strangest argument used to decry Browning's *Dracula* comes as a result of cardboard: to be precise, a single piece of cardboard snuggly fitted in between a lamp and headboard in Mina's bedroom at the Seward Sanitarium. And it represents a major mistake in the eyes of some of *Dracula*'s critics. However, under careful examination, it becomes apparent that it was not in fact an error at all. Instead, it represents a curious instance in which critics have (unintentionally) manufactured a "mistake" to bolster their own negative critiques of the film.

Onscreen mistakes occur in many films. They happen, time and again. *Ben-Hur* (1959) famously features tire tracks in the sand, apparently made by a camera dolly. But then there are mistakes made by careless viewers who hope to be more clever than filmmakers. For years, some audience members have claimed that Charlton Heston wears a wristwatch in *Ben-Hur*, but no visual evidence supports the rumor. None whatsoever. It is a myth.

As for *Dracula*, it is undeniable that a piece of cardboard (for lack of a better term, as the object could actually be made from some other kind of material) appears in Mina's bedroom, sandwiched between a lampshade and the headboard of her bed. Those who see the cardboard as a mistake believe it was left on set accidentally (or, in an even more bizarre and completely unfounded suggestion, that cinematographer Karl Freund left in on set intentionally to exact "revenge" on Tod Browning for being an inattentive director).[29] What is undeniable is the fact that the cardboard had to have had *some* purpose. It is not as if it had been left randomly on the floor. Someone deliberately positioned it between the lamp and headboard. It simply would not stay in place otherwise.

If this is a mistake, as some would suggest, it was because the cardboard acted as an improvised "flag" used to block or limit the light on a shot – in this case, presumably a closeup of actress Helen Chandler ("Mina") – and it was then forgotten. As a result, it is visible in wide shots seen in the film. But numerous evidentiary problems emerge for that point of view. One problem is that the cardboard is used on a lamp, not a movie light. If the lamplight was a distraction, it could have been turned off or backed away from the actress.

If the lamp was meant to be out of frame in such a presumed closeup, the shade could have been tilted to direct light in the desired direction. A lower wattage bulb could also have been used.

Aside from those issues is an even bigger problem. There is no known closeup of Chandler in which light directed from the lamp exists. None appears in the film. Medium shots show Chandler in bed sleeping, but they do not feature any light from the lamp, or its general direction, whether flagged or otherwise. If the lamp was even present on set when these closeups of Chandler were shot, it does not appear to have been a factor in the lighting. The slight glare apparent in the cloth on the headboard suggests that a more diffuse light placed higher than the table lamp was used. [See Figure 11E.]

Any hope of understanding the cardboard means charting its onscreen appearances. It first appears during Dracula's initial visit to Mina's bedroom, approximately 37:30 into the running time.[30] The composition presents a medium long shot of Dracula entering Mina's room and creeping towards her bed. The lamp is turned on, but it is not a factor in the lighting of the room. Instead, it is merely a visual accent [See Figure 11F.]

The cardboard shot appears twice in this scene, broken up by the image of Mina as depicted in Figure 11E. Its point of view is curious, as Karl Freund has placed the camera behind Mina's headboard in a manner akin to an over-the-shoulder shot. The frontal shot of Mina in bed clearly shows that her headboard is placed against a bedroom wall, so that very same set wall had to be moved physically in order for Freund to obtain the shot within which we see the cardboard. The cardboard is quite visible in the lower half of the screen, with the top of it nearly in the center of the frame. As Dracula begins to crouch down towards Mina, it even blocks part of the left side of his body. [Again, see Figure 11F.]

Someone has placed both the cardboard and the lamp for use in this particular shot. The cardboard is only held up by having been carefully fitted between the lamp (which sits on a table) and the headboard; the two pieces of furniture appear to be only a few inches apart. But in the shot of Mina sleeping in her bed, neither can be seen. [Again, see Figure 11E.] At a minimum, to screen left of Mina's bed, at least a small amount of the table should be visible. Its tabletop is quite ornate, and it appears to have a diameter almost as large

Chapter 11 – CRITICAL BACKLASH

as the bottom of the lampshade. This spatial disconnect between the two shots underscores the fact that the lamp has not been used to light Mina sleeping in her bed.

The cardboard next appears in a medium long shot at approximately 64:00. The lighting of Mina's room appears the same as the prior scene, even in character (save for that thrown off by the lamp) and slightly dim, as if to suggest that the lamp is the only light source. Close examination reveals that the cardboard is in a *different* position than the earlier scene, and the table and lamp are further from the bed than they are in Figure 11F. The position of the cardboard now casts a harsher light directly onto the screen left side of Mina's pillow, and it extends from the side of the headboard, something that cannot be seen in Figure 11E. [See Figure 11G.]

At approximately 66:30, Mina can once again be seen sleeping in her bed. The table holding the lamp is not visible, but it seems possible that both were present for this shot, as there is downward light being cast onto her pillow at screen left, light which is particularly noticeable by a diagonal shadow on the headboard. The light appears on less of Mina's pillow than in Figure 11G and 11H, which suggests that the cardboard has been moved yet again, allowing light from the lamp to be present, but directed just to the side of Mina's face. [See Figure 11I.] This would suggest that, in terms of the story, a character – perhaps the nurse or maid attending to Mina – has left the lamp turned on so as to be able to see while entering her room to check on her. However, the character has also used the cardboard to prevent light from shining directly onto the patient's face and thus disrupting her sleep. At any rate, it is clear that the lamp is not used to light actres Helen Chandler's face, as her face rests in dimmer and completely even light.

The cardboard next appears at approximately 67:00. In silhouette, a hypnotized nurse who has been staring at Dracula through the terrace door lifts her arm to remove wolfbane hanging insde the door. Through the curtain, light from the lamp, as directed by the cardboard, illuminates the scene enough so that the film viewer can see inside the room. Without the lamplight cast upwards thanks to the cardboard, the shot would be too dark to see anything. [See Figure 11J.]

Figure 11G

Figure 11H

324   Chapter 11 – CRITICAL BACKLASH

Figure 11I

Figure 11J

Figure 11K

Soon thereafter, at approximately 67:45, the nurse opens the terrace door, with Dracula entering Mina's room. The room appears noticeably darker than during Dracula's earlier visit, or during the Van Helsing/Seward sequence. The light from the lamp is crucial at this point, with the cardboad not only shielding lamplight from beaming onto Mina's face, but also directing it upwards onto the wall, thus creating an eerie visual effect. [See Figure 11K.]

To believe that the cardboard is an accident, it is necessary believe that everyone on the set, from Browning and Freund and various other crewmembers to actors like Lugosi and Chandler, has either not noticed or has forgotten the cardboard for *two* different lighting setups. That is in addition to believing that they forgot or did not notice the cardboard even as someone has moved the table, lamp, and the cardboard at least twice. And if this was an accident, the cardboard also accidentally kept light off Mina's face in each instance, as well as directing it to places in the set that were helpful. [Again, see Figure 11K.]

Can all of this really be a mistake, even though the London sequences are replete with other illumınated lamps in other scenes (including Lucy's bedroom, Seward's library, and Seward's laboratory)? If so, the mistake was far worse than has been previously suggested. Three publicity stills exist depicting Mina in bed with the cardboard on the lamp. In one, Dr. Seward and a nurse stand, watching Mina from a distance. In the other, the maid is absent, with Seward sitting at Mina's bedside. He places wolfbane on her neck while she sleeps (an action not depicted in the film's footage). Here is yet a different lighting setup, higher key than the aforementioned film scenes. A third still depicts Dracula advancing

Figure 11L

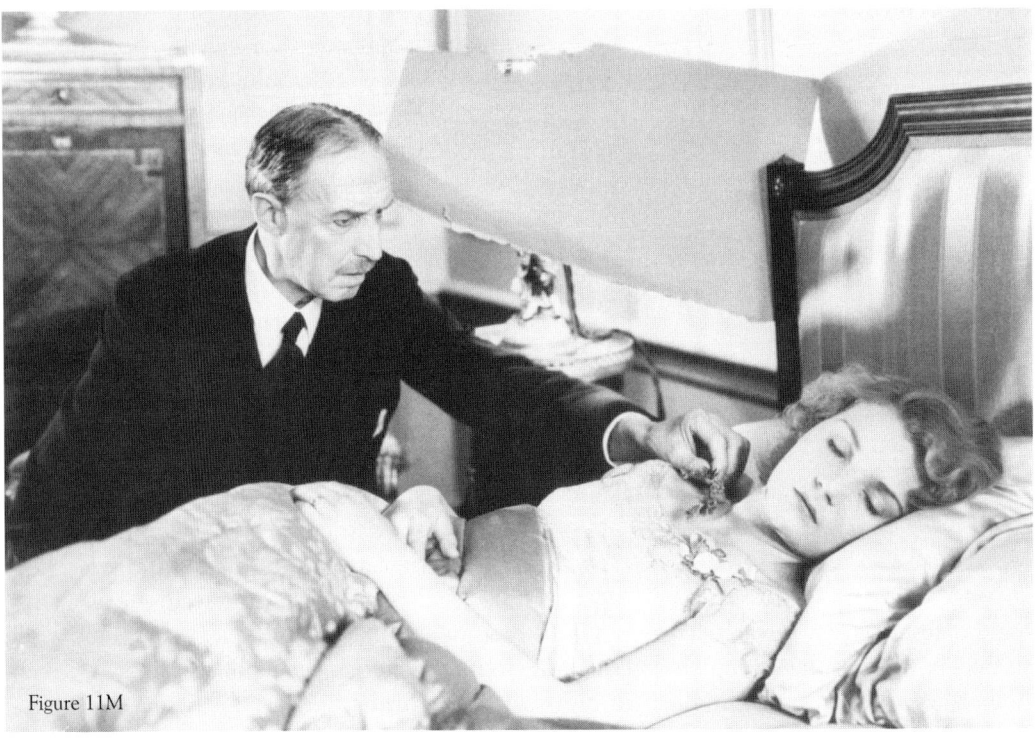

Figure 11M

Figure 11N *(Courtesy of Fritz Frising)*

on a helpless Mina with a hypnotized nurse in the room; the lighting setup is dramatically different from the aforementioned two still photographs. So now, the mistake has been made *several* times. Added to those who have not seen the cardboard are the skilled photographer Roman Freulich and actor Herbert Bunston, who certainly should have noticed it, as in one photograph his face appears to be only a couple of inches from it, with his own head creating a shadow upon it. But upon reflection, it is clear that at least someone did see it, because in the publicity stills, the cardboard itself appears quite *different* than in any shot used in the film. At a minimum, it has obviously been repositioned yet again. However, close comparison suggests that it might even be a different piece of cardboard than the one used in the film. [Figures 11L, 11M, and 11N offer images of these three publicity stills.]

Believing that the cardboard is a mistake thus means believing that several accidents occurred, given the various light setups and cardboard repositioning that occured, with it always "accidentally" working to keep the light from an sick character's eyes. Either that, or it means that Karl Freund took vengeance on Browning and also required others on the set to be complicit, including a stills photographer. Evidence exists for neither view, and both strain credulity under the slightest scrutiny. (Indeed, Karl Freund and his wife even invited Tod Browning to their home for Freund's birthday party in 1933.)[31]

Indeed, it is quite apparent that the cardboard was *not* a mistake. One could argue that Browning (or, more likely, an art director) did not make a wise choice in using a potentially distracting prop. Or, one could argue, it was a good choice, as it appears like a realistic, improvised aid for characters attempting to assist an ill Mina, characters who need to care for her through the night even while she slumbers. At any rate, no critics mentioned the cardboard prior to the 1990s, which suggests that the film's earlier detractors either were not bothered by it or – like the bulk of viewers for the film's first sixty-odd years – had not even noticed it.

Chapter 11 – CRITICAL BACKLASH

Figure 11O.

Figure 11P.

Sleight of Hand

The cardboard is not the only element in *Dracula* that has generated adverse comment. When the coach arrives at the Transylvanian inn, its horses are pointed in the opposite direction of the gate; when it is time for Renfield to leave, the coach is pointed towards the gate. The film does not show the coach turning around around, but this does not strike me as a problem. Ten shots and nearly two minutes of screen time unfold in which we do not see the coach at all, and so enough time passes for an offscreen driver to have moved it. After all, Hollywood films do not usually depict every single movement that its characters undertake. True, we do not hear background noise of the coach moving, but to complain about that fact would be asking too much in my view. *Dracula* is an early talkie produced in an era before multitrack sound recording, and so to have tried to feature noise from an unseen source could have proved distracting. No, this is not a mistake so much as it is the intentional avoidance of depicting unnecessary onscreen action.

Other criticisms focus on Dracula's appearance when disguised as the coach driver who transports Renfield to the castle. Lugosi wears a hat and garment around his head, but most of his face is visible. [See Figure 11O.] Here the complaint is that Renfield seems not to recognize Dracula upon meeting him formally at the castle, even though he has caught a clear view of his face as the coach driver. But two considerations should be made on this point. One is that F. W. Murnau's *Nosferatu* (1922) does much the same, concealing its vampire with a hat and collar but little else, allowing his face and exaggerated features to be in clear view. [See Figure 11P.] The second point – which is related to a similar requirement in *Nosferatu* – is that the audiences in 1931 needed that visual information so that *they* could identify the coach driver as being Dracula, as many of them would not have been as familiar with the story as their modern counterparts.[32] In short, this is not a mistake either.

One of the most obviously false comments made about *Dracula* is the incessant repetition of the "fact" that the film depicts human blood only once: Renfield pricking his finger on a paper clip in Dracula's Chambers. Here are reverberations in an echo chamber, as even many viewers who have watched the film only once can immediately attest otherwise. Van Helsing mixes Renfield's blood with another chemical in a test tube in his laboratory. The blood appears right in front of our eyes, and we hear the word "blood" being used in the dialogue, in English and also in Latin ("sanguine"). Hence, we see blood *twice* in the film. The mistake is again one made by latter-day critics, not the 1931 film.

Figure 11Q

Figure 11R

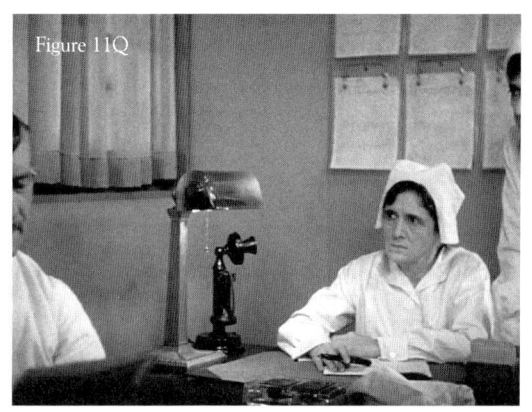

Does *Dracula* feature actual mistakes? It does indeed. It features numerous errors, which makes the cardboard debacle all the more of a distraction. For example, an opening title card misspells the word "President" (in reference to Carl Laemmle, Sr.) as "Presient." As Renfield leaves the inn, the arrangement of the villagers who wave goodbye to him changes from one shot to the next, as can be seen at the edit at approximately 5:04. At roughly 50:00, a camera shadow appears in the scene of Martin reading a newspaper article about the Woman in White. [See Figure 11Q.] More problematically, a film light can momentarily be seen on the floor behind a couch during a right-to-left pan at approximately 59:50. [See Figure 11R.]

Of course continuity errors and typographical errors in opening credits occur in many films, including some that would be considered extremely important. For example, director Stanley Kubrick has long held a reputation for being a perfectionist. But the credits of Kubrick's *Dr. Strangelove* (1964) contain a misspelling with their reference to the film being "base on the book *Red Alert*," rather than "based." And continuity errors occur in various Kubrick films, including the intricately-planned *2001: A Space Odyssey* (1968).

But there is also, as they say, the illusion of the cinema. The line between continuity errors and successful editing – which can operate a bit like sleight-of-hand magic tricks – is blurred. For well over eight decades, even *Dracula*'s detractors have not noticed some of its continuity errors, which speaks to how minor they are.

Indeed, the fact that both of *Dracula*'s most glaring continuity errors have gone hitherto unnoticed might also speak to the lack of careful attention the film's critics have paid to it. Consider Figure 11E, which we can now examine clearly without it being surrounded by the fog of the cardboard nonsense. The image shows Mina sleeping in bed on the *first* night that Dracula bites her. Van Helsing has just arrived at the Seward Sanitarium. He has not yet heard about her "dream," and he has not yet ordered wolfbane to be placed in her room. But what is resting on Mina's neck in this image? Wolfbane, which does absolutely nothing to discourage Dracula's approach towards her, or his biting of the neck where it rests. Figure 11E is actually footage shot for use on Dracula's *second* visit to Mina's room – footage similar to that which appears at approximately 66:30, though framed a bit wider – but which was edited into the scene of Dracula's *first* visit.

And then there is *Dracula*'s greatest magic trick, for its most obvious error is one that went unnoticed, even after all the years of scrutiny, even after all the efforts to decry it, until I discovered it (along with the aforementioned shot of Mina with wolfbane) in 2006.[33] *Dracula*'s critics – some of whom have not noticed their own errors of observation – have

Chapter 11 – CRITICAL BACKLASH

Figure 11S

Figure 11T

Figure 11U

Figure 11V

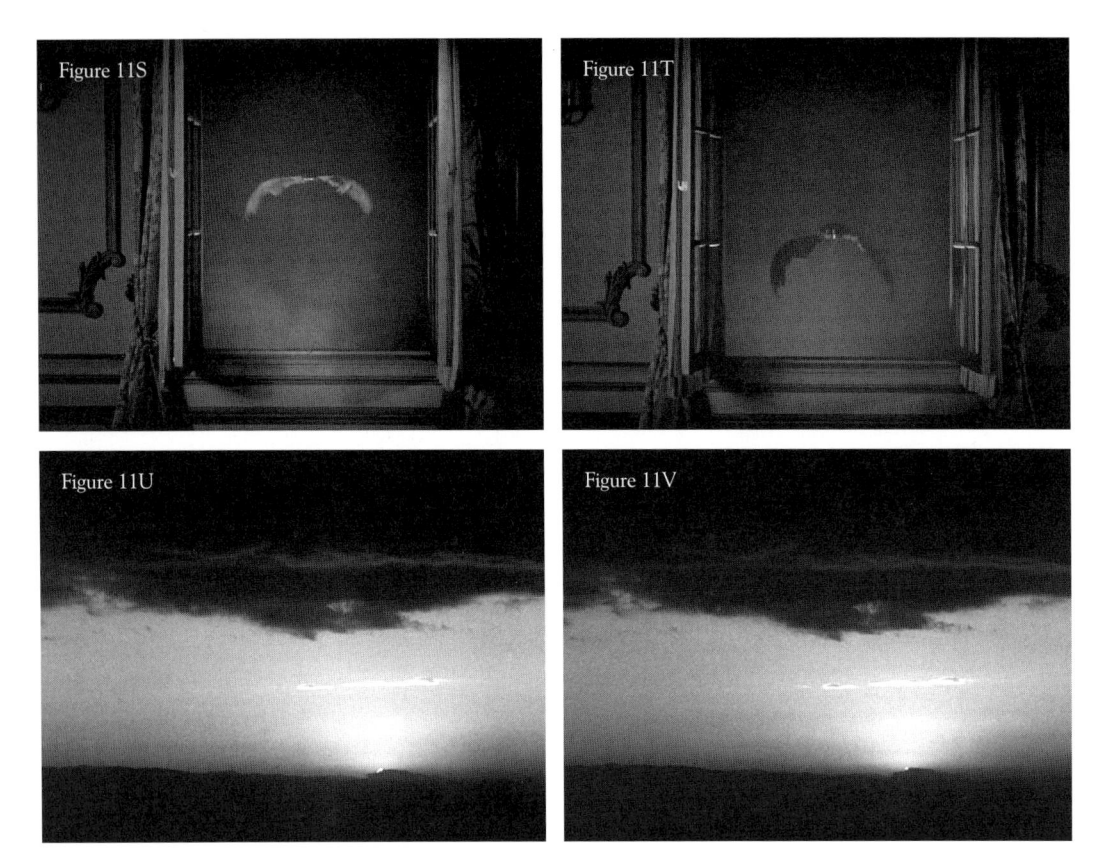

not seen this trick either. And if no one sees these tricks, then they are not so much errors as they are examples of successful editing.

Consider Lucy's London apartment, which features a large window. Before retiring to bed, she opens the window, not realizing that Dracula is on the sidewalk below. At approximately 28 minutes into the film, we see a shot of her window from the interior of her room. A bat is flapping just outside it, about to enter the room. [See Figure 11S.]

Nearly ten minutes later, Dracula makes his first visit to Mina's bedroom in Whitby. She is asleep in her bed. Then, at approximately 37:30, we see a shot of the window from the room's interior. A bat is flapping just outside the window. It is footage from the same shot used to represent Lucy's London apartment. [See Figure 11T.]

The two different rooms in two different buildings in two different cities have the *same* window. If that is not enough, reusing the window for Mina's bedroom is particularly strange, as other shots in the film indicate that Mina's bedroom does not have any windows at all. Instead, it has terrace doors.

To add to these two key examples, I can add one more that I have never mentioned in print until this book. Three different images of sunsets appear in the film, the first being a foreboding sunset in Transylvania at approximately 4:10. The next appears during the Whitby sequence at approximately 34:20; it too is ominous, with heavy, dark clouds filling the upper third of the frame, but it pictures a clearly different landscape from its predecessor. [See Figure 11U.] The final sunset appears at approximately 54:00. [See Figure 11V.]

Publicity still illustrates the signage at the Transylvanian inn.

A comparison of Figure 11U and 11V reveals another trick, as Figure 11V not only (appropriately, given the consistent narrative setting) repeats the same landscape, but also offers an image of the *very same* sunset, the footage filmed only seconds after Figure 11U, as a comparison of the cloud formation discloses.

Conclusion

Are there things in *Dracula* that may or may not be problematic? The answer would vary from viewer to viewer, of course. The spider at Dracula's castle is clearly a prop, and is the least effective special effect in the film. I am not fond of the fact that the shots below deck in the *Vesta* – which do show some movement, as if to mimic a sea voyage – appear distinctly at odds with the much rockier voyage depicted in old footage repurposed from an earlier film. I am also disappointed by the wooden sound of Carfax Abbey's "stone" steps. But minor flaws are minor, and they are small components of a larger whole.

The films of Stanley Kubrick reveal extraordinary deliberation and careful attention to detail, something which is not undermined by their occasional lapses of continuity. Similarly, it would be wrong to let a small number of continuity errors in *Dracula* limit an investigation of its attention to detail. The sets are stunning, carefully and thoroughly dressed. Consider, for example, the fact that the handles on Dracula's coffin are more ornate than those of his wives. Gaze at the otherwordly pockets of fog emerging from the ground near Dracula's coffin. Witness the breath that lifts from the mouths of Martin and the Maid as they stand outside in the dark of night. Examine the packing label on Dracula's "box" at Carfax Abbey. Ponder the intricacies of Dracula's medallion, which appears to be an amalgam of an Ottoman Order of Merit award with a Turkish coin, quite appropriate given the vampire's war-like past.[34] Scrutinize Dr. Seward's monkey bookends, which are seen in his laboratory and library. Such bookends were popular in Victorian England, and they seem particularly appropriate for a man of science.

And then there is the use of language. Let us think about the toast that Lucy recites at the concert hall. The first half seems to have originated with one of the film's screenwriters. But then Lucy offers the line, "Quaff a cup to the dead already! Hurrah for the next who dies!" It seems to be a prophecy of her own pending doom. Those words stem from Irish writer Bartholomew Dowling's *The Revel*, composed in the mid-1800s. The poem was famous in Victorian England, having been included in editor E. C. Stedman's *A Victorian Anthology, 1837-1895* (1895). By that time, *The Revel* had been set to music as well.

Or consider the use of the Hungarian language at the inn. We hear a prayer in Hungarian, as well as Hungarian dialogue while Renfield lobbies to venture to the Borgo Pass. The coach has Hungarian words written on it, as does the front of the inn. In addition to having a Hungarian name, the inn advertises "Hites Szesz Pálinka Kimérés," an indication that they sell an authorized brand of palinka, as opposed to a locally-distilled home brew. Another sign claims, "Bor Sor és Pálinka," meaning "Beer, Wine, and Pálinka." The reference to pálinka is accurate: it is a plum brandy still popular in the region. However, in addition to advertising different drinks, the phrase "Bor Sor és Pálinka" is a common, welcoming phrase in Hungarian. That it can be seen so clearly on the inn's exterior is ironic, as the warnings that Renfield receives (and his eventual fate) are wonderfully, dramatically out of sync with such a welcoming phrase.

What do all of these examples mean? Collectively, it is clear that *Dracula*'s critics have sought to provide evidence to substantiate their claims that it is a problematic film, one that was (in part or whole) poorly directed. However, two factors emerge from a meta-analysis of their work. Firstly, issues like the cardboard reveal that they have at times relied on faulty evidence, even while ignoring the film's overall attention to detail.

Secondly, I would argue that some of *Dracula*'s critics may not as clever as they believe, and have not viewed the film as closely as they have imagined, as they have never noticed continuity errors like the reuse of Lucy's window, Mina's wolfbane, and the Whitby sunset. The absence of these examples from their work requires us to question whether a continuity error is in fact an error if no one notices it. In other words, these are examples of where the term "sleight of hand" trumps the term "mistake."

1. Geltzer, George. "Tod Browning." *Films in Review* (Oct. 1953): 415.
2. Everson, William K. "Horror Films." *Films in Review* (Jan. 1954): 15.
3. Everson, William K. *Classics of the Horror Film* (New York: Citadel, 1974): 194.
4. Clarens, Carlos. *An Illustrated History of the Horror Film* (New York: Capricorn Books, 1967): 61.
5. Brosnan, John. *The Horror People* (New York: St. Martin's, 1976): 30.
6. Halliwell, Leslie. *The Dead that Walk* (London: Grafton, 1986): 35.
7. Weaver, Tom. "*Dracula* (1931)." In Brunas, Micheal, John Brunas, and Tom Weaver. *Universal Horrors* (Jefferson, NC: McFarland, 1990): 13.
8. Skal, David J. *Hollywood Gothic: The Tangled Web of Dracula from Novel to Stage to Screen* (New York: W. W. Norton, 1990).
9. Halliwell, p. 37.
10. Skal, David J. and Elias Savada. *Dark Carnival: The Secret World of Tod Browning, Hollywood's Master of the Macabre* (New York: Anchor, 1995): 155-156.
11. Tudor, Andrew. *Monsters and Mad Scientists: A Cultural History of the Horror Movie* (Oxford: Basil Blackwell, 1989): 161.
12. See, for example: Salt, Barry. "Statistical Style Analysis of Motion Pictures." *Film Quarterly* Vol. 28, No. 1 (Fall 1974): 13-2; Bordwell, David. "Intensified Continuity Visual Style in Contemporary American Film." *Film Quarterly* Vol. 55, No. 3 (Spring 2002): 16-28. See also http://www.cinemetrics.lv.
13. The twenty films in this study include: *Sin Takes a Holiday* (Pathe) and *The Bat Whispers* (United Artists), both of which were released in November 1930; *Hook, Line and Sinker* (RKO), *Morocco* (Paramount), and *The Devil to Pay!* (United Artists), all three of which were released in December 1930; *Little Caesar* (Warner Bros.), *Other Men's Women* (Warner Bros.), and *No Limit* (Paramount), all three of which were released in January 1931; *Cimarron* (RKO), *Kept Husbands* (RKO), *Millie* (RKO), *Illicit* (Warner Bros.), *Dance, Fools, Dance* (MGM), *Parlor, Bedroom and Bath* (MGM), *Resurrection* (Universal), and *Reaching for the Moon* (United Artists), all eight of which were released in February 1931; *The Drums of Jeopardy* (Tiffany) and *Ten Cents a Dance* (Columbia), both of which were released in March 1931; and *Dirigible* (Columbia) and *The Secret Six* (MGM), both of which were released in April 1931. For this study, I have examined the 35mm flat version of *The Bat Whispers*, as it represents the version that most audiences would have seen in 1930 and 1931.
14. The individual ASLs for the twenty films in this study are as follows: *Sin Takes a Holiday* (13.8 seconds), *The Bat Whispers* (9.8 seconds), *Hook, Line and Sinker* (8.5 seconds), *Morocco* (11.4 seconds), *The Devil to Pay!* (10.3 seconds), *Little Caesar* (9.5 seconds), *Other Men's Women* (9.7 seconds), *No Limit* (16.5 seconds), *Cimarron* (11.3 seconds), *Kept Husbands* (8.7 seconds), *Millie* (15 seconds), *Illicit* (8.3 seconds), *Dance, Fools, Dance* (15.9 seconds), *Parlor, Bedroom and Bath* (10.3 seconds), *Resurrection* (10.2 seconds), *Reaching for the Moon* (14.9 seconds), *The Drums of Jeopardy* (8.7 seconds), *Ten Cents a Dance* (16.5 seconds), *Dirigible* (6.9 seconds), and *The Secret Six* (9.5 seconds).
15. Skal, David J. *The Monster Show: A Cultural History of Horror* (New York: W. W. Norton, 1993): 124.
16. See, for example: "Jump Cuts and Blind Spots." *Wide Angle* Vol. 6, No. 1 (1984): 4-11.
17. For example, *Dirigible* includes over fifty cuts of less than thirty degrees on the axis.
18. Lennig, Arthur. *The Count: The Life and Films of Bela "Dracula" Lugosi*. (New York: G. P. Putnam's Sons, 1974): 100.
19. Skal, *Hollywood Gothic*, p. 130.
20. One should approach Arthur Lennig's observations with a degree of caution. For example, in his book *The Immortal Count: The Life and Films of Bela Lugosi* (Lexington, KY: University of Lexington Press, 2003), he states that "Browning has been blamed for not allowing Freund a free hand in the shooting, but one must remember that when Freund directed *The Mummy* two years later, he didn't move the camera very much either" (p. 107). The phrase "very much either" is qualitative, to be sure, but it implies a degree of commonality between the two films with regard to the amount of camera movement in them. However, that is not the case. *Dracula* features 43 camera moves, 28 pans, and two tilts. In stark contrast, *The Mummy* features 62 camera moves, 59 pans, and 24 tilts. It should be added that *The Mummy*'s running time is approximately 90 seconds shorter than *Dracula*'s.
21. Indeed, it would seem that Van Helsing's curtain speech in the film (absent from prints since 1938) also unfolded in a crane shot.
22. One of them – perhaps not coincidentally given that it was also made at Universal and used the very same crane – is *Resurrection*.
23. Barry Salt observes that the other Hollywood studios "acquired large camera cranes in imitation of Universal" (p. 26). See "Film Style and Technology in the Thirties." *Film Quarterly* Vol. 30, No. 1 (Autumn 1976): 19-32.
24. "Phil Goldstone Drops 'All Talkies' Phrase." *Hollywood Filmograph* 16 Aug. 1930: 7.
25. "25 Per Cent Dialogue Reduction Ordered for Universal Pictures." *Motion Picture Herald* 29 Oct. 1932: 12. In this article, the trade notes that Junior Laemmle had ordered that dialogue in Universal films be cut to the "bare necessity."
26. The twenty films feature a combined total of 181 examples of music, which results in an average of 9.05 per film. In all of these cases, I am counting opening and closing music (where it exists).
27. The individual ASLs of these four films are as follows: *Svengali* (7.1 seconds), *Murder by the Clock* (11.5 seconds), *Frankenstein* (8.5 seconds), and *Dr. Jekyll and Mr. Hyde* (13.2 seconds).

28 According to Universal's final cue sheet for *Frankenstein*, which I have viewed courtesy of William H. Rosar, the film's five musical selections are: *Main Titles* (written by a Universal staff composer), *Old Tyroleon Folk Song* (public domain), *Polka in F* (public domain), *Laendler No. 1* (ie, *Ländler*, public domain, heard twice in the film), and *Grand Appassionato* (written by Guiseppe Becce, and published by Belwyn).

29 Skal, *Hollywood Gothic*, p. 139.

30 Of necessity, the use of minutes and seconds to specify given shots in this chapter is approximate. Different prints on different home video formats vary, ranging from the inclusion of modern studio logos and FBI warnings as a preface to the film's original credits to the minor variance in frame rates for different media and in different regions of the world. I offer these approximations merely as a rough guide for the reader to find given shots within the film.

31 "Freunds Observe Karl's Birthday." *Los Angeles Examiner* 22 Dec. 1933.

32 Various persons have drawn attention to Lugosi's appearance as the coach driver, including Skal in *Hollywood Gothic*, p. 163.

33 I first discovered the re-use of Lucy's window when analyzing *Dracula* for a book I wrote with Richard Sheffield entitled *Bela Lugosi, Dreams and Nightmares* (Collectables, 2006). I subsequently mentioned the window and the shot of Mina with wolfbane in an essay entitled "The Curious Undead Life of Tod Browning's *Dracula* (1931)" in *Monsters from the Vault* (Summer 2011): 5-33.

34 Here I am thankful to the careful research of Jeff Carlson.

Chapter 12
THE SPANISH-LANGUAGE DRACULA

As Chapters 3 and 5 discussed, Universal produced a Spanish-language version of *Dracula* in addition to the Tod Browning film. Using the same sets and script, George Melford directed a different cast, headed by Carlos Villarias as Dracula. Horror-film historians occasionally mentioned the film in the sixties and seventies, but it was largely forgotten until a screening sponsored by the Museum of Modern Art in August of 1977.[1] Though the print was an incomplete copy on loan from the Library of Congress, Melford's film fascinated many of the viewers, in large measure because it represented something of a discovery, a largely-unseen Universal horror movie.

William K. Everson's *More Classics of the Horror Film* (Citadel, 1986) offered the first major analysis of the film, claiming to readers that the film made a better use of sets like Dracula's Chambers than the Browning version. Everson also praised the film for the mist that arises out of Dracula's coffin when it opens, its depiction of Dracula's journey to England, and the "suprisingly erotic" qualities of its leading lady, Lupita Tovar.[2] Tovar's allure had earlier drawn attention at the MOMA screening.

Subsequent discussions of the film appeared in an essay by George E. Turner published in *American Cinematographer* in 1988, as well as in an essay coauthored by Turner and Philip J. Riley that accompanied the publication of *Dracula*'s shooting script in 1990.[3] Both texts generated further interest in Melford's film.

Soon thereafter, David J. Skal's book *Hollywood Gothic* (W. W. Norton, 1990) explored the Spanish-language *Dracula* in a lengthy chapter, offering numerous still photographs from it, as well as information gleaned from a print of the film archived at the Cinemateca de Cuba, which included important footage missing from the Library of Congress copy.[4] While Everson enthused about certain aspects of the Spanish version, Skal went to great lengths to promote it as being superior to the English version. Never before had such a beleaguered film as the Browning *Dracula* had to contend with a shadow version of itself.

In 1992, Universal released a restoration of the Spanish-language *Dracula* to home video, which rightly created much excitement. Here was essentially a "new" Universal horror movie from the classic era. All of the others had been viewed and reviewed *ad nauseum*. But this was different, a fresh film released with analysis in *Hollywood Gothic* having already paved the way to its acceptance. Being shot at night with arguably fewer resources, the film assumed the position of an underdog status to the Browning version. That Lupita Tovar, who had played Eva ("Mina" by another name), was alive and participating in the rediscovery festivities created even more fanfare. The restored footage from the Cuban print also intrigued many viewers, as it revealed that Dracula's Transylvanian wives were depicted as more overtly sexualized than their counterparts in the Browning film. Titillation was a key reason that many responded favorably to what Universal and others imprecisely but repeatedly referred to as the "Spanish Version."

With little debate, numerous critics suggested that the Spanish-language version (hereafter the "Melford version") was better than the Browning version in every way, save perhaps for the fact that Bela Lugosi gave a more memorable performance as Dracula than Carlos Villarias. Consider, for example, Skal's comments in *Hollywood Gothic*, which claim the Melford version was "nothing if not ambitious, and today can be read as an almost shot-for-shot scathing critique of the Browning version." He adds:

Cinematographer George Robinson brought a highly developed visual sensibility to the assignment, employing a highly mobile camera, complex compositions, and deep shadows. ... The American compositions are remarkably flat, like a play performed on a narrow stage apron. Robinson's camera work is distinguished by multiple planes of focus and action.[5]

After the restoration was released on home video, these arguments – as repeated by various critics and fans, concretized. The Melford featured a striking and mobile camera, as compared to what Carlos Clarens had earlier called the "static, pedestrian, and uncinematic" Browning film.[6] Its story was more developed, as some scenes were longer than in the Browning version. The editing was faster paced. It was a lost classic, back from its cinematic grave to take its rightful place as a classic horror film.

Certainly at least that was what many persons quickly and confidently proclaimed in the early nineties. But there were two key voices who offered opposing views. One was a critic at *Variety*, who viewed both the Browning and Melford versions when MCA released them on VHS in October of 1992:

Contrasting the works, Dracula's entrance is more dramatic in the Spanish, beginning with a wide shot before going to a dolly and zoom, but in general, the film is far less ambitious technically [than the Browning] with fewer dolly or tracking shots. Images are more static with less tension, and shots tend to be wider with fewer closeups and less involvement in the individual characters.
Although both films share the same cutaways, the Spanish version lacks extras, making it look stagebound. ... Dialog has also been trimmed in the English version, picking up the pace. ... While the Browning clocks in at a brisk 75 minutes, Melford's creeps along to 104 minutes with ponderous pauses and plodding dialog.[7]

Overall, this critic made his final judgment known by pronouncing that Browning had directed the "superior" film.

The *Variety* review was little-read outside of those in the film industry, and certainly not by the bulk of persons buying or renting the Melford version on home video. However, some of those persons – particularly those who were horror movie fans – might well have seen

Publicity still of Carlos Villarias in the Spanish-language version of Dracula *(1931). (Courtesy of Buddy Barnett)*

film historian Tom Weaver's review in *Fangoria*. Weaver cautioned that deliberations about which was the better film could only be at an early stage, because the "foremost" asset of the Melford film was that it was something fresh, something different than the overly familiar Browning version. "Is it actually a better film than Lugosi's, or will it just *seem* better until the novelty wears off?", he importantly asked.[8] But Weaver's careful discriminations were not heeded.

"Better" is a personal judgment, and everyone has a right to their opinion. Melford's opening credits, featuring a burning candle and billowing cobwebs, offer a different approach to the art deco bat artwork used in the Browning. The vampire women who approach Renfield are more overtly sexualized in their behavior and appearance than those depicted in the Browning. The sequence aboard the *Vesta* is handled quite differently. In the Melford version, Renfield screams mainiacally as frightened crewmembers watch Dracula emerge on deck, as opposed to Browning's more subtle approach, in which Renfield does not rave and in which Dracula quietly surveys a crew that does not yet see him. In these instances, I do not know which is better. They are simply different interpretations of the same scenes; judgments on them would surely be no more than personal opinions.

In the Melford, we actually see Eva/Mina bite Harker, even if just for a moment, with his scream heard emanating from offscreen space. Two atmospheric shots show Dracula with top hat approaching the sanitarium for his announced visit. Each image has eerie light cast through the trees, though both are slightly marred. In the first, actor Villarias seems to have a bit of trouble finding his footing; in the second, editor Tavares strangely begins the shot before Villarias has begun walking, which appears odd in view of the fact that we have just seen Villarias walking in his previous shot.[9] At any rate, these choices also represent a different artistic approach from Browning's.

However, some of Melford's decisions are quite questionable. At the film's conclusion, Dracula carries Eva/Mina on the stairs of Carfax Abbey. In the Melford, Dracula has to rest her on the steps to kill Renfield, and then has to pick her back up. Neither action looks particularly memorable, and they involve unnecessary screen time. By contrast, the Browning film has Mina walking slowly, her apparel featuring a long train. As a result, she visually echoes the wives seen at Dracula's castle, a subtle indication that she may soon become one of them.

Other aspects of the Melford seem even less wise. Unlike the Browning, his version does not show a closeup of the crucifix given to Renfield at the Transylvanian inn. In the Melford (especially if we wish to judge the film on its own merits, rather than relying on narrative/visual information we know from the Browning or from other sources), the crucifix is not particularly visible, in part because Melford's Renfield quickly pokes it into his clothing. Moreover, Melford treats the nighttime, outdoor banter between Martin and Seward's maid noticeably differently from Browning. In the Browning, the maid tentatively agrees with Martin that she may be crazy like all the others. But in the Melford, she huffily walks out of the frame, upset by what he has said. Her acting – like a good deal of the acting in the Melford version – seems quite overdone.

And then there is the breaking of the fourth wall. During the nickelodeon era, it became increasingly taboo for actors to look directly into the camera. When it occurred on rare occasions in the Classical Hollywood Style, it was usually for a clear purpose: for example, Oliver Hardy staring at the audience in hopes of gaining sympathy after Stan Laurel has made a mistake. Browning has Lugosi stare directly into the lens, particularly when we see his face for the first time. It is as if we, the audience, are a potential victim; Victor Halperin would explore this device again in *White Zombie* (1932). Melford also chose to have Dracula look directly into the camera lens, such as in his confrontation with Van Helsing. But he has Van Helsing look directly into the camera as well, which muddles an effect that otherwise would have been reserved for the hypnotic vampire. [See Figure 12A.]

Figure 12A

The Melford version's use of Browning outtakes is also unfortunate, even if Melford had little choice but to incorporate them. Lugosi and Carlos Villarias (Melford's Dracula) do not look alike. Lugosi is taller and thinner, and his eyes and hands appear noticeably different. But the Melford version has to rely on Lugosi footage for a number of images. Some of them appear in the London sequence when Dracula walks to the outside of Lucy's window, staring up before transforming (offscreen) into a bat and flying into her room. In the Browning, we see Dracula staring upwards at Lucy, who can clearly be seen at the window from his exterior vantage point on the sidewalk. Melford combines footage of Lugosi with closeups of Villarias' eyes, and has Dracula stare upwards four times. However, Lucy ("Lucia," in this version) has moved away from the window *before* Dracula looks up the *first* time, meaning that he repeatedly stares at what, for him, has always been an empty window. In other words, the problems extend beyond the ill-matching footage of the two actors.

Other Browning outtakes also suffer in the Melford. Consider for example, Browning's underrated medical classroom scene in which Seward finds the bites on Lucy's neck. It unfolds in three shots, each showing medical students watching the examination from tiered seating. In one of Browning's most subtle and yet most eerie uses of German Expressionism, the students are all arranged in different poses, and each is frozen (so much so that in a high angle shot, they also seem to be mannequins). This is akin to what Lotte Eisner would call an "expressionist" handling of crowds, and in the Browning it is an effect that deserves praise.[10]

By contrast, the Melford version opens his hospital scene with an outtake of the high-angle shot from Browning, but, for reasons that seem unclear, he shot his own actors from a different angle that does not depic the student seating.[11] He does include a fascinating closeup of the bitemark on Lucy's neck (another Browning outtake, it would seem, given the hair color of the victim), but the coherence of the entire scene is harmed by Melford combining Browning's footage with his own.

Another outtake from the Browning footage in the Melford film is as extremely problematic narratively as it is unnecessary visually. During the film's climactic scenes, Van Helsing and Harker follow Dracula and Mina to Carfax Abbey. They rush in their efforts to save Mina, while Dracula is rushed to stay ahead of the onset of daylight. In a staggeringly poor choice – one that has surprisingly gone without mention until now – the Melford version opts to use a Browning outtake of what is indisputably a *sunset*, rather than a sunrise, at this critical moment in the plot. Here the (quite pronounced) mistake belongs to the Melford version, not the outtake, as the sunset footage should simply not have been incorporated.[12]

These are my reactions, which may be very different from those of other viewers. Every filmgoer will have their personal preferences, and hopefully – as Weaver implied audiences should do in his *Fangoria* review – they will (or at least should) return occasionally to both films with an open eye. But many things said when the Melford version re-emerged are not personal opinions. They were objective claims about the Melford in comparison to the Browning, and many of these claims are notably false.

To begin, much has been made of Melford's use of moving camera. Moving camera synthesizes space; editing fragments it. Filmmakers often have clear reasons to do one or the other, or both in combination within a single sequence. If more moving camera is inherently "better," whatever that means, then Sokurov's *Russian Ark* (2002) – which was filmed using a single, 96-minute steadicam shot – must be the most important film in history, at least from a visual standpoint. But that is not the case, even though *Russian Ark* is certainly a fascinating film.

Moving camera and how much it should be used in a film is a debatable topic, and one that might vary for different films and different scenes within them. Such was true during the Classical Hollywood period. For example, in 1944, *Motion Picture Daily* wrote:

> *Years ago, cameras became restless because of thos two famous German imports,* Variety *[1925] and* The Last Laugh *[1924]. It got so bad for a time that sitting in a theatre anticipating enjoyment was like experiencing an extreme case of seasickness. Quiet was restored finally, but it took time.*[13]

As a result of the perceived overuse of camera movement, the same trade chided Hollywood filmmakers for being too "impressionable."

That said, all of the many critics who have claimed that the Melford version of *Dracula* employs more moving camera are wrong. They are, without doubt, mathematically incorrect. Whatever one makes of that fact, it is indisputably a fact. The Browning film uses more moving camera than the Melford version. Specifically, the Browning features 43 camera moves, whereas the Melford features only 37. Moreover, the Browning film features 28 camera pans, whereas the Melford features only 13. The Browning film features 2 camera tilts (in addition to tilts used in combination with pans), whereas the Melford features no tilts. These ratios become even more stark when considering that the Melford film runs approximately 29 minutes *longer* than the Browning.

How then could this myth have arisen, initiated and repeated by reputable scholars? One reason perhaps is the fact that the Melford version features three crane shots, as

Figure 12B

Figure 12C

Figure 12D

opposed to only two in the Browning version as it currently exists.[14] However, two of the three crane shots in the Melford are in fact alternate takes shot by Browning's crew. Indeed, the impressive and singular crane shot introducing the Seward Sanitarium in the Browning exists in the Melford as *two* discarded shots from the English-language version which had to be stitched together. Here is not a reason to heap praise on Melford.

No, it is the third crane shot in the Melford that is responsible for the moving-camera myth. A skillful image that comes at Dracula's castle, the camera moves past Renfield (who has just swung his cane at a bat) and ascends the old staircase to introduce Dracula holding a candle. As he does throughout the film, Carlos Villarias bugs his eyes as opposed to Lugosi's more subtle, piercing gaze. While well-achieved and certainly to be admired, the shot unfortunately precedes a troubled sequence. For example, Renfield sees Dracula, but then he walks up the steps to be at relative eye level to Dracula before either character speaks. That action takes approximately twelve seconds, resulting in an odd pause where two persons have acknowledged one another, but neither speaks a word.

When Renfield reaches the same step as Dracula, they are depicted in a two shot with Dracula on screen left and Renfield on screen right. At approximately 11:30, the shot crosses the 180-degree line, a violation of Classical Hollywood norms. As a result, all of a sudden, for no apparent reason, their positions are reversed, with Renfield on screen left and Dracula on screen right. That this was a last-minute, poorly-made choice is made all the more clear when we note that the two are not properly lit in the second of the two shots; in fact, as Dracula's head moves, we see some problematic shadows on his forehead. [See Figures 12B and 12C.]

Thus, whatever is gained by the impressive crane shot is largely lost by the poor lighting and editing that follow, as well as by the delayed introduction of the characters to one another. Moreover, not only does the Melford version *not* use the classic dialogue "I bid you welcome," it loses the geography that separates the two characters in the Browning version, in which Dracula on the staircase literally towers high above the man who becomes his slave, a position later echoed aboard the *Vesta* when Renfield kneels before his "master."

If there is any other reason that viewers mistakenly believe the Melford features more moving camera than the Browning, it is due to a lengthy mobile shot inside Dracula's Chambers (the "more comfortable" room in Dracula's castle where Renfield drinks wine). At a glance, the central camera movement might appear striking, but viewing it under scrutiny reveals three problems. One is that it is actually very bumpy, which serves to draw attention to the artifice of the cinema; in other words, it looks unprofessional. Another is that midway through the shot a shaft of hard light from a movie light is noticeable in the middle of the top of the frame, particularly odd for a room allegedly lit by candles. [See Figure 12D.] Thirdly, and perhaps most significantly, no reason exists for the camera to be moving. The result shows the scope of the room, but the castle's size is revealed through numerous other shots. Here the move backwards from Dracula and Renfield serves only to take the viewer *away* from their action. This lack of purpose becomes even more noticeable when compared to the Browning version. Its key moving-camera shot in the scene – which is smooth, rather than bumpy – makes a U shape around Renfield, encircling him geographically to underscore how trapped he is.

The Browning version is also a faster paced film. Whatever we make of this, it too is an undeniable mathematical fact. For one, it unfolds in 466 shots in approximately 73 minutes,

7 seconds (excluding the opening and closing credits, which takes prints of the film closer to approximately 74 minutes, 17 seconds). By contrast, the Melford version features 496 shots in a running time of approximately 102 minutes (excluding the opening and closing credits, which take the film to just over 103 minutes). These figures are striking, but we can take them even further. The Average Shot Length (ASL) for the Browning film is just over 9 seconds; the ASL for the Melford is just over 12 seconds. As a result, on average, the Melford lingers on each individual shot for about 25 percent longer than the Browning. Even aside from its additional 29 minutes of running time (a factor that cannot be ignored), the Melford is a considerably slower paced film.

Not only is the Browning film faster paced, but it is far more economical in its storytelling. We can note this difference in specific scenes. The Melford depicts the interior of the opening carriage ride in a single, proscenium arch shot that lasts approximately one minute and nineteen seconds; Browning conveys the same scene with four different shots in approximately thirty seconds. Later, for no particular reason, Dracula pours wine on *two* different occasions for Renfield in the Melford version, with Renfield drinking it both times, thus creating unnecessary repetition.

Some have argued that the sheer length of the Melford version allows it to develop the plot more thoroughly. That is a debatable point, but what is not debatable is that in some ways the Melford film – despite its dramatically longer running time – does not cover all of the narrative ground that Browning's does. We do not see the three bats (apparently Dracula's wives) flying outside Dracula's castle, as we do in the Browning. Nor does the Melford visualize Dracula's first visit to Mina's (Eva's) bedroom, which makes her subsequent behaviour somewhat less understandable. The Melford also does not let us hear the cries of the child who is bitten by the Woman in White. Instead, we simply see a cemetery gate and then an outtake of actress Frances Dade, Browning's Lucy. Here the image is so badly lit that it is dark and murky; it is easy to see why Milton Carruth, Browning's editor, avoided it.

Despite its longer running time, the Melford also does not include one very crucial scene that does appear in the Browning: Dracula's walk through London and his biting of the flower girl. Its absence not only foregoes the one chance for Dracula to bite a random victim, but it also creates

Figure 12G

a narrative problem in the Melford, as during the medical examination Lucia is referred to as "another victim," who bears the "same symptom" as another case. But without the flower girl, there has not actually been "another" victim in either London or Whitby.

Even aside from questions of pacing and narrative, Arthur (Arturo) Tavares' editing of the Melford film is sometimes clumsy and confusing. Even under minimal scrutiny, the opening sequence of Dracula emerging from his coffin at the Transylvanian castle is highly problematic. Shot 1 of this scene is a moving-camera shot taken from Browning's alternate takes, one that the Browning version wisely did not use. Just before the camera begins to move towards the coffin, the viewer readily notices water dripping from castle steps seen on the screen right. The water is noticeable because it is lit by an offscreen movie light. But to keep the camera from making its own shadow once it passes in front of that same light, someone simply turned it off after the camera began moving. Perhaps the effort was to suggest the vanishing rays of the sun, but to the viewer, it looks like exactly like what it is: someone has quite abruptly switched off an electric light within the catacombs of an ancient crumbling castle. The camera then moves towards the coffin, its lid opening slightly thanks to Dracula's hand.

Shot 2 then depicts a coffin covered in cobwebs, and then Shot 3 goes back to Lugosi's hand opening the coffin. Shot 4 shows an insect, and then Shot 5 returns again to Lugosi's hand opening the coffin. We know the coffin contains Dracula in part because we recognize the shot as being an alternate take from the Browning. Even aside from that external reference point, we know it contains a male vampire (rather than one of Dracula's wives) because – in addition to having seen the male hand on three occasions – Tavares lets the shot run until we glimpse a male face (Lugosi) inside it (at 7:07). [See Figure 12E.]

It is at Shot 6 that major trouble occurs. Now we see three coffins together in a different part of the castle. In fact, they are not actually coffins, but are instead the wooden crates that Dracula later ships to Carfax Abbey. The lid on the one near the back of the frame opens to release a foggy mist and Dracula. Either there are two male vampires in the castle or there is a major continuity error. [Compare Figure 12F with Figure 12E.]

New troubles begin in Shot 7, which features a medium shot of Dracula moving to screen right with the same wall behind him, which then cuts at to Shot 8, a long shot of him walking parallel to the castle wall, devoid of depth. By the end of the shot, he has turned the corner of his wooden crate. Shot 9 is an image of Dracula's wives, an alternate take from Browning. Shot 10 shows Dracula standing beside a wooden crate at screen right; its lid is clearly open, though it is in the process of closing of its own accord. But no one has got out of it. Dracula has already emerged from a different wooden box, and we have already seen Dracula's three wives elsewhere in the castle. It makes no sense whatsoever. [See Figure 12G.] At any rate, by the end of the shot, Dracula is increasingly far away from the first wooden box. Shot 11 then offers more footage of Dracula's three wives.

Chapter 12 – THE SPANISH-LANGUAGE DRACULA

Shot 12 presents a repetition of Shot 7, even though we have already seen Dracula move quite far from this position in the set. In other words, for no reason, Dracula is now back where he began after emerging from the first wooden crate. [See Figure 12H, which represents Shot 7, and Figure 12I, which represents Shot 12.] More strangely, footage of this same shot reappears much later in the film at Carfax Abbey, where it appears even more out of place, given that its background clearly does not match that of the shot that follows it.

David J. Skal's contention that the Melford version employs a greater cinematographic use of "multiple planes of focus and action" is also highly questionable.[15] Rather, the film features quite a number of visual problems. For example, when Renfield tells the carriage driver not to take his luggage down, the Melford version depicts this from over Renfield's shoulder, hardly the optimum place to show him. The fact that this image is not captured with a shorter depth of field is also a hindrance, as immediately on the other side of Renfield are background characters in relative focus, causing him to be lost in the frame. Karl Freund never allows for such clutter in the Browning film, and he appropriately varies the focal landscape, whether in the sentimentally soft-focus closeup of the crucifix as given to Renfield ("for your mother's sake"), or in the shallow depth of field in Renfield's cell when Martin throws out his spider. Freund's shots also show careful planning. For example, consider the final scene at Carfax Abbey when Harker and Mina embrace; here Freund intentionally uses a shallow depth of field, causing the background – unlike the other shots in the same scene – to go softly, appropriately, romantically out of focus. [See Figure 12J.] These kinds of tricks, common to so

Figure 12H

Figure 12I

Figure 12J

344   Chapter 12 – THE SPANISH-LANGUAGE DRACULA

many cinematographers of the period, are not employed in the Melford film, which does not feature an interplay with depth of field or soft focus.

Indeed, George Robinson's cinematography in the Melford film is far more flat than Freund's in the Browning. Freund regularly utilizes the z-axis space (meaning the depth of the set), as can be seen when he places us literally under the carriage when it drives over us on the way to Dracula's castle. By contrast, the Melford has a diagonal carriage entrance from screen right, which features some depth, but then has the carriage arrive at the castle by entering parallel to it from screen right, thus removing all depth. Later, at Carfax Abbey, Melford's Dracula walks parallel along the back wall, corners his wooden crate, and then walks parallel to the back wall in the other direction. Such limited use of the z-axis space and such reliance on movements parallel to the backs of sets seem to manifest a drive towards a lack of depth, however unintentional.

Figure 12K

A particularly clear comparison between the Melford and Browning can be made by examining the scene in which Renfield approaches a maid who has fainted. In the Melford, after proscenium framing depicts both characters, Renfield emerges into a static frame from screen right. Until he turns to come closer to the maid, he is moving parallel to the back of the set, again creating a lack of depth. By contrast, in the Browning, Renfield approaches the frame by crawling through the z-axis space (in other words, from near the back of the set towards the maid, who is in the foreground). Freund also carefully times his camera to tilt downward at a pace commensurate with actor Dwight Frye's movements.

In *Hollywood Gothic*, Skal applauds Robinson's use of "foreground objects" to create tension and depth," but examples of that are difficult to find.[16] Freund makes a much greater use of the foreground, and he avoids blatant errors that Robinson commits. Consider for example the use of the candelabra at Dracula's castle. In the Melford, Dracula pours wine for Renfield, a pivotal moment in the narrative, and his face is obscured by a candelabra. It is not in the foreground, used as an artful framing device to build depth. Instead, it is mere inches in front of Dracula, clumsily blocking his face. [See Figure 12K.]

The notion that the Melford film features "complex" compositions is particularly problematic, even startlingly so. One is tempted to blame Tavares for the repetitious ABA structure that is used in so many scenes, particularly in that the B shot often constitutes an awkward cut, but thanks to Melford and Robinson, Tavares may have had no other footage with which to work. In fairness to all of them, limited time might have driven them to a repeated reliance on the ABA structure, as avoiding angle changes meant the camera did not have to be moved or had to be moved only slightly; as a result, no changes to the lighting or sound equipment were required. To be sure, Melford and Robinson and Tavares worked together again on *East of Borneo* in 1931, a film that does not rely on a repetition of the ABA structure. At any rate, it is necessary to explore specifically how this occurs over and over again in the Spanish-language *Dracula*, even if it was a by-product of limited production time.

To begin, Robinson repeatedly relies on proscenium framing, far more than Freund. This is a mathematical certainty. Proscenium framing marked the early years of cinema, as it attempted to capture what might be considered the "best seat in the house" for live theatre. The camera is directly in front of the action, at a ninety-degree angle to the back wall of the theatre, or, in the case of cinema, the set. Such framing appears particularly theatrical if the composition is loose, showing full-body shots and large areas of the set at once. Proscenium framing can also appear quite flat, especially if: A) it is not enlivened by cuts to alternate camera angles of at least thirty degrees, in keeping with the Classical Hollywood Style, which move the point of view further inside the set, and/or B) if the actors stay in relatively the same place as one another, rather than being positioned or walking through noticeably different zones in the z-axis space. And yet, the Melford commits these mistakes in its ABA structure on repeated occasions.

We first see this structure in Dracula's castle. Dracula and Renfield are depicted in a long shot with proscenium framing (Shot A, in other words). Then, we see a two-shot of Dracula and Renfield for roughly two seconds (Shot B); the angle change is only slight, a few degrees. Then, we return to the proscenium long shot (Shot A). Out of two minutes and three seconds, we have one minute and fifty-three seconds of the *same* long shot. [See Figures 12L, 12M, and 12N.]

Figure 12L

Figure 12M

Figure 12N

346   *Chapter 12 – THE SPANISH-LANGUAGE DRACULA*

Figure 12O

Figure 12P

Figure 12Q

As another example, a proscenium long shot appears at approximately 42:45; it lasts for some 39 seconds, then finally cuts inward to show Renfield on the floor, the angle changing by only a few degrees. The scene then cuts back to the original proscenium framing. The ABA structure is finally broken at 44:09 (after approximately one minute and thirteen seconds) with an angle change of approximately thirty degrees. [See Figures 12O, 12P, and 12Q.]

The ABA structure appears again at approximately 47:42, when (in proscenium framing) Dr. Seward consoles Eva/Mina; they are flanked on screen left by Van Helsing and screen right by Harker. At 47:58, the shot changes to a two shot of Seward and Eva, featuring no noticeable degree change in the angle. It is a jump cut, which then cuts back at 48:23 to the proscenium framing long shot, completing the ABA structure. [See Figures 12R, 12S, and 12T.]

Repetition of these matters might not be exciting, but they are evidentiary of a structural repetition on which the Melford version sadly relies. Proscenium framing can be seen at approximately 52:21 (Shot A), which then jump-cuts inward to Renfield at 51:27 (Shot B), which then jumps back outward to proscenium framing at 57:36 (Shot A). After a break of only thirty seconds in the film, the Melford then presents yet another version of the ABA structure. Proscenium framing occurs again from approximately 58:06-58:18 (Shot A); then Shot B jumps inward, with a degree change of only a few angles. It lasts for five seconds, and then (at approximately 60:04) we return to Shot A for 28 seconds. Similarly, proscenium framing occurs at approximately 70:39 (Shot A). A jump cut inward, this time

Chapter 12 – THE SPANISH-LANGUAGE DRACULA

to the nurse and Van Helsing, occurs at approximately 70:52 (Shot B), which then jumps outward back to the original proscenium framing at approximately 71:02 (Shot A).

The same happens again at approximately 78:21 (Shot A, of Seward, Renfield, Harker, and Van Helsing), approximately 78:41 (Shot B, of Renfield, which stays on screen for a staggering 1 minute, 18 seconds), and then approximately 79:59 (which takes us back to Shot A). The aforementioned Shot A ends at approximately 80:14 and is replaced by a left-to-right pan of Martin entering the room. The shot pans until we are back to nearly the same proscenium framing from where we started, the focal length not having changed.

Melford's reliance on proscenium framing is quite consistent, including at key moments in the action, such as when the looseness of framing does not at all take advantage of Eva/Mina's wild-eyed gaze at Harker. Similarly, at approximately 53:49, we see full-body shots of (from screen left) Seward, Dracula, Van Helsing, and Harker. It is here that Dracula sees the mirror in the cigarette box, which he smashes with a cane. The use of the cane is different from the Browning, which may or may not be "better": that is a matter of personal opinion. But the sequence does not show Browning's planning or expertise.

Specifically, the Browning film features Dracula smashing the mirror in what begins as a medium long shot showing, from screen left, Van Helsing, Harker, Dracula (walking into frame), and Dr. Seward. As Dracula approaches Van Helsing, Harker and Seward exit screen right, and the camera moves inward to a two shot of Van Helsing and Dracula. That they are depicted together at this point is interesting,

Figure 12R

Figure 12S

Figure 12T

348   Chapter 12 – THE SPANISH-LANGUAGE DRACULA

not only because Van Helsing needs to show the cigarette box to Dracula, but also because Dracula has tried to ingratiate himself with Van Helsing. After Dracula smashes the box, Freund moves the camera again, accentuating Dracula's physical action and serving to change the shot to a single. Dracula is now visually alone, just as he is narratively alone in the room, separated from Van Helsing, who knows he is a vampire, and Harker and Seward, who have just witnessed his violent behavour. In addition to his outburst, Dracula realizes that Van Helsing knows he is a vampire. With an appropriate change of angle, we see a confident Van Helsing standing by himself. After another single medium shot of Dracula, there is an image of Harker and Seward together, both in shock at Dracula's actions, but also jointly unaware that he is a vampire. It makes sense that they are linked visually in the two shot. Robinson's camera in the Melford version does not at all reveal such clear planning.

Other kinds of problems occur in the Melford version as well. A proscenium-framed long shot appears from approximately 53:05 to 53:14, which is followed by a jump cut inward, in typical Melford-Robinson-Tavares style. Harker, who is in the middle, stands both slightly behind and between Dracula and Van Helsing. At the edit, in a minor lapse of continuity, he is physically closer to the other two men. While the continuity problem is negligible, the result means that Harker's forehead features unattactive shadows from the heads of both Dracula and Van Helsing.

Or consider the sequence that begins at approximately 36:33, in which Seward and Van Helsing are seated in Seward's office (as opposed to the Browning film, in which Van Helsing, the man empowered with knowledge, stands, which visually suggests that he is the one in control). After being static for some eleven seconds, Robinson's camera moves backward. The move ends at 37:12, by which time Renfield and Martin have entered the room. The camera's movement has performed the function it has elsewhere, as at Dracula's castle: to reveal large spaces for no other apparent reason. In this example, the moving camera has accomplished nothing more than being repositioned into proscenium framing.

Proscenium framing marks numerous other scenes as well.[17] In some ways, it is the sheer length of time for which Tavares allows these loosely-composed shots to linger that underscores the sense that we are viewing a live stage play, as many of them last for twenty or thirty seconds. For example, at approximately 50:51-51:44, a single proscenium shot lasts for some fifty seconds. Even when Dracula hurls Renfield off the stairs at Carfax Abbey, Robinson depicts the action in proscenium framing. And then, when Dracula and Eva/Mina leave the room at approximately 51:43, a bizarre crossing of the 180 degree line occurs to depict Van Helsing. The 180-degree line is also crossed at approximately 54:53-54:55. The shot shows the backs of Seward, Harker, and Van Helsing as they watch Dracula. Then, in yet another example of a lack of depth, Dracula walks across the lawn from screen right to left, rather than at an angle that would take advantage of z-axis space.

Unlike comparisons of moving camera and shot lengths, it is difficult to compare the Browning to the Melford in terms of proscenium framing, because Freund uses it so sparingly. For example, Freund avoids the looseness of composition that Robinson employs in the Whitby section of the film, presumably because he knows that with interiors such an approach can too easily make sets appear stagey. Freund also generally adheres to the thirty-degree rule, rather than awkwardly jumping straight forward or backward without noticeable angle changes. When Freund does use loose framing, he usually avoids its potential pitfalls by employing tactics like placing the camera slightly off center and placing objects carefully in the foreground, as he does at Dracula's castle, in which a table appears in the foreground on screen left and a dinner table appears screen right at a different place in the z-axis; in between the two pieces of furniture are Renfield and Dracula. Here is a true use of multiple planes. [See Figure 12U.]

Consider also approximately 55:52-56:05 in the Browning, when Seward walks at an angle through the room to make a phone call on screen left, his body providing depth accentuated by Renfield and Van Helsing, who also walk in z-axis space. [See Figure 12V.] In other cases, Freund presents a proscenium shot, but only as the starting point for a more complicated shot. For example, Renfield and Dracula are nicely positioned off center in a proscenium shot at approximately 12:49, but that image is merely the basis for what becomes a moving camera shot that follows Renfield to the dinner table.

Returning to the Melford, it must be said that the film mathematically features a greater number of continuity lapses than the Browning, some of which are particularly noticeable. However "erotic" Dracula's vampire wives in the Melford might be, they have quite different hairstyles from their counterparts in the Browning. The problem is of course that in the Melford we have seen alternate takes of Dracula's wives from the Browning *before* seeing Melford's version of the same. Either Dracula has at least six wives, or he has three who have all changed their hairstyle on the very evening that Renfield arrives. More curious still is that the wives as directed by Melford descend upon Renfield as the scene fades to black, rather than being made to leave him alone, as Dracula requires in the Browning. It is as if Dracula's wives bite Renfield in the

Figure 12X

Figure 12Y

Figure 12Z

Melford, which makes Dracula's subsequent hypnotic control over Renfield difficult to explain.

Other continuity errors are minor, but – given the attention levied on those in the Browning version – they are worth mentioning. At approximately 17:04, Dracula looks at the crucifix around Renfield's neck. He appears unhappy, as if he has bitten into a lemon, but he strangely does not shrink away or avert his eyes; instead, he keeps staring at it for aproximately three seconds. [See Figure 12W.] But when Tavares cuts to the next shot, Dracula's eyes are closed and his head is not even positioned in Renfield's direction.

Van Helsing and Dr. Seward meet with Renfield at approximately 37:09 in the Melford version. At 37:37, Van Helsing sits down, with his right hand resting on Seward's desk; in the next shot, his hand has changed position, pointing at Renfield. Then, at 41:07, Dracula is staring at screen right. In the shot that follows, he is looking (in profile, no less) directly screen left. Much more noticeable is Van Helsing at 60:31. In the previous shot, Harker stands in front of Van Helsing on screen right as they (along with Seward, on screen left) confront Renfield. But at 60:31, Van Helsing points at Renfield, Harker having strangely and completely *disappeared*. [See Figures 12X and 12Y.]

But these are not the only problems in the Melford. At approximately 15:39, Dracula *spills* wine on the table while pouring it for Renfield. And then there is Dracula's walk to Lucia's London apartment, during which he passes a policeman. In the Browning, the bobby notes that the fog is decreasing. In the Melford, the policeman suggests the fog is getting "thicker," even though almost no fog can be seen in the shot. This leads to

Chapter 12 – THE SPANISH-LANGUAGE DRACULA

another continuity error only moments later in a shot of Lucy's window from inside her bedroom, with extremely thick fog visible just outside of it. Even worse is the bat that comes to her window. Melford elects to visualize the bat entering through the window, rather than just flapping outside it. At approximately 31:49, the bat clearly bumps into the window and has to back up in order to enter the room. [See Figure 12Z.]

Without even getting into a more in-depth comparison, it is fair to say that the Melford version will continue to have champions, just as the Browning will. But personal opinion and emotional reactions aside, the Melford version does not live up to many of the aesthetic arguments or "factual" claims that were made about it at the time and that have since been repeated over and over again, despite Tom Weaver's advice that the film should be re-examined outside of the cloud of its "newness" (and, one might add by extension, titillation over its leading leady and vampire wives).

In the end, the Melford version is a derivative work, a movie that could not have existed without the Browning film, either when it was produced in 1930 or when it was first restored some sixty years later. This element poses a final consideration that cannot be easily dismissed.

1 "Going Out Guide." *New York Times* 27 Aug. 1977: 14.
2 Everson, William K. *More Classics of the Horror Film* (Secaucus, NJ: Citadel Press, 1986): 28-32.
3 Turner, George. "The Two Faces of Evil." *American Cinematographer* (May 1988): 34-42; Riley, Philip J. and George Turner. "Production Background." in *Dracula (The Original 1931 Shooting Script)*. Ed. by Philip J. Riley. (Absecon, NJ: MagicImage, 1990): 19-88.
4 Skal, David J. *Hollywood Gothic: The Tangled Web of* Dracula *from Novel to Stage to Screen* (New York: W. W. Norton, 1990): 152-177. Skal also published a two-page article on the Spanish-language *Dracula* in *American Film* (1 Sept. 1990): 40-41.
5 Skal, *Hollywood Gothic*, p. 160.
6 Clarens, Carlos. *An Illustrated History of the Horror Film* (New York: Capricorn Books, 1967): 61.
7 "Archive Review." *Variety* 5 Oct. 1992: 66.
8 "*Dracula.*" *Fangoria* 119 (1992): 38.
9 As endnote 30 for Chapter 11 explains, the use of minutes and seconds to specify given shots is approximate.
10 Eisner, Lotte H. *The Haunted Screen* (Berkeley, CA: Univ. of CA, 1973).
11 A publicity still for the Spanish-language version does show some extras in the front row of the auditorium, but not in the rows behind them.
12 Here I am thankful to Carter B. Smith, DVM.
13 Kahn, Red. "Insider's Outlook." *Motion Picture Daily* 16 Feb. 1944: 2.
14 Edward Van Sloan's curtain speech in Browning's *Dracula* was apparently filmed as a single crane shot. As previously discussed, versions of the film from 1938 onwards, including restorations, have not included this shot.
15 Skal, *Hollywood Gothic*, p. 160.
16 Ibid., p. 160.
17 See, for example, Melford's use of proscenium shots at approximately 24:09, 41:40, 41:52, 45:55, 46:34, 49:11, 49:31, 54:37, 54:59, 58:06, 62:13, and 62:24, 63:24, and 65:54

Chapter 13
ENDINGS

Archaeologists do not excavate photocopies. They excavate parchments, scrolls, and tablets. Browning's *Dracula* is no photocopy. It is an original. It might be informed by the novel and stage play that preceded it, but it is an original, incorporating elements of various prior texts into a unique film that features its own additions and innovations. And our distance from it historically should allow us to re-engage with it critically.

Dracula shows the aesthetic hallmarks of the period in which it was created. As Andrew Sarris once noted, films are ultimately judged in the "realm of now," and life in the twenty-first century is so distant and removed from 1931 that everything about the film has become old.[1] Even its then-modern accents – ranging from art deco opening titles to its automobiles – seem increasingly antique in the twenty-first century. If the film creaks, it creaks like the old doors of Dracula's castle. It is as if *Dracula* has been excavated from an ancient tomb, or that it represents a nightmare dreamt not by ourselves, but by someone who walked the earth in the far distant past.

Implicit in much of the negativity about the Browning *Dracula* is a disappointment that it was produced when it was. So much of the discussion has revolved around what the film did *not* show. Critics like Carlos Clarens – who regrets the film does not depict the "red mist" that Renfield describes – know that the use of color was rare in films produced in 1930.[2] It is as if some of these critics do not want to address the specific film *Dracula,* but rather express their desire that it was produced in, or at least features the cinematic norms of, say, 1935, or 1945, or even much later. With regard to some of these complaints, one could just as easily add disappointment that *Dracula* does not feature CGI red mist accompanied by a rock soundtrack in digital surround sound.

Cinematically, Browning's *Dracula* represents an austere brand of horror. Offscreen space is used repeatedly, not only for vampire bites and the death of Dracula, but for Dracula in wolf form running across the lawn. The same is true for the Whitby harbormaster, who speaks from offscreen space when we see only a lonesome dock and the shadow of a dead sea captain. In the Browning film, offscreen space allows Browning to create a pattern in which danger is regularly hidden from view, much as how Dracula hides behind a tree when Harker and Van Helsing find Mina outside at night. Danger lurks just beyond the frame, with horror thriving in an unseen space, a space too horrible to reveal.

Much the same is also true when Renfield recounts the rats he has seen. To lose this dialogue delivered with such zeal by actor Dwight Frye would be unfortunate, and what could possibly be gained? Special effects as they could be delivered in 1930. After all, *Dracula* benefits increasingly from its lack of special effects. Shots depicting a red mist on the lawn, or blood spattered over Mina, or a stake plunging into Dracula's body are the kinds of images that temporarily please some horror fans. But whatever effects could have been mustered would only have dated the film in a very different and less successful way, as graphic special effects generally do. For example, the grisly effects of splatter films of the 1960s appeared dated to many audiences of the 1980s' splatter films, whose special effects appear dated to audiences of splatter films of the twenty-first century.

Overall, the few special effects that *Dracula* does employ remain effective. The glass paintings of the mountains and of Dracula's castle are stunning and imminently believable within the dreamscape that is the film's Transylvania. The minimal use of the bats is judicious, as are their limited flight patterns. The trio seen through a window at Dracula's castle hardly move from their position, and the bat at Lucy's window wisely flaps in one position. Even when pausing on every frame in which they appear, no strings can be seen.

While much has been written about specific aspects of Browning's *Dracula*, I believe it is worth returning to a number of key issues surrounding its narrative,

Publicity still of Bela Lugosi as the title character in *Dracula* (1931). *(Courtesy of Buddy Barnett)*

cinematography, and soundtrack to understand why its critical reputation is evolving, and to underscore the fact that its evolution is leading towards a more positive understanding of one of Hollywood's most important and enduring horror films.

Time and Space

In many respects, ranging from its brooding pace to its lack of a background score, *Dracula* unfolds much like a nightmare. Its characters are locked in a particular time and place, both of which seem otherworldly and distinctly unreal. As a result it is not problematic that the film's Whitby is "near London," whereas the actual Whitby is over 200 miles away from the city. Nor does it seem problematic that at times *Dracula* evokes a Victorian England, and at other times it suggests the time period in which it was produced. This is not England of either the late nineteenth century or of 1930, but instead an oneiric setting that defies the spatio-temporal.

Dracula takes place at the Seward Sanitarium for approximately 37 minutes, 40 seconds of its approximately 74:30 running time. The only change of location during that time frame comes in the form of two shots depicting the "Woman in White" narrative. However, these two shots are followed by the attendant Martin reading about her in the newspaper. While we could view them as distinct and separate from the sanitarium, we could also see them as visualizations of the story Martin is reading at the sanitarium. Both interpretations seem valid, but in either case, the film revolves around the sanitarium location for roughly half of its running time, not the two-thirds that has often been claimed.

The terrace at the Seward Sanitarium, which is under siege in *Dracula* (1931). *(Courtesy of Anthony Osika)*

At any rate, the sanitarium sequence relies on an important plot device that continues to be duplicated in modern horror films. The characters are trapped in a single location, a near-claustrophobic environment with a monster stalking them. Fleeing, in this case to London, would be even more dangerous. The night outside of the Seward Sanitarium reveals another space, a transgressive environment where vampires (Dracula and the Woman in White) are in control, where guns are of no value, and where no one is safe. The sanitarium terrace becomes a nether region, where a woman who has tasted the blood of a vampire languishes as if between two worlds.

Many horror movies have focussed on a single location to place their characters under siege, ranging from *Night of the Living Dead* (1968) and *The Shining* (1980) to dozens of others. And the characters in *Dracula* are not merely under siege in an old house, but in an insane asylum.

The final night at the sanitarium is long and dangerous. For example, a clock reveals that it is approximately 4:40AM when Dracula appears on the terrace to visit Mina's bedroom. He may be the master of Renfield and, to a degree, Mina, but he is a slave to his own passions. His lust outweighs his concern that Van Helsing knows he is a vampire; his lust also outweighs the approach of dawn. Indeed, when Dracula and the others leave the sanitarium, the film's narrative reverses, becoming a mirror opposite of itself. It is Dracula who is under siege at Carfax Abbey. He has perhaps foreseen trouble because, at some point, he has moved his earth box into the cellar, as earlier scenes show it elsewhere in the abbey. But no hiding place or locked door can protect Dracula from the onset of daylight and two vampire-hunters.

Whatever its detractors have insinuated, *Dracula*'s cinematography achieves some of the most haunting images in film history: painterly, and imbued with a strong sense of depth. The Browning film features an array of lighting setups that explore not the monochromatic

A publicity still of Van Helsing and Harker entering the gate of Carfax Abbey.

but rather the panchromatic, from the heavy blacks and whites at Dracula's castle to the rich range of grays at the Seward Sanitarium.

Tracing the film's use of moving camera is intriguing, as much of it is judiciously reserved for Dracula and those under his control. It repeatedly pushes inward, sometimes with surprising speed, to depict Dracula, Renfield, and the increasingly vampiric Mina. The camera moves are particularly transgressive when associated with Dracula and his power, ranging from a shot that moves backwards in Dracula's chambers to reveal the dinner table (with Renfield unknowingly soon to provide the vampire with nourishment, a point underscored by his pricking his finger soon thereafter) to a subsequent camera move in the same scene that encircles the hapless Renfield. And then there is camerawork at the concert hall that first tracks screen right to reveal Dracula in the auditorium only then to track back screen left to follow his movements.

Consider also the film's penchant for panning from right to left at particular moments. Pans in the Classical Hollywood Style are most commonly left to right, echoing the direction in which we read. But *Dracula* relies on pans in the opposite direction to underscore moments in which danger is at hand. For example, a shot pans left (and tilts downwards) to Renfield, who asks for his baggage to remain on the carriage at the inn, and then the camera pans right (and tilts upwards) to the worried porters, who fear Walpurgis Night. Soon thereafter, we see a right-to-left pan from Dracula's coach to the one that abruptly leaves Renfield at the Borgo Pass. Dracula's emergence from his coffin at Carfax Abbey is also conveyed in a right-to-left pan to a castle window, then back left-to-right to reveal Dracula standing.

Soundscapes

Dracula's austerity extends to its soundtrack. It has no background musical score. The only music heard in its running time (after the usage of Tchaikovsky's *Swan Lake* in the opening credits) is diegetic music. As Robert Spadoni has rightly noted, "A different way to approach the quiet is to regard it in the context not of post-1931 horror films, as we might, but of earlier sound films, as *Dracula*'s first audiences did."[3] In addition to understanding the historical context, we can also consider the fact that some modern movies – likes the Coen Brothers' *No Country for Old Men* (2007) – have been lauded for not using background music.

With regard to the music that is heard in *Dracula*, Skal and Savada claim in *Dark Carnival* that it is "arbitrary," but that is not an accurate description.[4] It should be noted that the concert-hall scene does not exist in the novel or play: it was created, at least in part, to insert diegetic music into the film. And then there are the particular musical selections. After Dracula arrives at the concert hall, we hear roughly four measures of Schubert's *Symphony No. 8*. When Dracula is inside the concert hall, the music abruptly shifts to Wagner's overture to *Die Meistersinger*. Then, after Dracula joins Harker, Mina, and Lucy, Schubert's *Symphoney No. 8* returns from its beginning, not picking up from where it was just heard.

It would actually have been easier to choose any single, random classical music and allow it to be the only selection heard at the concert hall, but here are two different pieces, with snippets arranged in a curious order that would never be programmed at a concert. Film-music historian William H. Rosar makes this point in an essay published in the *Quarterly Journal of the Library of Congress*.[5] I agree with his assertion that this particular music was chosen and arranged in the sequence for dramatic effect.

In this publicity still, the vampire count approaches the concert hall in Dracula *(1931). (Courtesy of Buddy Barnett)*

Both selections were extremely popular in Victorian England. *Die Meistersinger* was ubiquitous at the time, Wagner's most performed work of the 1890s. That it plays while we are visually introduced to Harker, Lucy, Mina, and Seward clearly postions them in the role of the urban, educated, middle-to-upper-class English, for whom the piece was extremely popular even into the twentieth century. To an extent, the selection may have been guided by the final shooting script, which indicates that the music inside the concert hall should be, "something rather impressive, perhaps almost Wagnerian, to sustain atmosphere of the scene's dramatic movement."[6] Here it seems that Universal's Music Director Heinz Roemheld selected (or at least approved) a specific composition of Wagner's to follow the script's more general suggestion.

Schubert's *Symphony No. 8* was also commonly performed in Victorian England, and it is heard when Dracula arrives at the concert. Immediately after Dracula delivers his dialogue about "far worse things awaiting man than death," the lights dim and Schubert returns. It is Schubert's "Unfinished." That symphony, like the character Dracula, is perpetually unfinished, immortal and yet incomplete. *Symphony No. 8* is twice linked with Dracula in a manner similar to what film music would often do in the years that followed: commenting on specific characters. This seems quite clear given that the Schubert is carefully timed to follow Dracula's dialogue about immortality being problematic. Indeed, the shooting script also provides a note in that very direction: "As he finishes speech, the box is in deep shadow – lights from stage casting dim, weird lighting on his face. The sound of music from stage starts to come over scene – a low prelude of woodwinds and strings, adding to the macabre quality of the scene as we FADE OUT."[7] Such a use of music was rather progressive for a film released in early 1931.

And then there is the *other* music that most critics seem not to notice, but that was also featured in the film and was also described in the final draft of the script. Depicting Lucy's bedroom, the film fades up to a closeup of a music box. The Fort-Browning script suggested that it should begin playing when Lucy removes a bottle of perfume from it. Instead, the scene begins with the music box already playing, which it continues to do until Lucy places a perfume bottle inside it. As the music ends, Mina chides Lucy for being "so romantic."

Music boxes flourished in England during the nineteenth century, but they had to be imported from such places as Switzerland, Germany, and Bohemia. In like fashion, the shooting script suggested that Lucy has a "Viennese perfume bottle." Sounds from the music box – an old French folk song – provide the background to Mina imitating Dracula's voice, which concludes with Lucy's sexualized insertion of the perfume bottle into the box. After touching the box tenderly, she stares down at the bottle inside it while telling Mina, "I think he's fascinating." Lucy is entralled by Dracula and the fact that he is a foreigner; such props in her bedroom underscore her passion for the European continent.

Elsewhere in the film, the lack of background music accentuates the intentional sound effects, such as the relentless bumping of the coach ride on its way to Dracula's castle, the castle doors creaking open and closed of their own accord, the wind and rough waters during the voyage of the *Vesta*, and the heroes' struggle to break into Carfax Abbey. That some of the sound effects emanate from offscreen space (such as the various howls of wolves, Van Helsing's breaking of a coffin lid to improvise a stake, and Dracula's death groans) serves to emphasize them and their potential eeriness.

Children of the Night

Occasionally modern writers mistakenly refer to the women at Dracula's castle as "brides," but the innkeeper's dialogue clearly informs Renfield that these women are Dracula's "wives." Lucy becomes another addition to that group. Then, at the film's conclusion, we see Mina entering Carfax Abbey, the train of her apparel dragging the ground in a visual echo of the Transylvanian wives. That Dracula takes multiple spouses is another of his transgressions, the violation of another taboo.

Much the same could be said of Lucy's nocturnal visits to Mina, which are plural, given Van Helsing's question about "the next time" Mina saw Lucy after the funeral. Mina recounts Lucy looking like a "wild animal," and compares her to a wolf, which by extension becomes a comparison to Dracula. And yet Mina hardly describes their meetings as sad visits from a friend condemned to vampirism. Instead, Lucy's behaviour speaks to lust, even if it is not consumnated. Perhaps she – in a repetition of Dracula's wives approaching Renfield – has to shrink away from Mina because of Dracula's designs on the same woman.

And there is Van Helsing's final dialgoue, "Not yet... presently," which implies he will remain at Carfax Abbey to stake Renfield, and possibly Lucy as well. Before entering Carfax Abbey, Harker and Van Helsing appear at the same cemetery gate where we earlier heard the cries of one of Lucy's victims. As a result of that gate (and her visits to Mina), we know Lucy has been in the nearby vicinity. She may well be cohabitating with Dracula at Carfax Abbey.

But vampires are not the only creatures that Browning unleashes. The trio of armadillos at Dracula's Castle have received the most attention, with the film's detractors pointing out that the animal is not indigenous to Transylvania. But few viewers in 1931 would have known that fact.

Aside from personally seeing armadillos in such American states as Texas, audience members in 1931 would have either been unaware of the creatures or perhaps would have known them through Rudyard Kipling's famous tale *The Beginning of the Armadillos*, in which he jokingly describes their creation at the Amazon River. First published in the *Ladies Home Journal* in 1900, the story reappeared in his popular collection *Just So Stories* (1902). Through such accounts, their origins seemed rooted in

13H = Dracula's trio of Transylvanian wives as shown in a memorable publicity still. *(Courtesy of Anthony Osika)*

a faraway place. Their preternaturally bizarre appearance was well-suited to the ancient qualities of Dracula's castle as well as to Dracula himself, given Harker's comparison of the Count to a "lizard" in Chapters 2 and 3 of Bram Stoker's 1897 novel.

The nocturnal armadillos underscore the vampire's relationship with such vile "children of the night" as wolves and bats. Consider the inaugural scene at Dracula's Castle. The first image of Dracula's hand emerging from his coffin cuts to a nocturnal possum beside a coffin covered in cobwebs, which cuts to a shot of one of Dracula's wives opening her own coffin. A cut reveals the shot of an insect, which cuts to another shot of one of Dracula's wives sitting upright in her coffin. A cut offers the image of another possum inside a coffin with a lifeless, skeletal hand reaching out from it, which then cuts to Dracula standing outside of his coffin.

These visual juxtapositions suggest that all of these disgusting creatures share much in common, not least of which is that they are nocturnal.[8] But the connections are deeper thanks to the soundscape. Once we see Dracula standing outside of his coffin, we hear a bizarre squeaking noise. It does not come from the insect, nor does it come from the possums (which are clearly meant to be read as possums, rather than rats, as Browning would have known many viewers would recognize them as such, and likely chose them because they are nocturnal). Possums hiss, but they do not squeak. The squeaks continue over the next image, which depicts three vampire wives in long shot, as well as over the start of its replacement, which shows Dracula walking towards some steps. Once he ascends them, a wolf's howl is heard.

Later, when we see a trio of bats flying outside of the castle window, the same squeaking noises return, with the bats being their apparent source; similar sound effects accompany the appearance of Dracula in bat form in England. To return to the earlier scene, we can imagine that the squeaks emanate from offscreen bats, much as the howl emanates from an offscreen wolf. But the question remains as to *which* bats, as the squeaks are heard in the earlier scene even while we see Dracula and his three wives in human form. Herein lies one of the great mysteries at Dracula's Castle. It makes us wonder if there are in fact other bats, and, by extension, other vampire wives that we do not see. Visually, there is at least one coffin shrouded in cobwebs, not in current use, with its skeleton inside representing the remains of what might have been another vampire, long since destroyed. And so it becomes easy to ponder whether the squeaks suggest the presence of unseen vampires, or whether the squeaks are non-diegetic, commenting on the unfolding and disgusting scene much as background music does.

A frame from *Dracula* (1931) depicts the insect that has provoked so much comment from viewers.

Within the same sequence at Dracula's castle is one of the film's most mystifying (and, as a result, most exciting) images. The fourth shot in the scene shows an insect, one that has become the source of much discussion. To begin, it is possible to identify the insect as a Jerusalem cricket, but *only* thanks to outtakes that appear in Melford's Spanish-language version of *Dracula*. As more than one entomologist has noted, the footage in the Browning film does not allow for positive identification because not enough of the insect's head is visible. As a result, the shot has led scholar Tony Williams to conclude that – in the world of *Dracula's* narrative – the insect is from "no known species, but is instead a Gothic bug."[9] [See Figure 13A.]

The insect crawls of out some object, which is the source of even greater controversy. It appears to be a coffin, but therein lies the problem. The insect does not appear larger than an ordinary insect. There is no low angle. There is no forced perspective. But there is a set piece behind it that could potentially be understood as a scaled-down version of a column in the catacombs. As a result, many viewers perceive the bug to be a monstrously-sized creature, if not a succubus. Such an interpretation might well make sense, particularly in view of Van Helsing's question in Chapter 14 of Stoker's novel *Dracula*: "Can you tell me why, when other spiders die small and soon, that one great spider lived for centuries in the tower of the old Spanish church and grew and grew, till, on descending, he could drink the oil of all the church lamps?"

By contrast, many other viewers see the insect as small, crawling out of a small object, but then the question is whether the object is meant to be some kind of loose, ornamental woodwork, or whether it is meant to be a tiny coffin. Certainly it does not appear similar to any of the other coffins seen in the castle, which might call into question whether it is supposed to be one, particularly if it was a prop created for the film. Another possiblity is that it is a small wooden object *and* a small coffin. Consider the following passage from Chapter 4 of Charles Dickens' *Oliver Twist* (1838):

> 'You'll make your fortune, Mr. Sowerberry,' said the beadle, as he thrust his thumb and forefinger into the proffered snuff-box of the undertaker: which was an ingenious little model of a patent coffin.

Snuff boxes are connected to the very aristocracy to which Dracula belongs, and snuff boxes shaped like coffins date to at least the eighteenth century.[10] Rather than someone having constructed a tiny coffin for a normal-sized insect, perhaps the insect is merely crawling out of a carelessly placed snuff box.

Perhaps. The Classical Hollywood Cinema to which *Dracula* belongs strived towards being excessively obvious in its storytelling. Through visual (or audiovisual, once the talkies arrived) film language, Hollywood movies gave audiences all the information they needed to understand the narratives they saw. That meant viewers shouldn't have to ask questions. That meant viewers not having to worry about "perhaps."

But Browning eschews that approach at appropriate moments in *Dracula*. After all, vampires are undead, a condition that is itself difficult to process intellectually, as it is neither one thing nor another. While individual viewers might reach conclusions that satisfy their own curiousity about the insect, the fact is that the shot cannot be read. It is an impenetrable totem. It cannot be processed under scrutiny, which makes us ponder how bizarre it must have seemed to viewers in 1931, who did not have the ability to pause or rewind. On the enormous movie screens of the day, the "gothic bug" appeared before their eyes for little more than two seconds and then disappeared, trapped inside a scene that is not only horrifying, but also challenging to the sensibilities.

Devils in the Details

Throughout this book, I have tried to illuminate Browning's direction of *Dracula*, ranging from his ten-year odyssey to transform the story into an official film adaptation to the various changes he clearly made to the shooting script during *Dracula*'s production. In Chapters 11 and 12, I further described cetain detailed features of his film, such as particular aspects of its set design. At this stage, I would like to shed light – literally, in fact – on Browning's attention to detail in *Dracula* using two final examples. I do not rest my case on such evidence, but rather view them as the culmination of my efforts throughout this text.

The mythology of the cardboard on Mina's lamp has dimmed our ability to laud one of the film's most fascinating and repeated flourishes, meaning the specific and planned usage of lamps in both Lucy and Mina's bedrooms. While Lucy sits at her vanity table, Mina gently chides her about Count Dracula. She goes so far as to predict a pending union by calling Lucy "Countess"; Mina also imitates Dracula's voice and words, as if she were him momentarily, at least for the sake of a joke between friends. Flanking Lucy's vanity are two lamps. One features a lamp stick with a sculpture of a single female; the other of a single male. The male bows from the waist, as if courting the female on the lamp opposite. They represent Lucy and Dracula. If one at first balks at such an interpretation, consider that Mina – who has in fact pretended to be Dracula in the same scene – stands and bows in the same pose as the male lamp, to the extent that she positions her left hand and arm just like the figurine. [See Figures 13A and 13B.]

After Mina leaves, Lucy goes to bed. The lamp in the corner of her room nearest the window that Dracula enters casts an eerie, bat-like shadow upon the wall, which hardly seems to be a mistake. Before falling asleep, Lucy reads briefly. Her bedside lamp stick features three frolicking women, which calls to mind Dracula's three Transylvanian wives.[11] [See Figure 13C.] By that point, Lucy is only moments away from becoming not *the* "Countess," but certainly a "Countess," meaning a fourth (so far as we know) wife of the vampire. From that point onward, she exists as the Woman in White. Not dead, not alive, but – like her counterparts in the polygamist nightmare – undead.

For the rest of the film, Dracula pursues Mina, who seems to be the object of his greatest desire. We know that in part due to the amount of running time devoted to his pursuit of her, as well as to the risks he takes so near sunrise when leading her back to Carfax Abbey, knowing all the while that Van Helsing is aware of his intentions. For some time prior to the scene, however, Mina languishes in a twilight state, not yet undead, but surely under Dracula's control. After all, he easily and successfully beckons her onto the sanitarium lawn, enveloping her body with his cape. Yes, there is cardboard on Mina's bedside lamp, discussion of which has darkened any chance thus far to revel in Browning's ongoing usage of lamps subtly to underscore the onscreen action. Mina's bedside lamp stick features a sculpture highly reminiscent of Lucy's, as if it could have been created by the same designer. We never see it until Dracula approaches Mina to bite her, thus initiating the process of vampirism. And so the lamp sculpture quite logically features a man and woman *together*, as Dracula and Mina have already become, or are at least in the process of becoming. [See Figure 13D.]

The pattern of repetition with lamps is difficult to deny. The usages would seem too coincidental otherwise. Was Browning responsible? We cannot say whether he developed such

Figure 13A

Figure 13B

Figure 13C

a notion or simply approved of choices made by an astute art director, but even if it was the latter, he did approve of it. How can we possibly know that is the case? It is quite logical to do so after carefully scrutinizing one final example of Browning's attention to detail, namely in Van Helsing's laboratory. Microscopes and books fill the room, while other artifacts speak volumes about the character's research interests and his imminent and certainly antithetical relationship with Dracula. In long shot with Van Helsing at his desk, we can see two skulls and an eerie face mask to screen right of his window. The visual connection to the Dracula of Transylvania is immediately clear, the skulls reminiscent of the skeletal remains inside one coffin at the Castle and the face mask – which seems only somewhat human in appearance – reminiscent of Dracula.

If such connections seem diffuse, consider the presence of the wall sculpture (for lack of a better term) to the screen left of the window. Like the aforementioned "gothic bug," we witness what appears to be a lobster-like insect. [See Figure 13E.] It echoes the opening scene at Dracula's Castle when the Creatures of the Night that dwell within waken from their unearthly slumber. But much like the bizarre and concocted creature that Browning used in *Mark of the Vampire* (1935), as described in Chapter 10, this hanging monstrosity is not a known entity. It does not exist. It has what appears to be the tail of a lobster, as well as antennae that appear reminiscent of a lobster or a cockroach. And yet, within the world of *Dracula*, it cannot be a lobster (even if the prop was constructed in part from an actual lobster) because it has no claws. It is yet another gothic mutation, an unearthly thing of superstition, one forged for the film, much in keeping with usages of other creatures and creations elsewhere in Browning's oeuvre.

Should this freakish invention, this subtle trick, not present a compelling argument to all readers, particularly insofar as Browning's choices go, then a final consideration becomes key. Melford filmed his Spanish-language *Dracula* rapidly, much more so than Browning did his version. It used the same script and sets and so many of the same props, and as Chapter 11 notes, Melford had little time to waste. But when shooting Van Helsing's laboratory on the night of

Figure 13D

Figure 13E

Figure 13F

3 November 1930 (as opposed to Browning, who shot the same scene during the daytime of 9 October 1930), Melford clearly opted to liberate Browning's mutant from the frame. Though the set is the same, the creature is not present. It has been removed.[12] [See Figure 13F.]

Evolutions

Though critical reaction to Browning's *Dracula* has been largely negative since George Geltzer's 1953 essay on the director, it has occasionally evoked more moderate opinions. In *Horror!* (MacMillan, 1966), Drake Douglas claimed: "*Dracula*, although masterfully directed by Tod Browning and boasting the brilliant camera work of the German Karl Freund, seems somewhat dated today and does not stand up as well as does *Frankenstein* [1931], but it is still an effective work."[13] Calvin T. Beck went further in his *Heroes of the Horror Film* (Collier, 1975), claiming, "Though it spawned several dozen sequels and hybrids, including the more commercial-looking *Horror of Dracula* (1958), there has never been anything to surpass Lugosi's *Dracula* or, for that matter, its brilliant predecessor, *Nosferatu* (1922)."[14]

In *Universal Horrors* (McFarland, 1990), Tom Weaver wrote, "The judgment of time has sadly gone against *Dracula*."[15] He was correct in a sense, but time is not static. It has marched onward from 1931, as well as from 1990. Audiences change, and with great regularity. We, the audience, as well as those who have come before and who will come after, are in flux.

Even one of *Dracula*'s most notable critics changed his views. In *More Classics of the Horror Film* (Citadel, 1986), William K. Everson informed readers that some enjoyment of

Lucy's bedside lamp – visible in this publicity still – depicts three frolicking women who call to mind Dracula's three Transylvanian wives. *(Courtesy of Buddy Barnett)*

Browning's *Dracula* occurrs when "one re-sees the film." He also emphasized that the film's interchange between Van Helsing and Dracula represented delights that were "increasing" over time.[16]

Increasing over time. Whether as individuals or as part of larger "audience," the ways in which moviegoers (and critics) engage with particular films certainly do change. Popular acceptance of *The Wizard of Oz* (1939) and *It's a Wonderful Life* (1946) grew over time; the same could be said about the critical appreciation of *Citizen Kane* (1941). Everson's opinion toward *Dracula* had changed from his first published views on the film in 1954 to his last in 1986. To be sure, time does not actually judge films. We do. We can change. We can be fickle. And, happily, we are plural. Not everyone need agree.

Consider the thoughts of Andrew Sarris, film critic for the *Village Voice* and America's leading proponent of auteur theory. In 1998, he wrote:

Browning's direction of Dracula *has been denigrated by later critics and historians for its allegedly static and stagey shortcomings. Mine may be a minority view, but I have always felt that the Browning style was appropriate for a mood piece, particularly one photographed by the incomparable Karl Freund.*
…The intensity of [its] performances gave this first American-made Dracula *a gravity and conviction none of its many sequels and derivatives could match.*[17]

Here was one of America's leading voices on the cinema rejecting the critical tradition initiated by George Geltzer and openly challenging allegations made against the film. Only months later, the *Los Angeles Times* echoed his views, noting: "this is a film that will scare you if given half a chance, but it needs to be taken on its own terms to do that."[18]

In 1999, Philip Glass' score to Browning's *Dracula* – written for the Kronos Quartet – made its debut. Nonesuch Records issued a soundtrack version that same year. Eight years later, Orange Mountain Music released a CD featuring solo pianist Michael Riesman playing the entire score, as well as a previously unrecorded track that did not finally become a part of the film soundtrack.

In the year 2000, the Library of Congress selected Browning's *Dracula* for preservation in the National Film Registry. Like others inducted before and after it, *Dracula* was deemed to be a "culturally, historically, or aesthetically significant" film. Dr. James H. Billington of the Library of Congress has said that the registry "stands among the finest summations of American cinema's wondrous first century."

Then, in 2006, Universal Home Video released a new version of *Dracula* (a "75th Anniversary Edition") on DVD. In addition to reissuing an audio commentary by David J. Skal that was first heard in 1999, the disc featured a second commentary, this time by Steve Haberman, one of the screenwriters of Mel Brooks' film *Dracula: Dead and Loving It* (1995). In it, Haberman argues in favor of the Browning film's superiority over the Melford.

The commentary's producer Constantine Nasr has described his motivation for hiring Haberman: "Skal's commentary was a very strong and informative one, but with a sensibility that I personally didn't agree with. I felt there was value in hearing a more positive approach that celebrated the film, as opposed to knocking it in favor of the Spanish version – and so did the good folks at Universal Home Video. Steve Haberman was a like-minded admirer of the film and of Browning, not simply an apologist but a true believer, and I asked him to do the commentary, which I felt was a good alternative to Skal's views."[19]

Reaction to both the Glass score and the Haberman commentary have been mixed. But along with the Sarris endorsement and the National Film Registry selection, they represent key points in a different critical trajectory for Browning's *Dracula*. Haberman offers praise for the film, something that has been sorely lacking for most of the past fifty years. Moreover, Glass is a highly respected modern composer who chose to engage artistically with the Browning film, stamping it with his own imprimatur. Few early talkies could lay claim to such an endorsement at the turn of the new millennium.

When I personally first saw *Dracula* at the age of four or five, I was enthralled. When I saw it again at the age of twelve, I was somewhat disappointed and remained so for several years thereafter. But by the time I was 28, I was convinced that – as Everson had already argued – its delights were increasing. Since then, each time I watch the film, I find it to be richer and more engrossing than before. The critical pendulum swung in one direction, but the Everson of 1986, the Sarris of 1998, the Glass of 1999, and the Haberman of 2006 suggest a change, however gradual.

Many persons will no doubt continue to find *Dracula* uninteresting. They may hate it. That is a wonderful thing. People love and hate films. They have visceral responses and gut reactions. If anyone finds the film vomitous, more power. Good health to them. Likewise, many will likely embrace Melford's Spanish-language *Dracula* for years to come. They will revel in delight at its female vampires or its lengthy running time or its lead actor. Fair play.

So often we react to films for reasons that are hard to understand. Perhaps we are bored with a film because we are not drawn to the genre in which it operates, or because we dislike one of its actors. Or maybe it is just because we have other plans later in the day that occupy our thoughts. We can grow restless at the movie theatre, fearing that we left the coffee pot on or forgot to lock the back door.

And sometimes we love a film just because we saw it on an important day in our life: a first date with a spouse, for example. Or we love it because of some particular line of dialogue or particular image that thrilled us. And sometimes we simply don't know why we like or dislike a film. So much the better. Life needs good mysteries.

More than anything else, if I have any single hope for Browning's *Dracula*, it is not that everyone comes to love it. After all, no matter how many critics *Dracula* has, I suspect it will outlast all of them. It already has a good track record in that regard. And like any unique work of art, it deserves, in the best sense of the word, critics.

But I do hope the next generation of critics offers new ideas to consider. Or that they will just admit that they wish that *Dracula* had been produced years after it was. Or that they will at least find fresh adjectives to describe how much they despise the film. Any of those kinds of critiques would be preferable to further rehash of "facts" about *Dracula* and its history that are not factual.

Dracula deserves such treatment, given its ongoing popularity and lasting influence. And the film deserves to be discussed as what it was and what it is. The film was not Karl Freund's *Dracula*, or Garrett Fort's *Dracula*, or even Bram Stoker's *Dracula*. For better or worse, it was and shall remain Tod Browning's *Dracula*.

1. Sarris, Andrew. *The American Cinema: Directors and Directions, 1929-1968* (New York: E. P. Dutton, 1968): 24.
2. Clarens, Carlos. *An Illustrated History of the Horror Film* (New York: Capricorn Books, 1967): 61.
3. Spadoni, Robert. *Uncanny Bodies: The Coming of Sound Film and the Origins of the Horror Genre* (Berkeley: University of California Press, 2007): 79.
4. Skal, David J. and Elias Savada. *Dark Carnival: The Secret World of Tod Browning, Hollywood's Master of the Macabre* (New York: Anchor/Doubleday, 1995): 155-156.
5. Rosar, William H. "Music for the Monsters: Universal Pictures' Horror Film Scores of the Thirties." *The Quarterly Journal of the Library of Congress* Vol. 40, No. 4 (Fall 1983): 393-395.
6. *Dracula (The Original 1931 Shooting Script)*. Ed. by Philip J. Riley. (Absecon, NJ: MagicImage, 1990).
7. Ibid.
8. Such nocturnal creatures even bear commonalities to other creatures who are not present in the film, despite suggestions to the contrary. For example, in his book *The Immortal Count: The Life and Films of Bela Lugosi* (Lexington, KY: University of Lexington Press, 2003), writer Arthur Lennig wrongly claims that an image of a "rat scurrying among the bones" appears in the film (p. 104).
9. Williams, Tony. Email to Gary D. Rhodes 11 Feb. 2013.
10. Here I must acknowledge the kind assistance of my friend Leonardo D'Aurizio, who drew my attention to the history of these kinds of snuff boxes.
11. This prop is reused in *The Mummy* (1932), where it appears on a bedside table when Helen Grosvenor (Zita Johann) is being kept under the protection of Doctor Muller (Edward Van Sloan) and Frank Whemple (David Manners).
12. It is also worth noting that no armadillos appear in the Melford version, another example of the differences in approach between Browning and Melford.
13. Douglas, Drake. *Horror!* (New York: MacMillan, 1966): 43.
14. Beck, Calvin T. *Heroes of the Horrors* (Collier, 1975):
15. Weaver, Tom. "*Dracula* (1931)." In Brunas, Micheal, John Brunas, and Tom Weaver. *Universal Horrors* (Jefferson, NC: McFarland, 1990): 18.
16. Everson, William K. *More Classics of the Horror Film* (New York: Citadel, 1986): 30.
17. Sarris, Andrew. *"You Ain't Heard Nothin' Yet": The American Talking Film, History and Memory* (New York: Oxford University Press, 1998): 80.
18. Turan, Kenneth. "Live Musical Accompaniment Drains *Dracula* of Its Scariness." *Los Angeles Times* 1 Nov. 1999: 11.
19. Nasr, Constantine. Email to Gary D. Rhodes. 11 Feb. 2013.

INDEX

Abbott and Costello Meet Frankenstein (1948) 294, 295
Abe Lincoln in Illinois (1940) 101
Abraham Lincoln (1930) 108
Ackerman, Forrest J 56, 287
Albee Theatre (Brooklyn, NY) 270, 271
Alhambra Theatre (Milwaukee, WI) 213, 270, 271, 272
Alibi (1929) 107
All Quiet on the Western Front (1930) 12, 45, 63, 64, 65, 73, 84, 85, 86, 87, 88, 92, 96, 102, 112, 114, 159, 174, 184, 197, 215, 222, 231, 244, 273, 278
Ames, Robert 159, 165, 172
Among the Living (1941) 135
Anderson, John Murray 152
Andrews, Del 197
Angelus Novus (painting) 15
Applause (1929) 75
Asher, E. M. 13, 87, 91, 93, 105, 106, 107, 111, 141, 142, 143, 150, 153, 154, 155, 161, 195, 203, 291
Ayres, Lew 60, 73, 86, 92, 96, 97, 98, 102, 103, 112, 159, 172, 189, 192

Bahn, Chester B. 58
Bakacs, Anna 100
Balderston, John L. 12, 13, 34, 40, 56, 89, 90, 119, 120, 121, 123, 124, 125, 127, 128, 129, 132, 133, 138, 139, 140, 143, 144, 179, 193, 291, 316
Ballet mécanique (1924) 131
Bara, Theda 10, 30, 31, 33, 36, 40, 91, 157, 158, 227, 233, 276
Bass, Saul 155
Bat, The (stage play) 79
Bat, The (1926) 79-80, 81, 84, 150
Bat Whispers, The (1930) 84, 106, 107, 140, 241, 319, 320, 333
Beahan, Charles 136
Beal, Scott R. 91, 148, 149, 154
Bear's Wedding, The (1925) 65, 66
Beaton, Welford 258-259
Beck, Calvin T. 365

Beginning of the Armadillos, The (short story) 360
Behind That Curtain (1929) 81
Bela, Nicholas 99-100, 101
Bell, Monta 87
Belmore, Daisy 99, 101
Ben-Hur (1959) 322
Benjamin, Walter 15
Benson Murder Case, The (1930) 81, 82
Bergerman, Stanley 87
Berman, Pandro S. 184
Better 'Ole, The (1926) 74
Big City, The (1928) 198
Big House, The (1930) 107
Big Pond, The (1930) 136
Billington, James H. 366
Birth of a Nation, The (1915) 9
Bishop Murder Case, The (1930) 81, 82
Black and Tan (1929) 132
Black Bird, The (1926) 53, 55
Blake, Michael 67
Blaze o' Glory (1929) 78
Blind Wives (1930) 112
Blue Mouse Theatre (Seattle, WA) 300, 301
Blues for Dracula (record album) 310
Boles, John 86, 87
Booth, Frank H. 155
Bordwell, David 316
Boucicault, Dion 22, 23, 24
Bozoky, Barbara 100
Boudoir Diplomat, The (1930) 86, 91, 98, 108, 109, 112, 152, 177, 184, 189
Bradford, Gardner 220

Bram Stoker's Dracula (1992) 310-311
Brannan, Margaret 56-57
Brats (1930) 77
Brent, Evelyn 62
Broadway (1929) 62, 92, 93
Broder, Jack 303

Broekman, David 213
Bromfield, Louis 12, 105, 106, 125-130, 131, 132, 133, 135, 136, 137, 138, 139, 131, 143, 152, 153, 163, 182
Brooks, Mel 366
Brosnan, John 315
Brotherton, Joseph 92, 115, 220
Brown, Porter Emerson 30
Browning, Tod
    Early Life 46
    Early Career 46, 47
    And cinematic trickery 52-54
    And *Dracula* (1931) vii, viii, 9, 10, 12, 13, 14, 15, 18, 19, 22, 24, 38, 43, 45, 69, 74, 88, 90, 91, 93, 102, 103, 104, 111, 122, 123, 125, 130, 133, 136, 137, 138, 139, 140, 141, 142, 143, 146, 147, 148, 149, 150, 151, 152, 153, 154, 155, 157, 158, 159, 161, 162, 163, 164, 166, 167, 168, 170, 171, 172, 174, 175, 176, 177, 178, 179, 180, 181, 182, 184, 185, 186, 187, 189, 190, 191, 193, 195, 197, 198, 199, 200, 202, 203, 205, 206, 208, 210, 211, 212, 216, 220, 221, 227, 231, 239, 245, 250, 251, 252, 253, 254, 256, 259, 261, 262, 263, 265, 274, 275, 280, 283, 284, 289, 310, 311, 313, 315, 316, 317, 318, 320, 321, 322, 325, 327, 333, 335, 336, 337, 338, 339, 340, 341, 342, 343, 344, 345, 348, 349, 350, 351, 352, 353, 354, 356, 359, 361, 362, 363, 364, 365, 366, 367, 368
    And *London After Midnight* (1927) 55-58, 67, 102
    And *Mark of the Vampire* (1935) 295-299, 310
    And pre-*Dracula* (1931) film career 43, 44, 45, 46, 47, 48, 49, 50, 51, 67, 68, 69, 71, 72, 77, 82, 86, 89, 93, 96-97, 102, 104, 116, 133, 197, 198, 199, 221
    And sound cinema 58-60
    Post-*Dracula* Career 60, 222
Bruce, Lenny 310
Bunston, Herbert 155, 167, 170, 176, 212, 327
Burgess, Dorothy 189
Burman, Ben Lucian 159
Burne-Jones, Philip 10, 12, 27, 28, 29, 30, 31, 33, 36, 40, 91, 158, 227

Cabinet of Dr. Caligari, The (1920) 38, 88, 137, 138
Calmson, Bertrand 261, 285
Canal, The (short story) 38
Canary Murder Case, The (1929) 81
Capitol Theatre (Atlanta, GA) 270
Capra, Frank 320
Captain of the Guard (1930) 197
Carew, Arthur Edmund 43, 44, 70
Carewe, Edwin 73, 77, 87, 96, 151, 152, 171, 177, 197, 219, 225
Carmilla (short story) 25, 41
Carol, Sue 184
Carroll, Moon 177
Carruth, Milton 197, 198, 199, 200, 203, 205, 208, 209, 210, 211, 212, 213, 342
Cat and the Canary, The (stage play) 79, 81
Cat and the Canary, The (1927) 64, 80, 81, 84, 88
Cat Creeps, The (1930) 64, 83, 84, 90, 93, 208, 215, 216, 222 231, 241, 244, 289
Cat Creeps, The (1930, Spanish-language version) 83, 84,
189, 203
Chandler, Geraldine 145
Chandler, Helen 13, 74, 98, 99, 100, 145, 167, 172, 175, 180, 183, 185, 186, 188, 189, 226, 231, 233, 240, 241, 242, 251, 261, 262, 322, 323, 324, 325
Chaney, Lon, Jr. 293
Chaney, Lon, Sr. 38, 39, 45, 50, 51, 52, 53, 55, 56, 57, 58, 67, 69, 83, 89, 102-103, 107, 114, 117, 149, 161, 169, 233, 253, 254, 265, 293, 315
Chaplin, Charlie 92, 270
Charlatan, The (1929) 83, 84
Chinese Parrot, The (1927) 88
Christensen, Benjamin 82
Churchill, Edward 164
Cimarron (1931) 274, 277, 320, 333
Citizen Kane (1941) 9, 155, 366
City Lights (1931) 270
Civjans, Gunars 316
Clarens, Carlos 313, 336, 353
Clarke, Mae 197, 223
Claw, The (1927) 141
Code of Ethics for the Production of Motion Pictures (1930) 112, 141, 142, 163, 166, 207
Cohen, Max 217-218
Collins, Wilkie 139
Colman, Ronald 167, 168, 182
Columbia Pictures 89, 177, 222, 304, 333
Confessions of a Nazi Spy (1939) 101
Conway, Jack 102
Costello Case, The (1930) 81
Count Chocula 310
Count, Count von 310
Courtenay, William 107, 109, 111, 112, 117
Crafton, Donald 73, 75, 77
Crawford, F. Marion 33, 34
Crosby, Bing 184
Curtiz, Michael 166
Czar of Broadway, The (1930) 103, 104

Dade, Frances 145, 164, 167, 202, 214, 231, 240, 309, 313, 342
Dance, Fools, Dance (1931) 319, 321, 333
Dangerous Affair, The (1931) 282
Dangerous Nan McGrew (1930) 136
Danse Macabre (1922) 131, 132
Darkened Rooms (1929) 81, 82
Davidson, John 58
Davis, Hubert G. 44
Dean, Priscilla 48
Deane, Hamilton 12, 13, 34, 40, 56, 58, 89, 90, 119, 120, 121, 123, 124, 125, 127, 128, 129, 132, 133, 138, 139, 140, 143, 144, 291, 316
Dell, Gabriel 310
DeMille, Cecil B. 131, 135, 243
DeMond, Albert 87
Destry Rides Again (1939) 302
Devil to Pay!, The (1930) 319, 333
Devil-Doll, The (1936) 53, 55, 60, 135
Dickens, Charles 362

Dickson, W. K. L. 74
Die Meistersinger (opera) 216, 316, 357-358
Dinner with Drac (song) 310
Dirigible (1931) 317, 320, 333
Disraeli (1929) 100
Dr. Jekyll and Mr. Hyde (1931) 321, 333
Dr. Strangelove (1964) 329
    Doctor X (stage play) 241
Don Juan (1926) 74
Donaldson, Bob 232
Doorway to Hell, The (1930) 95
Douglas, Drake 365
Downtown Theatre (Detroit, MI) 277
Dracula (acrobat) 26-27
Dracula (novel, 1897) 17, 18, 20, 22, 24, 25-27, 33, 34, 36, 38, 39, 40, 43, 44, 56, 57, 58, 64, 66, 69, 70, 88, 89, 90, 105, 119, 120, 121, 122, 123, 124, 125, 126, 127, 128, 129, 130, 132, 135, 142, 143, 219, 231, 232, 238, 245, 246, 250, 251, 253, 261, 262, 274, 275, 278, 293, 315, 353, 357, 360, 361
Dracula (novel, 1931 edition) 232, 245, 246
Dracula (1979) 310
Dracula: Dead and Loving It (1995) 310, 366
Dracula of the Hills, A (poem) 34
Dracula–The Vampire Play (stage play) 13, 34-37, 38, 40, 56, 69, 74, 88, 89, 90, 91, 95, 97, 103, 104, 105, 106, 107, 119, 120, 121, 122, 123, 124, 125, 127, 128, 129, 132, 133, 134, 138, 139, 140, 141, 142, 143, 144, 155, 176, 179, 184, 189, 191, 206, 231, 232, 233, 241, 244, 245, 246, 251, 252, 254, 248, 262, 267, 269, 270, 274, 276, 277, 278, 279-280, 283, 291, 295, 315, 316, 353, 357
Dracula's Daughter (1936) 135, 193, 290-293, 294, 295
Dracula's Guest (1914) 138
Drake, Frances 150
Drifting (1923) 221
Drinkwater, John 62, 179, 182
Drums of Jeopardy, The (1931) 241, 320, 333
Du Maurier, George 236
Dvorak, Geraldine 100, 101

Eadie, Arlton 38
Early Autumn (1926) 126
East Is West (1930) 86, 141
East Is West (1930, Spanish language version) 84, 203
East Lynne (1931) 249, 255
East of Borneo (1931) 345
Ellington, Duke 132
Everson, William K. 197, 313, 335, 365, 366, 367
Eyes of Mystery, The (1918) 48

Famous Players 135
Faust 138
Fazenda, Louise 81
Fejos, Paul 61, 62, 319
Fighting Thru (1930) 98
Film Daily, The (trade publication) 51, 61, 62, 68, 76, 82, 93, 99, 103, 110, 130, 134, 135, 171, 172, 174, 177, 195, 203, 205, 206, 208, 226, 227, 229, 231, 232, 236, 237, 241, 249, 252, 259, 261, 273, 280, 284

Film Fun (fan magazine) 262
First National 82, 173, 174, 177, 192, 203
Fithian, Ted 141
Fletcher, Bramwell 241
Florescu, Radu 17
Floyd, John 79
Fool There Was, A (novel) 30
Fool There Was, A (stage play) 30
Fool There Was, A (1914) 30
Fool There Was, A (1915) 30, 31
Fool There Was, A (1922) 31
For the Blood is the Life (short story) 33
Forest Vampires, The (1914) 27
Fort, Garrett 68, 135-141, 142, 143, 144, 154, 180, 181, 186, 199, 210, 216, 299, 316, 359, 367
14 Minutes in Darktown (comedy skit) 46
Foucault, Michel 10
Fox, William 30, 74
Foy, Bryan 82
Frankenstein (1818) 21
Frankenstein (1931) 105, 135, 197, 273, 278, 289, 300, 301, 302, 303, 304, 305, 307, 311, 321, 322, 333, 334, 365
Frankenstein Meets the Wolf Man (1943) 293
Freaks (1932) 54, 60, 198, 321
Free Love (1930) 171, 222
Freedman, Harold 89, 105, 110
Freulich, Roman 93, 327
Freund, Karl 13, 91, 92, 93, 115, 147, 148, 149, 150, 151, 154, 155, 163, 164, 190, 191, 203, 219, 220, 252, 261, 318, 319, 322, 323, 325, 327, 333, 344, 345, 346, 349, 350, 365, 366, 367
Friedman, Phil 93, 95
Frozen Ghost, The (1945) 305
Frye, Dwight 95, 96, 99, 101, 116, 156, 157, 164, 168, 185, 200, 206, 212, 226, 241, 261, 315, 345, 354
Fuseli, Henry 231

Gaige, Crosby 136
Galeen, Henrik 39
Garson, Harry 93
Geltzer, George 197, 313, 365, 366
Gente Alegre (1931) 282
Gerrard, Charles 168, 261
Gershwin, George 246, 277
Ghost of Frankenstein, The (1942) 293
Ghost Talks, The (1929) 82
Girls Demand Excitement (1931) 245
Glass, Philip 307, 308, 366
Goethe, Johann Wolfgang von 138
Gold Rush, The (1925) 92
Goldstone, Phil 98, 320
Goldwyn, Samuel 125, 164, 168
Golf with Johnny Farrell (1931) 280
Goodman, Frank 213
Gorilla, The (1927) 80
Gorilla, The (1930) 82
Gray, King 92, 220
Green Bay Tree, The (1924) 125
Greene Murder Case, The (1929) 81

Grey, King *see* Gray, King
Griffith, D. W. 108
Griffith, Raymond 73
Guerrero, Carmen 161, 170
Guffey, Robert 15

Haberman, Steve 308, 366, 367
Hall, Charles "Danny" 92, 93, 174, 186
Hall, Gladys 233
Hall, Manly P. 295
Hall, Mordaunt 102, 249, 250, 251
Halliwell, Leslie 315, 316
Hamilton, George 310
Hamrick, John 300, 301
Harder, Anita 170
Hardy, Oliver 77, 82, 338
Harlow, Jean 189, 190
Hart, William, S., Jr. 197, 198
Hays, Will H. , 141, 152, 225
Hays Office, The 141, 142, 200, 206, 225, 289
He Male Vamp (1920) 33
Hello New York (stage show) 246-248, 255
Henley, Hobart 69, 171
Heston, Charlton 322
Hidden Hand, The (1917) 141
Hippodrome Theatre (New York, NY) 272
Hoffman, Gertrude 26
Hoffman, John 93
Holden, Gloria 54, 291, 293
Holiday (1930) 159, 161
Holloway, Clark J. 223
Hollywood Filmograph (trade publication) 14, 78, 91, 92, 93, 94, 96, 106, 107, 111, 125, 136, 137, 143, 149, 152, 157, 171, 189, 205, 220, 256, 259, 261
Hollywood Reporter (trade publication) 10, 78, 95, 97, 98, 99, 112, 132, 138, 143, 145, 152, 155, 174, 177, 179, 182, 190, 195, 203, 206, 218, 220, 232, 242, 243, 244, 249, 278, 282
Hook, Line and Sinker (1930) 320, 333
House of Dracula (1945) 294, 308
House of Frankenstein (1944) 292, 293, 294, 295, 312
House of Horror, The (1929) 82, 100
House of Secrets, The (1929) 82
House of Wax (1953) 313
Hull, Henry 99
Hume, Cyril 175
Hunchback of Notre Dame, The (1923) 43, 64, 86
Hunter, C. Roy 92
Huntley, Raymond 57, 106
Hurlock, Madeline 33
Huston, John 150

I Stole a Million (1939) 302
Illicit (1931) 320, 333
Invisible Man, The (1933) 135
Invisible Prince! Or, the Island of Tranquil Delights (stage play) 27
Iron Man (1931) 54, 60, 189, 190, 194
Irving, Sir Henry 25

It's a Wonderful Life (1946) 366

Janis, Elsie 165
Januskopf, Der (1920) 149
Jazz Singer, The (1927) 9, 74, 75
Jessel, George 74
Jim Bludso (1917) 46
Johann, Zita 368
Johnston, John LeRoy 137
Jolson, Al 74
Jones, Philly Joe 310
Jones, Ray C. 46
Journey's End (1930) 112, 147, 172
Joy, Colonel Jason 141, 142, 144, 206
Jukes, Bernard 95
Julian, Rupert 64, 84, 87
Just So Stories (1902) 360

Kael, Pauline 155
Kaelred, Katharine 30
Kalich, Bertha 26
Karloff, Boris 105, 292, 301
Katz, Sam 75
Keith, Ian 108, 109, 110, 111
Kept Husbands (1931) 320, 333
King of Jazz (1930) 62, 63, 79, 84, 85, 93, 99, 114, 152, 282
Kingsley, Grace 103, 110
Kipling, Rudyard 10, 12, 27, 28, 29, 31, 33, 36, 40, 91, 158, 227, 360
Kismet (1930) 148, 177
Kiss, The (1962) 202, 310
Klee, Paul 15
Kohner, Paul 78, 79, 90, 168, 177, 184, 189, 242
Komic Kompany 46
Kronos Quartet 307, 308, 366
Kubrick, Stanley 329, 332

La Plante, Laura 82
Lady to Love, A (1930) 78
Lady of Scandal, The (1930) 167
Laemmle, Carl, Jr. 12, 13, 14, 43, 45, 60-65, 66, 67, 68, 69, 73, 74, 76, 77, 78, 79, 84, 86, 87, 88, 89, 90, 91, 93, 94, 96, 99, 103, 105, 106, 110, 111, 112, 113, 114, 121, 125, 126, 130, 135, 137, 138, 141, 142, 143, 144, 150, 152, 153, 154, 155, 156, 157, 159, 161, 163, 171, 174, 177, 178, 179, 184, 187, 190, 195, 197, 200, 203, 206, 222, 227, 229, 243, 244, 257, 273, 283, 284, 297, 320, 333
Laemmle, Carl, Sr. 12, 43, 44, 60, 61, 62, 67, 84, 86, 99, 111, 155, 179, 182, 184, 195, 197, 200, 213, 214, 218, 219, 227, 228, 239, 242, 243, 244, 254, 261, 273, 281, 329
Laemmle, Carla 66, 99, 101, 155, 156, 157
Laemmle, Junior *see* Laemmle, Carl, Jr.
Lang, Fritz 92
Langella, Frank 310
Lasky, Jesse L. 75
Last Laugh, The (1924) 340
Last Performance, The (1928) 61, 78, 93, 117
Last Warning, The (1929) 62, 82, 83
Laurel and Hardy 77, 82, 338

Laurel-Hardy Murder Case, The (1930) 82
Lawrence, Edmund 82
Lawrence, Florence 111
Le Fanu, J. Sheridan 25
Lease, Rex 98
Lee, Christopher 310
Léger, Ferdinand 131
Legion of Death, The (1917) 48
Leni, Paul 82, 88,
Lennig, Arthur 200, 202, 311, 318, 333, 368
Lesser, Sol 273
Life and Adventures of Carl Laemmle, The (1931) 62
Life of the Party, The (1930) 177
Lights of New York, The (1928) 75
Little Caesar (1931) 189, 319, 320, 321, 333
Liveright, Harace 34, 89, 90, 133, 189, 241
Loff, Jeanette 86, 97, 98, 99, 109
Logue, Charles A. 141
London After Midnight (1927) 12, 38, 45, 52, 53, 54, 55-58, 67, 70, 102, 198, 265, 295, 297, 299
Lonesome (1928) 61
Love Sublime, A (1917) 48
Lowell, Amy 34
Lucky Transfer, The (1915) 46
Lugosi, Bela viii, 13, 18, 21, 34, 36, 37, 38, 53, 57, 74, 75, 79, 88, 90, 95, 102, 103, 104, 105, 106, 107, 110, 111, 112, 114, 116, 117, 120, 133, 135, 136, 145, 146, 147, 149, 150, 154, 161, 164, 165, 169, 171, 172, 174, 175, 176, 177, 179, 185, 199, 200, 202, 206, 214, 220, 226, 228, 231, 233, 235, 238, 241, 242, 245, 250, 252, 254, 256, 258, 259, 261, 262, 268, 272, 274, 276, 277, 283, 287, 288, 289, 290, 292, 293, 294, 295, 296, 298, 299, 302, 303, 306, 307, 308, 309, 310, 311, 313, 314, 315, 325, 328, 334, 336, 337, 338, 339, 341, 343, 354, 365

McAvoy, May 81, 83
McNally, Raymond T. 17
Mace, Junior 232
Mad Love (1935) 150
Mainstreet Theatre (Kansas City, MO) 274
Male and Female (1919) 131
Mamoulian, Rouben 75
Man Who Laughs, The (1928) 88, 93
Manners, David 13, 147, 148, 149, 150, 151, 154, 155, 165, 172, 173, 174, 176, 180, 182, 183, 186, 187, 189, 191, 226, 241, 274, 368
Manon, Hugh 10, 53
Many a Slip (1931) 205, 222
Mariana (stage play) 26
Mark of the Vampire (1935) 12, 53, 55, 191, 203, 295-299, 310, 311
Mayer, Louis B. 67, 102
Maynard, Ken 98
Maywood, Robert Campbell 21
MCA/Universal Home Video 306, 307, 336
Medvezhya Svadba see *Bear's Wedding, The*
Melford, George 15, 83, 84, 161, 168, 347, 348, 349, 350, 351, 352, 361, 364, 365, 366, 367, 368
Mephistopheles at Play (vaudeville act) 27

Metro-Goldwyn-Mayer (MGM) 38, 45, 46, 51, 56, 67, 68, 70, 78, 82, 89, 90, 102, 143, 190, 198, 219, 222, 295, 333
Metropolis (1927) 92
Metzger, Lou 257
Midnight Faces (1926) 92
Midnight Girl, The (1925) 135
Midnight Mystery, The (1930) 81
Midwest Theatre (Oklahoma City, OK) 270
Milestone, Lewis 63, 64, 73, 87, 92
Millie (1931) 172, 272, 276, 277, 320, 333
Miracles for Sale (1939) 53, 54, 60
Mitchell, Johnny 232
Modern Dracula, The (Proposed Sequel) 289
Modern Screen 234, 235, 262
Monster, The (stage play) 79
Monster, The (1925) 79
Moran, Dade 145
Morocco (1930) 177, 320, 333
Morris, Chester 106, 117
Motion Picture Classic (fan magazine) 149, 233, 263, 268
Motion Picture Daily (trade publication) 226, 227, 239, 242, 243, 252, 253, 273, 274, 340
Motion Picture Herald (trade publication) 190, 205, 206, 232, 233, 241, 280, 283, 284, 299, 333
Motion Picture Monthly (trade publication) 269
Motion Picture News (trade publication)
Motion Picture Producers and Distributors of America 141, 143, 206, 207, 225
Mummy, The (1932) 148, 215, 333, 368
Muni, Paul 107, 108, 111, 117
Murder by the Clock (1931) 278, 282, 321, 322, 333
Murder on the Roof (1930) 81
Murder Will Out (1930) 81
Murders in the Rue Morgue (1932) 215, 273, 278
Murnau, F. W. 13, 38, 39, 69, 90, 92, 122, 132, 143, 149, 250, 328
Murphy, Donald 116
Murphy, Dudley 105, 106, 130-135, 136, 137, 138, 143, 163, 182
Murray, Charlie 46
Mysterious Dr. Fu Manchu (1929) 81
Mystery of King Tut-Ankh-Amen's Eighth Wife, The (1923) 217
Mystic, The (1925) 53, 54

Nasr, Constantine 308, 366
National Association of Radio and Television Broadcasters (NARTB) 305
National Screen Service 237, 264
Navarro, Ramon 166
Nelson, Jerry 310
New Movie Magazine (fan magazine) 262
Nielsen, Leslie 310
Nigh, William 98
Night Ride (1930) 106, 197
Nightmare, The (painting) 231
No Limit (1931) 317, 333
Nolan, Mary 59, 69, 96, 98, 152, 177, 178
Nosferatu (1922) 13, 38, 39, 40, 65, 69, 90, 122, 123, 130,

132, 133, 138, 143, 159, 170, 250, 328, 365

Oates, Joyce Carol 10
O'Brian, Jack 289
Oldman, Gary 310-311
Oliver Twist (1838) 362
Other Men's Women (1931) 333
Outside the Law (1920) 45, 49, 50, 55
Outside the Law (1930) 12, 54, 55, 59-60, 68, 69, 71, 77, 86, 93, 96, 97, 136, 174, 197, 198, 199, 221
Outward Bound (stage play) 98
Outward Bound (1930) 98-99

Palmer, A. Arnold 198,
Pantages Theatre (Hollywood, CA) 261, 280
Paramount Pictures 75, 78, 89, 90, 101, 135, 136, 141, 177, 189, 190, 222, 278, 282, 333
Parker, William 45
Parlor, Bedroom and Bath (1931) 320, 333
Parsons, Louella O. 60, 61, 72, 96, 102, 111, 159, 172, 174
Pascal, Ernest 136
Phantom, The (stage play) 22, 23, 24
Phantom of the Opera, The (1925) 43, 83, 182, 213,
Phantom of the Opera, The (1930) 83, 102, 103, 231
Photoplay (fan magazine)
Pickford, Mary 243
Picture Play (fan magazine) 262, 263
Pierce, Jack 93, 94, 161
Pivar, Maurice 197, 198, 200
Planché, James Robinson 22
Poe, Edgar Allan 26, 45, 250, 303,
Polidori, John William 22, 23, 24, 41
Prisoners (1929) 75
Proctor, Jack 232
Production Code Administration (PCA) 301
Psycho (1960) viii, 150

Raffles (1930) 168
Rapee, Erno 246
Rapf, Harry 46, 67
Rapf, Maurice 46
Reaching for the Moon (1931) 272, 319, 333
Realart Re-Releasing 303, 313
Reisman, Phil 113, 243
Remarque, Erich Maria 63
Resurrection (1931) 73, 77, 87, 92, 93, 96, 151, 152, 154, 161, 171, 174, 177, 197, 205, 215, 218, 219, 222, 225, 231, 244, 255, 319, 320, 333
Return of Dr. Fu Manchu, The (1930) 81
Return of Dracula, The (proposed sequel) 289
Revel, The (poem) 332
Reynolds, Harry 198
Rhapsody in Blue 246, 247, 255, 277
Rialto Theatre (Washington, DC) 213, 269-270
Riesman, Michael 366
Right to Love, The (1930) 147, 182
Riley, Philip J. 335
Rinehart, Mary Roberts 79
RKO Keith's (Boston, MA) 280

RKO Orpheum (Los Angeles, CA) 277
RKO Orpheum (New Orleans, LA) 280
RKO Orpheum (Portland, OR) 271
RKO Orpheum (San Francisco, CA) 277
RKO Orpheum (Seattle, WA) 272
RKO Orpheum (Tacoma, WA) 270
Roadhouse Nights (1930) 136
Robinson, Edward G. 60, 64, 68, 189
Robinson, George 336, 345, 346, 349
Roemheld, Heinz 213, 358
Rogers, Will 243
Rosar, William H. 357
Rosen, Al 95
Rosse, Herman 93
Rothafel, S. L. "Roxy" 244, 245, 248, 249, 255
Roxy Theatre (New York City) 244, 245, 246, 247, 248, 249, 254, 255
Rubio, Pablo Alvarez 161
Run for His Money, A (stage play) 167

St. Clair, Malcolm 87, 152
St. Louis Blues (1929) 131, 132
Salt, Barry 316, 333
Sarris, Andrew 10, 353, 366, 367
Savada, Elias 116, 191, 193, 194, 255, 285, 286, 316, 357
 Scared Stiff (1930) 170
Scarface (1932) 107
Schade, Peter 309
Schildkraut, Joseph 106
Schreck, Max 38, 39
Screen Book Magazine (fan magazine) 262
Screenland (fan magazine) 262
Screenplay (fan magazine) 262
Schubert, Franz Peter 216, 308, 316, 322, 357, 358
Schulberg, B. P. 89, 190
Second Floor Mystery, The (1930) 81
Secret Six, The (1931) 333
Seiler, Lewis 82
Sennett, Mack 91
Sesame Street (television program) 310
Seven Faces (1930) 107, 108
Seven Keys to Baldpate (stage play) 79
Seven Keys to Baldpate (1917) 79
Seven Keys to Baldpate (1929) 81
Shelley, Mary 21
Shock! Television Package 304-305
Show, The (1927) 53
Silver Nails (stage play) 100
Silver Screen 233, 240, 262
Simon Called Peter (stage play) 167
Sin Takes a Holiday (1930) 177, 333
Skal, David J. vi, 71, 110, 114, 116, 117, 147, 151, 152, 153, 172, 191, 192, 193, 194, 255, 285, 286, 307, 308, 315, 316, 317, 318, 334, 335, 336, 344, 345, 352, 357, 366, 367
Slander (1916) 95
Smith, Bessie 131, 132
Smitch, Carter B., DVM vi, 193, 352
Soanes, Wood 105

Solomon, Matthew 10
Son of Dracula (proposed sequel) 289
Son of Dracula (1943) 293, 294, 308
Son of the Gods (1930) 100
Son of Kong, The (1933) 300
Soul of the Cypress (1920) 131
Spider, The (stage play) 107, 140
Spider and Her Web, The (1914) 236
Spreckel's Theatre (San Diego, CA) 267
Standing, Joan 170
Standing, Wyndham 170
Stanley Theatre (Philadelphia, PA) 272
Stanley Theatre (Pittsburgh, PA) 271
Star Wars (1977) 9
State-Lake Theatre (Chicago, IL) 275, 276
Stephani, Frederick "Fritz" 122-125, 130, 132, 133, 136, 137, 139, 140, 141
Stedman, E. C. 332
Steve Allen Show, The (television program) 310
Stoker, Bram 10, 12, 13, 17, 18, 20, 22, 25, 26, 27, 30, 33, 34, 36, 38, 39, 40, 43, 44, 55, 56, 57, 58, 65, 70, 89, 90, 102, 105, 119, 120, 121, 122, 123, 124, 125, 127, 128, 129, 130, 132, 134, 138, 139, 140, 142, 143, 198, 219, 232, 245. 246, 250, 261, 262, 293, 310, 360, 361, 367
Stoker, Florence 89, 90
Stolen Heaven (1931) 274
Stolen Jools (1931) 277, 280
Storm Breaker, The (1925) 208
Studio Murder Mystery, The (1929) 81
Sullivan, C. Gardner 31
Summers, Montague 40
Summerville, Slim 110, 172
Sunrise (1927) 250
Svengali (1931) 321, 322, 333
Szekeler, Al 243

Tavares, Arthur (Arturo) 203, 338, 343, 345, 349, 351
Tell-Tale Heart, The (stage play) 303
Ten Cents a Dance (1931) 319, 333
Terror, The (1928) 81, 83, 140, 214, 215, 289
Thalberg, Irving 51, 67, 71, 190, 243
That Awful Mrs. Eaton (stage play) 167
Thaw, Cornelia 100
Thirteenth Chair, The (stage play) 79
Thirteenth Chair, The (1919) 79
Thirteenth Chair, The (1929) 51, 53, 58, 59, 67, 72, 82, 92, 102, 104, 116-117, 177, 198
Thomas, Ed 229
Thompson, Kristin 316
Tibbetts, Lawrence 165
Tichner, Fay 46
Tiffany Productions 320
Tilden, William 37
Tovar, Lupita 79, 84, 155, 161, 189, 283, 335, 336
Three Faces East (1930) 107, 109
Trilby (1895) 236
Trilby (1923) 43
Tryon, Glenn 62
Tsivian, Yuri 316

Tudor, Andrew 316
Turner, George E. 93, 143, 155, 335
Tree, Dorothy 101-102
Twelvetrees, Helen 84
2001: A Space Odyssey (1968) 329

Under Two Flags (1922) 55
Unholy Night, The (1929) 78, 81
Unholy Three, The (1925) 51, 53, 55
Unholy Three, The (1930) 102
Universal Pictures 12, 13, 43, 44, 45, 47, 48, 50, 60, 61, 62, 63, 65, 66, 67, 68, 69, 70, 73, 76, 77, 78, 79, 82, 79, 82, 83, 84, 86, 87, 88, 89, 90, 91, 92, 93, 95, 96, 97, 98, 99, 100, 102, 103, 105, 106, 107, 108, 110, 111, 112, 113, 116, 117, 119, 121, 122, 125, 127, 130, 132, 135, 136, 137, 141, 142, 143, 151, 152, 153, 155, 159, 161, 164, 165, 167, 168, 170, 171, 172, 173, 174, 175, 177, 178, 179, 180, 182, 184, 188, 189, 190, 192, 195, 197, 198, 199, 203, 205, 206, 208, 213, 214, 215, 216, 217, 218, 219, 220, 221, 222, 223, 225, 227, 228, 229, 231, 232, 233, 235, 236, 237, 238, 241, 242, 243, 244, 245, 246, 249, 252, 254, 255, 256, 257, 258, 259, 261, 266, 270, 273, 277, 278, 280, 281, 282, 283, 287, 289, 290, 291, 293, 294, 295, 300, 301, 302, 303, 304, 305, 306, 307, 308, 310, 311, 319, 320, 333, 334, 335, 336, 358
Universal Studios *see* Universal Pictures
Uris, Michael 101
Unknown, The (1927) 53, 54

Vasco, the Vampire (1914) 27
Vamp Cure, The (1918) 33
Vamping the Vamp (1918) 33
Vampire, The (burlesque) 25
Vampire, The (painting) 27-33
Vampire, The (poem) 27-33
Vampire, The (1910) 30
Vampire, The (1912) 30
Vampire, The (1913) 30
Vampire, The: His Kith and Kin (1928) 40
Vampire, The, or, A Ghost in Spite of Himself (stage) 24
The Vampire of the Desert (1913) 30
The Vampire's Trail (1914) 30
"The Vampires" (men's club) 17, 40
Vampires of the Coast (1909) 27
Vampires of the Night (1914) 27
Vampyr, Der (opera) 23
Vampyre, The, A Tale (1819) 21-22
Vampyre, The, or the Bride of the Isles (stage play) 22
Van Sloan, Edward 95, 96, 144, 147, 175, 180, 186, 191, 201, 206, 216, 226, 228, 237, 261, 290, 291, 292, 300, 320, 352
Vane, Sutton 98
Variety (trade publication) 38, 65, 67, 68, 69, 78, 81, 83, 86, 91, 92, 93, 96, 98, 112, 117, 125, 127, 131, 174, 177, 179, 182, 190, 208, 213, 225, 241, 244, 247, 248, 253, 261, 269, 276, 277, 278, 281, 286, 287, 305, 306, 336
Variety (1925) 340
Varney the Vampyre, or the Feast of Blood (1847)
Veidt, Conrad 79, 88

Veiller, Bayard 58
Velez, Josephine 177
Velez, Lupe 86, 87, 177
Victor, Henry 60
Viennese Nights (1931) 245
Villarias, Carlos 155, 161, 335, 336, 337, 338, 341
Virgin of Stamboul, The (1920) 45, 48, 50, 53, 55, 68, 198
Visaroff, Michael 100, 156, 157, 158, 187, 188, 296-297

Wagner, Richard 216, 316, 317, 358
Wallace, Edgar 81, 136
Walsh, Raoul 108
Walsh, Robert E. 61
Warhol, Andy 202, 310
Warner Bros. 74, 75, 78, 81, 98, 102, 172, 173, 177, 189, 214, 241, 257, 333
Watts, Richard, Jr. 55-56
Waxworks (1924) 88
Weaver, Tom vi, 315, 337, 339, 352
Webster, Aileen 145
Webster, Nicholas 145
Wegener, Paul 92
Weight, Harold 259, 261, 285
Weird Tales (magazine) 38
Welles, Orson 155
West, Roland 80, 84, 106, 107
West of Zanzibar (1928) 51, 53, 55, 94, 198
Whale, James 105
When the Daltons Rode (1940) 302

Where East Is East (1929) 198
Whirl of Mirth, The (variety show) 46
Whitbeck, Frank 225, 227
White, Courtney 244, 245, 280
White Tiger, The (1923) 53, 68
White Vampire, The (short story) 38
Wicked Darling, The (1919)
Wilson, Harry 225
Wilson, Lois 182
Witzel, Albert 95
Wizard of Oz, The (1939) 366
Wolf Woman, The (1916) 31
Woman in White, The (novel) 139
Women of All Nations (1931) 241
Wooden Kimono, The (stage play) 79
Worrell, Everil 38
Wrangell, Basil 198
Wray, John 85, 103, 104, 106, 111
Wright, Dudley 33

You Can't Cheat an Honest Man (1939) 302
Young, Robert 53
Young, Roland 166
Young, Waldemar 56
Zacherle, John 305, 310
Zacherley, John *see* Zacherle, John
Zinn, John 164-165